CONSPIRACY ENCYCLOPEDIA

First published in 2005 by Collins & Brown
The Chrysalis Building
Bramley Road
London W10 6SP

An imprint of **Chrysalis** Books Group plc

British Library Cataloguing-in-Publication Data:
A catalogue record for this book is available from the British Library.

ISBN 1843402874

The author and publishers have made every reasonable effort to contact all copyright holders. Any errors that may have occurred are inadvertent and anyone who for any reason has not been contacted is invited to write to the publishers so that a full acknowledgement may be made in subsequent editions of this work.

Produced by Conspiracy Books
PO Box 51726, London NW1 9ZH

Project Management: Will Steeds
Design: Barbara Doherty, Mark Stevens
Editorial: Mal Peachey, Fiona Screen, Christine King, Lesley Levene, Victoria Richards, Nina Sharman, Julia North
Index: Diana LeCore

This book has been compiled by a panel of writers and contributors:
Thom Burnett, Nigel Cawthorne, Richard Emerson, Mick Farren, Alex Games, John Gill, Sandy Gort, Rod Green, Emma Hooley, Esther Selsdon, Kenn Thomas

Printed and bound by SNP Leefung, China

CONSPIRACY ENCYCLOPEDIA

the encyclopedia of
conspiracy theories

COLLINS & BROWN

CONTENTS

AL-QAEDA

ASSASSINATIONS

DISINFORMATION

GLOBAL CONSPIRACIES

INTELLIGENCE

KEY FIGURES

MEDICAL CONSPIRACIES

MILITARY CONSPIRACIES

RELIGIOUS CONSPIRACIES

ROYAL CONSPIRACIES

SECRET SOCIETIES

UFOs

introduction

Conspiracy Theory is big business. Look at the number of book titles, TV documentaries, and Hollywood films dealing with the genre. Oliver Stone's 1991 blockbuster *JFK*, detailing the theories of district attorney, Jim Garrison, caused such a public uproar that the US government had to release declassified files in an attempt to correct the increasingly public misconception about the John F. Kennedy assassination. President Clinton appointed Kermit Hall to head a five-man team of scholars to sift through all the evidence made available to the Assassinations Records Review Board. Hall frequently quoted Benjamin Franklin's famous comment: "In order for three people to keep a secret, two must be dead." But this did little to dissuade the estimated 75 percent of Americans who believed Lee Harvey Oswald was part of a conspiracy.

A climate ripe for conspiracies

Declassified files on this and other topics have clearly shown that governments work in very secretive and deceptive ways in the defence of what is perceived as national security. The orthodox views of history and current events as reported by historians and journalists are no longer accepted as the final word. Amateur investigators have decided to form their own conclusions about events that they feel the professionals are misrepresenting. The advent of the internet has opened up opportunities for such amateurs to publish their theories to the world, in a format that is almost indistinguishable from that of the professionals. The internet has also allowed access to information and source materials upon which new conspiracy theories can be built by anyone willing to spend the time to do so. Nevertheless, thankfully, the field is dominated by professional journalists and publications such as Kenn Thomas of Steamshovel Press and Rob Sterling of The Konformist, whose investigative works are necessary strongholds in a cyberspace where hoaxers can operate freely.

In the past, some popular beliefs have been effectively debunked then naively resurrected by the next generation. An example is the medieval secret society of the Priory of Sion, first exposed to the English-speaking world by the 1982 publication of Baigent, Leigh, and Lincoln's, *Holy Blood, Holy Grail*. It was almost instantaneously debunked but has found a new generation of believers who read Dan Brown's recent, *The Da Vinci Code*. That author promotes it as a real entity, even though it was shown to be a hoax perpetrated by Pierre Plantard and Gérard de Sède in the 1950s. Does the conspiracy now lie not with the medieval Priory of Sion but with the postmodern hoaxers?

Structure of the encyclopedia

This encyclopedia is organized into 12 thematic sections covering the following ranges of conspiracy theory: al-Qaeda, Assassinations, Disinformation, Global conspiracies, Intelligence, Key Figures, Military conspiracies, Medical conspiracies, Religious conspiracies, Royal conspiracies, Secret Societies, and UFOs.

Links can be found between these sections and the reader is directed to some of them. It is part of the conspiracy theorist's arsenal to have the ability to form links between apparently distinct pieces of information in a way known as cognitive mapping. Critics such as Frederic Jameson have described conspiracy theory as "a poor person's cognitive mapping," implying that it betrays the same lack of understanding that a poor person has of the workings of the international banking system. But these connections between people and events often provide evidence of an underlying structure to history that academic historians wish to ignore. It is therefore left to the conspiracy theorist to discover and publicize these links. An example of how this works will be given here, using one of the founding fathers of the US and a key conspiracy personality, Benjamin Franklin.

How conspiracies grow – an example

In 1730, Franklin wrote the first documented article exposing American Freemasonry in his newspaper, the *Pennsylvania Gazette*. The next year he became a Freemason himself, rising swiftly to the position of Provincial Grand Master of Pennsylvania by 1734. After publishing the first Masonic book in the US, Franklin went on to join other Masonic lodges in France where he made important contacts with revolutionary leaders.

The dollar bill is clearly Freemasonic — an all-seeing eye in a triangle above a thirteen-stepped pyramid, beneath which a scroll proclaims the advent of a "new secular order," one of Freemasonry's long-standing dreams.

In 1773, while in England, Franklin co-produced a new revised version of the *Book of Common Prayer* with Baron le Despencer, otherwise known as Sir Francis Dashwood, a member of Adam Weishaupt's Illuminati and the founder of the notorious Hellfire Club. Based at the Abbey of Medmenham, this group of British rakes revelled in drunken orgies and worshipped Satan. Among its elite membership were Frederick, Prince of Wales, the Prime Minister Lord Bute, the First Lord of the Admiralty the Earl of Sandwich, and Franklin himself. As an example of a secret society of powerful men, the Hellfire Club must rank as the template for all subsequent demonic conspiracy groups. Remains of children's bodies recently found under the basement of Franklin's London home have been "explained away" as neither Satanic sacrifices nor grave-robbing but cadavers purchased by Franklin's housemate for medical research.

It has even been suggested that Franklin was a British Intelligence agent from 1772 onwardswho betrayed many of Pierre de Beaumarchais' gun-running missions from France to the US. With Freemasons fighting on both sides of the American War of Independence, conspiracists see the outcome being fixed by the powerful lodges of both countries. Through people like Franklin, the British chose to "lose" the war. Military ineptitude was the deliberate action of the secret brotherhood to establish a Masonic state.

It is claimed that Franklin gave this speech during the Constitutional Convention in Philadelphia in 1787:

> There is a great danger for the United States of America. This great danger is the Jew. Gentlemen, in every land the Jews have settled, they have depressed the moral level and lowered the degree of commercial honesty ... If they are not expelled from the United States by the Constitution within less than one hundred years they will stream into this country in such numbers that they will rule and destroy us and change our form of Government for which we Americans shed our blood and sacrificed our life, property and personal freedom.

This was an elaborate hoax, although it was claimed to be the speech recorded in the journal of Charles Pinckney, the revolutionary delegate from South Carolina, and stored in the Franklin Institute, Philadelphia. With the latter denying the existence of the manuscript, investigators have attempted to trace its real source. The Franklin Prophecy, as it is known, was first published in William Dudley Pelley's, *Liberation,* in February 1934 and soon found its way into the 1935 edition of the Nazi's, *Handbuch der Judenfrage,* (Handbook on the Jewish Question) by Theodor Fritsch.

It appears to have been a piece of anti-Semitic propaganda along the lines of the far more infamous, *The Protocols of the Learned Elders of Zion*. Its relevance to the post 9/11 conspiracy-filled world is through its continued ability to fool those not well versed in the art of conspiracy theory. One such believer is Osama bin Laden. In his November 2002 "Letter to the American People," the terrorist leader states:

> The Jews have taken control of your economy, through which they have taken control of your media, and now control all aspects of your life, making you their servants and achieving their aims at your expense, precisely what Benjamin Franklin warned you against.

Madman or voice of reason?

What Franklin actually warned against at the convention was that the US government "can only end in despotism, as other forms have done before it, when the people shall become so corrupted as to need despotic government, being incapable of any other." Writers such as Gore Vidal see this

Who is really in charge? This is the question at the root of most conspiracy theories.

real prophecy being fulfilled in present times and filmmaker, Michael Moore, has given maximum exposure to similar claims. Anti-Americanism and anti-Zionism are promoted by academics such as the 1999 Benjamin Franklin Medal winner, Noam Chomsky, who himself is accused of conspiring to deny the Nazi Holocaust with long-time associate Robert Faurisson and fellow neo-Nazis. Chomsky defined conspiracy theory as the "intellectual equivalent of a four-letter word … used by people who know that they can't answer arguments and that they can't deal with evidence." To be a conspiracy theorist is to be paranoid, marginal, crazy and uninformed. No wonder that Mel Gibson played the stereotypical role in the 1997 film, *Conspiracy Theory*. But to be uninformed is no longer the case. Conspiracy theorists can inform themselves and cut through the official disinformation, to arrive at conclusions which dare to confront the orthodox versions of events. From such theories, real criminal conspiracies are often revealed and the methods of conspiracy theory have become a modern tool in investigative journalism. The failure of the mainstream press to cover such matters, proves to some that it has become corrupted by the other three Estates: the Church, the Aristocracy, and the Capitalists. Investigative journalism and conspiracy theory have now become the Fifth Estate, protecting freedom of thought and freedom of speech.

But how are we to explain the crazier theories taking root? Theories are used in the sciences, and stand a good chance of being proved through rigorous investigation. Alas, this is not usually the case in theories about conspiracies. Perhaps the problem lies in the use of the word theory. The Germans have a word, *Verschworungsmythos*, which translates as "Conspiracy Myth" and this has more going for it. Perhaps the conspiracy world is an updated version of ancient myths where monsters and the gods of Olympus and Valhalla have been replaced by aliens and the Illuminati of Washington and Buckingham Palace. To some conspiracy theorists, such as David Icke, Benjamin Franklin represents the evil Reptilian aliens from another dimension that have controlled Earth's history. Is this an example of a "poor person's cognitive mapping?" Think of this the next time you stare at Franklin's face on a $100 bill.

The emergence of al-Qaeda as a political force can only be understood within the historical origins of Islam and the development of Islamic society. The western press has a tendency to portray Islam as a violent, repressive religion. However, Mohammed's main message was, on the contrary, the importance of a unified, egalitarian society.

The term "jihad" was coined to mean the effort of human beings to live in the way God intended. After Mohammed's death, Islamic society divided into two main groups. One, the Shia-i-Ali, was led by Mohammed's son-in-law, Ali, and its members believed that this direct connection to the Prophet made them the true Muslims. The other group, whose members later became known as Sunnis, believed that, despite their lack of blood ties to Mohammed, they far surpassed the Shias in the quality of their faith. These historic and theological hostilities continue to this day.

The Muslim Brotherhood

By 1928, the European powers had colonized one Islamic country after another. In Cairo, a Sunni schoolteacher called Hasan al-Banna saw the luxury in which the British lived and was appalled. He founded a group called the Muslim Brotherhood which accepted that, while Muslims needed western European technology, this must go hand in hand with spiritual reform. He stated that Islam was not so much a religion as a way of life and, therefore, Muslims must fight to liberate Muslim countries from foreign domination.

The West saw this struggle as a frightening direct threat to their secular and financially dominant way of life. As a result, it began to report on "Islam's conspiracy to destroy the West." By 1948, the Muslim Brotherhood had millions of members and the founding of the state of Israel that year was seen by them as yet another powerful symbol of Islam's humiliation by the West, creating even more members for the movement. It was into this sweeping historical tide that Osama bin Laden, another Sunni, was born in Saudi Arabia on March 10th, 1957.

In 1979, the Islamic revolution took place in Iran and an Islamic secular leader was deposed by his people. The millions of members of the Muslim Brotherhood saw that mass movements could be extremely effective and many existing regimes, including the USSR, which had by this time invaded Islamic Afghanistan, and western powers with a multitude of financial and military interests to protect in the region, were very anxious about both the trend towards people power and the Islamists' radicalized realization that this could work as a powerful weapon.

The origins of al-Qaeda

The name al-Qaeda derives from Arabic root letters meaning "the base" or "the foundation" and first appeared in the mid-1980s, when it began to be used by a variety of radical Islamic leaders all over the Muslim world. It was most publicly employed in Afghanistan, where Arab militants were now fighting alongside the local Mujahideen rebels to get rid of the Soviet invaders. Abdullah Azzam, the chief ideologue for these Arab militants, wrote: "We are the vanguard...which constitutes the strong foundation [*al-qaeda al-sulbah*] for the expected society." As is clear from his wording, at this stage the term "al-Qaeda" merely referred to an idea rather than any particular organization.

Osama bin Laden had set up his own small militant group in the Pakistani town of Peshawar, on the border with Afghanistan, some time around August 1988. During the war, Muslim radicals from all over the world had gathered in the region to support the fight against communism. After the Soviet defeat, these men began to splinter into defined ethnic groupings.

Bin Laden felt very strongly that this dispersal was the antithesis of the philosophy behind the Muslim Brotherhood, which wanted to create one unified Islamic uprising. He left the region and returned to Saudi Arabia in 1989, determined to continue the global battle and to create a truly "international" army. In 1990, when Saddam Hussein invaded Kuwait, he offered to form an army of Islamic militants to protect Saudi Arabia from the secular infidel. The Saudis rejected his offer. Humiliated, Bin Laden fled to Sudan in 1991.

At this stage, a number of militants in Pakistan began compiling an 11-volume standard reference work for militants entitled *The Encyclopaedia of Jihad* and al-Qaeda is not mentioned. Bin Laden is personally thanked for his work in Afghanistan but not as the leader of any independent organization. In 1993, however, a militant called Ahmed Ajaj was arrested at JFK airport in New York. In his luggage he had a terrorist training manual called *Al-Qaeda*. The CIA concluded that this title referred to the name of an organization rather than "the fundamentals" of terrorist training.

Bin Laden to the fore

By the mid-1990s, Bin Laden was one name on a CIA list which included thousands of suspects. The CIA knew that, between 1996 and September 2001, a number of radical Islamic militants had gone back to the relatively lawless region of Afghanistan to create Islamic training camps within a cave complex called Tora Bora in the east of the country. Many local groups in Afghanistan may have trained or had some association with the al-Qaeda hardcore at that time, as Bin Laden was well funded and it was a good place to share information, trade weapons, and exchange views. This did not mean, however, that they were all part of the same single organization. At this time, no one group was more influential than any other. Most of the participants in these training camps were dedicated to violent action long before they arrived in Tora Bora and all already subscribed to a similar world view. This was not a world view created by Bin Laden or even developed by him, it just happened to be one that he and his followers shared with a number of other individuals and groups from any number of different countries. Having misappropriated the name, however, the CIA now began to use the term "al-Qaeda" to refer to the dozens of military and terrorist camps in Afghanistan of which Bin Laden's was merely one minor element.

In 1998, after the US embassy bombings in East Africa, President Clinton referred to the protagonists as "the Bin Laden network" and never mentioned "al-Qaeda." It was during this FBI investigation, however, that the term first started to be used publicly, and "al-Qaeda" was referred to in a State Department report at that time as "an operational hub, predominantly for like-minded Sunni extremists." Much of the evidence for the existence of this "operational hub" came from the testimony of an unreliable witness called Jamal al-Fadl, who had earlier been expelled from Bin Laden's circle for stealing funds. He received large sums of money from the US for his evidence and it is no coincidence that the term started to gain common currency in the security services during this period. Under US law, in order to convict suspects of the offence of conspiracy, it is necessary for them to be members of a coherent organization. The evidence that al-Qaeda was a physical entity with subscribing members suddenly became extremely important to the FBI, which had, until that moment, barely remarked on the group's existence. By pulling together a variety of loosely connected individuals under the name "al-Qaeda," it would become much easier to prosecute them for a wide range of offences. It would also make public relations for the security services much easier by creating a "bogeyman." During this period, US investigators constantly asked all terrorist suspects if they had ever been a member of a group called "al-Qaeda." Most replied that they had never heard of such a group, but the question continued to be asked.

Until 2001, Osama bin Laden himself had never been known to use the term "al-Qaeda" and neither had any of his colleagues. Even as late as 2001, one former member of the group, when interviewed by ABC TV, stated that he had spent eight months at Tora Bora but had never heard the name "al-Qaeda." Though this is not to deny that a network of like-minded individuals existed, the cohesiveness of this group appears to have been entirely defined by external forces, such as the US security services. The name of the ideology that connected all these individuals was simply derived from that of one of its most highly publicized subsets, but Bin Laden, who had proved himself to be an extremely efficient organizer and fund-raiser during the war in Afghanistan, soon realized the potency of the new terminology. Through the idea of an amorphous grouping with a single title, he could create both enigma and power. The level of negative but secretive publicity that Bin Laden began to garner for himself as "Global Bogeyman Number One," and into his group, thereby strengthened his cause.

On an international level, it was also extremely convenient for large numbers of governments to have access to such a neat label to pin on all political opposition. These opponents could now be tackled as part of the "War on Terror." However, to label all local groups as part of the "al-Qaeda" movement is simply to misunderstand the way in which the organization works. Even in any one country or any local area, some groups might be associated with Bin Laden while others might not. Kurdistani rebels, for example, apparently have no interest in any external regions, the Algerians have consistently rejected advances from Bin Laden, and the Indonesians do not ally themselves with anyone beyond a general ideological interest. This does not stop the western press, the CIA, or Bin Laden himself from subsuming any terrorist outrage under the al-Qaeda banner, as this explanation of events suits all these groups in

different ways. Bin Laden himself constantly uses the Occupied Territories as a cause to rouse global Islamic feeling, but it seems that his practical involvement with Hamas and Islamic Jihad is, in fact, extremely limited because the Palestinian groups feel that his involvement would have a negative impact on both their publicity and their funding.

The splintering of al-Qaeda

Since 9/11 and the American-led invasion of Afghanistan, an important part of the network's flow of information and funding has been profoundly disrupted. Partly because of this, a huge number of splinter groups have sprung up all over the world, some with almost no direct connection to Bin Laden save, possibly, a few ex-trainees and a shared ideology. The amorphousness of this new form of the movement makes it almost impossible to defuse as there is no longer any genuine hierarchical structure to be taken apart. Tashkent has now labelled its rebels as members of al-Qaeda, as have Beijing, Macedonia, Tunisia, the Philippines, and Kashmir. There is no evidence that Bin Laden has ever been actively engaged in the politics of any of these regions, particularly Kashmir, yet the Indian secret services are constantly claiming to have found al-Qaeda cells in the area and occasionally even leak reports that he has been spotted there. The London newspaper the *Daily Telegraph* has even reported that British secret services have actively hunted Bin Laden in Kashmir. There is no evidence for this, but the claim neatly coincides with India's political interests and its ongoing territorial dispute with its nuclear-powered neighbour, Pakistan – the country most closely associated with harbouring al-Qaeda terrorists.

Al-Qaeda and the West

Spreading the enigmatic power of al-Qaeda, the British government's intelligence dossier on the group in October 2001 stated that Bin Laden was responsible for much of the drug trade in Afghanistan. There was no evidence for this. Indeed, many of the local traders actively refuted the claim. It also stated that, between 1989 and 1996, Bin Laden was based in Afghanistan, Pakistan, and Sudan, but failed to mention that he spent almost two years of that period in Saudi Arabia. Presenting information to the British public in this way helped

FBI TEN MOST WANTED FUGITIVE

MURDER OF U.S. NATIONALS OUTSIDE THE UNITED STATES;
CONSPIRACY TO MURDER U.S. NATIONALS OUTSIDE THE UNITED STATES;
ATTACK ON A FEDERAL FACILITY RESULTING IN DEATH

USAMA BIN LADEN

Date of Photograph Unknown

Aliases: Usama Bin Muhammad Bin Ladin, Shaykh Usama Bin Laden, the Prince, the Emir, Abu Abdallah, Mujahid Shaykh, Hajj, the Director

DESCRIPTION

Date of Birth:	1957	**Hair:**	Brown
Place of Birth:	Saudi Arabia	**Eyes:**	Brown
Height:	6' 4" to 6' 6"	**Complexion:**	Olive
Weight:	Approximately 160 pounds	**Sex:**	Male
Build:	Thin	**Nationality:**	Saudi Arabian
Occupation:	Unknown		
Remarks:	Bin Laden is the leader of a terrorist organization known as Al-Qaeda, "The Base." He is left-handed and walks with a cane.		

CAUTION

USAMA BIN LADEN IS WANTED IN CONNECTION WITH THE AUGUST 7, 1998, BOMBINGS OF THE UNITED STATES EMBASSIES IN DAR ES SALAAM, TANZANIA, AND NAIROBI, KENYA. THESE ATTACKS KILLED OVER 200 PEOPLE. IN ADDITION, BIN LADEN IS A SUSPECT IN OTHER TERRORIST ATTACKS THROUGHOUT THE WORLD.

CONSIDERED ARMED AND EXTREMELY DANGEROUS

IF YOU HAVE ANY INFORMATION CONCERNING THIS PERSON, PLEASE CONTACT YOUR LOCAL FBI OFFICE OR THE NEAREST U.S. EMBASSY OR CONSULATE.

Bin Laden was already on the FBI's ten most wanted list, over two years before the 9/11 attacks took place.

US ground combat marines on the first day of Operation Rio Bravo, a mission designed to find Taliban insurgents and weapons in south-central Afghanistan.

to justify the war in Afghanistan and built up propaganda against "the enemy" without creating negative publicity for an important trading and military partner (Saudi Arabia).

Similar dossiers began to be used to build up a case against Saddam Hussein. If the security services could only implicate al-Qaeda with this regime, then half the battle for hearts and minds would be won. In late 2001, the CIA stated that Mohammed Atta, the leader of the 9/11 bombers, had met an Iraqi agent in Prague just before the attacks. He was in the US at that time. George Bush and Tony Blair referred to "broad linkages" between al-Qaeda and Saddam, but it was an indisputable fact that Bin Laden reviled the Iraqi regime and consistently rejected Saddam's approaches. A cursory examination of CIA material also shows that several figures named as key al-Qaeda members in this context were actually members of rival organizations. Much of this erroneous information was leaked by key Iraqi dissidents with strong political agendas of their own – namely, the desire to promote an American invasion of Iraq – but the security services rapidly incorporated it because it suited their own purposes.

Meanwhile, though Bin Laden has praised many militant Islamic acts, he has never admitted direct responsibility for any terrorist attack. This adds considerably to the confusion. He is a sophisticated tactician and extremely careful never to dwell on the fact that his movement is a minority belief group within Muslims as a whole. It suits him to give the impression that a grand uprising of an entire people is taking place and that, therefore, unconnected "brothers" are springing up all over the world. The myth of the great unpublicized power of al-Qaeda is extremely useful for Bin Laden and in this way too the aims of both the CIA and al-Qaeda neatly coincide.

Contemporary Islamic militancy is extremely complex. During the late 20th century, a network of militants formed, of which al-Qaeda was just one strand. After the events of 9/11, it was extremely convenient for the US to name a specific group with a single leader, Osama bin Laden, as the "enemy," as this implied that his removal, together with that of a finite group of members, would make the world a more secure and safer place. After the US-led invasion of Afghanistan, these militants scattered over the entire globe. It was then necessary for repressive governments to persist with the myth of the single "enemy." This allowed for the use of unlimited or illegitimate force on any number of financial or political opponents without provoking international condemnation simply by claiming that these opponents were connected to the "enemy." The existence of this mythical group was also extremely useful politically as it could be labelled as the source of all unidentified global ills. The fact is that the network of individuals commonly referred to as al-Qaeda is not a cohesive force of global militants dedicated to an international uprising, challenging current western Judaeo-Christian capitalist value systems. And never was.

1930s
OIL IN SAUDI ARABIA AND
THE HOUSE OF SAUD

The Saudi royal family struck a deal to share the
country's oil wealth with the US

Saudi Arabia is ruled by the House of Saud, all of whose
members are Wahhabis – a "pure" form of Islam based on a
literal interpretation of the Koran. The family has selec-
tively used this religion, which was founded in the region
in 1750 by Mohammad Ibn Abd al-Wahhab, as a means to
maintain their wealth and control their people.

The conspiracy theory
The House of Saud conspired with the US government to
divide the country's oil wealth between them and then to
use some of the profits to suppress any political opposition.

The evidence
In 1923, the chieftain in Saudi Arabia was Abd al-Aziz ibn
Saud, whose income depended almost entirely on pilgrims
making the *hajj* (holy pilgrimage) to Mecca. After the British
left the area, Ibn Saud auctioned the country's oil rights
in 1933 to the Standard Oil of California Company for
$250,000. Local oil was so underexploited that, even in
1939, the Arabian-American Oil Company (ARAMCO) still
used 700 camels to do most of its transportation work. As
it gradually became clear that huge quantities of oil could
be obtained easily in the region, the House of Saud and the
US began to work together to control its flow. Throughout
the period of World War II, production increased, so that
by the end of the war Saudi Arabia was producing 300,000
barrels of oil a day. The fuel went straight to the US for the
war effort and the income went directly into Ibn Saud's
personal bank account. When the war finished, Ibn Saud
was the only Arab leader to meet President Roosevelt in
Egypt. Roosevelt explicitly committed the US to protecting
the power base of the House of Saud.

The US never interfered with the internal politics of Saudi
Arabia despite the fact that none of the $400 million paid
by the US to Ibn Saud for oil between 1946 and 1953 was
used for development. The only students sent abroad were
relatives of Ibn Saud. In 1946, the country spent $150,000
on building schools and $2 million to build the royal garage.
All aeroplanes required Ibn Saud's personal permission to
land and take off.

By 1950, the US and the Saudis were inextricably linked
militarily and financially. US Strategic Air Command had
built a huge airbase in the region, ostensibly to protect the
oilfields but actually to protect the House of Saud against
any opposition. Ibn Saud promoted the House of Saud above
other Arabs, and Saudi Arabia was the only Arab country
which did not send troops to fight in the Israeli War of
Independence of 1948. Ibn Saud died in 1953, by which
time Saudi Arabia and the US were utterly dependent on
each other. By 1955, Saudi Arabia had overtaken Iraq as
the world's leading oil supplier.

Saudi citizens began to express admiration for the liberal rule of President Nasser of Egypt and the House of Saud
became worried. They decided to promote conservative
Wahhabism, as the more "religious" they could persuade
local citizens to become, the less "Arab" they would feel. In
these circumstances, the people would be much less likely
to threaten the House of Saud. In 1959, an Egyptian magazine called *Al-Musawar* published a detailed account of the
ways in which the CIA was cooperating with Saudi Arabia to
create Muslim political groups all over the country. This was
sure to lessen local support for Nasser. The CIA, in turn, was
keen to support this because the US was now dependent on
Saudi oil and access to oil would remain unlimited only
under the House of Saud. In 1975, King Faisal told *Time*
magazine: "US relations are a pillar of Saudi policy."

The verdict
It seems almost certainly true that the US and Saudi Arabia
have manipulated the flow of oil to support each other. A
very pro-US foreign policy helps keep the House of Saud
wealthy. A very pro-House of Saud foreign policy helps keep
the US factories and war efforts up and running.

1930s
THE ORIGINS OF THE WEALTH
OF THE BIN LADEN CLAN

The Bin Ladens acquired their wealth by means of a
secret agreement with the Saudi ruling family

Saudi Arabia is ruled by the House of Saud. The origins of
the Bin Laden clan's wealth are historically and financially
linked to the House of Saud. This relationship has developed symbiotically.

The conspiracy theory
The Bin Ladens and the House of Saud constantly conspire
to promote each other's wealth and power and then to retain the benefits of Saudi Arabia's natural oil wealth within
the two families.

The evidence

Osama's father, Sheikh Mohammed bin Oud bin Laden, was a peasant from Yemen who is thought to have been born around 1911. He left his native province, Hadramut, in the early 1920s and eventually settled in Hejaz, Saudi Arabia, in 1932. There he began working in the Jeddah docks, but later he started a small construction company. This prospered until it became one of the area's leading building firms; in fact, Bin Laden was contracted to build the first royal palace in Jeddah. The firm's assets grew so rapidly that on one occasion, when the Saudi treasury apparently had cash-flow difficulties, Bin Laden was asked to help. For six months he paid all the salaries of the country's civil servants. Soon afterwards, he acquired the contract to rebuild a number of the country's leading mosques. Later, the Bin Laden group was also awarded the contract to rebuild the al-Aqsa mosque in Jerusalem.

Cannily, the Bin Ladens now had an area of expertise which was both highly lucrative and deeply praiseworthy. The family – which ran to some 300 members – were very popular with local citizens because of their prestigious work, in the process of which some of them had cultivated incredibly close ties with the government. At one stage Sheikh Mohammed combined the roles of chief national builder and chief national commissioner and became King Faisal's Minister for Public Works. As national commissioner he was in charge of deciding who should receive engineering contracts, so effectively he commissioned himself. He also made sure that his children mixed with children from the royal family, sending many of his sons to the same top public schools – primarily Victoria College in Alexandria, Egypt, but also Millfield in the UK.

Osama bin Laden was born in 1957. When his father died in a helicopter crash 11 years later, 10,000 people attended the funeral and, immediately afterwards, King Faisal met the Bin Laden clan and informed them that he was placing the company under royal decree. The estate would now be controlled by a committee appointed by the king and the board would consist primarily of members of both families. Individual sons now gained their inheritance and Osama's is generally calculated to have been around $30 million.

The company expanded further and became known as Bin Laden Brothers for Contracting and Industry. National contracts were never awarded by public tender but rather by official notification direct from the Head Chamberlain of the House of Saud. Any publicity led to the immediate termination of a contract and secrecy, therefore, surrounded every business deal. It was at this stage that the Bin Laden

group acquired its most lucrative contract and became the official arms intermediary between Riyadh and the West. They were also chosen to represent the Audi and Porsche concessions in Saudi Arabia.

The Bin Ladens were so involved in the affairs of the House of Saud that they became business and financial mentors to the royal children. Two princes in particular, Mohammed bin Fahd and Saud bin Nayef, were taught the ins and outs of international finance by the Bin Ladens and the two families now share controlling interests on the boards of many foreign oil-based conglomerates. In November 1979, the Bin Laden construction company had the exclusive contract for repairs to the Holy Palace and were therefore the only people to have detailed architectural and engineering drawings of Islam's holiest site. When the mosque was suddenly seized by terrorists, police used the Bin Laden drawings to find secret paths into the cellars. Shortly afterwards, Mahrous bin Laden was arrested, as there was evidence to connect him directly with the terrorists. The Saudi secret services subsequently declared him innocent of all charges and Mahrous now heads the Bin Laden group's office in Medina.

The Bin Laden group rebuilt large parts of Beirut and maintains offices in London and Geneva. In 1980, Salem bin Laden, who had been involved in many of the company's arms deals, attended a meeting between Iranians and Americans in Paris. In 1988, he was killed in a mysterious plane crash in Texas. The Bin Ladens also have an office in the Dutch Antilles which, in collaboration with a number of American companies, was awarded many of the reconstruction projects in Kuwait after the first Gulf War.

The verdict

The power and wealth of the House of Saud and the Bin Laden group are inextricably linked. The two families depend upon each other to maintain and promote their financial dealings through whatever means necessary. It is imperative for neither party to publicize this fact.

1980
THE SAUDI GOVERNMENT
FUNDED AFGHAN JIHAD
The Saudi government secretly funded the Afghan rebels to stabilize their own position at home

In 1980, the Saudi government identified two clear threats. First, internally, Islamic extremists considered the House of Saud to be secular and corrupt. Second, externally, the

Iranian revolution had increased the power of Shia Islam. Both might destroy the wealth of the predominantly Sunni House of Saud. The government determined to pour oil money into Afghanistan in order to increase the power of Saudi Islam (Wahhabism) and, simultaneously, to make the Saudis seem more actively "Islamic."

Saudi intelligence agents were given enormous sums of money by the Saudi government to distribute among Afghan rebels. They chose reliable Saudis, such as Osama bin Laden, to manage the funds. This money paid for rebel Afghans to obtain Saudi passports, visit the country, and develop a sophisticated funding network through a variety of lightly disguised charities.

Abd Sayyaf, an Afghan Wahhabi, built up his power base from almost nothing. With Saudi money, he became a major player, using his influence to create Sayyafabad – a refugee camp with military facilities, mosques, and religious schools, which in turn taught Wahhabism. This became the favourite camp for many foreign volunteers, established Wahhabism as Afghanistan's pre-eminent theology, and also became Bin Laden's first military base. At the start of the war, Wahhabism barely existed in Afghanistan; by its end, Sayyaf and his Saudi allies were in total control.

The Saudis used their banking networks to promote not only Islamic fundamentalism, but also their own power, in Afghanistan.

1980s
OSAMA'S BANKING NETWORK
AND THE MUSLIM BROTHERHOOD

Bin Laden channelled money to terrorist groups via charitable foundations

After school in Jeddah, Osama bin Laden attended King Abdulaziz University, where he studied economics and management. He abandoned plans to join the family business and began to focus on Islamic studies at university in Jeddah, where he was taught by Mohammed Qutb, the brother of Syed Qutb, who founded the modern Muslim Brotherhood. Syed had followed Hasan al-Banna's original ideas on Islam but added to them the theory that the aim of *jihad* should be to tackle "political power resting on racial, class, social and economic oppression." He was executed in Egypt in 1966. Bin Laden was also taught at this time by Dr Abdullah Azzam, a Palestinian member of the Jordanian Muslim Brotherhood. When the PLO was expelled from Jordan in 1968, Azzam began teaching Islamic jurisprudence at al-Azhar University in Cairo, but again

he was expelled. Both Qutb and Azzam had been given sanctuary by the Saudis as part of the House of Saud's self-interested campaign to counter the atheistic socialism that was now spreading across the Middle East, particularly in Egypt.

The conspiracy theory
Osama bin Laden channelled money from Islamic charities to help fund a variety of Mujahideen groups through a complex set of heavily disguised charitable donations. Much of this funding came directly from an unsuspecting West, while other money came from the CIA and a number of highly secretive Saudi sources.

The evidence
Through various educational influences, Bin Laden had become radicalized and, within a month of the Soviet invasion of Afghanistan in December 1976, he left for Pakistan. There he met and worked with a number of Afghan and Arab commanders who were leading the fight against communism. They were funded by a multinational coalition organized by the CIA. Other contributors were the UK, Saudi Arabia, Pakistan, and China. They all felt they were fighting the Cold War and did not care that, as a by-product, they were supporting radical Sunni Islam . Together with Azzam, Bin Laden set up Maktab al-Khidamar (MAK) in 1984. Azzam was the *emir* (leader) while Osama was his deputy. They had close contacts with the Saudi government and the Muslim Brotherhood, both of whom channelled vast funds into MAK. Also known as the Afghan Service Bureau, or the Office, it played a decisive role in anti-Soviet resistance. In addition to recruiting, indoctrinating, and training tens of thousands of Arab and Muslim youths from all over the globe, MAK disbursed $200 million of Middle Eastern, US, and British aid, most of which came from NGOs for unspecified Islamic relief work. Bin Laden and Azzam also developed relationships with the ISI, the Pakistani secret services. This was the CIA's conduit for arms supplies and the American secret services provided weaponry, ground-to-air missiles, and satellite information systems for the Islamic terrorists. Azzam travelled widely under the auspices of the Muslim Brotherhood and visited both Germany and the US, where he was welcomed with open arms. At a meeting in Fort Worth, Texas, in 1982, he even inspired a student called Essam al-Ridi, who later became Bin Laden's personal pilot.

Azzam and Bin Laden used some of the massive amounts of funding to build training camps on the border between Pakistan and Afghanistan. At this time the Pakistani

238   THE 9/11 COMMISSION REPORT

American Airlines Flight 11

Left to right,
Mohamed Atta, pilot;
Waleed al Shehri,
Wail al Shehri,
Satam al Suqami,
Abdulaziz al Omari,
hijackers

The five plane hijackers of the 9/11 attacks on the World Trade Center are all believed to be products of al-Qaeda training camps in Afghanistan.

government wanted to exert some control over the two men and asked the Saudis to send a military leader to coordinate proceedings. The Saudis sent Prince Turki ibn Faisal ibn Abdelaziz, their chief of security. While Bin Laden's training as a construction site manager was perfect for overseeing the building of roads and cave complexes in hostile territory, Prince Turki worked closely with two Saudi banks, Dar al-Mal al-Islami, founded by his brother, and Dalla al-Baraka, founded by his uncle, to channel funds to Arab fighters in Afghanistan through 20 NGOs, including the International Islamic Relief Organization.

The verdict
Osama bin Laden used a variety of pseudo-charitable sources from an extensive global banking network in a number of countries to fund terrorist activities.

1980s
OSAMA WAS FINANCED, TRAINED, AND ARMED BY US
Bin Laden was effectively set up by the US in order to assist in their battle against communism

In April 1978, the People's Democratic Party of Afghanistan (PDPA) seized power. They were committed to reform and rule by Soviet-style communism. Washington feared the spread of communism in the region and the CIA offered funding and military support to anyone who could help them defeat the PDPA.

Between 1978 and 1992, the US government poured at least $750 million, and possibly as much as $1.5 billion, into assisting the rebel groups in Afghanistan. Zbigniew Brzezinski, President Carter's national security advisor, developed a plan to spread Islamic fanaticism into Soviet Central Asia and thereby destabilize the USSR. The US-run radio station Radio Liberty constantly broadcast Islamic fundamentalist lectures across the region and, in 1986, CIA chief William Casey committed support to at least 100,000 Islamic militants in Pakistan, who were trained in CIA-sponsored camps.

The CIA was not allowed to enter Afghanistan, so its money was distributed by the local agency of ISI, the Pakistani secret services, via a local organization called Maktab al-Khidamar (MAK), the Afghan Service Bureau, or the Office. In 1989, Bin Laden took overall charge of MAK and used the CIA money to build his headquarters inside a natural cave complex called Tora Bora.

Tora Bora was the headquarters for al-Qaeda until it was demolished by the Americans in 2001. This was ironic, as they had given the money to build it in the first place.

1990
AL-QAEDA HAD MEN IN IRAQ
DURING FIRST GULF WAR

A deliberate lie was circulated by the CIA in order to justify the later invasion of Iraq

After the first Gulf War, the CIA deliberately leaked information connecting Saddam Hussein to al-Qaeda. On October 27th, 2003, the US under-secretary of defence sent a 16-page memo to the Senate Intelligence Committee, stating that the FBI, the CIA, and the National Security Agency had produced "conclusive" evidence that al-Qaeda had fighters working for Saddam Hussein during the first Gulf War.

The memo claimed that, in 1991, Iraq sought Sudan's assistance to establish links to al-Qaeda via the Sudanese leader. Iraq needed this relationship because al-Qaeda could assist with the transportation of proscribed weapons through Afghanistan.

In late 1989, Osama bin Laden was in Saudi Arabia, warning the government that Saddam Hussein was the apotheosis of a corrupt secular leader. As such, he was the single most immediate threat to the country that contained the two holiest places in Islam. When Iraqi tanks moved into Kuwait City in September 1990, Bin Laden went to see Prince Sultan, the Saudi minister of defence, accompanied by a group of senior Afghan Mujahideen leaders. He submitted a detailed proposal to the government, explaining the need for an international Islamic army to fight Saddam, and he asked to be its commander. He was promptly dismissed and soon placed under house arrest in Jeddah.

He spent no time in Iraq during that period.

1992–6
OSAMA BIN LADEN IN SUDAN

Bin Laden funded and planned terrorist activities with the Sudanese government

In June 1989, Hassan al-Turabi and General Bashir staged an Islamic coup d'état in Sudan. Al-Turabi wanted his country to become the spiritual focus of the Sunni Islamic world. He therefore invited Osama bin Laden and prominent al-Qaeda member Ayman al-Zawahiri into Sudan to set up 23 military bases as well as a joint construction company with the government. This was used to fund the construction of the "Challenge Highway" from Khartoum to Port Sudan, an airport, a bakery, and a peanut farm. In 1993, members of al-Qaeda took crate-loads of ammunition from al-Zawahiri's farm to Port Sudan, using the highway that Bin Laden's money had built. These arms were shipped to Yemen in a deal supervised by the Sudanese government.

By February 1996, however, sanctions had been imposed on Sudan and Bin Laden was a liability. President Bashir contacted US officials and offered to arrest and extradite him to Saudi Arabia. The Saudis knew that Bin Laden would plot to overthrow them and President Clinton rejected the offer. The Sudanese expelled Bin Laden in May 1996. Al-Turabi wrote to President Clinton to offer him secret service dossiers on all al-Qaeda members. President Clinton rejected this offer, as radical Islam was a convenient national security threat, while for the Saudis it was an actual one.

The US could have captured Bin Laden at this stage but chose not to do so.

February 26th, 1993
RAMZI YOUSEF WAS AN
IRAQI AGENT

The man behind the first World Trade Center bombing was not an Al-Qaeda member but an Iraqi secret agent

Ramzi Yousef was born in Kuwait City in 1968. He studied electrical engineering in Swansea, Wales, before returning to Pakistan in 1991. On August 31st, 1992, he flew to New York and began attending the al-Farouq mosque in Brooklyn, which was an MAK (Maktab al-Khidamar) office. Yousef entered the US on an Iraqi passport and was known locally as "Rashid the Iraqi." On February 26th, 1993, a bomb in the World Trade Center killed six people, after which Yousef disappeared. In 1995, he accidentally set off an explosion in Manila which eventually led to his arrest by Pakistani/US agents in Pakistan.

One of his co-conspirators in New York made 46 calls to Iraq during the run-up to the bombing and, as all Baghdad phones at that time were bugged, Iraqi intelligence may have had some prior knowledge of the affair. In addition, the bomb went off on the second anniversary of the ending of the Gulf War and Yousef led a secular lifestyle with a Filipina girlfriend.

On the other hand, the husband of one of Osama bin Laden's half-sisters had funded the bombers and Yousef had stayed in one of Bin Laden's safe houses in Pakistan. Bin Laden himself stated that he did not know Ramzi.

Yousef was almost certainly a roving free agent and the conspiracy lies in the attempt to connect him to the interests of broader groups.

November 13th, 1995, and June 25th, 1996
AL-QAEDA RESPONSIBLE FOR
SAUDI TERRORIST ATTACKS
Al-Qaeda was behind the bombings in Riyadh and Dhahran

On November 13th, 1995, a 90kg (200lb) car bomb exploded in Riyadh in a car park outside a building rented by the Pentagon for use by American military contractors. This was the first such incident in Saudi Arabia's history, and it resulted in the deaths of five Americans and two Indians, as well as injuries to sixty others. The following year, on June 25th, 1996, a bomb in a fuel truck outside an American base in Dhahran exploded, killing 19 US soldiers and wounding 400 others.

In the mid-1990s bin Laden was not a well-known figure but was about to become an icon for Muslim radicals.

The conspiracy theory
Al-Qaeda militants were responsible for these two attacks but the Saudi authorities hid the proof because it would weaken the House of Saud.

The evidence
By April 1996, the security services had extracted confessions for the first incident from four men in their twenties. Saudi citizens of modest means, they had all fought under the overall command of Osama bin Laden in Afghanistan. They spoke with local accents and were well known in their respective villages. They had returned from the successful fight against communism in Afghanistan expecting to receive national recognition or, at least, generous financial reward. The Saudi Arabian authorities, however, had no desire to advertise any radical Islamic victory, as this would only undermine their own power. They, therefore, completely ignored the men's claims for military recognition.

Bin Laden was not yet a well-known figure in his native country. By 1994, he had been stripped of his Saudi citizenship and his assets had been frozen. He had also begun to make tapes that called for violent action against the Saudi regime. The indictment that the security services drew up, however, mentioned neither Bin Laden nor al-Qaeda. Instead it claimed that the four accused men were sponsored by unnamed "outside forces," by which the Saudis were implying Iraq or Iran, as any suggestion of a radical Islamic uprising might destabilize the government. Provoking a public outcry against the four men by connecting them to unpopular foreign powers would avoid the risk of turning them into martyrs and possibly igniting further popular unrest. All four men, however, made state-ments that were broadcast on Saudi TV, in which they flatly denied any foreign connections. They claimed links to radical Islamic leaders, including their personal icon, Osama bin Laden, and they had in their possession material that he had written. They were all executed.

Early in 1996, the Sudanese government offered to extradite Bin Laden to Riyadh but the Saudi authorities rejected the proposal, as by this stage they considered his very presence on their soil a threat. On May 18th, 1996, Bin Laden, therefore, returned to Afghanistan. On June 25th, 1996, the bomb in the fuel truck parked outside an American base in Dhahran exploded, killing 19 US soldiers and wounding 400 others. Once again the Saudi authorities immediately put the blame on Afghan veterans backed by "foreign influences." Some 600 of these former fighters were immediately arrested. Investigations by the security services "conclusively proved" that an Iranian-backed Shia group within Saudi Arabia was responsible. This was an extremely convenient analysis for the Saudi government, as the Shias were the enemies of the Sunni House of Saud. They had undergone a long history of both repression and violent resistance within the country. The Americans, who had vested interests in propping up the Saudi regime, indicted 13 members of Saudi Hizbollah (a Shia organization), including as evidence phone calls from senior Iranian officials to the conspirators as well as apparently detailed descriptions of the bombers' movements. No evidence connecting Bin Laden, or indeed any other Sunni radical, to the bombings ever emerged from this second incident and indeed, in an interview for CNN in 1997, Bin Laden himself stated: "What [these men] did is a big honour that I missed participating in."

The verdict

Osama bin Laden may not have ordered the bombings himself, but to suggest that he might have done so is a misunderstanding of the nature of al-Qaeda. The Saudis deliberately obscured evidence that this was the case.

August 7th, 1998
ATTACKS ON US EMBASSIES
IN EAST AFRICA

Al-Qaeda provoked Clinton into bombing Afghanistan, so boosting its popularity in the Arab world

On August 7th, 1998, two simultaneous bomb attacks on the US embassies in Nairobi, Kenya, and Dar es Salaam, Tanzania, killed a total of 225 people and injured over 4,000 others. One of the bombers survived and confessed to having acted on orders from al-Qaeda. Perhaps even this confession was carefully calculated by Osama Bin Laden.

By February 1998, Bin Laden had realized that moving the focus of his attacks from Middle Eastern rulers to US targets would help unite the whole of radical Islam behind him. He therefore declared an international war against the American-Zionist crusaders and began to plan the attacks on the US embassies to provoke President Clinton into attacking a Muslim state. Sure enough, 13 days later, Clinton ordered missile strikes on six al-Qaeda training camps in Afghanistan, as well as a pharmaceutical factory in Sudan which, the US claimed, was producing chemical weapons.

Most Wanted Terrorists

MURDER OF U.S. NATIONALS OUTSIDE THE UNITED STATES; CONSPIRACY TO
MURDER U.S. NATIONALS OUTSIDE THE UNITED STATES; ATTACK ON A FEDERAL
FACILITY RESULTING IN DEATH

FAZUL ABDULLAH MOHAMMED

Aliases: Abdalla

Fazul Abdullah Mohammed remains on the FBI's most wanted list as ringleader of the US Embassy attack.

These attacks immediately united different radical groups behind Bin Laden, and established him as their dominant leader. He gained cult status and valuable new recruits, money, and prestige. On a practical note, US missile strikes against two independent Muslim states also ensured that the Taliban allowed Bin Laden to remain in Afghanistan, where his position had previously been precarious.

The al-Qaeda attacks on the US embassies in East Africa were deliberately designed to provoke President Clinton into bombing Afghanistan.

See also: *Enron's Collapse p.128*

Late 1990s
THE FUNDING OF THE
TALIBAN

The Taliban was funded by both Pakistan and the Saudis, in conjunction with Osama Bin Laden

The Taliban was a parochial movement in Afghanistan with limited knowledge of the outside world. It did not invite Osama bin Laden into the country, but it could not have continued without him or without military and financial support from a variety of foreign countries.

The conspiracy theory

The Pakistani and Saudi secret services colluded to keep the Taliban in power.

The evidence

By 1996, the Taliban had captured Kabul, but Mullah Omar, its leader, had not actually invited Bin Laden into the city. The Taliban had control of most of the country but real power was vested in local tribal groups and their support was tenuous. From his base in the east of the country, Bin Laden began to use the same methods that he had in Sudan to consolidate his position. He extended his power base by constantly praising Mullah Omar and offering him unconditional financial support. He poured money into the Taliban coffers and at the same time offered multiple straightforward sweeteners to Afghans, including several hundred second-hand Toyota estate cars, which he distributed to the families of Taliban members who had died in the fighting. This largesse was gratefully received.

Saudi Arabia, meanwhile, donated millions of dollars to help prop up the Taliban. After the House of Saud had agreed to allow US troops into Saudi Arabia following the first Gulf War, King Fahd had been forced to make political concessions to large numbers of discontented groups within his borders. It had been necessary, in particular, to increase the authority of the local Wahhabi religious police in the country. In a reciprocal move, it was this same religious police which now helped to create the Taliban's Ministry for the Propagation of Virtue and Suppression of Vice. The Saudis felt that this financial and political aid would help secure their position both at home and in Afghanistan, as well as making them generally more popular in the Arab world.

Mullah Omar met Prince Turki ibn Faisal ibn Abedlaziz, the head of the Saudi secret services, in June 1998, as part of a secret deal to hand Bin Laden over for trial in Saudi Arabia. After the US bombings on training camps in Afghanistan, however, Mullah Omar reneged on his promise. Prince Turki threatened to withdraw Saudi donations to the Taliban coffers, but this simply infuriated the mullah, who accused him of collaborating with the US. There was little the Saudis could do to maintain their position apart from continue to donate funds.

Pakistan, meanwhile, had its own reasons for supporting the Taliban. Small cells of radical Muslims were now active in the more lawless parts of the country, stoking up anti-government aggression and attacking places of public entertainment. Almost all the Pakistani radical groups now had offices in Kabul and most of the training camps were instructing Pakistanis. Publicly, Pakistan complained about this militarization of its alienated youth. In reality, though, it was pouring funds into the Taliban's military training camps because it had run out of fighters for its own territorial disputes. The militants trained in Afghanistan were now being used by the government to fight as paramilitaries against India in Kashmir. Hundreds of Afghan-trained Pakistani fighters were employed in Operation Kargil in 1999 and Pakistani troops made great inroads into Kashmir.

It was not a coincidence, therefore, that Pakistan, the UAE, and Saudi Arabia were the only three countries which recognized the Taliban as the legitimate government of Afghanistan. A former senior Pakistani civil servant stated that, in Afghanistan: "The US provided the weapons and the know-how, the Saudis provided the funds, and we provided the training camps for the Islamic Legions in the early 1980s and then for the Taliban."

The verdict

The Saudis supported the Taliban because they believed they could use the group to take control of Afghanistan, the Pakistanis because they were short of manpower, and Bin Laden simply because he needed somewhere to live.

The USS *Cole* after the attack in the port of Aden, Yemen, which crippled the ship and killed 17 sailors.

October 12th, 2000
USS COLE WAS BLOWN UP BY ISRAELI SECRET SERVICES

Mossad, not al-Qaeda, was behind the attack on the USS *Cole* in order to portray Yemen in a negative light

On October 12th, 2000, a small boat packed with explosives powered into the side of the USS *Cole* as it was anchored off the coast of Yemen. It killed 17 US sailors as well as the two bombers, who saluted as they plowed into the ship's side.

A variety of internet sites soon claimed that the bomb, known as D4, was so sophisticated it must have been produced by either the US or Israel. Mossad, the Israeli secret services, had been worried about improving American–Yemeni relations and had, it was argued, planned the attack in order to paint Israel's enemies in a negative light. Yemeni police, however, soon arrested six men, all of whom had fought in the Afghan war. The suspects' leader told investigators that he had trained in Osama bin Laden's "Jihad Camp No. 1" in Afghanistan and had been following specific telephone instructions from an al-Qaeda commander in Dubai. Satellite records confirm that the suspects made dozens of calls to known Bin Laden associates in Africa during this period. One member of the FBI team which arrived in Yemen within hours said that he had seen evidence of links between the suspects and Saudi Arabia but was unable to investigate further as his team had been asked to leave Yemen in order to protect international relations.

The USS *Cole* was blown up by al-Qaeda operatives.

September 11th, 2001
US GOVERNMENT KNEW ABOUT
9/11 ATTACKS IN ADVANCE

The US government had reasons for allowing the
World Trade Center attacks to proceed

At the height of New York's morning rush hour on Tuesday,
September 11th, 2001, a hijacked plane flew straight into
the north tower of the World Trade Center. As smoke and
flames poured from the building and rescue workers struggled to save those trapped inside in what was initially
assumed to be an accident, a second plane hit the south
tower. As both towers collapsed shortly afterwards and the
death toll rose, it became clear that the US had just suffered its worst terrorist attack.

The conspiracy theories

Numerous theories have sprung up around the attacks on
the World Trade Center but each revolves around the idea
that the US government either planned the attacks or simply allowed them to happen in order to advance its own
foreign policy agenda in a bid to control the world's fuel
supplies by invading oil-rich countries.

The evidence

The conspiracy theorists argue that American wealth and
power, and in particular the wealth and power of the Bush
clan, were directly threatened by the exhaustion of the
world's oil supplies. Once it became clear to the administration that Afghanistan was the best possible location for
a natural gas and oil pipeline to supply the US with all the
recently available, ex-Soviet fossil fuels from the Caspian
Sea, it was imperative for President George W. Bush to invade and control Afghanistan. The US would then also have
a monopoly on the export of fuel to massive new markets in
East Asia. Popular support for an invasion of Afghanistan
would be considerably greater if "the enemy" could be
shown to have committed an atrocity on US soil. President
Bush, Dick Cheney, and an "energy task force" were also
convening almost daily meetings in 2001 to try and rescue
Enron, the troubled fuel company which was one of the
Republican Party's biggest backers. Energy from the Caspian
Sea might help Enron recover some of its losses, as with access to the Caspian Sea it could transfer its interests away
from oil and into natural gas.

Much of the evidence, however, suggests that the 9/11
attacks were in fact orchestrated by hardcore al-Qaeda
members in Afghanistan, in collaboration with members of
a self-supporting al-Qaeda cell in Hamburg led by an
Egyptian called Mohammed Atta. At Hamburg University,
Atta met Marwan al-Shehhi from the UAE, Ziad Jarrah from
Lebanon, and Ramzi bin al-Shibh from Yemen. The four men
rented a flat and, according to German prosecutors, by mid-
1998 the "Hamburg cell" was fully formed. The university
granted them a "prayer room" into which they installed a
telephone and a computer. German intelligence reports suggest that the group then travelled to Afghanistan to get
financial help for a plan they were hatching, evidence for
which lies in internet records and flight simulators. Other
sources state that the Hamburg computer merely contained
a few computer games. The cell's arrival in Afghanistan,
meanwhile, was mutually fortuitous. In late 1999, al-Qaeda's
strategists had decided to carry out a spectacular attack on
the US mainland; the Hamburg cell had a partially developed plan but needed $500,000 to effect it.

By July 2000, the entire Hamburg cell was in the US except Ramzi bin al-Shibh, who could not obtain a visa. He
selected a Frenchman called Zacarias Moussaoui to replace
him. It is confirmed that al-Shehhi opened a joint current
account with Mohammed Atta at SunTrust bank in Florida
and that a total of $109,500 was transferred into this from
Dubai. In the meantime Moussaoui had joined a flying
school in Minnesota, where he registered as Zuleiman Tango
Tango. He failed his pilot's examination and, by August
2001, he was arrested for immigration offences. He later
confessed to membership of al-Qaeda but denied any participation in 9/11. He asked for a satellite link to conduct
a defence interview with Bin al-Shibh, who was in custody
in Pakistan, but this was turned down on the grounds of
national security.

A leading al-Qaeda official, Khalid Shaikh Mohammed,
gave al-Jazeera a long interview after 9/11 in which he confirmed that, between April and June 2001, a number of
Saudi volunteers had arrived in the US. They were selected
as it was relatively easy for Saudis to obtain visas. Satellite
data records that, at 3am on August 29th, 2001, Atta called
Bin al-Shibh in Hamburg and confirmed the date of the attack. Following this call, al-Shibh vacated the flat.

Between 7.58am and 8.42am on September 11th, 2001,
four planes left three different East Coast airports and were
hijacked by a total of 19 Arab-speaking men. The black
boxes record that the first plane crashed into the north
tower of the World Trade Center at 8.35am and the second
into the south tower half an hour later (the other two planes
headed for the Pentagon and Pennsylvania). Some 3,000
people are thought to have died as a result of these attacks.

The New York skyline fills with smoke as the second terrorist plane hits the south twin tower of the World Trade Center on September 11th, 2001.

This pattern of activity was in keeping with previous radical Islamic policy. In 1993, Ramzi Yousef had led an attack on the World Trade Center. In 1994, he had planned to hijack a plane and fly it into CIA headquarters in Virginia, while Algerian terrorists had attempted to hijack an Air France plane and then fly it straight into the Eiffel Tower.

To support their views, conspiracy theorists also point to the fact that, after the attacks, Mohammed Atta's passport was found intact in around 1.6 million tons of debris in a matter of hours. So extremely fortuitous for the US investigating authorities was this that it must, they claim, have been planted. But it is the case that a number of other passports were also found intact in the rubble. Then there were the Arabic-language flight manuals left rather surprisingly in one of the hijackers' cars. Such manuals could have served

no useful purpose so late in the day and, it is suggested, must also have been planted deliberately in order to place the blame squarely on Islamic activists. There can be no answer to this accusation, however, as anyone who could confirm or deny it is now dead.

The verdict

The 9/11 attacks were carefully planned by al-Qaeda operatives, directed by Osama bin Laden. However, this does not mean that events did not also turn out extremely well for the US president and the American oil industry.

See also: *Ramzi Yousef was an Iraqi Agent p.20; Pentagon Attacked by Cruise Missile p.26; World Trade Center p.262*

September 11th, 2001
PENTAGON ATTACKED BY
CRUISE MISSILE

The Pentagon was hit by a cruise missile rather than hijacked Flight 77

Conspiracy theorists have suggested that Flight 77 never actually crashed into the Pentagon on September 11th, 2001, but rather that the damage was caused by a cruise missile fired by the US itself. Blame would be placed on al-Qaeda and the US would then have a perfect excuse to invade Afghanistan.

This hypothesis does not explain what happened to Flight 77, which took off from Washington DC that morning, even though it is claimed that photographs of the damaged Pentagon apparently show no evidence of a crashed plane. In addition, theorists suggest that it would be impossible for such a huge plane as a Boeing 757 to crash straight into the ground floor of the building and not damage its interior. Furthermore they say that no aeroplane debris was found and that there is no evidence of wing damage to the sides of the building.

The fact is that while Flight 77 appeared to hit the ground floor of the Pentagon, it actually crashed between the first and second floors. When the plane hit the building at 560kph (350mph), there was, of course, damage to all five rings of the Pentagon. Its limestone protective layer shattered but its internal protection, which had only recently been coated with reinforced steel, remained intact for another 35 minutes. It was designed, at great expense, to do just this. Basic aeronautical engineering also suggests that, at such speeds and in such heat, all identifiable pieces of aeroplane would have caught fire and burnt up instantly. The outer portions of the wings would also have snapped off on impact and similarly been reduced to ashes.

September 2001
AL-QAEDA TARGETS
LONDON'S DOCKLANDS

British government invented news of an al-Qaeda-style attack that was foiled by intelligence services

In March 2004, sources in Whitehall leaked information that British intelligence services had uncovered a plot to blow up Canary Wharf, in London's Docklands, possibly on the very same day as the 9/11 attacks in New York. Over 60,000 people work in Canary Wharf, which houses some of the world's leading banking corporations. Since December 1995, it has been owned by an international consortium which includes Canadian orthodox Jews and Prince Saud of Saudi Arabia.

Pakistani intelligence officers in Lahore had apparently arrested and then searched the computers of an al-Qaeda operative called Mohammed Khan. His job had been to encrypt and transmit messages between international al-Qaeda activists. One of the files contained detailed plans of Canary Wharf drawn from reconnaissance information and included vehicle height restrictions for the complex's underground car parks. Other details were sketchy and it was unclear how British intelligence was involved. Downing Street declined to comment.

This news broke at the very moment that the British government was unveiling plans for its new anti-terrorism laws. An atmosphere of fear was sure to help pass this legislation. The news would also improve government public relations, particularly as it was common knowledge that on 9/11 itself, instead of fighting terrorism, the UK had been playing host to one of the world's biggest international arms fairs – at Canary Wharf.

September 2001
INSIDE DEALING IN AIRLINE
AND INSURANCE STOCKS

The shrewdness of certain stock exchange trading suggests prior knowledge of the 9/11 attacks

Between September 6th and 7th, 2001, the Chicago Options Exchange received 4,744 "put options" that United Airlines shares would imminently fall. On September 10th, 4,516 of these bets were placed on the likelihood that the value of American Airlines shares would also fall. No other airline showed such brisk activity.

Two tenants of the World Trade Center, Morgan Stanley and Merrill Lynch, also saw extraordinary "put options" on their shares. In all, 12,215 bets were placed on the fall of Merrill Lynch's shares on the days immediately preceeding the attacks. The previous daily average had been roughly 250 "puts." The profit on this betting was $3.17 million and, after September 11th, the authorities investigated the possibility that traders had had prior knowledge of the attacks. The firm which was found to have placed most of the bets was Alex Brown, Inc. Until 1998, this company had been headed by "Buzzy" Krongard, who was now executive director of the CIA. The CIA might have informed Alex Brown of the attacks in advance or even planned them in order to make a profit.

The huge profits made on these bets remain unclaimed. Perhaps Alex Brown declined to take advantage of such a tragedy. Or perhaps the company was thwarted by the fact that the US stock markets were suspended for four days after September 11th and they could not cash in their profits before investigations began.

The coincidence of the connection and the potential profit seems highly suspicious.

2001
THE BUSH FAMILY AND AL-QAEDA

The relationship between the leading family in the US and al-Qaeda is involved and longstanding

George W. Bush's first business, Arbusto Energy, received $50,000 from a Texas businessman called James Bath. Bath was the sole US business representative of Salem bin Laden, the head of the Bin Laden clan and brother of Osama. By 1987, Arbusto had become Harken Energy Corporation and a further $25 million had been invested in the company via a transaction in Geneva. This was a joint venture between the Union des Banques Suisses and the Geneva branch of the Bank of Commerce and Credit International (BCCI), with whom James Bath also had extensive connections. The BCCI was the bank later accused of laundering money for clandestine CIA activities, including the funding of the Afghan Mujahideen.

The conspiracy theory

The Bush family has received billions of dollars of investment from the Bin Laden clan. This helps the Bin Ladens directly influence US foreign policy and funds al-Qaeda.

The evidence

By 1992, James Bath was under investigation by the FBI, accused of channelling Saudi money through Texan companies in order to influence US foreign policy. George W. Bush initially denied knowing James Bath, despite the fact that he had funded Bush's campaign to become governor of Texas. After Salem bin Laden died in 1988, another Saudi businessman called Khalid bin Mahfouz inherited his Houston portfolio. By April 1999, Khalid bin Mahfouz had been accused of transferring $3 million from a Saudi pension fund and into BCCI accounts in New York and London, which were linked to Bin Laden operations.

By the mid-1990s, meanwhile, George Bush Senior had begun working for the Carlyle Group. This was a $12-billion private equity company based in Washington DC and Bush was senior advisor to its Asian fund plan. James Baker, the former US defence secretary, was the firm's senior counselor and Frank Carlucci, President Reagan's defence secretary, was the chairman. The Carlyle Group built itself up into the US's 11th largest defence contractor. Bush Senior went to Bin Laden headquarters in Jeddah to represent the Carlyle Group at least twice. The Bin Ladens, alongside 11 other Saudi families, invested heavily in the Carlyle Group.

With George W. Bush in the White House, it was easy for Frank Carlucci, an old college friend of Donald Rumsfeld, to meet the secretary of defence on numerous occasions. They discussed the awarding of billion-dollar defence contracts to the Carlyle Group. These would directly benefit George Bush Senior and, therefore, President George W. Bush. Aside from the personal connections, the Carlyle Group was in an extremely strong position as it was also a leading contributor to President Bush's electoral campaign. Also on Carlyle's advisory board is Sami Baarma, director of a Pakistani institution called the Prime Commercial Bank, which is based in Lahore and owned by Khalid bin Mahfouz.

On the morning of September 11th, 2001, the Carlyle Group was holding its annual investor conference in the Ritz Carlton Hotel in Washington DC. Frank Carlucci, James Baker, George Bush Senior, and Shafiq Bin Laden, Osama's half-brother, all watched together as the attacks took place. By September 26th, the US army had signed a $665 million contract with a division of the Carlyle Group called United Defense Industries to develop a cannon called the Crusader. In October that year, the Carlyle Group filed to make UDI a public company and, when it was floated in December 2001, it made a profit of $237 million dollars in one single day. George Bush Senior retired from the board in October 2003 but still retains investments in it. The Bin Ladens have all discreetly bowed out.

In the aftermath of the World Trade Center attacks, President Bush was asked to appoint a chairman for the 9/11 Investigation Commission. He chose a man called Thomas Kean, whose business partner just happened to be a member of the Bin Laden family.

The verdict

The Bush family has extensive business links with the Bin Laden family. The Bin Ladens are still in contact with Osama and, therefore, with the al-Qaeda organization.

October 12th, 2002
THE BALI BOMBING

> The bombs were planted by the CIA to provoke a war
> in Iraq or the Indonesian army to invoke military rule

On October 12th, 2002, three bombs went off in Bali, killing 202 people but relatively few Americans. Some 12 hours earlier, the US embassy in Indonesia had issued a warning to US citizens to avoid public places. If the CIA was behind the bombs, it could blame Jemaa Islamiyaah – a splinter group of al-Qaeda. Investigations into the attacks would also allow the CIA, and more US troops, into Indonesia.

Alternatively, since the fall of Suharto, there was an increasingly tense power struggle going on between the Indonesian military (TNI) and the police. If the TNI could provoke terror on the scale of the Bali bombing, they could then arrive and re-establish order, making themselves more popular. In addition, al-Qaeda would not want to cause trouble in Indonesia when they were being hunted down in Singapore, Malaysia, and the Philippines.

In fact, a group of Islamic activists, based around Jemaa Islamiyaa, was probably responsible. Many of them were first-time activists of local origin and, therefore, banned from Bali's nightclubs, which they saw as part of the West's secular assault on the Islamic world. Jemaa Islamiyaa had received some help from senior al-Qaeda operatives in Afghanistan but, by 2002, there was no assistance left and only one member of the group had ever been to Afghanistan. Inconveniently for the US, the perpetrators of the Bali bombing were merely heavily influenced by al-Qaeda methods but were not members of al-Qaeda itself.

March 11th, 2004
THE MADRID BOMBS

> ETA, not al-Qaeda, was responsible for the train
> station attacks

On March 11th, 2004, ten bombs detonated simultaneously in and around Madrid's Atocha railway station, killing nearly 200 and injuring around 2,000. Spain had been one of al-Qaeda's declared targets since the day Prime Minister Aznar sent troops to Iraq as part of the Allied coalition. Upon hearing the news, the ruling People's Party at once realized that any suggestion of al-Qaeda involvement would be extremely detrimental to their election campaign so, moments after the bombings, its spokespeople began to make statements blaming ETA rather than any Islamic organization. Three days later, the People's Party lost the general election.

The conspiracy theory

The Basque separatist group ETA was really responsible for the Madrid bombings, but the left-wing Spanish media falsely blamed al-Qaeda so that the ruling People's Party would lose the forthcoming general election.

The evidence

Ex-Prime Minister Aznar soon started to claim that the Basque separatist group ETA was the real culprit behind the bombings. In order to save political face, he still felt the need to refute claims of deliberate deception. Police statements, however, continued to maintain that there was not a shred of evidence for any involvement outside the dozen Islamic radicals who had been arrested and the seven who had blown themselves up when surrounded by police a few weeks later. Aznar, however, continued to claim that the coincidences connecting ETA to the attacks were too numerous to ignore.

It was common knowledge that ETA had been planning attacks in the capital and had previously attempted to blow up trains. Intelligence suggested that they had the technology to use mobile phones to do so. It is also undisputed that police in the northern region of Asturias later tried to hide evidence that they had ignored a tip-off, just before the bombings, stating that local dynamite dealers had sold stolen explosives to Basque terrorists who intended to use them imminently. Al-Qaeda had not been mentioned but the dealers might have been trading simultaneously with both groups or with one on behalf of the other. It is also true that a vanload of ETA explosives was seized a few weeks before the attacks as it travelled along a route that coincidentally led to the Madrid bombers' hideout near Toledo. In addition, a car used in an ETA bombing two years prior to the Atocha incident was stolen from the very street in Asturias in which one of the dynamite dealers lived.

There were a number of very well-publicized reasons, however, why Spain was a prime al-Qaeda target. Prime Minister Aznar had been highly vocal in his support for the US-led coalition, both before and during the invasion of Iraq, and Spain had been specifically singled out as a terrorist target in statements made by Osama bin Laden before the war. Also, historically Spain holds a special place in the Islamic world, as it was once part of the Moorish empire.

On the other hand, al-Qaeda bombings had traditionally involved the suicide of the bomber, which was not the case here. Nor was Atocha station a particularly symbolic target, either financially or politically. It also true that the short-termism of the attacks – to affect the result of the

Spanish election – was unusual for a traditional al-Qaeda operation. It did, however, achieve the withdrawal of Spanish troops from Iraq. Most of the Moroccan bombers were later arrested and confessed that there had been almost no involvement from Bin Laden himself. This was certainly not a standard al-Qaeda operation and was so far removed from "hardcore" al-Qaeda activities as to barely qualify for connection to the organization.

The verdict

An autonomous radical Islamic group was responsible for the bombings. This autonomy merely proves, however, how diffuse, widespread, and hard to contain radical Islamic militancy has now become.

Present day
THE ATTACKS ON FORCES IN AFGHANISTAN AND IRAQ
Al-Qaeda is behind attacks in Afghanistan and Iraq

The Afghan war failed to achieve a single confirmed "kill" of an al-Qaeda member and Osama bin Laden has not been seen in person since November 2001 (although he appeared in a video released in October 2004). Though the Taliban regrouped after 2001, it consisted mainly of small units along the border with Pakistan, considerably weakened and with little popular support. Two-thirds of the original al-Qaeda leadership was probably eliminated and the group has been deprived of its permanent base. On the other hand, the mass exodus of members has now spread the methods of Islamic terrorism over the globe, creating a new and radicalized international network of militants. Many of these fled through Iran to northern Iraq and possibly settled there.

The conspiracy theory

Most of the attacks on troops in Afghanistan and Iraq are by insurgents unconnected to al-Qaeda. The UK and US governments try to disguise this as it implies the "War on Terror" has not simply failed but been counterproductive.

The evidence

The war in Iraq further increased the recruiting power and morale of a wide range of radical Islamic groups, of which Abu Musab al-Zarqawi's is reputed to be the most active. Al-Zarqawi, a Jordanian, was specifically cited by then US secretary of state, Colin Powell, as being a leading al-Qaeda member when he argued the case for the invasion of Iraq at the UN. CIA reports, said Powell, had indicated that

Al-Zarqawi was now in Baghdad. This implied that Saddam Hussein was working with al-Qaeda and justified the war.

Back in Afghanistan, Al-Zarqawi had never worked with al-Qaeda but had run his own camp near Herat. After losing a leg during a US missile strike in 2001, he fled to Iran. US officials maintain he then moved to northern Iraq, where his job was to establish links between al-Qaeda and Ansar al-Islam – a group of Kurdish Islamists. Other intelligence suggests he was simply expelled from Iran and fled. A number of Al-Zarqawi's followers were soon arrested in Germany, where they stated unequivocally that Al-Zarqawi was not an ally but a rival of Osama bin Laden. They told German interrogators that their group had been created "especially for Jordanians who did not want to join al-Qaeda."

Once the war in Iraq began, Washington laid the blame for any number of spectacular suicide bombings, kidnappings, and assassinations on the al-Zarqawi group and so on al-Qaeda. The CIA believed with a "high degree of confidence" that it was Al-Zarqawi who had read the statement on a video of the beheading of Eugene Armstrong in September 2004 and that he had personally carried out the murder.

The $25-million bounty on Al-Zarqawi's head had increased after American authorities intercepted a letter in February 2004 which, they claimed, confirmed that he was working with al-Qaeda to drive the US out of Iraq. In it, the author described a plan to ignite sectarian violence in Iraq as a way to undermine the US troops. He claimed to already have undertaken 25 successful attacks against the enemy.

In March 2004, an apparent attempt to try and stir up civil war between Iraq's Shias and Sunnis began to emerge. Iraq's defence minister accused Iran of supporting al-Zarqawi, referring to them as "al-Qaeda in Iraq" and stating that Iran wanted "turbaned clerics to rule in Iraq." He knew that this was sure to appeal to both the US administration and its public. He claimed that, according to intelligence accounts, he now knew that the key to terrorism was Iran.

A body of evidence was rapidly building up against the US's next named target, despite the fact that al-Zarqawi's Sunni followers had never before chosen to seek help or model themselves on Shia Iran. It may be that the Iraq war has been so counterproductive that Sunni terrorist groups are now cooperating with Shia terrorist organizations against a common enemy – the US.

The verdict

To date, no evidence has emerged that any terrorist organization, operating in either Afghanistan or Iraq, is directly related to al-Qaeda.

Death has been used as an extreme solution to a spectrum of problems from the very start of human history. Genesis, the first book of the Bible, rapidly followed the creation of the world and the expulsion of Adam and Eve from the Garden of Eden with its first murder – the assassination of Abel by his brother Cain.

From that biblical point onwards, and for the rest of recorded time, murder for material, religious, or political gain has been the option to be used when all others failed, or proved themselves too difficult or inconvenient.

Mercifully, murder, most of the time, has always been viewed as a somewhat radical means to an end; not something that is undertaken lightly. Even today, killers still use euphemism for their chosen trade or profession. Victims are "whacked," "rubbed out," "liquidated," "disappeared," "sanctioned," "terminated with extreme prejudice," "subjected to executive action," or "sent to sleep with the fishes." The most bloodthirsty tyrant or the most deviously ruthless conspirator still hesitates to speak plainly about implementing the death of another human being. Joseph Stalin, the despot who ruled the USSR through the first half of the 20th century, came closer than most when he cynically declared: "One death is a tragedy. A million deaths is a statistic."

The natural order

For many centuries, assassination was primarily the sport of kings. The slaying of a king, queen, or any hereditary nobleman was not only the death of an individual but it could also change lineage and threaten dynasties. In a political system where power was handed down from father to eldest son or daughter, and marriages were arranged to cement alliances, reinforce treaties, or combine rival families, assassination was nothing more than the other side of the same coin. The murder of the royal father, or the son and heir, changed the inherited order and could rearrange the affiliations of nations. England's Henry VIII took eight wives, and either divorced or executed them because not one was able to bear him a son. Richard III fought and won the first phase of the Wars of the Roses for the House of York, but found himself a distant sixth in line for the crown. His only way to gain ultimate power was to murder or have murdered all who stood in his way until he finally ascended the throne, and it would take another war to bring him down.

The political order

When democratic elections replaced the rule of hereditary monarchs, the basics of assassination did not cease to be a political last resort, but the reasons for the kill profoundly changed. The coming of the ballot box meant that death ceased to be the only way to remove an unpopular or unsuitable ruler. Prime ministers and presidents could, sooner or later, be voted out of office, and no son or daughter would automatically rule in his or her place. Although some would claim that royal conspiracies and assassinations continue today, citing the conspiracy allegations that have surrounded the 1997 deaths of Princess Diana, Dodi Fayed, and driver Henri Paul in the Place de l'Alma tunnel in Paris, and how they might have been the work of the British secret intelligence service MI6 with the collusion of French officials. Diana, having divorced Prince Charles, was already an inconvenient woman, and the thought that she might further embarrass the House of Windsor by marrying/being pregnant by Fayed was – in the opinion of Prince Philip, the prime suspect in most conspiracy theories – too unthinkable for her to be allowed to live.

For the most part, though, assassination became the expedient tool of those in a democracy who were in too much of a hurry to wait for an election, and of any group who distrusted the will of the people and wanted to circumvent the process and impose a minority agenda. A prime, 20th-century example of such a negation of democracy happened in Chile in 1973, when Chilean president Salvador Allende appeared to be leading his country too swiftly in the direction of socialism for the tastes of some of his generals, and also those of the Nixon administration and the Central Intelligence Agency in the United States. Unwilling to wait for an election, or to take the chance that the Chilean people might not vote Allende out of office, a palace coup was implemented. Allende died as tanks and infantry stormed the presidential palace, and Chile was subsequently ruled by a military junta led by General Augusto Pinochet for almost two full decades. This was a repressive dictatorship that tortured and "disappeared" thousands of its citizens.

The JFK labyrinth

In Chile in 1973, the objective of the assassination was clear for all to see. The only question has ever been about the degree of US involvement in the coup d'état that removed Allende. When, however, the conspiracy of assassins is more covert and shadowy, even their ultimate goals remain a matter for speculation. This was certainly the case in the death of President John F. Kennedy. The truth has been so well concealed and the facts have become so blurred in what has to be the most famous assassination of the 20th century, almost every part of it remains open to question. All we know for sure is that the president of the United States was shot dead, a little after noon on a sunny November day, while riding in a motorcade in an open-topped limousine through the city of Dallas, Texas. As the angry and seemingly insoluble debate continues to rage as to whether Kennedy was slain by Lee Harvey Oswald, the supposed lone gunman, or by the Mafia, or by a shadowy power elite of his political enemies and their allies in the intelligence community, we are left totally unable to see the purpose of his death, because we have no way of really knowing what might have been had Kennedy lived. Some theorists claim that the Kennedy administration, had it continued, would have avoided the US's costly 12-year involvement in the Vietnam war. But we cannot be sure, and indeed, we may never know, as the hope that one or more of JFK's killers will finally make a deathbed confession grows fainter with the passage of time.

In his 1991 movie *JFK*, director Oliver Stone has one of his characters state a simple rule for at least tentatively deciding who or what was behind a political assassination. Ask the question "who benefits?" Like or dislike Stone and his work, and agree or disagree with his politics, the usefulness of the question cannot be disputed. Once the question "who benefits?" has been answered, one at least has a working hypothesis of the "why" of an assassination if maybe not the full and complete "wherefore." History records that Philip II of Macedonia was stabbed to death by his lover Pausanias, at a lavish farewell feast before leading combined Greek armies on an invasion of Persia. Not unlike Lee Harvey Oswald, Pausanias was immediately killed before he could reveal the motive behind his crime. It might have been a lovers' quarrel, but history, invoking Stone's simple test, has always blamed the murder on Philip's son Alexander. With his father dead, it was Alexander, later known as Alexander the Great who led the Greeks into Persia, brought down the Persian empire, and went on to conquer the known world, while Philip remained little more than a footnote in history.

Who benefits?

The only problem with the principle of "who benefits" is that, in some cases, the concept of "benefit" may only really exist in the mind of the assassin or the conspiracy behind his actions. When a tubercular student called Gavrilo Princip shot the Archduke Franz Ferdinand in Sarajevo, in June 1914, it has always been assumed that he was protesting at the Austro-Hungarian occupation of Serbia. If this was the case, the long-term results were a long way from anything Princip may have intended. His executive action touched off a chain of events that rapidly involved Britain, France, Germany, Italy, Russia, the United States, plus numerous far-flung colonies, and sparked off the bloody carnage of World War I, causing the deaths of tens of millions, and such peripheral upheavals as the Russian Revolution, and the rise of fascism in Italy and Nazism in Germany. "Benefit" may also be an abstract concept like revenge, as it would appear to be in the case of the assassination of US president Abraham Lincoln. Although some more material reasons have been advanced by Lincoln conspiracy theorists, the weight of evidence would appear to indicate that John Wilkes Booth and his co-conspirators were seeking revenge for the defeat of the Confederacy in the Civil War by the Lincoln-led Union. Wilkes and the other plotters may have hoped that the slaying of Lincoln would inspire the exhausted South to carry out a desperate and spontaneous uprising, and a fresh round of hostilities, but the real outcome was a fast death for Booth, the slightly slower trial and execution of his associates, and far harsher treatment of the Southern states during the period known as Reconstruction. To paraphrase the Rolling Stones, assassins don't always get what they want.

Madman or murderer?

In this modern age of mass media, what the assassin wants may also prove so intangible that it can only be categorized as madness. In 1973, Arthur Herman Bremer shot – but failed to kill – Alabama governor George Wallace because he wanted to be famous. In 1980, and 1981, scarcely three months apart, Mark David Chapman shot dead former Beatle John Lennon, because he thought Lennon had become a phoney, and John Hinckley attempted to kill President Ronald Reagan because Hinckley had a crush on the movie actress Jodie Foster, and wanted to impress her. All three seemed to be playing out the "lone nut" role that – rightly or wrongly – has been assigned to killers like Oswald in the shooting of JFK and to Sirhan Sirhan

Lee Harvey Oswald is arguably the most notorious figure in the history of assassinations.

in the later murder of the younger Kennedy brother, Bobby. In the latter half of the 20th century, so many assassinations have been committed by "lone gunmen," or "lone nuts," that a large section of the public have ceased to believe this explanation, and the death of any prominent figure is immediately surrounded by conspiracy theories. (In the death of JFK, polls have revealed that only 30 percent or less of the American public believe that Oswald acted alone.) Not only do conspiracy theorists refuse to believe any lone-nut story without considerable forensic and psychiatric evidence, but they even charge that, since the end of World War II, the intelligence community has devoted years of effort and millions of dollars to highly secret research – like that of the CIA's MKULTRA operation – to the creation of plausibly deniable, mind-controlled assassins (known as Manchurian Candidates) and techniques to make a murder look like a suicide. This last idea has even given rise to the verb "suicided" as a part of conspiracy jargon.

The Mafia

The labyrinthine complexity of political assassination – with its drugs, poisons, brainwashing, and spy satellites looking down from the edge of space, makes the machinations of another section of society, where murder continues to be a prime stock in trade, seem comparatively homely. While the public watches movies like *The Godfather* and TV shows like *The Sopranos*, organized crime, aka the Mafia, goes about its often lethal business with little need for elaborate smokescreens, convoluted cover stories, or hypnotized hit men. When, in 1985, Big Paul Castellano was murdered outside Sparks Steak House in Manhattan, it seemed that no-one in the entire city of New York entertained any doubts as to who was responsible. Walk into any tavern and the overheard gossip made it clear that mobster John Gotti had organized the hit in cahoots with a gang of discontented young wiseguys, and was now the new boss of the Gambino crime family. The problem for prosecutors was to prove this to a jury (and a jury that had not been tampered with by Gotti and his men). This piece of Mafia business was so smooth and uncomplicated that it almost made one nostalgic for those ancient times when, in order to get rid of Julius Caesar, a group of senators simply whipped out their daggers and stabbed their victim to death on the floor of the Senate.

Conference Room Technique

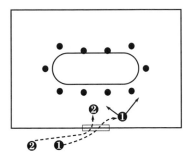

❶ Enters room quickly but quietly.
❷ Stands in doorway.

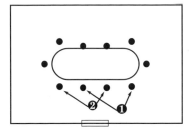

❷ Opens fire on first subject to react. Swings across group to centre of mass. Times burst to empty magazine at end of swing.

❶ Covers group to prevent individual dangerous reactions, if necessary, fires individual bursts of rounds.

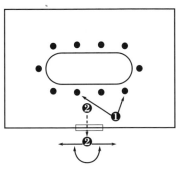

❷ Finishes burst. Commands "Shift". Drops back through door. Replaces empty magazine. Covers corridor.

❶ On command "Shift", opens fire on opposite side of target. Swings to include whole group.

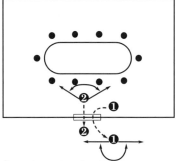

❶ Finishes burst. Commands "Shift". Drops back through door. Replaces magazine. Covers corridor.

❷ On command "Shift", re-enters room. Covers group. Kills survivors with two-round bursts. Leaves propaganda.

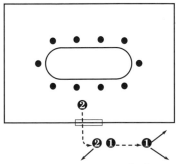

❷ Leaves room. Commands "Go". Covers rear with nearly full magazine.

❶ On command "Go", leads withdrawal, covering front with full magazine.

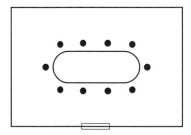

A page from the 1954 CIA assassination manual showing how two men can enter a room and kill everyone inside without killing each other.

1323 BC
TUTANKHAMUN
b. 1341 BC/1340 BC, Egypt
d. 1323 BC, Egypt
    Pharaoh of the 18th dynasty of Egypt

Tutankhamun is best known to the modern world as the only Egyptian pharaoh whose tomb has been discovered almost intact – and for the wealth of art treasures and other objects the tomb contained. While still in his teens, "King Tut" ruled at a time of massive religious upheaval and political intrigue. He succeeded the pharaoh Akhenaten, who had attempted what is now called the "Amarna" revolution, in which he tried, by royal edict, to supplant the existing priesthood and gods and convert the entire country to the worship of a single sun god.

On ascending to the throne, Tutankhamun's task was to restore the old pantheon of gods together with their temples, but he died at about the age of 19. It is likely he was assassinated: X-rays of his mummy show an injury to his head – a dense spot at the lower back of the skull, maybe a subdural hematoma. If the young pharaoh was murdered, his successor Ay, a commoner and a former advisor, is the logical culprit. Ay may have thought that the return from monotheism was not happening sufficiently quickly, and perhaps wanted to control it directly himself. To strengthen his claim, Ay appears to have married Tutankhamun's widow Ankhesenpaaten and, maybe out of a sense of guilt, arranged for the creation of the Boy King's lavish tomb. Ay ruled Egypt for four years, consolidating the return to the old religion.

336 BC
KING PHILIP II
b. 382 BC, Pella, Macedonia
d. 336 BC, Pella, Macedonia
    King of Macedonia

An ambitious father and an even more ambitious son can prove to be a fatal combination. Philip II is best known to history as the father of Alexander the Great, but although the son would conquer the known world, the father would achieve the previously impossible task of conquering Ancient Greece and unifying the warring city states against the threat from the Persian empire. The only real opposition to Philip was from the city of Athens. The Athenians temporarily halted him at Thermopylae in 352 BC but, after 14 years of intermittent warfare, Philip finally defeated an alliance of Thebans and Athenians at Chaeronea in 338 BC, and forced the creation of the League of Corinth, a federation of Greek states pledged to wage war on Persia. After two years' preparation, Philip was about to embark on his invasion of Persia when he was assassinated by a servant/lover named Pausanias, who stabbed Philip during a vast and lavish farewell feast for the departing armies. Pausanias was immediately killed before he could reveal his motive, but it is likely that the assassination was engineered by Alexander, perhaps aided by his mother, Philip's estranged wife Olympias. The reason for the assassination? So Alexander, rather than Philip, could be the one to lead the Greek armies to glorious victory against the Persians.

44 BC
JULIUS CAESAR
b. 100 BC, Rome, Italy
d. 44 BC, Rome.
    Roman emperor

An assassination that is planned to achieve a specific political objective often produces results that are completely the opposite of what the assassins or conspirators intended. The most famous example of this must be the dramatic, Ides of March assassination of Gaius Julius Caesar in 44 BC. Caesar's killers claimed that they were protecting the Republic from Caesar's alleged monarchical ambitions, but instead of returning Rome to democracy, the murder sparked a series of civil wars that marked the end of the Roman Republic and the start of the Roman Empire.

As a military leader Caesar defeated the Gauls in what today is France, extended Roman territory all the way to the Atlantic, and even launched the first Roman invasion of Britain. When, under pressure from the Senate and his major rival Pompey (who feared his power), Caesar was ordered to disband his army, he did the unthinkable and took his troops directly into the city of Rome, triggering a civil war that he fought, and won. This victory made him undisputed master of Rome and, effectively, dictator for life. He began extensive reforms of Roman society, and centralized the government of the weak Republic. But, believing that Caesar's form of dictatorship was little short of absolute monarchy, Gaius Trebonius, Decimus Junius Brutus, Marcus Junius Brutus, and Gaius Cassius Longinus decided that the only way to restore power to the people of Rome was to assassinate him. Caesar was duly stabbed to death at a meeting of the Senate, sustaining 23 stab wounds before falling, dead, at the foot of a statue of his life-time rival, Pompey.

AD 41
CALIGULA
b. AD 12
d. AD 41
Roman emperor

When a ruler has absolute power, assassination may be the only way to remove him, or her. History has condemned Caligula (Gaius Caesar Germanicus) as one of Rome's worst emperors, although lately this verdict has been somewhat mitigated by accounts of a childhood during which he was a mascot for the Roman army, and an adolescence in which he feared for his life during the infighting over who would succeed the ageing Emperor Tiberius. When Tiberius died in AD 37, the Roman Senate proclaimed Caligula Emperor, but not before Tiberius's young grandson, Tiberius Gemellus had been murdered, and Caligula's grandmother Antonia had committed suicide. Caligula was happily accepted by the people of Rome simply because he was a descendant of Julius Caesar, and a great-grandson of Marc Antony.

Although he initially attempted to reform the Imperial tax system, he quickly lapsed into the excesses that have become legend: how he made his horse Incitatus a senator, his incest with his sister Drusilla, his elaborate orgies, his "war" with the sea god Neptune, and his attempt to declare himself a deity. After three years and ten months in power, Caligula's own Praetorian Guard conspired against him. He was trapped in a corridor and stabbed by Cassius Chaera. Caligula's wife Caesonia was also killed, along with their infant daughter Julia Drusilla, whose head was smashed against a wall. His elderly uncle Claudius was then declared Emperor by the very same Praetorian Guards who had assassinated his 28-year-old nephew.

453
ATTILA THE HUN
b. 406, probably somewhere in Hungary
d. 453 probably near Belgrade
King of the European Huns

For 1600 years, the rumour has persisted that Attila the Hun was murdered, almost certainly because most found it hard to believe that anyone dubbed the "Scourge of God" could die of anything so prosaic as a drunken nosebleed, as was suggested by the historian Priscus. At the height of his powers, Attila was the absolute ruler of a vast territory that stretched from Central Europe to the Black Sea and from the Danube River to the Baltic, and his nomadic Hun horsemen struck fear into both the Eastern and Western Roman Empires. He invaded the Balkans twice, marched through France as far as Orleans and, moving south into Italy, he drove the Emperor Valentinian III from his capital at Ravenna. In 452, advancing on Rome, Attila finally halted at the River Po, where only a personal plea by Pope Leo I (and, according to legend the direct intervention of Saint Peter and Saint Paul) convinced him to turn back – although an epidemic among his troops may also have been a contributing factor. In 453, Attila was planning an assault on Constantinople when he died during a wedding feast celebrating his marriage to a Goth woman named Ildico. Although the nosebleed story is the most popular, it is possible that Attila was stabbed, either by one of his numerous other wives, or as part of a conspiratorial power grab by one of his three sons, Ellak (his appointed successor), Dengizik, and Ernak who would fight over, and ultimately destroy, the nomad empire that Attila left them.

1090
HASAN-I SABBAH
b. 1034, Yemen (?)
d. 1124, Iran
Leader of the Hashasheens

According to legend, Hasan-i Sabbah performed executions with his private army of heavily drugged young killers, the Hashasheens, who were transformed into highly efficient assassins through a combination of ritualized hashish-smoking and brainwashing.

Most serious research has shown that the so-called Hashasheens may have started out in the 8th or 9th century as brigands on the medieval Silk Road to the Far East. It was a time when the Islamic Middle East was under pressure from the crusaders from the West and Mongol invaders from the East, and the simple bandits gradually evolved into a militant religious cult of Ismaili Muslims. Their own name for the sect was *al-da'wa al-jadßida* which means the "new doctrine," and they called themselves *fedayeen* "one who is ready to sacrifice their life for a cause." (The term used today by fundamentalist "suicide bombers.") The group used murder as a way of maintaining the balance of power in the area, but were careful to kill only the individual who had been targeted, without causing any other collateral casualties. They therefore favoured a close kill, and their weapon of choice was a dagger.

The conspiracy theory

Stories of Hasan-i Sabbah – "The Old Man of the Mountain" who wielded deadly political power from his stronghold at Alamut in the hills of Northern Iran – go back thousands of years. According to legend, a would-be assassin was subjected to the same rites as other mystery cults in which the subject was made to believe that he was in imminent danger of death. Hassan's followers drugged their recruits to convince them that they were "dying," but later had them awakened in a garden where they feasted in the company of attractive young women, leading them to believe they were actually in heaven, that Hasan was in direct contact with God, and that his orders should be followed, even to death. Ever since, the Hashasheens, having given the world the word assassin, have been favourites of conspiracy theorists, who believe that their organization provided a model for the Knights Templar; the Priory of Sion, the Freemasons, and the Rosicrucians.

The evidence

Contemporary sources indicate that the real reputation of the Hashasheens was created in 1090 when Hasan-i Sabbah established his mountain stronghold. His initial aim was to destroy the Abbasid Caliphate of Baghdad, a dynasty that was marked by perpetual strife but also noted for its scientific knowledge, support for the liberal arts, and a love of luxury that offended opponents such as Hasan-i Sabbah.

At first the assassins were largely sectarian, and most of their victims were Sunni Muslims, but soon they were inspiring fear out of all proportion to their power, and became a shadowy threat that put all power elites in the area on their guard. It also seems that they were prepared to accept commissions to carry out assassinations, to order, for money. Records indicate that they may even have staged assassinations for Christian crusaders such as Richard the Lionheart and Conrad of Montferrat. The power of the Hashasheens was destroyed by the Mongol warlord Hulagu Khan in 1256. Sadly, during the Mongol assault, the library of the sect was destroyed, and thus much information about them was lost.

The verdict

The story of the Hashasheens is shadowy, but there is little doubt that they represented a formidable force in the Middle East in the 13th century. The idea that smoking hashish made them what they were, on the other hand, is plainly absurd. Hashish has many properties, but not even the staunchest foes of marijuana would claim that it can turn the user into a suggestible, homicidal zombie. The ex-

plorer Marco Polo claimed to have visited Alamut in 1273, and describes the drug being used in the programming of Hasan's followers. However, Polo's reliability is questionable as other accounts allege that Alamut was destroyed by the Mongols in 1256. At the same time, this is not to say that Hashasheen training techniques did not employ religious hysteria, drugs, and sex.

See also: *MKULTRA p.143; Knights Templar p.243; The Priory of Sion p.246; Rosicrucians p.283; Society of Jesus p.283; Freemasons p.284*

1327

EDWARD II

b. 1284, Caernarvon, Wales
d. 1327, Berkeley Castle, England
King of England

The head that wears the crown is always uneasy, but when the heir to the throne fails to measure up to his predecessor, his head is even less easy. King Edward II of England, the son of Edward I, was a ruthless but powerful king, popularly known as "Longshanks" and the "Hammer of the Scots," who conquered Wales, kept Scotland under English domination, and institutionalized anti-Semitism to avoid paying debts. The son, however, was too weak to hold the kingdom together, preferring instead the company of a coterie of young men, giving rise to rumours that he was homosexual.

By 1311, England had come under the control of a committee of barons, who constituted an early form of Parliament. In-fighting immediately broke out among rival factions of the nobility and, to complicate matters, the Scottish King Robert Bruce defeated Edward II's army at the Battle of Bannockburn and regained Scottish independence. In 1326, Edward's wife Isabella took matters into her own hands and, with a group of powerful barons led by Roger Mortimer of Wigmore, imprisoned Edward in Kenilworth Castle, and forced him to give up the crown. Unfortunately, the position of Isabella and Mortimer was too precarious to leave the deposed king alive. Edward was removed from Kenilworth and secretly put to death on September 21. The popular legend is that a red-hot poker was the murder weapon, thrust up his anus through a hollow tube. Apart from the obvious and brutal symbolism of this method of assassination, there would have been a practical reason for killing Edward in this way: it would show no outward signs of violence. It was announced that Edward had died a natural death. He was buried in St Peter's Abbey, Gloucester.

1400
GEOFFREY CHAUCER
b. 1343,

d. 1400, exact locations unknown

English author, philosopher, diplomat, and poet

To have friends in high places may not always be an advantage. Geoffrey Chaucer is best remembered as the author of *The Canterbury Tales*, a collection of stories told by fictional pilgrims on the road to Canterbury Cathedral. His other works include *Troilus and Criseyde*, the *Parlement of Foules*, the *House of Fame*, and *Chanticleer and the Fox*. Having travelled extensively in Europe, he also translated a number of contemporary works from French and Italian. To survive as a writer in the 14th century invariably required the ability to attract aristocratic patronage and Chaucer would appear to have been quite skilled at this, ultimately coming under the protection of King Richard II, with an income from the post of Comptroller of the Customs for the Port of London. Unfortunately, when Richard was deposed by his cousin, Henry Bolingbroke (later Henry IV), and placed in Pontefract Castle, to be starved to death, many of those under his patronage suffered similar fates.

Terry Jones (of *Monty Python* fame, and now a bestselling popular medievalist) makes the case that Chaucer, who vanished in the same year as Richard (1400) would, as the former king's poet (and as his prime propagandist, in 14th-century terms) have been one of the first on any list of those

Chaucer may have been the victim of the wrong sort of royal patronage.

to be liquidated by Henry and the cabal of nobles led by Archbishop Thomas Arundel, who ushered in an era of repression that Jones compares to "Russia under Stalin." Chaucer's fate may have been further sealed by the possibility that he acted as Richard's personal spy during his European travels, or simply because, in *The Canterbury Tales*, Chaucer ridiculed the Church. He is buried in Westminster Abbey, London. In 1556 his remains were transferred to a more ornate tomb in the Abbey, making Chaucer the first writer interred in the area now known as Poets' Corner.

1450
ASSASSINATIONS OF THE RENAISSANCE

In Carol Reed's 1949 acclaimed film, *The Third Man*, Orson Welles, who plays the unscrupulous Harry Lime, aptly if rather cynically sums up the Italian Renaissance: "*In Italy for 30 years under the Borgias they had warfare, terror, murder, bloodshed – but they produced Michelangelo, Leonardo da Vinci and the Renaissance. In Switzerland they had brotherly love, 500 years of democracy and what did that produce – the cuckoo clock!*"

The golden age of the conspirator
The Italian city states of the 15th and early 16th centuries were under the control of powerful, competing families. This has prompted the drawing of comparisons with the 20th-century Mafia, but this hardly does justice to the ruling families of the Italian Renaissance. Although both were organized on principles of family power – and both used assassination to enforce that power – today's Mafia work according to a basic framework of shared rules that at least contain the worst possible excesses of its members. However, the Renaissance families such as the Medici, the Orsini, the Colona, and the notorious Borgias actually made the law in their city-states. At times they even controlled the Church, and various members of each family made themselves pope. They also had armies at their disposal that turned 15th-century Italy into a theatre of continuous invasion and siege warfare.

The Medici family, who ruled Florence, used banking as their power base with their most important client being no less than the Catholic Church. The Medici bank collected ten percent of earnings for the church. If anyone defaulted on a debt or failed to keep up the payments, they faced excommunication. Lorenzo de Medici (1449–92) – "Lorenzo the Magnificent" – first shared power with his younger

Portrait of Cosimo de Medici by Pontormo. Italian Renaissance families wielded incredible power.

adventurers, assassins, prostitutes and informers; murder and robbery were committed with impunity, heretics and Jews were admitted to the city on payment of bribes, and the pope himself shamelessly cast aside all show of decorum, indulging in dancing, stage plays and indecent orgies." Constantly at war and constantly in need of funds, Rodrigo began a series of papal confiscations, and any cardinal, nobleman or official who was known to be rich would be accused of some offence, then imprisoned, frequently murdered, and his property seized. His victims included Cardinal Michiel, who was poisoned, Cardinal Orsini, and even Troccio, who had previously been one of the family's most faithful assassins.

Rodrigo's son Cesare Borgia (1475–1507), did all he could to emulate his father, and his absolute and deadly pragmatism was greatly admired by Niccolo Machiavelli, who knew him personally. Machiavelli used many of Cesare's tactics as examples in his classic book *The Prince*. Among these tactics was the murder of the Duke of Bisceglie, Cesare's half-sister's husband, when the marriage ceased to be of political advantage. The sister in question was Lucrezia Borgia (1480–1519), the daughter of Rodrigo Borgia and his mistress Vannozza de Cattanei. By the time she was 11, Lucrezia had been betrothed twice. She was reputed to be an expert poisoner who wore a hollow ring which she used frequently to poison drinks. Her brother Cesare was also alleged to be the father of one of her children.

But like the Medici, the Borgia's were also leading patrons of the arts, and artists such as Michelangelo and Leonardo da Vinci worked in their courts. Without them, the world today would be a very different place.

See also: *Niccolo Machiavelli p.178*

1533
ATAHUALPA
b. 1500
d. 1533, Cajamarca, Peru
12th and last Incan emperor of Peru

The Spanish conquest of South and Central America has always posed the question of how a relatively small number of European adventurers and mercenaries could overthrow large, well-organized native empires. The simple answer has always been that the Spanish had superior weapons and the element of surprise, but other factors may also have to be considered, including internal strife and outbreaks of smallpox unknowingly carried by the invaders from Europe.

brother, Giuliano then, after his brother's assassination, became sole ruler. Lorenzo is known to history for his patronage of the arts, supporting both Leonardo da Vinci and Michelangelo. Other members of the family were famed for less noble pursuits. Lorenzo's brother, Giuliano de'Medici, impregnated his mistress before his brutal murder in 1478. Their child, Giulio de'Medici, was later crowned Pope Clement VII. Clement took a black slave girl as a mistress and their child, Allessandro, became the first black head of state when he was made Duke of Florence in 1530. But he was stabbed to death after an argument over a woman. The tastes of Giovanni de' Medici (1475–1523), who became Pope Leo X, were exotic even for the times. When the new pope entered Florence in triumph, he had a young boy painted gold from head to toe; he was paraded through the streets as a symbolic herald of a new golden age, but the boy died shortly afterwards, poisoned by the paint on his skin. Meanwhile, Catherine de'Medici, who became Queen of France, monitored the intrigues of her court via a network of attractive young courtesans.

No family, however, was equal to the Borgias in ruthlessness. Originally from Aragon in Spain, Alfonso Borgia elected himself as pope, taking the name Calixtus III, and his nephew Rodrigo 1431–1503, became Pope Alexander VI in 1492. Under Rodrigo, Rome "swarmed with Spanish

Certainly the politics of the Incan empire contributed to the downfall and death of Atahualpa, the last Incan emperor of Peru. When the gold-hungry Spanish arrived under the command of Francisco Pizarro, Atahualpa had just concluded a costly and protracted civil war with Huayna Capac, his half-brother and rival to the throne. This, on the other hand, hardly condones the behaviour of the Spanish. When they arrived in Peru, Atahualpa met peacefully with Pizarro and his men in the town of Cajamarca; there, believing the Spanish might be gods, he arranged a lavish feast in the town square for them. Thousands of native nobles and soldiers came to meet the visitors, and Pizarro's troops, with the aid of horses and cannons, took this opportunity to slaughter their hosts. Atahualpa was captured alive and held for ransom. The emperor himself offered to fill a large room with gold, and two smaller rooms with silver, in exchange for his release. Pizarro agreed. Couriers came from all parts of the empire to fill the rooms with treasure worth an estimated $100 million today. Having collected the ransom, Pizarro broke his word and had Atahualpa executed on August 29th, 1533. According to legend, a last-minute conversion to Christianity saved Atahualpa from being burnt alive, and permitted him a more humane death.

1593
CHRISTOPHER MARLOWE
b. 1564, Canterbury, England
d. 1593, Deptford, England
British playwright

Christopher Marlowe is one of the most mysterious figures in all of English literature. During his life he was suspected of atheism, blasphemy, subversion and homosexuality when all were capital crimes. He is a major contender for being the "real" author of Shakespeare's plays. It was also rumoured that he was an Elizabethan "James Bond," working for the highly efficient English spy network run by Sir Francis Walsingham. Claims are made that while still studying at Cambridge University, he took time off to carry out a secret mission for the government. Marlowe began writing plays after leaving Cambridge; *Tamburlaine the Great*, his first play, was performed in London in 1587. This was followed by *The Jew of Malta*, *The Tragical History of Doctor Faustus*, *Edward II*, and a number of others. Marlowe's mysterious death in Deptford in Eleanor Bull's house, when he was stabbed in the eye by his friend Ian Frizer – nominally over who should pay a bill – may have had a political cause. Research suggests that he was murdered by an agent of Walsingham, for reasons unknown, or that his death was faked so that he could work anonymously as a spy again. This idea is strengthened by the fact that Marlowe was buried two days later in an unmarked grave, while his killer pleaded self-defence and quickly received a pardon from Queen Elizabeth I.

See also: *Walsingham and Mary Queen of Scots p.268*

1606
GUY FAWKES
b. 1570, York, England
d. 1606, London, England
Mercenary and conspirator

Four hundred years after the event, the exposure of Guido Fawkes and his "Gunpowder Plot" are still celebrated in England with fireworks every November 5th. It was on that day in 1605 that a group of Catholic conspirators attempted to blow up the staunchly protestant King James I, plus all members of both branches of the English parliament while they were assembled for that year's formal opening. The plotters had filled a cellar under the House of Lords with sufficient barrels of gunpowder to reduce it and a number of surrounding buildings to rubble. They believed that the death of James, plus all of his ministers and senior clergy, would help them to return England to Catholicism. The plot, however, was discovered and Fawkes, a mercenary soldier and explosives expert who had fought on the Catholic side in Europe's sectarian wars, was arrested as he was about to set the fuses. He was taken to the Tower of London where, after two days of torture, he revealed the names of his co-conspirators – Robert Catesby, Thomas Percy, John Wright, Robert Keyes, Thomas Wintour and Robert Wintour. After a very swift trial, the plotters were hung, drawn and quartered in the Old Palace Yard in Westminster.

1865
ABRAHAM LINCOLN
b. 1809, Hardin County, Kentucky
d. 1865, Washington DC
US president

Abraham Lincoln was shot dead by actor and Southern sympathizer John Wilkes Booth while watching the play *Our American Cousin* at Ford's Theatre, Washington DC.
On April 9, 1865, Union General Ulysses S. Grant accepted the surrender of Confederate forces by General Robert E.

Lee at Appomattox. The Civil War was over and slavery was duly abolished in the US. Five days later, in Washington DC, the president who had led the North to victory through the agonizing and bloody conflict was dead. This killing of "Honest Abe" – a national hero – changed the path of history in ways that cannot even be imagined. It certainly slowed any healing process between North and South, and traumatized the nation in the 19th century much as the assassination of President John F. Kennedy did in the 20th.

The conspiracy theories

The details of Lincoln's murder are not in dispute. Any debate about the Lincoln assassination concerns the nature and extent of the plot. The major theories are as follows.

The first theory is that Wilkes Booth was the leader of a small band of co-conspirators. Booth was motivated by his racist fury at Lincoln's plans to extend voting rights to certain blacks. The second theory is that Lincoln was killed as part of a conspiracy of Confederates who refused to accept Lee's surrender and who wished to rekindle hostilities. The third is that Lincoln was killed at the behest of a cartel of international bankers whose loans to finance the Civil War he had declined. Booth was only the "hired gun." The fourth theory is that Secretary of War Edwin Stanton masterminded the assassination. He was against Lincoln's Reconstruction policies and wanted more radical reprisals against the South. Again, Booth was simply the "trigger man."

The evidence

On the afternoon of April 15th, 1865, after a drink in an adjoining saloon, Booth entered the theatre and made his way to the State Box where Lincoln and his wife were sitting with Clara Harris and Henry Rathbone. Booth opened the door to the State Box, shot Lincoln in the back of the head at near point-blank range, struggled with Rathbone, and then jumped approximately 3.5m (11ft) to the stage below, breaking his leg, but still yelling *Sic Semper Tyrannis* ("As Always to Tyrants") to an audience of more than 1,000. Booth escaped and Lincoln would never regain consciousness. Pausing only for a Dr Mudd to set the bone in his leg, Booth headed south. Federal authorities caught up with him at Garrett's Farm, Virginia. Booth hid in a barn, and this was promptly set on fire by the pursuers. Before he could give himself up, he was shot dead by Sergeant Boston Corbett.

A diary that was found on Booth's body, and other evidence, left no doubt that Lincoln's assassination was the work of a conspiracy by Booth, plus Samuel Arnold, Michael O'Laughlen, John Surratt, Lewis Powell, George Atzerodt,

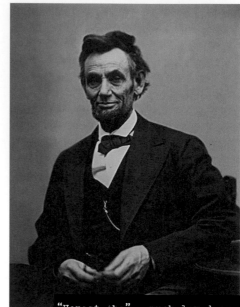

"Honest Abe" – much-loved president and victim of John Wilkes Booth.

David Herold, and perhaps Dr Samuel Mudd and Mary Surratt, whose boarding house they used for their meetings. Within days, all Booth's co-conspirators were arrested, except for John Surratt who escaped to Canada. They were tried by a military tribunal, and found guilty. Mary Surratt, Powell, Atzerodt, and Herold were all hanged on July 7th, 1865. Dr Mudd, O'Laughlen, and Arnold were given life in prison, but since that time the legitimacy of the convictions of Mary Surratt and Dr Mudd have often been challenged. One year earlier, the same group had concocted a never-to-be-realized scheme to kidnap Lincoln, take him to Richmond (the Confederate capital), and hold him in return for Confederate prisoners of war.

The verdict

Even after 140 years, the debate shows no signs of being resolved. The standard history text is that Booth and his gang killed Lincoln as some grandiose payback for the Confederate defeat, and no hard records of the plot extending beyond the group survive, but much hinges on the motives of John Wilkes Booth. These, however, are obviously now unknowable, and his death and the haste of Federal authorities to try and execute the assassins made investigation of wider links impossible.

1881
JAMES GARFIELD
b. 1831, Cuyahoga County, Ohio
d. 1881, Elberon, New Jersey
US president

James Garfield was the first left-handed president, and the second US president to be assassinated and, with little exaggeration, these have always been his main claims to fame. Elected as a political compromise, he held office for just six months and 15 days, and most of his term was devoted to internal Republican party politics.

His assassin, Charles J. Guiteau, shot him because he had been passed over for the post of US consul in Paris and he believed Garfield was involved in a conspiracy to keep Guiteau out of public office. Garfield didn't even die immediately. One of Guiteau's bullets lodged in Garfield's back and could not be found, and he lingered for more than two months before succumbing to infection. (Inventor Alexander Graham Bell devised a metal detector in an attempt to find the bullet, but it was thwarted by a metal bedframe.) Garfield might even have lived had his doctors not been totally inept – they punctured his liver while hunting for the bullet. Guiteau was found guilty of assassination, despite claiming insanity as a defence, and was sentenced to death. He was hanged on June 30th, 1882 in Washington DC, and the case seemed to be closed.

Then, 100 years later, David Icke, and others who see the dread hand of the Illuminati in everything, blamed that all-pervasive secret society for the assassination. They claim that, under the guise of making modest civil service reforms, Garfield had planned to take over the Federal Reserve – and thereby control of the US economy, as the Federal Reserve, and not the president, regulates interest rates and money supply, and this had been in the hands of the Illuminati since the founding of the US.

1881
BILLY THE KID
b. 1860 location unknown
d. 1881, Old Fort Sumner
US Western outlaw

As civilization came to the Old West, many of the original desperadoes were systematically eliminated. Billy the Kid, also known as William Bonney or Patrick Henry McCarty, might have remained one of the many unknown frontier outlaws in the American South West had he not been involved in what became known as New Mexico's Lincoln County War. The violent vendetta between cattle barons William Tunstall and John Chisum, and the merchant monopoly of J.J. Dolan and John Riley was extensively reported in the eastern press. The Kid, one of the quasi-legal Regulators fighting in the pay of Tunstall, was presented as a romantic figure.

Shootings and arson ran unchecked throughout 1878, including the murder of Billy's patron William Tunstall, until retired Union general, Lew Wallace (probably best remembered for his book *Ben-Hur*), became territorial governor and attempted to restore order by proclaiming amnesty for those involved in the conflict. Unfortunately a combination of the Kid's own recklessness and the political interests of the Lincoln County Ring, who preferred to see him dead, exempted Billy from a pardon. With extreme irony, a former friend, Sheriff Pat Garrett was sent to bring him to trial. Billy was captured after a brief siege at aptly named Stinking Springs, and was then sentenced to hang by Judge Warren Bristol. Billy escaped from the town jail at Mesilla, killing guards James Bell and Bob Ollinger in the process.

Tracking Billy to the ranch of Pete Maxwell in Old Fort Sumner, Garrett staged a night ambush. The Kid's last words were *"Quién es? Quién es"* (Who is it? Who is it?), before Garrett fired two shots killing him outright.

1890
SITTING BULL
b. 1831, Grand River, South Dakota
d. 1890, Standing Rock Reservation, South Dakota
Native American leader

Even a defeated enemy can continue to pose a threat. Sitting Bull ("Tatanka–Lyotanka"), Lakota medicine man and chief, was generally considered the last of the Sioux nation to surrender to the US government and, as such, was viewed by whites with deep distrust. Although a legendary figure in the Native American battle against white expansion into the Western United States, Sitting Bull did not participate in the resistance until late in the struggle. After the 1868 gold rush into the Black Hills broke the Treaty of Fort Laramie, which was designed to protect Indian lands, he had his famous mystic vision that correctly foretold the crushing defeat by the Lakota of the 7th Cavalry under General George Armstrong Custer. Although victorious against Custer, Sitting Bull and his people could not stem the tide of white settlers, and in the harsh winter of 1881, he finally gave himself up to the US army. He was held prisoner for two years before he was moved to the Standing

Rock Reservation although, in 1885, officials allowed him to tour Europe with Buffalo Bill's Wild West Show.

The rapid emergence (and huge popularity) of the Ghost Dance cult among Native Americans in 1890 spooked the US authorities – the ceremony promised to rid the land of white people and restore the Indians' way of life – and the Indian agents called for troops. Fearing that Sitting Bull would join the Ghost Dancers, 43 Lakota policemen burst into his cabin at Standing Rock before dawn on December 15th, 1890, and dragged him outside. His followers gathered to protect him, and in the ensuing gunfight, one of the Lakota policemen put a bullet through Sitting Bull's head.

1901
WILLIAM MCKINLEY
b. 1843, Niles, Ohio
d. 1901, Buffalo, New York
US president

William McKinley, a two-term president who led the country into the Spanish-American war, was shot at point-blank range by a young anarchist, Leon F. Czolgosz, on September 6th, 1901 while meeting and greeting well-wishers at the Pan American Exposition in Buffalo, New York. McKinley died eight days later. Czolgosz would appear to have been attempting to emulate his hero Gaetano Bresci, who had murdered Italy's King Umberto a year earlier. When Czolgosz was arrested, police found a folded newspaper clipping about Bresci in his pocket. He was tried, and sentenced to death, becoming one of the first victims of the newly introduced electric chair. His last words were "I killed the president because he was the enemy of the good people – the good working people. I am not sorry for my crime."

Although McKinley's death is usually viewed as part of the wave of anarchist violence at the start of the 20th century, some evidence points to a higher level of organization than Czolgosz on his own would have been able to achieve. For example, why was McKinley's security chief, Charles Foster, moved from his usual position, next to the president? And how was Czolgosz able to be in exactly the right place at the right time when McKinley's meet-and-greet was a spur-of-the-moment decision? And, finally, how was Czolgosz able to move (carrying a gun) through more than 80 police, secret service, and military personnel? Either the anarchist movement of the time was more pervasive, connected, and efficient than we have ever been led to believe, or other – unknown – political forces were at work.

1914
FRANZ FERDINAND
b. 1863, Graz, Austria
d. 1914, Sarajevo, Bosnia
Archduke of Austria; heir to Austro-Hungarian throne

The assassination by Gavrilo Princip of the Archduke Franz Ferdinand and his wife Sophie Duchess of Hohenburg on June 28th, 1914 in Sarajevo, in Austrian-occupied Bosnia-Herzegovina, was the spark that ignited World War I. Before the drama that resulted from Franz Ferdinand's assassination had played out, 9 million soldiers had died, millions more civilians had lost their lives or livelihoods, monarchies had been destroyed, and the entire power-structure of Europe had been turned on its head. Historians even suggest that World War I was nothing more than the first phase of a single conflict lasting from 1914 to 1945. Had the Archduke not been the nephew of Emperor Franz Josef I of Austria and next in line to the crown, the repercussions of his death might not have engulfed the world; but unfortunately for those millions of people, he was.

Franz Ferdinand had come to the throne following the suicide of his more flamboyant cousin Crown Prince Rudolph, who had allegedly battered his mistress to death before killing himself. Gavrilo Princip was a tubercular and a somewhat inept revolutionary, but his Serbian connections were enough to precipitate an Austrian declaration of war against Serbia, a war that then dragged in the other nations of Europe.

The conspiracy theory
That the assassination of Franz Ferdinand was organized by members of "Young Bosnia" and the notorious criminal/political Black Hand – the Serbian nationalist mafia – is hardly disputed. That any of the conspirators anticipated that the horror of World War I would be precipitated by their single bullet is highly unlikely.

The evidence
The crowds thronging the streets of Sarajevo for the June, 1914 visit of the Archduke provided ample cover for six Serbian assassins, members of revolutionary youth organization, Young Bosnia, an offshoot of the Black Hand – the Serbian nationalist mafia. These boys from Young Bosnia were equipped with pistols and bombs supplied by the Black Hand, and also cyanide capsules so they wouldn't be taken alive. The four cars carrying the Archduke and his party passed them at approximately 10.15am. One assassin threw

his bomb, but the Archduke saw it and tossed it away (it landed in a car behind, injuring several of his entourage). Meanwhile, believing the attack to have failed, one of the Serbians, Gavrilo Princip, had made his way to Schiller's, a café nearby. Next, by what seemed to be a miracle, the Archduke's limousine appeared right in front of the café – the driver had taken a wrong turn. Princip pulled out an automatic pistol and fired two shots from close range. One bullet struck Franz Ferdinand in the neck, the other hit the Duchess in the stomach. Both died within 30 minutes. Princip tried to kill himself with his cyanide pill, but vomited the poison up, and the police wrestled his gun away from him before he could shoot himself. Princip would later die in jail of TB.

From the moment of the fatal shot, coupled with an explosive political situation in the Balkans, a machine-like complexity of long-established treaties and alliances ground into action. Armies mobilized as though to a railway timetable. France, Germany, Great Britain, Russia, Italy, and Belgium all became involved; Japan and Turkey took sides, and only the US would remain aloof, at least until 1917. Imperial powers brought their empires into the conflict and battles were fought as far apart as Togoland, and New Guinea. The final irony was that the shooting, which had triggered the subsequent horror, only happened because of an extraordinary coincidence.

Franz Ferdinand, Archduke of Austria. His assassination sparked off the beginning of World War I.

The verdict

Princip had no real idea of what he might be starting, but once his Serbian connections had come to light, it was all Austria needed to declare war on Serbia. The spread of the conflict truly became an inevitable sequence of events that no-one could prevent. The bullet Princip fired at the Archduke – "the bullet that started World War I" – is on show in Konopi Castle in the town of Konopi in the Czech Republic.

See also: *Rasputin p.43*

1916
RASPUTIN
b. 1869–71 (?), Tyumen, Siberia
d. 1916, St Petersburg
   Russian mystic

The so-called "Mad Monk" Grigori Yefimovich Rasputin may not have caused the Russian revolution that ended the autocratic monarchy of Tsar Nikolai II and gave birth to the USSR, but he was certainly a symbolic figure in the upheaval, and his murder did nothing to slow down the process.

Over the centuries, the vast expanse of Russia spawned hundreds of *starets* (religious pilgrims) who existed on the fringes of the Orthodox Church. Some claimed to be psychic, others to possess healing powers; many were charlatans, and a few plainly crazy. Rasputin may well have been all of the above, as well as being a drunkard and lecher, with a deft theological line about divine grace through acts of sin that worked remarkably well on a large number of women, from peasant girls to society ladies. What really separated Rasputin from the average *starets* was his ability to penetrate the highest levels of Russian society.

Although nicknamed the "Mad Monk," Rasputin never held holy orders. His early life is shrouded in mystery, and exactly how his reputation as a healer reached Tsar Nikolai II and his wife, Tsaritsa Alexandra, is a matter of speculation. Their only son, Tsarevich Alexei, the heir to the throne, suffered from hemophilia, and the tsaritsa, who was both desperate and something of a religious extremist, summoned Rasputin in 1905, as a last resort in an attempt to save her son. Although his methods have long been disputed, it cannot be denied that Rasputin did help the tsarevich, and very quickly he became part of the royal circle, with Alexandra describing him as "a man of God," and "a religious prophet" – she completely ignored his drunken sexual rampages. Even before World War I, Rasputin's profound influence on a weak tsar and his superstitious wife was distrusted on all levels of society, but once Russia was at war with Germany, the tsarina, who was of German descent, became increasingly loathed by the people.

The conspiracy theory

It is more proven fact than theory that, when rumours spread that Rasputin and Alexandra were sleeping together, Prince Felix Yusupov, Vladimir Purishkevich, and the tsar's cousin, Grand Duke Dmitri Pavlovitch Romanov, finally resolved to murder Rasputin, maybe with the help of the British Secret Service. It has also been suggested that Rasputin had been "planted" at the court of the tsar by outside forces to weaken and discredit the monarchy.

The evidence

On the night of December 30th, 1916, the plotters threw a party for Rasputin in St Petersburg, serving him wine and cakes laced with cyanide. He ate and drank well but proved unnaturally hard to kill. When the cyanide failed, the plotters shot him three times in the chest, back and head, then beat him with an iron bar. They tied him, still struggling, in a sheet and dropped it into the frozen River Neva, where he finally drowned. But the assassination came too late to avert the October revolution of 1917. Within three months Nicholas II had been overthrown and, on July 16th, 1918, the tsar and his family were executed in Yekaterinburg by a detachment of Bolsheviks led by Yakov Yurovsky. In the early 1990s, following the fall of the USSR, the bodies were located, exhumed, formally identified, and reinterred in the Romanov family crypt in St Petersburg's Peter and Paul Cathedral on the 80th anniversary of the execution.

The verdict

Books and movies have woven a larger-than-life legend around Rasputin, who was a larger-than-life figure. No evidence exists, however, that he was in any way manipulated from the outside. If anything, his progression through the ranks of society only serves to confirm the cultural isolation and ignorance of the Russian aristocracy at the beginning of the 20th century. Even that he was supernaturally hard to kill seems be borne out by independent witnesses. Like Gavrilo Princip who set the spark for World War I by assassinating Archduke Franz Ferdinand in Sarajevo, Rasputin was an individual who played a pivotal role far beyond his apparent capacity to influence history.

See also: *Franz Ferdinand p.42*

1922
MICHAEL COLLINS
b. 1890, County Cork, Ireland
d. 1922, County Cork, Ireland
   Irish revolutionary leader

Even when revolution has been achieved, assassination can become a tool in the power struggle between the victors. Following the 1916 Easter Uprising in Dublin, Michael Collins and Eamon de Valera emerged as the leading figures in the IRA armed resistance to British rule in Ireland. Initially allies and then rivals, the two men became bitter enemies during the 1922 Irish Civil War between factions that supported the Anglo-Irish Treaty of 1921, which had established the Irish Free State, and those who opposed it. Collins, originally the IRA "hard man," who created a special assassination squad called The Twelve Apostles to kill British agents, had negotiated the treaty as a necessary compromise, while de Valera so opposed the deal, under which Northern Ireland remained under British rule, that he attempted to establish his own rival government. Fighting broke out in the spring of 1922 and Collins, as head of the newly formed National Army, was forced to crush de Valera's insurgents, first in Dublin and then in the countryside. Collins himself became the victim of anti-Treaty militants when at *Beal na mBlath* (Gallic for "the Mouth of Flowers") in County Cork, he was shot dead in an ambush. Collins must have foreseen the possibility. When signing the disputed treaty with the British he remarked. "I may have signed my actual death warrant."

1923
PANCHO VILLA
b. 1878, Durango, Mexico
d. 1923, Chihuahua, Mexico
   Mexican revolutionary and folk hero

Pancho Villa was an illegitimate peon, bandit and outlaw, who nevertheless came to play a vital role in the series of revolutions that rocked Mexico in the early years of the 20th century. In 1911, he used the power of his guerrilla army to make Francisco Madero president but, in the next shift of power, the military junta under General Huerta sentenced him to death. In 1916 US president, Woodrow Wilson, sent 12,000 troops, led by General John J. Pershing, into Mexico to apprehend Villa, but to no avail. Pershing telegraphed his failure to Washington – "Villa is everywhere, but Villa is nowhere." Villa, also known as Francisco Villa or José

Doroteo Arango Arámbula, depending on the account, remained elusive until 1921, when the Mexican government accepted his surrender and retired him on a general's salary. However, on July 20th, 1923, Villa was killed when his car was riddled with bullets while driving back from a christening in Parral, Chihuahua. A local politician named Jesus Salas Barraza took credit for masterminding the plot to kill Villa, but the incoming president, Plutarco Elías Calles, has always been the prime suspect, and the gunmen certainly used government-issue ammunition. The theory is that Calles feared Villa might enter legitimate politics as he was already practicing a form of cooperative socialism on the land that he had been given in Durango as part of his "retirement" settlement.

1929
THE ST VALENTINE'S DAY MASSACRE

The St Valentine's Day Massacre of 1929 is credited to Al Capone as part of his Chicago mob war to eliminate George "Bugs" Moran and his gang. The groundwork for the spectacular killing was undertaken by Capone's lieutenant, Jack "Machine Gun" McGurn. McGurn's plan was to lure Moran and his top men to a warehouse on Clark Street with an offer he could not refuse – in this case, a load of bargain hijacked whiskey. A team of Capone's killers would then enter the building disguised as policemen, appear to arrest Moran and his men, but then kill them. McGurn himself would be safely elsewhere, and Capone would conveniently be "on vacation" in Florida.

Unfortunately, the plan misfired. The Capone crew drove up to the warehouse in a stolen police car at around 10.30am on February 14th, 1929. Seven of Moran's men (plus an ophthalmologist who happened to be in the wrong place) were lined up against a wall in the garage of the S-M-C Cartage Company and shot. Moran, however, got away. He had been approaching the warehouse, but the arrival of Capone's "cops" in their police car had scared him off. The dead men were James Clark, Frank and Pete Gusenberg, Adam Heyer, Johnny May, Reinhardt Schwimmer and Al Weinshank.

The widely held assumption has always been that the murders could not have been accomplished without the complicity of the notoriously corrupt Chicago police, and that the latter may have even supplied the uniforms and vehicle used in the massacre. A year later, the tommy guns used in the St Valentine's Day Massacre were found in the

Michigan home of professional hit man Fred Burke, but Burke was never extradited to Illinois for trial – supposedly because he might have implicated the police who were in on the conspiracy.

1935
HUEY LONG
b. August 3rd, 1893, Winnfield, Louisiana
d. September 10th, 1935, Baton Rouge, Louisiana
 US politician

Huey Pierce Long, a powerful, Depression-era populist politician (governor of Louisiana, then senator) was assassinated by Carl Weiss in the Louisiana Capitol building in Baton Rouge.

Populism can be a dangerous business, and the US has never seen a greater populist than Huey Long. Known as "The Kingfish," a name borrowed from the popular radio show *Amos 'N' Andy*, Long's radicalism and massive consolidation of power in the state caused many to accuse him of attempting to set up a personal dictatorship. Coming to power on the slogan "every man a king, but no one wears a crown," Long financed a wide-ranging programme of public works; over 19,000km (12,000miles) of road were paved, and education funding was greatly increased, all financed by increased taxes on the rich and big business. Although a vociferous champion of the underdog, Long was ruthless in his methods and so determined to have his own way that he frequently bypassed state legislature, and made sure his own hand-picked loyalists controlled every level of the political system. He was the subject of an intensive IRS investigation after he increased annual state government expenditure three-fold and the state debt more than ten-fold. In 1929 he survived an attempt to have him impeached and in 1930 was elected to the Senate. While in Washington DC he continued to maintain effective control of Louisiana and even though he had no constitutional authority to do so, carried on pushing bills through the Louisiana legislature, which remained wholly controlled by his supporters. On September 8th, he was shot by Carl Weiss in the Capitol building at Baton Rouge. Weiss – the son-in-law of Judge Benjamin Pavy, a long-time political opponent of Long – was, in turn, immediately shot dead by Long's bodyguards.

Dr Carl A. Weiss, Jr, the Baton Rouge physician who shot and killed Senator Huey Long.

The conspiracy theories

The death of Huey Long set off the third most notable set of conspiracy theories in US politics after those surrounding the deaths of Abraham Lincoln and the Kennedy Brothers. Rumours persist that Weiss actually had no gun and only struck Long with his hand, and that the Senator had in fact been accidentally shot by his own guards when they opened fire on Weiss. Or perhaps the action of the guards was no accident? Had one or more of them been bought off by a conspiracy of some of the wealthiest men in Louisiana? For, in 1934, Long had created the Share Our Wealth programme, which proposed heavy new taxes on the super-rich; this provided more than sufficient motive to have him killed.

Franklin Delano Roosevelt also came under suspicion. Long had made vigorous efforts to combat the ravages of the Great Depression, and had started out as a vocal supporter of FDR; but when the Kingfish was not offered a federal post, he positioned himself to run against Roosevelt in the 1936 elections, announcing his bid in August, 1935.

The Kingfish also did not die at once, but lingered on for two days, finally succumbing to internal bleeding that many claimed was caused by the inept treatment provided by Long's attending physician, Dr Arthur Vidrine, who had failed to close Long's wounds properly after the shooting. Some theories take this further, claiming that Long would have recovered easily but was deliberately killed by his doctors.

The evidence

The primary, if scant, evidence in the case is the story repeated by the Pavy family that Weiss, enraged by a racial slur against his wife, was unarmed and only threw a punch at Long, hitting him on the lip. Carl Weiss did have a gun in the glove compartment of his car that was removed by Louisiana State Troopers. The story of Long being punched in the mouth is supposedly confirmed by a Mrs Melinda Delage, who was present at the Baton Rouge hospital when Long was brought in. She saw a cut on his lip and heard him tell a doctor "That's where he hit me." K.B. Ponder, an investigator for the Mutual Insurance Co., which insured Long, said he was in no doubt Long was killed by his own bodyguard, probably one Joe Messina, who covered Long's back.

The verdict

The politics of Louisiana are noted for their corruption, and in a context where the supposed assassin did not survive the assassination, and the State's most senior politician failed to receive adequate medical treatment, the almost complete lack of hard evidence means that, after 70 years, the question of who was behind the murder will never be answered satisfactorily. Long had made many enemies and any one of them could have commissioned his death. Certainly, those who benefited most obviously from Long's death were the state's wealthy elite – his death meant that Long's planned new tax on the rich never came into effect.

See also: *John Fitzgerald Kennedy p.54*

1940
LEON TROTSKY
b. November 7th, 1879, Yanovka, Ukraine
d. August 21st, 1940, Coyoacán, Mexico
Russian revolutionary

When a rival has been stripped of all power and forced into exile, it may still be safer to have him murdered to prevent any return, or to stop him becoming a focus for dissent. That was certainly the course of action taken by Stalin with regard to his arch-rival Leon Trotsky. Trotsky (born Lev Davidovich Bronstein) was a hero of the 1917 Bolshevik revolution. By 1920 he had risen to the post of people's commissar for foreign affairs and was recognized as the founder of the

Red Army. But he would prove the loser in a deadly power struggle with Stalin, after which he was expelled from the Communist Party and deported from the USSR.

After living uneasily in Turkey, France, and Norway, Trotsky settled in Mexico City (finding refuge for a while with the painters Diego Rivera and Frida Kahlo). In Mexico he wrote *The Revolution Betrayed* (1936), a scathing critique of Stalinism in which he argued that the Soviet state would either be overthrown or revert to capitalism. In May 1940 he survived an attack on his home by Stalinist assassins but, on August 20th in the same year, Soviet agent Ramón Mercader infiltrated Trotsky's home and killed him with an icepick as he sat at his desk. Mercader testified at his trial. "With my eyes closed, I dealt him a terrible blow on the head." Trotsky's house in Coyoacán is now a museum.

See also: *Joseph Stalin p.50*

1942
REINHARD HEYDRICH

b. March 7th, 1904, Saxony-Anhalt, Germany
d. June 4th, 1942, Prague, Czechoslovakia
German SS Obergruppenführer

Sometimes an individual is truly deserving of assassination – and none could be considered more so than Reinhard Tristan Eugen Heydrich. Nicknamed *The Butcher of Prague*, *The Blond Beast* and *Der Henker* (German for *the hangman*), Heydrich was handsome, arrogant, and homicidally ruthless; in all respects the ideal Nazi. An early and total devotee of Adolf Hitler, he rose rapidly in the party and ultimately became one of the main architects of the Holocaust, chairing the ultra-secret Wannsee conference at which the plans for extermination camps were first formulated.

In September 1941 he was appointed the Protector of Bohemia and Moravia, and – acting as a de facto dictator – often drove in an open car to demonstrate the complete subjugation of the Czech people. Unfortunately, for Heydrich at least, the Czechs were not as subjugated as he supposed. On May 27th 1942 he was killed by four British-trained agents of the Czechoslovak government-in-exile – Adolf Opalka, Josef Valcik, Jan Kubis, and Josef Gabchik.

Aware of Heydrich's flamboyant weakness for open cars, and knowing that he would be travelling on a particular road at a particular time, the hit team waited at a sharp bend on the route. As the SS Mercedes approached, Gabchik fired his Sten gun, but it jammed. Kubis then threw an anti-tank grenade at the car, severely wounding Heydrich. The Czech agents were pursued to a nearby church by Heydrich's guards, but managed to avoid capture by committing suicide. Heydrich later died in agony in a Prague hospital. Nazi retaliation for his assassination was savage. On June 10th, the village of Lidice, 22km (14miles) north-west of Prague, was burnt, and all males over the age of 16 were executed.

1943
WLADYSLAW SIKORSKI

b. 1881, Galicia, Poland
d. 1943, Gibraltar
Leader of the World War II Polish government-in-exile, assassinated by the Allies

In April 1943, just as the tide of World War II appeared to be turning, the Germans claimed that they had unearthed the graves of 4,300 Polish officers in Katyn Wood near Smolensk; the Germans said that the Poles had been taken prisoner and executed during the Soviet invasion of Poland in 1939. The International Red Cross confirmed that the victims had been killed with Soviet weapons, but the Soviet government – seemingly caught red-handed in a major atrocity – accused the Germans of fabricating the whole thing. Desperate to keep Russia in the alliance against Nazi Germany, the US and the UK accepted the implausible Soviet explanation, but the Polish government-in-exile, led by Wladyslaw Sikorski, totally refused to do so, and threatened to cause a disastrous rift among the Allies.

Sikorski was a hard line anti-communist who had fought the Soviets in 1921, during the Russian Civil War. He had been elected premier of post-World War I Poland, but was removed in a military coup in May 1926. Seen as too much of a right-wing radical, he was refused a command by the Polish army when Poland was invaded by Germany in September 1939. After the defeat, Sikorski escaped to London and established the Polish government-in-exile. In the wake of the Katyn massacre, and even under extreme pressure from Churchill and Roosevelt, Sikorski insisted that further relations with Russia were impossible. Then, in July 1943, just as matters seemed hopeless, he was killed in an air crash over Gibraltar, and was replaced by the less forceful Stanislaw Mikolajczyk. The timing of his death was so convenient for Britain, the US and USSR that rumours have persisted that the British Secret Service, on the orders of Churchill, conspired to arrange Sikorski's assassination.

See also: *Roosevelt and Churchill let Pearl Harbor Happen p.213; Churchill, Coventry, and the Enigma Secret p.225*

1945
ADOLF HITLER
b. April 1889, near Linz, Austria
d. April 1945, Berlin, Germany
Leader of Nazi Germany

When "Adolf Hitler" and "assassination" are mentioned in the same breath, the immediate thought is of the famous July 20th, 1944 bomb plot by senior army officers against the World War II Nazi fuhrer. Led by General Ludwig Beck, and inspired by the successful Allied D-Day landings in Normandy, the plotters planned to remove Hitler by blowing him up in one of his many headquarters. The actual planting of the bomb was delegated to Claus Schenk, Count von Stauffenberg, a combat veteran who had lost his left hand and fingers from his right hand fighting in Tunisia. After two failed attempts in Obersalzberg, von Stauffenberg smuggled a briefcase containing a bomb inside Wolfschanze ("Wolf's Lair"), Hitler's command post for the Eastern Front in Rastenburg, Prussia. Von Stauffenberg placed the bomb under a conference table and left. When the explosive detonated as planned, he and the other plotters believed Hitler was dead and prepared to seize Berlin. Unfortunately, Hitler was far from dead. He had been miraculously shielded from the blast by the heavy leg of the conference table and, although injured, was already issuing orders for revenge. Stauffenberg was subsequently shot but many conspirators tried to save their lives by informing. Erwin Rommel, who had been approached by the plotters but did not join, took poison. Eight of the conspirators were hung on meathooks and their death agony was filmed and shown to Hitler. Over the following nine months, before he committed suicide in his Berlin bunker, with the Red Army just streets away, Hitler used the July 20th plot as an excuse to destroy anyone in the army that he feared would oppose him.

The plot of July 20th was far from being the only attempt on Hitler's life. Throughout his political career, attempts had been made on his life. The following is a list of all the known assassination plots:

July 1921 shots were fired at Hitler during a rally at the Hofbräuhaus in Munich.
1923 shots were fired at his car in Leipzig.
March 1932 shots were fired at a train car in which Hitler, Joseph Goebbels and Dr Wilhelm Frick were riding in Munich.
June 1932 an ambush failed on a road near Stralsund.
30 July 1932 another attempt failed in Nuremberg.
March 1933 Kurt Luttner was arrested for planning to kill Hitler with a bomb at a rally in Köningsberg.
1933–4 at least ten attempts or plots came to the attention of the authorities, but no additional details are known.
1933 a man in a SA-leader's uniform was arrested and a gun was found on him in Obersalzberg.
1934 SA Chief Ernst Röhm and Julius Uhl allegedly plotted to kill Hitler, but this charge may have only been an excuse for Hitler eliminating them.
1936 Helmut Hirsch, a Jewish student, confessed to having been sent by Otto Strasser to kill Hitler with a bomb in Nuremberg.
1937–8 émigré groups mainly in Czechoslovakia, but also in Switzerland and the UK, plotted to kill Hitler, but nothing came of it.
November 1937 Josef Thomas, a mentally ill man from Elberfeld, was arrested by the Gestapo who claimed he had travelled to Berlin to shoot Hitler and Hermann Göring.
April 1938 Alexander Foote, an Englishman working as a spy for the USSR investigated the possibilities of assassinating Hitler, and succeeded in getting close to him in his favourite restaurant, Osteria Bavaria, in Munich without any problem.
1938 in Munich, Maurice Bavaud, a Swiss theology student, made several attempts to shoot Hitler, but failed and was arrested when trying to leave the country by train without a valid ticket.
1938–9 Colonel Noel Mason-MacFarlane, the British military attaché, investigated the possibilities of assassinating Hitler, but his ideas were rejected in London.
November 1939 in Munich, Georg Elser planted a bomb in the Bürgerbräukeller. Hitler left at 9.07pm and the bomb went off at 9.20pm, killing eight people
November 1939 Dr Erich Kordt, head of Joachim von Ribbentrop's personal secretariat, planned to kill Hitler in Berlin, the day before the planned offensive against France.
1939 Generaloberst Franz Halder, chief of the general staff, repeatedly went to see Hitler with a loaded gun planning to shoot him.
July 1940 Oberleutnant R. Fritz-Dietlof, Graf von der Schulenburg, and Dr Eugen Gerstenmaier planned to kill Hitler during the victory parade in Paris.
1943 General der Gebirgstruppen Hubert Lanz, Generalmajor Dr Hans Speidel, Oberst Hyazinth Graf Strachwitz planned to arrest Hitler when he visited the troops near Poltawa.
March 1943 Major Friedrich König planned to shoot Hitler during his visit to Smolensk.
Also March 1943 Generalmajor Henning von Tresckow, Leutnant Fabian von Schlabrendorff, and Oberst Rudolf-

Christoph Freiherr von Gersdorff placed a bomb disguised as a liquor bottle on Hitler's aircraft, a Focke-Wulf 200 Condor, but it failed to explode. Also Oberst Rudolf-Christoph Freiherr von Gersdorff attempted to kill Hitler with a bomb during an exhibition of captured Soviet equipment at the Berlin Zeughaus.

December 1943 in Wolfschanze, Hauptmann Axel Freiherr von dem Busche-Streithorst planned to kill Hitler with a bomb, but the show at which the explosion was to take place was postponed. In 1944, also at Wolfschanze, Ewald von Kleist also failed to kill Hitler with a bomb.

March 1944 Hauptmann Eberhard von Breitenbuch planned to shoot Hitler in Obersalzberg but could not get access to him.

July 1944 Oberst Claus Schenk Graf von Stauffenberg made his first attempt to blow up Hitler in Obersalzberg. On the 11th of that month, von Stauffenberg brought a second bomb to Obersalzberg, but as Hermann Göring and Heinrich Himmler were not present, it was not used. Finally on July 20th at Wolfschanze, he placed the bomb in the situation room that killed four people, but only wounded Hitler.

April 1945 at the very end of the war, Albert Speer planned to kill Hitler in his Berlin bunker using gas.

1948
MAHATMA GANDHI

b. 1869, Gujarat, India
d. 1948, New Delhi
   Non-violent theorist and charismatic mass-movement leader. Founder of modern India.

Albert Einstein said of Gandhi: "Generations to come, it may be, will scarcely believe that such a one, as this, ever in flesh and blood walked upon this earth." The ultimate irony is that the most effective and well-known advocate of non-violent political change in the 20th century – and perhaps in all of history – should be felled by an assassin's bullet.

Since his assassination by a Hindu fanatic in 1948, Mohandas Karamchand Gandhi has been elevated to a form of sainthood. His *satyagraha* model of non-violent protest was able, by means of tactics such as passive resistance and hunger strike, to bring an end to British colonial rule in India, once considered the "jewel in the crown" of the British Empire. He inspired protest movements throughout the world, and also generations of democratic and anti-racist activists, including Martin Luther King, Jr. and Nelson Mandela. A child of the merchant class, Gandhi went to the University of London at the age of 19 to train as a lawyer.

After being admitted to the British bar, an Indian firm sent him to South Africa, where he began protesting about legal and racial discrimination against Indians in South Africa, and was arrested leading a march of Indian miners.

During World War I, Gandhi returned to India, where he joined the Indian National Congress and the independence movement. In the 1920s and 1930s, he attracted world attention for his use of fasting and civil disobedience as forms of protest, as in incidents such as the 1930 Dandi March, when he led thousands of Indians to the sea to collect their own salt rather than pay the British salt tax. After World War II, and the British withdrawal from India, Gandhi responded to deadly clashes between Hindus and Muslims with a threat to go on a complete and final hunger strike unless the violence ceased. He was vehemently opposed to any plan which partitioned India into two separate countries. Nevertheless, the plan was eventually adopted, creating a secular but Hindu-majority India, and an Islamic Pakistan. On the day of the power transfer, Gandhi did not celebrate but mourned.

The conspiracy theory
Partition would also be indirectly responsible for Gandhi's death, as both the successful assassin, Nathu Ram Godse, and, Madan Lal, who attempted to blow up the Mahatma just ten days earlier, belonged to the same right-wing, upper-class Hindu group, who violently opposed a separate state being given to Muslims, and who irrationally held Gandhi responsible.

The evidence
Lal's bomb exploded in Birla House in New Delhi where Gandhi was conducting a prayer meeting, but Gandhi himself took no notice of the explosion; Madan Lal failed in his assassination attempt. Godse, a fellow conspirator, came to another of Gandhi's prayer meetings on the evening of January 30th. After bowing to the Mahatma, Godse pulled out a semi-automatic pistol and, in front of hundreds of witnesses, fired three times. Gandhi fell instantly with the words "He Rama" (Oh! God). Godse was later tried, convicted, and executed.

The verdict
No mystery surrounds the death of Mahatma Gandhi; it was simply a great and tragic loss to humanity.

В Колонном зале Дома Союзов 8 марта 1953 года. На снимке слева направо: В. М. Молотов, К. Е. Ворошилов, Л. П. Берия, Г. М. Маленков, Н. А. Булганин, Н. С. Хрущев, Л. М. Каганович, А. И. Микоян у гроба товарища И. В. Сталина.

Izvestia shows Soviet officials standing by the body of Stalin lying in state (left to right): V. Molotov, K. Voroshilov, L. Beria, G. Malenkov, two soldiers, N. Bulganin, Nikita Khrushchev, L. Kaganovich, and A. Mikoyan.

1953
JOSEPH STALIN

b. 1879, Gori, Georgia

d. 1953, Moscow

General Secretary of the Soviet Communist Party

Joseph Stalin (born Iosif Vissarionovich Dzhugashvili) was more than deserving of assassination. Murder was one of the tools he used to maintain his iron grip on the people of the USSR; the death toll over the four-decade span of his tyranny ran into millions.

As a result of Stalin's political purges, more than one million people were shot in the periods 1935–8, 1942 and 1945–50, and millions more transported to Gulag labour camps. When, in the 1920s, his policy of collective farming failed, Stalin blamed it on kulaks (rich peasants), who resisted collectivization. Therefore, those defined as "kulaks," "kulak helpers" and later "ex-kulaks" were to be shot, placed in the Gulag or deported to remote areas of the country. Even his combat soldiers in World War II were not exempt from his homicidal paranoia. Stalin's Order No. 227 of July 27th, 1942 was an example of his total ruthlessness: all those who retreated or otherwise left their positions without orders were to be summarily shot. In battle, advancing troops, were followed by "Smersh" units (battlefield NKVD squads dedicated to rooting out "traitors, deserters,

spies, and criminal elements") that would machine-gun anyone who turned back. Even Stalin's former revolutionary comrades were targets for arrest and execution, and with the murder of Leon Trotsky in August 1940, Stalin eliminated the last of his old opponents.

At first, there was nothing particularly unusual about the night of February 28th, 1953 for Joseph Stalin and his closest political cronies – Lavrenty Beria, Nikita Khrushchev, Nikolai Bulganin and Georgi Malenkov. These men – effective rulers of the vast expanse of the USSR – watched a film together in the Kremlin and then retired to Stalin's country home, ten minutes outside Moscow, for a night of revelry and drinking.

The usual routine only changed when, in the early hours of the morning, the normally security-obsessed Stalin dismissed his guards and ordered that he was not to be disturbed. The order was relayed by the head guard, a man named Khrustalev. When Stalin had not appeared by noon of the following day, concern began to grow, but no one dared enter his rooms. Finally a guard called Lozgachev was sent in. He reported that Stalin was lying incoherent, in his own urine. The guards rushed to call Beria, Khrushchev, Bulganin and Malenkov at the Politburo, but both they and medical help were surprisingly slow to arrive, almost as though they either knew Stalin was beyond help, or that they had no desire to help him.

The conspiracy theories

The political memoirs of Stalin's Foreign Minister, Vyacheslav Molotov, published in 1993, claim that Beria had boasted to Molotov that he had poisoned Stalin, and in 2003, a joint group of Russian and American historians announced their view that Stalin had ingested warfarin, a powerful rat poison that thins the blood and causes strokes and hemorrhages. As it is flavourless, warfarin is a plausible murder weapon. Other stories claim that Stalin had been injected with poison by the guard Khrustalev, under the orders of his master, Stalin's own security boss and hatchet man NKVD (later KGB) chief Lavrenty Beria.

But why would Beria have wanted to kill him? One theory is that Stalin was killed because Beria, Khrushchev, Bulganin and Malenkov believed that Stalin was about to precipitate a full scale nuclear war with the West. Stalin felt that the USSR had much less to lose than the highly prosperous US in the event of nuclear engagement. Also, he was supposedly on the verge of instituting a new wave of purges, this time mainly against Jewish doctors and other professionals, as a first provocation to the US. Beria, as head of the secret police, allegedly had secret orders to start deportations of Jews from Moscow as early as March 5th, 1953. Realizing that no-one would survive a nuclear war, the conspirators made their move.

The verdict

Although Beria is generally accepted to have played the major role in organizing Stalin's death by calling off his security guards, this did not help achieve his ultimate aim: to replace Stalin himself. For, in the next three months, a struggle between Lavrenty Beria and Nikita Khrushchev would lead to a power play by Khrushchev in June. While Beria, as head of the KGB, was being distracted with anti-communist unrest in East Germany, he was denounced as a traitor "working for the British", arrested and executed, making Khrushchev Stalin's ultimate successor.

The Soviet people were only told about Stalin's death on March 5th, when it was announced that he had died peacefully in his bed at 9.50pm. The great majority saw him as "Uncle Joe", the infallible leader and the victor in the war against Hitler, and went into hysterical mourning. Millions came to view his body as it lay in state in the Hall of Columns, a few streets from Red Square, and several hundred were rumoured to have died in the crush.

See also: *Leon Trotsky p.46; Adolf Hitler p.48*

1954
GAMAL ABDUL NASSER
b. 1918, Alexandria, Egypt
d. 1970, Cairo
President of Egypt

Not all attempted assassinations are what they appear, and considerable doubt has been cast on the authenticity of the 1954 attempt on the life of Egyptian president, Gamal Abdul Nasser. Throughout his political career, Nasser was a contradictory figure. For some, he was one of the most important Arab leaders in history. He led the military coup against King Farouk I of Egypt and ended the corrupt monarchy, but then replaced it with a police state, where mail was opened, the press was censored and political enemies sent to concentration camps in the desert. He is viewed as a leader who reformed his country and re-established Arab pride, but his relentless militarism led Egypt to repeated defeat at the hands of Israel, and his massive public works project, the Aswan Dam, proved an ecological disaster.

What has never been disputed was Nasser's flair for the dramatic, and some have claimed that the attempt on his life on October 26th, 1954 was staged, to solidify his hold on power after two years as president, and to provide an excuse for a crackdown on the growing power of Muslim fundamentalists. While delivering a speech, Nasser was shot eight times from close range by Mahmoud Abd al-Latif of the Muslim Brotherhood. All of the shots missed, and Nasser continued: "Let them kill Nasser. What is Nasser but one among many? My fellow countrymen, stay where you are. I am not dead, I am alive, and even if I die all of you is Gamal Abdel Nasser." Suspicions that the "assassination" had been pre-arranged were intensified by the lack of response by Nasser's bodyguards, and his later manipulation of national anger to eradicate the Muslim Brotherhood. Nasser would actually die in 1970 of a perfectly natural heart attack.

1961
PATRICE LUMUMBA
b. 1925, Onalua, Belgian Congo
d. 1961, Jadotville, Katanga Province
Prime Minister of the Democratic Republic of the Congo

On 17th January 1961, Patrice Emery Lumumba, the first and only elected prime minister of the Congo, was murdered six months after coming to power. He had co-founded the National Congolese Movement, the MNC, and had emerged as Congo's prime minister after elections in June 1960. However, the post-World War II European powers were not prepared to give up their colonies so easily. At the Independence Day celebrations of June 30th, Lumumba made a speech denouncing the brutalities of the departing Belgians. From that point on, Belgium, abetted by the CIA, who feared Lumumba would "go communist," did everything in its power to undermine him. Within days the army mutinied. The mineral-rich Katanga province in the south declared independence, under Moise Tchombe, a longtime enemy of Lumumba, aided by Belgian mining companies. Without Katanga's copper, gold and uranium, Congo's economy was ruined. Finally Lumumba was arrested after a coup d'état headed by Colonel Joseph Mobutu, again with the assistance of the CIA. Lumumba was shuttled from prison to prison and brutalized in front of TV cameras. He became a cause célèbre and, at the UN, the USSR demanded his release, but the CIA decided to end the embarrassment. Lumumba and his fellow prisoners, Maurice Mpolo and Joseph Okito were shot by a firing squad of Katangese soldiers, while Tschombe looked on.

See also: *CIA Plot to Depose President Sukarno p.144*

1961
FIDEL CASTRO
b. 1926, Biran, Cuba
President of Cuba

Almost as soon as Fidel Alejandro Castro Ruz and his revolutionary 26th of July Movement had overthrown the government of Fulgencio Batista in 1959 and turned Cuba into the first socialist state in the western hemisphere, plots were being hatched to kill him.

The conspiracy theories
The US government, Cuban exiles who had fled to the US with Batista, and the Mafia who had considerable interests in Havana's casinos, were all involved in hatching plots to bring down Fidel Castro. His assassination was approved by the Eisenhower administration and this approval was carried over to President John F. Kennedy's White House. The thinking behind all the plots was the same: remove "the Beard" (as Castro was code named) and Cuba's socialist regime would fall. These plans ranged from the deadly to the bizarre. The CIA and the Mafia, in collusion with various anti-Castro and anti-communist groups, repeatedly but unsuccessfully attempted to humiliate and then kill Castro.

The evidence
The first ideas were non-lethal and focused on exposing Castro to ridicule rather than murdering him. One of these involved contaminating the air of the radio station where Castro broadcast his speeches with an aerosol spray of lysergic acid (LSD), causing Castro to start ranting nonsense. Another was to dust Castro with the depilatory, thallium, so as to destroy his image by causing his beard to fall out.

The first plan to assassinate him was to contaminate Fidel's trademark cigars with botulin toxin, a virulent poison that produces a fatal illness some hours after being ingested. The Mafia came into the picture, meanwhile, when Mafioso Johnny Roselli became a go-between connecting the CIA with Chicago crime boss Sam Giancana. The agency hoped that Giancana would organize a gangland-style shooting in Havana, but the mobster vetoed the idea, pointing out that to shoot Castro in Cuba would be a suicide mission for the hit man. Instead, Giancana recommended a lethal pill, which one of New Orleans boss, Joe Trafficante's Cuban contacts could slip into Castro's drink. The poison was to be "stable, soluble, safe to handle, undetectable, not immediately acting, and with a firmly predictable end result." (IG Report, p.24) Again, the ever-useful botulin met all the requirements. The deed was to be done by a low-level official, Juan Orta, but Orta was fired from his government post and fled to Florida before he could complete the mission.

From this point on, the plots grew truly outlandish. The CIA knew Castro was a skin-diving enthusiast, so they prepared a very special wet suit for him, containing a fungus that would produce a chronic skin disease and scuba gear contaminated with tubercle bacilli. The closest any group came to success was when Rolando Cubela, a CIA contact on Castro's staff, formed a three-man sniper team to shoot him at the University of Havana. The scheme was foiled when Castro's security detail caught them red-handed.

Attorney General Robert Kennedy, and almost certainly President Kennedy himself, were aware of earlier assassination plots, but in October 1963, John F. Kennedy pulled the plug on "whacking the Beard," hoping to quietly normalize relations with Cuba. In a matter of days, however, Kennedy was dead himself, and the CIA assassination attempts resumed with a plan to kill Castro with an explosives-rigged sea shell. "The idea was to take an unusually spectacular sea shell that would be certain to catch Castro's eye, load it with an explosive triggered to blow when the shell was lifted, and submerge it in an area where Castro often went skin diving." (IG Report, p.77) This plan also failed as did all subsequent ones, and Fidel Castro is alive today, now in his late seventies.

The verdict

The 1976 revelations before congress on the part of CIA director, William Colby, in the *Inspector General's Report on Plots to Assassinate Fidel Castro*, leave little doubt that all of the alleged attempts on Castro's life really did take place. The only possible concealment could be of worse failures.

See also: *John Fitzgerald Kennedy* and *Robert Francis Kennedy p.54; Che Guevara p.55; The Mafia p.281*

1962
MARILYN MONROE (NORMA JEANE MORTENSEN)

b. 1926, Los Angeles 1926,
d. 1962, Brentwood, California
   Actress, sex symbol and pop icon

Marilyn Monroe, born Norma Jeane Mortensen, had been the luminous star of such films as *Gentlemen Prefer Blondes*, *Some Like It Hot*, and *The Misfits*, but towards the end of her life she had become erratic and unreliable due to her use of barbiturates and alcohol. When she was found dead on August 5th, 1962 by her housekeeper, Mrs Eunice Murray, from what appeared to be an overdose, it came as little surprise, and might have been dismissed as either an accident or suicide had rumours not been rife that she was the mistress of President John F. Kennedy, and may also have had an affair with his brother Robert Kennedy. The Kennedy connection was enough to generate a plethora of conspiracy theories. The most common being that Marilyn was eased into a drug-induced death by a Kennedy insider because, having been dumped by JFK, she was threatening to go public with their affair.

Contradictory autopsy findings, gaps in the time line on the night of her death, the disappearance of her diary and phone records, and witnesses who claimed the FBI joined the investigation for no valid reason were all cited as evidence of orchestrated foul play. The flames of conspiracy were also fanned by her hairdresser, Sidney Guilaroff, who claimed that Marilyn knew a lot of "dangerous secrets about the Kennedys." And a friend, Jose Bolanos, supposedly received a phone call from Marilyn on the night of her death, during which she threatened to reveal "something that would shock the whole world," but, hearing a disturbance at her door put down the phone without hanging up.

Marilyn's death will always remain a mysterious sidebar to the JFK assassination, but the reported comment of Jackie Kennedy to her husband adds some credence to the idea that Monroe was killed because she knew too much. "She's different to the others [mistresses and girlfriends]. She's unstable and dangerous."

See also: *John Fitzgerald Kennedy* and *Robert Francis Kennedy p.54*

1963
NGO DINH DIEM

b. 1901, Hue, Vietnam
d. 1963, Saigon, Vietnam
   First President of South Vietnam

When a national leader has outlived his usefulness but refuses to abdicate gracefully, assassination may be the only way to get rid of him or her. Such was the case with Ngo Dinh Diem, prime minister of Vietnam when the US first became involved in Vietnam.

Born into an aristocratic, Roman Catholic family, Diem had served the French colonial administration but, after World War II, as a staunch anti-communist, he rejected an offer to serve in Ho Chi Minh's brief postwar government. As insurgent forces – first the Viet Minh and then the Viet Cong – battled the French, he spent several years in exile gaining crucial American support. He became prime minister of South Vietnam in 1954, just as the defeated French forces were leaving; for the next seven years, he presided over a corrupt and repressive regime.

Communist guerrillas backed by North Vietnam launched a new rebellion, but a civil disobedience campaign led by the country's Buddhist monks contributed more directly to his downfall. Brutal persecution of the dissident monks in 1963 damaged the regime's, already shaky, international reputation. Declassified documents indicate that the US tacitly supported the military coup d'état that overthrew and executed Diem and his younger brother (Dinh Nhu) on November 1st, 1963, and show that Lucien Conein, a CIA operative, provided the group of generals with $40,000 to carry out the assassination. One common theory is that President Kennedy saw Diem as an obstacle to a rapid US disengagement in Vietnam, but this was not to be. A little over two weeks later, Kennedy himself was assassinated.

See also: *John Fitzgerald Kennedy p.54; CIA Plot to Depose President Sukarno p.144*

1963/8
JOHN FITZGERALD KENNEDY
b. 1917 Brookline, Massachusetts
d. 1963, Dallas, Texas
  US president

ROBERT FRANCIS KENNEDY
b. 1925, Brookline, Massachusetts
d. 1968, Los Angeles, California
  US senator

The assassination of President John F. Kennedy is the Great American Conspiracy, and an undying preoccupation of all conspiracy theorists. The death of his brother, Robert F. Kennedy, less than five years later only served to compound the trauma and the fascination for theorists.

John F. Kennedy's assassination
Psychologists theorize that the multitude of conspiracy theories are the product of a mass refusal to accept that anyone as powerful and charismatic as John (Jack) F. Kennedy who, along with Nikita Khrushchev, had stepped back from the very brink of nuclear war, could be extinguished by anyone as insignificant as the supposed lone gunman Lee Oswald. On the other side of the coin, there's the grim possibility that the murders of both Jack and Bobby Kennedy were part of a secret coup d'état in the US.

Initially the Kennedy murder was a tragedy that resonated across the world, as it vividly played out on TV. For almost 48 hours after November 22nd, 1963, simple grief prevailed. A suspected assassin was arrested and JFK's body was flown back to Washington DC for a state funeral. Then, on November 24th, at 11.21am CST, the suspect – identified as Lee Harvey Oswald (1939–63) – was transferred from Dallas Police Headquarters to the nearby County Jail, while millions watched on TV. Viewers saw a figure dart forwards and fire, and were later told that Oswald was dead on arrival at Parklands Hospital – where Kennedy had died two days before. Oswald's killer turned out to be Jack Leon Ruby (1911–67), a Dallas nightclub owner. At first these were just names but, when more was learnt, a sense of unease set in. Lee Oswald was an ex-Marine who, at the height of the Cold War, had defected to the USSR, but then returned to the US, apparently (and surprisingly) avoiding both retribution and any kind of major investigation. Oswald declared himself to be a Marxist-Leninist, but associated with extreme right-wing anti-Castro Cubans, and lived his life in a weird twilight zone where organized crime and

political extremists interacted with the CIA. As for Jack Ruby, his cheap strip club, the Carousel, was frequented by Dallas cops. In his youth, he had run with the Capone mob in Chicago, and still had Mafia acquaintances.

Unease slowly turned to distrust as rumours circulated that anywhere between 20 to 40 individuals linked to Kennedy's assassination had mysteriously died. The first was Karyn Kupcinet, discovered strangled on November 30th, 1963. In his book, *Forgive My Grief*, W. Penn Jones writes: "A few days before the assassination, Karyn Kupcinet, 23, was trying to place a long distance telephone call from the Los Angeles area … the long distance operator heard Miss Kupcinet scream into the telephone that President Kennedy was going to be killed." Ex-CIA and a consultant to *Life* magazine, Gary Underhill, was found shot in the head on 8th May 1964; he had confided to friends that Oswald was correct when, on the night of his arrest, he had told reporters that he was "just a patsy." Other journalists showed up dead, including Bill Hunter of the *Long Beach Press Telegram* and Jim Koethe of the Dallas *Times Herald*. The London *Sunday Times* wrote in 1967 that the odds for so many witnesses dying were "one hundred thousand trillion to one."

Even in September 1964 when, after a ten-month investigation, the Warren Commission published its finding that it "could not find any persuasive evidence of a domestic or foreign conspiracy involving any other person(s), group(s), or country(ies), and that Lee Harvey Oswald acted alone", the national mood was such that "lone gunman" became a disparaging term. President Lyndon Johnson's attempt to allay fear was a failure. The Warren commission had ignored many possible witnesses, and Earl Warren himself had even refused Jack Ruby's plea that he would "come clean" if moved from jail in Dallas to Washington: "My life is in danger here. I want to tell the truth, and I can't tell it here."

Mercifully the Warren Commission was not the only official investigation. In 1969, New Orleans District Attorney, Jim Garrison, prosecuted businessman, Clay Shaw, for conspiring to murder the president, although two witnesses, Guy Bannister and David Ferrie, died suspiciously. Shaw was acquitted, but the jury was convinced regarding the conspiracy. Garrison also forced the first showing of the 486-frame, 8mm home movie shot by Abraham Zapruder of Kennedy's last 26.6 seconds in Dealey Plaza, which shows him being hit on the right side of his skull, with a horrific backwards puff of blood and brains. To the untrained eye, the Zapruder film suggests the President had been shot from the front, and by someone other than Oswald. In 1978, the House Select Committee on Assassinations concluded that

Jacqueline Kennedy leans over to assist her husband John F. Kennedy just after he is shot as the presidential motorcade passes through Dealey Plaza on Elm Street, Dallas, Texas, on November 22nd, 1963.

there was "a high probability that two gunmen fired at President John F. Kennedy," and that "President John F. Kennedy was probably assassinated as a result of a conspiracy." The House Committee also unearthed a Dictabelt that had accidently recorded, from a Dallas motorcycle policeman's radio, the sound of four shots rather than the three supposedly fired by Oswald.

The conspiracy theories

Discarding the truly outlandish theories that JFK was the victim of time-travelling aliens or an elaborate, neo-pagan fertility sacrifice, the mystery, in broad terms, has three contenders for a possible solution:

First, JFK was shot by Lee Oswald alone, as stated by the Warren Commission, and supported more recently by Gerald Posner in *Case Closed*. It continues to be doubted. A 2003 ABC TV news poll showed that only 32 percent of Americans believe that Oswald acted alone. A Discovery Channel poll gave 21 percent and the History Channel 17 percent. Second, JFK was murdered by the Mafia; the hit organized by Chicago boss Sam Giancana along with Santos Trafficante, Carlos Marcello, and Johnny Roselli in revenge for Attorney General Robert Kennedy's crusade against organized crime. The main objection to this theory is that the JKFK shooting does not resemble a gangland hit. Mafia assassins like to get in close (like Jack Ruby) and then vanish in the confusion. Also Giancana, Trafficante, Marcello, and Roselli had been involved in a CIA plot to kill Fidel Castro, a complication that

leads to the third theory: JFK was assassinated by a coalition of right-wing elements inside the CIA (who wanted to halt his moves for détente in the Cold War and disengagement in Vietnam), anti-Castro Cubans (who felt that he had betrayed the Bay of Pigs Invasion of Cuba that was supposed to oust the Castro regime), and the Mafia bosses (who joined the coalition for the reasons given in theory two). The CIA organized the hit with a militarily precise set-up of triangulated snipers in the Book Depository, on the Dealey Plaza grassy knoll in front of the target and maybe a third in another building. The Mafia would take care of the clean-up, killing Oswald, the patsy, and any inconvenient witnesses. This is the conclusion of Garrison's investigation, and the thrust of Oliver Stone's film *JFK*.

The verdict

The third theory is likely to be closest to the truth.

Robert F. Kennedy's assassination

Sirhan B. Sirhan (born 1944), a 24-year-old Palestinian, shot RFK as he was making an exit through the hotel kitchen after addressing supporters at the Ambassador Hotel in Los Angeles. It was June 4th, 1968 and Bobby was running for President. He had been JFK's campaign manager, and then his Attorney General, working with him during the Bay of Pigs Invasion and the Cuban Missile Crisis. He was a populist and against the war in Vietnam. Sirhan had suddenly appeared out of nowhere, and fired from point blank range.

Rosey Grier of the Los Angeles Rams and Olympic gold medalist Rafer Johnson subdued Sirhan, but Bobby died early in the morning of June 6th, 1968 at the age of 42.

The conspiracy theories

Authorities claimed that Sirhan was another disturbed "lone gunman," but public credulity sank to an all-time low as serious anomalies in the evidence emerged, especially over the question of how 11 slugs had been recovered even though Sirhan had used an 8-chamber Iver-Johnson .22 revolver. There were also the five witnesses who saw a woman in a polka-dot dress fleeing the scene shouting, "We shot him!"

The verdict

Fingers were again pointed at the CIA, and the theory was advanced that Sirhan was a "Manchurian Candidate" assassin, programmed to kill Kennedy and to forget that he had done so. Dr Eduard Simpson, who examined Sirhan, said that he was easily hypnotizable and unusually susceptible to post-hypnotic suggestion. Sirhan's memory has always been totally blank about the night of the killing, and only the evidence had convinced him of his guilt. Despite these and other problems, Sirhan was convicted and sentenced to death, but never executed. After his conviction, the Los Angeles Police Department destroyed most of the evidence from the case, making any reinvestigation impossible.

See also: *Fidel Castro p.52; The Manchurian Candidate p.223; The Mafia p.281*

1965
MALCOLM X
b. 1925, Omaha, Nebraska 1925
d. 1965, New York City
Black American activist

By the time he was assassinated at the Audubon Ballroom in Manhattan, Malcolm X had evolved from being a streetwise hoodlum, to one of the most prominent militant black nationalist leaders in the US.

Born Malcolm Little, he was the son of an outspoken Baptist minister who was murdered by the Black Legion, a white supremacist group in Lansing, Michigan in 1931. In 1965, Malcolm Little would himself be assassinated. By this time he was known around the world as Malcolm X, and was by far the most eloquent speaker of the movement that preached how most African-Americans were Muslims before arriving in the US as slaves, and should reconvert to Islam

to reclaim their heritage. He called for black separatism, black pride, and black self-dependence, and rejected the non-violent resistance of Martin Luther King.

As a young man Malcolm Little had been a street hustler, involved in drug dealing, gambling, prostitution, racketeering, and robbery (referred to collectively by Malcolm as "hustling"); he even faked insanity in order to avoid World War II draft. Sentenced to eight to ten years for robbery, Malcolm had converted to Islam in jail, taken the name El-Hajj Malik El-Shabazz, and become a devotee of Elijah Muhammad. His conversion had been absolute, so his faith was shaken when he later learnt that Elijah Muhammad was engaging in illicit sexual affairs.

By this point Malcolm was a leading figure in The Nation of Islam, almost eclipsing Elijah Muhammad himself. It was no secret that Malcolm's success had aroused jealousy within the Black Muslim hierarchy. The Nation of Islam wanted him gone. He knew too much and could not be controlled. In the wake of the Kennedy assassination, he gave them their chance. Malcolm described the Kennedy murder as "chickens coming home to roost," that it was the same violence whites had long used on blacks. Elijah Muhammad duly suspended Malcolm, who formed his own organization. Violence then followed. On February 14th, 1965, Malcolm's New York home was firebombed, but no one was hurt. Just a week later he was dead.

The conspiracy theory

The assassination was initially assumed to be a violent finale to the running feud between Malcolm's Organization of Afro-American Unity and Elijah Muhammad's Nation of Islam, but later the story began to circulate that his death had been orchestrated by no less than the Federal Bureau of Investigation and its notorious director, J. Edgar Hoover, who had a phobic fear of what he termed a "black messiah."

The evidence

On February 21st, 1965 a brief scuffle and a voice yelling, "don't be messin' with my pockets!" was heard during a speech Malcolm was giving to a New York crowd of 400 people. His bodyguards were distracted and a man rushed forwards and shot Malcolm in the chest with a sawn-off shotgun. Two other men charged the stage firing pistols, then the crowd grabbed the assassins as they tried to flee. Nation of Islam members Talmadge Hayer, Norman 3X Butler, and Thomas 15X Johnson were convicted of first-degree murder.

However, an FBI memo, uncovered later during investigations into the FBI's COINTELPRO (Counter-intelligence

Program), takes credit for the Malcolm assassination, and states that at least one of Malcolm's bodyguards was an undercover NYPD police officer working for the FBI. COINTELPRO was used to infiltrate and neutralize groups like the Black Panthers, the Students for a Democratic Society and the movement against the war in Vietnam. Some investigators have also accused current Nation of Islam leader Louis Farrakhan of also playing a major role in the assassination, although Farrakhan strongly denied this in 1998 on the CBS TV show *60 Minutes*.

The verdict

COINTELPRO was Hoover's own domestic political spynet of the 1960s; infiltration and provocation were two of its favourite techniques, and there is a strong likelihood that undercover FBI agents fomented the existing hatred between the two Islamic factions, and deftly eased the Nation of Islam into committing the assassination.

See also: *John Fitzgerald Kennedy p.54; Martin Luther King p.58; FBI v Black Panther Party p.59; J. Edgar Hoover Blackmailed by the Mob p.148*

1967
CHE GUEVARA
b. 1928, Rosario, Argentina
d. 1967, La Higuera, Bolivia
Marxist revolutionary

During an ill-conceived and badly organized 1967 attempt to foment a worker/peasant revolution in Bolivia, Ernesto Rafael Guevara de la Serna was captured in a joint operation by the CIA and Bolivian Rangers. The CIA wanted to keep Guevara alive for interrogation and propaganda purposes, but the Bolivians went ahead and executed him.

Born and educated in Argentina, Guevara initially studied to be a doctor, but an innate and rebellious restlessness spurred him to take a year off and travel the length of South America on a beat-up motorcycle. This trip was an education of a different kind. Horrified by the hardship and poverty he witnessed in the countries he visited, and the exploitation of the poor by US-controlled corporations, Guevara began to embrace a form of Pan-American Marxism. He met and joined Cuban exiles Fidel Castro and his brother Raúl in Mexico City, where they were preparing to return to Cuba to overthrow the US and Mafia-backed regime of Fulgencio Batista. Guevara and 80 other guerrillas sailed with Castro to Cuba aboard the cabin cruiser *Granma* in November 1956.

Initially the uprising was a complete disaster, but through two long years in the Sierra Maestra mountains, the rebels slowly gained strength and support. When they finally came down from the mountains to oust Batista, *El Comandante* Che Guevara led the column that took the city of Santa Clara. Once the new Cuban government had been installed, Che served under Castro as an official at the National Institute of Agrarian Reform, President of the National Bank of Cuba, and Minister of Industries. However, he chaffed under the routines of power, and also began to find himself at odds with Castro over the close Cuban relationship with the USSR. Guevara left Cuba in 1966 to sow the seeds of revolution in other countries, first in the Democratic Republic of the Congo and later in Bolivia.

The conspiracy theory

The plan to kill Che and its implementation was never any secret. When President René Barrientos of Boliva learnt that Che and 120 guerrillas were operating in the mountainous Camiri region, he is reputed to have wanted Che's head displayed on a pike in downtown La Paz, and ordered the Bolivian Army to hunt him down. In Bolivia, Che had expected to face poorly prepared troops but found himself pursued by elite Rangers trained by the CIA and US army special forces. He also failed to receive expected assistance from Bolivia's Moscow-oriented Communist Party.

The evidence

Betrayed by a deserter in October of 1967, Che was encircled at his camp and captured near the village of La Higuera. President Barrientos immediately ordered his execution, but Che's legend was sufficiently powerful to make the officers on the ground reluctant to kill him themselves. Eventually a sergeant was dispatched to the schoolhouse where Che was being held, to kill him with a machine gun. The man was so nervous, however, that he only wounded Che in the legs, at which Che allegedly shouted "Shoot, coward, you are only going to kill a man." The senior CIA agent hunting Guevara was Felix Rodriguez, a veteran of the failed Bay of Pigs invasion and other anti-Castro covert actions. Rodriguez had the decency to note Che's courage in his report, but after the execution, he took Che's Rolex watch, proudly showing it to reporters, and then removed Che's hands to verify his identity.

The verdict

Sometimes, a political assassination can rebound on the assassin – instead of destroying the threat posed by the victim, it turns him or her into a martyr. Che Guevara is the most obvious example of this phenomenon in the 20th century. Barrientos and the CIA could not have made a worse mistake. After his death, Guevara became a symbol of international revolution, both as a charismatic face on posters and T-shirts, and as a respected theorist on land reform and asymmetric warfare.

See also: *Fidel Castro p.52; The Mafia p.281*

1968
MARTIN LUTHER KING

b. 1929, Atlanta, Georgia
d. 1968, Memphis, Tennessee
Civil rights activist, Baptist minister and Nobel laureate

Martin Luther King made a unique contribution to the struggle for African American civil rights. He embraced the philosophy of non-violent civil disobedience used successfully in India by Mahatma Gandhi and, with the most bitter of ironies, like Gandhi he too was assassinated.

The Reverend is perhaps most famous for his "I Have a Dream" speech, given in front of Washington DC's Lincoln Memorial in 1963. He organized and led marches for the right to vote, to end desegregation, in support of fair hiring, and to promote other basic civil rights. On October 14th, 1964, he became the youngest recipient of the Nobel Peace Prize, but he had also earned the hatred of many southern whites, and in addition, the enmity of FBI director, J. Edgar Hoover. The FBI planted bugs in King's home, office, and in hotel rooms. The bureau also informed Attorney General Robert F. Kennedy of King's alleged "communist connections," although King was adamant that "there are as many communists in this freedom movement as there are Eskimos in Florida" – to which Hoover responded by calling King "the most notorious liar in the country."

From 1965 King also began to express doubts about the American role in the Vietnam war. The FBI responded by shifting the focus of its investigations to discrediting King through exposing supposed weaknesses in his private life. The bureau distributed reports and, allegedly, tapes, proving King's extramarital sexual affairs, to friendly reporters, his supporters, and even to his own family.

He was shot dead by a sniper on April 4th, 1968, on the balcony of the Lorraine Motel in Memphis, Tennessee. Associates (including the Rev Jesse Jackson) heard the shot and ran to the balcony, but were too late. King was

pronounced dead a few hours later. In the hours that followed, cities across the US exploded with vicious riots, and singer James Brown went on radio and TV to appeal for calm, as did Robert F. Kennedy, who would be shot himself exactly two months later. A decade and a half after his 1968 assassination, Martin Luther King Day was established in his honour.

The conspiracy theory
Martin Luther King was killed on the orders of J. Edgar Hoover after he had not been deterred from his political goals by prolonged FBI intimidation. A "small-time crook" called James Earl Ray (1928–98) was arrested and confessed to the shooting, but he was a brainwashed, "Manchurian Candidate" assassin, probably supplied by the CIA, who were also happy to see King gone given his increasingly vocal opposition to the war in Vietnam.

The evidence
The idea that James Earl Ray was a "lone nut" was first brought into question after his arrest in London. That a supposed psychotic was capable of single-handedly fleeing Memphis might be credible, but that he was sufficiently well organized to leave the country was not. His subsequent confession that he acted alone became the basis of Ray's conviction for murder and the resulting 99-year jail sentence. The fact, however, that he recanted three days after his conviction rekindled doubts. His rambling jailhouse statement that King had in fact been shot by Ray's brother Johnny, and a mysterious figure called "Raoul", seemed like the ravings of someone crazy or brainwashed. Ballistic anomalies, and the fact that, by 1968, King was under constant surveillance by both the FBI and local police (who, at the least, would have had to turn a blind eye to the assassination), further amplified doubts about the official story.

Ray spent the rest of his life attempting unsuccessfully to withdraw his guilty plea, and even testified to the House Select Committee on Assassinations in 1977 that he did not shoot King. To complicate matters, shortly after testifying, Ray and six other convicts escaped from Brushy Mountain State Prison in Petros, Tennessee, but were recaptured after a week on the run. Ray died from kidney disease in 1998, caused by hepatitis C, probably contracted from a blood transfusion after a prison stabbing at Brushy Mountain.

The verdict
On December 8th, 1999, a jury in Memphis, Tennessee, decided that the long-held official version of Martin Luther

King Jr's assassination was wrong, agreeing that the assassination was too complex for one person to handle, and implicating a retired Memphis businessman, Loyd Jowers, and government agencies in a conspiracy to kill the civil rights giant. This judgement was reversed, however, the following year when then-Attorney General Janet Reno, presumably sticking to the politically safe lone-gunman theory, launched a probe that concluded that there was no credible evidence to support the conspiracy claim.

See also: *Robert Francis Kennedy p.54; J. Edgar Hoover Blackmailed by the Mob p.148*

1970
FBI V BLACK PANTHER PARTY

The Black Panther party was formed in Oakland, California in 1966 by Huey P. Newton and Bobby Seale, and within a year, FBI director, J. Edgar Hoover, called it "the greatest threat to the internal security of the country."

At best the Black Panther party played a short, if extreme, role in the civil rights movement. The Panthers believed that Martin Luther King's non-violent campaign had failed and that "revolutionary war" was the only option. Obviously such convictions were bound to draw the attention of the FBI, and when the Panthers staged their famous demonstration at the California State Capitol (at which they paraded in berets and black leather jackets, carrying rifles and shotguns), it struck a nerve in the US. Yet even the most cursory of investigations would have revealed that the Panther's talk of violence was more street theatre than armed uprising, and much of their energy was directed to inner-city projects like their Free Food Program and Free Health Clinics. J. Edgar Hoover was, though, the man who had denied the existence of the Mafia for years, and who once forwarded a list to Vice President Spiro Agnew of rock 'n' roll bands who were supposedly being funded by communist China. For him to see the Black Panther party posing a threat of armed insurrection was infinitely possible. His great fear was of a "black messiah" and of a major African-American political movement disrupting the US system.

The conspiracy theory
Just as Hoover had allegedly orchestrated the events leading to the assassination of Malcolm X, and as he had moved against civil rights leader Martin Luther King and was suspected of being involved in his death, so he ordered field operatives of the FBI to take whatever measures might be needed to crush the Black Panthers. As the FBI campaign to neutralize them played out, it became clear to many observers that the agency would not shrink from killing key members if need be. That Hoover should consider the BPP such a threat says much about his mindset and how he frequently operated according to prejudice and illusion rather than a command of the facts.

The evidence
Hoover had the ideal weapon to neutralize the Panthers: COINTELPRO (the FBI's Counter-intelligence Program). Designed to neutralize political dissidents, COINTELPRO had been used against the supposed "Red Menace" in the 1950s and, in the mid-1960s, it was being used against the Vietnam-era peace movement and radical political organizations. COINTELPRO's stock in trade was infiltration, provocation, and disinformation. In the case of the Panthers, assassination was apparently added to the menu. Maybe FBI agents didn't carry out executions themselves, but they certainly created a climate in which local law enforcement officers could mount a raid on the Panthers, go in with guns blazing, and not be too concerned if any suspects failed to come out alive. One of the first victims of just such a raid was 17-year-old "Little" Bobby Hutton, who was killed on April 6th, 1968 in West Oakland; he was shot ten times after his house was set ablaze, which forced him to run into police fire. But the most notorious incident occurred on December 4th, 1968. At 4am, acting on an FBI tip, Chicago police raided the apartment of Black Panther, Fred Hampton. Hampton was shot twice in the head while sleeping. Mark Clark, who was asleep in the living room, was also shot dead. Hampton's pregnant wife was shot too, but she survived. Four Panthers sleeping in the apartment were wounded, while one other escaped injury. According to a Federal Grand Jury, a total of 90 bullets were fired, all but one by police.

The verdict
This was not the first time that J. Edgar Hoover had resorted to summary execution. He had used the same tactics against the mid-west outlaws during the Great Depression of the 1930s. When bank robber and escape artist, John Dillinger, was shot dead outside the Biograph Theater in Chicago, it had not been an FBI attempt at arrest, but slaughter, pure and simple. The only problem was that the Black Panthers, although they talked tough and many had ghetto rap sheets, were not engaged in armed robbery, but political dissent, and were proof that Hoover believed that assassination was a legitimate weapon for the US government to

use against its own citizens if their political beliefs were deemed sufficiently extreme.

See also: *Malcolm X p.56; Martin Luther King p.58*

1972
GEORGE WALLACE
b. 1919, Clio, Alabama
d. 1998, Montgomery, Alabama
  US politician

George Corley Wallace was elected governor of Alabama four times, and also ran for US president four times, but lost on each occasion. At the start of his career he was a liberal, particularly on questions of race, but after a crushing election defeat in 1958, in what was a totally calculated move he became a hard-line segregationist, and won his first gubernatorial race in 1962 on the slogan: "Segregation now, segregation tomorrow, and segregation forever." A year later he stood in front of the University of Alabama, attempting to block the enrollment of two black students, Vivian Malone and James Hood. When, ten years later in 1972, he was shot on live TV while campaigning in Laurel, Maryland, the initial assumption was that the would-be assassin, Arthur Herman Bremer, was politically motivated. Bremer's diary revealed, however, that the shooting had simply been an attempt to "become famous," and that President Nixon had also been a possible target.

The mention of Nixon, however, prompted some speculation that this might be an attempt at homicide by the "Watergate team," as Wallace posed a political threat to Nixon just as Bobby Kennedy had been four years earlier. Although one of Bremer's bullets had lodged in Wallace's spine, leaving him paralyzed and confined to a wheelchair, Wallace continued his career in politics. His final run for president was in 1976 when he was defeated in the Democratic primaries by Jimmy Carter. In the late 1970s, he became a born-again Christian, and apologized to black civil rights leaders for his earlier segregationist views.

1973
SALVADOR ALLENDE
b. 1908, Valparaíso, Chile
d. 1973, Santiago, Chile
  President of Chile

On September 11th, 1973 a military coup d'état overthrew and murdered Chilean president, Salvador Allende Gossens,

and ushered in the repressive military dictatorship of General Augusto Pinochet.

The images of antiquated jet fighters strafing and bombing the Presidential Palace, and then of the palace being stormed by tanks and infantry – all to unseat Chile's democratically elected leader – is indelibly etched in the memories of those who saw them on TV. The justification for the coup d'état has always been – from no less than US National Security Advisor, Henry Kissinger, down – that Salvador Allende wanted to establish a Cuban-style dictatorship that would have destroyed human rights and economic prosperity.

Although Allende had indeed been a Marxist since his student days, and although he was on good terms with Cuba's Fidel Castro, his claim that he wanted to create a socialist state by means of free elections rather than violent revolution was more than borne out by his actions. Chile had been a democracy since 1932, and Allende won the presidency in what was a free and fair election. In addition, the idea of preserving democracy by instituting a dictatorship was absurd, as was the so-called defence of human rights by a repressive junta that ordered widespread and well-documented torture and "disappearances." One such grisly incident was the murder of Chilean songwriter Víctor Jara, (dubbed "Chile's Bob Dylan"), whose hands were hacked off before he was murdered in the National Stadium immediately after the coup.

The conspiracy theory
The primary question has always been the degree of US involvement in the coup.

The evidence
Documents, which were declassified during the Clinton administration, show that the United States government and the CIA had sought the overthrow of Allende in 1970, immediately after he took office, but direct involvement is neither proven nor contradicted.

Many potentially relevant documents still remain classified. The Nixon administration certainly did all it could to cripple Chile's economy and divide the population under Allende by discouraging investment and blocking credit from the International Monetary Fund, World Bank, and Interamerican Development Bank. In addition, the CIA secretly sent at least $10 million to Chilean groups that opposed Allende. The CIA claims that it was notified of the impending Pinochet coup two days in advance, but contends that it "played no direct role" in it. Henry Kissinger told President Richard Nixon that the US "didn't do it" but had "created the conditions." The CIA had also backed an earlier botched coup attempt in which Chilean army chief of staff General René Schneider, who opposed Allende's overthrow, was murdered. The details of Salvador Allende's death are unclear: his personal doctor said that he committed suicide with a machine gun given to him by Fidel Castro, and an autopsy labelled his death as suicide. Others insist that he was murdered by Pinochet's military forces while defending the palace.

The verdict

There is no question that the United States provided material support to the military regime in Chile both before and after Allende's death; neither is there any doubt that key Pinochet officers were paid contacts of the CIA or the US military, even though they were known to be involved in human rights abuses.

See also: *Watergate – A Pentagon Coup D'état p.148; Watergate – Presidential Abuse of Power p.150*

1975
JIMMY HOFFA
b. 1913, Brazil, Indiana
d. 1975, unknown location
US union leader

James Riddle Hoffa is probably more famous for the mystery surrounding his still-unexplained disappearance and presumed death than for his achievements as a labour organizer. The son of a coal miner, Hoffa proved himself to be a natural leader in the union movement and its fight for better pay and working conditions. At the age of 20, he organized his first strike, and then advanced rapidly through the ranks of the Teamsters union which organized truck drivers. Unfortunately, in the violent early days of the union he formed ties with organized crime that would dog him for the rest of his life.

Hoffa became president of the Teamsters in the 1950s, but only with help of mobsters like Antonio "Tony Pro" Provenzano. When US Attorney General Robert Kennedy began his early 1960s crusade against organized crime, Hoffa was an obvious target, and the enmity between the two men developed into something that was highly personal. In 1967 he was convicted of bribery and sentenced to 15 years in prison but, after 4 years, President Richard Nixon commuted his sentence on condition he take no

further part in union business. Hoffa, however, was planning a comeback when he disappeared on July 30th, 1975 from the Machus Red Fox restaurant in Bloomfield Hills, Michigan, where he had planned to meet Provenzano and mob boss Anthony "Tony Jack" Giacalone. His death continues to be a mystery, but various theories claim that his mob-executed body is buried in Michigan, under the New Jersey Turnpike, and under the end zone at Giants Stadium outside New York. Another theory is that Hoffa was actually put in a cement-mixer and ground into concrete. No theory has been proven and his body has not been found.

See also: *Robert Francis Kennedy p.54*

1977
ELVIS PRESLEY
b. 1935, Tupelo, Mississippi
d. 1977, Memphis, Tennessee
US musician

The conspiracy theories that gathered around the death of rock 'n' roll legend Elvis Aron Presley were always more a matter of fan denial than actual fact. Early, albeit inept, attempts were made to suppress autopsy findings that the demise of "the King" was heavily drug related. However, subsequent media investigations have left little doubt that Elvis's death – on an upstairs toilet in his Memphis Mansion, Graceland, in August 1977 – was a result of physical collapse brought about mainly by his massive and prolonged abuse of prescription drugs. Elvis was a "pillhead" from as far back as the 1950s when he scandalized a generation as the great driving force behind rock 'n' roll. Little credence can be attached to the story published in some UK tabloids in the 1990s that he was the victim of a mob hit, after his father, Vernon Presley, had bungled the deal while purchasing the private jet "Lisa Marie" from on-the-run financier/swindler Robert Vesco.

At best, the accusation of a conspiracy-by-neglect can be levelled at Presley's life-long manager Colonel Tom Parker and some of the Graceland entourage, who it would appear did nothing to rescue Presley from a lifestyle that was clearly going to end in his premature death. Perhaps Colonel Parker had calculated that there was more money to be made from a dead legend than from a live, but unstable and often incoherent one.

Mystery surrounds the death of Prime Minster Aldo Moro. His body was discovered in the back of a car.

1978
ALDO MORO
b. 1916, Maglie, Italy
d. Rome, 1978, Italy
Prime minister of Italy

What makes the 1978 assassination of Italy's Aldo Moro so unique is that he was kidnapped and held for ransom for 55 days before he was murdered.

The leader of the Italian Christian Democrats and one of Italy's longest-serving prime ministers, Aldo Moro, held power for a combined total of more than six years. Moro was considered an intellectual and a skilled mediator who was willing to compromise with the powerful Italian Communist Party, which made it grimly ironic – and, to some, less than plausible – that he should be kidnapped and killed by terrorists from the Red Brigades.

On March 16, 1978 Moro was kidnapped on Rome's Via Fani as he was being driven to the House of Representatives for a vote of confidence debate on the new government led by Giulio Andreotti that was, for the first time, being supported by the Communist Party. After killing Moro's five-man escort, the Red Brigades' team, led by Mario Moretti, vanished with Moro. The Red Brigades, a splinter group of 1960s radicalism, had been formed in Milan and Turin,

where they claimed to support labour unions against the far right. Its members – mainly workers and students, but never numbering more than about 50 – sabotaged factory equipment and broke into factory offices and trade union headquarters. In 1972, for the first time, they executed their kidnapped victim – a factory foreman who had been held for some time. Subsequently, they rapidly advanced to bigger and better targets, culminating in the ex-prime minister, Aldo Moro.

The conspiracy theory
Not everyone believed that the extreme left were responsible. It has even been suggested that Moro's murder could have been orchestrated by the Italian P2 Masonic lodge. P2 (Propaganda Due) had been deemed, by a special commission of the Italian parliament, to be a secret criminal organization, with ties to the Vatican Bank scandal, the collapse of Banco Ambrosiano, and the death of its president, Roberto Calvi; it also, allegedly, had links to the CIA. Another theory claims that the Red Brigades themselves had been infiltrated by the CIA, and that they had Moro killed because he had such a rapport with the communists. However, no concrete proof of this has ever come to light.

The evidence
Shortly after the Moro snatch, the Red Brigades supposedly made their demands. Moro's life would be spared if a number of imprisoned terrorists were released. This was the start of 55 tense days of hostage crisis, during which Moro wrote several letters to leading Christian Democrats, and to Pope Paul VI, in which he reasoned that the state's primary objective should be to save lives, urging the government to give in to his kidnappers' requests. Despite impassioned pleas by Moro's family, the politicians claimed that the letters could only have been written under duress and that a deal with terrorists was out of the question. Pope Paul appealed directly to the Red Brigades to release Moro "without conditions" but to no avail. On May 9th, 1978–55 days after the kidnapping – Moro was murdered in or near Rome. His body was found the same day in the boot of a parked car, at a spot on the Via Caetani that was – despite heavy police surveillance throughout the city – close to the headquarters of both the Christian Democrat and the Italian communist parties. The murder of Moro prompted an all-out assault against the Brigades by the Italian police and security forces. The murder of a popular political figure also drew condemnation from left-wing radicals, and even from the imprisoned ex-leaders of the Brigades. The Red Brigades

lost their grassroots support and public opinion turned strongly against them.

The verdict

Mystery still surrounds many of the details of Moro's murder, and it has been frequently asked why the Red Brigades should kill a man who had done so much to include the Communist Party in a coalition cabinet. That the CIA had infiltrated the Red Brigades was certainly one plausible explanation; it is also possible that the agency – either alone or in concert with P2 – orchestrated the Moro kidnapping with the definite notion that it would end in his death.

See also: *Pope John Paul I p.63; Calvi and the Vatican Bank p.256*

1978
POPE JOHN PAUL I
b. 1912, Forno de Canale, Italy
d. 1978, Rome, Italy

When John Paul I, born Albino Luciani, was found dead in his bed on August 26th, 1978 he been pope for just 33 days. Rumours immediately began to circulate that his death was not merely untimely, but also suspicious.

John Paul is remembered for his friendliness and humility, qualities not, at the time, much associated with popes, but doubts remain that his death may not have been natural, not allayed by a series of inept, inexplicable, and easily disproved lies circulated by Vatican officials in the aftermath of his death. John Paul had also clashed with the Vatican Bank over their sale of a subsidiary church bank in Venice some years earlier, and a major scandal was brewing around that organization, which went all the way back to World War II. These involved the laundering of funds confiscated by the Nazis from Holocaust victims, and the setting up of "rat lines" by which, after the war, high-ranking SS and other war criminals escaped with their fortunes to South America. The Bank was also reputed to have more recent ties to organized crime. Other behind-the-scenes tensions had been created after John Paul had openly considered a softening of the Catholic position on contraception after meeting with UN delegates on world population.

The conspiracy theory

The suggestion was that an alliance of the institutionally corrupt and the ultra-conservative could create enough pressure, and also provide the means, to have the new Pope murdered in his bed, before he could dismiss senior Vatican officials for corruption at the Vatican Bank; at the same time, the Church would rid itself of a potential reformer on the sensitive subject of birth control.

The evidence

The Vatican stated that John Paul's body was found by papal secretary, John Magee, when, in fact, it was discovered by a nun in the papal household, Sister Vincenza, who had brought him some coffee. A false time of death was issued. His personal property, including his glasses, his will, and the documents he was working on when he died, were all alleged to be missing when in fact they were in the possession of his sister's family. Conflicting stories were told as to his health, with the Vatican attempting to convey an exaggerated image of a sick man, physically unable to withstand the pressures of the papacy. It was hinted at that he suffered from ailments related to his heavy smoking, when the truth was he never smoked. The Pope's body was embalmed within one day of his death, but no postmortem was conducted. If the Vatican had been subject to Italian law, this would have broken it; however, the Vatican insisted that a papal postmortem was prohibited under Vatican statute. (This too was later revealed to be incorrect. In 1830 a postmortem was carried out on the remains of Pope Pius VIII that produced evidence of a possible poison plot.)

As the Vatican's disinformation campaign was refuted in every case, the rumours grew more outlandish. The death of a visiting prelate during an audience with the Pope some days before John Paul himself died was blamed on "poisoned coffee" intended for the Pope.

The verdict

If the conspiracy was real, its alleged plan worked perfectly on one level. John Paul I was replaced by the ultimate hardliner, John Paul II, although nothing could keep the lid on the Vatican Bank scandal, which, in 1982, blew apart after the corpse of Roberto Calvi was found hanged beneath London's Blackfriars Bridge. Calvi was head of the elite Banco Ambrosiano, at the time the largest privately owned financial institution in Italy. When a British coroner pronounced his death a suicide – despite the victim being weighed down with 14 pounds of brick and stone, and his hands tied behind his back – a second inquest was demanded by Calvi's family, that lifted the lid on a Pandora's box of financial and political corruption.

See also: *Aldo Moro p.60*

1979
LOUIS MOUNTBATTEN
b. 1900, Windsor Castle, England
d. 1979, Sligo, Ireland
British statesman

On August 27th, 1979, while at his summer home in Sligo in the Republic of Ireland, Lord Louis Mountbatten – cousin of Queen Elizabeth II, and the last Viceroy of India – was killed by an IRA bomb planted in his boat in Donegal Bay. Simultaneously, 18 soldiers were killed by two bombs at Warrenpoint on the Northern Irish border. For a while, rumours circulated that the bomb that killed Mountbatten was of KGB origin, but although the Provisional IRA made use of training camps in Libya, and had communists among its members, direct Soviet involvement was unlikely. The IRA has always been capable of carrying out its own assassination plots – as it had a few months earlier when, on March 30th, Airey Neave, a leading figure in Margaret Thatcher's Conservative Party, was killed by a car bomb as he was leaving the House of Commons car park. Then, six years later, the IRA also took credit for the bombing at the Grand Hotel in Brighton, England, on October 13th, 1984. Tons of rubble dropped through seven floors of the hotel, barely missing Prime Minister Thatcher and most of her cabinet, who were attending their party conference. The Conservative MP, Sir Anthony Berry, and the wives of two other MPs were killed. Despite the devastation, Thatcher continued with the conference, describing the attack as "an attempt to cripple our Government."

See also: *Michael Collins p.44*

1980
JOHN LENNON
b. 1940, Liverpool, England
d. 1980, New York City
Musician and ex-member of the Beatles

When kings, presidents, and politicians are assassinated, a certain logic may be seen behind the tragedy, but the murder of John Lennon singer, songwriter, and Beatle, appeared to be simply mindless. On December 8th, 1980, at 10.50pm, Lennon and his wife Yoko Ono arrived home at The Dakota, New York's landmark apartment building on Central Park West when a fan, Mark David Chapman called out "Mr Lennon!" then pulled out a Charter Arms 38 pistol, dropped into a "combat stance," and fired five shots. A security guard

called 911; but Lennon was bleeding to death, and died at nearby Roosevelt Hospital. Chapman, a former mental patient, drug-addict, and born-again Christian, had asked Lennon for an autograph earlier in the day. After the shooting, he paced up and down until police arrived, reading J.D. Sallinger's *The Catcher in the Rye*. Although Chapman has never given a lucid reason for the killing, beyond that Lennon was "a phoney," he was found competent to stand trial, and is currently incarcerated at Attica State Prison, New York. Although seemingly irrational, conspiracy theorists claim that Chapman was/is a "Manchurian Candidate" (assassin programmed to kill on post-hypnotic command), who was possibly abandoned as unusable. A connection between Chapman and a religious organization called World Vision – an alleged CIA front organization that also had links to Jim Jones's People's Temple whose followers committed mass suicide in Guyana – is cited as evidence.

See also: *The Jonestown Mass Suicide p.154; The Manchurian Candidate p.223*

1981
RONALD REAGAN
b. 1911, Tampico, Illinois
d. 2004, Bel Air, California
US president

Ronald Wilson Reagan began his varied career as a radio announcer for the Chicago Cubs. He later became a movie actor, president of the Screen Actors Guild, TV host, governor of California, and finally president of the United States. He was also the first US president to be the victim of an assassination attempt and to survive.

On March 30th, 1981, a young man named John Hinckley fired six times at Reagan as he left an AFL-CIO conference at the Hilton Hotel in Washington, DC Reagan was hit in the chest; Press Secretary James Brady, police officer Thomas Delahanty, and Secret Service agent Timothy McCarthy were also wounded. Reagan survived after surgery at George Washington University Hospital where he told his wife Nancy: "Honey, I forgot to duck." At his trial Hinckley – who was arrested at the scene of the shooting – was found not guilty by reason of insanity. His defence was that he had shot the president in order to impress the actress Jodie Foster, who he had watched repeatedly in the movie *Taxi Driver*. The fact has rarely been mentioned that Hinckley's brother, Scott Hinckley, was vice president of his father's Denver-based firm, Vanderbilt Energy Corp. The Hinckleys

Bodyguards smother the body of President Ronald Reagan after he was hit in the chest after leaving the Hilton Hotel, Washington, 30th March, 1981.

and the family of the then US vice president, George H.W. Bush, also interacted both socially and in the oil business through Neil Bush, the brother of current president, George W. Bush. From these connections a theory has been woven, on the principle of "who benefits," that the attempt on Reagan's life was a Bush family conspiracy to oust Reagan, who the Bushes loathed and distrusted. George H.W. Bush was, of course, a former director of the CIA. There is no evidence to support the theory, of course.

In 1994, Reagan was officially diagnosed with Alzheimer's. He died on June 5th, 2004 of pneumonia at the age of 93.

See also: *The Bush Family and al-Qaeda p.27*

1981
ANWAR SADAT
b. 1918, Mit Abu al-Kum, al-Minufiyah, Egypt
d. 1981
Egyptian president

On October 6th, 1981, Egyptian President Mohamed Anwar El-Sadat was shot by gunmen who opened fire at a military parade for the eighth anniversary of the Yom Kippur war.

Winners of the Nobel Peace Prize are not, as a rule, assassinated, but there is always the fatal exception. Anwar Sadat is best remembered as the first Arab leader to make an official visit to Israel, where he met with Israeli prime minister Menachem Begin and spoke before the Knesset in Jerusalem on November 19th, 1977, creating an unprecedented rapport between former enemies. He had not, however, always played the peacemaker. His ascent to world renown began when, as a career officer in the Egyptian army, he took part in the 1952 coup which dethroned King Farouk and led to the appointment of Gamal Abdal Nasser as president of Egypt. He was a key figure in the wars with Israel in 1950s and 1960s and, after Nasser died in 1970, succeeded him as president. In 1973, he launched the final Yom Kippur War against Israel, and although Israel emerged victorious, some initial successes helped restore the Egyptian morale, and paved the way for the peace settlement several years later that would be both Sadat's crowning historical achievement and also the direct cause of his death.

The conspiracy theory
Few doubt that the assassination of Anwar Sadat was anything but what it appeared. He was killed by Islamic

fundamentalists, furious that he had established a rapport between Egypt and Israel, but it has been mooted that members of Sadat's security were part of the plot, and deliberately allowed the gunmen to get close to their target.

The evidence

Sadat visited Israel in 1977 at the invitation of Menachem Begin, in a radical and deliberate move towards forging a permanent peace settlement, which led to the 1978 Camp David Peace Agreement, brokered by US President Jimmy Carter. Sadat and Begin both received Nobel honours for their efforts, but the peace agreement was most unpopular in the Arab World, particularly to Muslim fundamentalists. Many believed that only a threat of force would make Israel negotiate over a Palestinian homeland, and the Camp David accords removed the possibility of Egypt, the major Arab military power in the region, from providing such a threat. The fundamentalist opposition grew so intense that in 1981 Sadat cracked down on Islamic organizations and student groups, making nearly 1,600 arrests. At the time, Sadat's support among ordinary Egyptians was also waning due to his heavy-handed methods, and because economic failures were widening the gap between the rich and the poor.

The assassins struck after Sadat had taken the salute, laid a wreath and was viewing an aerial display by the Egyptian air force. First, two grenades exploded, then gunmen leapt from a military truck in front of the presidential reviewing stand and ran towards the spectators, raking officials with automatic gunfire. Despite the presence of many security personnel, the attackers continued shooting for well over a minute. By the time the president's bodyguards returned fire at least ten people lay seriously injured or dead inside the stand. Security forces then shot and killed two of the attackers and overpowered the rest, as crowds of military and civilian spectators scrambled for cover. President Sadat was airlifted by helicopter to a military hospital, and died about two hours later. A number of other dignitaries, including foreign diplomats, were killed or seriously wounded.

The verdict

The Islamic Jihad organization, who opposed Sadat's negotiations with Israel, as well as his brutal use of force in the September crackdown, claimed credit. No evidence exists to suggest anyone else was responsible. Ayman al-Zawahiri, the leader of the assassins, is credited with having recruited Osama bin Laden into the movement.

See also: *Gamal Abdul Nasser p.51*

1984
HILDA MURRELL
b. 1906, location unknown
d. 1984, Shrewsbury, England.
   British peace activist and rose grower

Hilda Murrell, a 78-year-old retired rose grower, went shopping in March 1984. Three days later, her body, slumped against a tree and partially clothed, was found in a remote wood, seven miles from her house in Shrewsbury, England. She had been stabbed repeatedly, although hypothermia was the actual cause of death. Why anyone would have wanted to target a mildly eccentric spinster has been the subject of at least three police investigations, plus documentaries, books and plays. Police claimed that Ms Murrell was killed by a burglar, but serious inconsistencies in the evidence, her anti-nuclear campaigning, and the fact that her nephew was a Royal Navy intelligence officer during the Falklands war led to speculation of plots by British intelligence (MI5), and claims that she had seen secret information about the sinking of the Argentine cruiser the General Belgrano at the very start of the Falklands. In 1983–4 it was rumoured that the ship was sunk by the submarine HMS *Conqueror* on direct orders of Prime Minister Margaret Thatcher to destroy peace talks. The most popular theory was that British security forces staged a raid on Murrell's home to see if she had proof of these claims, accidentally killed her, and then faked a burglary/sex murder. A fresh "cold case" investigation was opened in 2004. In May 2005 Andrew Harold George was charged for her kidnap and murder. The killing was described as a "burglary gone wrong." Conspiracists remain unconvinced.

See also: *Sinking of the Belgrano by British Royal Navy p.228*

1985
PAUL CASTELLANO
b. 1915, Bensonhurst, Brooklyn
d. 1985, Manhattan New York
   Capo of Gambino crime family

The murder of Paul Castellano (Big Paulie) was more than just a classic New York mob hit. It was a full scale coup d'état by young Turks in the Gambino crime family. When driver, Tommy Bilotti, chauffeured his boss, Paul Castellano, through the Christmas rush hour in a black Lincoln Continental to Sparks Steak House on East 46th Street, no fewer than eight hit men waited for the boss's arrival, all wearing identical trench coats and fur hats. Castellano's car arrived at 5.30pm. As Big Paulie got out he and Bilotti took six bullets each. Castellano toppled into the gutter, while the assassins walked quickly to waiting cars. All that witnesses could say was that they saw the identically dressed men. A few weeks later, the New York newspapers declared John Gotti, the leader of this internal conspiracy who had organized the hit, as the new boss of the Gambino family. Paul Castellano had assumed leadership of the Gambino family when Carlo Gambino's health began to fail in the 1970s, despite a general rank-and-file feeling that Big Paulie was selfish, greedy, and stupid, something he totally confirmed by living in an unforgivably ostentatious mansion on Staten Island, actually modelled on the White House. He also refused to mingle with his family underlings, and had an open affair with his wife's maid, Gloria Olarte, who would ultimately betray him by helping the FBI bug the house. Rising young underboss, John Gotti, finally dared to make the case to his fellow *capos* that Big Paulie was a dangerously weak and inept leader and had to go. By the end of 1985, Gotti's view had prevailed and the transfer of power was carried out with ruthless efficiency.

See also: *The Mafia p.281*

1986
OLOF PALME
b. 1927, Stockholm, Sweden
d. 1986, Stockholm, Sweden
   Prime minister of Sweden

The murder of Swedish prime minister, Sven Olof Joachim Palme, and the wounding of his wife Lisbet, put a terrible end to the belief that Sweden was such a well ordered and civilized country its leaders could walk the streets of the capital without the need for bodyguards. Before the Palme murder, Sweden's most recent assassination of a head of state had been the killing of King Gustav III in 1792.

Olof Palme, who was mainly educated in the US, was a confirmed socialist and a dominant figure in Swedish politics. Close to midnight on February 28th, 1986, he was walking home from a cinema with his wife Lisbet on the central Stockholm street, Sveavägen. The couple were attacked by a lone gunman who fired two rounds with a .357 magnum. The first bullet killed Palme, the second left Lisbet wounded; the attacker escaped on foot. Christer Pettersson, a small-time criminal and alcoholic, was arrested in

December 1988, tried and convicted of the murder, but later acquitted on appeal. After additional evidence against him surfaced in the late 1990s, attorney general Klas Bergenstrand filed for a new court hearing, but in May 1998 the Swedish Supreme Court turned down the demand. Although police never found the murder weapon, Pettersson was picked out from a police line-up by Lisbet, but the appeals court questioned her accuracy. Pettersson was even awarded about $50,000 in compensation for his time in prison. Despite being cleared, the highly unstable Pettersson confessed to shooting Palme in an interview with Swedish writer Gert Fylking in 2001: "Sure as hell it was me who shot [him], but they can never nail me for it. The weapon is gone." Later still he retracted the statement and said he was not involved. An extensive manhunt, an $8.6 million reward and over 14,000 tips, all failed to come up with another suspect.

The conspiracy theories
The Palme assassination remains unsolved, but it has generated a range of conspiracy theories blaming everybody from Kurdish militants to right-wing Swedish police officers. The difficulty is that Palme was so determinedly unaligned that it is hard to isolate a single political enemy.

The evidence
Palme was a controversial political figure with strong views. He criticized the United States for the Vietnam War and its policies in Central America, and the USSR for the invasion of Afghanistan; he fought nuclear proliferation, and condemned the apartheid politics in South Africa.

The greatest suspicions have always fallen on the pre-apartheid government of South Africa, and recent testimony by former secret police agents testifying before the Truth and Reconciliation Commission seems to add weight to these. Dirk Coetzee, allegedly a senior officer in the police murder unit, claims that the assassination of Palme was part of an operation called "Long Reach," carried out by a unit of the South African secret police headed by Craig Williamson. Williamson admits he was involved in three other murders, but denies this one. According to the Swedish news agency TT, 80 or 90 South African agents participated in planning the murder, and it was carried out with the tacit connivance of the CIA while the Reagan administration and the Thatcher government turned a blind eye.

The verdict
The popular South African theory hinges on whether Dirk Coetzee is to be believed.

1986
BARRY SEAL
b. 1943, Baton Rouge, Louisiana
d. 1986, Baton Rouge
Drug smuggler

On February 19th, 1986, Adler B. (Barry) Seal was getting out of his white Cadillac in the car park of the Salvation Army Community Treatment Center in Baton Rouge when he was shot to death by a Colombian firing a small machine gun. Seal was reputed to have made more than $50 million smuggling drugs into the US from South America between 1977 and 1986.

The death of Barry Seal marked the start of an unravelling process that would reveal crucial details of the Iran-Contra conspiracy and involve many of the power elite of the Reagan administration including George H.W. Bush, Oliver North, Dewey Clarridge, John Pointdexter, Caspar Weinberger and even the young Bill Clinton who was, at the time, governor of Arkansas.

At the time, right-wing Contra guerrillas were attempting to bring down the Marxist Sandinista government in Nicaragua. In 1984 Congress had cut off funding for the rightist Nicaraguan resistance, but Reagan's hardliners and the CIA wanted to keep the fight going, and quickly figured out an obvious means of paying for it. The CIA station chief in Costa Rica, Joe Fernandez, knew that the FDN (Nicaraguan Democratic Force) – the Contras – needed alternative funds, and that those alternative funds would come from the already thriving Central American drug trade. Cocaine was obtained from Colombia and moved to Panama, where it was protected by Panamanian defence forces. From Panama, the drugs were moved through Costa Rica, where the shipments were personally guarded by the minister of public security. Flights to the final destination in the US were handled by the FBI and CIA, and the small airport in Mena, Arkansas was set up as a covert entry point, free from interference by US customs or the Drug Enforcement Agency (DEA).

Chosen by the CIA because it considered Arkansas a banana republic right in the US – where politicians could be bought on the cheap – Mena rapidly became the American hub of Iran-Contra operations. The clandestine training of Contra guerrillas took place nearby, and consignments of weapons were shipped out in the same planes that returned with the cocaine. The final piece of the conspiracy was handled by organized crime. Mena's small First National Bank was even purchased to launder the drug money, eliminating any financial middleman. Iran-Contra even outdid the Bay of Pigs invasion of Cuba in terms of the bizarre cast of characters needed for its operation. CIA and FBI agents worked with right-wing guerrillas, black-operations hired-gun mercenaries, illegal arms suppliers, plus cocaine dealers, and experienced drug smugglers with a background in aviation. Barry Seal was one of the latter, and may have been selected because he had an earlier history of flying explosives for anti-Castro Cubans and a reputation for being able to fly "anything with wings."

The conspiracy theory
Barry Seal was already deeply involved in a very dangerous game when he decided to run his own private conspiracy-within-a-conspiracy; at this point, the waters of world events mercilessly closed over him, and all of those around him decided that he posed too much of a risk to be allowed to continue to live.

The evidence
The death of Barry Seal might have remained just one more unexplained casualty of the drug-running world had not a C-123K military cargo plane with nose art that read "Fat Lady" crashed in Nicaragua on October 5, 1986, six months after his murder. For the plane was carrying weapons and CIA employees. There was clear evidence that it originated from Mena airport. Matters were further complicated by the fact that "Fat Lady" had been owned and registered to the late Barry Seal.

As investigators backtracked, it emerged that Seal had been running more games and playing many more sides against the middle than anyone – even his employers and co-conspirators – could have imagined. On the one hand, he was organizing the supply of cocaine that was ultimately funding the Contras, and had become a trusted associate of Cali cartel leader Jorge Ochoa-Vasquez. On the other hand, Ochoa was pioneering a new cocaine distribution route through Nicaragua with the help of the Sandinistas – clearly conflicting with the CIA plan.

If that wasn't complicated enough, Seal was also a snitch for the US Drug Enforcement Agency (DEA), who were using a relatively minor 1984 Florida indictment for quaaludes and money laundering to control him. The DEA was fighting the war on drugs, while the CIA was bringing in the coke. It turned out that "Fat Lady" had actually been given to Seal by the DEA so that he could document Sandinista complicity in cocaine trafficking; the plane was equipped with hidden cameras that took photos of key Nicaraguan government officials loading the plane with cocaine. Thus Seal found himself running coke for the CIA and the Contras while working a DEA sting on the Sandinistas – who were the Contra's opponents in the Nicaraguan civil war. Maybe Seal figured out that he could just keep slipping and sliding, but when the DEA sting went down, and the story was about to be told in open court, it blew Seal's cover to all of his multiple associates. He must have known then that he would not be allowed to live long enough to testify against Ochoa and the Sandinistas.

The verdict

By the start of 1986, there was a $500,000 contract out on Seal, but who was actually behind his murder is academic. Everyone from the CIA to the Colombian cartels needed Seal silenced, and he might have stayed that way had the "Fat Lady" not gone down, making further cover-up impossible. In an odd coincidence, a luxury Beechcraft King Air (N6308F) that once belonged to Barry Seal was later used by Texas Governor George W. Bush.

See also: *Iran Contra p.228*

1988
MUHAMMAD ZIA-UL-HAQ
b. 1924, Jalunder, India
d. 1988, near Bhawalpur, Pakistan
President of Pakistan

Occasionally a national leader will be assassinated, and a conspiracy suspected, but, aside from his immediate followers, the world hardly bothers to speculate because it feels better off without him. One such was Pakistani general and later president, Zia-ul-Haq, who ruled his country from 1977 to 1988. A veteran of the British and Pakistani military, he was appointed chief of army staff on April 1st, 1976 by Prime Minister Zulfiqar Ali Bhutto, but just over a year later, he staged a coup, overthrowing Bhutto's government and enforcing martial law. He promised elections within three months, and released Bhutto, but as Bhutto's popular support actually increased under Zia's military junta, the army rearrested Bhutto and charged him with ordering the murder of a political opponent. Bhutto was convicted, sentenced to death and, despite international protests, hanged in April 1979. Zia continued to promise elections but instead staged an impossible-to-lose referendum that secured him the presidency. He also cynically rode the rising tide of militant Islamic fundamentalism and

laid the foundations of Pakistan as a nuclear power, and for a possible confrontation with India. In early 1988, an anti-Zia movement was growing around Benazir Bhutto, the daughter of the executed PM, and it seemed as though Zia would again duck an election. Then Zia-ul-Haq died in an aeroplane crash on August 17th, 1988. Many refuse to believe that it was an accident, and hold either the United States or the USSR responsible, but few outside Pakistani appear to care.

1990
JONATHAN MOYLE
b. 1961, location unknown
d. 1990, Santiago, Chile
British journalist

In March 1990, Jonathan Moyle, the editor of Britain's *Defence Helicopter World*, was found hanging in a hotel room in Santiago, Chile, where he had been covering the Santiago air show as a guest of the Chilean air force. Chilean police initially ruled that the cause of death was either suicide or due to a mishap occurring during autoerotic asphyxiation. A Chilean judge later reopened the case and it was found that Moyle had been drugged, by being injected in the heel with a lethal substance.

It is theorized that Moyle was killed in response to his investigation of arms trafficking between Iraq and Chile, particularly his investigation of Carlos Cardoen, a Chilean arms manufacturer with ties to Saddam Hussein. Cardoen had devised a conversion that could transform the Bell Jet Ranger, a popular civilian machine, into a low-cost attack helicopter for nations in the developing world and those internationally barred from obtaining more sophisticated aircraft. According to defence industry sources, Saddam Hussein ordered more than 50 of these customized Jet Rangers as part of his build-up to his invasion of Kuwait (an invasion that subsequently triggered the first Gulf War). Cardoen had sold illegal cluster bombs to Iraq during the Iran-Iraq War in the 1980s, and Moyle may well have come too close to the details of his more recent deals, and the identities of Saddam's secret corporate backers in the United States and Europe.

See also: *Project Babylon: Iraqi Supergun and Gerald Bull p.159*

1991
DANNY CASOLARO
b. 1947, McLean, Virginia
d. 1991, Martinsburg, West Virginia
    US journalist

The Holy Grail of all conspiracy theorists has to be a unifying factor that links all the plots, cabals, secret societies, and shadow governments that they believe to be running the planet. The goal is to prove beyond doubt the existence of an underground power elite that covertly hands down power from one generation to the next, maintaining its unseen grip on world politics and the global economy. This unified and omnipotent master conspiracy has been given many names. One is the Octopus, and writer Danny Casolaro thought he was hot on the trail of the Octopus when he was found dead in a West Virginia hotel in 1991. He thus became part of possibly the most extraordinary political tale of the 1990s.

Casolaro first began to suspect the existence of the Octopus as a transnational power bloc pursuing its own interests through subversion and the overthrow of governments, dirty money and extra-electoral manipulation, when he was researching the "October Surprise." This is the as-yet unproven theory that members of the 1980 Ronald Reagan presidential campaign arranged a deal with the government of Iran to continue holding 52 American hostages in Tehran until after the election, in order to prevent President Jimmy Carter from benefiting politically from their release.

Researching a cast of players that included Iran-Contra spooks, Middle-Eastern weapons merchants, double-dealing politicos, bankers, terrorists, and oil tycoons, he came to believe that apparently unrelated events, for instance, the Inslaw affair – the theft of super-surveillance software used to spy on criminals and police alike – banking scandals such as BCCI, the Keating Five, and Silverado Savings and Loan; gun-running; illegal arms sales; bogus mineral oil investment scams; and drug smuggling to fund intelligence community black operations; were all interconnected. Furthermore, that top-ranking Justice Department officials, New York organized crime figures, and Medellin Cartel drug traffickers were all arms of the Octopus.

The conspiracy theory
Danny Casolaro was close to the truth and, therefore, could not be allowed to live. One of the arms of the Octopus organization "suicided" him.

The evidence
The conventional media largely dismissed Casolaro as a nut, even when some of his findings – for example, his work on Oliver North and Iran-Contra – were revealed to be correct. Thus, when his body was discovered, on August 10th, 1991, in room 517 of the Sheraton Hotel in Martinsburg, West Virginia, his death was used to prove that he was so obviously crazy he had killed himself. The only problem was that Casolaro's suicide looked like a case of self-overkill. Both arms and wrists had been slashed a total of at least 12 times; one of the cuts went so deep that it severed a tendon. The accordion file containing his recent research was missing. He had already told his family to be gravely suspicious if he was the victim of any kind of "accident." Furthermore, the four-sentence suicide note hardly seemed plausible, and when local police allowed a hasty, unauthorized, and illegal embalming, it added to suspicions that there was a cover-up. And then, in a bizarre final flourish, mourners at Casolaro's funeral were amazed to see two unknown figures appear. One of them placed a medal on Casolaro's casket and saluted, although Casolaro never served in the military.

In an odd postscript, Jim Keith, who co-wrote *The Octopus Secret Government and the Death of Danny Casolaro* with Kenn Thomas, died in 2004 at Washoe Medical hospital. He had gone into hospital for simple knee surgery but died when a blood clot entered his lung.

The verdict
If Casolaro was killed and his death made to look like suicide, he provides a grim warning to conspiracy researchers.

See also: *Gary Webb p. 79*

1992
BILL CLINTON
b. 1946, Hope, Arkansas
    President of the United States

Operation Mount Rushmore was the code name given to an alleged and incredible assassination plot against yet-to-be-elected presidential candidate, William Jefferson Clinton. It was planned to be executed during a campaign visit to San Francisco in the summer of 1992.

These allegations are primarily made by author, Rodney Stich, and while they might seem fanciful, he is praised on the internet as "an activist or crusader against hard-core government corruption for the past 30 years, starting as an FAA [Federal Aviation Administration] air carrier operations

Was a JFK-style hit planned for Clinton by Bush supporters to stop him winning the 1992 election?

inspector responsible for air safety at several major airlines, especially United Airlines. He documented hard-core corruption at UA and within the FAA."

The conspiracy theory

A JFK-style hit was commissioned on the still-unelected Clinton by a conspiracy of various interests who wanted a second term for George H.W. Bush, and who so actively feared a Clinton presidency that they were prepared to kill to avoid it. It allegedly involved agents and officials of the Central Intelligence Agency (CIA), the Office of Naval Intelligence (ONI), the Republican Party, and Mossad, Israel's intelligence service. The financing of the operation supposedly came from a mysterious figure called Chan Wang.

The evidence

The information in Stich's *Defrauding America* comes mainly from two sources, both from the intelligence community, who independently revealed the same details. The primary source was, at first, just called "Agent X," but it was later revealed to be a Lieutenant Commander Robert Hunt, from the Office of Naval Intelligence. According to Hunt, the Clinton assassination was to be a virtual rerun of the Kennedy assassination, with snipers taking down the candidate outside the Ritz Carlton Hotel. A hit team was to be assembled at the San Francisco military base at the Presidio. As Hunt told the story: "I was ordered last summer [July,

1992] to go to San Francisco by Graham Fuller, CIA; Dick Pealer, ONI; and John Kaplin, CIA. These people were my handlers. I was told to go to the Bay Area. I flew from NAS [Naval Air Station] Norfolk to NAS Alameda, where I was to meet another agent. He was the CIA station chief for SF [San Francisco]. His name is Robert Larson. He made arrangements for me at the Presidio. The next day the team arrived, and I wondered why this hit team was in town. I got a call from a woman who said she was Mossad and we needed to meet. So we did; we had lunch. I asked her her name, and she said it was Anna Colburn. I later found out her real name was Yossi Jameir. We talked about why I was in town, and I asked for what reason. She said they wanted to hit Clinton."

Of the operation itself, Hunt alleged: "Knowing Clinton was coming to town in the next few weeks, we set up shop. Weapons, escape routes, rendezvous, etc. Clinton was expected to come and stay at the Ritz Carlton. That's when we were going to do it. My men and I took up a position across the street from the Carlton before Clinton's arrival. We photographed the whole area for best possible results. Anyway, three weeks before he was due to arrive, word had it there was a leak. Where, was unknown. So my team and I pulled out in fear of being caught. That night we were told to eliminate all factions involved, including the Mossad agents."

Faced with the task of killing everyone involved on the operation, Hunt seemed undaunted but, just in time, the slaughter was called off: "I get a call on my pager ... stop operations. When I asked the reason why, they said they found the leak." The story was that one of the Mossad agents was dating a security guard and both had talked too much. "Our job was to, of course, take care of it. So that night when he got off work at midnight, and he went to catch the BART [Bay Area Rapid Transit] train at Market [Street] to go home, my friend and I grabbed him and threw him in front of a BART train on Market Street. They thought he committed suicide."

The verdict

When contacted by independent researchers, the Secret Service Branch in Los Angeles declined to comment on the story, referring the enquiry to the public affairs office in Washington DC. An official there denied any knowledge of the story, and stated that if the San Francisco office were contacted, that they too would refer back to public relations office. As the assassination was aborted the story remains basically unprovable.

See also: *John Fitzgerald Kennedy p.54*

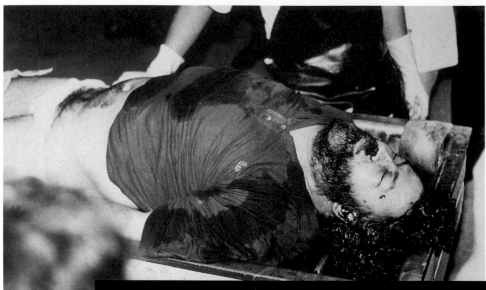

Notorious Colombian drug king, Pablo Escobar, was shot dead while trying to flee from police on December 2nd, 1993.

1993
PABLO ESCOBAR
b. 1949, Medellín, Colombia
d. 1993, Medellín, Colombia
Colombian drug lord

Perhaps both the Colombian authorities and the CIA concluded that the only way to stop Colombian cocaine kingpin Pablo Escobar was, simply, to kill him. Pablo Emilio Escobar Gaviria had risen from being a teenage car thief in his home town of Medellín to become the head of *El Cartel de Medellín* (the Medellín Cartel), gaining a worldwide reputation as one of the most ruthless and powerful drug dealers in history, and making billions smuggling cocaine into the US in the process. At the height of his power, he kept a herd of rhinoceroses in the grounds of his heavily guarded estate, and was suspected of having ordered more than 100 murders, including the killing of three presidential candidates in Colombia, one aboard an Avianca jet in 1989. Despite his crime, though, Escobar was a hero to poor Colombians, and was looked on as a Robin Hood figure who gave freely to the poor when it suited him.

A war between Medellín and Colombia's other main drug cartel, *Cartel de Cali*, however, took a major toll on his organization, and Escobar brokered a deal with the Colombian government whereby he would spend five years in *La Catedral*, a luxurious private prison he designed and built

himself. He escaped in 1992, fearing extradition to the US. After this a police task force was created to capture or kill Pablo Escobar, while a criminal death squad known as *Los Pepes* (People Prosecuted by Pablo Escobar), went on a bloody rampage killing 300 of Escobar's followers. Los Pepes were widely credited with sharing information with local law enforcement and the CIA. Escobar himself was killed on December 2, 1993, while trying to run from police in Medellín. Some claim snipers of the US Special Operations Command may have taken part in the kill.

1994
KURT COBAIN
b. 1967, Aberdeen, Washington
d. 1994, Seattle, Washington
American musician

Musician Kurt Cobain – who achieved superstar status with the band Nirvana – supposedly killed himself with a shotgun on April 5th, 1994, but rumours that he was murdered refuse to fade. Although some stories have to be subscribed to an Elvis Presley-style fan denial, certain facts appear to conflict with the suicide verdict which was the officially stated reason for his death.

It is claimed that no legible fingerprints were found on the fatal shotgun Cobain reportedly used, nor on the pen used to write the "suicide note," or on the box of shotgun shells from which the gun was loaded. Cobain is claimed to have died with three times the lethal dose of heroin in his bloodstream, which would have been enough to knock over even the most tolerant addict. The last four lines of his "suicide note," beneath the signature, appear to have been written by a third party. The final supposed anomaly is that Cobain's credit card was used twice between the time he died (as determined by the medical examiner) and when his body was found. A Los Angeles private investigator named Tom Grant, who claims to have extensively investigated Cobain's death, suggests that Cobain's wife, the singer Courtney Love, headed a conspiracy to kill Cobain. His dubious and mainly hearsay evidence centres on a singer named "El Duce," from a band called The Mentors. Before he was killed by a train in 1997, "El Duce" made a name for himself by alleging that Love offered him $50,000 to kill Kurt Cobain. There is no proof for any claims that Cobain was murdered. The official cause of death was suicide.

See also: *Elvis Presley p.61*

1995
YITZHAK RABIN
b. 1922, Jerusalem
d. 1995, Tel Aviv, Israel
   Prime minister of Israel

Cynicism regarding the political assassinations by "lone gunmen" had reached such a point that, by 1995 and the assassination of Israeli prime minister, Yitzhak Rabin, the official story of the assassination was widely disbelieved from the very start.

Born in Jerusalem, and trained on a kibbutz, Yitzhak Rabin had been chief operations officer of the Haganah underground during the Israeli war of independence, then chief of staff in the Israel Defence Forces (IDF) in the victorious Six-Day war. Following his retirement from the IDF, he became ambassador to the US, was elected to the Knesset, and finally succeeded Golda Meir as prime minister.

The government-appointed Shamgar Commission stated that Rabin was shot dead by right-wing zealot Yigal Amir on November 4th, 1995. Amir had waited in an adjoining car park after a peace rally in Tel Aviv's Kings of Israel Square, and then shot Rabin with a 38 calibre Beretta as he was about to get into his car. Amir fired three times, hitting Rabin twice, and also wounding a bodyguard. Rabin was rushed to the nearby Ichilov Hospital where he died on the operating table. Amir apparently considered Rabin a traitor for his role

in establishing the Oslo Accords – for which Rabin was awarded the 1994 Nobel Peace Prize, along with Yasser Arafat and Shimon Peres – that created the Palestinian Authority and granted it partial control over parts of the Gaza Strip and West Bank of the Jordan River. The Oslo Accords had polarized Israeli society; some people saw them as a welcome advance towards the cause of peace while others, like Amir, believed that Rabin had given away land that rightfully belonged to Israel. Amir was caught at the scene and was sentenced to life imprisonment, with six additional years for injuring the security guard.

The conspiracy theory
To consider Yitzhak Rabin a traitor to Israel, however, was clearly absurd, and a general sense of disbelief, coupled with various anomalies in the evidence presented by the Shamgar Commission, caused many to start talking about Rabin's murder as the Israeli version of the John F. Kennedy assassination. One of the most vexing questions – in a country that has lived with terrorism for over half a century and is one of the most security conscious places on Earth – is how Yigal Amir was able to penetrate the safe zone where Rabin's bulletproof car was parked.

The evidence
In an exact parallel with the John F. Kennedy conspiracy furore, an amateur video tape of the Rabin assassination surfaced, and many people who had seen this believed they saw Rabin continuing to walk on, apparently unharmed, to his car, and some of them drew the conclusion that Rabin had not been killed by Amir, and that possibly Amir had been firing blanks. Opposing and, in some cases, truly bizarre conspiracy theories began to circulate. The primary theory is summarized by Victor Ostrovsky, a former Mossad case officer now based in Canada, who claims that: "Rabin was murdered in a well-orchestrated assassination carried out by extremist right-wing officers of the Shabak (the Israeli security service). The man sitting in jail is only a puppet triggerman."

The verdict
As with the Kennedy assassination, the Rabin controversy continues, with no possible resolution presenting itself. However, as the Kempler tape appears to be authentic, the Ostrovsky theory does deserve some credence, unless, of course, this is merely covering up a similar conspiracy by renegade elements in Mossad, or even possibly in the Jewish right-wing of the Russian mafia.

1996
ADMIRAL JEREMY BOORDA
b. 1938, South Bend, Indiana
d. 1996, Washington DC
    US chief of naval operations

Admiral Jeremy "Mike" Boorda joined the US navy as an enlisted sailor and rose through the ranks to become a four-star admiral and chief of naval operations – the navy's most senior military officer and commander of all its active-duty and reserve personnel. He hardly appeared to be the kind of man who would commit suicide, yet, on the afternoon of May 16th, 1996, he went home, supposedly for lunch, and shot himself (twice, according to some reports).

The first explanation for the suicide was that Boorda was embarrassed that he had worn medal ribbons to which he was not entitled. When it transpired that Boorda was in fact entitled to wear the decorations, a new story emerged: he was suffering from stress about downsizing plans for the navy. Boorda had supposedly left two suicide notes, but neither of these was ever released. In this atmosphere of doubt and implausibility, a bizarre story – never either confirmed or refuted – circulated on the internet. Boorda was the leader of a group of 24 US admirals and generals who planned to arrest President Bill Clinton for treason as authorized by the US uniform military code. Clinton had allegedly supplied classified information to the head of the Red Chinese Secret Political Police, but Boorda's death pre-empted the action of these senior officers.

See also: *Bill Clinton p.70*

1996
WILLIAM COLBY
b. 1920, St Paul, Minnesota
d. 1996, Rock Point, Maryland
    Director of Central Intelligence Agency

When a former director of the CIA dies mysteriously, conspiracy theories will inevitably surface. William Egan Colby was not just a CIA director, but had been an insider on many of the CIA's most notorious excesses, ever since beginning his career as a World War II agent for the CIA's precursor, the Office of Strategic Services (OSS). Colby launched the Accelerated Pacification Campaign and Operation Phoenix during the Vietnam War, and was involved in the overthrow of Salvador Allende in Chile. In 1976, he revealed a mass of CIA secrets to Congress, including CIA drug trafficking,

and attempts to assassinate Fidel Castro. He was fired by President Gerald Ford and replaced with George H.W. Bush. After going canoeing on the night of April 29th, 1996, Colby vanished; he had not mentioned his highly unusual plan to go night-time canoeing to his wife. A week later, his body surfaced in a marsh near his home. Local police quickly closed the case as an accident, stating he had suffered an aneurism, which caused him to drown. Two opposing theories immediately circulated. One was that Colby was killed on the orders of the Clinton White House because he knew the "truth" about the 1993 suicide of Vince Foster, the attorney who worked for Bill and Hilary Clinton. The other was that he was executed to settle old scores, perhaps because he was allegedly the informant "Deep Throat" during the Watergate scandal.

See also: *Fidel Castro p.52; Salvador Allende p.60; CIA Running Heroin in Vietnam p.141; Watergate – A Pentagon Coup D'etat p.148; Death of Vince Foster p.162*

1996
AMSCHEL ROTHSCHILD
b. 1955
d. 1996, Paris, France
    US banker

On occasion, the circumstances of an assassination are so murky that the background becomes totally impenetrable. When, in July 1996, Amschel Rothschild, chairman of Rothschild Asset Management, was found dead by a maid in the luxurious Bristol Hotel, a new episode in a banking saga that goes back more than 200 years was uncovered. The Rothschild family gained prominence by financing such projects as the construction of European railways and the British military campaign that led to the final defeat of Napoleon at Waterloo in 1815. However, Amschel Rothschild had been embroiled in a gathering scandal that was linked to a spectrum of dubious banking interests that ranged from the Vatican to the Cali cocaine cartel. Rothschild Asset Management had suffered huge losses because of his miscalculations, the Rothschild family were facing a financial disaster to the tune of almost a trillion dollars, and the European Commission had launched a series of investigations into a number of suspicious transactions associated with Crédit Lyonnaise.

Police claimed that Amschel had taken his own life, but only after the news had been withheld by the family for several days, and the suicide method – tying one end of a belt to a towel rack, the other around his neck and then jerking backwards – was wryly described by one investigator as "very innovative." The general consensus would appear to be that, if the Rothschilds themselves did not organize the removal of an "inconvenient" family member, they facilitated the covering of the real killer's tracks.

See also: *Pablo Escobar p.72; Pope John Paul I p.63*

1996/7
TUPAC AMARU SHAKUR
b. 1971, New York City
d. 1996, Las Vegas, Nevada
  Rap artist

BIGGIE SMALLS (THE NOTORIOUS B.I.G.)
b. 1972, Brooklyn, New York
d. 1997, Los Angeles, California
  Rap artist

When rap superstars Tupac Shakur and Biggie Smalls were gunned down in drive-by shootings just six months apart, the hip-hop community treated the linked events as though they were a combination of the death of Elvis Presley, the murder of John Lennon, and the Kennedy assassination.

Although the killings remain unsolved, conventional wisdom argues that the two rappers, former friends, fell out when Tupac signed with the notorious Marion "Suge" Knight's Death Row Records and Wallace joined Sean "Puffy" Combs's Bad Boy Records. As the rivalry between the "West Coast rap" (with links to the infamous Bloods gang of LA) and the "East Coast rap" (with similar connections to the Bloods' rivals the Crips) escalated, it turned deadly. Tupac was fatally shot in Las Vegas, Nevada on September 7th, 1996 – following the highly publicized prizefight between Mike Tyson and Bruce Seldon – and died in the University of Nevada Hospital six days later. The prime suspects were Crips gang members connected to Combs. Then, on March 9th, 1997, Biggie was shot and killed in Los Angeles, in what was seen as an act of retribution.

The conspiracy theories
The less than complete evidence has caused numerous stories to circulate. Among the many claims, one of the most recurrent is that Suge Knight may have orchestrated both murders (even though Tupac was one of his artists); that he enlisted the help of corrupt black cops to kill Biggie;

that the police investigation was shut down when it got too close to these cops; that the FBI may have been fomenting the hatred between Biggie and Tupac; and that the FBI had Biggie under surveillance when he was killed. It has also been suggested that Tupac faked his own death; and that the shooting was a government assassination. The government conspiracy buffs cite the fact that Tupac's mother, Afeni Shakur, was a member of the Black Panther Party, and questions were also asked as to why Tupac was not wearing his usual bullet-proof vest on the night of the shooting, and how his close friend Yafeu "Kadafi" Fula, told police he could identify the assailants, but was shortly after killed in New Jersey.

The most extreme conspiracy is the Seven Day Theory, culled from lyric references in Tupac's *Makaveli* album, and the amount of number sevens surrounding his death. Tupac was shot seven months after *All Eyez on Me* was released. He was shot on September 7th. He survived for seven days after the shooting before being pronounced dead. At the time of his death he was aged 25, two and five equal seven. The numerological list goes on and on, and The Seven Day Theory ultimately promised that Tupac would return in September 2003, exactly seven years after his death, but, unfortunately, he never appeared.

The evidence
The scenario of gangsta rap tit-for-tat killings is to some degree borne out by a *Las Vegas Times* investigation that pointed out how Tupac and the crew at Death Row generally depended on members of the Bloods gang for security, while Biggie and the Bad Boy Crew depended on Crips' members for security when visiting California. An unnamed source claimed that Biggie – who was also in Las Vegas for the fight – offered to pay the Crips to murder Tupac, and it was noted by the LAPD's Compton Gang Unit that the Crips were bragging about the killing soon after returning to Los Angeles.

The verdict
The murders are unlikely to be resolved, especially as they are not only a matter of legend, but money-making legend.

See also: *FBI v Black Panther Party p.59*

1999
EDMUND SAFRA
b. 1932, Beirut, Lebanon
d. 1999, Monaco
  International banker

In the world of international banking, the rewards can be fabulous, but the price of failure is equally extreme. When Edmund Safra, one of the world's richest and most powerful men, became involved, along with Russian prime minister, Mikhail Kasyanov, in the 1998 disappearance of a $4.8 billion International Monetary Fund loan designed to prop up the failing rouble, he seemingly paid with his life. Investigations by the FBI and Swiss officials revealed that the $4.8 billion was transferred from the New York Federal Reserve to accounts at the Republic Bank of New York, controlled by Safra, before the Russian Central Bank defaulted on most of its short-term debt. In the ensuing chaos, Safra had transferred money to other foreign accounts through a tortuous series of transfers, but had later decided to cooperate with the FBI, detailing how the Russian mafia had been using US banks to launder money. Safra's death soon afterwards, in a fire in his luxury Monaco home, was initially blamed on his nurse, Ted Maher, but uncomfortable evidence such as the fact that his bodyguards – former Israeli intelligence agents – were given the night off by his wife Lily, who escaped the fire, caused the chief prosecutor in Geneva to theorize that the murder was a result of Safra's decision to help the FBI. In an ultimate irony, Safra died from carbon monoxide fumes while firefighters were unable to penetrate the elaborate security system of his penthouse.

See also: *Amschel Rothschild p.74*

2000
WOLFGANG HULLEN
Date and place of birth not known;
d. January 20th, 2000
  German politician

When a key player in an ongoing scandal suddenly commits suicide for "personal reasons," suggestions that it might have been arranged are hardly surprising. When the death is also that of a powerful and influential politician, the same suspicions take a quantum leap, as they did in Germany in 2000 when Wolfgang Hullen, the chief financial officer of Chancellor Kohl's formerly ruling party, the Christian Democratic Union, was found hanged in his apartment.

Hullen's suicide came just as a parliamentary commission of enquiry was looking not only at the secret accounts through which former Chancellor Kohl had admitted channelling more than one million dollars in illegal campaign contributions, but also at whether money paid to Mr Kohl's party in secret – as much as $4.5 million of unknown origin – could have influenced subsequent political decisions. As other players in the drama included international arms dealer Karlheinz Schreiber, and the Saudi Arabian military, even more scepticism surrounded Hullen's death when it was revealed that he had left a note admitting to embezzling party funds. In the 1998 German election, the CDU were voted out of power and, after Hullen's death, the party's executive committee asked Kohl to resign from his post as honorary party chairman. Kohl stepped down but kept his seat in parliament after 16 years as chancellor.

2001
AHMED SHAH MASSOUD
b. 1953, Jangalak, Afghanistan
d. September 2001, Khvajeh Ba Odin, Afghanistan
  Leader of Afghanistan's Northern Alliance

That the leader of the most effective anti-Taliban force in Afghanistan should be assassinated on September 9th, 2001, just two days before the al-Qaeda attack on New York's World Trade Center, has been interpreted by many to have been a house-cleaning operation by the Islamic fundamentalist alliance between al-Qaeda and the Taliban to eliminate any possible supporters of an American retaliation against Afghanistan for the attacks. Ahmed Shah Massoud was a Kabul University engineering student who became an Afghan guerrilla leader, and played a leading role in driving the Soviets out of his country in the 1980s. In the early 1990s, he became defence minister under President Burhanuddin Rabbani. Following the collapse of Rabbani's government and the rise of the Taliban, Massoud retreated to the hills to lead the Northern Alliance, a coalition of Afghani opposition groups that controlled the mountainous areas in the north – some ten percent of Afghanistan's territory and perhaps thirty percent of its population. The apparent intention of the suicide attack by two men posing as journalists was to wipe out most of the Northern Alliance ruling council with a bomb supposedly hidden in a video camera, but Massoud and Mohammed Asim Suhail, a Northern Alliance official, were the only victims. One attacker was killed by the explosion, and the other was shot while attempting to escape.

Daniel Pearl, the first hostage to be executed on video.

2002
DANIEL PEARL
b. 1963, Princeton, New Jersey
d. 2002, Karachi, Pakistan
    American-Israeli journalist

As the shadow of Islamic terrorism darkened the start of the 21st century, the video image of a hostage or hostages pleading for their lives before their taped execution had become horribly familiar. *Wall Street Journal* reporter, Daniel Pearl, had the regrettable role of being the first. On January 23rd, 2002, Pearl, while investigating the case of convicted shoe bomber Richard Reid, was on his way to an interview with a supposed terrorist leader when he was kidnapped by that militant group, The National Movement for the Restoration of Pakistani Sovereignty. Using the almost unbelievable email address *kidnapperguy@hotmail.com*, his captors issued demands, including the freeing of all Pakistani terror detainees, and the release of a halted US shipment of F-16 fighter jets to the Pakistani government. When these demands were not met, Pearl's throat was cut, live on video, and then he was decapitated. Edited versions of the tape were shown on TV networks across the globe. Three months later Ahmed Omar Saeed Sheikh and three other suspects were charged with his murder. Conspiracy theorists alleged that Pearl was an Israeli secret agent who infiltrated the al-Qaeda network and was beheaded for betraying Osama bin Laden, but with little or no foundation.

2003
DR DAVID KELLY
b. 1944, Rhondda, Wales
d. 2003, Oxfordshire, England
    British scientist

Dr David Christopher Kelly was part of the team that assembled a British government dossier on possible weapons of mass destruction (WMD) held secretly by the regime of Saddam Hussein; the dossier would be used as justification for the 2003 invasion of Iraq. After he talked to a reporter about possible fabrications in the dossier, Kelly was found dead near his home, apparently having committed suicide.

In 2002, Dr David Kelly was working for the Defence Intelligence Staff on the dossier the British government had commissioned in preparation for what later became the 2003 invasion of Iraq. Kelly was eminently qualified to do this work. His experience with biological weapons at Britain's Porton Down research station had led to his appointment as a United Nations weapons inspector in Iraq after the Gulf War, and his uncovering of Iraq's biological weapons programme had earned him a Nobel Peace Prize nomination. He was, however, not happy with a claim that Iraq was capable of firing battlefield biological and chemical weapons within 45 minutes of an order to use them, but his superiors had been assured that this was the case by the British Secret Intelligence Service (MI6).

Kelly was even less happy when, after the US-British invasion, no WMD whatever were found. In May 2003, Kelly met with BBC reporter Andrew Gilligan, agreeing to talk without attribution, and told Gilligan that the 45-minute claim was of dubious authenticity and had been inserted in the dossier at the instance of Alastair Campbell, the director of communications for Prime Minister Tony Blair. The story caused a political storm, with the Government denying any involvement in the intelligence content of the dossier, and pressing the BBC to reveal its source. Kelly reported his conversation with Gilligan to his superiors, but was surprised when the Ministry of Defence went public with a confirmation that Kelly was the insider who had talked.

The conspiracy theory
Kelly was "suicided" by British government assassins, both to silence him and to deter others from talking to the media.

The evidence
Kelly was summoned to appear as a witness before two committees of the House of Commons which were investigating the situation in Iraq. When he was questioned by a foreign affairs select committee on July 15th, Kelly appeared to be under severe stress. He told the committee that he had not said the things Andrew Gilligan had reported his source as saying; members of the committee came to the conclusion that Kelly had not been the BBC's informant.

Two days later, however, matters took a sinister turn. On the morning of July 17th, Kelly was working at home in

Oxfordshire. At about 3.pm, he told his wife that he was going for a walk. He appears to have gone directly to an area of woodland about a mile from his home, where he took a quantity of the painkiller co-proxamol and then allegedly cut his left wrist with a knife. Kelly's wife reported him missing shortly after midnight, and he was found dead early the next morning. After a five-month investigation, the government-appointed Hutton Enquiry reported that Kelly had committed suicide as a result of the strain created by the WMD furore and the resulting investigations.

Although suicide was officially accepted as the cause of death, some medical experts have raised doubts about the veracity of the verdict, including three doctors who wrote to the *Guardian* newspaper arguing that the autopsy finding of a transection of the ulnar artery could not have caused fatal blood loss. They also contended that the co-proxamol Kelly had taken amounted to only a third of what would have been required for a lethal dose. Further, two paramedics at the scene of Kelly's death raised questions about the quantity of blood they found at the scene; they told the *Guardian* that they saw only a small amount of blood on plants near Kelly's body, and a patch of blood the size of a coin on his trousers. They said they would expect to find several pints of blood at the scene of a suicide involving an arterial cut.

The verdict

The findings of the Hutton Enquiry stand and, lacking any fresh evidence, Dr David Kelly's death joins the other murky issues that surround the inception of the war in Iraq. The questions raised about Kelly's death by the paramedics and doctors who wrote to the *Guardian* have not been answered.

See also: *British Broadcasting Corporation (BBC) p.84; Blair and the Missing Iraq WMDs p.170*

2003
ANNA LINDH
b. 1957, Stockholm, Sweden
d. 2003, Stockholm
Swedish minister for foreign affairs

It was inevitable that conspiracy theories should form around the murder of Anna Lindh, the Swedish Social Democrat who was tipped to succeed Göran Persson as prime minister of Sweden. Lindh was stabbed on the afternoon of September 11th, 2003, while shopping at Stockholm's Nordiska Kompaniet department store. The killer was able to escape, but not before surveillance cameras had recorded

images of Mijailo Mijailovic, a Serbian living in Sweden, who had been released from a mental institution just five days before the killing; he was supposedly enraged by Lindh's support for the US-led military campaign against Serbia during 1999. Mijailovic confessed, and a report concluded that he was not criminally insane at the time of the murder, and he was sentenced to life imprisonment; on appeal he was transferred from prison to a closed psychiatric ward. The most popular theory, among those who refuse to accept the lone assassin story, is that Persson had been "programmed" by Mossad – who perhaps had MKULTRA-style programmers working on his "Serbian rage" while he was institutionalized – to remove Lindh as one of the architects of a Swedish foreign policy less than sympathetic to the government of Israel and its treatment of Palestinians. Right-wing elements in SÄPO, the Swedish security service may also have been part of the plot.

See also: *Olof Palme p.67; MKULTRA p.143*

2004
KENNETH BIGLEY
b. 1943, Everton, England
d. 2004, Iraq
British contractor

Kenneth Bigley was kidnapped on September 16th 2004, along with Americans, Jack Hensley and Eugene Armstrong; all were subsequently beheaded. The tapes of Bigley, pleading with Prime Minister Tony Blair to meet the captors' demands to release Iraqi women prisoners, forcefully demonstrated how much more sophisticated the hostage-takers had become in their manipulation of the international media since the assassination of Daniel Pearl in 2002.

Tapes are now prepared with an instant translation and produced so quickly that they have effectively become a means of conducting a proxy dialogue between Abu Musab al-Zarqawi himself and world leaders such as Blair. It was unavoidable that the Bigley tape should prompt serious consideration of a supposed conspiracy between the kidnappers and the Al Jihad-friendly media, who colluded in making all news coverage of the kidnapping reflect badly upon the US and British governments. When Al Jazeera TV broadcast the tape, which showed Bigley squatting in an iron cage, dressed in an orange jumpsuit of the sort worn by Muslims detained at the US military detention centre in Guantánamo Bay, begging for his life, it went beyond reporting on a kidnapping; it was participating in an act of psychological warfare. Ever

Kenneth Bigley's pleas could not prevent his eventual execution.

since the murder of Daniel Pearl, the counter-allegation that hostage tapes, such as the one of Bigley, are the work of western intelligence agencies – the CIA, Mossad, MI6, or even Donald Rumsfeld's Office of Special Plans. These theories are lent weight by the presence of background furniture in some videos that closely resembles US military issue.

See also: *Daniel Pearl p.77*

2004
GARY WEBB

b. 1955, Corona, California
d. 2004, Carmichael, California.
US investigative journalist

The news that Gary Webb, who shocked the world with his allegations linking the CIA to crack cocaine trafficking,had suddenly committed suicide, was greeted with scepticism.

In August 1996, investigative reporter Gary Webb wrote a series of articles called *Dark Alliance* for the *San Jose Mercury News* that exposed links between the CIA and the drug trade. He ultimately won a Pulitzer Prize for his stories of how Nicaraguan drug traffickers had sold tons of crack cocaine in Los Angeles and funnelled millions of dollars in profits to the CIA-supported Nicaraguan Contras during the 1980s. On Friday, December 10th, 2004, however, Webb was found dead in his home outside Sacramento. At 8.20am, "A Better Moving Company" arrived at Webb's home and discovered a note posted to his front door. The note read: "Please do not enter. Call 911 and ask for an ambulance." Inside, Webb lay dead from gunshot wounds to the head.

The conspiracy theory
First reports stated that Webb had died of two shotgun blasts to the face. This was later changed to a "single gun shot wound" when people began to question how or why a man would (or could) shoot himself in the face twice. Media stories also told how Webb's body was found by removal men, but none of them seemed to question why a man who was about to commit suicide would plan a house move. These two seeming contradictions were enough to start questions being asked, but they were only the beginning of a rapidly unfolding puzzle. But while conspiracy theorists looked to simple shotgun murder, others were piecing together a slightly different, but equally dark story. According to Webb's ex-wife, Sue Bell, Gary Webb had been distraught in the weeks before his death over his inability to land another job at a major newspaper.

The evidence
Credible sources close to Webb told how he had been receiving death threats, was regularly followed, and was concerned about strange individuals seen on multiple occasions breaking into and leaving his house before his apparent suicide. Ricky Ross, one of Webb's primary sources, had spoken to Gary in the days before his death. Webb told Ross that he had seen men scaling down the pipes outside his home and that they were obviously not burglars but "government people." It was also mentioned that Gary was working on a new story concerning the CIA and drug trafficking. At the same time, however, some evidence would seem to exist for Webb being deeply depressed. Although most of the claims in *Dark Alliance* had, in the end, been confirmed by independent investigations and government inquiries, he had been mercilessly attacked by much of the mainstream press when the CIA/crack cocaine story broke. His life had been made miserable by media pundits who seemed more concerned with killing the messenger than understanding the message. The death threats and surveillance – from and by the "government people" – might be more his paranoia than tangible reality. In his final year, Webb had paid for his own cremation, named Bell as the beneficiary of his bank account, and sold his house because he could no longer afford the mortgage payments.

The verdict
Some people have reasonably made the point that, if the government so desired, they had more subtle ways at their disposal of killing a nosey, gadfly journalist than by shooting him in the head with a shotgun.

See also: *Barry Seal p.68; Danny Casolaro p.70; The CIA Flooded Ghettos with Cheap Crack Cocaine p.165*

One thousand, five hundred years after the death of Christ, his name dominated the western world. Christendom ruled. Although its power was based on doctrines that the preacher of peace, love and understanding would have struggled to sanction. But while he may not have approved, he'd have recognized the template. For the Church ruled with an all embracing brutality that even the most despotic of Roman Caesars would have struggled to maintain.

Church control of information

Central to the control that the Holy Roman Catholic Church exercised over the medieval world was the manipulation of the flow of information. The policy was easy to implement, of eventually impossible to preserve. At the centre of each community was a church. Each church was controlled by a clergyman who took his orders directly from the head of the organization, the incumbent pope. The congregations were told that the Bible was the one true word of God, and that they should do everything that was written therein. They were also told that the Bible said their pope was head of the Church, infallible and to be obeyed without question.

No one could argue with that. Literacy was the sole province of the clergy and a few privileged scholars. Even if an ambitious merchant or inquisitive yeoman taught himself to read in his native tongue, the literature available to him was predominantly written in Latin. Books were hand-written by hand-picked monks in the official language of the Church. There were few of them, and they were concerned predominately with pro-papal propaganda.

Of course there was the occasional dissenting voice. The 14th-century theologian John Wyclife, for example, who was the first to translate parts of the Bible into English, and proposed – to the horror of his prosperous colleagues – that followers of Christ should eschew earthly riches. He also pointed out that he had found no mention of a "Pope" in any part of the New Testament, calling for all men to: "Shake away all ye lawe that ye pope hath maad."

The Church's response to troublesome voices like Wyclife's was to declare them heretics. Heresy, the people were told, was the most heinous sin listed in the Bible that they weren't allowed to read. The punishment for that sin was burning at the stake. Wyclife luckily died before the papal officers could catch up with him, but they exhumed his body and burnt it anyway. His biblical translations were deemed heretical and all copies of them were also burnt. For almost a century afterwards mere possession of an English translation of the holy scriptures would result in a person being burnt alive at the stake.

The advent of printing

The Church maintained its grip on the flow of information until the mid-1400s when there occurred what is for many the single most important invention since the wheel. Sometime around 1448 a German goldsmith by the name of Johann Gutenberg married the technologies of moveable metal type and oil-based inks to produce the world's first printing press. In 1456 he printed 300 copies of the first mechanically produced book – a Bible.

In a world unhampered by patent or copyright laws, the technology quickly saturated the rest of Europe. By the turn of the century there were printing presses operating in every major city. Translators were working to produce books in their native tongues, and the price of books fell from the equivalent of a year's wages for a brewer to a level whereby he could afford one after a day's work. Entranced by the new opportunity to read, and to do so in their vernacular, people from all walks of life sought out scholars who could help them master the skill.

The Church knew it was facing a potential catastrophe and clamped down accordingly. Licences were issued to printers that forbade them from printing books not in Latin. A papal decree in 1502 ordered the destruction of all books in any way critical of the Church or the pope. For a while they got away with it. The initial interest in reading came largely from those who wanted to better their position. There was high demand for technical and scientific works, and while religious works were popular, the threat of martyrdom ensured that they contained nothing controversial.

Then in 1517 the radical German theologian, Martin Luther, famously nailed his 95 Theses to the door of a church in Wittenburg. "Print," he is quoted as saying, "is the best of all God's inventions," as translations of his critique of the Church infiltrated the whole of Europe. In the face of continual persecution Luther went on to publish the first German edition of the Bible. Meanwhile, in England, a priest by the name of William Tyndale was determined to complete the work that Wyclife had started. Tyndale is reported as telling one of the senior clerics who initiated his subsequent trial: "If God spare my life, 'ere many years I will cause a boy that driveth the plow to know more of the Scriptures than thou dost." He did it. Or at least completed the New Testament in 1525, and started work on the Old Testament. Unlike his predecessor Wyclife, Tyndale was also able to circulate substantial numbers before the clergy caught up with him. As they had done with Wyclife, they burnt Tyndale. But this time before he was actually dead.

But Tyndale's mission was complete. The boy who drove the plow could now look into the scriptures. And therein learn that there was no such thing as an infallible pope; there were far worse sins than heresy; one of the far worse sins was Love Of Money; and that he was under no obligation to fund the sumptuous lifestyle of the clergy.

The new information age led to a perpetual conflict between those in authority who wanted to control what was written, and those who wished to write whatever they wanted. The appearance of daily newspapers in England, for example, coincided with – and was partly precipitated by – the outbreak of the Civil War in 1648. For a while the pioneering press ran amok as both sides started to grasp the importance of the medium as a recruiting forum and propaganda tool.

The temporarily victorious Republican, Oliver Cromwell, devoted considerable energy and legislative power to clamping down on printed media. Only books that he had personally read and approved were allowed into print and any illicit publication would result in the printer's door being kicked in by Roundhead troops, ensuring destruction of presses and likely imprisonment. Nevertheless, a network of underground newsletters flourished, and when the

monarchy was finally restored in 1660 many of these developed into the forerunners of what we now know as newspapers. Charles II, however, was no more keen on a free-speaking press than Cromwell had been.

In 1662 the Printing Act was passed and Surveyor O The Press, Sir Roger L'Strange, was put in charge of enforcing its draconian remit. L'Strange made his motives very clear on the suppression of news:

> It makes the multitude too familiar with the actions and counsels of their superiors, too pragmatical and censorious, and gives them not only an itch but a kind of colourable right and licence to be meddling with the government.

By the end of the century it was clear, even to the government, that there was no chance of holding back the tide of information. No legislation was ever going to be equal to the ingenuity of those who wished to put their printed opinions before the eyes of inquisitive readers, and for a further 300 years the world learnt all that was new via the printed word. It was not until the 1920s, over 400 years after Gutenburg pressed his first page, that a new medium arrived which would change the way we found out about things.

Information via the airwaves

In 1894 Italian inventor and card-carrying fascist Guglielmo Marconi started experiments with wireless broadcasting from England. In 1914, as World War I commenced, the technology required to broadcast speech was perfected and the British Government immediately banned all radio broadcasts on the grounds that they would interfere with military communications. The Navy effectively commandeered the new technology, and the "wireless" was denied to the British public until the British Broadcasting Company (BBC) was handed a monopoly to exploit it in 1922.

In the US the invention was a lot less constrained. The Hungarian electrical engineering genius, Nikola Tesla, had pipped Marconi to the post and made his first broadcasting demonstration in 1893. It meant that by the time speech broadcasting was a practical reality, more development work had taken place in the US than in Europe. There was also a much stronger commercial impetus, unimpeded – albeit temporarily – by government control. By the end of 1922 there were 460 radio stations broadcasting around the US, householders were buying up millions of sets, and Tesla and Marconi were waging war in the courts.

While the British were tentatively exploring the new medium, and the US was allowing it to proliferate with little regulation, the Germans were acting quickly to ensure that the state had complete control of all radio broadcasting. By the mid-1920s the German Post Office controlled both the national broadcasters and the radio transmitters. Ten years later a shrewd and ambitious Nazi grasped the potential of a state-run radio network as a tool and moved quickly to incorporate it into his panoply of propaganda.

Goebbels' art of disinformation

Hitler's Minister For Propaganda, Dr Joseph Goebbels, had already proved himself fastidious in his duty to spread and control the Nazi communication machine. His street posters were radical exercises in economy of word and image. He had mastered the forum of oratory to the point of making it an art. His newspaper *Der Angriff* (The Attack) was nothing less than a masterclass in twisting the political point until it became populist opinion. He pressurized motion picture makers in order to ensure that he had input on both the style and the content of their product through his Reich Film Chamber. He even managed to stop German comedians telling funny jokes about him and his cohorts.

Throughout the 1930s Goebbels not only expelled foreign journalists who were critical of the Nazi regime but dispatched hundreds of compliant German journalists around the world to act as spies, and to disseminate pro-Nazi disinformation. He became convinced that the written word was close to defunct as a medium for the spread of information, and that the recorded, and broadcast, word was destined to be mightier than the pen. He took his inspiration from his Fuhrer's own thoughts on propaganda in his fascist manifesto Mein Kampf:

> The great masses of nation will always and only succumb to the force of the spoken word ... every

great movement on this earth owes its growth to great speakers and not to great writers.

Accordingly, Goebbels had already produced the world's first multi-media mail shot when in 1932 he sent out 50,000 copies of a gramophone record small enough to fit into a standard envelope. A year later, when Hitler was in power, it was Goebbels who initiated the mass burning of books in towns and cities all over Germany. Libraries and bookshops were ransacked by party members who built bonfires in the streets of books by Jewish, Communist and "subversive" authors.

But the control of radio broadcasting was Goebbels very first and highest priority. He ordered the manufacture of millions of cheap Volksempfanger, or People's Radios, so that virtually every home could afford a set. He filled the National Broadcasting Company with Nazi propagandists and commenced to broadcast the party line to the nation. He even appointed "wireless wardens" to ensure that every time there was a major broadcast it was pumped through loudspeakers in all public places. "With the radio," he boasted, "we have destroyed the spirit of rebellion."

As war with Germany became inevitable, the British Government took note of Goebbels' information machinery and established its own Ministry Of Information, an entirely ineffective organization run by a series of hapless civil servants, all of whom were lampooned and vilified by the media. Quite justifiably. As late as 1940 an internal memo was circulated to Controller Lord Davidson suggesting that all postmen be reminded that they had a duty not to repeat idle rumours. The memo stated:

> I gather that the Express Dairy and the United
> Dairies have already been approached and that
> their roundsman have acted as disseminators,
> leaving copies of leaflets with each bottle of milk.
> Owing to paper shortage, I feel we ought to
> concentrate on the milk roundsman himself and
> get him fully instructed so that he can pass on
> the correct message by word of mouth.

While the MOI was asking the milkman and the postman to head up their propaganda team, Goebbels was typically ahead of the

Joseph Goebbels, the master of Nazi wireless propaganda, pictured during a radio broadcast on April 28th, 1939.

game. If he could destroy the spirit of rebellion in Germany through radio broadcasting, could he not achieve similar results in the UK? His masterstroke was to hire one, William Joyce, to broadcast his version of the news to the British people. Joyce was a New Yorker, who was raised in the UK where in the early 1930s he became enamored with fascism, eventually fleeing to Germany in 1939 where he offered his services to the Nazis. Goebbels took personal responsibility for Joyce's broadcasts, and between them they came up with a style, and content, that actually struck a chord among the dispirited and underinformed British public. They created an array of satirical characters who were stereotypically upper class, patronizing, corrupt, stupid or just out of touch with the majority of the populace. Not entirely dissimilar to the men in charge of the MIO. Joyce was dubbed "Lord Haw Haw" by the *Daily Express* and in 1940 was drawing an estimated six million listeners across the UK.

When Winston Churchill was appointed Prime Minister in 1940, he initiated a shake-up of the MOI, demanding a much more sophisticated and less patronizing system of delivering information to the masses. He also ensured that the BBC came

on side to broadcast to the world the Allied version of events. So subtle and effective was the subsequent campaign that apparently even Goebbels came to be impressed.

Joyce was hanged as a traitor in 1946. Nine months earlier, holed up in a Berlin bunker, Russian troops advancing, Goebbels poisoned his six small children, shot his wife in the head and then committed suicide. The Third Reich was smashed, but with a legacy of carnage and depravity that lives with us.

Doctor Goebbels was one of a handful of men responsible for transforming the Nazi Party into a force of evil that changed the world. As the world sifted through the literal and psychological debris of the Second World War, it became apparent that his role was of paramount significance. Every time a government, political party or an organization engages in a cover-up, seeks to mislead, spins bad news or endeavours to manipulate the media, they owe a debt to Joseph Goebbels for creating the art of disinformation.

In turn, every time we are misinformed, misled or manipulated by those same people, we owe a debt to Johan Gutenberg for creating, what some would argue, remains the most efficient and reliable medium of information – the printed word.

1922
BRITISH BROADCASTING
CORPORATION (BBC)

"Independent" broadcaster was involved with espionage and propaganda

The BBC was established in 1922 by a consortium of businesses involved in new broadcast technology, to establish a national radio network in the UK. In 1927 the BBC was granted a Royal Charter of Incorporation, and its unique structure was put in place. The BBC is ostensibly an independent broadcaster; however, it is funded by compulsory public subscription, which is collected by the government. The board of directors are all appointed by the current government, the directors in turn appoint a director general, with overall responsibility for running the corporation.

The first director general was Sir John Reith, a man of high principal who saw the BBC's role as: "Contributing consistently and cumulatively to the intellectual and moral happiness of the community." Reith is often reported as being dedicated to maintaining the corporation's independence from the government, but in reality was very much a man of the establishment. During the General Strike of 1926, for example, he wrote the prime minister's speeches on the subject, refusing to allow opponents of government policy any airtime until after the dispute had been settled.

As governments have come and gone, and director generals have done the same, relationships between the BBC and the government of the day have never been consistent – although invariably the ruling party will claim anti-government bias, while the BBC complains of unnecessary political interference.

As recently as 2004 Director General Greg Dyke, Chairman of Governors Gavyn Davies, and journalist Andrew Gilligan were all forced to resign over The Hutton Report. The report, which many believe to be a cover-up, fiercely criticized the BBC over the way they investigated government claims that Iraq had developed weapons of mass destruction.

The conspiracy theory

Although the BBC is generally regarded as a bastion of incorruptible truth, its reputation is tarnished by past involvement with intelligence agencies. This inevitably leads to accusations that its news agenda is sometimes influenced by the intelligence community.

The BBC employs thousands of people, and it would be wrong to give the impression of an organization teeming with espionage agents. However, many theorists remain convinced that British intelligence continues to hold a powerful influence within the corporation.

The evidence

The infamous spy, Guy Burgess, worked as a reporter for the BBC from 1936 to 1944. He was given the job, apparently by Prime Minister Neville Chamberlain, of delivering secret messages to French premier, Edouard Daladier and Italian dictator, Benito Mussolini. While in the employ of the BBC, Burgess worked as a double agent on the payroll of both the British and Russian governments.

During World War II the BBC made invaluable contributions to the war effort by broadcasting Allied propaganda, coded messages to resistance fighters in occupied Europe, and by training secret agents in broadcast techniques.

The intelligence services had some success during the Cold War in convincing the government to use the BBC to carry on some of those clandestine wartime activities. As early as 1946, the head of the BBC's European Services, and former wartime spy Sir Ivone Kirkpatrick recommended getting the BBC on board to assist in anti-Soviet propaganda. By 1949 the Foreign Office had established the Information Research Department (IRD), a propaganda tool which acted as a conduit for information about the USSR. According to Stephen Dorril's 2001 book MI6: Fifty Years of Special Operations: "The IRD regarded its relationship with the BBC as perhaps its most important, and it became, according to one former IRD operative, 'the official source for Bush House's (BBC Foreign Language Headquarters) East European Services.'"

It was also during the 1940s that the practice of vetting all BBC staff by "the special assistant to the director of personnel" was initiated. Their job was to provide a list of all job applicants to MI5 who then provided clearance, or declared the applicant a "security risk." The procedure was stopped in 1985, after an exposé in the Observer newspaper, which also revealed that no government had ever given permission for such vetting.

The verdict

The British intelligence services have always maintained a strong presence within the BBC and undoubtedly continue to do so. And, as its founder, Sir John Reith, showed during the UK's General Strike in 1926, if the establishment is perceived to be under threat, those running the corporation can be quick to abandon the independent line.

However, the BBC has on occasion distinguished itself by standing up to the government of the day. For example, in 2004 many believe that the BBC, and journalist Andrew Gilligan, were vindicated by the *Butler Report,* a second enquiry into government claims over WMD in Iraq. There was a feeling that the *Hutton Report* had been a whitewash, and that Dyke, Gilligan and Davies were victimized for daring to criticize the government. Unfortunately, the BBC governors failed to back Dyke, Gilligan and Davies, indicating again that the establishment protects its own.

See also: *Dr David Kelly p.77; Cambridge Spies p.138; The Smearing of Colin Wallace p.158*

1958
JOHN BIRCH SOCIETY
Right-wing organization disseminated global conspiracy theory

The John Birch Society was started by businessman Robert Welch in Indianapolis in 1958. Welch was a committed Christian, a patriot, and dedicated anti-communist. In 1954, he wrote a biography, entitled *The Life of John Birch,* about a missionary who, while preaching in China, worked for American intelligence. Birch was killed in 1945 by Chinese troops and Welch believed that he was the first American martyred by communism. He honoured his memory by naming his organization after the spy, and dedicating his life to fighting communism. At the Indianapolis launch of the society, Welch and 12 other "patriotic and public-spirited men" worked out their philosophy, and Welch published their thoughts in *The Blue Book of the John Birch Society.*

Welch was a hard worker, avid recruiter and persuasive speaker. By 1961 the society claimed to have more than 100,000 members and was starting to get its voice heard, mainly through the publication of their magazine *American Opinion.* Since its inception the society has functioned as a pressure group and publishing house.

Welch died in 1985 and, although the organization subsequently declined slightly, the past few years have seen a revival, which some commentators have put down to their pioneering conspiratorial views.

The conspiracy theory
The central tenet of the John Birch creed is that there is a global communist conspiracy. Robert Welch traced this back to the German Masonic secret society, the Illuminati. He believed that Karl Marx, author of the Communist Manifesto, was in the pay of the Illuminati, and that they had started both the French and Russian Revolutions.

Web page of the John Birch Society, showing the exposure of a "new world order" as its first objective.

In his 1963 book, *The Politician*, Welch accused an extraordinary array of people of being part of the conspiracy. They included ex-presidents, Truman and Roosevelt, CIA director, Alan Dulles, and the president at the time, Dwight D. Eisenhower, of whom he said: "He is a dedicated conscious agent of the communist conspiracy."

After the Cold War, the John Birch Society shifted its emphasis away from a communist conspiracy, although some of its writers warn that it is still a significant threat. Society author John Stormer wrote in the 1998 introduction to his reissued multi-million seller *None Dare Call It Treason*: "Communism, which some believe (or hope) died in the Soviet Union, is alive and on the march in Asia, the Middle East, Central and Southern Africa and through guerrilla groups in Central and South America."

Today, the Society spends a lot of its time criticizing the United Nations for its part in orchestrating world affairs.

The evidence
Much of Welch's evidence of a communist conspiracy within the US was based on his observations of what he felt was a degeneration of society. For example, in a 1970 bulletin, he says: "I believe that at least 90 percent of all the hippies, young criminals, and heartbreaking misfits, who are now

ruining the wonderful minds and bodies and opportunities for permanent happiness which nature gave them, would never have fallen for the cleverly deceptive and cruelly destructive communist line if parental authority had seen that they were given pats on the back, often enough, hard enough, and low enough while they were still at the right age for such discipline."

He was also keen to point out that there were others, not necessarily affiliated with the John Birch Society, who also believed in the conspiracy. Former FBI director, J. Edgar Hoover, for example, who said of communism in 1956: "The individual is handicapped by coming face to face with a conspiracy so monstrous he cannot believe it exists."

In more recent times, President George Bush caused excitement among those who think as the John Birch Society do. In his 1991 State of the Union address he said: "What is at stake is more than one small country, it is a big idea – a new world order, where diverse nations are drawn together in common cause." Bush has used the phrase "New World Order" on several occasions, and this is seen as proof that he is part of a global conspiracy.

The verdict

Since the end of the Cold War, the spectre of an international communist conspiracy has proved to be invalid. The John Birch Society has been, to a large extent, overtaken by those events, and only recently started to make an impact again with its theories on Bush's New World Order. When Bush refers to a NWO, it is less likely to be a reference to an international conspiracy, however, than a desire to see US style democracy practised in those countries that he has on his famous "Axis of Evil" list – so the John Birchers are likely in for further disappointments in their search for a grand anti-American world conspiracy.

See also: *Carroll Quigley p.179; Freemasons p.284; The Bavarian Illuminati p.285*

1958
THE REALIST
Satirical magazine which was the first to publish conspiracy theories
First published 1958, New York City
Publication ceased 2001

The publisher of *The Realist*, Paul Krassner, describes himself as an "investigative satirist," *People* magazine referred to him as: "The Father of the Underground Press." An FBI

agent subsequently wrote to *People* saying: "*The Realist* is an unimportant, smutty rag. To classify Paul Krassner as some sort of social rebel is far too cute. He's a nut. A raving, unconfined nut."

The Realist was launched in the offices of teen comic, *Mad Magazine*, and for many was merely an adult version of that publication. But Krassner was keen to mix social relevance in among the satire. The magazine was the first to provide a forum for legendary conspiracy researcher, Mae Brussell, who used it to propound her theories on the kidnapping of newspaper heiress, Patty Hearst; The Watergate scandal and the 1963 assassination of President John F. Kennedy, among others. *The Realist* also published political commentary from a range of important writers including Norman Mailer, Ken Kesey and Joseph Heller.

When the magazine ran into financial difficulties in the 1970s, it was the conspiracy theory element that attracted ex-Beatle John Lennon to donate. He once told Krassner: "If anything ever happens to me … it won't be an accident."

The last issue of *The Realist* maagazine appeared in 2001, but Krassner continues to write about conspiracies. His 2002 book *Murder at the Conspiracy Convention* included examinations of President Clinton's well-documented affair with intern Monica Lewinsky, and the 1995 bombing of a federal building in Oklahoma City. His 2004 book, *Magic Mushrooms and Other Highs*, deals with one of the author's other areas of expertise.

See also: *Mae Brussell p.181*

1960
LIBERTY LOBBY
Right-wing publishing and pressure group

The Liberty Lobby was set up by reclusive publisher Willis Carto as a "pressure group for patriotism." It evolved into a nexus of publications dedicated to conspiracy theory and political philosophy. Carto was initially a member of the John Birch Society, and friend of founder Robert Welch. But the two fell out, it is believed because Welch found Carto's views too extreme. He is quoted as saying: "If Satan himself, with all of his superhuman genius and diabolical ingenuity at his command, had tried to create a permanent disintegration and force for the destruction of the nations, he could have done no better than to invent the Jews."

One of Carto's first publishing ventures was the 1962 reprint of *Imperium: The Philosophy of History and Politics* by his hero Francis Parker Yockey. Yockey had worked on the team that prosecuted Nazi war criminals after World War II, but had resigned, believing that the Nazis were actually in the right. *Imperium* was effectively a manifesto for fascism, and it had a profound influence on Carto. He said that Yockey was: "A great force of atomic power."

For many years Liberty Lobby's flagship newspaper was *Spotlight*, which was launched in 1975 and known for its investigations into secret societies, such as The Bilderberg Group and the Skull & Bones Society. The weekly tabloid was one of the most popular ever to deal with conspiracies, and at its peak was selling over 300,000 copies an issue.

In 1978, *Spotlight* faced closure after publishing an article by an ex-CIA agent, claiming that another of his ex-colleagues, Howard Hunt – imprisoned for his part in the 1972 Watergate scandal – was involved in the 1963 assassination of President John F. Kennedy. Hunt sued the paper for libel, and in 1981 won damages of $650,000. The judgement was overturned in 1983 when Liberty Lobby hired JFK expert and trial lawyer Mark Lane to defend them. *Spotlight* subsequently claimed that Lane: "Proved to a jury that Hunt was connected to the assassination and that the CIA had killed Kennedy."

Among the panoply of other publications founded by Liberty Lobby was the *Journal of Historical Review* – the magazine of the Institute for Historical Review (IHR), which he cofounded in 1978. The IHR is an organization predominantly concerned with denying that Hitler exterminated six million Jews.

The relationship between Carto and his partners at the IHR was tempestuous, and issues of editorial and financial control came to a head in the mid 1990s. The IHR sued Carto for fraudulent practices, specifically over the disbursement of millions of dollars that had been bequeathed to the IHR by a descendent of the inventor Thomas Edison. In 1996, Carto was instructed to repay the IHR $6.43million, the judge said: "Much of his [Carto's] testimony in court was different from his previous testimony; much of his testimony was contradicted by other witnesses or by documents. By the end of the trial I was of the opinion that Mr Carto lacked candor, lacked memory, and lacked the ability to be forthright about what he did honestly remember."

Carto continued to fight both the IHR, and numerous other organizations in court throughout the 1990s and 2000s. He has not had great success, and alleges that there is a conspiracy against him involving the CIA, corrupt court officials, Mossad (The Israeli Secret Service), and the equally litigious cult of Scientology. In 2003, officials in Switzerland issued a warrant for Carto's arrest on charges of financial crimes, including money laundering in connection with the IHR case.

One of the consequences of the heavy legal fees and expensive judgments against Carto and the Liberty Lobby, was the closure of *Spotlight* magazine. Carto has since launched two publications dealing with similar conspiratorial themes, *The Barnes Review* and *American Free Press*.

Both of these publications have alleged that the *Journal of Historical Review* is controlled by the Anti-Defamation League (ADL), the organization that campaigns against anti-Semitism. The ADL itself says that Carto is: "One of the most influential American anti-Semitic propagandists of the past 50 years."

See also: *John Birch Society p.85; The Anti-Defamation League p.249; Holocaust Denial p.253*

1961
PRIVATE EYE
Fortnightly British satirical magazine that exposes cover-ups
First published 1961, London, England

The British magazine *Private Eye* was started by a group of ex-public school boys in the early 1960s. Its provenance has led to accusations of elitism, snobbery and even racism, nonetheless, it has flourished as a fortnightly publication with a reputation for attacking a wide range of targets. *Private Eye* maintains secrecy about its ownership, but one of its renowned owners was the British comedian and satirist Peter Cook.

Although the magazine is essentially a satirical organ – providing a platform for the UK's best humorists and cartoonists – it also plays a vital role in exposing scandal and financial irregularities. Many of the stories it breaks are specific to the UK, detailing local government corruption and lampooning British media figures. Paul Foot, a leading left-wing investigative journalist, was a regular contributor to the magazine until his death in 2004.

Over the years it has also tackled a series of global issues, and had extraordinary success in pioneering alternative theories that prove more credible than the official versions. The corrupt financial practices of media mogul Robert Maxwell; the blowing up of an aeroplane over Lockerbie, Scotland; and the controversy surrounding the safety of the measles, mumps, and rubella vaccine (MMR) are some of the stories it has investigated. Often in fuller detail than the mainstream press.

One of the *Eye's* strengths is that it allows journalists to write stories anonymously, which their legitimate editors would never allow into print. This policy has resulted in the magazine being in an almost perpetual state of litigation against those who seek to use the libel laws to keep it quiet.

See also: *Pan Am Flight 103 p.158; Measles, Mumps, Rubella Vaccine p.204; MOSSAD Killed Robert Maxwell p.258*

1965
SEARCHLIGHT

British anti-fascist monthly periodical that was infiltrated by the security services
First published 1965, London, England

Searchlight is a UK magazine dedicated to exposing activities of far-right organizations, racists and anti-Semites. Started by former Communist Party member, Gerry Gable, it is inevitably the source to which the mainstream media turn when they require information on right-wing extremists. Its two main targets are the extremely right-wing National Front and British National Party. However, many left-wing organizations refuse to cooperate with *Searchlight* because of their suspected links with British Security Services.

The roots of the conspiracy go back to 1963 when Gable and two associates were arrested for breaking into the home of renowned Holocaust denier, David Irving. They were subsequently fined for impersonating telephone engineers. Their lawyer claimed that they had effected the break-in hoping to find documents to give to Special Branch, the covert arm of the UK police force.

In 1977, when Gable was a producer for London Weekend TV, he sent a memo to his employers detailing the subversive activities of some of his colleagues. The following references led to accusations that Gable had a close relationship with the security services:

> ... according to my top level security service sources, they inform me in the strictest confidence ... I have now given the names I have acquired to be checked out by British/French security services, especially the French and German connections and the South American stuff is being checked by Geoffrey Stewart-Smith's institute. He has strong CIA links. I may try somebody in the Israeli Foreign Office that I know for some checks.

See also: *Holocaust Denial p.253*

1973
FORTEAN TIMES

Monthly magazine that investigates the paranormal, conspiracy theories and strange phenomena
First published 1973

The *Fortean Times* has a level of popularity and newsstand distribution that rivals mainstream magazines. Its original founders, Bob Ricard and Paul Sieveking, started it in 1973 as a small magazine dedicated to furthering the research practises of Charles Fort. Fort was a native of Albany, NY who became determined to accumulate truthful scientific information left out of mainstream journal reporting because it did not fit the belief paradigm of modern science. This included such anomalous realities as frogs jumping from the trunks of felled, centuries-old trees, strange rocks and fish falling from the sky, and UFOs.

Beginning in the late 1800s, Fort ferreted out research on such things, first at the New York Public Library, and later at the British Museum library. His work culminated in the publication of four books: *The Book of the Damned* (1919), *New Lands* (1923), *Lo!* (1931), and *Wild Talents* (1932). Ricard and Sieveking drew inspiration from his work to create a regularly produced catalog of articles on cryptozoology and the paranormal.

Fort was among the earliest to recognize unknown aerial phenomena as possible space visitors – even inventing such terms as "teleportation" – and firmly believed that a great deal of reality was screened out of authoritative sources. For this reason, the original Fortean Times became as much sought after for the peek it offered underneath official cover-ups, as it did for the latest catalog of UFO and Loch Ness monster sightings.

Today, the magazine is owned by conglomerate, Dennis Publishing, but retains a gawking admiration for weirdness and still runs regular columns examining conspiracy, uniquely bridging a conceptual gap between the paranormal and the parapolitical.

1976
THE INTERNET

Computer software reveals key to hidden world government

The World Wide Web that connects all the computers on the planet, and allows them to communicate with each other, developed from early experiments by the US Defense Department in the late 1960s. The military needed a

Tim Berners-Lee, at the Massachusetts Institute of Technology (MIT), in 2000.

system that ensured computers could still share data in the event of nuclear war, or natural disaster.

They came up with the ARPANET (Advanced Research Projects Agency) a forerunner of the internet. In the mid 1980s The National Science Foundation developed the NSFNET as a centrally linked communications tool for academic institutions.

In 1991, British computer programmer, Timothy Berners-Lee, built the first web page, accessible from any other computer, and is often credited as being the man who invented the World Wide Web. Berners-Lee also insisted that the components he had developed to create web pages should be free of charge. It was this that would ensure access to the internet for all.

By the mid-1990s the internet was a resource available to the whole world, whereby anyone could use a web of connected computers to send electronic messages, cyber-chat, and access millions of pages of information.

There is no governing body regulating the internet, and the explosion of information, easily produced by anyone, makes it a highly volatile medium. The personal, commercial and official information stored on computers has been compromised as experts develop new ways to access other people's information. This can range from simple theft of a user's credit-card details, to attacking a large corporation's vital networks through computer "viruses."

The leading computer software company in the world, and provider of the bulk of our internet technology, is the renowned Microsoft Corporation. The head of Microsoft, Bill Gates, is the richest man in the world worth, according to *Forbes Magazine,* a massive $46.6billion in 2004. There is no doubt that Gates has accumulated such a fortune by being totally ruthless in business, and accusations of sharp practice have always dogged the Corporation. A common accusation is that they patently leave computers vulnerable to external access.

The conspiracy theory

The very fact that the internet was developed by the military is enough to convince most conspiracy theorists that it must serve their interests. The existence of the "Echelon" project, the 1947 agreement between the US, UK, New Zealand, Canada and Australia which allows them to monitor communications on each other's behalf, adds fuel to the fire of paranoia. Initially the project was concerned with eavesdropping on telephone and radio communications, but since the advent of the World Wide Web, a surveillance system was put in place that uses a "virtual dictionary" to catalog word-specific emails and, if enough suspect words are used in conjunction, it refers them to a human monitor. It has been estimated that Echelon can sift through three billion emails an hour. Many countries excluded from the

Echelon agreement have alleged that the system is used in industrial and commercial espionage.

In 1999, Andrew Fernandez, a scientist working for a Canadian security firm, claimed that he had found evidence that Microsoft were colluding with the National Security Agency to allow the latter to spy on personal computers. He said: "The result is that it is tremendously easier for the NSA to load unauthorized security services on all copies of Microsoft Windows, and once these security services are loaded, they can effectively compromise your entire operating system." The claims were vehemently denied by Microsoft, but most suspicious computing magazines appeared to have no trouble finding other experts who concurred with Fernandez's theory.

Microsoft itself is at the centre of one of the most fantastic theories of the modern age. It is alleged that their involvement with the internet is entirely satanic and Bill Gates is the "Antichrist" or the Beast of Revelation which the Bible foretells will come in the last days. St John's beast carries the number 666 on its forehead. Revelations 13 says: "And he causeth all, both small and great, rich and poor, free and bond, to receive a mark in their right hand, or in their foreheads: and that no man might buy or sell save that he had the mark of the beast, or the number of his name."

The all-pervasive presence of Microsoft products, allied with the ever-increasing use of the Internet as a commercial tool, indicates that Gates is about to bring that prophecy to fulfillment.

The evidence

Gates' money has clearly brought him power, making him a prime suspect for being part of a hidden world government. He is a member of the Bilderberg Group, the conclave of powerful men who meet once a year in secret and provoke much speculation among conspiracy theorists. Some even have Gates down as the head of the modern-day descendents of the 18th-century German secret society, the Illuminati. The founder of the original Bavarian Illuminati was Adam Weishaupt. There is a school of thought that his name is actually a cipher. Adam was the first man and Weishaupt means "Wise Head" in German. The First Wise Man.

Similarly the name Bill Gates is a cipher. B. Ill gives the initials and stands for Bavarian Illuminati, and Gates refers to the fact that he is the keeper of the Gate through which a New World Order will arrive.

When it comes to connecting Gates with the Beast of Revelation, however, the theorist has to rely on the fuller name Bill Gates III. Using a complex numeric system, allied

A European Parliament investigation of the ECHELON system was prompted by concern over rights and freedoms.

to the Microsoft operating language, ASCII, it can be shown that both Bill Gates III and Windows 95 (a Microsoft product) will add up to 666. By the same code alignment, the names Adolf Hitler and Josef Stalin may also add up to the number of the Beast.

By following a complex system of procedures using another Microsoft product, EXCEL 95, it is possible to find a hidden window entitled, "The Hall of Tortured Souls", through which one can see the "proof" that Gates and Microsoft are agents of the Devil. Either that, or proof that Microsoft software designers had too much time on their hands.

The verdict

It is possible that the whole ASCII code for Gates/Microsoft equals Satan conspiracy, originated as a joke. Apparently the numbers also take some manipulation before they produce the 666 required. But a surprising number of people take it very seriously. Gates is clearly a powerful man who wields tremendous influence. Time will tell if he is also planning to precipitate the Apocalypse.

See also: *The Echelon Dictionary Exposed p.165; Daniel Brandt p.187; The Bavarian Illuminati p.285*

1983
CLASS WAR

Anarchist group (infiltrated by MI5) and magazine
First published 1983, Swansea, Wales

Class War – the name of both the magazine and the organization which publishes it – was started by an anarchist group in Swansea, Wales. The group have always taken an antagonistic line towards what they see as a conspiracy between the ruling class and the police to keep the working class subservient. Their stated policy is: "Class War doesn't shy away from violence … We feature people fighting back in the paper to show that it happens all the time (it's ignored or marginalized by everyone else), and to show that it works … the ruling class aren't just going to roll over and give up their power – it will have to be taken from them."

In 2002 former MI5 agent David Shaylor ran into trouble when he started talking to the press about the intelligence agency's activities, at one point serving time in prison.

One of Shaylor's claims was that while he was responsible for monitoring the activities of groups like Class War, he had advised against continuing the practice, believing resources would be better deployed in fighting terrorism. He also claimed that in the early 1990s a police officer was placed with Class War who was so efficient he was able to streamline the anarchist's operations and increase membership. Shaylor inferred that once the officer was reassigned, Class War suffered a decline in fortunes.

Class War themselves accept that they were infiltrated by an officer, who they appointed as treasurer of their London branch. They also claim he was no good at the job and disappeared having stolen some of the branch's funds.

1983
LOBSTER

British magazine investigating state espionage, conspiracies and the abuse of governmental power
First published 1983, Hull, England

Although it does not appear on newsstands, the UK's *Lobster* magazine remains one of the most influential publications in the parapolitical underground. Its select subscribers look to it for the most insightful reporting about interconnections between the intelligence services and public affairs in the UK and the US, and it has even been spied upon by MI5 and denounced in the House of Commons.

Interestingly, *Lobster* began when editor/publisher Robin Ramsay decided to wed his magazine-making skills with an interest in an American parapolitical phenomenon, the Kennedy assassination. He met a fellow assassination buff named Steve Dorril in 1982, and founded *Lobster*. "We started," says Ramsay, "because that's what people were doing: it was the golden age of D-I-Y or punk publishing in the UK. And we'd seen US newsletters on JFK and such. So, starting a mag with zero money – hey, why not?"

Dorril remained a major contributor until the tenth issue, and went on to write books. *Lobster's* first print run of 150 was done on a friend's offset machine that was held together with rubber bands. Today it sells 1,200–1,300 copies.

Lobster has included reviews of historical controversies, such the Jonestown massacre as seen by such noted conspiracy critics as John Judge and Jim Hougan, as well as current ones, such as the intellectual origins of the war on terrorism found within Benjamin Netanyahu's Jonathan Institute. Despite the staid presentation of its format, *Lobster* does not shy away from sober analysis also of such subjects as UFOs and remote viewing, especially seen as products of the covert world.

1986
NEXUS

Australian magazine reporting on suppressed science, the unexplained, and government cover-ups
First published 1986, Mapleton, Australia

Nexus magazine began in Australia in 1986 when publisher Duncan Roads successfully transformed a New Age news magazine into a warhorse of underground/conspiracy information by adding to its content his own favourite subject areas: the unexplained, future science, health alternatives – and conspiracies. *Nexus* maintains a globalist perspective on parapolitics, with editions published in the USA/Canada, UK/Europe, and New Zealand, with translated editions in Italian, French, Greek, Polish, Croatian, Russian, Japanese, Swedish, and Spanish.

According to Roads: "*Nexus* breaks all the traditional rules of publishing by presenting long, in-depth, referenced articles; few glossy, irrelevant pictures; the same boring, blocky layout every issue; non-glossy paper stock inside the magazine, and no inside colour pages." Nevertheless, it has been at the forefront of reporting upon such transnational conspiratorial phenomena as the Octopus cabal; American dominance of the Australian government under Gough Whitlam; the Nugan-Hand bank scandal; and the US help in developing the USSR's postwar atomic weapons programme (the artificial creation of the Cold War).

Health issues also characterize *Nexus'* content, with editorial attention often paid to cancer treatments suppressed by the medical and pharmaceutical industries, including some reference to Wilhelm Reich's orgone. Roads, and his partner Catherine, own *Nexus* and run it from their home/office in Australia and keep the magazine non-aligned with any political or religious ideology or organization. It also organizes regular conferences around the globe that have provided speaking platforms for such popular conspiracy writers as Jim Marrs and David Icke.

See also: *FBI v Wilhelm Reich p.144; David Icke p.188*

1988
STEAMSHOVEL

Leading American-based conspiracy theory magazine
First issue 1988; but published regularly (quarterly) since 1992, St Louis, MO

The founder of *Steamshovel*, Kenn Thomas, prefers to call himself a "parapolitical researcher" believing it sounds less marginal than "conspiracy theorist." Nevertheless, the tagline for his periodical: "All Conspiracy and No Theory," coupled with a highly eclectic editorial policy make *Steamshovel* essential reading for those who want to explore those margins. Thomas traces his interest in conspiracy back to the 1963 assassination of President John F. Kennedy: "When I was five years old they shot JFK. It guaranteed that one of my strongest early memories always would be of conspiracy."

Thomas started his magazine as an irregular bulletin to send to publishers so that he could convince them to send him free books for "reviewing." He also claims that early copies of the magazine were surreptitiously photocopied in the print room of the Monsanto Corporation, a food and chemical production conglomerate who have attracted their own share of conspiracy theories.

In 1992, *Steamshovel* emerged as a regular magazine for the first time, and continues to be a primary source for those eager to learn the latest theories on everything from UFO activity to the death of Princess Diana.

Thomas is also a prolific author with a string of books fleshing out stories that appeared first in *Steamshovel*. In 1999, Thomas' long time collaborator Jim Keith, died under mysterious circumstances, followed by colleague Ron Bonds in 2001. Thomas is investigating the deaths of both men, and is given to making a toast: "You are drinking with the last of the three."

Steamshovel publisher Kenn Thomas is a contributor to *The Conspiracy Encyclopedia*.

See also: *John Fitzgerald Kennedy p.54; Jim Keith p.187; Ron Bonds p.189; Genetically Modified Food p.202*

1992
PARANOIA

US conspiracy magazine published tri-annually
First published 1992 in Providence, RI

Paranoia magazine began as an offshoot of the "I Am Providence" Conspiracy League in Providence, Rhode Island in the early 1990s. This was a conspiracy discussion club primarily run by the pseudonymous Joan D'Arc and partner Al Hidell, whose nom de plume is the name that Lee Harvey Oswald used to purchase a gun through mail-order.

Paranoia took its place among the underground magazines of the period as an outlet to disseminate ideas about conspiracies and various alternative explanations for current affairs. As early as 1996, it included the work of Ron Patton, who became well-known as the publisher of *MKZine*, a magazine devoted exclusively to mind control. Other notable contributors to *Paranoia* include UFO researcher Scott Corrales; Michael Ruppert, who later won renown for his book on 9/11 entitled *Crossing The Rubicon*; shadow government author Len Bracken; and noted alternative-energy activist Remy Chevalier.

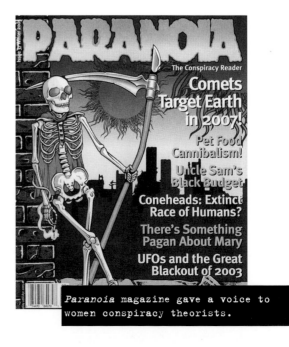

Paranoia magazine gave a voice to women conspiracy theorists.

However, from its inception *Paranoia* reflected an emphasis on conspiracy writing by and about women, including reprints of articles by the widely respected parapolitical researcher Mae Brussell; a UK counterpart named Mary Seal; religious conspiracy critic Acharya S; and it produced a special "all girl" issue. That proclivity culminated in the 1996 publication of an anthology by D'Arc entitled *Paranoid Women Collect Their Thoughts*.

Paranoia attained a degree of commercial success that eluded other underground publications, at one point developing an offshoot book catalog and actual shopfront in Providence. Today it remains a well-circulated, three times a year, newsstand magazine that provides readers with a broad look at the gamut of current conspiracy theories without the specialization of similar internet offerings.

2004
CONSPIRACY RADIO
Radio broadcasts rich source of conspiracy theory

The first conspiracy researcher to broadcast on a regular basis was Californian housewife Mae Brussell. She was invited, in 1969, to appear as a guest on local, privately owned station KLRB, enthralling listeners with her meticulously researched views on political assassinations and the Freedom of Information Act. Brussell was invited back on a weekly basis and, by 1971, she had been given her own show, *Dialog: Conspiracy*, which was quickly picked up by many other radio stations on the west coast of the US.

In 1975, Brussell received her first death threat. She had broadcast an item about serial killer Charles Manson, and The Manson Family, in which she claimed they had committed mass murders in collusion with the LA Sheriff's Department. A note arrived in her mail saying: "You are thinking yourself in a circle of madness ... and all that BS you are running is only a reflection of what the news and books have programmed your soul's mind brain to ... it seems as if you are looking for your death wish in the Family."

Brussell passed the note on to the FBI, who advised her to change her telephone number, but declined to investigate the threat. It was the first of many threats to her life, and in 1988, some months before she died, Brussell finally decided to quit broadcasting, although she continued to mail out tapes to her subscribers.

Brussell left two important legacies, her pioneering show proved that conspiracy theory was popular radio and, more tangibly, she also left her massive filing system, specifically to researcher John Judge. This fact seems to have really annoyed fellow researcher Dave Emory. Both men had been loyal colleagues of Brussell, but they had entirely different ideas about what should happen to the archives.

Judge did attempt to set up a foundation to house the files, and ensure that the public could access them, but Emory had taken Brussell's other legacy and was broadcasting his own syndicated show. He conducted a vitriolic campaign over the airwaves, in which he accused Judge of collaborating with the CIA. Judge lost listener support for his foundation idea and the dispute remains unresolved.

Dave Emory's broadcasting style couldn't be more different from that of his mentor. While Brussell's words tumbled breathlessly, often making her tricky to follow, Emory delivers his theories in calm, measured and authoritative tones. Despite having broadcast on the Liberty Lobby-owned right-wing station, *Radio Free America,* Emory bills himself as an anti-fascist researcher. He specializes in finding evidence of fascist conspiracies within the American government. His gentle and composed delivery apparently belies the fact that, off mike, Emory is a fiery and unpredictable character who has alienated many former allies in the conspiracy community.

Another controversial character in conspiracy radio is Coast to Coast FM's quasi-legendary Art Bell. Former radio technician Bell attracts more than a million listeners and, as well as conspiracy theory, he likes to deal with valid, scientific news. In 2004, he wrote *The Coming Global Superstorm*, an examination of current weather phenomena. Bell was also the radio presenter who lent credence to the theory that the 1997 Hale-Bopp Comet was possibly accompanied by a spacecraft. He did all he could to distance himself from the story when it emerged that 38 members of the Heaven's Gate cult had committed suicide, on the basis that they were going to meet the Hale-Bopp aliens.

In 1998, Bell also caused consternation, and speculation, among his fans when he inexplicably announced that he was quitting broadcasting forever. Two weeks later he was back in the studio, but retired for good again in 2000. Less than a year later he was once again broadcasting, explaining that he had had to attend to confidential family matters. This time he lasted two years before the next permanent retirement. September 2003 saw him back behind the mike once more. He currently remains at *Coast to Coast* providing listeners with incisive, and occasionally caustic, opinions on the latest conspiracy and supernatural news.

See also *Liberty Lobby p.86; Mae Brussell p.181; Heaven's Gate p.295*

> The force of the modern global conspiracy lies in the power of communication. Planes can fly people, goods, plans, and plots from one corner of the planet to another while the internet has enabled these potential traders and conspirators to communicate with each other instantly and effectively. E-mail has allowed rumours about these conspiracies to spread just as fast, exposing them, multiplying their force, or creating new conspiracy networks of their own.

A plot can be hatched in Tokyo, its component parts purchased in Karachi, and then carried out in Houston. An internet site that has unearthed any part of this global chain can be translated, copied, and pasted onto a million other websites all over the world. Suddenly, "everyone knows" that the website's thesis is true because the website's "thesis" is so widespread.

But with the onslaught of mass information also come further layers of complexity. For example, during the second Iraq War hundreds of websites appeared to demonstrate that the US and UK governments had conspired to exploit people's fears in order to start a conflict. Immediately, hundreds of rebuttal websites then appeared claiming new conspiracy theories of their own – Laura Mylroie's, for example, claimed that the entire situation in Iraq had arisen as a result of a secret services' conspiracy to discredit the Bush administration. Or, perhaps, the whole thing was a Defense Department conspiracy with the aim of selling more arms. While many of these conspiracy theories may well be based on fact, they are all displayed on the internet as if they are true. And, whether they are true or not, in our world of instant communication, all such claims now have global dissemination.

Extreme wealth or power will always give rise to global conspiracies. There must be something underhand going on. How can one organization or one individual have acquired so much legitimately? For the former, the cases of Howard Hughes and Aristotle Onassis, with the attendant myths that have grown up around them, are typical. For the latter the Bilderberg Group certainly ticks all the boxes, and the same could be said, to a lesser degree, of the Trilateral Commission, Chatham House, and the Council for Foreign Relations.

Whatever the particular organization, the charge is the same – they plan to control the world. Any organization that draws together so many of the world's most powerful political figures cannot fail to be the source of numerous conspiracies, goes the logic. Yet whether the Bilderberg Group is actually more than a cosy talking shop of the super-elite is open to question.

Corporate conspiracy

Globalization has brought with it the possibility for corporate fraud on an unprecedented scale. Long before the greatest of these scandals – Enron – finally became public we had those of companies like BCCI, Guinness, Barings, and BRE-X, where fake accounting with no management counter-checks led to appalling misconduct and, ultimately, to the loss of investors' money.

Enron was the first company to demonstrate how international this kind of fraud had become. It was so much easier to carry out this type of financial corruption when complex transactions crossed borders and were subject to different regulations in each territory. Had Nick Leeson, of Barings Bank, been located in London not Singapore, his actions might well have been more closely monitored. Or perhaps his location in a distant outpost, yet within easy communication, was perfect for his directors since Leeson maintained a high-profit profile and yet a large public distance.

Fifty-one of the world's top 100 economies are now corporations. In other words, a company like Wal-Mart is now more powerful than a country such as Indonesia in terms of gross domestic product – and its financial tentacles are more numerous. It is a corporation's business to make as much profit as possible and, simultaneously, to ensure that the right political environment exists in which to pursue these economic goals. The company can afford to buy influence all over the world, safe in the knowledge that there will be investors in every country who want its business to succeed because they, too, want a share of the huge, potential profit. The truth remains, though, that the ultimate power behind these trillion-dollar fortunes is still within the hands of a few, ultra-powerful plutocrats.

While it is undoubtedly true that more internal regulation of multinationals would be desirable, it is also true that governments are dependent upon the financial backing of corporations in order to effectively run their political campaigns. And so, in return for economic support and advantage, governments promise to leave businesses alone or, as in the Jonathan Aitken affair, they actively collude to make even more money to support even more corrupt political regimes. It's a very cosy circle.

Superpower conspiracies

Once upon a time it was the United States or it was Russia. It was communist or capitalist, black or white (or vice versa, depending on where you were standing). Unsurprisingly therefore, a number of global conspiracies have this polarization of the world at their heart. Did the USSR intend to establish a completely communist world, as suggested by its determined drive to export communism internationally, not just to neighbours Czechoslovakia, Hungary, and Poland but to less accessible corners of the globe such as Cuba and North Korea?

In the United Kingdom, there was certainly a level of communist infiltration into political society and this was particularly in evidence in the trade union movement from the 1960s onwards. This is hardly surprisingly given that Karl Marx and Friedrich Engels spent a considerable length of time both living in the UK and writing about the conditions of the English working classes. What is more difficult to establish, however, is whether the USSR had any real influence over politics in the UK.

On the capitalist side of the equation, conspiracy theorists suggest that the CIA spent a considerable amount of time and money funding the European socialist movement to enable the United States to enforce its own capitalist agenda there. The CIA is also believed by many to be the controlling force behind the powerful Bilderberg Group.

The US and the World

Among most conspiracy theorists there is a consensus that a shadowy collection of elite bankers, politicians, and military leaders have plans to control the world with a single government and in this way to create a New World Order. This New World Order forms part of a grand right-wing "Project for a New American Century" (PNAC) – a programme built on the political philosophy of Leo Strauss and centered on the public figure of George W. Bush.

The internet throws up all sorts of connections around the topic which apparently interweave to keep the Project safe amongst a few trusted allies. And, as this inner circle is based in the United States, it has complete control over the world's only remaining superpower. Even the Bay of Pigs debacle was organized, so claim the conspiracists, by members of Skull and Bones, the powerful secret society at Yale University whose membership has included three generations of the Bush family.

Whatever the truth behind these claims, it is indisputable that defending its interests in foreign oil reserves is one area that has been a crucial element in US foreign policy for many years. Evidence tends to suggest that any individual who attempts to theaten US dominance in this field, as did Hugo Chávez of Venezuela in the late 1990s, will be relentlessly targeted and pursued by the US administration. Similarly, American oil companies apparently doubled their quarterly profits in the months before the Iraq invasion, leading to more suspicion about the war's ultimate motives, and the PNAC has now reinforced its foreign policy position by nominating one of its key members as the new director of the World Bank.

The tentacles of the US plot by a very few to take over the governance of almost everyone stretch remorselessly over the web. Most of the conspiracy theories, however, extrapolate that the one link between control of the oil industry, the discrediting of Bill Clinton, the New World Order, and the unfound "weapons of mass destruction" is always George W. Bush. The figure of George W. looms large over nearly all military, intelligence and international conspiracies. An internet search in these areas will almost inevitably lead back to him.

Biological and chemical weapons

Since 9/11, there have been roughly 2,500 Anthrax alerts in the US but not one gram of Anthrax has actually been found. But that is precisely the point.

Terrorist groups have learnt that death by chemical warfare is not their prime objective. Chemical weapons are, actually, relatively inefficient but that is not important as their power lies not in the violence they create but in the fear of violence they stir up. It remains basically true that, despite media attention, the effective mass use of chemical or biological weapons in any western-style democracy today is extremely unlikely. The Japanese cult movement, Aum Shinrikyo, for example, had over 50,000 members, and huge financial resources, but, even with this array of advantages, it could not develop and effectively deploy a successful biological weapon.

Firstly, developing "pure" materials is extremely technologically complex. Secondly, distributing the materials effectively is tremendously challenging. Aum tried to kill its victims on more than a dozen occasions before it, eventually, managed to release a chemical agent called Sarin on the Tokyo underground. Even then, it succeeded in killing only 12 of the intended thousands.

Yet in other ways Aum succeeded in its aims. The conspiracy, it appears, is not in the physical use of weapons of mass destruction but in their political capability. Terrorists have used biological and chemical weapons to terrify people while the United States and the United Kingdom have looked to them as an argument for war. Saddam Hussein, meanwhile, used them to declare that there was a "wicked American conspiracy" to remove him from power in Iraq and to refuse the UN

A former Enron employee protests outside the corporation's Houston headquarters, January 28th, 2002. The case of Enron showed the world how widespread international corporate fraud had become.

A UN inspector measures the volume of nerve agent in a container at Muthanna, Iraq, 1991. Despite over a decade of inspections, UNSCOM failed to locate any chemical or biological weapons in Saddam Hussein's Iraq.

weapons inspection team (UNSCOM) immediate access to certain presidential sites. In this way, the weapons ultimately worked to everyone's advantage.

Further to the realization that nation states are the only bodies with sufficient scientific and economic clout to be able to use biological and chemical weapons effectively, it follows that the US and Russia have the world's biggest reserves of chemical weapons, though both nations are committed to destroying them all. While the Convention on Chemical Weapons (1993) provides the right to carry out quick inspections, so far no such inspections have actually been performed and, in the Middle East, only Israel and Jordan have signed the treaty, but neither has ratified it.

The 1972 Biological and Toxin Weapons Convention bans the development, manufacture, and use of biological weapons but, in practice, it has been widely violated. The Clinton administration was enthusiastic for a strong BTWC, but the Bush administration has distanced the US from enforcement policy on the basis that this would be an open door to intrusions into US defence laboratories. It would be a lot easier to hold corporations responsible for the deaths of individuals like Karen Silkwood – who died, it is claimed, because she knew too much about plutonium contamination at the corporation where she worked – if the US were a more active player in the ratification of international treaties. But as it has already disengaged from the Kyoto treaty, no-one in the field has much hope of any major action from the US on this front.

1564
THE "REAL" WILLIAM SHAKESPEARE

The works of William Shakespeare were not written by him but by other authors/writers

This theory holds that William Shakespeare's plays were the work of others, such as Sir Francis Bacon; Christopher Marlowe; Roger Manners, Earl of Rutland; William Stanley, Earl of Derby; Edward de Vere, Earl of Oxford, and others. These writers, it is claimed, published the works anonymously – via Shakespeare's theatre company – because the subject matter was politically dangerous.

The conspiracy theory

Theorists dispute the fact that Shakespeare, or "Shakspere" as his birth name is recorded in Stratford-upon-Avon, Warwickshire, was the true author of *Hamlet* (1601), *Macbeth* (1606), and other plays published under his name. Writers including Walt Whitman, Mark Twain, Charles Dickens, Nathaniel Hawthorne, and Ralph Waldo Emerson have all lent their names to the Shakespeare conspiracy theory over the centuries.

The evidence

Shakespeare's identity has never been proven beyond his birth certificate, a few legal documents, and anecdotes. More importantly, what little is known of Shakespeare seems at odds with the authorship of the plays. The playwright is clearly well-educated, worldly, and generous-spirited, with a wide knowledge of arts, literature, medicine, seafaring, warfare, and much more – seemingly too much for one man.

Yet there is no evidence that Shakespeare was even educated, let alone able to amass this knowledge. It is known that he left Stratford for London – leaving his wife destitute – to become actor and later manager with a theatrical group. When he returned, he refused to honour his wife's debts, and got embroiled in shady business deals and legal wrangles. He did no writing and left no books or manuscripts in his will. His national reputation as a writer was established only after his death. Some plays once said to be his were, in fact, written by others.

This lack of convincing evidence leaves the authorship issue wide open. Prime candidates include Sir Francis Bacon, author of *The Advancement of Learning* (1605), and Christopher Marlowe, who was born the same year as Shakespeare. Marlowe was a scholar, poet, and dramatist – responsible for at least five of the greatest dramas of his

An impression of William Shakespeare from an undated engraving. How many of "his" plays did England's most famous dramatist actually write?

era, including *Tamburlaine* (1587) and *Faustus* (1589) – and Queen Elizabeth's spy. Apparently killed in a tavern brawl in 1593, he is said by some to have faked his death and lived on to author the "Shakespeare" plays.

During the Elizabethan era, all printed works were censored, but theatrical performances offered a clandestine means of promoting controversial views. *Richard II* (1595), a "Shakespearean work," is an example. The play deals with a monarch's downfall and was regarded by Elizabeth I as a personal attack on her. One scene was banned outright – a writer was jailed for life for mentioning it in print.

When the Earl of Essex led an armed rebellion against the Queen in 1601, he had the play staged throughout London to win the public to his cause. After the revolt was crushed, all those involved with the play were interrogated. Shakespeare was not among them. The Earl of Rutland, however, only distantly linked to the plotters, was tried and sentenced to death – no one knows why. Curiously, Shakespeare's gloomiest plays were written while the Earl was facing the death sentence. (He was later released.) He is also known to have visited Elsinore, in Denmark, where *Hamlet* is set.

The verdict

Shakepeare's era was a time of political intrigue and religious turmoil. Plays were opinion-formers as well as entertainment, and playwrights could risk hanging if they angered authority in any way. Bacon, Marlowe, the Earl of Rutland, and others, belonged to secret societies and held controversial views. Shakespeare, as actor-manager, desperate for new plays, was well placed to stage their works anonymously. If he also took the credit, the "true" authors could not object. Perhaps, in a dusty attic somewhere, lies an old document that, if ever discovered, will solve the issue – one way or another.

1720
THE SOUTH SEA BUBBLE

18th-century speculators lost millions on shares in non-existent businesses

"No Ships unload, no Looms at Work we see,
But all are swallow'd by the damn'd South Sea."

So declared revered poet, Alexander Pope (in "Rape of the Lock"), referring to the South Sea Bubble scandal of 1720, which was perhaps best described as the first City-of-London scam, where thousands of people were duped into investing in shares in non-existent businesses in the southern Atlantic. Profit fever boosted investments in phantom South Sea businesses by almost 100 per cent – at one point taking shares with a value of £128 up to £1,050 – only for the shares to crash back to £128 just days later, leading many to debtors' court and prison, and not a few to suicide. Some ended up in the Tower of London. (This being the 18th century, the speculators tended to be of a class that might find itself in the Tower of London, rather than strung up at Newgate.) Some say that the South Sea Bubble was the ruin of an entire generation of speculators.

What compounded the South Sea Company disaster was the fact that it was fully endorsed by both parliament and indeed royalty. Speculation in projects linked to the South Sea Company led to a rush of investment by people hoping to make a quick fortune from the scheme (the aforementioned poet, Pope, allegedly among them). The businessmen who had launched the South Sea Company quietly left town. It is estimated that between £9–20 million were lost in the scandal – a figure equivalent to billions of dollars today.

1789
THE FREEMASONS AND THE FRENCH REVOLUTION

A powerful secret sect was behind the violent overthrow of King Louis XVI

Conspiracy theories about the French Revolution (1789–99) perhaps inevitably focus on the alleged involvement of the Freemasons and the Illuminati. Theories claim that, rather than a popular uprising by the poor, the Revolution was fomented by Masons and Illuminati members pitched against the despised Catholic church.

This uprising against King Louis XVI is alleged to have been hatched by these secret societies, abetted by the Duke of Orléans and Napoleon Bonaparte. Theories also hold that the storming of the Bastille was orchestrated by gangs of thugs brought to Paris from elsewhere, and that among others, Marat-Sade and Robespierre, were Freemasons who had been "Illuminized" by infiltrators from Adam Wieshaupt's sinister German group.

What is actually known is that thousands died during France's Reign of Terror, not least Louis XVI and his queen, Marie Antoinette, at the guillotine. The Reign of Terror ended in 1799, when Napoleon assumed power and established a republic.

There is no doubt that rival factions would have been manoeuvring in the events that led up to the Revolution. Some historians and writers have lent credence to the possibility that the Masons and the Illuminati might have had reason to destabilize French society. It is uncertain, however, what these groups would have stood to gain in the aftermath of a 10-year civil uprising, particularly given that economic control would have remained in the hands of the landowners. Conventional opinion still holds that this was a popular uprising by the poor against appalling social conditions.

1832
SKULL AND BONES

Yale student secret society rules the world

There seems to be little doubt that Skull and Bones, formed by Yale University students in 1832 and probably inspired by similar student groups in Germany, does have genuine power in the world. Both George W. Bush and John Kerry are members, but sworn to secrecy about the group. Most of the more powerful north American Yale politicians and businessmen of the 20th century were members. Nowadays, however, the society accepts women, black people and gays.

There are only 800 members all-told, and only 15 people are "tapped" – literally, on the shoulder – each year. George W. Bush has tapped numerous people.

The society meets in a windowless building, called The Tomb, near the Yale campus. Its rites are the subject of much speculation, but are said to involve coffins, darkened rooms, skulls, hazing of new members, and the obligatory revelation of personal sexual histories. The organization is even said to have desecrated the grave of legendary American-Indian chief, Geronimo, and stolen his skull, which is used in its bizarre rituals.

Its base at Yale means that Skull and Bones is a magnet for intellectual high-flyers destined for positions of power and influence. As well as Bush and Kerry, former alumni include William Howard Taft, 27th president of the Union, Henry Luce, founder of *Time* magazine, and W. Averell Harriman, an advisor to several presidents. It is obvious that members network and do each other favours, but their influence on matters of world affairs is unfathomable.

1854
THE KNIGHTS OF THE GOLDEN CIRCLE
Yankee group who supported the south during the US Civil War

The existence of the Knights of the Golden Circle is an unambiguous fact; many histories and articles have been written about them. They were chiefly democrats who opposed the Civil War but, at the same time, were also opposed to the abolition of slavery.

The organization was formed in Cincinnati, largely to promote these ends but also to seize control of land in New Mexico. Founder, Dr George L. W. Bickley, nicknamed them the Copperheads, after a venomous indigenous snake. While they resisted anti-social behaviour, some of their members supported anti-war activity such as offering refuge to draft resisters and deserters.

The group was reformed in 1863 as the Organization of American Knights, and again in 1864 as the Order of the Sons of Liberty. Its much-vaunted ambitions would founder, however, as the Civil War ground on and its plans were thwarted, despite monetary support from wealthy southerners. Following various battles in Kentucky, Indiana, and Ohio, the group was suppressed by the authorities. It disbanded shortly afterwards.

An essentially democratic – if still pro-slavery – group who opposed what they thought was a wrong-headed war, the Knights were wrong-footed from the start, and eventually suppressed by the victorious Yankee government. Part of their motivation was financial, but they were also driven by the belief that the war was immoral. Vainglorious and naive, perhaps, but probably one of the least sinister secret organizations in recent north American history.

1910
THE US FEDERAL RESERVE
The Rothschild family orchestrated a cartel among the world's bankers

This theory is given credence by the fact that the foremost author on the story, Eustace Mullins, also worked for the US Library of Congress, and wrote the key text on the subject, *Secrets of the Federal Reserve*. Unfortunately, it is also somewhat undermined by the fact that Mullins was introduced to this theory by the poet, Ezra Pound, at a time when Pound had been sectioned in a mental hospital after being arrested for broadcasting pro-Nazi propaganda from Italy during World War II.

The conspiracy theory
Jekyll Island is a popular resort off the coast of Georgia in the southern United States. The island had been bought some years earlier as a millionaires's exclusive resort by the noted multimillionaire and philanthropist, J.P. Morgan. Mullins's thesis holds that, in November 1910, a group of US financiers left New York in a private train, with the window shutters down, to spend a week on Jekyll Island to plot to take over the country's Federal Reserve System as a means of controlling the US economy.

By colluding with European financiers, including the Rothschild and Warburg families, and bankers in the City of London, they also began to manipulate the world finance market. The Rothschild family alone controlled banks in Frankfurt, London, Paris, Vienna, and Frankfurt. They were, allegedly, complicit in the Wall Street Crash of 1929 and have been involved in financial scandals until the present day, and were even alleged to have had connections to Adolf Hitler's Third Reich.

Mullins's theory points out that the Federal Reserve System is not "federal," but private; the US government does not run its own financial system, rather a cartel of privately owned banks does. That cartel, he says, has put the US three trillion dollars in debt, and is charging the country fantastic amounts of interest every day. He also claims that the cartel was complicit in both World Wars I and II.

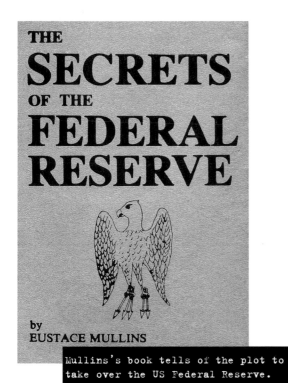

THE SECRETS OF THE FEDERAL RESERVE

by
EUSTACE MULLINS

Mullins's book tells of the plot to take over the US Federal Reserve.

The theory further holds that the US was debt-free until the Federal Reserve System was established and, hence, that the Federal Reserve System established the private bankers's control of the US economy and is little more than a money-making device for a powerful elite. The corollary is that the US banking system is milking the population of millions every day, and the senate is simply unwilling to do anything about it.

The evidence

Historians and journalists have provided plenty of corroboration for the notorious Jekyll Island meeting and the involvement of the mentioned financiers. The secretive 1,610km (1,000miles) journey by private train to Jekyll Island did indeed take place, other members of the exclusive resort were asked to stay off the island during the meeting, and the Federal Reserve Act, passed in 1913, was drafted during the intensive nine-day meeting. The chief author of the Act was businessman and senator, Nelson Aldrich. It led to the establishment of the private Federal Reserve System still in operation today. Many economists have claimed that the Act is directly responsible for the Great Depression, the economic boom-bust cycle, and inflation in general.

The verdict

Much of the detail behind the conspiracy theory is well established. What remains in question, however, is the supposed power of the cartel, particularly outside the US, where other legal systems might be thought to be in place to regulate fiscal dishonesty and where independent journalists would be keen to expose such cartels. There is no doubt that businesses collaborate and perhaps even conspire together. But recent scandals, from the collapse of the BCCI to Enron, and the activities of various whistle-blowers, would suggest that such a cartel would not go unexposed. It might also be expected that in post-Watergate north America, enough journalists would be pursuing such a nefarious conspiracy as to reveal such a conspiracy to be implausible – although not impossible.

See also: *BCCI Fraud p.124*

1917
BOLSHEVIK WORLD ORDER

Communist Russia planned to take over the world and impose socialism around the globe

The case for a conspiracy to establish a Bolshevik world order is undermined by a number of fairly compelling factors. It is interesting, however, to consider the claims made by its promoters.

The conspiracy theory

Soviet expansionism was an unquestionable fact, as its outposts in north Korea, Cuba, and elsewhere testify. The zeal with which it spread its message of collectivization and other practices in the name of a spurious "communism" is equally undoubted. While the project may have been derailed by Stalinism, it is clear that the USSR's founders saw their philosophy, however misguided, as something that would benefit humanity. It might, therefore, be assumed that they would want to export this philosophy around the globe. Others see a darker conspiracy of global domination behind this and, what is more, a hostility to western ideas of liberty and freedom. It might further be expected that the USSR would see the domination of other countries, perhaps even the entire world, as a means of bolstering its own economy, which we now know was in fact crippled by Russian expansionism. The USSR couldn't feed its own people. As one (admittedly Chinese) communist philosopher put it, rather over-ambitiously: "In the future, America will be our bread-basket, Europe our boutique."

The evidence

From its earliest days, and from the writings of its key theorists – Bakunin, Marx, Lenin, Engels, Trotsky, et al. – it was demonstrably clear that this was not merely a local democratic movement formed with the aim of changing the government in Russia and its associated satellites. It was a vision of a new world order, and the USSR exported it wherever it could – to Czechoslovakia, Hungary, Poland, the Balkans, and Cuba.

As reds-under-the-bed witch-hunts on both sides of the Atlantic proved, the USSR was also busily proselytizing its cause in the US and the UK, and in other continental European democracies. The USSR became a rival in the space race, and in the competition to build nuclear arms, and was notorious for its espionage activities in every country where it established an embassy or diplomatic presence. And like the West, it also meddled in African politics. It recruited figures in positions of power, such as Alger Hiss and Ethel and George Rosenberg in the US, and Kim Philby, Guy Burgess, Donald McLean, and Anthony Blunt in Britain, as well as many other European intellectuals.

The desire to spread the communist word led to the formation of the Communist Party of Great Britain, and communist parties in France, the US, and elsewhere. In the US, this led to the Cold War House UnAmerican Activities Committee hearings of the 1940s and 1950s, in which actors and writers were effectively put on trial for alleged communist affiliations. Western fears of a Russian invasion survived into the late 20th century; as recently as 1984, for example, film-maker John Milius made a movie, *Red Dawn*, about a Russian invasion of the north American mid-west by parachutists.

The verdict

The theory is undermined by at least three profound contradictions. From the end of World War II in 1945 and up to the fall of the Berlin Wall in 1989, the USSR maintained an uneasy but pragmatic equilibrium in its geopolitical balance with its key opponent, the US, with the obvious exception of the Cuban Missile Crisis of 1962, which itself led to an impasse.

During the same period, it also remained in a stand-off with its other global rival, China. As was also revealed in the post-Berlin Wall events, while the USSR may have been the first to put a man into space, Yuri Gagarin aboard *Soyuz 1*, its economy was in fact in tatters. It is worth noting that even internally, the USSR was fractured; some regions of the East were and some remain little more than medieval fiefdoms run by corrupt warlords. Simply, the USSR did not have the ability to take over the world.

See also: *Cambridge Spies p.138*

1917
THE OCTOBER REVOLUTION
Western, especially north American, big business was involved in fomenting the Russian Revolution

This is possibly one of the most outrageous of all conspiracy theories: that western capitalism, more specifically, Jewish businessmen in the US and Europe, were behind the origins of the Russian Revolution of October 1917.

The conspiracy theory

There had been unrest in Czarist Russia since the 1840s, and a famous revolt against the iniquities of Russian social inequality in 1905. Romantic history holds that the unsuccessful 1905 revolt – sparked by a sailors' strike in Petrograd, part-influence for Sergei Eisenstein's famous film, *Battleship Potemkin,* and the iconic Odessa Steps sequence where a woman in glasses is shot in the eye and a baby in a bassinet bounces down the flight of steps – was a genuine workers' uprising. But subsequent writings on the more famous, October 1917 revolution, which ushered in the Bolshevik dictatorship, have suggested a more complex cause to the revolution.

While the 1917 uprising was, again, thought of as a people's revolt inspired by poverty and oppression, it is now alleged by some that several factions were implicated in its origin and planning. These include German and north American bankers, who are said to have transferred funds to the communist revolutionary Menshevik and Bolshevik forces via banks in Europe.

While this might seem an extraordinary claim, those who promote the theory say that the reason for this bizarre alliance between Wall Street and the Bolsheviks is quite simple: incredibly wealthy north American magnates saw Russia simply as a vast untapped source of revenue. An emancipated former peasant society would be clamoring for north American consumer goods, and in the absence of a Russian consumer culture, beyond beets and vodka, the US could move in on the action unhindered.

The evidence

It is alleged that much of this was organized from offices at 120 Broadway in Manhattan, which was the identified base for a number of organizations implicated in the Wall-Street-Bolshevik connection. The J.P. Morgan, Rockefeller, and Guggenheim families are also implicated, as is, perhaps unsurprisingly, the privately run Federal Bank Reserve, which was also based next door to 120 Broadway. The Guggenheim corporation, General Electric, and the Bankers' Club also had headquarters in the same skyscraper. One individual banker, it is claimed, gave the Bolsheviks $1 million to fund the uprising, a considerable sum in the 1910s.

Some even put forward the idea that the famous US activist, John Reed, a great supporter of the revolution and the subject of the Warren Beattie film, *Reds*, was funded by Wall Street in his efforts to promote the revolutionary cause. The conspiracy is alleged to have gone deep into the heart of north American finance and politics, and with the complicity of the Senate. It is even claimed that Leon Trotsky was funded by Wall Street, so keen was big business to exploit the potential Russian market. Trotsky, the theory goes, having left the country, entered Russia again using a north American passport. He died, of course, an exile in Mexico, famously attacked by an assassin using an ice pick. There is also evidence of complicity by banks in Sweden and even the British establishment.

Crowds of revolutionaries gather on the Avenue Niglini in Petrograd, on May 15th, 1917.

The verdict

The seasoned conspiracy collector should be prepared for anything, and this certainly boggles the imagination. It is indeed conceivable that north America's vastly wealthy robber barons would want to exploit a market as large as the USSR, but the gamble strikes the reasoned thinker as possibly too high. There does indeed appear to be – perhaps conjectural – information that some of these things did in fact take place. But a number of factors jar: not least that deep-rooted racism in the US, and resistance to left-wing politics (the revolution happened just a decade before the illegal executions in the US of immigrant left-wing Italian activists, Nicola Sacco and Bartolomeo Vanzetti, in 1927, on a trumped-up murder charge) would seem to militate against any enthusiasm for Bolshevik politics. It also seems likely that western businesses would have found it easier to deal with the pre-communist, Czarist system.

There are a few other crimps in the theory. The red "menace" was well known even before the beginning of the 20th century: even rural peasants in Spain were being taught the radical theories of Mikhail Bakunin as early as the 1860s. It is also difficult to see how collectivization, state control, and a bitter opposition to western capitalism would have somehow opened up the Soviet market to western business.

As Josef Stalin demonstrated, Sovietization brought only misery to millions, and, as the collapse of communism amply illustrated, ruin to the USSR economy. No shrewd businessman or woman would have seen the USSR market as a golden opportunity.

See also: *Leon Trotsky p.46; Nicola Sacco and Bartolomeo Vanzetti p.138*

1920
CHATHAM HOUSE

Renowned debating society is a front for politicians and business leaders seeking secret global influence

The idea that Chatham House, the former Royal Institute for International Affairs (RIIA), might have a manipulative agenda is one of the most subtle of conspiracy theories.

The conspiracy theory

Founded in 1920, Chatham House ostensibly serves as a forum for uninhibited debate on politics, economics, business, the environment, and world affairs. The society is based in Chatham House in London's Mayfair. The building gives its name to the organization's famous Chatham House Rule, which states that any meetings held under its auspices should allow anyone the right to speak their mind, off-the-record, and without fear of reprisal or criticism. It is a membership-based organization, currently charging nearly £300 per individual per year, and hosts a variety of conferences and seminars on issues of world importance. Past and present members have included British prime ministers Harold MacMillan, Harold Wilson, and John Major. Its conferences have been addressed by British media figures such as Jeremy Paxman, Andrew Marr, John Simpson, and Janet Street-Porter.

The subtext to the theory is that it is in effect a front for an unofficial international cabal of back room policy-makers working outside the democratic process and influencing matters of world importance. There is a further subtext that in its dealings with politicians and big business the organization might in fact be providing a forum for certain vested interests to promote their own agendas, and that these agendas might in fact lean towards the right wing. Certain arcane blogs on the internet have implied connections to disgraced figures, such as Henry Kissinger and, even more outrageously, convoluted connections that could link the organization to the US far right. Perhaps inevitably, Israel, the Freemasons, the Bilderberg Group and, shockingly, Germany's original Hitlerian Nazi Party, also feature in some of these allegations.

The evidence

The secrecy that lies at the heart of Chatham House has led some to suggest that it is a cabal of politicians and business people with their own agendas to pursue. The organization may insist that its meetings are held in-camera, but membership is, in theory, open to anyone who can afford it. Its offices in London are listed on its own website, staff are identified, jobs advertised, and publications and a number of magazines are published regularly. Conspiracists argue, however, that it has an entirely different agenda to that proclaimed in its publicity. Some see the membership of powerful British and international politicians as a sign that Chatham House is somewhat more than a think-tank on world matters.

The verdict

The fact that British prime ministers, MacMillan, Wilson, and Major, have all been members lends credence to the theory that the RIIA/Chatham House has some international influence. It is impossible to measure its power in

the global arena, although there is one incontrovertible fact undermining the conspiracy theory about Chatham House: no shadowy organization would invite such a firebrand journalist as Briton Jeremy Paxman to address its meetings. It is possible that a second-order manifesto is at work behind its facade, but the organization strives to present a semblance of transparency. It would also seem to be the case that no global conspiracy would offer membership to anyone interested for just a few hundred pounds.

See also: *Council for Foreign Relations p.104; The Bilderberg Group p.108*

1921
COUNCIL FOR FOREIGN RELATIONS
North American think-tank exerts an unusual influence on world affairs

The Council for Foreign Relations is perhaps unique and certainly unusual in admitting that other people think it constitutes a conspiracy; its publicity joshingly refers to the fact that some people might not find it as conspiratorial as others claim.

The conspiracy theory

The Council was formed in 1921, just a year after the foundation of the UK's Royal Institute of International Affairs. A think-tank and discussion forum, its remit is to address "American internationalism based on American interests." Its key publication, the magazine *Foreign Affairs*, has published articles by a diverse range of commentators, from the influential black thinker and newspaper publisher W.E.B. DuBois, to Vietnam hawk, Henry Kissinger. An early reader of *Foreign Affairs* was one V.I. Lenin.

Allegedly non-partisan, with a mixture of Democrat and Republican members, the Council also welcomed Jewish and black members at a time when both were normally excluded from most political elites.

Early members included FBI boss John Foster Dulles and W. Averill Harriman, a confidant to many a president, as well as other political figures. The Council's proceedings were and remain secret and confidential.

It is said by some to be directly linked to the UK's RIIA/Chatham House, Canada's Institute of International Affairs, and two shadowy groups, the Round Table and the Secret Team, formed specifically to influence US public opinion. Links are also alleged to exist with similar organizations in the Netherlands, Japan, China, and Russia. It is further believed to be involved in CIA activities, particularly PSYOPS exercises, and, in the further reaches of conspiracy theory, to have links with the Bilderberg Group.

The council convened, according to its own history, over "brandy and cigars," but as well as radical figures such as DuBois it also courted the opinion of labour activists. It claims to have identified the Nazi menace as early as the 1930s, and to have reported its horror at Hitler's philosophy following an interview with him shortly after he came to power. Its magazine published some of the earliest attacks on the Nazi movement, as well as articles rousing the US to oppose fascism in Europe and the Far East. Contributors have included Germany's Konrad Adenauer, England's Hugh Gaitskell, Anthony Eden, and Clement Attlee, Russia's Nikita Khruschev, Egypt's Gamal Nasser, and Cambodia's Norodom Sihanouk – a fairly stellar masthead for any small magazine to boast.

The verdict

Even by its own admission, the Council for Foreign Relations has a reputation for influence among the American upper echelons that seems to be gold-plated. Organizations such as J.P. Morgan, Henry Stimson, President Taft's war secretary and President Hoover's secretary of state, and the Warburg, Dulles, and Coolidge families, have all been involved. At one point the Council was being bankrolled by the Andrew Carnegie foundation. With uncanny prescience, the Council liquidated $300,000 of its assets shortly before the Wall Street Crash of 1929, enabling it to purchase property in mid-town Manhattan, right next door to Franklin D. Roosevelt's town house.

The editorial policy of *Foreign Affairs*, and its willingness to embrace Third World, black, Jewish, and anti-Fascist concerns, would seem to cast the Council for Foreign Relations in a libertarian mode, one ready, it would appear, to entertain oppositional attitudes. It clearly has connections with the international diplomatic A List – Condoleezza Rice featured on a recent *Foreign Affairs* cover – and both organization and magazine appear to operate as a super-charged chat room for politicians, businesspeople, academics, and general movers and shakers. A glance at the names of individuals involved in the Council's activities confirms its position at the centre of western political intellectual activity, as does a browse through *Foreign Affairs*. As with many semi-secretive think-tanks, however, it is difficult to gauge its actual influence on internal or overseas policy, or its effect on how Joe or Jane Public votes.

1933
DUPONT, ICI AND IG FARBEN
Chemical company wants to rule the world

The DuPont story has led to accusations that Ronald Reagan was a communist, George W. Bush is a gay activist, and Queen Elizabeth II is in fact a Nazi sympathizer.

DuPont was founded outside Wilmington, Delaware, in 1802. It specialized in gunpowder and explosives, and by 1902 had a 75 per cent share of the explosives market. It is believed that DuPont supplied 40 per cent of all explosives fired during World War I, some 684 million kg (1.5 billion lb) of it. After that war, it moved into developing plastics, most notably inventing Nylon and clingwrap, and other man-made materials. Most people who own a toothbrush brush their teeth with a DuPont product.

DuPont was troubled by accusations of monopolization almost from its original incorporation as a company. Colorful figures such as the Rockefeller family and Senator Nelson Aldrich – the man behind the controversial Federal Reserve Act (1913) – have also been associated with its business affairs. Its business links with German industrial giant IG Farben, its purchase of General Motors, and ICI's nylon business has consolidated its position as one of the major players on the world stage.

It is almost inevitable that a corporation of this size will wield considerable political power. It controls 30 percent of all artificial textile manufacture, and its chemical and petrochemical business alone is worth in excess of $30 billion a year. Global companies have the ear of global leaders – but as most of DuPont's meetings with world governments take place in secret it is impossible to measure the full extent of its influence.

1937/1938
WALL STREET AND THE NAZIS
North American bankers funded the growth of National Socialism in pre-war Germany

This is a conspiracy theory promoted largely by fundamentalist Christians but, if true, could be one of the most shocking conspiracies of all time, not least because of the deaths of more than six million people.

The theory holds that after the German defeat in World War I, the US and its Allies demanded reparations from the German state of over 100 billion German marks, equivalent to a quarter of the country's annual industrial output. This beggared the German economy. Subsequently, the J.P. Morgan bank and other investors made available loans approaching $800 million, which were in turn used to found IG Farben and steel company, Vereinigte Stahlwerke, among other industrial concerns. Between them, they would provide most of the materials employed by Germany during World War II.

This economic disaster is said to have driven many Germans into the arms of National Socialism, and Adolf Hitler's Nazi party. Millions of Germans were made unemployed, and one of Hitler's key theories under National Socialism was a promise to end unemployment. It is also alleged that north American bankers made a healthy profit on the loans to Germany.

There were definite connections between the US banking system and pre-World War II Germany. Whether a direct link can be established between those bankers and the rise of fascism, which could be said to have been set in train after World War I, is probably impossible to prove.

1942
DE BEERS AND THE NAZIS

Diamond monopolists helped to fund the growth of Nazism in Germany

The world's largest diamond dealers De Beers has long been accused of operating a cartel in the international diamond industry and supplying "blood diamonds," today also known as conflict diamonds, to the Nazis.

De Beers was founded in 1888 and now controls around 60 per cent of the world's diamond trade from its headquarters in Southdale, South Africa. Much of the diamond excavation work is done in third world countries and in appalling conditions by workers who are punitively policed and poorly paid.

The conspiracy theory is based on the premiss that the company dealt in diamonds with the Nazi government of Germany. One thesis claims that an arrested spy was found carrying a letter relating to a source of cutting diamonds for German industry, which identified De Beers as the likely supplier of a substance called "boart," a diamond residue necessary for industrial grinding. Until the start of World War II, the UK and its subsidiaries in Africa had been Germany's key source of "boart" and diamonds in general. With the onset of hostilities, Germany had to look elsewhere for supplies. Allegedly, De Beers was happy to supply them.

De Beers has built such an enormous empire in the diamond trade that it has attracted any number of anti-trust cases in the US and concomitant accusations of monopoly and conspiracy. Its collusion with Nazi Germany is so far unproven, but if proven De Beers would not be alone in being one of the many non-German corporations to have supplied the Hitler regime.

1945
FDR AND THE HOUSE OF SAUD

President Roosevelt made a secret oil deal with Saudi Arabia

In 1933, the US established formal diplomatic relations with Saudi Arabia, barely a year after the kingdom had been founded by its ruler, King Abdul Aziz. The connection was made for perhaps not entirely innocent reasons: significant amounts of oil had already been discovered there.

The kingdom signed a deal with Standard Oil of California in the same year, hoping that the company would uncover the oil wealth that had been discovered in neighbouring Iraq some years earlier. In 1938, the US dispatched teams of scientists to the kingdom, ostensibly to assist the desert plateau country to find water resources. Instead, they discovered large deposits of oil. While the kingdom remained resistant to outsiders, the royal family negotiated a number of deals with American oil suppliers through its home-grown company, Aramco.

Following World War II, the US began discussions with the Middle Eastern oil producers in an attempt to secure a regular supply. It is said that in 1945 Franklin D. Roosevelt and Abdul Aziz met in secret on a boat moored in the Suez Canal to strike a secret deal in which, in return for a regular supply of oil, the US would provide military security, training, and arms.

The friendship continues to this day, and helps to explain George W. Bush's close ties with the House of Saud, and also the curious reluctance of the US to acknowledge the fact that the majority of the 9/11 terrorists were in fact Saudis.

See also: *Oil in Saudi Arabia and the House of Saud p.16; The Origins of the Wealth of the Bin Laden Clan p.16; The Bush Family and al-Qaeda p.27*

1945
NATO AND THE WORLD ORDER
The North Atlantic Treaty Organization controls international politics

The NATO agreement was signed between north American and European countries on April 4th, 1949, a result of discussions aimed at securing peace in the north Atlantic region after World War II. In continental Europe, it is also known as OTAN, roughly, in English, the "Organization of the Treaty of the Atlantic North."

NATO/OTAN was formed in the early years of the Cold War, to unite both the US and Canada with Europe against a perceived threat from the East, be it Russia, China, or any number of permutations of eastern countries. A key event was western Europe's response to Russia's take-over of East Berlin and the subsequent construction of the Berlin Wall.

One of NATO's founding ideas was that its members would consider that an attack on any one member would be seen as an attack on all its members, and respond accordingly. Thus NATO/OTAN established what is in effect an international standing army, ready to be dispatched to hotspots around the world to intervene in conflict. NATO/OTAN is mandated to be non-partisan and impartial. Some believe, however, that the organization is a back door method of allowing certain political factions to take control of destabilized societies.

The very nature of NATO/OTAN would probably militate against it functioning as a conspiracy; few conspiracies are launched by committee, less still 26 different countries, the number of signatories to the NATO/OTAN agreement.

1945/6
LESTER PROUTY
Lester Prouty and the American involvement in the Korean and Vietnam Wars

Lester Fletcher Prouty was a retired US Air Force colonel and some-time CIA operative who, between 1955 and 1963, was co-ordinator of the CIA's Covert Activities operations. He was also the author of a book about the John F. Kennedy assassination, *JFK: The CIA, Vietnam, and the Plot to Assassinate John F. Kennedy*, published in 1992. Prouty is portrayed as the anonymous "Mr X" at the beginning of director Oliver Stone's film *JFK*.

Prouty had been involved in CIA covert operations since 1943, when he advised General Dwight Eisenhower about the threat of the military-industrial complex. He was a jet pilot and a professor of aeronautics at Yale University, and served as an advisor at a number of key World War II strategy conferences. However, he did not go into print until 1970, in a Washington news magazine. Prouty was highly sceptical about the US's decision to enter into combat with north Korea. In both cases, he felt that shadowy forces in the military-industrial complex had taken the US into war for the wrong reasons. Prouty's circumspection, his position in the military establishment, and his decision to go public, only in 1970, all lend credence to his theories, not least that JFK was assassinated because he wanted to restrict the activities of the CIA and stop the US's growing involvement in Vietnam. Tellingly, his revelations came at the height of the Vietnam War.

1947
THE CIA AND EUROPEAN DEMOCRACY
CIA had puppet socialists in post-World War II Europe

This theory holds that the CIA funded the European socialist movement to ensure that it followed the North American agenda for its new world order. Curiously, if perhaps unsurprisingly, the conspiracy identifies the very busy Prince Bernhard of Holland and the Bilderberg Group as principal agents in keeping European left-wing activists on-message with the US and its plans for the rest of the world.

CIA funds were invested in liberal magazine, *Encounter*, so as to provide a forum for diverse left-wing politicians such as Britain's Anthony Crosland, Dennis Healey, and Hugh Gaitskell. Conspiracy theorists claim that such "perspicacious" intellectuals should have known that the impoverished magazines that were publishing their opinions were being funded by shadowy forces outside the conventional left. Cynics of the conventional left might have similarly argued that if the shadowy forces outside the conventional left wanted to throw money at politicians who supported the Campaign for Nuclear Disarmament, then they would be more than happy to catch it.

The one disturbing possibility about the CIA's interference in European politics is that it used part of its $2 billion annual budget in the post-war years to destabilize left-wing organizations of which it disapproved, perhaps fearing that these were a front for the Soviet Union. It can be argued, however, that a competent intelligence agency should have recognized the impotence of the USSR.

See also: *The Bilderberg Group p.108*

1950

THE USSR/CHINA COALITION

The two great communist powers conspired against the West

While they might be seen as prickly co-habitants, histori-ically there has been a certain interaction between the USSR as was and China. Mao Zedong's communism was influenced by Russian ideologues, such as Lenin and Trotsky, and it has been assumed by some western observers that policies in Beijing were led by the Kremlin.

In 1944, near the end of World War II, the uneasy truce that had existed between Japan and Chinese Nationalists since 1938 ended with an invasion of northern China by Japanese forces, in a last desperate attempt to destroy US bomber air bases. Nervous about its own borders, particu-larly in the regions of Manchuria and Sinkiang, the USSR stepped in to assist its neighbour. In such a vast region – parts of the USSR were lawless medieval fiefdoms – it was assumed by some that areas such as Manchuria in fact fell under the control of Moscow.

While relationships between the two superpowers may have been tense, there are suggestions that the USSR took the pragmatic decision to ally itself to its neighbour. The US had in fact begun tentative negotiations to offer China financial aid from 1947, perhaps sensing that this largest country in the world would become, if not a force to deal with, then a market to exploit.

In the see-sawing balance of geopolitics that took place between the three superpowers, it is highly likely that the USSR might have developed a cautious friendship with China. But China's resistance to outside culture, the phi-losophy of Maoism, the Cultural Revolution, and the Great March, would have certainly opposed it to any meaningful collaboration with the USSR.

1954

THE BILDERBERG GROUP

Shadowy international policy discussion group is suspected of manipulating the global economy

If conspiracy it be, the Bilderberg Group is the first organi-zation to be documented by investigative journalists. It was launched, some say, under the auspices of the CIA, in 1954, with the intention of creating a forum for debate and collaboration between north American and European politi-cians, business people, and other movers and shakers. It is named after the Hotel de Bilderberg, in the Dutch border town of Oosterbeek, where the first meeting was held, spon-sored by Dutch royal, Prince Bernhard.

The conspiracy theory

The Bilderberg story is probably one of the best recorded in the history of conspiracy theories. Chief among its concerns, in the years after World War II, was the need to defend western democracy against what it perceived to be the threat of the Soviet Union.

The Bilderberg Group is said to meet twice a year. Prince Bernhard of Holland was the chairman of the first meeting, and ran the European arm of the organization, while C.D. Jackson, a special assistant for psychological warfare at the CIA, became the organizer of the US branch.

The evidence

Attendance is by invitation only. Membership is drawn from mainly NATO-supporting countries. It is chiefly a forum for the like-minded; there is no agenda, no issues to be voted on, no policy decisions made or carried out. Even its critics point out that the organization has no formal philosophy or unifying motives.

Conferences are in secret and never held in the same place. They are organized at different times of the year, usually in remote hotels. Other guests are barred and the venue's normal staff are replaced with Bilderberg Group hirelings; maids, cooks, waiters, receptionists, telephone operators, administration, and so on.

Some of the earliest invitees included presidential advi-sor Averell Harriman, David Rockefeller of the Rockefeller banking family, and Bedel Smith, head of the CIA from 1950–53. Yet the meetings also invite figures from less pow-erful or glamorous professions, such as health, education, and even trades unions. Debate is said to be open and wide-ranging, from across the spectrum of political beliefs – US meetings feature both Democrats and Republicans. Even though the media is barred, certain powerful figures in the largely US-based media, such as *Washington Post* owner Katharine Graham and columnist William F. Buckley Junior, have been invited.

The Bilderberg Foundation, which actually has offices in Manhattan and Amsterdam, asks host countries to provide armed military protection for its meetings, and is said to recompense them for the cost of this security. It is alleged that members are exempted from immigration, visa, and even passport requirements, and that local police are de-ployed as their personal bodyguards. The cost of this, too, is reimbursed by the organization. There also seems to be

Was Prince Bernhard head of the Bilderberg Group? Here he enjoys a joke with ex-president of Zaire, Joseph Mobutu, during a 1973 visit to the country.

an overlap with the north American think-tank, the Council on Foreign Relations.

Anyone attempting to infiltrate a Bilderberg Group meeting can expect to be manhandled, interrogated, and handed over to the police, although it is unknown what the police might do with someone who has merely gatecrashed a bunfight of international eggheads.

The verdict

That Bilderberg Group conferences do take place is too well documented to be in doubt. What is unquantifiable is the scope of the group's influence, and its remit on the international stage. A sympathetic reading of its philosophy might compare it to the think-tanks that are held yearly at the Swiss resort of Davos.

The Bilderberg meetings clearly have as their objective the defence of western, pro-capitalist values. It is similarly clear that the Bilderberg Group sees NATO as its unifying structure, and that it is committed to so-called "supranational" government. It is also claimed that the group is still steered from the back room by the CIA. Interestingly, however, conspiracy theory bloggers have singularly failed in their attempts to prove or even charge the group with any nefarious acts beyond being a twice-yearly freebie for

politicians, businesspeople, economists, publishers, and assorted freeloaders.

See also: *Council for Foreign Relations p.104; The CIA and European Democracy p.107*

1960
BRITISH TRADE UNION LINKS TO USSR

British union activists had links to and possibly were influenced by the Soviet Union

Given that two of communism's greatest theorists, Karl Marx and Friedrich Engels, spent much of their lives living in Britain, both using the British working class as a model for their theories (notably Engels's *The Condition of the Working Classes in England*), it is hardly surprising that the British trades union movement had links with the Soviet Union.

Until communism fell from favour there was a regular traffic between the British trades union movement and eastern Europe. The house publications of the British left – *Tribune, New Statesman, Nation, Morning Star* and, later, *Workers News, Marxism Today,* and *Socialist Worker* – acted as platforms for the theories of Russian left-wing philosophers since as early as the 1860s, and the writings of such figures as Mikhail Bakunin.

Keen to proselytize its philosophies, in all their various guises – Marxism, Leninism, Trotskyism, Stalinism, and the later ameliorative policies of Khruschev and others – the USSR and its satellites frequently played host to visits from British politicians, trades union activists and even youth activists from organizations such as the Co-operative Society and Young Socialists.

Links between the British trades union movement and eastern Europe between the period of the 1917 October Revolution and the fall of communism are an indisputable fact. What is arguable, however, is whether eastern Europe had any overt influence on trades union policies or activities beyond the political opinions they already espoused.

1963
CODEX ALIMENTARIUS
The "food code" rules world food standards

The Codex Alimentarius commission, a fairly arcane Latinism for "food code," was formed under the aegis of the UN, the World Health Authority, and the US Food and Agriculture Organization, in 1963. It aims to regularize food production standards across the globe.

The CA sets standards under its dual Agreement on the Application of Sanitary and Phytosanitary Measures (SPS) and the Agreement on Technical Barriers to Trade (TBT). Essentially, it tells food producers how they should prepare a pre-cooked chicken or any other foodstuff. However, critics claim that it is an unpoliced, self-regulating body in the service of the food multinationals. It is argued that its rules restrict small, independent food producers; organic farmers, for example.

It is also claimed that it is in direct competition with the vitamins industry, going against recommendations in the *American Journal of Medicine* that adults should take some sort of daily multivitamin and, by implication, that it is in the service of the fast food industry. It seems likely, however, that the vitamin industry itself – most experts recommend vitamin intake from fruit or vegetables, rather than tablet form – is smarting from the competition.

In the era of avian flu and BSE, and the global pandemic of obesity and other food-related problems, a conspiracy surrounding the CA might actually be beneficial. There are, however, clear divisions in the opinions of the countries that attend the Codex conferences, and there is evidently a need for an independent regulator to monitor its dictats.

1963
THE PROFUMO AFFAIR
British government sex scandal that ushered in the swinging '60s

In March 1963, during the conservative government of Prime Minister Harold MacMillan, the Secretary of State for War, John Dennis Profumo, was forced to admit that he had lied to the Houses of Parliament about a relationship with a young nightclub showgirl, Christine Keeler.

Keeler had left home at 16 after an unhappy childhood and had found work as a showgirl at Murray's nightclub in London's West End. At Murray's she met Marilyn "Mandy" Rice-Davis, who introduced her to Stephen Ward, said by some to be a procurer, and possibly a drug dealer. Ward then introduced Keeler to John Profumo at a society party. Keeler and Profumo embarked on an affair, which Profumo kept secret. Not secret enough, however, to prevent the FBI from investigating it, inspired largely by Keeler's parallel affair with Russian naval attaché, Eugene Ivanov.

Profumo was forced to apologize for lying to Parliament and eventually resigned in June, 1963. Both Keeler and Rice-Davies were prosecuted for prostitution, Keeler serving a short sentence. Ward was also prosecuted for pimping, but committed suicide on the last day of his trial. At the time of writing, both Profumo and Keeler are still alive; Profumo later dedicated himself to charitable work in London's East End and was awarded a CBE in 1975. Keeler published a salacious memoir in 2001.

The affair is undeniable, and ushered in a new type of media scandal. Whether their behaviour constituted any threat to national security is doubtful, but the scandal occurred at the height of the Cold War.

1968
THE PARIS UPRISINGS
France and Europe teetered on the edge of a latterday revolution

The *événéments* (events) of May 1968 in Paris, France represent one of the most explicit conspiracies in history. Sparked by a student rebellion at the University of Nanterre, the Paris revolt spread to workplaces across the country. It would also emigrate: to London, and Berlin, perhaps inspiring German terrorists, Andreas Baader and Ulrike Meinhof, to launch the Red Army faction.

The Nanterre uprising was a protest against the arrest of members belonging to the National Vietnam Committee,

A diver tries to raise the car that plunged into a pond with Edward Kennedy at the wheel. Mary Jo Kopechne was killed in the crash, July 17th, 1969.

who opposed the Vietnam War. With a backdrop of rising unemployment and falling wages, and under the rule of patrician President Charles de Gaulle, this was a recipe for disaster. The disaffection spread, and not just to other universities, but factories and workplaces too. Hundreds of thousands marched against the government. Certain forms of food production ceased, cross-channel ferry services were halted, and tourists bussed to other countries. Students and workers made barricades in the streets, adopting whimsical slogans, such as "Beneath the cobbles, the beach," while they ripped up the cobbles to throw at charging police. The police, in turn, were vicious in their reprisals.

Paris 1968, one of the most extraordinary uprisings in 20th-century history, fell apart due largely to left-wing disorganization and dispute. It is difficult, however, to imagine how the student revolution would have fared beyond the events of that spring.

1969
EDWARD KENNEDY AND
CHAPPAQUIDICK

The Kennedy clan protected Edward Kennedy from criminal proceedings following a fatal accident

On the night of July 17th, 1969, senator Edward "Teddy" Kennedy was at a party at a house on the small island of Chappaquidick, off Martha's Vineyard, Massachusetts. Also present were the "Boiler Room Girls," six young researchers who had worked for his older brother Robert until his assassination the year before. Among them was 29-year-old Mary Jo Kopechne.

Kennedy and Kopechne left the party at 11.15pm, although their car was observed some hours later by a local police officer. Ostensibly, Kennedy was taking her to a ferry landing to transfer to Martha's Vineyard and return to her hotel, yet their car was seen some time after the last ferry had left. It is commonly assumed they left to have sex in a secluded setting.

Although he had travelled along the road twice that day, Kennedy claimed that he was confused when he took a wrong turning, accelerated, and drove off a bridge into a tidal pond. The car flipped over, Kennedy was able to escape, but Kopechne wasn't. He claimed to have attempted to save her, but gave up and returned to his hotel, where he and friends constructed an alibi. When the accident was discovered the next day, it was estimated that Kopechne had perhaps lived another two and a half hours before finally asphyxiating as a pocket of air in the car expired.

Kennedy pleaded guilty to leaving the scene of an accident, but went unpunished.

1969
THE PINAY CIRCLE, AKA
LE CERCLE
The death of Diana, Princess of Wales, was
an assassination

Le Cercle takes its name from 1950s French premier, Antoine
Pinay, and is believed to be a direct-action offshoot of the
Bilderberg Group. Pinay was at the original Bilderberg Group
meeting at the Hotel de Bilderberg in Oosterbeek, Holland,
in 1954. He formed his *Cercle* in 1969, allegedly with the
express intent of carrying out direct actions on behalf
of the Bilderbergs. It was supported by the French secret
service and members of the Austrian royalty.

Le Cercle is said to comprise international spooks, members of the military, politicians, and others on the right. Its
critics claim that it destabilized the governments of both
Harold Wilson and Ted Heath in Britain, Gough Whitlam in
Australia, and François Mittérand in France. Its dependence
on the so-called military-industrial complex, particularly in
Britain and France, has led to links with shadowy organizations such as Opus Dei and even, it's claimed, the Moonies.
It is accused of being responsible for the assassination of
pacifist Swedish premier, Olof Palme, and, controversially,
the death of Diana, Princess of Wales and her boyfriend Dodi
Fayed, because her anti-landmine campaign threatened the
profits of the multimillion-dollar mine industry.

Diana died in August 1997 in a high-speed paparazzi
car chase. She was being driven by a driver who, the authorities claimed, had consumed excessive amounts of
cocaine and alcohol (this has since been disputed, adding
to the mystery surrounding Diana's death). Whether or not
the accident was "arranged" and if so by whom, remains
shrouded in mystery.

See also: *Olof Palme p.67; The Bilderberg Group p.108;
Prince Philip ordered Diana's Murder p.274*

1970s
CROWN AGENTS
Shadowy role of a quasi-governmental organization

Despite its name, the Crown Agents is in fact a private company that is hired by the British government's Treasury as
a consultant on various policy issues. It works with developing countries from Serbia to South Africa, as well as with
over 100 consultancy client governments around the world.
It was originally founded in 1833; in the mid-1970s the

organization went bust due to poor property investments
and had to be bailed out by the government. In 1996, it
was privatized and the name changed to the Crown Agents
for Overseas Government and Administrations Ltd.

Crown Agents is paid millions of pounds a year for its consultancy services and has been targeted with accusations of
secrecy and collusion. The EU, the International Monetary
Fund, and the World Bank are said to be surprised that the
British government has hired the private company to advise on issues of international policy. Among various other
concerns, Bulgarian politicians and its media have complained that reports on Bulgaria's customs infrastructure
by Crown Agents amount to a furtive privatization of the
customs service.

The organization has fingers in an untold numbers of
pies: from tsunami relief projects in the Philippines to HIV
awareness programmes in Rwanda, and from earthquake relief in Algeria to national debt management in Vietnam. As
a private company, it takes on these projects on a paid,
commercial basis.

The number and breadth of the projects undertaken
by Crown Agents, and the fact that it is a private, profit-
making company, are the seed-bed for suspicions about
its actual role on the global stage. Crown Agents argues
that it is more a facilitating body, enabling countries to
address issues such as HIV or debt management, by applying international expert knowledge. Conspiracy theorists
argue, however, that its influence in numerous countries
around the world represents an unofficial, back-room, and
business-oriented, world government.

1973
THE LONRHO AFFAIR
The mining company condemned as the
"unacceptable face of captialism."

The Lonrho – London and Rhodesia Mining and Land
Company – scandal in 1973 gave the world the resonant
phrase, in the words of the then British Conservative prime
minister Edward Heath, "the unacceptable face of capitalism." Its chairman, the late businessman, Roland "Tiny"
Rowland, replied that he would not want to be the acceptable face of capitalism anyway.

The Lonrho scandal was, essentially, the exposure of
the swashbuckling Rowland's repeated breaches of international sanctions placed on what was then Rhodesia, under
the rule of premier Ian Smith. Smith had made a unilateral
declaration of independence from Rhodesia's colonial

governors at the time, Britain. Smith's regime was vilified around the world.

Ironically, Rowland, who became director of Lonrho in 1961, was considered a charming and charismatic figure who knew that liberalized African nations would move on to the international business stage. He befriended many African leaders, including Robert Mugabe, and later the freed, Nelson Mandela. After Rowland's death in 1998, former Zambian leader Kenneth Kaunda also praised his efforts to help African states engage in the international economy.

Rowland's visibly pro-African policies sparked a failed attempt to sack him by fellow Lonrho board members in 1963, but he clung on until being ousted in a boardroom coup in 1994. It seems clear, however, that his dealings with certain African governments did stray into illegality, not least bribery and back-room dealing with questionable governments. The Lonrho story remains a curious tale of western capitalism mixed with pro-African sentiments.

See also: *Harrods Affair and Tiny Rowland p.120*

1973
THE TRILATERAL
COMMISSION

International think-tank is attempting to steer global democracy

The Trilateral Commission, a group formed in 1973, is an invitation-only group of north American, European and Asian business people, entrepreneurs, media, trades unionists, and individuals of all political persuasions. Its original remit was to promote communication between the nations at a time when the Vietnam War, student unrest and labour disputes seemed to be threatening the fabric of society.

The conspiracy theory

The Commission was set up by a number of north Americans, including David Rockefeller and presidential advisor, Zbigniew Brzezinski, who became its first director, in 1973. The group specifically excludes acting politicians, although democrat senator Jimmy Carter was asked to join before he became US president in 1977, allegedly because of his interest in Japanese and European cooperation, which was one of the Commission's diplomatic objectives.

Originally, Japan was the only eastern member, but that has since been expanded to form the Pacific-Asian Group, which, like Europe and north America, holds a separate conference once a year.

The evidence

The Commission claims that, while its conferences are held in secret, its processes and membership are a model of transparency. Its publications are made available free to anyone who asks, as is its membership list; its website lists key members, and a full list of its 450 invited members is also available. The Commission is at pains to explain that it is not linked to the Council for Foreign Relations or any other international think-tank. It should be pointed out, however, that other Trilateral commissioners currently include Alan Greenspan of the non-governmental north American Federal Reserve, which effectively runs the US economy via a cartel of the big banks, Vice President Dick Cheney (fingered in the Halliburton/Iraq scandal) and George Bush Sr, are among influential figures from the business and political fields. Katharine Graham, publisher of the *Washington Post*, Walter Mondale, and even Bill Clinton, are said to be members. Secretary of state during the Vietnam War, Henry Kissinger, a hated figure among anti-war activists, was also an early member.

Critics claim, however, that the Trilateral Commission is little more than a front for the personal financial interests of alleged Bilderberg member, David Rockefeller, owner of the Chase Manhattan Bank, and also a member of the Council for Foreign Relations. It is said that Rockefeller was spurred into proposing the Trilateral Commission after reading Zbigniew Brzezinski's book, *Between Two Ages* (1982), written when Brzezinski was a professor at Columbia University. The book warned of a sea change in international politics and economics, and the need for the US to respond to this change. Chiefly, it pointed out the growing international clout of Japan – for centuries a closed society with little interest in the ways of the rest of the world – and the post-war economic growth of Germany and other European countries.

Former US republican senator Barry Goldwater, now retired, has been quoted as saying that the Trilateral Commission under the Rockefeller aegis effectively manufactured Carter's election to the White House in 1973. And the *Washington Post* has quoted right-wing activist, Lyndon LaRouche, as saying that the Commission is behind the international drugs trade. The paper has similarly quoted another right-wing figure, fundamentalist Christian, Pat Buchanan, claiming that the Commission is linked to Freemasonry and even witchcraft. In an unlikely alliance, the black rap group, Public Enemy, joined Lyndon LaRouche's team when, during a concert in the US, they accused the Commission of being a "wicked" Zionist conspiracy.

The verdict

As the *Washington Post's* journalist, perhaps not entirely unbiased, pointed out, the Commission is a "club for people who run the world anyway," which suggests that figures such as Bush and Rockefeller don't need to hatch a conspiracy if they already own the shop. The criticisms from the north American far right range from the insane to the anti-Semitic, but the "shadow world government" has been criticized by the far left as well. Clearly, many of its members have held positions of considerable power internationally, and there are a great many powerful industrialists involved – executives from AT&T, ITT, Exxon, Enron, Xerox, Mobil, Pepsico, Nabisco, and Goldman Sachs among them. What political clout these companies might have is debatable, but they clearly have the ear of governments the world over.

As the *Washington Post* perspicaciously points out, everyone knows that big business rules the world. It is notable, however, despite the power some of its members might wield, that most of the Commission's star public figures – Carter, Kissinger, Mondale et al – are considered political has-beens in the 21st century. Conspiracy theorists might better consider identifying a newer, younger, generation of Masters of the Universe. A certain William Gates with offices in Seattle might be a good starting point.

See also: *The US Federal Reserve p.100; Council for Foreign Relations p.104; Freemasons p.284*

1974
KAREN SILKWOOD

b. 1946, Longview, Texas
d. 1974, Crescent, Oklahoma
Union activist, Silkwood, was assassinated on nuclear industry orders

Karen Silkwood was a union activist who fought for better health and safety conditions at the Kerr-McGee plutonium processing plant in Oklahoma. She died in an unexplained car crash in 1974; she was on her way to deliver documents revealing evidence of spills, leaks, and missing plutonium at the plant to a union representative and a *New York Times* investigative reporter.

The conspiracy theory

Silkwood was deliberately contaminated with plutonium by agents of the Kerr-McGee Corporation. If she had survived these incidents, it is highly likely that she would have developed cancer from radiation. Her sudden death in a car crash in November 1974 was deliberately planned and formed part of a larger conspiracy to maintain a silence about nuclear contamination in the US which stretched from the Atomic Energy Commission to the FBI and the CIA.

The evidence

Karen Gay Silkwood was born on February 19, 1946, in Longview, Texas. She studied medical technology and, in 1965, married William Meadows, with whom she had three children. In 1972, she left her husband and went to live in Oklahoma City, where she began working as a metallography laboratory technician at the Cimarron River plutonium fuels production plant. This plant was owned by the Kerr-McGee Nuclear Corporation. While there Silkwood became interested in working conditions for herself and her fellow employees – she joined the Oil, Chemical, and Atomic Workers Union at a period when little was known about nuclear contamination and most people were unaware of its consequences. There were almost no security measures in place to prevent the removal of plutonium from the plant.

By 1974, Silkwood had become the first female on the local union's negotiating committee and, by November, employees at the plant felt they had sufficient evidence about poor maintenance and leaks at the plant to consider taking legal action against Kerr-McGee. Silkwood began monitoring herself for radiation activity on November 5th. Readings from the meter in her workroom identified Plutonium-239 on her hands as well as down the right side of her body. She had, apparently, been exposed to a low level of airborne plutonium. Strangely, there appeared to be no leaks in Silkwood's gloves and no plutonium on the relevant work surfaces or in the air.

The following day, Silkwood measured her radiation levels for a second time. Although she had not worked in the apparently contaminated zone that morning, she now had even higher radiation levels on her right side. At her request, her locker and car were measured but no radiation was found. By November 7th, her radiation levels were dangerously high but, again, no activity was identified in her locker or car. At her apartment, a team of investigators found significant levels of radiation in the bathroom and kitchen. The levels in Silkwood's home urine samples were far higher than those taken at the Kerr-McGee plant.

On November 12th, a Dr George Voelz of the Los Alamos Laboratory Health Division concluded that Silkwood's flatmate, who also worked at the plant, and her boyfriend had very insignificant amounts of plutonium in their bodies

Karen Silkwood may have paid heavily for her interest in the workings of the nuclear industry.

the inner and outer parts of Silkwood's lung were also roughly equal, which would indicate that the exposure had been extremely recent.

During preparations for the subsequent trial against Kerr-McGee, several significant witnesses died or disappeared. In addition, a number of Silkwood's lawyers claimed to have received death threats and to have been tailed. After the first trial, in 1979, the jury awarded the estate $10.5 million but this was later reversed by the Federal Court of Appeals in Denver, which awarded $5,000 for loss of personal property. The matter was eventually settled out of court for $1.3 million and the Kerr-McGee nuclear fuel plants closed in 1975.

The verdict

Karen Silkwood might have died of radiation and had the evidence to prove it. The events surrounding her rather more premature death seem, in the circumstances, highly suspicious. There was no investigation into her death because Silkwood officially died in a one-car crash. A Hollywood film, *Silkwood*, released in 1983 and starring Meryl Streep brought her case to the public eye.

1975
ARISTOTLE SOCRATES ONASSIS

b. 1906, Smyrna, Turkey
d. 1975, Neuilly-sur-Seine, nr Paris, France
Tycoon, and Greek shipping and oil magnate, Onassis, influenced economies and governments

while Silkwood had roughly half the maximum permissible lung burden for workers. Dr. Voelz assured Silkwood that this would not affect her health or her fertility levels but Silkwood and her flatmate were restricted from further radiation work.

After work on November 13th, Silkwood went to a union meeting in Crescent, Oklahoma. Afterwards she drove to a secret meeting with an Atomic Energy Commission official and a *New York Times* reporter. During the drive, her car crashed into a concrete ditch, though no other vehicle was involved and the weather was clear. Silkwood died from multiple injuries. She had earlier intimated that she was carrying important document to this meeting, one of which contained proof that 19kg (42.5lb) of plutonium was missing from Kerr-McGee's Cimarron plant. This was enough to make three nuclear bombs.

The Atomic Energy Commission and Oklahoma State requested a specialist autopsy. It concluded that Silkwood must have ingested plutonium prior to her death and that her levels of plutonium contamination were well above average. She also had twice the recommended dosage of a sedative called Quaalude in her blood which would definitely induce drowsiness. The plutonium concentrations in

Onassis's family fled from Turkey to Greece at the beginning of the 20th century. Aged 17, he moved to Argentina, where he established joint Greek-Argentinian nationality. The Onassis myth holds that he was poor and worked variously as a dishwasher and a telephone operator. It is alleged that drug smuggling, specifically opium, is what made him a millionaire within the space of three years.

Onassis used his profits to move into the shipping industry. He struck lucrative deals with the US Navy during World War II, and invited international scorn when his fleet of whaling ships broke international boundary rules for fishing and the types of whale that could be fished. He also moved into the airline industry, relaunching Greece's ailing TAE airline as Olympic Airways.

It is alleged that he began to seduce Jacqueline Bouvier Kennedy, wife of John F. Kennedy, prior to JFK's assassination in 1963, inviting her aboard his yacht without JFK.

Aristotle Onassis and Jacqueline Kennedy Onassis relaxing on a ten-day tour of Egypt, just a year before the shipping magnate's death.

Perhaps the worst allegation is that he arranged the assassination of Robert "Bobbie" Kennedy in 1968, when the senator became close to Jackie Kennedy after JFK's death.

Onassis married Jackie Kennedy in 1968, but their marriage would only last until his death in 1975. At least one respected biography has rehearsed these claims in print, but given its posthumous, libel-proof nature, the Kennedy assassination theory, and the allegations of drug smuggling, it will probably remain unproven.

See also: *John Fitzgerald Kennedy p.54*

1975
THE GEMSTONE FILE
The conspiracy to run the US by big business and the Mafia

The Gemstone File conspiracy first surfaced in 1969 with the appearance of the initial papers. The complete papers were uneared in 1975. It alleges that an attempt was made by Aristotle Onassis, Howard Hughes, the Mafia, and assorted others to take over the US. It also claims that there were no less than four gunmen in Dallas the day John F. Kennedy was assassinated.

This conspiracy begins with Onassis sealing a deal with Joe Kennedy and criminal Meyer Lansky to ship illicit alcohol into the US. Onassis is also said to have agreed with David Rockefeller to secure oil supplies from the Middle East to the detriment of the eastern economies. In the meantime, multimillionaire Howard Hughes was bribing politicians, not least Richard Nixon. Castro was taking control of Cuba, as well as the Onassis/Lansky gambling empire based there, which spurred Onassis on to manipulate the US into mounting the Bay of Pigs invasion fiasco of 1961.

In 1960, Gemstone author Michael Roberts showed the Hughes Corporation his "Gemstones" – synthetic rubies that were used in laser technology – and they were stolen by the corporation. Between them, Onassis, Hughes, and the Mafia assumed control of the government of the US.

Nixon was indeed indebted to Hughes, in the form of an unpaid $200,000 loan to a relative, and Onassis was also involved with the Kennedys. But the Gemstone File reads too much like a novel and is undermined by inaccuracies – namely that Hughes was buried at sea off Onassis's private Greek island Skorpios; in fact he was buried in Houston.

See also: *John Fitzgerald Kennedy p.54; Aristotle Onassis p.115; Howard Hughes p.117*

1976
HOWARD HUGHES
b. 1905, Houston, Texas

d. 1976, in his jet en route to a Houston hospital
Secretive multimillionaire tycoon who invited untold conspiracy theories about his private life

Born into a wealthy Texas oil family, Hughes is said to have been a painfully shy person, even though he was later seen at movie premiers and nightclubs with stars such as Ava Gardner, Katharine Hepburn, Jane Russell, and Lana Turner. He became an expert flyer, at one point holding all the records for feats of flying recognized in the US. With his inherited wealth, he built a vast, multimillion dollar empire out of two key US industries, oil and cinema.

This appears not to have been without its problems, however. In 1966, the secretive Hughes moved into the Desert Hotel Inn in Las Vegas, bought it, and converted a floor into his own private, off-limits quarters. Here Hughes began to show signs of the manias that would affect him until his death in 1975: a phobia about germs and sunlight, paranoia, and intravenous drug addiction following a course of painkillers taken after an earlier plane crash.

Hughes was never seen again. One of the more outlandish conspiracy theories was that on his disappearance he had in fact been kidnapped and drugged by rival businessman Aristotle Onassis, and an actor hired to replace him.

Hughes's wealth, power, and evident paranoia are unquestioned. So are his youthful bravery, commitment to the US war effort, and his skills in the film industry. Many of the conspiracy theories, however, are probably pure fiction.

1980
THE NUGAN HAND BANK SCANDAL
CIA-funded bank was involved in drug-running and the war in Indochina

The Nugan Hand Bank, set up by former US marine Mike Hand and Australian businessman Frank Nugan, dissolved in 1980 when Hand disappeared. He is believed to have fled Australia on a flight to Fiji under an assumed name. Shortly before Hand disappeared, Nugan was found dead in his car on a country road outside Sydney, with a single shotgun wound. Neither man had previous banking experience.

The conspiracy theory
Hand was awarded a Silver Star, a Purple Heart, and a Distinguished Service Cross for his bravery in Vietnam. These are believed to have won him a job as a special agent for the CIA in Vietnam and the covert US war in Laos. The Nugan Hand Bank was formed in Australia in 1973, and there is strong, if circumstantial, evidence that it was used to launder money and supplies of drugs and arms to finance illicit CIA actions in countries neighbouring Vietnam.

Journalists in Australia and the US have made several allegations about Hand, not least that he returned to the US to undergo CIA training, and that he was involved in covert actions in what was then Rhodesia (Zimbabwe as is now) and Panama. A known dealer in drugs and gambling equipment, Bernie Houghton, was also employed by the Nugan Hand Bank.

The Nugan Hand Bank was similarly reported to be striking drug deals with warlords in Burma and further alleged to be soliciting large deposits from other figures on the Asian mainland, Saudi Arabia, and from US servicemen.

The conspiracy actually widens out in Australia, with claims by certain members of the Australian Labor Party that the US may have also used its networks to destabilize the government of Gough Whitlam in 1975. Certain politicians have gone on record as saying that the CIA influenced the Australian ex-governor John Kerr to sack Whitlam, giving the north Americans more clout in the region's politics.

Australian journalists maintain that a FBI file on the Nugan Hand Bank was withheld from disclosure, even under the Freedom of Information Act, and that it was not even shown to the Australian security forces, as it was claimed that this would endanger US "national defense or foreign policy." The bank is said to have connections with Hong Kong business people, companies in Lebanon, and certain figures working in Washington. One Sydney employee has sworn on oath that if staff did not obey orders, they were told that their wives would be kidnapped, chopped up, and sent home in boxes.

The evidence
It has been established that Hand was helped when he fled Australia in 1980 by a figure known as "Charlie" and later identified as James Oswald Spencer – a former special services operative and CIA agent. In 1991, Australian journalist Brian Toohey found a letterbox for Hand in Bellevue, a town in the Cascades mountain range, near Puget Sound and the Canadian border in Washington state, where he was believed to be living with his equally fugitive wife, Helen. Both vanished shortly after Toohey located the letterbox.

Another writer, author Jonathan Kwitny, who wrote a book about the Nugan Hand affair, *The Crimes of Patriots*, in 1987, actually went as far as preparing a dossier on the story. The dossier was used as part of an in-camera enquiry by the Senate and Congress Intelligence Committee on the Iran-Contra scandal, which heard closed-door testimony from CIA chief William Casey, among others. The details of the Nugan Hand interrogations were never released. Hand is still missing.

The verdict

For leading national journalists to go into print with such allegations lends no uncertain force to the conspiracy theory. That such an establishment as US publishing house Simon and Schuster should repeat them in a book by a respected author, a book which furthermore would have to have been read by a paid libel lawyer to protect the publishers from libel action, only lends further force to the tale. As the Iran-Contra scandal proved, a lot of very strange things took place in this period of north American history. The disappearance of Hands and his wife, and his enduring reluctance to appear in public to either refute the claims or confront his accusers, is more coal on this particular fire. There is no proof of the allegations of drug dealing or money laundering for covert CIA actions in South East Asia, but seasoned conspiracists will no doubt form their own opinions on the Nugan Hand Bank affair. It would also be safe to speculate that, with so many journalists on the trail of this tale, it might only be a matter of time before the definitive story of this alleged CIA front is established and placed in the public domain.

See also: *Gough Whitlam p.152; Iran Contra p.228*

1980
THE OCTOBER SURPRISE

Presidents Carter, Reagan, and Bush and the scandal of the 1980 Iranian–US hostages affair

The October Surprise took place against the backdrop of the 1980 US election campaign that saw standing Democratic president Jimmy Carter challenged by Republican candidate Ronald Reagan. It is alleged that Reagan and running partner, George Bush Sr, negotiated with Iranian politicians to delay the release of US hostages being held in Iran, expressly in order to derail Carter's campaign.

The conspiracy theory states that, in October 1980, during the build-up to the election, William Casey, who was then head of the CIA, and Bush Sr, himself a former CIA boss, held negotiations with Iranian officials with a mission to delay the release of 52 captives in the American embassy in Tehran. This would pull the carpet from under Carter's plans to have the captives freed after 444 days of negotiations – the so-called "October Surprise" that would win Carter the election.

Papers, said to have been discovered in the White House during the Clinton presidency, apparently contain a message sent by the Kremlin to the US congress in the early 1990s outlining the plot. Casey and Bush Sr are said to have met Iranian representatives in Madrid and Paris, outbidding Carter in their offers of weapons and military support should the Iranians comply with Bush Sr and Reagan.

Carter lost the election, the hostages were not released until 1981, and the US under Reagan supplied hundreds of millions of dollars-worth of weapons to Iran via Israel. Whether this proves that a conspiracy existed is debatable, but it fulfils the claims of the conspiracists.

1981
PROPAGANDA DUE (P2)

Illegal Masonic group rules Italy in secret and masterminds political assassinations

The Propaganda Due scandal – Propaganda Due being the full name of the secret Italian former Masonic lodge P2 – has the hallmarks of a classic conspiracy: Masons, Mafiosi, the Vatican, CIA, the international drugs trade, and senior politicians were all said to be involved. It is also alleged to encompass the murder, in 1978, of Italian prime minister Aldo Moro, and Swedish premier Olof Palme.

The conspiracy theory

Much of the theory is well-established fact. Propaganda Due was founded (or "consecrated," as it is known in Masonic circles) in 1895. By the 1960s (and probably earlier), P2 was infiltrated by the Mafia and its tame (intimidated) politicians – some in government. In 1976, the Italian Masonic authorities were forced to close P2 down because of its involvement in criminality, and to expel its master Licio Gelli, an ex-Mussolini fascist and alleged CIA officer.

From then on P2 (sometimes also known as P7) met in secret. P2 was implicated in the misuse of Vatican funds, and power by Archbishop Marcinkus, who notoriously was unable to leave the Vatican for fear of automatic arrest should he leave the protection of the Vatican State. It is widely believed to have had close connections with at least two Italian prime ministers, Giulio Andreotti and Bettino Craxi, both with proven Mafia links and both subsequently convicted on corruption charges. Left-wing activists, including journalists on the respected anti-fascist magazine, *Searchlight*, have even alleged that current Italian prime minister Silvio Berlusconi is a member of P2. An independent commission described P2 as a "government within the government," a subversive movement, and a military coup waiting to happen.

As recently as 2002, *Searchlight* was speculating whether P2 had launched a new wave of political terror in Italy, using a network of "second generation Red Brigades," following a series of political assassinations.

Other elements of the conspiracy theory, especially those involving the CIA, are more open to debate. P2 was not only believed to be involved in the international drug trade but also – via Gelli and others – closely connected with the CIA. Some have claimed that CIA involvement was, like the Iran-Contra and other scandals, suggestive of US manipulation of the global drugs trade to influence geopolitical balance.

It has also been alleged that the CIA paid P2 to foment political revolt in Italy, and to do its dirty work in Europe. This included the death in 1978 of Italian prime minister Aldo Moro, claimed by some to have been killed by CIA operatives who had penetrated the left-wing revolutionary group the, Brigado Rosso, Red Brigade. Moro's body was found in the boot of a bullet-riddled car abandoned in a Rome back street. The CIA has also been implicated in the 1986 assassination of Swedish premier Olof Palme – a fierce critic of US foreign policy – because of his interference in the Iran-Contra affair.

The evidence

P2's criminal links are well known. After his expulsion, Licio Gelli continued to run P2 until 1981, when he fled his home just before it was raided by police. A search of the premises revealed papers that connected Gelli with other P2 members, among them Michele Sindona, a banker with proven Mafia connections, who was under investigation for embezzling money from the Vatican, and Roberto Calvi, president of the Banco Ambrosiano, which handled the Vatican's financial affairs. Sindona fled to the US where he was caught and tried for fraud and jailed for 25 years.

Calvi stole an estimated $1.3 billion from his own bank, and was said to be passing it on to P2 when he was found hanged under Blackfriars Bridge in London, in 1982. When discovered, Calvi had 6.5kg (14lb) of bricks and stones in his pockets and his hands were tied behind his back, yet bizarrely a City of London inquest declared that he had committed "suicide."

Many have read his death as a ritual Masonic killing. His body was found inside the Square Mile of the City of London, under a bridge near the site of a former monastery of the eponymous Black Friars, all symbols of Italian Freemasonry.

Calvi's family insisted on a second inquest, which declared an open verdict on his death. His body was exhumed in 1998 at the order of an Italian court, and laboratory tests on his clothing proved that he had been murdered. In 2005, British police arrested two men in connection with Calvi's murder who are now awaiting trial.

The verdict

Many of the facts in the Propaganda Due story are indisputable. The organization was a front for the Mafia. Successive Italian leaders have been shown to be corrupt. Roberto Calvi was murdered, as high-tech tests on his clothing proved. He had also been stealing large sums of money from his bank, which folded after his death.

The wilder accusations are virtually impossible to prove, however, although an individual claiming to be a CIA operative spoke on national TV claiming that the organization had paid P2 to have Olof Palme assassinated. As more facts come to light in relation to Calvi and P2, the full story may eventually be known.

See also: *Aldo Moro p.62; Olof Palme p.67; Searchlight p.88; The Mafia p.281; Freemasons p.284; Calvi and the Vatican Bank p.256*

1982
HENRY KISSINGER ASSOCIATES

The power-broker and kingmaker, who is also known as the "Milosevic of Manhattan"

Former diplomat Henry Kissinger (born 1923, in Fürth, Germany) has been assiduously collecting enemies ever since he helped mastermind American covert operations in Vietnam, Cambodia, and Laos during the Vietnam War in the late 1960s and early 1970s. The highly respected libertarian journalist Christopher Hitchens has been pursuing Kissinger for decades, calling for him to be tried for war crimes in several continents. Respectable publications, such as *Vanity Fair* and *Harper's* have published his pieces, directly accusing Kissinger of war crimes, while Oxford University Press has published *The Lost Crusade,* by John Prados, which included references to Kissinger's activities being on the periphery of legality.

The conspiracy theory

The theory begins in 1970, when Kissinger, then President Nixon's secretary of state, is alleged to have chaired a meeting on American covert operations in Vietnam and neighbouring countries. The trail warms up, however, in 1973, when the US engineered the overthrow of democratically elected socialist Chilean prime minister Salvador Allende, who died during a military coup led by General Augusto Pinochet. Allende fatally believed Pinochet to be his friend. (Pinochet was, in fact, a friend of Kissinger's.) Pinochet subsequently established a right-wing dictatorship that ruled the region with the help of Washington, DC.

The expedition undertaken in the Far East by the US was an unmitigated disaster, ending with the ignominious Fall of Saigon in 1976. Yet Kissinger managed to move effortlessly into private political and business consultancy. He is, and was, a friend of powerful politicians, and his firm Kissinger Associates, formed in 1982, has been called a secret agency for electing puppets of the US far right. But anti-war activists, among them the young Hitchens, were already on his heels.

The evidence

One group of student protesters who proposed a citizen's arrest of Kissinger for war crimes committed during the Vietnam War found their mail intercepted and were rounded up and jailed for plotting to "kidnap" the US secretary of state. American complicity in the murder of Allende is unquestionable, as are its numerous crimes against humanity in Vietnam and neighbouring countries in that apocalyptic period in the region. Kissinger is alleged to have once said: "It is an act of insanity and national humiliation to have a law forbidding the President from ordering assassination" (quoted in The Lost Crusade). He is believed responsible for ordering the assassination of a Chilean army general, René Schneider, in a deliberate ploy to scare centrist politicians into resisting the appointment of Allende.

Recently declassified state department documents from 1976 show that Kissinger was involved in Operation Condor, an international plot by the right-wing governments of Argentina, Brazil, Chile, Bolivia, Paraguay, and Uruguay to kidnap and murder exiled dissident politicians. He is now wanted for questioning in several countries, including Argentina, Spain, and France, in connection with the Condor conspiracy and disappearance of numerous foreign nationals in Chile and other South American countries. As a consequence, he can no longer travel to these – and many other – countries with impunity. Kissinger is also known to

be a close ally of the Republicans and, in particular, the Bush family. He is a popular figure in Washington, and his company still advises many major right-wing politicians. He appears regularly at society dinners and other events, publishes columns, and appears on TV.

The verdict

The evidence against Kissinger, and his Teflon-like ability to avoid blame-sticking, is pressingly convincing. He has also managed to amass a small army of media-savvy opponents simply with his air of serene and imperious arrogance. As Richard Nixon's number two man, Kissinger would have had the imprimatur to authorize the atrocities that the US committed in Vietnam and elsewhere. Critics such as Christopher Hitchens have amassed vast amounts of information detailing his almost exclusive complicity in secret but often outrageous police actions in untold countries across the world.

The surprise is that the so-called "butcher" of Cambodia, who helped Richard Nixon push on with the Vietnam War to the extent that a further 35,000 young north Americans are believed to have perished unnecessarily as a result, was never asked to explain his actions. The only explanation, if the theories are true, is that Kissinger got off scot free because he has information that would incriminate powerful figures in the American establishment.

See also: *Salvador Allende p.60; The Trilateral Commission p.113; Operation Condor p.147*

1984
HARRODS AFFAIR AND TINY ROWLAND

Two warring tycoons joined battle over England's most famous department store

The Harrods affair is one of the murkiest scandals in recent decades, involving two multimillionaire businessmen, Mohammed Al-Fayed and Roland "Tiny" Rowland, controversial boss of the Lonrho corporation. The scandal also ensnared British politicians, not least former prime minister Ted Heath, whom both sides accused of favouritism towards the other.

The scandal centered on both men's unusually passionate desire to acquire Harrods in Knightsbridge, London, possibly the smartest upmarket store in Britain. Al-Fayed beat Rowland in the bid. It is alleged that Al-Fayed purchased the Harrods parent company House of Fraser from funds of £1.5 billion loaned by the Sultan of Brunei, which he denied. Rowland, who had built the Lonrho (London and Rhodesia Mining and Land Company) empire, worth over £250 million, and had purchased the British Sunday newspaper *The Observer*, spent an estimated £20 million competing with and later attacking Al-Fayed. At one point in 1987, the Sunday newspaper actually printed an extraordinary one-off mid-week edition specifically aimed at criticizing Al-Fayed.

The two men struck a rapprochement in the early 1990s, but the tension between them took a bizarre twist when a safety deposit box at Harrods owned by Rowland and his wife was broken into and an estimated £200,000 worth of his wife's jewelry was stolen. Al-Fayed was acquitted, but he admitted the responsibility of former Harrods security personnel in the robbery.

See also: *The Lonrho Affair p.112*

1987
THE CARLYLE GROUP
Influential private investment bank with tentacles that reach around the globe

The Carlyle Group came into public view in the wake of the Iraq war of the early 21st century, due largely to the heavily publicized involvement of figures such as George Bush Sr and John Major. It is also said to have connections to the Bin Laden family and other powerful dynasties in the Middle East.

It is alleged that the Carlyle Group was in conference with members of the bin Laden family on the morning of 11th September 2001. Famously, days later, a 747 Jumbo jet packed with members of the bin Laden family, who had been flown across the US despite the air lock-down, was flown out of the country, to the incredulity of pilots and air traffic control staff.

The Carlyle Group has, since its formation in 1987, built up an estimated $25 billion business in the interface between weapons, security, and technology. It has close ties with the Saudi Arabian empire, which pays it $20 million a year to train its troops. Its weapons deals with South Korea have led responsible trade organizations in the US to accuse it of conflicting business interests and undue influence on foreign policy.

The rogues' gallery of mountebanks involved lends weight to the suggestion that the Carlyle Group might indeed be a fully fledged and active conspiracy. Some misguided

investments in military technology and failed communications projects might suggest, however, that it is less successful than the conspiracy theorists claim.

1988/9
PROJECT HAMMER
Global alliance created "black" money for illicit purposes

The numbers involved in the so-called Project Hammer conspiracy are so large they make one's eyes water: one perhaps over-zealous conspiracy theorist claims the sums run to hundreds of trillions of dollars. Essentially, Project Hammer is a "ghost" global economy run by government and big business for their own ends.

The conspiracy
The Project Hammer theory holds that the United States government and banking system, with the collusion of other governments and banks around the world, simply "invents" money for nefarious ends such as drug smuggling and weapons deals to fund international covert actions. This fictional financing is said to help the US and big business

Ferdinand Marcos, here with Reagan in 1982, is said to have benefitted from Project Hammer black money.

to effectively rule the world in secret, and shore up governments and individuals it wants to influence. One theory holds that some $13 trillion of this "black money" ended up in a Crédit Suisse bank account opened under the name of Howard Hughes. The late president of the Phillipines, Ferdinand Marcos, is also said to have been a beneficiary of this black money, largely to keep him sweet while the US pursued its own agenda in the Far East.

These phantom bank accounts, held, it is claimed, by the Citibank corporation, among others, are secured against gold and other valuables illegally acquired from Europe in the closing months of World War II. As these valuables cannot be legally liquidated on the open market, they sit in a sort of escrow, securing the ghost trillions that are used in a form of barter as a means to manipulate global politics, the international drug trade, and shipments of weapons.

The Project Hammer conspiracy, which has many proponents, is frequently linked to the Nugan Hand Bank, the alleged CIA front that funded guns/drugs for arms deals during the Vietnam War. Also implicated in the theory are former East German leader Erich Honecker, South African financiers, the Chinese military, and French and British intelligence. East Germany's secret service Stasi and the South African government are also claimed to have been involved.

The evidence

As conspiracy theorists might expect, the actual evidence for the existence of Project Hammer is fairly sparse. Apart from unfounded allegations about the Nugan Hand Bank, Honecker, China, and Britain and France, the evidence for the conspiracy resides solely in one document, itself of dubious provenance. This is a statement by the late Brigadier General Erle Cocke, who claimed to have been a major fixer for every US president since Truman.

Cocke, cited in most Project Hammer theories, was a black arts specialist who had worked in banking before joining the CIA and, it is said, the Agency's front banking operation Nugan Hand. The Nugan Hand Bank was alleged to be responsible for organizing drug and weapons deals during the Vietnam War and complicit in covert actions in neighbouring Cambodia and Laos. His family opened a bank in Georgia, Carolina, in the 1920s, and Cocke trained in the family business. He gave a statement in 2000 revealing his involvement in Project Hammer just ten days before dying of cancer. In it, he is said to outline a vast system of bankers and politicians inventing money out of thin air to fund clandestine activities serving military, industrial, and narcotic interests. Given the US's proven complicity in the Iran

Contra affair and the coke-for-carbines scams run through Manuel Noriega's Panama, it is not surprising that theorists invest credibility in Project Hammer.

The verdict

Erle Cocke was just ten days away from dying of pancreatic cancer when he is said to have given his statement about Project Hammer and the complicity of those individuals mentioned above. If claims about Cocke's statements are accurate, he was a Deep South braggart and not averse to boasting about what a multitrillion banking conspirator would normally prefer to keep secret. Conversely, someone dying of cancer would likely be on medication, painkillers, or simply in an altered mental state from the onset of terminal illness. These facts have to give question to the veracity of his claims.

Questions also arise as to the final destinations of all these hundreds of trillions of black dollars. Iran Contra did indeed prove that murky deals went on under the aegis of the CIA and its accomplices, but so far no one has explained exactly what these trillions were used for. Any healthy sceptic would allow themselves to believe that governments and the banking system are capable of anything, but, to date, nobody has established proof of the existence of Project Hammer. Conspiracy theory publications and websites feed off each other's unproven theories, which ultimately weakens rather than strengthens their arguments.

See also: *The Nugan Hand Bank Scandal p.117; Iran Contra p.228*

1990
THE GUINNESS AFFAIR
The scandal surrounding insider dealing within the Guinness business empire

The Guinness affair is utterly unique in the history of conspiracies for involving the first-ever recorded instance of someone miraculously "recovering" from Alzheimer's disease. Ernest Saunders, one of four Guinness directors jailed in 1990 for insider dealing over the 1986 purchase of British-based drinks conglomerate United Distillers plc, managed to convince doctors and a court that he was suffering from Alzheimer's disease, normally an irreversible degenerative condition that eventually leads to the victim's death. A judge reduced his sentence of five years to just ten months on the "probability" that he was suffering from a pre-senility condition.

Shortly after his release, Saunders was seen enjoying a holiday on his yacht in the Caribbean. Fit and healthy, he had made an extraordinary recovery from the diagnosed Alzheimer's; he claimed the symptoms were the effect of a cocktail of painkillers and sleeping tablets he had been given in prison. He actually telephoned for an on-air apology for the suggestion that he had faked his Alzheimer's diagnosis from the British satirical television programme *Have I Got News For You*, only for the show's host Angus Deayton to promptly call him a "swindler and con-artist" after making the apology. No further apology was forthcoming, nor any further legal action from Saunders.

After a short recuperation, Saunders returned to the world of business, where he became a much-sought-after consultant, notably to the biggest in-car phone company in Europe, Carphone International. Meanwhile, his co-directors languished in jail.

1991
KUWAIT AND BLOOD FOR OIL
The West's complicity in Middle Eastern conflicts and its greed for oil

The Kuwait "Blood for Oil" controversy is a symptom of the increasingly muddy story of western connivance in geopolitical events in the Middle East. Not least, it has been alleged that the US played fast and loose with the lives of hundreds of thousands of people to secure a cheap and plentiful supply of petrol.

The conspiracy theory
Kuwait is a region of what was previously referred to as the Persian peninsula; it was declared an independent state by the region's British protectorate in 1899. In geographical terms, it blocked neighbouring Iraq's access to the Persian Gulf with a British-friendly "emirate," which would have disastrous political consequences when the region began to exploit its oil fields. Not least, it established a fierce enmity between Iraq and Kuwait, which would explode into open warfare a century later.

Conspiracy theorists claim that the US was playing both sides against each other in order to maintain its supply of petroleum. They further claim that, not for the first time, the US's disastrous misreading of local political conditions allowed a tension to develop between impoverished Iraq and oil-rich Kuwait that would result in the 1990 invasion of Kuwait by Saddam Hussein. Worst, however, is that US manipulation of the situation directly inspired Hussein,

responsible for horrendous massacres of Iraq's northern Kurdish communities, to invade Kuwait. A popular uprising by the Iraqi people against the tyrannical Hussein was left to fizzle out with no support from the US or the West, with appalling consequences for the people who had launched the uprising.

The evidence
What appears to have tipped the balance in the Kuwait-Iraq dispute is an unexpected glut in Kuwaiti oil production, which drove the price of oil down throughout the world markets. This further impoverished the Iraqi economy, which, as has been established, had been beggared by the Hussein family and its cronies. It has been claimed that ten days before Hussein invaded Kuwait, in 1990, the American state department was still assuring him that it had no military interest in defending Kuwait, virtually inviting him to invade the emirate. At the same time, American diplomats were warning the Saudis that Iraq was planning to invade Saudi Arabia and was massing hundreds of thousands of troops on its borders.

Certain journalists, however, were suspicious of this claim; the US government refused to release or even show satellite images said to show Iraqi forces massing on the border. Journalists on the *St Petersburg Times* acquired commercial satellite images of the region with no evidence of troop movements whatsoever, and even the national ABC News network began to question the government's claims. Nevertheless, the Saudi government allowed an estimated half a million US troops on to its soil, establishing a first, and vital, American bridgehead in the Middle East. In 1991, the bombings of Baghdad began. An estimated 200,000 civilians are believed to have died in the invasion.

The verdict
Oil is one of the unholy trinity of commodities – along with weapons and drugs – that recur in many of the conspiracy theories involving the US and third world countries with either access to or interest in those commodities. There is no doubt that Saddam Hussein and his murderous sons were thugs and monsters, and that his Ba'athist party colluded in effectively looting the economy of Iraq. There is also filmed documentary evidence of his appalling gas attacks on the Kurdish population in Iraq's northern marshlands. On the other side of the coin, however, is the fact that the people's uprising in 1991 was fatally betrayed by western politicians and military, who left the Iraqi people to fend for themselves when Hussein retaliated horribly. Worse, he

Saddam Hussein ordered retreating Iraqi forces to set Kuwati oil fields ablaze, even though by that time there was no chance of victory.

1991
BCCI FRAUD

The 1991 collapse of the international banking empire BCCI

The case of the Bank of Credit and Commerce International (BCCI) was described by New York District Attorney Robert Morgenthau in 1991 as "one of the biggest criminal enterprises in world history." Morgenthau sat in judgement on an investigation conducted between 1988 and 1991 and led by, among others, John Kerry into the criminality at the heart of this international bank.

The conspiracy theory

The BCCI story also involves George W. Bush, who was involved in a deal with the bank in 1987, and Henry Kissinger's consultancy, Kissinger Associates, among others. The bank was founded in 1972 by Pakistani banker Aghar Hasan Abedi with an initial outlay of £2.5 million, profits from earlier banking operations in Pakistan, but was estimated to be worth £4 billion by 1980. It is alleged that these funds came from deals on the international drugs market and that billions vanished from the bank's coffers, probably into the directors' pockets, but also into the shadowy drugs-for-arms network. Following investigations, BCCI and its offices in seven countries were closed down, its directors indicted, and criminal proceedings begun against those involved in its operations. George W. Bush is said to have obtained a $25 million loan from a subsidiary of BCCI. Osama bin Laden held an account with the company.

The evidence

This information is remarkably complex in nature, but would appear to pivot on the influence of democratic senator and presidential hopeful John Kerry. In 1987, the US congress launched its famous Iran Contra drugs-for-weapons enquiry. While John Kerry was not involved in this particular enquiry, he was asked to head another into the related drugs-for-weapons deal. His investigators soon discovered, in 1988, that BCCI was acting as a money-laundering agent for Panama's Manuel Noriega, who was trafficking drugs, allegedly with illicit US cooperation – using US airforce aircraft, for example – for the Medellín cartel in Colombia. It has been said that the CIA informed Ronald Reagan's administration of links between BCCI and the Medellín cartel, but that it declined to act on this.

was left to terrify, torture, and murder his own people for the next decade.

This feeds into the conspiracy theorists' claims that another agenda was at work in the Middle East during this period. There is a certain cynicism about the US's reluctance to back the people's uprising against Hussein in 1991 when it later committed trillions of dollars to the second invasion of Iraq after 9/11.

There is no evidence of a link between Saddam Hussein and Osama bin Laden, although there is plenty of evidence of a link between the Bush family and the House of Saud. Most of the 9/11 bombers were Saudi nationals, a fact elided by the Bush administration. The movement of US military on to Saudi soil would have benefitted both parties prior to an invasion of Iraq. Given its thirst for oil, the US would benefit immensely from finessing geopolitics in the Middle East. That it was caught lying about the Iraqi "threat" to Saudi Arabia points to a certain dishonesty in this escapade.

See also: *Oil in Saudi Arabia and the House of Saud p.16; The Bush Family and al-Qaeda p.16*

In 1989, John Kerry's investigations were stalled, some might say deliberately, by the Justice Department. This is when Kerry approached Morgenthau with evidence that BCCI was handling the accounts of the Medellín cartel, among others, and that funds were being diverted to revolutionary groups by banker Aghar Hasan Abedi with the aim of countering the "evil" non-Muslim West. Subsequent investigations led to the American and British governments ordering the closure of BCCI, and, after the discovery of massive transfers of funds from the bank, the collapse of the business itself. Staff went unpaid and investors made fruitless attempts to retrieve funds from the closed bank's branches in London and elsewhere.

The verdict

Aghar Hasan Abedi's political opinions may be open to debate, but the actions of his bank are not. BCCI, formed on the back of earlier, smaller, Asian banking operations, was found to have laundered money for the Medellín cocaine cartel and others besides. A French intelligence investigation uncovered the fact that Osama bin Laden had a BCCI bank account, and there are strong suggestions that both the Reagan and George Bush Sr White House administrations turned a blind eye to its shadier deals.

It also seems probable that other offices of the US administration preferred to ignore what was going on until John Kerry began his investigation and Morgenthau came on board. It is unquestionable that billions went missing from BCCI, a fact proven by television footage of disgruntled customers queueing in vain to retrieve their money from the collapsed bank's offices. (There is a hint, however, that BCCI clients may have been in on the deal with advantageous remunerations on investments.) It is difficult to trace a link from the BCCI embezzlement to Bin Laden, but his account with the bank lends more than circumstantial evidence to the conspiracy theory.

See also: *The Bush Family and al-Qaeda p.16; Overthrow of Panama's General Manuel Noriega p.230*

1993
ASIL NADIR AND POLLY PECK

Fugitive businessman wanted for the £2 billion collapse of Polly Peck business empire

The Cypriot, Asil Nadir, is still listed as "wanted" by the British Metropolitan Police and the Regulatory Intelligence Agency. He is alleged to have milked 23,000 investors in Polly Peck, the British-based textile, electronics, and domestic goods group, of £2 billion before making a daring escape to northern, Turkish-dominated, Cyprus in 1993. Nadir is himself a Turkish Cypriot, and northern Cyprus does not have an extradition treaty with Britain, so he is in effect a free man so long as he stays in Cyprus.

Nadir's family and friends claim that he was not able to prepare a defence of his actions when accused of embezzlement. His sister, Bilge, wrote a book, *The Turquoise Conspiracy*, alleging that Nadir was the victim of a conspiracy by senior officers of the serious fraud squad and the British judiciary.

This is hard to square with certain facts in the public domain, some of them repeated by *The Times* of London. Nadir jumped bail of £3.5 million in May 1993, and was flown out of the country by a friend in a light aircraft. It's said that he celebrated his escape with champagne and caviar. The pilot was later jailed.

Using funds that had been salted away in Cayman Island banks, Nadir proceeded to rebuild the empire that had collapsed in the UK. He was voted man of the year by the Turkish Cypriot business community in 1997, and is said to have offered $3 billion to an environmental project in Turkey.

1994
BROOKHAVEN NATIONAL LAB

US Department of Energy laboratory caused plane crashes in the vicinity of Brookhaven

Established in 1947 on Long Island, NY, Brookhaven is a multi-programme science centre run by the US Department of Energy. Locals suspected it was being used for top-secret, illegal activities after a variety of unexplained events near the site. TWA 800 crashed on July 17th, 1996, around 24kms (15miles) away while John F. Kennedy Jr's plane crashed on July 16th, 1999 around 160kms (100 miles) away. An inquest into the Kennedy crash stated that it was due to pilot error, but radioactive leaks were found in the nearby Peconic River. A high-energy ion collider and a particle accelerator had been built on the premises and it was known that the lab had been working on the Star Wars project.

On November 22nd, 1992, a number of locals saw three separate green lights above their heads. Fire stations were alerted and all roads towards Brookhaven were blocked off. The locals were convinced that these must have been UFOs shot down by the Particle accelerator. There is no independent evidence to corroborate this rumour.

On July 17th, 1996, TWA Flight 800 was flying over the same area when it, too, crashed inexplicably. Locals claimed that military manoeuvres had been conducted in the area and that a heat-seeking nuclear missile had been fired. This was aimed at a target which malfunctioned and which caused the missile accidentally to lock onto Flight 800. Salvage teams must have been aware of this as they wore radiation suits and several French intelligence agents were, coincidentally, aboard Flight 800.

Information given to the investigators in early 1999 shows that TWA Flight 800 could have been shot down by one or more shoulder-fired missiles though this has never been pursued by federal investigators.

1995
BARINGS BANK COLLAPSE
Barings Bank was brought down by its entire board of directors

Barings Bank was the oldest merchant bank in the UK, founded in 1762. On February 26th, 1995, it collapsed due to the exploits of Nick Leeson who lost the company $1.4 billion gambling on the futures market on the Singapore Exchange. It seemed incredible that he could, single-handedly, have masterminded such a fraud. But the bank claimed that, though Leeson was working for them, his mismanagement of funds was entirely his own doing.

In 1993, Nick Leeson became the general manager of Baring Bank's Futures division in Singapore. He made record profits and was appointed manager of both the trading and the "back office" divisions in Singapore. He was in total control of the Singapore operation and made large profits by trading on derivatives in high-risk ventures (he effectively gambled on the future value of shares). When he began to make losses, Leeson opened a secret account, "88888," in which to hide these losses. The haemorrhaging of funds inevitably increased until he lost over $1 billion. Leeson then disappeared. At the Bank of England's enquiry, Leeson was single-handedly blamed and no governors were deemed responsible. Baring Bank officials permitted investigators only limited access to documents in Singapore at this time. James Bax, the Singapore-based general manager for Baring's entire South East Asian operations, had warned the bank about Leeson but the enquiry was "unable" to interview him. It established that Barings instantly complied with Leeson's requests for loans. The BIB chief, Peter Norris, stated that any allegation that he might have known about events was "baseless and inconceivable."

The conspiracy appears to lie, not in a corporate plan to make illicit money, but in the governors' complicity through ignorance and greed. Since they all stood to make millions, standard banking procedures were not put in place and adhered to. No one questioned Leeson, even though he had never held a trading licence, and no individual at Barings was ever held accountable.

1995
THE OMEGA AGENCY
A small group of elite individuals is running the world

The whole world is run by ten to twelve select members of a secret organization called the Omega Agency. George Bush Sr, Alexander Haig, and Gerald Ford have all been prominent members. Colin Powell, apparently, still is. Their plan is to form a "New World Order" in which people of all races, both human beings and extraterrestrials, will live side by side in peace. The Omega Agency members know that there are aliens living on earth but will conceal this information until the human race is emotionally ready to receive it.

Members of the Omega Agency have been aware for over 50 years that there are aliens living under the city of Albuquerque, New Mexico, conducting scientific experiments. Their main reason for being on Earth is to help the Omega Agency to curtail the endless cycle of violent behaviour on our planet. The aliens realized that it was only a matter of time before man travelled into space and began to destroy civilizations on other planets. There are both grey and green aliens but the grey ones are mainly vegetarians, though they do seem to have a taste for fish and chicken. Believers in the theory maintain that they particularly enjoy mango.

Evidence for the existence of the Omega Agency consists primarily in the fact that President Bush used the words "New World Order" in a speech on 6 March 1991, just after the end of the first Gulf War – and that dozens of internet sites claim that evidence exists to prove it. There is, however, not a shred of real evidence, nor a single credible witness to prove that the Omega Agency actually exists.

1995
TEMPLE MOUNT PLOT
Elite group aims to take control of Jerusalem

The Temple Mount in Jerusalem is a holy place for Jews, Muslims, and Christians. It was the site of the first and second Jewish temples, but is also the site of the Islamic "Dome of the Rock." It is currently in Israeli-controlled East Jerusalem and is a highly contentious location.

The conspiracy theory

The movement to reclaim this plot of land for the Jews and to use the site to build a Third Temple is heavily sponsored, if not organized, by British Freemasons and US Christian fundamentalists. They have been conspiring to destroy the Al-Aqsa mosque and to reclaim the land for Christian/Jewish use since the late nineteenth century.

The evidence

Prince Edward Albert, the future King Edward VII, visited Jerusalem in 1862 and became very interested in the archeology of the Old Testament lands. He launched an organization called the Palestine Exploration Fund. He was also the nominal head of the Quatuor Coronati Lodge of the UK Freemasons who were part of the Imperialist/Royalist movement and were very keen to expand British Christian influence in the Middle East. Under their funding, a number of early archeological digs were carried out in the area.

On June 5th, 1967, the Israeli Six Day War began and East Jerusalem, and the Dome of the Rock site, came under Jewish control for the first time in almost 2,000 years. Just weeks later, a massive gathering of Freemasons took place in England to commemorate the 250th anniversary of the founding of the United Grand Lodge of England. It was claimed that a large number of archeological organizations then moved into the site for the first time and that some of these had sprung directly from discussions at the 250th anniversary meeting. One of the main expeditions was led by Dr Asher Kaufman who was an active member of the Quatuor Coronati Lodge. It is also claimed that one of the leading architects at the site was partially funded by groups connected to the Lodge.

On September 28th, 1995, Ariel Sharon appeared at the Temple Mount site hours before a new Middle East peace treaty might have been signed in New York. This was a highly provocative gesture. On October 16th, both orthodox Jewish members of the Temple Mount and members of the "Land of Israel Faithful Movement" (which was directly connected to the Freemasons) attempted to enter the Dome of the Rock and to anoint the cornerstone of a Third Temple. This simultaneous action, which was repelled by members of the Israeli army, apparently proved claims that both Ariel Sharon's walkabout and the invasion was part of a larger US- and UK-sponsored conspiracy to take over the site.

Around December 1995, a dedicated "Jerusalem" branch of the Freemasons was established immediately next to the Temple Mount. Its leader was the Grand Master of Italian Freemasonry, Giuliano di Bernardo, who had extensive links with the UK branch. At the launch ceremony, Di Bernardo was said to have stated that: "the rebuilding of the Temple is at the center of our studies." In June 1996, Di Bernardo published a book entitled, *The Reconstruction of the Temple*.

The verdict

There is no demonstrated link between the Jewish members of the Temple Mount movement and the Land of Israel Faithful Movement. No documents have ever been provided to show that there is a link between the Temple Mount incident and the British Freemasons. The published accounts of the Quatuor Coronati Lodge show that the only money they have ever given to archeological expeditions in Israel was a prize of £100 for an essay. The British Freemasons have never stated any public intention to rebuild the Third Temple, or, indeed, any particular interest in the matter. There is no discussion of the rebuilding of the Third Temple in Giuliano Di Bernardo's book and it was not, in fact, secretly published by the British Freemasons as conspiracy theorists claim. There is not a shred of credible evidence for this theory.

See also: *Freemasons p.284*

1997
THE BRE-X SCANDAL

Canadian mineral company invented massive gold discoveries in Indonesia

Bre-X Minerals Limited was a small Alberta-based company owned by a Canadian called David Walsh. It bought property near Busang, Indonesia and, in March 1995, the company's Filipino geologist reported that he had located deposits equivalent to eight percent of the world's gold there. Bre-X's shares, previously valued at one penny, soared to $286.50. Between April and September 1996, David Walsh, his wife, and the company's vice-president sold $50 million worth of shares. No-one questioned this train of events.

By February 1997, a number of big corporations had invested in the company. The Toronto Stock Exchange, Indonesia's President Suharto, his daughter, and his son all got involved. In fact, there was no gold. In March 1997, the Filipino geologist apparently jumped to his death from a helicopter. Bre-X's shares collapsed and the company filed for bankruptcy. Laboratory tests soon showed that the Busang gold had been shaved from jewelry. It also emerged that no locals had ever seen any gold and that the geologist had personally taken the samples to the lab.

The Canadian public sector had invested over $200 million (Canadian dollars) in Bre-X. These companies insisted that they were victims, but it had taken them over two years to carry out any independent tests. All standard industry procedures had been ignored. In 1999, the Canadian federal police terminated its investigation with only one charge for insider trading. There is no evidence to suggest that this was any more than a simple fraud perpetrated by three main players, but the victims in the drama did nothing to protect themselves.

1997
CHEMTRAILS

American climate control and biological warfare experiments caused death and illness

The US Department of Defense has been releasing biological weapons into the skies above the US for several decades. These chemicals are released from aeroplanes and cause coloured trails to appear in the sky. They are commonly referred to as Chemtrails.

In 1994, a scientist named Dr Cole testified before the US Senate that the Department of Defense had been conducting experiments into biological warfare, weather modification, and earthquake induction. He stated that, during the summer of 1994, the inhabitants of Oakville, California, had noticed US military aircraft dropping a gel-like substance onto their town. Some inhabitants became ill and said that their pets had unexpectedly died. Dr Cole claimed to have analyzed this gel and found it to contain human blood cells and pseudonomas fluorescens – an experimental biowarfare bacterium. In May 1997, Oakville received further publicity when its citizens began to report that unidentified officials had now arrived in town claiming to be intelligence personnel from Fort Hood, Texas. The Oakville residents stated that they were repeatedly visited, questioned about their health and told not to contact any broadcasters – which they immediately did.

In a separate incident which occurred that same year, William Wallace from Kettle Falls, Washington, claimed that he had been sprayed with a fine mist while ploughing his fields. Wallace became so ill that he lost his job and his cat died. He, too, attempted to sell his story to CBS. The US may have conducted experiments on biological weapons, but there is no evidence to corroborate these Chemtrail stories of 1997.

See also: *Biochemical Weapons p.197*

1997
JONATHAN AITKEN AND ARMS
SALES TO SAUDI ARABIA

British cabinet minister was guilty of perjury

In 1997, Jonathan Aitken, a Conservative MP, went on trial for not declaring his bill at the Ritz Hotel, Paris, in 1988, to a public accounts committee. He could not do so because it would then have been obvious that he had visited the hotel to meet the Crown Prince of Saudi Arabia and to discuss the commissions that British and Saudi representatives would receive on arms sales to the country.

In 1986 and 1988, the British government under Margaret Thatcher had signed Al Yamamah I and Al Yamamah II, the two biggest arms deals ever with a foreign country. Saudi purchasers and British enablers paid themselves "commissions" of an estimated £15 million for the purchase of each of the 48 Tornado jets that formed part of this deal. Jonathan Aitken was the Minister for Defence Procurement at that time and had personally supervised the supply of each of these Tornados.

The British government stated that the Saudi market was extremely important for jobs and, therefore, public accountability was less rigorously enforced than in other cases. Jonathan Aitken, naturally, had to remain silent about all aspects of the negotiations or he might have faced losing his massive personal commission. In fact, it appeared that the UK made very little real profit from the Al Yamamah deals. It would seem logical that the real profit went into the deal-makers as commissions were an essential part of the system.

Jonathan Aitken was sentenced to 18 months in jail for perjury in June 1999. No substantive government enquiry was ever mounted.

1998
KENNETH STARR AND THE
IMPEACHMENT OF CLINTON

Starr was part of a vast right-wing conspiracy against President Clinton

After the election of Democrat President Bill Clinton in 1992, the Republicans were determined to get back into power in the US. In January 1998, a scandal broke in which the President was accused of having an extra-marital affair with a 22-year-old White House intern called Monica Lewinsky. The entire matter was investigated by a team of prosecutors led by a lawyer called Kenneth Starr, who had originally been appointed in August 1994 by the US Court of Appeals as the Independent Counsel to investigate whether either President Bill, or Mrs Hillary Clinton had violated any law with regard to their business or other relationships. This action eventually led to the President's humiliation and impeachment.

The conspiracy theory

President Clinton's affair with Monica Lewinsky was brought to light as part of a greater right-wing conspiracy in the US to bring down the President and, thereby, to discredit all Democrats. The investigations were primarily funded by a billionaire conservative called Richard Mellon Scaife. He directly paid for most of the activities of the state prosecutor. The debate was fuelled by Hillary Clinton who specifically talked about "this vast right-wing conspiracy against my husband."

The evidence

Richard Mellon Scaife is a billionaire from Pittsburgh who inherited the Mellon oil fortune. He now owns *The Pittsburgh Tribune-Review* and runs the Sarah Scaife Foundation – primarily a Republican lobbying group. By 1994, this was one of the US's most active political lobbying foundations and it gave heavily to the Republican election campaign that year. After Clinton won that election, Scaife was disgusted, particularly as he had personally funded Newt Gingrich's campaign for a Republican takeover of Congress that same year.

Scaife spent the next few years funding projects which might help to discredit the Clintons. In 1997, he donated $550,000 to the organization Judicial Watch, whose director eventually filed 18 lawsuits against the Clinton administration. He also paid for a dedicated reporter from *The Pittsburgh Tribune-Review* to undertake an investigation into the deaths of Vince Foster (a lawyer who worked for Bill Clinton and was found dead in a Virginia Park in July 1993) and Ron Brown (Clinton's Commerce Secretary and fundraiser who died in a plane crash in Bosnia on April 8th, 1996) and to try to uncover any evidence that might implicate the Clintons in their deaths. It is claimed that he also donated $2.4 million to enable the right-wing American *Spectator* magazine to set up the "Arkansas Project," the aim of which was to expose shady incidents in Clinton's past. It later emerged that the only substantive witness prepared to give evidence of Clinton's misdemeanours following the investigations of the Arkansas Project was a man called Patrick Dozhier who had received money from Scaife. After Dozhier's girlfriend, Caryn Mann, and her 17-year-old

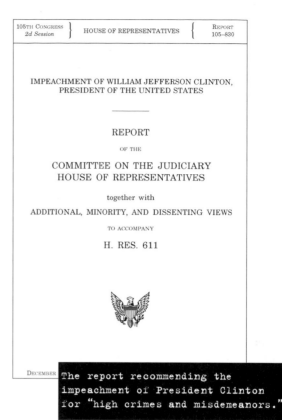

The report recommending the impeachment of President Clinton for "high crimes and misdemeanors."

son attempted to give evidence to this effect, they reported that Dozhier had threatened them both with violence.

There also appear to be many specific links between Scaife and Kenneth Starr. Between 1988 and 1996, Scaife donated $3 million to the Washington Legal Foundation on whose board Starr sits. Scaife also donated $920,000 to the "Federalist Society," of which Starr is a member. Starr himself prepared a legal brief (for a sexual harassment suit against Clinton) by Paula Jones (who sued Clinton for sexual harassment in May 1994, and later acquired tapes in which Monica Lewinsky apparently discussed the Clinton affair with her friend, Linda Tripp). This suit was supported by the Independent Women's Forum which receives much of its funding from Scaife.

It is also an undisputed fact that, in 1997, Kenneth Starr was offered a job as the Dean of the School of Law and Public Policy at Pepperdine University in Malibu, California. Initially he chose to accept the post, despite the fact that Scaife had donated nearly $13 million to the institution. It appeared that Starr only decided to turn the new post down once the fact of Scaife's donation became common knowledge.

Starr himself says that he has never met Scaife and that, when he had the opportunity to trap Clinton in a lie by surprising him with forensic evidence about the stains on Lewinsky's infamous blue dress, he encouraged Clinton to tell the truth. Starr claims that the idea to include graphic, and highly prejudicial, sexual details in his final report on the Lewinsky affair was not his own but came from his fellow lawyers. All other links are, he says, coincidental.

The verdict

It is in the corporate interest of the US not to have a Democratic president. Several organizations, and especially the Scaife Foundations, have clearly funded the Republican Party. It is unclear whether the subsequent undermining of President Clinton was, therefore, coincidental or deliberate.

See also: *Sexgate p.166*

1998
LOBBYGATE AND DEREK DRAPER

Political access in the UK was controlled by high-profile lobbyist

After Tony Blair became Prime Minister of the UK in 1997, a number of his former associates set up a selection of political lobbying firms. For a large fee, these firms' clients could gain advance access to government documents and, possibly, even influence policy.

In 1998, an undercover journalist working for the British newspaper, *The Observer,* approached a number of lobbyists with close ties to Blair's government. One of these was a man named Derek Draper who informed the journalist that he knew the "17 people who count." In exchange for a large fee, he could enable his clients to have lunch at 10 Downing Street, obtain early drafts of government documents, and even influence the selection of personnel on government boards. As a result of "inside information" he had, apparently, informed one of his banking clients of a rise in interest rates a week ahead of the public announcement.

The undercover journalist next met Lawson Lucas Mendelsohn (LLM), a firm created just months after Labour came into power, which employed at least 19 individuals formerly associated with the Labour Party. One of its partners correctly claimed that the Chancellor would soon announce the creation of a new housing inspectorate. This information could be extremely valuable to building companies who wished to build on greenbelt land. A third

company offered a pre-release copy of a potentially valuable document about government policy on energy.

None of this was illegal and Draper may have wildly exaggerated his influence, but the whole affair eroded public confidence in the democratic process.

2000
ENRON'S COLLAPSE

Friends in high places failed to save the energy giant

In 1985, a natural gas producer called Houston Natural Gas merged with another gas producer to form a new company called Enron. Houston's boss, Kenneth Lay, was named Chief Executive Officer. Enron was burdened with large debts and the price of natural gas was falling. In January 1987, the company was alerted to serious financial misdeeds by two of its oil traders in New York: Louis Borget and Thomas Mastroeni.

The conspiracy theory

Enron's directors knew about the company's debts for years and deliberately conspired to cover them up. Enron was a major sponsor of the Republican Party which attempted to assist the company in its recovery. The company then built a new oil plant in India which could only ever become profitable if it could obtain cheap gas from the Caspian Sea via Afghanistan. President Bush invaded Afghanistan partially in order to gain Enron access to such a pipeline.

The evidence

In January 1987, Apple Bank in New York noticed that two Enron traders on the oil futures exchange called Louis Borget and Thomas Mastroeni had been receiving $100,000 transfers into bank accounts in the UK's Channel Islands and then transferring them to Apple accounts in New York. They had, apparently, been writing cheques to themselves. Enron boss Kenneth Lay was told but did nothing, as this division of the company made $30 million a year – one third of the company's entire annual profit.

When Lay met the two men in Washington, they were, apparently, questioned about mysterious transfers to an "M. Yass" in Lebanon. Borget and Mastroeni replied that he was an important dealer and were not questioned further. M. Yass was, in fact, Mastroeni's personal accountant and spelt "my ass."

The auditors told Lay to fire the two men immediately but he took no action. Lay claimed that he had limited their powers but, between April and October 1987, they gambled with around 1.2 billion Enron dollars. They were not fired until October 1987. Borget later served five months in prison and Mastroeni was given a suspended sentence. The losses were tentatively acknowledged and Enron managed to reduce its debt to $142 million by transferring money between companies.

In 1992, Lay decided to invest $3 billion in a new oil plant called Dabhol in Mumbai, India. This was intended to supply a fifth of India's energy needs but it became apparent that India's citizens could not afford to buy such expensive energy. The project would only work if Enron could find a cheaper source of gas.

In 1996, a leading energy company called Unocal won a contract to exploit the massive oil reserves of Turkmenistan. In 1997, Enron announced that it would be investing over $1 billion in the supply of gas from Dabhol into India's pipelines. If a pipeline from Central Asia could be built, it would suddenly provide the cheap natural gas to India's homes that Enron so desperately needed for its own ends. The main hindrance to the plan now was that the pipeline would have to run through Afghanistan, which was under Taliban control.

In December 1997, Unocal invited representatives of the Taliban to Texas to discuss the pipeline. The plan was finally abandoned in 1998 after two simultaneous bomb attacks on US embassies in East Africa on August 7th, 1998, which were reputedly masterminded by al-Qaeda. By January 2001, however, George W. Bush had been elected President, with Dick Cheney as his deputy. It is known that, early on in the Bush presidency, Kenneth Lay was called in to the White House on three or four separate occasions to discuss the company's difficulties and the feasibility of constructing the new pipeline. The cheapest way to run this pipeline would still be through Afghanistan. In February 2001, Vice-President Cheney met Kenneth Lay to discuss the awarding of the contract for the actual construction of this pipeline to a company called Halliburton. Halliburton had previously been run by Cheney himself.

The matter came to a head in May that year when the Indian state of Maharashtra stopped paying for Dabhol's power, and the plant was closed. The company could now only be saved if the Indian government bought the plant or if cheap gas could suddenly be supplied from another source. In October 2001, the US invaded Afghanistan but the invasion was too late to save Enron. On November 8th that year, the company disclosed that it had overstated earnings dating back to 1997 by $600 million. Enron was declared bankrupt.

The verdict

It seems highly likely that Enron's directors knew much more than they publicly acknowledged about the company's disastrous affairs. High-level discussions clearly took place about the ways in which an oil pipeline through Afghanistan might facilitate Enron's financial situation. The timings suggest that these discussions occurred too late to save the company but it remains true that the invasion of Afghanistan would have been extremely convenient for Enron if the directors had not been guilty of such serious earlier mismanagement.

See also: *Attacks on US Embassies in East Africa p.22*

2001
DONALD RUMSFELD AND THE US EMPIRE
The "Project for a New American Century" is a plan to create an American Empire

The Project for a New American Century (PNAC) is a think-tank founded in 1997 by William Kristol, the editor of a magazine called *The Weekly Standard*. Its critics suggest that it has a secret agenda for global US military dominance in a "New American Century."

Kristol was part of the Neo-Conservative (Neocon) movement in the US, founded during the Cold War by a group of anti-communist intellectuals, which included his father, Irving. In 1997, Kristol rallied a group of these Neo-Conservatives, including Jeb Bush, Donald Rumsfeld, Dick Cheney, and Paul Wolfowitz, to form the PNAC. Their website (www.newamericancentury.org) states that "American leadership is good both for America and for the world." As early as 1998, PNAC members, including Donald Rumsfeld and Paul Wolfowitz, wrote to President Clinton urging him to invade Iraq.

After George W. Bush was elected in January 2001, Dick Cheney was picked as vice-president and he immediately gave jobs in the Defense Department to Rumsfeld and Wolfowitz. In September 2000, the PNAC issued a report entitled "Rebuilding America's Defenses." This suggested that the US had a post-Cold War duty to deploy permanent military bases around the world and that there was "immediate justification" for a US military presence in Iraq.

Just a few weeks after 9/11, under advice from Rumsfeld and other PNAC members, President Bush stated that any hostile nation would be regarded as an enemy. This implicitly accepted PNAC policy and would inevitably lead to an invasion of Iraq despite the lack of any connection with 9/11. The PNAC had finally got their way.

2001
SADDAM HUSSEIN AND WORLD TERRORISM – LAURA MYLROIE
The CIA kept WMD evidence from the US government

The CIA and the FBI deliberately conspired to hide crucial information about Saddam Hussein's weapons of mass destruction from President Bush because they had earlier claimed that there weren't any and they were embarrassed to be proved wrong.

Laurie Mylroie wrote several books on Saddam Hussein and terrorism and is connected to a right-wing think-tank in Washington called the American Enterprise Institute. In 2003, she published a book, called *Bush vs the Beltway: How the CIA and the State Department Tried to Stop the War on Terror*. In it, Mylroie claimed that, after the 1993 World Trade Center bombing, the CIA abandoned the idea of state-sponsored terrorism. She went on to claim that only "the unwavering vision of President Bush" had broken through the conspiracy which the CIA had placed in the way of "liberating Iraq." The CIA, she said, had deliberately hidden evidence about Saddam's links to al-Qaeda and to his development of nuclear weapons. She claimed, as a Washington insider, that the CIA were more concerned with looking good than with national security, and that real information about al-Qaeda's links to Saddam Hussein had been buried or dismissed without adequate investigation. She rapidly became a regular spokesperson for the radical right and Richard Perle, senior advisor on the Middle East to President Bush, suggested that she be put in charge of "quality control" at the CIA.

Subsequent events have proved that there were no weapons of mass destruction in Iraq and, therefore, that the CIA had nothing to hide.

See also: *Al-Qaeda had Men in Iraq During First Gulf War p.20; Iraq WMD Conspiracy p.234*

2002
HUGO CHAVEZ
US backed a coup against the Venezuelan president

In Autumn 1998, former paratrooper Hugo Chávez was unexpectedly elected as Venezuela's president on a programme of deliberate opposition to US-style free market economics.

Venezuela is the world's fifth largest oil-producing country and its political regime is, therefore, a matter of great importance to other oil-producing countries and, in particular, the US. President Bush's administration immediately signified that it considered the Chávez administration to be a major threat to the entire region.

The conspiracy theory
President Chávez's policies and, particularly, his stated intention to nationalize the lucrative oil industry were very unpopular in Washington, DC. The CIA, therefore, sponsored and organized a coup against him on April 11th, 2002.

The evidence
Hugo Chávez first came to political prominence in February 1992 when he led an attempt to overthrow President Carlos Pérez. He subsequently went to jail and became a minor celebrity amongst left-wing radicals. In late 1998 he was, unexpectedly, elected as President of Venezuela and immediately began a programme of radical economic and political change. The oil industry was nominally state owned but effectively run by a few elite Venezuelan families. Under Chávez, over 70 percent of the population voted for a new constitution which criminalized any attempt to privatize the oil industry. Other new laws increased government control over the industry, created stronger trade unions, and enforced human rights.

In 2000, Chávez was reelected and began a scheme in which members of the armed forces helped around one million citizens to build homes, install clean water, and construct sewage systems for the first time. He also became the first head of state to visit Saddam Hussein after the first Gulf War and, much to the irritation of the US, began a friendship with Fidel Castro. In May 2001, Chávez announced the formation of "Bolivarian" circles – local neighbourhood groups which would be armed by the state to help "support government reforms."

On February 10th, 2002, Chávez told listeners to his weekly radio and TV show *Hello Presidente* that he had uncovered evidence that the US was working to overthrow him. A new website, www.venezuelafoia.info, had used the Freedom of Information Act in the US to post hundreds of documents revealing that US government departments were funding a wide range of anti-Chávez groups.

At around the same time, the head of the Venezuelan Business Association (Fedecamaras), Pedro Carmona, began making regular visits to senior government personnel in Washington, DC. At the White House, he met Bush's key

Pedro Carmona is escorted out of
court in Caracas, April 15th, 2002.

policy-maker on South America, a Cuban-American called
Otto Reich. It was later claimed that the military and financial details of a possible coup were discussed in some
detail at these meetings. Records show that meetings were
also attended by other senior officials, many of whom had
worked in Nicaragua under President Reagan to overthrow
the Marxist regime of the Sandinistas there. There was little doubt that they had helped supply illegal weapons to
rebels while under the direct command of the discredited
military commander, Oliver North, in the 1980s and 1990s.

On April 11th, 2002, a military coup led by General Felipe
Rodríguez attempted to overthrow Chávez and his "socialist" policies. Pedro Carmona claimed power and Reich
instantly summoned South American ambassadors to his
office to report that Chávez had resigned and that the US
would support Carmona's government. Within 48 hours,
however, Carmona's government had been overthrown by
a combination of the army and the new Bolivarian circles,
which now involved around two million people.

A US State Department spokesman, Richard Boucher,
rejected any accusations of US involvement in the coup as
"baseless and irresponsible," while the Venezuelan opposition and the US administration now continually refer to
Chávez as Fidel Castro's "man in Caracas."

The verdict

The evidence in the Chávez case certainly suggests that the
Bush government was delighted that Hugo Chávez had been
overthrown. The administration appears to have given
direct funding to groups which assisted in the coup. It is not
possible to say whether they took part in any military action but they certainly appear to have assisted it financially
whenever possible.

See also: *Iran Contra p.228*

2003
THE SYNARCHIST AGENDA

Secret international right-wing cabal aims to
dominate the world's political and financial agendas

In 2003, a weekly magazine called *The Executive International
Review* published a series of articles claiming that the Bush
administration, the Nazis, and Leo Strauss, a leading neo-
Conservative US philosopher, were all linked to a shadowy
network of right-wing activists, the Synarchist movement.

The Movement for Synarchist Empire (MSE) began in
France in the 1930s when (so the articles claimed) it was
a network of businessmen and civil servants who all
supported Adolf Hitler. The central figure in modern US
Synarchy was Leo Strauss—the influential neo-Conservative
philosopher. In Germany, in 1928, he had met a Russian
called Alexandre Kojève who now lived in Paris. Strauss
now sent all his protégés to Paris to study under Kojève
who worked in the French Economics Ministry and gave
occasional seminars to such leading European young
"Straussians" as Francis Fukuyama, the author of the bestselling book, *The End of History*. Strauss's leading protégé
was the US political philosopher Allan Bloom who taught
primarily at the University of Chicago. He, too, visited Paris
frequently and later taught Paul Wolfowitz.

The Executive Intelligence Review is published by Lyndon
LaRouche, a man who has been disowned by the Democratic
Party and has been imprisoned for both tax evasion and
fraud. He has also stood for President of the United States
eight times.

There is evidence that members of elites club together
to form groups. There is no other credible evidence to support the idea of the existence of the Synarchists.

See also: *Lyndon LaRouche p.183*

Espionage has been an integral part of warfare for as long as there has been warfare – and man has been at war almost since the first primate stood up on his hind legs, looked over the long grass, and did not like the other primate that was looking back at him.

Initially the spy and the scout were one and the same. They observed and reported on enemy strength and deployment, and maybe went so far as to infiltrate the camps or villages of the foe to ascertain their supplies and morale. As war developed and became more sophisticated, so the arts of espionage and intelligence gathering developed in parallel with it. By the 4th century BC, the legendary tactician Sun Tzu showed that he was well aware of the crucial importance of military intelligence: "If you know yourself and know others you will win a hundred times in a hundred battles."

When exactly the spy made the advance from being a mere observer to playing a proactive role, performing sabotage and assassination, and even spreading rumours to undermine the enemy will to fight, is less than clear. Again, Sun Tzu seemed to advocate such actions when he stated that the "battle is best won without being fought at all." The kind of institutionalized conspiracies that are now known as "black" operations were well known to the Roman military, and although much was lost in the dark ages after the fall of the Roman Empire, they were rediscovered with great rapidity. By the 13th century, Hassan i-Sabah had turned the Hashasheens into a highly specialized murder-for-hire organization in the Middle East, and around the same time the Ninja were fulfilling the same function in Japan. The Mongol conqueror Tamar the Lame (Tamerlaine) was a master of psychological warfare, while intrigue, murder, and skulduggery were refined to an art by the Borgias and the Medici during the Italian Renaissance.

Espionage gets serious

The first national spy network was established in 16th-century England, by Sir Francis Walsingham during the protracted hostilities with the Spanish Empire of Philip II.

Although Walsingham remained absolutely loyal to Elizabeth I, he more than once pursued his own agenda even when it did not exactly conform to the government policy he was officially supposed to serve, and this is where the great danger of such operations lies. A nation can become too dependant on the gatherers of its intelligence and thereby vulnerable to their manipulation.

In 17th-century France, Cardinal Richelieu took the spy game to a new level and, declaring, "I have never had any [enemies], other than those of the state," established a formidable intelligence system, both foreign and domestic. This network enabled Richelieu to centralize the entire system of government; strip political power from the nobility, and local autonomy from the cities; brutally suppress religious dissent; slow the development of a middle class, and vest all authority in the Monarchy and the Church, although much of King Louis XIII's power also came through Richelieu. Cardinal Richelieu turned France into an early version of a totalitarian police state, in which sedition was a capital crime. His boast: "If you give me six lines written by the most honest man, I will find something in them to hang him", might, as a concept, be described as positively modern, and an early lesson in what can happen when the running of a country is handed over to its spymaster. On the other side of the coin, however, Richelieu also laid the foundations of injustice that would, a century later, trigger the French Revolution and the bloody terror of the guillotine and then set the armies of Napoleon Bonaparte marching across Europe.

In the comparative peace of post-Napoleonic Europe, when war was primarily confined to the colonies of the great empires, and aberrant skirmishes such as the Crimea War, espionage became a major tool of national policy. The European powers, especially the UK, France, Russia, Prussia and Turkey engaged in what became known as the Great Game. Individuals like Sidney Reilly (an early, real-life model for Ian Fleming's James Bond) were able to move from plot to conspiracy like fish through water, manipulating governments for their own often mysterious ends. At this time the US, with its 19th-century wariness of "foreign entanglements" stayed fairly isolated. During the Civil

War, Allan Pinkerton became head of the Secret Service, and founded an efficient spynet for the Union, even foiling an 1861 assassination attempt on President Abraham Lincoln. By not being given control on the ground in Washington, however, he was not able to prevent John Wilkes Booth and his group from killing Lincoln four years later. After the war, instead of remaining in government to maintain a peacetime intelligence service, Pinkerton returned to the Pinkerton National Detective Agency which, although a private company hired primarily by the railroads, in many ways foreshadowed the work of the FBI in the next century. Subsequently, Pinkerton's men acted as though they were part of what came close to being a national law-enforcement agency, pursuing such high-profile outlaws as Jesse and Frank James, the Reno Brothers, the Hole-in-the-Wall Gang, and the Missouri Kid and Butch Cassidy. The Pinkerton Agency also established the first database of criminal activity, which included early use of both mugshots and fingerprints.

The birth of spying institutions

The start of World War II took the US by total surprise as far as its intelligence capabilities were concerned. Although the FBI, under its notorious director-for-life, J. Edgar Hoover, was reasonably efficient at combating enemy spies, fifth columnists, and saboteurs, a coordinated response to threats from abroad was wholly lacking. Debate continues as to whether President Franklin Roosevelt concealed advance knowledge of the Japanese attack on Pearl Harbor, but, with a more efficient intelligence system, the disaster could possibly have been averted anyway. To make up for lost time, the Office of Strategic Services (OSS) was created under the leadership of Colonel William (Wild Bill) Donovan, and based largely on the British Special Operations Executive (SOE). The OSS had responsibility for collecting and analyzing information, but it also organized guerrilla fighting, sabotage and espionage. Donovan's motto was *"give 'em hell,"* and he relished covert operations, dirty tricks, and gadgets. His agents were mainly bright athletic young men from Ivy League colleges who he trained to be upper-class thugs.

The Cold War

The patterns that Donovan established in the OSS – the sense that it was acceptable to cut corners, the "give-'em-hell" mentality, and with the operatives recruited from good schools – were largely adopted by the Central Intelligence Agency when it was founded in the aftermath of World War II. These meant that the agency started out with a sense of superiority and of being above the law as it commenced Cold War operations against the USSR and Communist China. But the CIA also started out with a more sinister attribute than the simple devil-may-care-attitude of the OSS. It inherited, by a very convoluted process, much of the intelligence structure of Nazism, many of its people, and by a kind of psychological osmosis, a few of its attitudes. Following the collapse of Nazi Germany, an operation codenamed Paperclip had been set up to spirit "useful" Nazis into the US before the Russians got them. The primary targets were rocket scientists such as Werner von Braun. But deals were also made with former German intelligence agents from the Abwehr, the Gestapo and the SS in the name of anti-communism, and in return for information they had on the Soviets, and communist-led resistance groups in other Allied countries, especially France.

One group, led by General Reinhard Gehlen, had even opened negotiations before Hitler's suicide and the end of World War II. In return for their cooperation, the former Nazis, many of whom were wanted war criminals actively being hunted by other Allied intelligence units, were given new identities and put on the OSS/CIA payroll. Assistance was also given to their Nazi friends and comrades to escape to safety in Argentina and other safe havens in South America. In addition to these human assets, captured files by the ton fell into the hands of Donovan and his successors, including those of the inhuman medical experiments at Dachau and other concentration camps. These "deals with the Devil" were justified, at least to the Cold War mindset, as a necessary and pragmatic evil. But somehow it seems to have placed a taint on the CIA that certainly lasted for 40 years – well into the Reagan era. And it maybe still lingers today, if the Iraq torture scandals and its accompanying conspiracies are any indication. As the US and the USSR emerged from World War II as the only viable superpowers, and their respective spies and agents in the CIA and KGB faced each other across what Winston Churchill called the Iron Curtain, it began to seem that they were becoming mirror images of each other. The only other contender in the field, the British Secret Service – despite the fictional exploits of James Bond – was effectively sidelined, in no small part by the way in which it had been compromised by double agents Guy Burgess, Donald Maclean, Kim Philby, and Anthony Blunt. It would be some years before Mossad, the formidable Israeli intelligence agency, became a global player.

The KGB and the CIA shared a sense of superiority, and of being above legal and, at times, basic civilized restraints. An ethic of total ruthlessness may have been actively encouraged in the USSR under Josef Stalin, but when President Harry Truman oversaw the formation of the CIA, he specifically had provisions included in the CIA charter that were supposed to prevent it becoming an "American Gestapo."

Within five years of its foundation, though, the CIA, again under the rubric of the ideological fight against communism, was ignoring all limitations and forming links with all manner of dangerous and non-democratic entities, from military juntas to organized crime. The overthrow of an elected socialist government in Guatemala in 1950 gave the agency a taste for destabilizing small nations and imposing handpicked CIA governments in their place. Showing a marked distaste for the kind of democracy that they were in fact pledged to defend, the agency frequently chose to install the most repressive right-wing dictatorships, and then chose not to see the ensuing brutality. Indeed, the agency did more than simply look the other way; it actually taught such refinements as torture and death-squad operations at The School of the Americas in Fort Benning, Georgia.

At times throughout the 1960s, 1970s, and 1980s, it seemed as though the CIA – or at least radical factions within it – might be attempting to destabilize the United States, which was at risk of having its intelligence community become its worst nightmare and actually usurp the function of government. This is certainly the core of one of the most popular theories about the assassination of John F. Kennedy, and became well documented during the Vietnam War, when the agency at times appeared to be running American foreign policy. As ultra secret units like MKUKTRA were finally revealed to the public, with their LSD experiments and mind-control research, and rumours circulated of black operations' think-tanks devising elaborate plans for an Orwellian mind-controlled society, the American public came to the point of believing anything of its intelligence agency. Meanwhile, in the real world of death and politics, the aftermath of the Iran-Contra conspiracy has revealed that the CIA had been embroiled in gun-running, cocaine smuggling, and the deliberate flouting of specific acts of Congress. It seems that, by the late 20th century, the bad guys were identical to the good guys.

This atmosphere of distrust contributed greatly to the curtailment of the CIA during the 1990s, when the Clinton administration brought it to heel. But this very curtailment also made it increasingly reliant on technology rather than on the rough and tumble of operations in the field. In the aftermath of the al-Qaeda attack on the World Trade Center and the Pentagon, the CIA actually took the rap for not spotting the elaborate hijacking conspiracy while it was still in the planning stages – something that would have been unthinkable 30 years earlier when Nixon, Kissinger, and the CIA were rigging elections at home, and overthrowing governments abroad. George Tenet resigned and it seemed that George Bush had brought the CIA to heel. The intention seemed to be to merge all the existing agencies into one mammoth super-agency, although warnings were issued that it would be an unworkable bureaucracy in which the right hand would never find out what the left was doing. At the same time, the once-fearsome KGB, which had already been tainted by the Soviet defeat in Afghanistan, became simply the intelligence service of the Russian Federation, and its power was so greatly reduced that it seemed unable to deal with its own Islamic terrorists. Rumour even claimed that it had been infiltrated, if not largely taken over, by the new Russian Mafia.

The post-Cold War era

Now the Cold War has receded into history, and the real or imagined threats to the West have shifted away from eastern Europe, and South and Central America. The focus is currently on the oil-rich Middle East, and terrorism by Islamic fundamentalists,

CIA Director George Tenet (standing) meets with President George W. Bush and Vice President Dick Cheney in the Oval Office, October 2003.

and a major new player has come to geopolitical prominence in the international spygame. Mossad (*Ha-Mossad le-Modiin ule-Tafkidim Meyuhadim*; Hebrew for the Institute for Intelligence and Special Tasks), the formidable Israeli secret service has become a power to be reckoned with, and the subject of increasing speculation by conspiracy theorists. Mossad has, of course, existed in its present form since 1951. Although known for its successes, such as the capture of Nazi arch-war criminal Albert Eichmann, and the 1976 hostage rescue at Entebbe airport, it previously managed to maintain a close grip on the secrecy of its operations – certainly far better than the CIA or MI6 ever managed. A chilling glimpse into the scope of Mossad's power was revealed, though, by a 2005 story on the mysterious death, in 1991, of billionaire publisher Robert Maxwell, the former owner of the London *Daily Mirror*, aboard his luxury yacht the Lady Ghislaine. It was the *Daily Mirror* itself that revealed how Maxwell had been a top Mossad operative for decades, with access to both 10 Downing Street and the White House. At the time of his death, he was formulating an almost unbelievable scheme to depose Mikhail Gorbachev, the reformist Soviet leader, and facilitate a return to the Cold War. The plan, however, was too crazy even for Mossad, and when Maxwell,

who had massive debts, demanded a quick-fix, hush-money bale-out of £400million for past services rendered, Mossad arranged his apparent suicide, fearing that he would go public with all he knew.

In this new century, the global chessboard has evolved, and the nature of the chessmen is in the process of changing accordingly. Some of the mighty, such as the CIA and KGB, appear to have fallen, not only to internal reorganization, but also to a globalization in which the spynets of multiple countries are needed to monitor the infinite volume of communications and world travel.

New players, for instance, the North Koreans, seem to be in the process of pushing to the centre of the game, and others, for example, India with its nuclear weapons, will have to be factored into the equation, as the old 20th-century systems and alliances undergo profound transformations.

But while much changes, much also stays the same. It should not be forgotten that Russian leader Vladimir Putin is an ex-KGB member, President George W. Bush's father was once a Director of Central Intelligence, and the old-school intelligence community, even in seeming eclipse, never strays far from the heart of power.

1920
NICOLA SACCO AND
BARTOLOMEO VANZETTI
b. 1891 and 1888 (respectively)

d. 1927

American/Italian convicted bank robbers who were executed to set an example

On April 15th, 1920, an armed gang shot dead a paymaster and his guard on Main Street, South Braintree, Massachusetts. Three weeks later, a shoe-worker called Nicola Sacco and a fish peddler called Bartolomeo Vanzetti were charged with the murders.

Sacco and Vanzetti were Italian immigrants who had become friends and political allies through a shared horror at American working conditions. They claimed to have been in Braintree purely to remove literature – anarchist in nature – which implicated some of their political sympathizers. The authorities, however, feared a perceived Red Scare. Vanzetti's alibi was more solid than Sacco's but, thanks largely to their inept defence counsel, both were found guilty of first degree murder and sentenced to death.

Many denounced the Sacco-Vanzetti verdict. Here, 12,000 workers protest in Union Square, NY City, August 1927.

The flaws on both sides of the court argument made this case one of the most controversial in US legal history. Six years of appeal hearings followed, prompting anti-US demonstrations in several European countries.

Most observers have concluded that Sacco and Vanzetti were denied a fair trial because they were anarchists with ties to criminals. However, in the teeth of impassioned intervention by leading artistic figures, from Dorothy Parker to George Bernard Shaw, the two men – by now symbols of the dignity and suffering of the working classes – were executed on August 23rd, 1927.

1930s–1950s
CAMBRIDGE SPIES
Donald MacLean **b.**1915, London; **d.**1983, Moscow

Guy Burgess **b.**1910, Devonport, England; **d.**1963, Moscow

Harold Adrian Russell (Kim) Philby **b.**1912, Ambala, India; **d.**1988, Moscow

Anthony Blunt **b.**1907, Bournemouth, England; **d.**1983, London

Soviet double agents drawn from the British upper classes

The Cambridge Spies were a group of Cambridge-educated British government employees who became Soviet double agents in the World War II. Four are known. The identity of the fifth man is still a mystery.

The conspiracy theory

The Cambridge spies were able to operate with relative ease because, in wartime Britain, few in the establishment believed that Cambridge-educated and, in some cases, Eton-educated men would conspire to betray their country.

At the beginning of World War II, Maclean was at the Foreign Office, Burgess at the BBC, Blunt was with MI5 and Philby with MI6. All had attained their positions through a combination of academic flair and old-fashioned connections. The group, however loosely the term is applied, was said to have been recruited at Trinity College, Cambridge, by Anthony Blunt who was a fellow there while the others were undergraduates.

As the war was nearing its conclusion, and with Churchill viewing Stalin's USSR with increasing concern, Philby, in many ways the arch-spy, was promoted to head MI6's anti-Soviet Section IX section. This department studied Soviet intelligence in the USSR and all over the world. Thus Philby was able to tell his Soviet bosses exactly how the UK was spying on them, as well as how the UK and the US were prosecuting the war against Nazi Germany. Blunt also had access to a welter of decrypted German radio signals from the UK's top secret Ultra system.

In the Cold War, Philby liaised with the newly created CIA in Washington, and Maclean became first secretary at the British embassy in Washington. He advised the UK government on nuclear warfare issues, as well as giving information to the KGB used to help build Soviet atom bombs. While Burgess and Blunt were transcribing top-secret Foreign Office and MI5 documents for their Soviet spymasters, Philby still had a senior position in MI6. Yet despite his political loyalty to the USSR, the KGB never fully trusted him – he was destined to remain a KGB "agent," not "officer." This rankled, but it revealed a suspicion on the part of KGB that its four super-spies might be *treble* agents, spying against them. This suspicion has never quite been erased. Burgess and Maclean, tipped off by Philby, fled to the USSR in 1951 causing up-roar in British political and intelligence circles. Ten years later, there were similar scenes when Philby followed them.

Blunt's position was different. He was unmasked in 1964, whereupon he revealed much useful information to the authorities. They took the view that if they exposed him publicly, his information against enemy agents would be redundant. So he retained his postwar position as a director of the Courtauld Institute and Surveyor of the Queen's Pictures – he was a Poussin expert – until 1979 when he was finally exposed in print. He thus had to live with the fact that he had betrayed agents on both sides.

The evidence

Philby's autobiography *My Silent War* was an unapologetic attempt to put his side of the story. Andrew Boyle's book *Climate of Treason* was the first to name Blunt in print, and set the story rolling again. By then, a number of ex-spies had speculated on the identity of the Fifth Man. Contenders included Guy Liddell, Goronwy Rees, and the former head of MI5 Sir Roger Hollis as well as Victor, Lord Rothschild.

The verdict

Without doubt the Cambridge five were effective spies, but how much damage did they do? The only person "with blood on his hands" is Kim Philby. Having organized for Balkan partisans to enter the USSR, he then tipped off the Soviets, effectively sending dozens to a certain death. And yet the Cambridge Spies have become, if anything, romantic and idealistic figures rather than shabby double agents.

See also: *Bolshevik World Order p.101*

1943
HENRI DERICOURT
b. 1909, France
d. 1962, Laos
World War II suspected double agent

Henri Dericourt was a French commercial pilot before the outbreak of World War II. Two years after the French capitulation to the Nazis he fled to the UK via the Middle East, arriving by boat with another French pilot, Leon Doulet. Dericourt claimed to be working for the UK commercial airline BOAC, but instead was employed by the Special Operations Executive (SOE) and in January 1943 was parachuted back to France.

His brief was to work for Winston Churchill's Prosper Network, arranging for the safe reception and transporting of Allied spies. Although he arranged passage for more than 67 SOE agents to enter and leave occupied France by plane, several arrests by the Gestapo in the summer of 1943 began to arouse suspicions that the Prosper Network had been infiltrated. Suspicion increased when it emerged that Dericourt was living in a flat in Paris next to the Abwehr agent Hugo Bleicher.

Dericourt continued working until February 1944, and his prospects improved when he arranged the successful recovery of a senior British SOE officer, Nicholas Bodington. He was arrested in 1946 but the case, brought in 1948, was inconclusive and Allied agents like Bodington stated that although he may have been a double agent, he had committed little actual harm. Dericourt's reputation never fully recovered, and he died in an air crash in Laos in 1962. As his body was never found, suspicion remained that Dericourt's death was faked to allow him to begin a new life under a different identity.

1947
THE CIA AND THE UFO MOVEMENT
US government concealed its investigations into the UFO phenomenon

On June 24th, 1947, a private pilot called Kenneth Arnold claimed to have seen nine "disk-shaped" objects in the air near Mt Rainier, Washington. They were travelling at a speed which he estimated to be greater than 1,000mph.

Arnold's report sparked a torrent of similar sightings, with commercial pilots and even military pilots and air traffic controllers all over the US adding to the craze. Confirmation that the authorities were taking these reports seriously came in 1948, when air force general, Nathan Twining, then head of the Air Technical Service Command, established Project Saucer (later SIGN) to investigate these rumours. The general's brief was to disseminate such information as existed within the government, but no information was to be made available to the general public, and nothing was made public until Gerald K. Haines, then chief historian of the CIA, revealed all that was known in 1997.

Project SIGN

Inevitably, there was anxiety that these flying objects might be Soviet missiles, and so the Technical Intelligence Division of the Air Material Command assumed control of Project SIGN on January 23rd, 1948.

Investigations soon discarded the Soviet missile theory, preferring to put the sightings down to mass hysteria and hallucination, hoax, or misinterpretation of known objects. But the archives show that the initial report urged the military not to abandon its surveillance work and, crucially, it did not rule out the possibility that extraterrestrial phenomena existed.

Although the military seemed to be losing interest, public curiosity was growing, and the authorities were being deluged with inquiries. The air force continued to collect and evaluate UFO data in the late 1940s under a new project, GRUDGE. This public relations campaign explained the UFO sightings as, variously, zeppelins, aircraft viewed from uncommon angles or through unusual filters, known planets, shooting stars, optical illusions and solar reflections.

GRUDGE officials accepted no talk of alien weaponry, whether Soviet or extra-planetary, and their verdict was that the unexplained flying craft were of no threat. Furthermore, the mere fact that the air force was taking an official line on it was fermenting public speculation, and so, on December 27th, 1949, the air force announced the project's termination.

Project Blue Book

But if their intention had been to dampen public expectations, it did not work in the fevered atmosphere of the Cold War and the Korean War. In 1952, US air force director of intelligence, Major General Charles P. Cabell, undertook a new UFO operation with the title Project Blue Book. It fell to the Air Technical Intelligence Center (ATIC) to persuade the public that it had nothing to fear from UFOs.

Yet despite the calm words, the CIA took pains to suppress any public acknowledgement that it was still taking UFO sightings seriously enough to monitor them, in spite of its outward (though not published) scepticism that such sightings amounted to anything. A series of unexplained radar blips at Washington National Airport and Andrews Air Force Base on July 19th and 20th, 1952 led fighter aircraft to be scrambled. Nothing suspicious was found, but the media had a field day despite the air force's hastily drawn-up explanation of "temperature inversions."

Partly in response to this, the CIA created a new group from the Office of Scientific Intelligence (OSI) and the Office of Current Intelligence to address the situation. Edward Tauss, from the OSI, warned against giving in to alarmism, but A. Ray Gordon of the OSI took over investigations, even, as he said, if "there was only one chance in 10,000 that the phenomenon posed a threat to the security of the country."

The air force officials explained the UFO reports as the misinterpretation of known objects or naturally occurring incidents, which had yet to be understood by science. Both sides, however, agreed that it was most unadvisable that anyone outside their restricted circle should find out about their investigations. It was, perhaps, this atmosphere of concealment more than anything else, which added to the general level of paranoia about UFOs.

1947
REAL "MEN IN BLACK" – MAJIC 12

US government committee was in contact with aliens

Majic 12, MJ-12 or Majestic is the name of a top-secret American government committee that served Presidents Harry H. Truman and Dwight Eisenhower. Its members are said to have included the secretary of defence and the first three directors of the CIA. The aim of the group was to allay public fears about reports of unidentified flying objects in the skies over the US.

The conspiracy theory

On June 24th, 1947, a civilian pilot spotted nine disc-shaped "aircraft" in the skies above the Cascade Mountains in the State of Washington. Several days later, a rancher reported seeing a flying object crash in an isolated region of New Mexico, 75 miles northwest of Roswell Army Air Base (now Walker Field). Reports in the media sparked dozens of copy-cat sightings. There were even reports that four human-like objects that had ejected, and which were found in an advanced state of decomposition a week later in a distant field, were "extraterrestrials". But all traces of

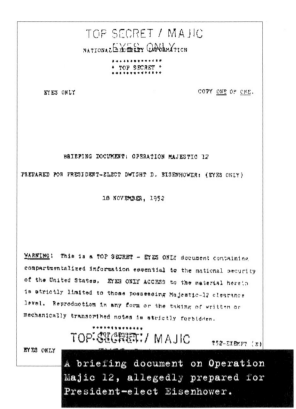

A briefing document on Operation Majic 12, allegedly prepared for President-elect Eisenhower.

the crash were scrupulously removed, and the official line was that the object had in fact been a stray weather research balloon.

In 1987, a former CIA pilot called John Lear claimed to have discovered a history of contacts between the Majic 12 group and extraterrestrials, stretching back to 1947. Lear claimed that the aliens carried out experiments on cattle in order to resolve disorders in their own gene systems. Abducted animals – and sometimes humans – would then be returned to Earth, having been implanted with tracking devices. Laboratories in New Mexico were working on alien-human hybrids.

Eventually, according to various arch-conspiracists, there was a grand falling-out with the aliens, and they retreated to wherever they had come from. The government, which was apprehensive that they might return with more aggressive intentions, developed the Strategic Defense Initiative or Star Wars, and sold it to Congress as if it were merely a rampart against Soviet Russia in the Cold War.

In 1988–9, one of the US's most prominent UFO controversialists, the late Milton William Cooper, claimed to have evidence of the activities of "Delta" teams. With the Cold War at its height, the authorities had evidently believed

that public order could not be guaranteed if evidence of this new threat from the skies were to leak out. Anyone who was in danger of breaching the wall of secrecy was liable to harassment or even assassination, usually by teams of two or three unnamed men, also known as "Men in Black" from their uniform.

The evidence

On December 11th, 1984, a Los Angeles-based film-maker and UFO investigator by the name of James Shandera claimed that he had been sent, anonymously, a roll of 35mm black-and-white film. When developed, this was shown to contain the photographic record of documents drawn up for President Dwight Eisenhower, and a memo from his predecessor, Harry Truman, to his defence secretary James Forrestal under the auspices of a top-secret government committee called, variously, Majic 12, MJ-12 or Majestic. Shandera's pages were made public in 1987. The veracity of these documents is still disputed. For example, the signature of President H. Truman in one memo has been proved to be a forgery.

Although John Lear's claims came with scant documentary proof, Milton William Cooper declared that he had seen a huge mass of UFO-related documents when he was in the navy. His steady stream of articles and claims was halted when he was shot in November 2001, in what the authorities claimed was an unconnected incident, but which has never been satisfactorily explained.

The verdict

Although Cooper went as far as to try and impeach Presidents George Bush Sr and Clinton because of their complicity in the cover-up, the stories about Majic 12 seem to be too redolent of post-World War II neurosis, Cold War hysteria and the growth of sci-fi literature to be taken that seriously. Nevertheless, they continue to proliferate.

See also: *The CIA and the UFO Movement p.139*

1950
CIA RUNNING HEROIN IN VIETNAM

US secret services were involved in covert drug operations in South East Asia

During the late 1940s, as the Cold War became axiomatic to White House thinking, the policy of the CIA was to subvert communism wherever it encountered it. In South East

Asia, this meant allying itself with any organization with which it could agree on this one goal.

The UN's predecessor, the League of Nations, prohibited the legal sale of opium or cocaine throughout the 1920s. By the second half of the 20th century, however, an extremely sophisticated cultivation and distribution system had been established, located along one of the major fault lines of the postwar global power lines. This 8,000km (5,000mile) zone took in Turkey, Laos, and the southern borders of the USSR and Communist China.

From the late 1940s onwards, the CIA was running covert operations along the border with the USSR and China. Its allies in these operations were tribal barons, whose actions went largely unchallenged. The first such operation was conducted against China in 1950, using Burma as its base. Without the connivance of the upland barons, no such military actions could have been contemplated.

The conspiracy theory

The local chiefs had always used opium as a currency. The annexation of CIA money and influence encouraged these drug lords to expand their operations without hindrance. In Chiang Mai, for example, which at the time was the heroin capital of South East Asia, staff of the US government's Drug Enforcement Administration (DEA) were prevented by their bosses from carrying out surveillance operations or seizures against local drug lords.

The evidence

One possible explanation for the apparent intimacy between the DEA and the CIA is that the CIA – in its previous incarnation as the Office of Strategic Services – had supplied a number of key staff to the DEA's forerunner, the Federal Bureau of Narcotics.

In 1955, Vietnam's US-backed, staunchly Catholic president Ngo Dinh Diem closed down its opium dens and expelled the French-backed opium barons. Three years later, faced with growing insurrection, the President's brother, Ngo Dinh Nhu, appealed to Washington for extra cash. Washington took the view that it was donating enough financial assistance for the time being. The result was that Nhu reopened Vietnam's opium trade in order to finance his repressive operations, and the market started up again with a vengeance.

Such was the infiltration of a new generation of drug barons that the main air route, from the poppy fields of Laos to South Vietnam, was run by a Corsican gangster called Bonaventure "Rock" Francisci. On the ground, Nhu's head

of the secret police, the Machiavellian Dr Tuyen, commanded a vast intelligence network that included the CIA-financed special forces. They were used to smuggle gold and opium into South Vietnam.

Throughout 1961 and 1962, overflights by the South Vietnamese army imported propaganda leaflets (and opium) into South Vietnam as part of the Kennedy regime's doctrine of increasing American influence in the region, but a power vacuum followed the removal of President Diem in 1963. One US operation, code-named "Operation Haylift" – intended to fly agents into North Vietnam under the direction of Vice-President Ky – degenerated into a gold- and opium-smuggling operation.

The seeds which earlier administrations had sewn were reaped by later generations. By 1968–9 the opium fields of Burma, Thailand and Laos – an area known as the Golden Triangle – were harvesting close to 1,000 tons of raw opium annually. The low-grade no. 3 heroin was superseded in late 1969 and early 1970 by the fine-grained, 80–99 percent pure no. 4 heroin, produced in laboratories by master chemists from Hong Kong. The benefits for local farmers were obvious. By mid-1971 US army medical officers estimated that about 10–15 percent, or 25,000–37,000 conscripts in Vietnam were heroin users, spending around $12 a day on four vials of heroin. That added up to around $130million a year for the local economy: a huge amount for a cash-strapped country torn apart by war.

The verdict

The DEA knew what was going on in Vietnam but were prevented from taking action; the CIA colluded in the drug trade for its own reasons.

1951
OPERATION ARTICHOKE

The CIA's experimental mind-control programme

The CIA programme, Operation Artichoke, was designed to develop "special and extreme methods of interrogation", which concentrated on ways and means of manipulating the human mind. It was essentially a response to rumours that the USSR and the communist Chinese had developed brainwashing techniques and that these were being put to use during the Korean War – a war that was, at the time, draining American resources.

In addition to techniques such as disorientation, sleep deprivation, psycho-surgery, electroshock, hypnosis and sensory deprivation, the programme focused on the use of drugs, for example, amphetamines and the recently discovered LSD-25. Experiments were conducted not only in CIA labs and safe houses but also in federal prisons and mental hospitals.

Operation Artichoke was also concerned with the problem of disposing of so-called "blown agents", and with finding a way to produce amnesia in operatives who had seen too much and could no longer be relied upon; such experiments spawned the first rumours of "Manchurian Candidate" assassins. Although rumours had circulated about Operation Artichoke for some time, the darker details of the programme's official existence were first revealed from declassified documents that came to light during a 1975 lawsuit brought by the family of army biochemist, Dr Frank Olson. In settling the lawsuit, the government paid $750,000 to Olson's family, after the CIA admitted dosing Olson with LSD just days before his fatal 1953 fall from a New York City building,

See also: *MKULTRA p.143; The Manchurian Candidate p.223*

1951
MKULTRA
The CIA's mass mind-control programme

In April 1953 CIA director Allen Dulles authorized the MKULTRA programme under the control of Dr Sidney Gottlieb. With six percent of the CIA's operating budget, this programme expanded the mind-control experiments of Operation Artichoke from "spy/counterspy" operations to the theoretical mass control of armies on the battlefield and whole civilian populations. An added advantage was that Gottlieb had almost complete files of inhuman Nazi medical research that had fallen into Allied hands after the liberation of Dachau concentration camp.

Experiments with drugs, radiation, and even ultrasonics, and microwaves were conducted mainly on prisoners or soldiers, but also the unwitting patrons of brothels set up and run by the CIA, with two-way mirrors for observation. It was rumoured that Gottlieb may even have triggered the 1967 "Summer of Love" and the whole psychedelic movement by allowing LSD to become a street drug.

Reviewing the experiments five years later, one secrecy-conscious CIA auditor wrote: "Precautions must be taken not only to protect operations from exposure to enemy forces but also to conceal these activities from the American public in general. The knowledge that the agency is engaging in unethical and illicit activities would have serious repercussions in political and diplomatic circles." Most MKULTRA records were accordingly destroyed in 1972 by order of then-director Richard Helms and, as a result, the details of only a fraction of more than 150 secret research projects are known.

See also: *Operation Artichoke p.142*

1952
OPERATION SPLINTER FACTOR
The CIA's destabilization campaign in eastern Europe

Operation Splinter Factor was one of the most ambitious – and disastrously unsuccessful – CIA operations ever carried out against non-Soviet communist regimes in eastern Europe. It began in the dying days of World War II when a British agent known as "Michael Sullivan" attempted to foment civil unrest by spreading rumours of food shortages and collectivization.

At the same time, the future head of the CIA, Alan Foster Dulles, was working under the cover of religious or charitable institutions so as to further his anti-Soviet ends. He recruited a well-placed Polish security chief called Jozef Swiatlo, who in turn hired an American NKVD (communist secret police: People's Comissariat for Internal Affairs) agent called Noel Field, a somewhat mysterious figure with numerous contacts beyond the Iron Curtain. Field was set up and arrested as an American spy in Czechoslovakia in 1949 and taken to Hungary. His wife and brother also disappeared at this point in time.

The Fields were held for five years and then released. During their captivity, Noel Field's address book served to implicate numerous eastern European Communist Party officials with the taint of collaboration with Washington. The fevered atmosphere, which characterized the depths of the Cold War from 1949 to 1953, led to dozens of show trials, during which thousands of party officials were imprisoned – or even killed – on trumped-up charges.

The CIA's domino theory was that the whole shaky edifice of non-Soviet communist states would topple as civil disharmony spread. In the end, thousands died, but communism survived for several more decades.

1956
CIA PLOT TO DEPOSE
PRESIDENT SUKARNO

US secret services planned to get rid of
Indonesian president
b. 1901, Surabja, Java
d. 1970

Achmed Sukarno was the first president of independent
Indonesia from 1949 until he was deposed in 1966. He was
a demagogue who, for a while, successfully played off the
communist PKI party against the army. But by 1956, his
brazenness at forging links, not only with the US but also
with the USSR and China, was worrying the CIA, and a
series of increasingly bizarre attempts were planned to
destabilize him.

A failed bomb plot on November 30th 1956, was wrongly
attributed by the CIA to the PKI, in an attempt to incriminate
its "Soviet paymasters." The CIA subsequently attempted
to make more out of Sukarno's womanizing. There was, for
example, the story of a blonde Soviet air hostess (or "spy")
who had accompanied him on several state visits. Their efforts were mostly too laughable to be convincing, though.

In early 1958, the CIA, using unmarked planes, were sent
in to support growing tribal unrest, but when American air-
man, Allen Lawrence Pope, was captured with incriminating
documents in his possession, he was paraded before the
world's press on May 27th, making a nonsense of President
Eisenhower's declaration of American neutrality. After that,
the CIA reduced its support of the rebels, and the insurrection subsequently died down. President Sukarno stayed in
power, tightening his grip until 1965 when the army, again
with the help of the CIA, ousted him at last.

1957
FBI V WILHELM REICH

Scientist hounded by Hoover's FBI

Wilhelm Reich (born Austria 1897, died USA, 1957) was
an Austrian psychoanalyst trained by Sigmund Freud. His
bioelectrical experiments demonstrated that what Freud
had called "libido" might be a measurable phenomenon.
According to Reich, microscopically small particles, "bions",
are a primordial cosmic energy, responsible for weather as
well as biological expressions of emotion and sexuality.
Reich argued that the well-being that humans feel after ex-
periencing a full sexual orgasm was due to the discharge of
bioenergetic tension. He attempted to apply his theories

to a range of problems from mental health to cancer, but the
connections he made between medicine and sexuality
caused him to fall foul of the Gestapo in pre-World War II
Germany, and then the FBI in the USA.

The notedly prudish FBI director, J. Edgar Hoover, took
pains to discredit Reich as a communist, but when investigations proved that quite the reverse was true, the case was
turned over to the American Food and Drug Administration
(FDA). They then arbitrarily condemned Reich's work as
pseudo-science and obtained court orders in order to force
him to cease his research and treatment. His books were
burnt, his laboratories and equipment destroyed, and technical violation of a questionable FDA injunction led to his
incarceration for "contempt of court", and his death in an
American prison. Today his work is widely viewed as a legitimate area of alternative medicine, especially with regard
to the human immune system.

1959
MURDER INC – OPERATION
40 IN THE US

US crime syndicate of the 1920s to the 1940s

Murder Inc is the story of the early years of organized crime
in the US from the late 1920s to the mid-1940s. The membership, originally mainly Jewish, became dominated by
Sicilian families whose management structure was, to some
extent, modelled on corporate lines. The syndicate was involved in protection rackets, narcotics, liquor smuggling
and gambling.

Murder Inc, as it became known, carried out somewhere
between 500 to 700 contract killings across the States. The
killings combined brutality with a lurid imagination. The
ice pick was a favoured instrument – often inserted into the
ear and beyond. But pinball machines were also involved,
as were quicklime, slow strangling and live burial.

Hit men seemed to have been well cared for, receiving
the equivalent of a salary, pension, legal and healthcare –
in stark contrast to their victims' treatment. Salvatore
Luciana, aka "Lucky Luciano", dominated it with his associates Meyer Lansky and Bugsy Siegel. The US police made
little penetration into these organizations: indeed, the only
state executions carried out was that of Louis (no relation
to Al) Capone, Mendy Weiss and Lepke Buchalter in 1942.

Murder Inc began to unravel when Abe "Kid Twist" Reles
went to assistant district attorney, Burton Turkus, with a list
of names before jumping (or falling) six floors to his death
on Coney Island. By the time Albert Anastasia was rubbed

Murder Inc. trigger men Harry Straus, Harry Malone, and Frank Abbadando were arrested after "Kid Twist" grassed them up before falling to his death.

out in a barber's chair in 1957, Murder Inc was finished. Thereafter, gangland in the US was more businesslike – and even more brutal.

See also: *J. Edgar Hoover Blackmailed by the Mob p.148; The Mafia p.281*

1968
FREEPORT SULPHUR

CIA-backed grab of world's mineral wealth

Freeport Sulphur is a US-based mining company with global connections. In 1959, one of its directors, top engineer, Forbes Wilson, located a huge source of copper on the remote island of Dutch New Guinea or West Irian, part of modern-day Indonesia.

At the time, political instability in the country could not allow mining operations to begin. In 1963, President Sukarno, with the support of President Kennedy, was trying to continue his pattern of limited nationalization and of establishing links equally with both western and eastern

powers. Contrary to the wishes of Freeport Sulphur's directors, the logical outcome of this policy was that the company would not benefit from Indonesia's mineral wealth. By 1965, however, with Lyndon Johnson in the White House, support switched to the military coup led by the anti-democrat pro-westerner, Colonel Suharto. The Freeport Sulphur board had excellent connections with the White House and the CIA sympathizers, and in April 1967, Freeport became the first foreign company to sign a contract with the new government.

The contract granted Freeport mining rights across the huge 250,000-acre site. The company paid nothing to the traditional Papuan owners of the land, nor did Freeport have to pay compensation. No environmental restrictions were placed on the mining operation. The contract lasted 30 years, and formalized mutually beneficial relations between Freeport Sulphur, the new government, and its arm of repression (TNI). Back in the US, Freeport became a defender and apologist for the regime. Suharto, for his part, made sure that the US company had become an integral part of Indonesia's patronage system.

1970
GROUP 13
Covert British Foreign Office assassination squad

Group 13: even the name is shrouded in secrecy. Certainly its existence has never been officially acknowledged, but those close enough to know, and distant enough to speak out, have claimed that Group 13 operates as something between an enforcement arm and a protection squad for SAS personnel engaged on highly secret missions. Its working methods may be paramilitary rather than political, but its agenda has always been set by British intelligence chiefs and in pursuance of the objectives – sometimes far to the right – of the British intelligence community.

The conspiracy theory
When WPC Yvonne Fletcher was shot dead during an anti-Colonel Gaddafi protest outside the Libyan People's Bureau in St James's Square, London, on April 17th, 1984, the reaction from both the British public and the press was understandable. Shock and anger merged with revulsion to produce an atmosphere in which almost any punitive action taken against Libya would be condoned. So when, 18 months later, permission was given for eight UK-based US war-planes to take part in a high-impact raid on Libya's capital Tripoli – in retribution, claimed the government of Ronald Reagan, for a Libya-backed bomb attack on La Belle Discotheque in West Berlin nine days earlier – few British tears were shed. More questions might have been asked had it been suggested that WPC Fletcher was killed not by a Libyan sharp-shooter but by a British special agent. Was this the hand of Group 13?

In March 1990, Jonathan Moyle, the editor of the British trade journal *Defence Helicopter World* was found hanging in a wardrobe in a hotel room in Santiago, capital of Chile. From the accumulation of plastic bags and extraneous underwear, the conclusion was drawn that he had died in the course of an increasingly frenzied attempt to heighten his own sexual pleasure. The image which that charge created was so bizarre that Moyle's reputation as a serious defence journalist was effectively rubbished. Subsequently, however, it has emerged that Moyle had come close to penetrating an arms ring that linked a British ammunition company, and plans to equip Chilean helicopters with an electronic guidance system for anti-tank missiles. The posthumous attempt to tarnish Moyle's name was typical of the sort of "dirty tricks" campaign of which the intelligence services were fond. Group 13 again?

The evidence
The bullet that killed WPC Fletcher was a "terminal round", designed to "throw" the sound of a discharge so as to give forensic specialists the idea that it had been fired from close range. The evidence for this claim came from the highly regarded, investigative TV programme, *Dispatches*, broadcast on Channel 4 in the UK, in 1996. A range of ballistics experts were consulted, though the blame for WPC Fletcher's death was laid equally with British and American intelligence.

One of the few arms industry insiders to have gone public about his experiences is Gerald James, the former head of the Astra fireworks/explosives company. In his 1995 book, *In the Public Interest,* he produces anecdotal evidence from government insiders, claiming: "the Foreign Office is said to draw Group 13 operatives from the SAS as well as from private security firms. Its duties involve 'service to the nation' of a kind given only to the most ruthlessly experienced SAS officers."

Author Gary Murray tried to bring the Group 13 story to light but it nearly cost him his life. In 1991, he was persuaded, at the point of a gun, that the book which he was intending to write about Group 13, might not be commercially viable. As he staggered, dazed, from the back of the van into which he had been bundled, he had already decided on an altogether less challenging title, and Group 13's enforcement squad – if indeed they were responsible – had achieved another cover-up.

The verdict
There is no solid proof that the two organizations are synonymous, but the evidence of *Dispatches*, together with Gerald James's book, are the most high-profile evidence we have that Group 13 does indeed exist.

1970
HAROLD WILSON WAS COMMUNIST STOOGE
b. 1916
d. 1995
British Prime Minister had KGB connections

When Hugh Gaitskell resigned suddenly as leader of the British Labour party in 1963 and died shortly after from a never-explained illness, one theory was that he had been poisoned by the Russians in order to clear the way for Harold Wilson to take over.

The smear against Wilson was that he was a communist and KGB agent. Former MI5 agent, Peter Wright, reopened the allegation in his 1987 book *Spycatcher*, in which he claimed that MI5 had tried to persuade Wilson's 1963 campaign manager George Caunt to spy on him, and had Wilson put under surveillance in the run-up to the 1974 election.

MI5's suspicions may have originated in Wilson's campaign to increase trade with the USSR when he was part of Clement Atlee's postwar government. Later, MI5's top brass became convinced that Wilson would respond to the news that it had failed to act on a tip-off about Anthony Blunt's double-agent activities a decade earlier by reorganizing the security services. Thereafter, despite meager evidence, MI5 maintained a relentless campaign against him.

In the 1970s, a British army information officer, called Colin Wallace, led an MI5 intelligence operation known as Clockwork Orange, which was a dirty tricks operation intended to smear both the Republican movement in Northern Ireland and the Labour government.

In 1976, Wilson resigned as unexpectedly as had Gaitskell in 1963. He went into mental decline, but the substance of the claims against MI5 was never officially admitted.

See also: *Harold Wilson, the CIA, and MI5 p.153*

1970
OPERATION CONDOR
US sponsored South-American terror plan

Under the guise of supposed counter-terrorism, Operation Condor was the code name that was given to a joint, "death squad" campaign of political murder – mainly of leftist sympathizers and their families – by the military governments of Argentina, Bolivia, Brazil, Chile, Paraguay, and Uruguay in the mid-1970s. These hit teams were placed as far afield as France, Portugal, and the US and were set up to locate and assassinate political opponents.

The Condor teams remained just an ugly rumour until 1992, when a judge in Paraguay, researching the fate of a former political prisoner, found what have become known as the "terror archives," a catalogue of hundreds of individuals secretly kidnapped, tortured, and killed by these combined security services. The theory was that Operation Condor had been given at least tacit approval by the US – attributable to the Nixon-era fear of Marxist revolution in South and Central America – and was implemented by Henry Kissinger, Nixon's secretary of state. No hard proof, however, was forthcoming until March of 2001, when *The New York Times* published the text of a recently declassified state department document that revealed how the CIA had organized and operated communications for the Condor killers. This 1978 cable from Robert E. White, the US Ambassador to Paraguay, finally provided "weighty evidence suggesting that US military and intelligence officials supported and collaborated with Condor as a secret partner or sponsor."

See also: *Salvador Allende p.60*

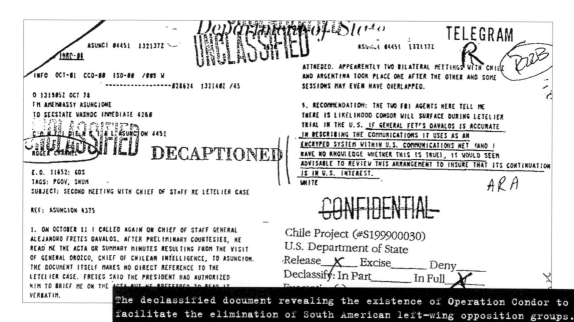

The declassified document revealing the existence of Operation Condor to facilitate the elimination of South American left-wing opposition groups.

1972
J. EDGAR HOOVER
BLACKMAILED BY THE MOB

Hoover denied the existence of the Mafia for so long because he was being blackmailed by them

One of the continuing enigmas of US law enforcement history has always been why, for more than 20 years, FBI director, J. Edgar Hoover, seemingly refused to believe in the existence of organized crime – the "Mob" or "Mafia".

Yet J. Edgar Hoover (1895–1972), who ran the bureau for 52 years, could be concerned to the point of paranoia over the activities of organizations such as the Communist Party and the civil rights movement. Even before he joined the fledgling FBI in 1921, he had made a name for himself at the US Department of Justice during what became known as the 1919 "Palmer Raids", when more than 10,000 communists and anarchists were arrested (many of them were later deported). During the 1930s, he moved against mid-West outlaws such as Baby Face Nelson, Pretty Boy Floyd and John Dillinger (although most of the actual manhunts were conducted by FBI Agent Melvin Purvis – the original "G-Man" – who was Hoover's only real rival for media attention). From the bootlegging days of Prohibition to the late 1950s, however, Hoover hotly denied that there was any "underworld crime syndicate." He only grudgingly conceded the fact of the Mob's existence after New York State police staged a raid on the infamous Apalachin Conference of Mafia dons in November 1957. The full press coverage that the raid received made it impossible for even Hoover to ignore the Mob any longer.

The conspiracy theory

Hoover maintained his power by almost obsessively amassing secret files on everyone, from ordinary citizens to politicians and presidents. That he could not know about characters such as Al Capone and Charlie "Lucky" Luciano seemed beyond belief, and many conspiracy theorists have drawn the conclusion that Hoover, certainly no stranger to the use of blackmail, was being blackmailed himself. Two possible weaknesses have been suggested that would have made Hoover vulnerable to blackmail. The first was that he was an inveterate gambler; the other that he was gay, and one or both gave the Mafia a hold over him.

The evidence

There is strong evidence that Hoover had a gambling habit. He was frequently seen (and even photographed) at race-courses within driving distance of Washington DC. He would boast to the press that he "only ever bet at the $2 window," but FBI agents have put on record that they were enlisted to place much larger bets on Hoover's behalf. On a more serious level, crime boss, Frank Costello, insisted that he passed Hoover lucrative racing tips via the gossip columnist, Walter Winchell, in return for Hoover's continuing myopia towards the Mob. The other story is that the syndicate possessed photographs of Hoover dressed as a transvestite, which kept him from investigating them. Public speculation that Hoover was both gay and a secret cross-dresser only started to circulate after his death. The most often-cited proof is his 40-year relationship with his right-hand man and constant companion Clyde Tolson. A more detailed tale of Hoover's cross-dressing comes from Susan Rosenstiel, a former wife of one-time bootlegger Lewis Rosenstiel, who claims that, in 1958, she was at a party at the Plaza Hotel where Hoover was wearing "a fluffy black dress with flounces, and lace stockings and high heels." Her ex-husband, and the notorious New York lawyer, Roy Cohn, himself a gay homophobe, were also present.

The verdict

The gambling story has proved hard to refute, although the only blackmail claims are made by mobsters such as Costello. The rumours about Hoover's homosexuality may well be true, but he remains such a hero to American conservatives that, any suggestion that he was anything but heterosexual and celibate, despite his lifelong intimacy with Clyde Tolson, is greeted with fury. Pictures of Hoover wearing dresses and lingerie have circulated on the internet, but all have proved to be computer-generated composites.

1972
WATERGATE – A PENTAGON
COUP D'ETAT

Watergate was engineered by the Pentagon to smear Nixon

President Richard Nixon of the US resigned on August 9th, 1974, forced from office as a result of the investigation into the break-in at the Watergate Hotel, which led to a stream of scandalous allegations involving illegal phone-taps, bugged rooms, nefarious political donations and dirty tricks campaigns. Against that, though, Nixon apologists maintain that Nixon was the victim of a smear campaign, and that the whole Watergate conspiracy was itself, a conspiracy conducted by his political opponents.

Were Bob Woodward (left) and Carl Bernstein (right) of the *Washington Post* duped by "Deep Throat" into disseminating a Watergate cover-up that worked?

The conspiracy theory

The five men who broke into the Democrat offices at the Watergate Hotel were CIA alumni engaging in CIA business. The CIA could have easily concealed their tracks. Instead, they sheepishly allowed the FBI to conduct whatever investigations it felt were necessary, and then allowed Nixon to take the wrap for the CIA's own illegal activities. Hardly surprising, given that the CIA feared that the occupant of the White House was becoming dangerously detached from reality. Put simply, the CIA decided that Nixon had to go, and they devised the means for his removal from office.

Woodward and Bernstein, the *Washington Post*'s investigative reporters, owed all their stories to CIA informants such as Watergate ringleader, E. Howard Hunt, whose "day job" was with the Mullen Company, a firm that provided cover for CIA agents. Woodward's mysterious source, known only as "Deep Throat", was named in 2005 as former FBI deputy director Mark Felt. Until then, Deep Throat had been thought by many to be Robert Bennett, the owner of Mullen, and by others to be General Al Haig, whom Woodward may well have briefed in his pre-journalism incarnation (1969–70) as a navy lieutenant. Deep Throat set up the whole story and Woodward and Bernstein swallowed it all.

Hunt was a CIA double agent, put there to spy on Nixon. And Robert McCord, one of the Watergate "plumbers" (the unofficial name for a member of Nixon's Special Investigations Unit), deliberately sabotaged the break-in in order to instigate an enquiry that would eventually nail Nixon. Prominent Nixon apologist, G. Gordon Liddy, claims

that former White House counsel, John Dean, dreamt up the Watergate burglary in order to remove documents linking his wife to an alleged prostitution ring.

In a 1977 interview with the *San Francisco Chronicle*, former CIA agent, Frank Sturgis, claimed that the raid on Watergate was part of an investigation by the CIA to see if the tycoon Howard Hughes was secretly bank-rolling the Democratic Party.

The evidence

The White House tapes, though muffled or even inaudible in places, are a powerful indictment of Nixon's presidency. All the players are there, and Nixon's centrality to the original break-in is hard to dismiss. But other clues have emerged since, such as the key which was recovered from Watergate burglar Roland Martinez. Since it fitted secretary Maxie Wells's desk, was that not an indication of the burglar's intentions? Also, Jim Hougan's 1984 book, *Secret Agenda,* revealed for the first time the FBI lab findings that the Democrat National Committee was never bugged. (What then was Watergate burglar McCord doing there in the first place? Was there a more sensitive secret from which he wished to divert attention?)

Much of Hougan's case is circumstantial in that he produces no actual evidence to support his claim that the break-in was a CIA plot. Nevertheless his arguments have attracted praise and demand to be taken seriously.

A final mystery remains. Given that the tapes provide such damning evidence, why didn't Nixon destroy them?

That question has never been satisfactorily answered, save to say that their existence doesn't provide black-and-white proof of his guilt.

The verdict

President Richard Nixon was a paranoid, corrupt and venal president but Carl Bernstein and Bob Woodward may not have given us the pure unblemished truth with the official account of their investigations, *All The President's Men*. But to agree with CIA agent Frank Sturgis that "it doesn't take a genius to figure out that Watergate was a CIA set-up" is asking us to disregard too much available evidence.

See also: *Watergate – Presidential Abuse of Power p.150*

1972
WATERGATE – PRESIDENTIAL ABUSE OF POWER

Nixon's paranoia led to his downfall

On August, 8th, 1974, Richard M. Nixon became the first president in American history to resign, having been weakened and backed into a corner by an agonizing trail of allegations which had lasted two years. The allegations brought Washington to a peak of paranoia, and brought low a president who, only two and a half years earlier, had won a landslide election victory unprecedented in modern politics in the US. Watergate is still one of the most controversial episodes in American political history.

The conspiracy theory

It all began to unravel in the early hours of June 17th, 1972 at the Watergate Hotel in Washington DC, when a security guard called Frank Wills noticed that a door lock in the Democratic National Committee's offices had been tampered with. The police made five arrests, one of whom, James McCord, was a Nixon campaign "security officer." Some reporters and politicians began to wonder where this was all leading. In fact, it had all begun a while earlier.

In 1969, Nixon secretly approved phone-tapping against critics of his policy of bombing Cambodia. In 1971, he fell foul of FBI director, J. Edgar Hoover, when the security services discovered that mail was being intercepted, allegedly to prevent "security leaks."

President Nixon's growing insecurity coincided with his creation of the Special Investigations Unit. The unit was known unofficially as the "plumbers", and its activities included raiding the office of psychiatrist, and anti-Vietnam

activist, Dr Daniel Ellsberg, in an attempt to collect incriminating material.

By the time of the Watergate break-in in 1971, the attorney general, John Mitchell, and John Dean, counsel to the president, had been working with Nixon's chief of staff, H.R. Haldeman, and Jeb Magruder and G. Gordon Liddy of the Committee to Reelect the President (CRP). Their work amounted to political espionage on Nixon's behalf.

Nixon believed that his more questionable activities could be disguised if he ordered Magruder and others to destroy sensitive documents or give false testimony to official investigators. On June 23rd, 1972, Nixon was heard trying to pit the FBI against the CIA, claiming that the FBI investigation into the wire-tapping was hindering CIA special operations. On July 1st, Mitchell left the CRP in protest.

Nixon's denial on August 29th that anyone in his administration had anything to do with Watergate was evidence of his growing alienation from reality. On September 15th, the five men from the break-in, together with Liddy and E. Howard Hunt, one of the "plumbers," were arrested.

In November 1972, Nixon was re-elected with the biggest landslide in US electoral history and yet the impressive victory did little to ease his paranoia. Two months later,

Fiddling while Rome burns? The President entertains at the White House, March 7th, 1974.

McCord and Liddy were convicted of conspiracy, burglary and illegal wiretapping. Amid mounting hysteria, the Senate voted to conduct an investigation.

On March 21st, 1973, former acting FBI director, L. Patrick Gray warned of "a cancer growing on the presidency." Nixon was becoming increasingly unpredictable, alternately urging aides to greater openness and new heights of concealment. On March 23rd, McCord implicated Dean and Magruder in the Watergate break-in. On April 30th, Nixon announced the resignations of Haldeman, Ehrlichman and Dean. Their evidence, under oath, revealed that the president was far from all-powerful, but rather, an embattled figure increasingly paranoid about dozens of "enemies" both within and outside the White House.

When the Senate's Selected Committee on Presidential Campaign Activities opened public hearings in May 1973, Dean's evidence linked Nixon to the cover-up. A young lawyer called Donald Segretti admitted in court that he had 28 agents working in 12 states carrying out "dirty tricks" against potential Democrat candidates for the presidency, ranging from disrupting public meetings to accusations of sexual misconduct.

Further accusations rained down, all seized on by an eager White House press corps. Leading the charge were Carl Bernstein and Bob Woodward of the *Washington Post*. In July 1973, former White House official, Alexander Butterfield, testified that Nixon had taped conversations in his office. Prosecutor Cox subpoenaed certain tapes but Nixon refused to release them on the grounds of executive privilege.

On July 24th, 1974, the Supreme Court rejected Nixon's claim that he had authority to withhold material from the prosecutor. As impeachment came closer, it emerged that on one tape, dated June 23rd, 1972, Nixon had discussed with Haldeman how they could thwart the FBI investigation. When this was published, Nixon's support in Congress evaporated. In the face of irresistible pressure, he resigned at noon on August 9th, 1974.

The evidence

Richard Nixon claimed that his motives for taping his conversations were archival, for he wanted his administration to be the "the best chronicled in history". In fact, his administration proved to be among the most meticulously documented in US political history, but as far as Nixon was concerned it had the worst possible outcome.

As well as the 261 hours of secretly recorded Oval Office audiotapes, the televised congressional Watergate hearings stretched to 250 hours. So much of the essence of that

```
TRANSCRIPT OF A RECORDING OF A
MEETING BETWEEN THE PRESIDENT
AND H.R. HALDEMAN IN THE OVAL
OFFICE ON JUNE 23, 1972 FROM
10:04 TO 11:39 AM

June 23, 1972 FROM 10:04 TO 11:39 AM                    3
**********

HALDEMAN:     okay -that's fine. Now, on the investi-
              gation, you know, the Democratic break-in
              thing, we're back to the-in the, the problem
              area because the FBI is not under control,
              because Gray doesn't exactly know how to
              control them, and they have, their
              investigation is now leading into some
              productive areas, because they've been able
              to trace the money, not through the money
              itself, but through the bank, you know,
              sources - the banker himself.  And, and it
              goes in some directions we don't want it to
              go.  Ah, also there have been some things,
              like an informant came in off the street to
              the FBI in Miami, who was a photographer or
              has a friend who is a photographer who
              developed some films through this guy,
              Barker, and the films had pictures of
              Democratic National Committee letter head
              documents and things. So I guess, so it's
              things like that that are gonna, that are
              filtering in. Mitchell came up with
              yesterday, and John Dean analyzed very
              carefully last night and concludes, concurs
              now with Mitchell's recommendation that the
              only way to solve this, and we're set up
              beautifully to do it, ah, in that and
              that...the only network that paid any
              attention to it last night was NBC...they
              did a massive story on the Cuban...
PRESIDENT:    That's right.
HALDEMAN:     thing.
PRESIDENT:    Right.
HALDEMAN:
```

The transcript of the "Smoking Gun" tape, which reveals Nixon and Haldeman's plotting.

case is on tape, for as H.R. ("Bob") Haldeman said to Nixon, "Once the toothpaste is out of the tube, it's hard to get it back in." The problem lies in knowing what sort of pattern the toothpaste makes on the bathroom sink.

The White House itself has a huge Watergate archive, which is publicly accessible via the internet. And yet, the debate still rages.

The verdict

Richard Nixon resigned more than 30 years ago, but at times it is as if we are still reeling from the full impact of the suspicion and paranoia aroused by the Watergate scandal. The man who said: "I am not a crook", is generally believed to have been just that. He may have claimed that he was taping conversations as a matter of record, but the fact is that the taping was done in stealth, with even his top aides unaware of what was being done. The stories that the tapes, often barely audible, reveal is an exercise in concealment on a massive scale. Could the public ever trust the president again? Not if that person willfully misuses power as brazenly as did Richard M. Nixon.

See also: *Watergate – A Pentagon Coup D'état p.148*

1975
LEONARD PELTIER
b. 1944

American Indian was imprisoned for killing two
FBI agents

On June 26th, 1975, two FBI agents, called Jack Coles and
Ronald Williamson, and Joe Stuntz, an American Indian,
were killed during a gun battle near Wounded Knee, South
Dakota. Leonard Peltier, a prominent spokesman for the
American Indian Movement (AIM), stood trial along with
Dino Butler and Robert Robideau. In April 1977, Peltier re-
ceived two life sentences for killing the FBI men but the
two others were cleared.

The trial was highly controversial. Peltier's defence lawyer
claimed that the agents were killed during cross-fire. Peltier
sympathizers suggested that the evidence of Peltier's girlfriend, Myrtle Poor Bear, was trumped up by the FBI.

The Pine Ridge reservation has been the site of trouble
ever since Custer's Last Stand in 1875. AIM claims that the
US government has installed a puppet local government,
which gives them easier access to the area's vast mineral
wealth. According to his supporters, Peltier was fighting
for his people's ancient land rights.

Detractors claim that a succession of appeal hearings has
yielded nothing, but the Free Peltier Movement claims
Peltier as a figurehead for AIM, and insists that his conviction was an act of collusion between the FBI and turncoat
non-traditional Indians. His defenders number among them
writers such as Peter Matthiessen, who posited the existence of the real killer (inevitably known as Mr X), and Robert
Redford, whose 1991 film, *Incident at Oglala*, was sympathetic to Peltier. Meanwhile, the next date for a full parole
hearing is 2008.

1975
GOUGH WHITLAM
b. 1914, Australia

Australian prime minister was overthrown by
CIA/MI6

On December 2nd, 1972, Gough Whitlam became Australia's
first Labour prime minister for 23 years with a radical man-
date to reform policy on censorship, women's rights and
Aboriginal issues.

For the CIA, however, the main concern was that nothing should in any way disturb the work of its Australian spy
and satellite station, Pine Gap. Work began on a project to

destabilize the government, with attention focused on
Whitlam's deputy prime minister, Jim Cairns, a former stal-
wart of the anti-Vietnam movement. To the CIA he was a
virtual terrorist.

Thus, Cairns was duped into signing a patently fraudulent finance package with a company called Commerce
International which had well-known links to the CIA. The
story was then leaked to the press, and Cairns was portrayed
as either inept or corrupt. Suddenly Cairns was a liability
and Whitlam had little option but to sack him, and another
minister, leaving himself dangerously exposed.

On November 2nd, 1975, an embattled Gough Whitlam
accused the opposition of being "subsidized by the CIA."
Then, fatally, he threatened not to extend the lease of the
CIA's bases, such as Pine Gap, in Australia. On November
11th, 1975, Governor General, Sir John Kerr – a staunch
monarchist and anglophile whom critics accused of taking
his orders directly from the CIA and/or MI6 – summoned
Whitlam to his office and dismissed him. The conservative
Malcolm Fraser took over as prime minister and, for the CIA
at least, business returned to normal.

On the very few occasions that Gough Whitlam – the only
Australian prime minister ever to be thrown out of office by
a governor-general – has spoken of the scandal since, he
has implied very strongly that his ousting was at the
hands of the CIA.

1976
BOSS AND LIBERAL LEADER
JEREMY THORPE
b. 1929, Surrey, England

British Liberal politician who resigned after
sex scandal

The Eton and Oxford-educated Jeremy Thorpe became leader
of the British Liberal Party on January 19th, 1967. He had
flair and energy, but he was also an ardent critic of the
apartheid regime in South Africa. It was in this latter respect that he may have come to the attention of the South
African security services, known as BOSS.

In November 1961, Thorpe became on friendly terms with
a groom called Norman Josiffe, who later changed his name
to Scott. Scott was a volatile character with constant monetary problems. When he claimed to a liberal MP that he and
Thorpe had been lovers, the claim was initially dismissed
as a ludicrous attempt at blackmail. But when he showed
a cache of letters from Thorpe, Thorpe's advisors became
seriously alarmed.

In January 1975, a man called Andrew Newton was paid by Thorpe to drive Scott to Dartmoor, to shoot his dog Rinka, and then to threaten Scott.

In March, 1975, Newton was tried and jailed for the attack on Scott. After the story appeared in the press, Thorpe resigned as Liberal Party leader on May 9th, 1976. Jeremy Thorpe's trial for conspiracy to murder began on May 8th, 1979. He was acquitted on June 22nd but never really recovered. Harold Wilson, who had resigned as prime minister in 1976, was convinced that the plot to smear Thorpe was inspired by the same BOSS squad that was attempting to smear him as a communist spy. The claim is, in the face of the other evidence, far-fetched.

1977
HAROLD WILSON, THE CIA, AND MI5
British prime minister was the target of smear campaign by UK and US intelligence

From 1974–6, British prime minister, Harold Wilson, was conspired against by MI5 and CIA agents. Spies bugged and burgled government offices and leaked disinformation to the press to discredit the Labour Party leader. Wilson was reelected when the previous Conservative government of Ted Heath was defeated following a national miner's strike, which MI5 claimed was communist backed.

Convinced that Wilson was a Soviet "plant," the spooks conspired to remove him from office. In 1977, Wilson briefed journalists about the smear campaign but his claims were given little credence. Corroboration came from former intelligence officers, Colin Wallace and Peter Wright. In his book, *Spycatcher*, Wright said that MI5 began monitoring Wilson during his time with an East-West trading organization, a job involving regular trips to the Soviet Union. Russian defector, Anatoli Golitsin, later claimed that during the 1960s the KGB's Assassinations Department 13 removed a European leader and put their man (that is, Wilson) in his place.

Wilson became Labour leader in 1963, following the sudden death of his predecessor, Hugh Gaitskill, from a mysterious disease. KGB defector, Oleg Lyalin, claimed that eastern-European émigré business tycoons, such as Lithuanian, Joseph Kagan, Wilson's friend and financial backer, regularly met Czech agents. According to Wright, US agents spread similar allegations from Czech defector Joseph Frolik. The CIA was opposed to Wilson's left-wing politics and his pledge to end the Polaris nuclear missile programme. Nothing was proved against Wilson. His political career ended in 1976, when he suddenly resigned as prime minister and retired into a life of obscurity. Harold Wilson died in 1995.

See also: *Harold Wilson was a Communist Stooge p.146; The Smearing of Colin Wallace p.158*

1977
PSI-WAR: OPERATIONS GRILLFLAME AND STARGATE
CIA Psi-ops programmes

That the CIA commissioned research into the possibilities of Psi-War – the use of psychic and paranormal phenomena for intelligence-gathering, and as psychological weapons – is not disputed. Nor is there any doubt that from around 1977, the agency actually ran a team, under the code names Grillflame and then Stargate, that used remote viewing (a form of psychic visualization). Rumours about these operations were finally confirmed in 1995 when the American Research Institute (ARI) compiled the report that debunked Stargate's usefulness.

The $20million price tag that the operations had run up over some 18 years was too costly, but Stargate operatives named in the ARI report, such as Joseph McMoneagle, protested publicly that their work – almost certainly a response to Cold War reports of Soviet Psi-War research – had produced results. He argued that: "It wouldn't have lasted 20 years if we weren't productive. Across the board, we probably had a success rate of 15 to 20 percent." Among those successes are what McMoneagle has claimed are exact predictions. These include the following: that Skylab would crash when it fell from orbit; the detection of North Korean plutonium; and the location of Brigadier General James Dozier, the American officer kidnapped when he was held hostage by the Italian radical group, the Red Brigades, in 1981. Anecdotal reports have also circulated about a Stargate remote viewer who, quite by accident, psychically penetrated Area 51, the American government's most secret military facility.

See also: *The Stargate Conspiracy p.168; Area 51 p.308*

1978
THE JONESTOWN MASS SUICIDE

Jim Jones **b.**1931, Lyn, Indiana; **d.**1978, Guyana
Instigator of mass suicide in Guyana

In November 1978, American congressman, Leo Ryan, led a small party to Guyana to get to the bottom of some alarming human rights allegations that he had heard about, concerning the People's Temple, and its leader, the "Rev" Jim Jones. Having inspected the jungle encampment, Ryan was about to return to the US, with 16 disillusioned camp members, when Jones's loyalists opened fire on him as he boarded a plane on November 18th. Ryan and some accompanying journalists were shot dead.

Meanwhile, Jim Jones's 900 followers, including 270 children, ingested potassium cyanide and tranquilizers in a fruit punch. Mass suicide was the verdict of American authorities. Others were less sure.

The conspiracy theory
The nomadic, neo-communist People's Temple came to its final resting place in Guyana, South America, impelled by its charismatic leader Jim Jones. The taped record of those last minutes suggests that, once Jones had announced the congressman's death, the only way out for the stricken community was a communal rejection of an inglorious, vanquished life under capitalism, and a calm acceptance of death. Or was it?

Speculation centered on how one man could have persuaded 900 people to take their own lives. Jones's followers may have been, mostly, lost people looking for strong leadership, who willingly took whatever drugs Jones gave them, but how could the US authorities not have known what was going on? Why did they not move to prevent the massacre? And were there other such communities elsewhere?

Conspiracist, Jim Hougan, claims that Jones initiated the killings because he feared that Congressman Ryan would unmask his links with CIA agent, Dan Mitrione. Veteran author, activist and agitator, John Judge, blames British Black Watch troops, on a training exercise with the American Green Berets, and says that the deaths were part of the CIA-sponsored mind control exercise known as MKULTRA. An amateur theorist, called Nathan Landau, referred to Jonestown as an anti-American concentration camp, established by Jones so that he could take over Guyana in

Jonestown, Guyana: hundreds of bodies are visible from the air near the People's Temple community hall.

preparation for launching an assault against the United States. And he used drugs to control and exploit his army of mainly black "slaves."

Many theorists point out that Leo Ryan was one of the CIA's sharpest critics in congress. The Hughes-Ryan Amendment would have forced the CIA toput a cap on spending, and to inform congress of its covert operational plans in advance. With Ryan's death, the amendment never came to pass.

More mysterious deaths followed the Jonestown debacle, such as the killings of San Francisco's, Mayor George Moscone, and supervisor, Harvey Milk. They were investigating Jones's Temple funds, and were shot by Dan White, a Temple novitiate.

Dr Peter Beter, another professional conspiracist, claimed that the massacre was secondary to the destruction of a Soviet rocket. And Jim Jones was, in reality, a Jew who survived the massacre and was flown to Israel to recuperate (but was pushed out of the plane *en route*). In his recent book, *Was Jonestown a CIA Experiment?*, Michael Meiers suggested that Dr Laurence Layton, a former Chief of the US army's Chemical and Biological Warfare Division, cultured the Aids virus to be tested and deployed in a CIA-backed experiment in Jonestown, Guyana.

The evidence

One overwhelming body of evidence is the audio tape – broadly agreed to be genuine – on which Jim Jones can be heard discussing the deteriorating situation with his wife, Christine Miller, and, shortly after, chillingly asking for "medication." Congress's report contained 782 pages, but some 5,000 pages were withheld. Some evidence is missing or partial, for example, the body-lift records. There are minor variations in the transcripted tape, although these don't throw up too many suspicions. The few survivors who have told their own stories have concentrated more on the last hours, their escape, and Jones's charismatic leadership than on the mass of dark theories which the event provoked.

The verdict

The authorities still have a great deal of explaining to do in order to pin the whole Jonestown massacre on Jim Jones, but amid a welter of conflicting theories, the lone, doped despot with a messiah complex, still seems the most acceptable explanation.

See also: *FBI v Black Panther Party p.59; MKULTRA p.143*

1982
JOHN STALKER AFFAIR
Shoot-to-kill investigator in Northern Ireland was thwarted by British authorities

John Stalker was deputy chief constable of Manchester police when he was asked to take on one of the most sensitive assignments in UK policing: investigating claims that the Royal Ulster Constabulary was conducting a shoot-to-kill policy in Northern Ireland. But, quite suddenly, he was transferred to other duties.

The period under investigation was late 1982, when a special Royal Ulster Constabulary anti-terrorist unit shot dead six unarmed men in Country Armagh over five weeks. Four of the dead men had been implicated in the murder of three policeman in an IRA land mine, only three weeks previously. Were the RUC shootings tactical, or purely a matter of revenge?

Stalker was appointed in 1985. In May 1986, just as he was about to interview RUC chief constable, John Hermon, allegations broke that Stalker was linked socially to the Quality Street Manchester-based criminal network, accused of arms-running for the IRA. Stalker was removed from the enquiry. At the time, it seemed transparently obvious that the Quality Street charge was trumped up. This view seemed vindicated when, three months later on August 22nd, 1986, all charges against Stalker were dropped.

In January 1988, Stalker's replacement, Colin Sampson of the West Yorkshire police, reported to Attorney General, Patrick Mayhew, that no charges would be made against the RUC. Stalker later complained that his suspension came because his revelations would be an embarrassment to the government and security services.

In fact, Stalker's reputation for telling the truth was enhanced by the affair, and he has since become a popular speaker and writer.

1983
EDWIN WILSON AND THE CIA
b. 1928, Nampa, Idaho
Ex-CIA maverick was set up and imprisoned by his former employer

Edwin Wilson was a classic old-school CIA type and a close friend of Theodore Shackley, the head of CIA's clandestine operations during the 1960s.

Wilson left the CIA in 1971 but continued to work for the secret American navy operation Task Force 157 until 1976.

By this time he had made millions dealing in arms. But in 1977 he sold 19,050kg (42,000lb) of high-explosive C-4 to Muammar Gaddafi.

As Libya was classified as "sponsoring terrorism" by the US, Wilson was now a wanted man. He lay low in Libya, but in 1982 an old colleague of his, Ernest Keiser – who was in the pay of federal prosecutor Larry Barcella – persuaded Wilson that if he followed him to the Dominican Republic to run a spy operation, all charges would be dropped.

The plan worked. Wilson was arrested on arrival in the Dominican Republic and flown to New York where he was tried four times in two years. Eventually he was damned with evidence from Charles Briggs, the CIA's No. 3, who signed an affidavit declaring that Wilson had had nothing to do with the CIA since 1971. That affidavit was crucial: Wilson was jailed for 52 years.

However, his luck may yet change. In 2003, a Houston federal judge agreed that the prosecutors had "deliberately deceived the court." Furthermore, he accused them of "double-crossing a part-time informal government agent." Edwin Wilson is currently up for parole.

Edwin Wilson may not be a saint, but that does not justify convicting him with perjured evidence.

1983
KOREAN AIR FLIGHT KAL007
KAL007 was shot down by the Russians, killing 269

On September 1st, 1983, Korean Airlines flight 007, travelling from Alaska to Seoul, strayed from its flight path and was engaged by Soviet fighter planes. Initial reports stated that the plane had landed safely but it later emerged that it had actually crashed into the Sea of Japan, killing all 269 passengers and crew.

In January 1988, the Soviet newspaper *Izvestya* interviewed Lieutenant Colonel Gennadiy Osipovich, who admitted bringing it down with two air-to-air missiles. But in 1996 ex-pilot Michael Brun wrote a book claiming that KAL007 was a clandestine US operation to get a closer look at Soviet air defences. From conflicting newspaper stories, black box recorder transcripts, and items pulled from the sea itself, Brun concluded that the Americans had gambled that the Russians would never fire at a civilian aircraft. Tragically, they were wrong. For other observers, suspicion has centered around the presence on board of out-and-out Soviet critic, Congressman Lawrence P. McDonald.

The conspiracist Robert E. Lee accepts that the plane was fired on, but is suspicious that hardly any debris was found.

He reckons the pilot steered the plane safely back to Sakhalin, where the survivors were removed – and then imprisoned. Lee claims that the mass-kidnapping had to be concealed because, in the light of the USA's appeasement programme towards the USSR, no-one in the administration wanted the reopening of trade links to be delayed by anti-Soviet demonstrations.

This theory is dismissed in most circles as fanciful.

1985
ARROW AIRWAYS DC8 CRASH AT GANDER
Oliver North implicated in a plane crash carrying US military personnel

An Arrow Airways DC8, heading for Fort Campbell and loaded with 8 crew and 248 members of the third battalion of the 101st Airborne Division, crashed six minutes after take-off from Gander International Airport in Newfoundland on the morning of December 12th, 1985. Its military passengers were on peacekeeping duties in the Sinai desert.

An amateur sleuth, called Jamie Sandford, became interested in the crash after hearing about it on a radio programme in 1992. Sandford has painstakingly collected a mass of eyewitness evidence about the tragedy. He has expressed concern that the crash site was ordered to be bulldozed before meticulous examination could take place. His conjectures focus on the mysterious character of Oliver North, who at the time was negotiating with Iran over the fate of seven American hostages that were being held by pro-Iranian groups in Lebanon.

The trail of suspicion starts when a pilot observed lax security during a stop-over in Cairo. The troops' luggage was being left periodically unattended, and non-US military were re-loading the plane. Moreover, several large wooden crates were included for the onward journey, but their presence has never been explained. Sandford thinks the crates were improvised coffins, in case a covert attempt to rescue the hostages was made but failed, or in case the Iranians discovered that the 18 HAWK missiles North was selling them were second-hand, and so murdered the hostages anyway. He claims that a bomb was placed in the hold to show the world the true global scale of the terrorist threat.

The theory may be over-ambitious, but only five members of the official investigation team concluded that the crash was due to an accumulation of ice on the wings. Four members dissented. Perhaps Jamie Sandford was closer than his critics think.

1985
VENDETTA – SINKING THE RAINBOW WARRIOR

French secret services destroy Greenpeace flagship

The *Rainbow Warrior* was the flagship of the environmental organization Greenpeace. On July 10th, 1985, it was in Auckland Harbour, New Zealand, preparing to lead a flotilla of vessels to protest at the French nuclear test site at Moruroa Atoll. Just before midnight, two bombs exploded on the hull of the *Rainbow Warrior*.

The ship sank within minutes. Most of the crew managed to escape but Greenpeace photographer Fernando Pereira – a 36-year-old father of two who was trying to recover his camera equipment when the second bomb went off – was drowned. The New Zealand police acted fast. Within 30 hours they had charged Dominique Prieur and Alain Mafart as they returned their rental car in Auckland. The pair were agents of Direction Generale de la Securité Exterieure (DGSE) – the French secret service.

Although France's President Mitterand denounced it as "a criminal attack," the French media was soon claiming that the sabotage was approved by the French government.

On November 4th, 1985, Prieur and Mafart pleaded guilty to charges of manslaughter and were given ten years imprisonment. France responded by threatening to impose trade sanctions against New Zealand. Eventually, United Nations Secretary General, Perez de Cuellar, agreed to mediate between the two countries.

In July 1986, France paid the New Zealand government $13million compensation, and Prieur and Mafart were removed to the island of Hao, in French Polynesia. However, within three years, they were back in France. Meanwhile, Greenpeace has a new nuclear patrol vessel, aptly called the *Rainbow Warrior*.

1987
SPYCATCHER

b.1916, Chesterfield, UK; **d.**1995, Australia
British government tried to stop publication of former spy's memoirs

The battle to silence former MI5 man Peter Wright was officially lost on October 13th, 1988, when the Law Lords told the British government that they could not prevent his book, *Spycatcher*, being serialized by the press.

The Thatcher government's dread of *Spycatcher* derived from the fear that an intelligence "insider" was drawing aside the veil of secrecy behind which the security services were accustomed to work.

The book had already been a publishing phenomenon in Australia and the US in 1987, where its allegations of incompetence in MI5, the plot against Nasser, and the conspiracy against Harold Wilson when he was prime minister, had helped sell 400,000 copies. The sight of the British government squirming – as when Cabinet Secretary Sir Robert Armstrong admitted in a Sydney court that he had been "economical with the truth" – was unedifying but rivetting. The attempted injunctions on the British press publishing extracts or summaries could only guarantee extra sales, and the *Observer*, *Guardian* and the recently founded *Independent* newspapers joined battle under the flag of free speech, while also relishing the rise in sales. On July 12th, 1987, the *Sunday Times* published lengthy extracts from the book.

The *Spycatcher* affair had far-reaching consequences. For one thing, the British Security Services Act 1989 formally acknowledged, for the first time, the existence of MI5. Stella Rimington (1992–6) was the first head of MI5 whose name was publicly known. Gradually the spooks were starting to come out from the shadows.

Peter Wright's *Spycatcher* revealed uncomfortable truths about MI5.

1988
PAN AM FLIGHT 103

A Libyan agent blew up a commercial airliner over the town of Lockerbie

At 7.02pm on December 21st, 1988, 38 minutes after take-off, at an altitude of 31,000ft (9,500m), a bomb exploded in the forward cargo hold of Pan Am flight 103. The plane, packed with people flying back to the US for Christmas, blew up over the town of Lockerbie, Scotland. All 259 on board were killed, as well as 11 residents of Lockerbie who were hit by shrapnel. A Scottish court was convened in the Netherlands on May 3rd, 2000. Abdelbaset Ali Mohamed al-Megrahi was found guilty and his co-defendant Lamine Fehima not guilty. Both were Libyans.

The conspiracy theory

Right from the start, two countries had a clear motive for the crime. Libya could be acting out of revenge for the American bombing of Tripoli and Benghazi in 1986. And in July 1988 an Iranian civil airliner was mistakenly shot down by a US warship, killing all 290 passengers and crew. Did Libya and Iran work singly or together to exact revenge?

Some observers believed that Al-Megrahi was a cover for the Palestinian terrorist leader Abu Nidal. Then in 2000, as the trial was about to start, a former Iranian intelligence official, Ahmad Behbahani, claimed to have been in charge of all recent terrorist operations carried out by the Iranian government, including Lockerbie.

Behbahani told CBS's *60 Minutes* that he had taken his plan to Ahmed Jibril, leader of the Syrian-backed Popular Front for the Liberation of Palestine. However the PFLP denied any involvement.

A respected British investigative journalist, the late Paul Foot, claimed in March 2004 to have "an explanation so shocking that no one in high places can contemplate it." He suggested that the Lockerbie bombing was carried out not by Libyans but by terrorists based in Syria and hired by Iran. Some observers claimed that Libya was only accused after the US took the heat off Syria, whose cooperation it needed to repel Iraq from Kuwait in August 1990. But Palestinian terrorists could still have been working out of Damascus without implicating the Syrian government. Amid conflicting reports about whether the bomb was planted in Frankfurt or Malta, an internal Pan Am theory posited that the bomb was not targeted at Americans in general but at a rogue CIA unit, active in Lebanon. One of the victims, Major Charles McKee of the US Defense Intelligence Agency,

was returning to the US from Beirut, where it was thought he was trying to locate some American hostages being held by the terrorist group Hezbollah.

Other Lockerbie-watchers speculated that the CIA were raising funds to free the hostages through a drugs ring set up by Israeli Mossad agents. This theory was accepted recently by 50 per cent of visitors to Al Jazeera's website: 42 percent doubted it.

The evidence

Those hoping that the Libyan conviction had sealed the matter got a jolt in an interview that the Libyan prime minister gave to the BBC on February 24th, 2004, six months after Libya had formally accepted responsibility and offered compensation of $2.7billion, or about $10million per victim.

Prime Minister Shukri Ghanem stated plainly that his country had paid the compensation as a "price for peace" and to secure the lifting of UN sanctions, which were indeed lifted on September 12th, 2003.

To anyone listening, it was pretty clear that Libya regarded Megrahi's imprisonment as a small price to pay for reopening trade links. Against such a background, it is no wonder that a mass of conflicting theories have grown up.

The verdict

Emotions are, understandably, still very raw about Pan Am 103. The bereaved families are faced with an appalling choice: to continue to grapple with the complex and seemingly insoluble geopolitical aftermath of the crash, or to concentrate on coping with their loss.

1989
THE SMEARING OF COLIN WALLACE

Former Northern Ireland information officer framed for killing in a bid to silence "dirty tricks" claims

Captain Colin Wallace worked for the British Army's Information Policy Unit in Northern Ireland, at the height of the conflict between Catholics and Protestants. Wallace's job was to brief the media and spread "black propaganda" – disinformation aimed at the IRA and its political wing, Sinn Fein. Wallace later alleged collusion between army intelligence and protestant paramilitary groups to assassinate IRA members. He also told of an MI5 smear campaign, "Clockwork Orange," falsely alleging links between members of Harold Wilson's Labour government and both the IRA and KGB, and of a plot by the USSR to destabilize

Northern Ireland. Wallace further reported on a child abuse scandal at Kincora Boys' Home, in Northern Ireland. This was covered up, he said, because the home was run by William McGrath, an extreme protestant paramilitary on MI5's payroll. Wallace refused to cooperate over the Wilson plot, which he regarded as "unconstitutional," and complained about the Kincora cover-up. He was subsequently framed for passing classified information to a journalist and sacked. Wallace later wrote to Wilson regarding the MI5 plot, but shortly after was arrested for killing a friend, Jonathan Lewis, who was found drowned in the River Arun with a head injury.

Wallace was convicted of manslaughter in 1981 and served six years of a ten-year jail term. His case was highlighted in the book, *Who Framed Colin Wallace?*, by journalist Paul Foot. In 1990, Wallace received £30,000 compensation for unfair dismissal from the army and, in 1996, an appeal court quashed the manslaughter conviction.

See also: *Harold Wilson was Communist Stooge p.146; Harold Wilson, the CIA, and MI5 p.153; John Stalker Affair p.155; Spycatcher p.157*

1989
OPERATION BLUEBOOK – CIA PLOT TO BUY NUKES

Conman claims US intelligence was behind secret plan to use plundered gold to buy Russian A-bombs

When American conman, John Patrick Savage, died of cancer in August 1995, aged 39, he left behind a complex web of claims and counterclaims of a multi-million dollar scam that involved intelligence agencies, law enforcement departments, and financial institutions on both sides of the Atlantic. Such was Savage's murky world of lies and deceit that the full facts may never be known. The claim is of an audacious CIA plot, codenamed "Operation Bluebook," to buy up Russian nuclear weapons expected to flood the market following the break-up of the USSR. The Russian mafias were feared to be planning to use corrupt military leaders to access Soviet nuclear stockpiles and sell them on to rogue states and terrorist groups. It was alleged that agents acting for CIA director, John M. Deutch, approached Savage to act as intermediary to obtain the weapons, while keeping the CIA's involvement secret.

Savage's shady past and underworld contacts made him an obvious choice. His business partner, Charles Deacon, a lawyer from Staffordshire, England, provided a veneer of respectability. As cover, Savage claimed to have access to illegal funds, including plundered Nazi gold and the wealth of former Philippine president, Ferdinand Marcos. Ready cash for the transaction was obtained from various sources, including $8million from Monarch Assurance plc, based in Isle of Man, and all were promised a huge return on their investments. The sale never went ahead. Following Savage's death, Monarch sued the CIA, but lost when the agency hid behind a cloak of secrecy, claiming national security.

1990
PROJECT BABYLON: IRAQI SUPERGUN AND GERALD BULL

Inventor Gerald Bull was murdered by Mossad

The development of ballistic missiles during World War II made the idea of giant, ultra-long range artillery largely obsolete, but British engineer Gerald Vincent Bull (1928–90) was obsessed by the idea of building a huge "supergun" that could launch a satellite into space.

Even though the major military powers had abandoned work on very large ordinance, Bull was determined to continue his research. This led him into the shadowy world of illegal arms dealing with nations who were internationally prohibited from purchasing advanced weapons technology. Following his dream of eventually building a "space gun", he had designed long-range guns for South Africa at the behest of the CIA. He also worked for Chile, Taiwan and China, creating the G5 howitzer that he sold to fund his research. In 1980, the G5 caused him to fall foul of the Carter administration, and Bull spent six months in jail for illegal arms dealing, but emerged just as determined to fire a shell into orbit. His ambition seemed about to be realized in the mid-1980s when he convinced Saddam Hussein that Iraq would never have superpower status without a space programme. A secret deal was made for "Project Babylon" or the "PC-2 machine"; a gun 150m (164yd) long, weighing 2,100 tonnes (2,066 tons), that could a put 2,000kg (4,409lb) projectile into orbit. Although it would have orbital capability, it could also drop a projectile on Tehran or Tel Aviv.

On March 22nd, 1990, before the project could come to fruition, Bull was shot dead by two gunmen from close range in Brussels. No-one was ever arrested and the generally accepted theory is that Mossad organized his murder because his secret project in Iraq constituted too much of a threat to Israel.

1990
LEO WANTA AND THE CRASH
OF THE RUSSIAN ROUBLE
US arms dealer was part of CIA plot to destabilize
Russia by undermining its currency

Arms dealer Leo Wanta claimed involvement in a CIA-backed
plot to destabilize the Russian economy. Wanta, president
of American-based weapons exporter AmeriChina Global
Management Group Inc, was jailed for eight years in 1995
for false accounting and tax evasion; charges, that he said
were trumped up by officials of the American Justice and
Revenue departments to discredit him.

Wanta claimed that he couldn't owe the government
money because at the time alleged he was abroad, working
for the CIA. Wanta's involvement in the Russian currency
plot was first aired in Claire Sterling's book on global organized crime, *Thieves World* (1994). Sterling said Wanta and
other white-collar crooks took advantage of the chaos left
by the USSR's collapse to obtain false export licences from
corrupt Russian bureaucrats and make huge profits by selling guns and raw materials. Wanta also sought control of
international rouble markets in order to depress the currency's value, a plot that Wanta claimed was CIA-inspired.
According to Wanta, the CIA reasoned that an economically
weakened Russia could no longer maintain its hold over
troubled states such as Chechnya, so removing any threat
of a resurgent USSR. Wanta was previously involved in the
abortive sale of assault rifles and semi-automatic pistols to
Panamanian military leader Manuel Noriega, just before the
general was ousted by a US invasion force in 1989. The sale
– revealed in a leaked memo – may have been a CIA scam
to suggest Noriega was planning a stand against US forces,
so justifying the need for immediate military intervention.

See also: *Operation Bluebook – CIA Plot to Buy Nukes
p.159; KGB Plot to Poison Yushchenko p.173*

1990
OPEN VERDICT
Authorities played down mystery fate of 25 British
scientists linked to US Star Wars programme

In the eight years to 1990, at least 25 electronics experts
working for the British defence industry died in violent or
mysterious circumstances. Over half the deaths were in
the period from January–June 1987: four in car crashes,
three from carbon monoxide poisoning, two suffocated "by

accident," one fell to his death, one drowned, and one
overdosed on drugs. Only one died of "natural" causes.
Subsequent inquests recorded "open" verdicts, or death by
"accident" or "misadventure." During this period, another
scientist survived a near-fatal fall. Yet another disappeared,
only to reappear months later "dazed and confused."

The rising death toll prompted calls for an enquiry from
relatives of the deceased, politicians and trade union leaders. Even the US Defense Department expressed concern.
But the UK government has refused all requests to investigate. To this day, the reason for this spate of fatalities
remains a mystery. However, strong links between the scientists have emerged. All worked for the UK's Ministry of
Defence, or defence contractors such as Plessey, Marconi
and its sister company Easams. Many were involved in high-
tech research for the US government's Star Wars programme
– a laser ray system intended to shoot down nuclear missiles
in space. If a conspiracy lies behind the deaths, no group
or motive has yet emerged. Predictably, some speculate
that extraterrestrial forces are at work, attempting to halt
a potential threat to their spacecraft. However, if the UK
or US governments have evidence of involvement by inter-
galactic aliens, they're keeping quiet.

See also: *Dead Microbiologists – the Toll Mounts p.169*

1993
FBI STORM BRANCH
DAVIDIANS AT WACO
The BATF and FBI over-reacted at Ruby Ridge
and Waco

After a siege that lasted 51-days, FBI agents stormed the
ranch compound of a religious sect known as the Branch
Davidians at Mount Carmel, near Waco, Texas. The compound
was completely consumed by fire, and 75 men, women, and
children were killed.

The story of the Siege of Waco could be said to have
started with the authorities' growing awareness, in the late
1980s, of the existence of a right-wing American underground in the US heartland that would later be dubbed the
militia movement. A loose coalition of motorcycle outlaws,
illicit gun dealers, survivalists, and neo-Nazis, members
of this underground believed that the federal government
was ultimately controlled by the international New World
Order, which planned to turn the US into a slave state.
Infiltration of these groups by the Bureau of Alcohol,
Tobacco and Firearms (BATF), and the FBI fed into this

FBI agents place Branch Davidian member, Ruth Riddle, on the ramp of a Bradley fighting vehicle during the fire at the compound.

climate of suspicion and conspiracy. At the same time, the BATF and the FBI showed a marked lack of responsibility in the way that they dealt with these often unstable and highly paranoid groups and individuals. This irresponsibility culminated in a massive show of force over a comparatively minor gun law infraction.

In 1992 at Ruby Ridge in rural Idaho, a force of FBI agents – it would eventually number several hundred, in full combat dress – attempted to serve a warrant on an individual named Randy Weaver. A religious survivalist, Weaver and his family had opted out of the mainstream, but Weaver had become involved in dealing some sawn-off shotguns to bikers. The attempt to apprehend Weaver ended in a standoff, in which the FBI allegedly fired first; Weaver's wife, son, and dog were subsequently killed. Although Weaver was found innocent of all serious charges, and the surviving members of his family won $3.1million in civil damages, the FBI's show of force confirmed the militia movement's belief that the federal government were out to get them, and would use any force necessary to do so.

Thus, when on February 28th, 1993, the BATF raided the Branch Davidian compound near Waco, those inside, with Ruby Ridge fresh in their memories, expected the worst.

BATF search warrants alleged that the sect – a breakaway group from the Seventh-Day Adventist church – might be converting semi-automatic weapons to full auto capability. Texas newspapers had also hinted that sect leader David Koresh had abused children, and that Koresh advocated polygamy, and had married several female followers. In this climate of mutual tension and suspicion, the BATF seemed deliberately to confirm that everything the Davidians feared was coming at them in deadly paramilitary force. A full-scale firefight ensued, leaving four agents and five Davidians dead, and with the BATF in full retreat. In a condition of armed standoff, the FBI took command, surrounded the building, established contact with Koresh, and began a siege that was to last for 51 days. During the siege Bradley Fighting Vehicles circled the building, helicopters almost continuously clattered overhead, and deafening music and noise were broadcast at the compound. Koresh, seriously injured by a gunshot wound, negotiated delays, but his biblical imagery alienated the FBI, and, on April 19th, US Attorney General Janet Reno approved a final assault after being told children were being abused inside the complex. Armoured vehicles retrofitted for gas warfare began smashing down the compound's walls. A few Davidians emerged but most remained even when fire engulfed the building. This spread at an alarming rate, consuming everything as the world watched on live TV.

The conspiracy theory

Many contend that first the BATF and then the FBI brutally overreacted, first at Ruby Ridge and then at Waco. The FBI had characterized Koresh and his followers as "insane'" but then used psych-war techniques to drive them crazy, and totally ignored biblical experts who might have made sense of Koresh's statements. When the final attack turned deadly, the two agencies conspired to close ranks and cover up their recklessness.

The evidence

Much hinges on the cause of the fatal fire. The government claims it was intentionally set by Koresh and his followers in an act of mass suicide. Others contend that the fire was started by the FBI's firing of flammable CS gas grenades into the wooden buildings of the compound. Critics note that CS gas was pumped into the buildings by armoured vehicles immediately before the fire broke out, while the FBI allegedly fired weapons and stun grenades into the compound. Bright flashes in aerial infrared recordings certainly resemble heat signatures of gunfire. That fire crews were prohibited access to the burning buildings until they had been reduced to ashes has also led many people to question the motivations of the FBI. Autopsies revealed that some of the women and children died of skull injuries; they had been behind a wall that was in the path of one of the Bradley Fighting Vehicles. The bodies of other children were locked in postures like those that would have been caused by cyanide poisoning produced by burning CS gas.

The verdict

Although the FBI continue to stick to their increasingly disbelieved story they must, at the very least, be held responsible not only for exacerbating an already volatile situation, but for creating a climate of rage and paranoia that may well have resulted in the Oklahoma bombing exactly two years later.

See also: *Oklahoma City Bombing p.163*

1993
DEATH OF VINCE FOSTER
Suicide of deputy White House counsel was suspicious

Vincent Foster, deputy White House counsel to Bill Clinton, committed suicide by shooting himself through the back of the head. His death triggered a welter of conspiracy theories from the far right.

Vince Foster was a friend of Bill and Hillary Clinton and a partner with Hillary in the Rose Law Firm in Little Rock, Arkansas. When Clinton became president in 1992, Foster was picked as deputy White House counsel. In his new job, he had found himself involved in various Clinton legal matters, including Whitewater, a shady and unprofitable land deal that probably would never have received any attention had not Clinton's political enemies (part of what Hillary dubbed "the vast right-wing conspiracy") attempted to use it against him. Foster found himself constantly fending off attacks on the Clintons, including a minor furor about corruption in the White House Travel Office. The strain of political life in Washington DC seemed to be taking its toll on the Arkansas lawyer. He was suffering from depression, but no-one expected that on July 20th, 1993, his body would be discovered in Fort Marcy Park, in Virginia, dead from a self-inflicted gunshot wound to the head. A scribbled note was discovered a week later. "I was not meant for the job or the spotlight of public life in Washington. Here ruining people is considered sport." The fact that no bullet fragments were found at the site, and very little blood was present, caused suspicions to mushroom that the body had been moved from somewhere else; the suspicions increased when the White House, allegedly, tried to restrict access to Foster's files.

The conspiracy theory

Theorists are divided into two basic groups on the issue of Foster's death. Some maintain that Foster committed suicide in a location or in such away that would have embarrassed the Clinton administration, and that government agents moved his corpse to the park. Others suspect that Foster was murdered, shot in the neck by a small-calibre pistol, to stop him revealing damaging information he held with respect to the Clintons and other high-level officials. At the far extremes, Foster was fingered as some kind of super-spy, an overseer of an NSA project to spy on banking transactions, and that he was murdered by the Israeli secret service, Mossad.

The evidence

Most of the above allegations of foul play in the Foster death originated with Christopher Ruddy, a reporter for a small-town newspaper in Pennsylvania owned by billionaire arch-conservative Richard Mellon Scaife, and the Western Journalism Center, a non-profit institution supporting "independent journalism," which is primarily funded by Scaife. Below is a sample of allegations seized on by independent counsel, Ken Starr, during his $39.2 million, four-and-half-year investigation of the Clinton administration:

1. Foster's head was moved after his death. (His head was indeed moved by rescue workers, as was consistent with a routine procedure to verify that he was, in fact, dead.) 2. Suspicious carpet fibres were found on Foster's clothes. (The fibres were tested and determined to have come from Foster's house.) 3. No fingerprints were found on the trigger of the gun. (The gun's handle was textured, not smooth; the FBI stated that this type of surface was unlikely to retain prints.) 4. Foster's car keys were not found on his person at the scene. (Foster's pockets were patted down briefly on the scene and the keys were not found. Police went to the morgue a few hours later and turned the pockets out, where they found the keys.)

The verdict

If, after spending $6 million on two separate law enforcement investigations, Kenneth Starr could not tie Clinton to Foster's death, and had to content himself with harassing Clinton via the Monica Lewinsky sex scandal, it may be safe to assume that Vincent Foster committed suicide.

See also: *Sexgate p.166*

1994
ALDRICH AMES: THE MILLIONAIRE SPY
CIA agent Ames sold secrets to the Russians

In a conspiracy based on nothing more than a wife's greed, Aldrich Ames (who was born in Wisconsin in 1941) effectively shut down CIA operations in the USSR in 1985 by selling the Soviets the names of every "human asset" the US had working there.

Twenty-four men and one woman were immediately arrested and ten were sentenced to what the KGB euphemistically referred to as *vyshaya mera* (the highest measure of punishment): each of the condemned was taken into a room, made to kneel, then shot in the back of the

head with a large-calibre handgun, and then buried in a secret, unmarked grave. For his services the KGB paid Ames, a second-generation CIA employee, more than $2million and held another $2million for him in a Moscow bank, making him the highest-paid spy ever.

Ames was no communist sympathizer, however; he was simply an alcoholic who could not keep up with the spending habits of his attractive Colombian-born wife, Rosario. The Russian money allowed them to enjoy a lifestyle far beyond a CIA officer's pay. The Ames were arrested on February 21st, 1994 by the FBI, and proved to be an acute embarrassment to the CIA – they had failed to notice obvious details indicating that something was amiss, such as Ames' habit of driving to work in a new Jaguar that cost more than his annual salary. Ames received a sentence of life imprisonment, while his wife received a five-year prison sentence for conspiracy to commit espionage and tax evasion as part of a plea-bargain by Ames.

1996
OKLAHOMA CITY BOMBING
Timothy McVeigh and Terry Nichols did not act alone

Prior to the September 11th, 2001 attack on the World Trade Center, the bombing of the Alfred P. Murrah Federal Building in Oklahoma City in 1995 was the most deadly peacetime attack on American soil. The bomb killed 168 people, including 19 children, and injured more than 500 others.

On April 19th, 1995, just before 9am, a yellow Ryder Rental truck stopped outside the Alfred P. Murrah Federal Building in Oklahoma City. The driver walked away, and at 9.02am, the truck, loaded with 2,200kg (4,850lb) of ammonium nitrate and fuel oil, exploded. It tore the front from the nine-story building, the north side disintegrated, traffic signs and parking metres were ripped from the pavement, and pedestrians were injured blocks away. Fifteen children died in the building's second-floor nursery, and rescuers took almost six weeks to recover all the bodies from the rubble.

Timothy McVeigh, a Gulf War veteran, was arrested by an Oklahoma highway patrolman within an hour of the explosion on minor charges. The attack was staged on the second anniversary of the deaths of the 82 Branch Davidians who died in their compound near Waco, Texas, whom McVeigh believed had been murdered by the federal government. McVeigh is thought to have modelled the bombing on a similar event described in *The Turner Diaries*, a novel by former American Nazi, William Pierce, writing under the name, Andrew Macdonald, in which the hero, Earl Turner, starts a

Nothing but rubble remains of the front side of the destroyed Federal Building in the Oklahoma City bombing aftermath, April 19th, 1995.

white uprising against "inferior races" by truck-bombing FBI headquarters. Timothy McVeigh was sentenced to death for the Oklahoma bombing, and executed by lethal injection at the federal penitentiary in Terre Haute, Indiana, on June 11th, 2001. An accomplice, Terry Nichols, was sentenced to life in prison.

The initial hunt had been for Islamic terrorists but, with McVeigh in custody, media and law enforcement turned their focus to the militia movement, and how they might constitute a major internal threat. Militia members, however, refused to believe that McVeigh and Nichols were the "lone bombers," and, as time has passed, more credible weight was added to the doubts that McVeigh acted alone, or acted at all.

The conspiracy theories

The accepted story is that Timothy McVeigh and Terry Nichols performed the final act in a drama that began with the attack on the Weaver family at Ruby Ridge, and escalated to the siege at Waco. But others find this less than satisfactory. Eminent author and commentator, Gore Vidal, summed up many of these concerns in a 2001 article in *Vanity Fair* titled The McVeigh Conspiracy. Vidal heavily criticized the FBI, who, he shows, failed to investigate many

promising leads that could have lead to the identity of McVeigh's accomplices, and argues that the McVeigh-Nichols scenario is unlikely and makes no sense. Vidal suggests that McVeigh could have been working with Arab terrorists, or anti-government terrorists, or even ("who knows?") government agents. He suggests that even the "grandest conspiracy theory of all" is a possibility – that McVeigh neither built nor detonated a bomb, and was a patsy, but that he wanted to be executed as a martyr rather than face the prospect of "living in a prison cell for 50 years with the threat of rape an everyday fear."

The evidence

A number of important questions concerning the McVeigh conviction remain unanswered and, until they have been answered, the various theories listed above cannot be dismissed. For example, how could McVeigh and Nichols have built a 2,177kg (4,800lb) ANFO bomb on the evening before the bombing – as the government claims – when bomb experts claim it would have been impossible? Why were no BATF or FBI agents in their offices at the time of the blast? Stories circulate of a classified Pentagon study proving that the Oklahoma bombing was caused by more than one bomb, perhaps as many as five. Seismograph readouts at the

University of Oklahoma, allegedly, indicate more than one blast impulse, and independent ordnance experts have claimed that a car-bomb with low intensity fertilizer explosives could not have inflicted such extensive damage to the building unless high-intensity explosives had been wired directly to its supporting columns.

The verdict

Timothy McVeigh was executed at Terre Haute federal prison in Indiana, and the government has very firmly decreed the case closed. With all that has happened since, it is likely to remain that way. The vital questions thus remain unanswered.

See also: *FBI Storm Branch Davidians at Waco p.160*

1996
THE ECHELON DICTIONARY EXPOSED

Software program was used to spy on telecoms traffic

For 40 years, New Zealand's largest intelligence agency, the Government Communications Security Bureau (GCSB) helped its Western allies to spy on countries throughout the Pacific region using the ECHELON system. Designed and coordinated by the American National Security Agency, ECHELON is used to intercept ordinary email, fax, telex, and telephone communications carried over the world's telecommunications networks and potentially effects every person communicating between countries anywhere in the world. ECHELON was first exposed in 1996 by journalist Nicky Hagar in his book, *Secret Power*.

Hagar revealed how ECHELON uses the dictionary computer program that reads every word and number in every single global message, seeking target keywords and numbers. The same is happening at the other satellite tracking stations run by the NSA – in Australia (Geraldton), England (Morwenstow), the US (Sugar Grove and Yakima). Although, at the time, Hagar created a storm of protest at spooks who considered themselves free to read anyone's email, it has since been shown that the volume of world communication is simply too vast even for ECHELON. As was proved in the aftermath of 9/11, the best that can be achieved is a recognition of spikes in "chatter" on specific subjects in specific areas, and the FBI were forced to admit to the American 9/11 commission that they had months of possibly suspicious correspondence backed up that needed to be read by human agents.

1996
THE CIA FLOODED GHETTOS WITH CHEAP CRACK COCAINE

CIA introduced crack cocaine into LA street gangs in the 1980s to finance the Nicaraguan Contras

In a series of 1996 articles published in the *San Jose Mercury News*, reporter, Gary Webb, chronicled the drug-dealing activities of the Nicaraguan Democratic Forces (FDN) – the Contras – who reportedly sold "tons" of cocaine to street gangs in South Central Los Angeles. Backed by a wealth of documentation, Webb recounted how raw cocaine, easily cooked into cheap, smokeable "crack" was imported by the Nicaraguans – totally protected from prosecution and supported by the CIA – and sold at cut-rate prices, helping to spark the explosion of crack use in Los Angeles and other American cities in the early 1980s.

Previously, cocaine had been processed into its very expensive powder form to be consumed by the wealthy elite of the drug culture, such as rock stars, movie actors, and big-time lawyers. However, the new development of selling the cheaper cocaine base as rocks that could be smoked was seen as offering a great financial opportunity by the Contras and their backers inside the CIA, and the Reagan administration. Unlike powdered coke, crack was cheap enough to be broken down and sold in five- and ten-dollar increments, making it ideal for street sale in poor neighbourhoods, and opening up a whole new market. After legal US funding to the FDN had been cut off, the CIA, unwilling to "allow" Nicaragua to be governed by the communist Sandinistas, were casting around for sources of covert funds, and the potential profits of this new drug trade were just too tempting to ignore.

The conspiracy theories

That the CIA was involved in drug trafficking was hardly a revelation. In the spy game, drugs had always represented an easy and untraceable form of currency. Heroin and cocaine are less bulky than gold, and more easily obtained than diamonds. By their very illegality, drugs left no paper trail, and had the added advantage of actually increasing in value each time a consignment changed hands.

The CIA has a long history of drug dealing. During the Vietnam war, agents in South East Asia, with planes chartered from the CIA front operation Air America, ran opium out of Laos and into Thailand; much of it was processed into heroin and was later used by US troops in the field. When the US backed the mujahadeen rebels in Afghanistan, the

CIA actively encouraged the sale of opium to help finance the battle against the Soviet occupation in the 1980s. Thus Gary Webb's revelations came as no surprise to anyone who was familiar with the CIA's methods, and they also reinforced conspiracy theories deeply held by some Afro-Americans, going back to rumours that the government had used heroin to weaken the Black Panther party and other black nationalist groups of the 1960s.

The crack epidemic was viewed by the CIA as being beneficial in two ways. First, it made money for the CIA – and it was money whose expenditure never had to be justified to any oversight committee. Second, the resulting addiction was effectively a way of maintaining a brutal social control over some of the poorest but potentially most volatile sections of the population.

The evidence

Gary Webb identified Danilo Blandon, a former Nicaraguan government official, as the conduit for thousands of kilos (pounds) of cocaine that flowed to the Los Angeles street gangs between 1982 and 1986. Blandon, who pleaded guilty to cocaine trafficking charges in 1992, and then went to work for the American Drug Enforcement Administration, recently testified in federal court that he sold the cocaine in the city's black neighbourhoods as a way to raise money for the guerrilla army seeking to overthrow a revolutionary socialist government. His biggest customer had been drug kingpin, Rick "Freeway" Ross. Ross is now in jail, having been set up by Blandon in a 1994 bust. The Blandon case dovetailed with early revelations of CIA involvement in the coke business that came after a C-123K military cargo plane, owned by cocaine runner Barry Seal, crashed in Nicaragua in 1986 with weapons and CIA employees on board. (This had exposed the CIA traffic centered on Mena, Arkansas, airport, from where weapons were being flown out to the Contras then sent back loaded with cocaine.)

The verdict

Gary Webb's exposé created a furor. The then-director of the CIA, John Deutch, ordered the agency's inspector general to look into the allegations, but he has also said that he did not believe they were true. A 1988 CIA study concluded that the CIA "neither participated in or condoned drug trafficking by Contra forces" but Eric Sterling, a Judiciary Committee staffer who oversaw drug policy during that period, said congressional staff members never had the time or resources to fully investigate leads on drug trafficking. The situation was complicated in December 2004

when Gary Webb committed suicide in what some considered to be less than plausible circumstances.

See also: *Barry Seal p.68; Gary Webb p.79*

1996
LIPPOGATE
Asian financial conglomerate bankrolled Democratic party in return for renewed Vietnam trading links

The Lippo Group is a huge banking, finance and real estate conglomerate based in Jakarta, Indonesia. From 1991 to 1996 Lippo made illegal contributions of up to $700,000 to the Democratic party to fund its 1992 and 1996 US presidential campaigns. The money was in return for the Clinton administration normalizing diplomatic and trade relations with Vietnam, where Lippo has real estate and investment holdings amounting to $6.9 billion. The 30-year-old trade embargo with Vietnam was duly lifted in 1994 and diplomatic relations were restored in 1995. Lippo was founded in the 1960s by Mochtar Riady, an Indonesia-born ethnic Chinese. Donations to the Democrats were controlled by Riady's son, James, and other businessmen with links to the banking group, such as Charles Yah Lin Trie, a longtime friend of the ex-president, and former restaurateur in Clinton's home town of Little Rock, Arkansas. Lippo has extensive interests throughout the Far East, including mainland China and Hong Kong. It also owns the former Bank of Trade, now Lippo Bank, in Los Angeles, and is in partnership with First Union Corp., which owns Boatman's Bank in Little Rock. James Riady is a director of Boatman's. Lippo has other links with Little Rock and the Clintons. A former partner of Hillary Clinton at the Rose Law Firm in Little Rock was hired by Lippo for a reported fee of $100,000. In 1997, following an investigation by the House Government Reform and Oversight Committee, the Democratic party was forced to refund most of the donation.

See also: *Clinton a "CIA Spy" at Oxford p.170*

1998
SEXGATE
Kenneth Starr and the right-wing anti-Clinton conspiracy

In 1995, Monica Samille Lewinsky (born 1973) was hired as an intern at the White House during President Bill Clinton's first term in office. She had apparently fantasized about the

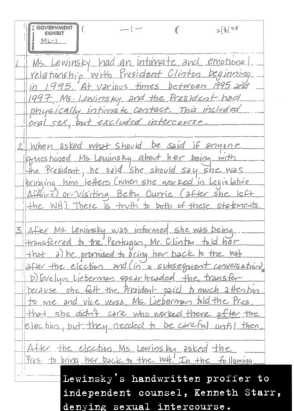

GOVERNMENT EXHIBIT ML-1 — 1 — 2/H/98

1. Ms. Lewinsky had an intimate and emotional relationship with President Clinton beginning in 1995. At various times between 1995 and 1997, Ms. Lewinsky and the President had physically intimate contact. This included oral sex, but excluded intercourse.

2. When asked what should be said if anyone questioned Ms. Lewinsky about her being with the President, he said she should say she was bringing him letters (when she worked in Legislative Affairs) or visiting Betty Currie (after she left the WH). There is truth to both of these statements.

3. After Ms. Lewinsky was informed she was being transferred to the Pentagon, Mr. Clinton told her that a) he promised to bring her back to the WH after the election and (in a subsequent conversation) b) Evelyn Lieberman spear-headed the transfer because she felt the President paid too much attention to me and vice versa. Ms. Lieberman told the Pres. that she didn't care who worked there after the election, but they needed to be careful until then.

After the election, Ms. Lewinsky asked the Pres. to bring her back to the WH. In the following

Lewinsky's handwritten proffer to independent counsel, Kenneth Starr, denying sexual intercourse.

president romantically, and after much flirting, the two engaged in oral sex. Lewinsky confided details of the relationship to her supposed friend Linda Tripp, a 48-year-old hold-over from the Bush administration. Tripp recorded their phone conversations, and eventually delivered the tapes to Kenneth Starr, the independent counsel appointed by Congress to investigate the president on various Arkansas land deals, including one known as Whitewater.

Hillary Clinton called the Starr investigation part of "a vast right-wing conspiracy", and other Democrats saw him as a repressed political zealot on a mission to remove President Clinton. Certainly, Starr had spent an estimated $39.2million attempting – but failing – to find evidence of Clinton wrongdoing, and the Lewinsky affair provided him with a final chance to justify his efforts.

Clinton denied having sexual intercourse with Lewinsky, stating that: "I did not have sexual relations with that woman, Miss Lewinsky." However, under intense FBI pressure, Lewinsky admitted that her relationship with Clinton involved oral sex in the Oval Office (including the infamous use of a cigar) and this eventually led to an attempt to impeach President Clinton on allegations of perjury. The

Senate, however, found Clinton not guilty on both counts on February 12th, 1999. Oddly, Clinton's approval ratings actually increased during the scandal.

See also: *Death of Vince Foster p.162*

1999
CIA BOMBED THE CHINESE EMBASSY IN YUGOSLAVIA
The CIA purposely targeted Chinese embassy in former Yugoslavia

When an American aircraft, acting as part of a Nato force, bombed the Chinese Embassy in Belgrade, Yugoslavia on May 7th, 1999, it was defended as having been an accident. The real target was the Yugoslav Directorate of Supply and Procurement, a military supply facility that occupied a building nearby. Many critics, however, including the British newspaper the *Observer*, have claimed that the bombing was intentional and engineered by the CIA. The *Observer* cited sources who alleged that the Chinese Embassy was deliberately targeted because the Chinese were providing communications support to the Yugoslav army, and possibly to the paramilitary group known as the Tigers, formerly led by Zeljko Raznatovic, "Arkan," who was later assassinated in a Belgrade hotel. Chinese officials accused the US of striking the embassy to punish China for representing Yugoslav diplomatic interests in Washington DC.

Another theory claims that the "accidental" bombing was part of an internal power struggle between the White House, the Pentagon, the CIA and other elements within the US political and military establishment. According to this claim, President Bill Clinton, who was in his final year in office (and disliked by many senior officers at the Pentagon), knew nothing about the attack. The bombing was designed to embarrass the Clinton administration, escalate the war, and force whoever followed Clinton, whether it be Vice President Al Gore or George W. Bush, the governor of Texas, to pursue an even more militarist agenda.

2000
STEALING THE ELECTION
The Florida result was fixed

November 7th, 2000 was election day in the US, and shortly before 8pm, the TV networks estimated that Vice President Al Gore had beaten George W. Bush in the key state of Florida. Later, however, the networks were forced to retract

In the Florida recount, an observer for the Republicans (or GOP – Grand Old Party) keeps an eye on the ballots as he looks through a chad hole.

the estimate. Gore conceded the election but when Bush's lead shrank dramatically, Gore retracted his concession. In the following days the Florida vote was counted and re-counted, until the Supreme Court finally declared Bush the winner in Florida and, therefore, president.

In the meantime, the nation's focus was on Florida and serious questions were being raised about the conduct of the election there. So many different examples of possible ballot rigging presented themselves: the punch card "but-terfly ballot"; the exclusion of black voters from polling places; the "scrubbing" of supposed felons from electoral roles; missing ballots that weren't even counted; and even that the entire voting process was overseen by Florida governor Jeb Bush (the candidate's younger brother and his protégées Sandra Mortham and Katherine Harris). Suspicions were rife that the Republicans and the Bush fam-ily had conspired to fix the presidential election, and with George H.W. Bush having been a former CIA director, the suggestion was made that the intelligence community might have been involved, although no solid evidence has ever been produced. Deliberate fraud has also never been proved, but the cloud over Florida was sufficient to make Democrat voters careful when going to the polls in 2004.

2001
THE STARGATE CONSPIRACY
Psi-op, or preparing humans for an alien takeover?

The Stargate conspiracy should not be confused with the CIA's remote viewing operation of the same name; this so-called Stargate conspiracy takes the sceptic and believer alike completely through the looking glass and attempts to be all things to all people.

The core of the conspiracy is that various elements of the intelligence community, especially the Air Force Office of Special Intelligence (AFOSI) have for a long time deliber-ately been feeding the public *X-Files*-type disinformation. This covered a range of cult subjects such as UFOs, Area 51, extraterrestrials, the Philadelphia Experiment, and the so-called "Majic 12" documents (claiming that a group of 12 Truman-era scientists had concealed the "truth" about the Roswell flying saucer crash). Stargate operatives, theorists claim, have even worked on the minds of UFO researchers: individuals such as Area 51 expert Paul Bennewitz, who was driven into a paranoid nervous breakdown.

The reasons for such a bizarre and long-running operation – and such a ludicrous expenditure of taxpayers' money –

vary according to whoever is making the claim. One school believes that it is an elaborate and continuing experiment in psychological mass manipulation, a test of human gullibility and its possible application in Psi-War. Another school argues that humanity is subtly being prepared for a future announcement that is far worse and more alien than anything conspiracists have imagined to date.

See also: *Real "Men in Black" – Majic 12 p.140; MKULTRA p.143; Psi-War: Operations Grillflame and Stargate p.153*

2002
FORGERY OF NIGER URANIUM DOCUMENTS

The French were behind the forgery of the documents that helped justify the invasion of Iraq

The charge that Iraq was seeking to buy nuclear material in Africa – used by the UK and the US as justification for the invasion of Iraq – was based mainly on documents that the International Atomic Energy Agency concluded in March 2002 were forged.

The director of the CIA and a senior national security advisor took the blame for allowing the allegation to be used as part of the rationale for going to war, despite the CIA's long-held doubts about its credibility.

For once the CIA's hands would appear to be clean, but the question remains: who created the forgery? According to Italian diplomats, France was behind the forged documents, which appeared to prove that Iraq was seeking "yellow-cake" uranium in Niger. The diplomats claim that France's intelligence service used an Italian-born middleman to circulate a mixture of genuine and bogus documents to "trap" the two leading proponents of war with Saddam Hussein into making unsupportable claims.

The papers found their way to the CIA and to MI6, and, in September 2002, British prime minister, Tony Blair, accused Saddam of seeking "significant quantities" of uranium from an "undisclosed African country." President George W. Bush made a similar claim in his State of the Union address four months later. The French made a counter-claim that the Italian government had forged the documents to help to justify the war in Iraq. The furor went on for some time until overtaken by events.

2003
DEAD MICROBIOLOGISTS – THE TOLL MOUNTS

World scientists killed to protect American government-backed killer germ programme

When scientist Ian Langford's battered body was found at his home in Norwich, England on February 11th, 2003, it was one more addition to a mounting toll of dead microbiologists. This remarkable run of mystery deaths may involve as many as 14 of the world's top germ experts. The first death to attract the world's press to this phenomenon was that of research scientist, Benito Que, aged 52, who died in hospital on December 6th, 2002. Less than four weeks before, his unconscious body had been discovered in a street near the University of Miami Medical School, where he worked. Four days later (December 10th), Robert Schwartz, aged 57, was hacked to death at his home in Leesberg, Virginia. The following day, December 11th, scientist Set Van Nguyen, aged 44, suffocated in the airlock of a walk-in fridge at his laboratory in Victoria State, Australia. On December 20th, the dead body of Don C. Wiley, aged 57, was found in the Mississippi River. He had been missing since November 16th, when his rented car was found abandoned on a bridge near Memphis, Tennessee. Like Langford, all four were microbiologists involved in cutting-edge research into deadly diseases. Their fates were soon linked to the deaths of other germ scientists, including Russian defector and bioweapons expert Vladimir Pasechnik, aged 64, found dead near his home in Wiltshire, England, on November 23rd, 2002, and up to ten Israeli scientists killed in separate incidents, including two aircraft crashes, between October 4th and November 24th, 2002. More mystery deaths occurred in 2003: Vladimir Korshunov, aged 56, on February 8th, bludgeoned near his Moscow home, and finally that of Ian Langford, aged 40. All had knowledge relating to the genetic make-up of diseases such as anthrax, smallpox and the ebola virus, or their prevention. In each case, the deaths were mysterious and/or violent.

The conspiracy theory

The deaths were soon being connected with a germ warfare programme allegedly being developed on behalf of the US military. Many of the dead microbiologists had expertise in gene sequencing, the branch of molecular science that identifies the genetic code of all living organisms, from bacteria to human beings. The knowledge can be used to produce antibiotics and vaccinations that target specific diseases and also create drugs tailored to an individual's genetic profile. By combining this information, it would be possible to clone diseases that only affect – or leave untouched – specific racial groups. The conspiracy theory states that the microbiologists either knew about the germ warfare programme or were working on treatments that would have nullified its effects. Several commercial enterprises with links to the US military and/or intelligence agencies are implicated, including the Howard Hughes Medical Institute, based in Maryland, which provides funds for various public and, allegedly, secret research programmes, and which employed one of the dead scientists: Dr Wiley. Another is Hadron Advanced Biosystems of Virginia, which carries out medical biodefence research for the army. Also implicated is Dyncorp of Washington, which provides wide-ranging US defence-related services. The work carried out by the scientists might have compromised the programme.

The evidence

The evidence is circumstantial. Critics of the theory say that you can connect deaths in any sphere if you cast the net wide enough. By looking as far afield as Australia, Russia, the UK and the US, links can be inferred where none exist. Also, it is suggested, the world of microbiology is so specialized that all its leading figures can be connected. Backing the theory is the close proximity in dates, mostly a matter of months and, in some cases, separated by weeks or days. The violent and/or mysterious nature of the deaths lends extra support.

The verdict

Until corroboration of a link with germ warfare is forthcoming, for example, in the form of written proof or witness statements, this must remain just a theory. However, the deaths are certainly mysterious and, if nothing else, they show that careers in microbiology should get a danger warning, on a par with bomb disposal.

See also: *Open Verdict p.160*

2003
CLINTON A "CIA SPY" AT OXFORD

Former president acted as an intelligence agent, informing on US anti-war students at UK university

Journalist Christopher Hitchens alleged, in 2003, that former US president, Bill Clinton, had been a CIA agent while studying at Oxford University in England in the early 1970s. Hitchens, a long-term critic of the ex-president, made the claim in an interview in the right-wing quarterly publication, *Doublethink*. According to Hitchens, a contemporary of Clinton at Oxford: "somebody was giving information [to the CIA] about anti-war draft-resistors, and I think it was probably him." Hitchens was giving his slant on a story that had been circulating as a rumour since 1992, and which later surfaced in print in Roger Morris's 1996 biography of Bill and Hillary Clinton, *Partners in Power*. Morris had been a senior official at the National Security Council until he resigned, in 1970, over the bombing of Cambodia. Morris quotes three intelligence sources as saying Clinton was "an asset" to the CIA at Oxford by informing on the American students who made up the bulk of the university's highly vocal anti-Vietnam war protest movement. At the time, Clinton would have been eligible to fight in Vietnam, but gained an exemption in order to pursue a Rhodes scholarship at Oxford. One of Clinton's university friends, Richard Stearns, was international vice president of the CIA-funded National Student Association. If the CIA allegation is true, it may have been Stearns who recruited Clinton. From 1969 to 1971, before beginning his studies, Clinton embarked on a series of trips to Norway, Russia, Czechoslovakia, and – with Stearns – Spain. Some claim that these trips were CIA-sponsored.

See also: *Lippogate p.166*

2003
BLAIR AND THE MISSING IRAQ WMDS

British government fabricated the threat of Saddam's weapons stockpile to justify Iraq invasion

Before the invasion of Iraq, in 2003, British prime minister, Tony Blair, claimed that Saddam Hussein posed an imminent threat to world security. According to Blair, the Iraqi dictator had huge stockpiles of nuclear, chemical and biological weapons – and the ballistic missiles needed to deliver them. The danger was so serious that it made the need for the invasion of Iraq and the toppling of Saddam's regime overwhelming. Yet the case for war was far from water-tight. The Iraq Survey Group, a team of UN weapons inspectors led by Dr Hans Blix, had spent six months trying to locate Saddam's Weapons of Mass Destruction (WMDs) without success. Blix firmly believed that Saddam had destroyed his weapons following the first Gulf War, more than ten years earlier. And a full-scale search of Iraq by US military inspectors, following the invasion in 2003, proved Blix right. They found no sign of "Saddam's WMDs." In fact, documentary evidence produced to back up the WMD "threat" had been wildly inaccurate, comprising forged documents, falsified reports, and unsubstantiated claims. Some military experts now believe the evidence was fabricated simply to justify the invasion. If so, why?

The conspiracy theory

Various theories have emerged to explain the discrepancy between British government claims and the absence of WMDs. American president, George W. Bush, had made it clear he was resolved to invade Iraq come what may. Some conspiracy theorists say Blair saw potential advantages for the UK in supporting Bush's plans and so the ends justified the means. One view is that Blair believed his backing would allow him to exert greater influence on US policy over the Middle East, international trade, and global warming. Another is that Blair hoped to gain privileged access to oil supplies from a US-controlled Iraq and to share in highly lucrative postwar rebuilding contracts. Blair maintains he simply followed the advice of security chiefs when claiming Saddam posed a serious threat to UK and world peace. Yet senior British intelligence sources had expressed doubts about the WMD threat. Chemical weapons expert, Dr. David Kelly, told BBC reporter, Andrew Gilligan, that he regarded the WMD allegations as exaggerated. Kelly was later found dead after his identity as Gilligan's "mole" was made public.

The evidence

A UK Government dossier on the Saddam "threat," published in February 2003, and said to be a considered appraisal by British Intelligence, included large chunks of text plagiarized from a ten-year-old thesis written by Ibrahim al-Marashi, a Californian postgraduate student. Much of the text was copied verbatim, or altered to make the threat more sinister. Documents purporting to show that Saddam had obtained uranium for his nuclear weapons programme from Niger, an African republic, had already been denounced as forgeries by Joseph C. Wilson, a retired US ambassador who had investigated the Niger link on behalf of the CIA during 2002. Wilson found no evidence that Saddam sought – let alone obtained – nuclear material, yet Blair's government continued to make the claim. An allegation that Saddam had "chemical and biological weapons, which could be activated within 45 minutes" came from a single uncorroborated source, and referred to battlefield weapons only.

Dr Brian Jones, a retired Defence Intelligence Staff (DIS) official, said that there was no evidence Iraq had produced chemical and biological weapons since the first Gulf War and that "advice from DIS experts had been over-ruled" by the government's Joint Intelligence Committee (JIC). Robin Cook, a senior British government minister, who later resigned in protest over the war, said that Blair had told him he did not believe Saddam had usable WMDs.

The verdict

Lord Hutton's report into the death of Dr Kelly suggested the JIC may have been "subconsciously influenced" by Blair's desire to have a dossier that was "as strong as possible in relation to the threat posed by Saddam." In other words, security chiefs said what Blair wanted to hear. As to why Blair wanted the public to believe that Saddam posed a threat, only time can tell.

See also: *Dr David Kelly p.77; Iraq WMD Conspiracy p.234*

2004
MARK THATCHER AND THE EQUATORIAL GUINEA COUP
Question marks over UK and US government links to plot to overthrow corrupt African president

In a plot echoing Frederick Forsythe's blockbuster *Dogs of War*, a coup attempt to overthrow the corrupt president of an oil-rich African state was foiled days before its launch. The plot drew in former British prime minister, Margaret Thatcher's millionaire son Mark, who funded the hire of helicopters for use in the coup. He has now been fined $150,000 with a five-year suspended jail sentence, although denies all knowledge. More mysterious is the role played by UK and USA governments. Both had advance knowledge, but chose not to act. Could this, as some allege, suggest tacit involvement? The plot, to kill President Teodoro Obiang Ngeuema M'basogo of Equatorial Guinea and install exiled opposition leader Severo Moto, involved over 80 mercenaries, mostly former South Africa 32 Buffalo Battalion soldiers, led by ex-SAS officer Simon Mann and arms dealer Nick du Toit. It was funded by an international business syndicate led by UK-based Lebanese millionaire Eli "Smelly" Calil. President Obiang was to be lured to an airfield to be given the gift of some luxury vehicles flown in by Russian cargo plane. Mercenaries would exit the plane, kill Obiang, and take over Equatorial Guinea. The plot was uncovered by former SA Special Forces commander (and advisor to

Obiang) Johannes Smith, who was alerted by mercenary friends. He wrote months beforehand giving full details to British Foreign Office minister, Jack Straw, and Michael Westphal, advisor to American defence secretary, Donald Rumsfeld. Both governments took no action. In the event, Zimbabwean and Equatorial Guinea authorities, probably alerted by Smith, intercepted the mercenaries en route.

2005
CIA TORTURE HISTORY
Abu Ghraib was an aberration

Evidence of torture of prisoners in Iraq by American troops serves as a reminder of the previous use of torture by the CIA, and other intelligence agencies in the free world.

When the world's media ran the first pictures of the Iraqis being tortured in the military detention centre at Abu Ghraib in Iraq, the first response of the US military and the Bush administration to the universal shock and revulsion that the photographs caused was to place the blame on enlisted personnel, and to claim that it was the work of a "few bad apples." Clear evidence to the contrary, however, was heard during the Senate confirmation hearing into the appointment of former White House counsel, Alberto Gonzales, to the post of US attorney general. In a memo dated August 1st, 2002 to Gonzales from Jay S. Bybee, a federal appellate judge, the legal definition of torture and the legality of its use in the "War on Terror" was specifically redefined.

The memo defines torture so narrowly that only activities resulting in "death, organ failure or the permanent impairment of a significant body function" qualify. It also states that Americans can claim self-defence if criminally prosecuted, based on the horror of the 9/11 attacks. Finally, the memo asserts that laws prohibiting torture "may be unconstitutional if applied to interrogations undertaken of enemy combatants pursuant to the president's commander-in-chief powers." In short, it advises that when acting as commander-in-chief, the president can go beyond the law.

The conspiracy theory
The use of torture by the US and its allies has been actively sanctioned at the highest level, including the Pentagon, the NSA, CIA and the White House. Abu Ghraib was not an aberration but planned and organized policy. Rumours also circulated that the CIA and military intelligence have sought the assistance of Israel's Mossad, and former Special Branch and SAS agents from Northern Ireland to advise on the current counter insurgency in Iraq.

The evidence
For the past 55 years the US, via the CIA, has been running what is now know as the Western Hemisphere Institute for Security Cooperation (Whisc) at Fort Benning, Georgia. Formerly it was called School of the Americas (SOA), and before that the International Police Academy.

Since 1946, this establishment has trained more than 60,000 Latin-American soldiers and policemen. Among its graduates are many of the continent's most notorious torturers, mass murderers, dictators and state terrorists as documented in hundreds of pages of documentation compiled by the pressure group SOA Watch.

In 1996, the US government was forced to release seven of the school's training manuals. Among other top tips for terrorists, they recommended blackmail, torture, execution and the arrest of witnesses' relatives.

The Abu Ghraib torture techniques have been field-tested by SOA graduates. Dr Miles Schuman, a physician with the Canadian Center for Victims of Torture, wrote in the *Toronto Globe and Mail*:

> The black hood covering the faces of naked prisoners in Abu Ghraib was known as *la capuchi* in Guatemalan and Salvadoran torture chambers. The metal bed frame to which the naked and hooded detainee was bound in a crucifix position in Abu Ghraib was *la cama*, named for a former Chilean prisoner who survived the regime of General Augusto Pinochet. In her case, electrodes were attached to her arms, legs and genitalia, just as they were attached to the Iraqi detainee poised on a box, threatened with electrocution if he fell off."

The verdict
Torture by US-trained thugs in Latin and Central America under the command of SOA graduates has been extensively documented by Amnesty International (in its 2002 report titled *Unmatched Power, Unmet Principles*). Evidence is also provided by books such as A.J. Langguth's *Hidden Terrors*, William Blum's *Rogue State* and Lawrence Weschler's *A Miracle, a Universe*. In virtually every report on human-rights abuses from Latin America, SOA graduates are prominent. It would be naive to believe the same was not true in Iraq.

See also: *Salvador Allende p.60; Guantánamo and Abu Ghraib Conspiracies p.235*

2005
KGB PLOT TO POISON YUSHCHENKO

Russian security forces planned to kill opposition leader on eve of Ukraine's presidential election

In January 2005, when Viktor Yushchenko was announced winner of Ukraine's re-run presidential election, his pock-marked face broke into a smile of joy – and relief. His badly scarred complexion was testament to an assassination attempt by a Russian hit squad to ensure their own man, Viktor Yanukovich, became leader. Yushchenko collapsed in September 2004 – at the height of the election campaign – during a dinner with officials from the Ukrainian Security Service and was rushed to hospital. Tests revealed that he had been poisoned with the deadly toxin, dioxin, and was lucky to survive. According to Oleg Gordievsky, ex-Soviet spy and British double agent, the assassination attempt bore the hallmarks of the dirty tricks department of the old KGB, now called the FSB. Gordievsky believes that the poisoning was ordered by Russian president Vladimir Putin, himself a former KGB head, concerned that election of pro-Western Yushchenko would end Russia's influence over the Ukraine. Worse still, Putin thought, Yushchenko was pushing for membership of Nato, which would bar access by the Russian naval fleet to the Ukraine's vital Black Sea ports. Writing in the London *Daily Mail*, Gordievsky said the job of removing Yushchenko was first given to Ukraine's own security services. Their failure prompted the head of the FSB, Nicholai Patrushev, to ask President Putin to sanction a hit by Russian agents. The KGB/FSB has a history of using poison to attack overseas "targets," usually favouring cyanide spray or, as with BBC journalist Georgi Markov, ricin injected from the sharpened point of an umbrella.

See also: *Operation Bluebook – CIA Plot to Buy Nukes p.159; Leo Wanta and the Crash of the Russian Rouble p.160*

2005
DONALD RUMSFELD'S OUTLAW SPYNET

US Defense Secretary runs his own covert unit

When, prior to the 2003 invasion of Iraq, the CIA did not produce the desired evidence for Saddam Hussein/al-Qaeda ties, or a genuine Iraqi security threat to the US, Defense Secretary Donald Rumsfeld secretly – and perhaps illegally – formed his own private intelligence, interrogation, and covert operations unit inside the Pentagon.

Rumours had been circulating about the existence of such a group for some time, especially in relation to the Abu Ghraib torture scandal. But in January 2005, journalist Seymour Hersh revealed that President George Bush had been authorizing secret commando groups and other Special Forces units to target ten nations in the Middle East and South Asia, and also to prepare for action against Iran. The resident's decision enabled Rumsfeld to operate outside the restrictions imposed on the CIA. Under current law, all CIA covert activities are reported to Senate and House intelligence committees. A former high-level intelligence official told Hersh: "They don't even call it 'covert ops' – it's too close to the CIA phrase. In their view, it's 'black reconnaissance.' They're not even going to tell the regional American military commanders-in-chief."

Washington insiders were doubly shocked by Hersh's revelations as this group, known as the Office of Special Plans, was found to be headed by Under Secretary of Defense Douglas Feith. The insiders recalled how, during the Iraq invasion, commanding General Tommy Franks, had called Feith the "f**king stupidest guy on the face of the earth."

See also: *CIA Torture History p.172; Guantánamo and Abu Ghraib Conspiracies p.235*

Was Vladimir Putin, former head of the KGB, responsible for Viktor Yushchenko's ravaged complexion?

key figures

"The Gods give us paranoia so that we
may occasionally glimpse something of
the truth."

                                    Socrates

Since the birth of the first civilized organizations, politicians, corporations, religious cults and intelligence groups
have all been involved in authentic, and historically proven,
acts of conspiracy against each other and their unwitting
constituencies. Whenever their deeds are examined and
detailed today, one name regularly emerges as the malevolent guiding spirit behind virtually all clandestine
behavior. The 15th-century philosopher Niccoló Machiavelli
had such an impact in the arena of political subterfuge that
his name has become synonymous with all that is covert
and duplicitous.

The fathers of conspiracy

In her 1924 book *Secret Societies & Subversive Movements*,
for example, the first lady of conspiracy theory Nesta
Webster quotes extensively from Machiavelli's *The Prince*.
She draws the convoluted conclusion that the world is in
grave danger of being ruled by an 18th Century Secret
Society, the Bavarian Illuminati. She then proposes
that their founder (Adam Weishaupt), the founder of
Communism (Karl Marx) and the founder of political manipulation (Niccoló Machiavelli) comprise the unholy trinity
on which all clandestine planet managers base their dogma.

Webster was well read and always drew from eclectic,
if occasionally esoteric, sources to support her assertions.
Yet she and the majority of conspiratologists who came
after her clearly hadn't read their Machiavelli properly. In
both *Discourses* and *The Prince*, he advises his students
against initiating conspiracies on the basis that they were
doomed to failure. In the former he argues that the inherent complexity of a conspiracy is likely to be its downfall.
In *The Prince* he points out that the more people involved
in a conspiracy, the more likely someone will talk about it:

For one man cannot carry on a conspiracy by
himself; and he can only find allies among those

whom he believes to be discontented; and as soon
as you reveal your plans to one of them, you will
give him the opportunity to improve his position
by denouncing you ... in short conspirators live in
fear, suspicion and apprehension of punishment ...

Machiavelli pointed back to historical examples of conspiracies that had failed because of the duplicity and
unreliability of the participants. As far back as the days of
the Caesars, he found examples of complex plots that had
foundered because someone had not been able to keep the
details of their particular conspiracy secret. Then of course
there is the small matter of conscience to consider for a
small band of conspirators.

The professional

Consider the case of Mordecai Vanunu, a technician who,
from 1975 to 1986, worked on a secret project to develop
Israel's nuclear capability. According to Vanunu he had a
crisis of conscience, as a result of which he decided to
reveal all he knew to a journalist. In a subtle twist of
Machiavelli's conspiracy principle, it was the exposer of the
conspiracy that lived in "fear, suspicion and apprehension
of punishment," however. After initially discussing the possibility of having him assassinated, Mossad, the Israeli
Secret Service, kidnapped Vanunu in Rome and brought him
back to Israel to stand trial. He served 18 years in prison,
11 of them in isolation and even on his release he was
submitted to stringent conditions. Among them was that
he should not talk to any foreigners or representatives of
the media.

They failed to shut him up, though. Vanunu's lawyer
said that the technician was: "the most stubborn, princi-
pled, and tough person I have ever met." Within weeks of
his release, Vanunu was talking to underground magazines
and radical websites about his treatment, alleging that he
knew more about Israel's nuclear programme; that the nuclear reactor he had worked at was unstable; that the CIA had
been involved in his abduction; and, most controversially,
that Mossad had been involved in the 1963 assassination of
the US President John F. Kennedy.

After 18 years in jail it was mighty unlikely that Vanunu had new, relevant information on his country's nuclear capability, though. Indeed, Dr Ray Kidder, a senior US nuclear scientist, said: "On the basis of this research and my own professional experience, I am ready to challenge any official assertion that Mr. Vanunu possesses any technical nuclear information not already made public." Neither did Vanunu offer any real evidence for any of his other accusations. The JFK allegation was based on what he called: "Near certain indications." Even though he was in a very vulnerable position, it was clear that Vanunu was not going to stop talking. His motivation to do so, however, is questionable.

Perhaps Vanunu had simply become a "whistle blower" – someone who calls a halt to what he (or she) sees as the wrongdoings of organizations who wield power and influence in the world – almost by profession. Here was an undoubtedly brave man, prepared to speak out on what he saw as morally wrong. It could be argued that the mere fact that he had no more moral wrongs to speak out on wasn't going to stop him and that after so long in prison, being forever regarded as a whistle blower became his reason for being. Whatever the reasons, Vanunu is in danger of becoming a Professional Conspiracy Theorist – an entity that Machiavelli was neither familiar with, nor perspicacious enough to predict.

Outside the tent

If a conspiracy was potentially doomed because of the volatility of the co-conspirators, what chance would it stand of remaining undiscovered with the advent of those mavericks who made it their business to actively expose it? The president who succeeded Kennedy, Lyndon B. Johnson, was apparently reluctant to sack the notoriously wily, political troublemaker, FBI director J. Edgar Hoover. When pushed on the issue LBJ apparently said:

I'd rather have him inside the tent pissing out
than outside the tent pissing in.

All of the people in this chapter are very clearly outside the tent. Their motives for giving it a soaking are manifold, but

Broadly speaking they fall into four categories. While the character definitions may blur from time to time it is likely that your conspiracy theorist is either: 1. The Altruist 2. The Political 3. The Professional 4. The Oddball

Beware the Political who tells you that everyone else is an Oddball, the Professional who tells you they're all Political except for the ones that are Altruists, the Altruist who tells you none of them are Oddball, and the Oddball who tells you they're all Oddballs except him.

Be also advised that all four groups will most likely be keen to point out that they are in no way even "Conspiracy Theorists." They would prefer to describe themselves as Analysts, Researchers, Activists or Sceptics.

The oddball

The traditional and much-cultivated view of the conspiricist is of a wild-eyed fanatic on the fringes of society struggling to remain out of the psychiatric ward. And in a lot of cases that may not be far from the truth. That image does a grave disservice, however, to a number of people who work in the area of looking at what goes on behind the things that happen in the world. It may also be argued that those people who are behind the things that happen deliberately cultivate that misconception. At the higher end of the conspiracy theory chain we find some of the most revered US writers – Noam Chomsky, Norman Mailer and Gore Vidal. All have written about the hidden agendas of contemporary government. And all have lamented the way in which any examination of hidden agendas instantly gets them branded as an Oddball. To paraphrase Gore Vidal, just because a person believes that there are suspicious circumstances surrounding a political assassination, it doesn't automatically follow that he believes Elvis was abducted by aliens. If all conspiracy theorists believe something as ludicrous as that, then all the theories they believe in must be ludicrous

The archetypal conspiracy theorist inhabits dark places exploring dark deeds, prepared to meet a darker end at the hands of the dark forces. The popular view is of people marginalized, dedicated to the point of obsession, and obsessed perhaps to the point of marginally insane. "The Truth is out there," was the tag line of the conspiracy-based 1990s TV show *The X Files*. And to the majority, the seekers of that Truth are way out there, far beyond the realms of reason and rationality. However, people from all four of the above categories have shown themselves more than capable of uncovering genuine conspiracies that might otherwise have remained hidden by the conspirators. Even the Oddballs.

British researcher David Icke, for example, believes that giant lizards are sending him messages, warning him of the activities of aliens masquerading as world leaders. Most senior politicians, the British royal family and, for some reason, a number of country and western singers, are really a race of Reptile Aliens who are able to take on the forms of humans.

He first wrote all about it in his book *The Biggest Secret: The Book That Will Change the World*. You can go to his website www.davidicke.com and read his reams of research, some of it pictorial, that went into providing his "evidence." There's some incredible stuff on there, for example, the corporate logos of Vodafone, Lindt Chocolate and Alfa Romeo all incorporate reptiles in their design, which "proves" that these corporations are in some way run by this "New World Order" or "Illuminati" of horrible lizard aliens. Ever since Icke started talking about his "Babylonian Brotherhood" of elite reptiles, he has invariably been laughed at by virtually everyone. Even among many ostensibly fringe theorists, Icke is considered too ridiculous to be included in the conspiracy canon. A look at the man's website, however, does reveal that along with the famously bizarre reptilian allegations, there is some serious research on some legitimate issues. Particularly enlightening are his findings in the field of medical conspiracies.

Obviously these are informed by Icke's agenda that it is in the interests of the lizard "Illuminati" to keep us all in a state of ill-health. Nevertheless, he has investigated a host of issues, from Aids to Zyban, and come up with facts that any sane person really should be aware of. Icke is certainly not the only person raising concerns about major pharmaceutical companies and their activities, or the cavalier attitude of health professionals, but he is one of the most diligent and meticulous as regards the collation of data. However, one can see how it would suit unscrupulous drug manufacturers to be able to deride anyone audacious enough to cite his work as authoritative criticism.

Not that Icke seems too perturbed by the disapprobation. He may well be classified as one of the conspiracy world's Oddballs, but he's no fool. All those years spent working in the media must have contributed to what amounts to a very savvy-looking career path. There is, literally, method in his madness. Booksellers report that the books he writes do a brisk business; he travels the world selling lots of seats for his lectures; and does all that's necessary to maintain the profile he needs to achieve success. He looks and acts like a professional. Icke's supporters see him as a lone crusader, under constant threat from the agents of the Babylonian Brotherhood against whom he rails. There's something romantic about the solitary theorist who fights to bring us the truth, despite the ridicule of the majority, or potential persecution by his targets.

The Altruist

Former Federal Aviation expert, Rodney Stich, for example, typifies the Altruist. He tells us he was so shocked at the dangerous practices, and subsequent cover-ups, within the airline business that he decided to wage a single-handed campaign to bring them to our attention. The more he found out, the more he fought, and the more he fought the more the system seemed to conspire to shut him up. But also, the more he fought, the more people approached him, told him he was doing the right thing and revealed what they knew about similar cover-ups.

Two things happened as a consequence of his becoming a lodestone for all this information and his attempts to try to get it out into the world. First of all, Stich opened up a whole new career as a writer on conspiracies that encompassed a wide range of corrupt organizations. Secondly, he believes that there is a concerted effort by the legal profession to ruin his life. Bankruptcy and prison were just two of the injustices he endured for refusing to keep quiet. Traditionally we see people like Stich as solitary, fearless and under-resourced, working overtime and under duress to expose the machinations of the unscrupulously powerful. Like many of his contempories, Stich is self-published and dependent on contributions to his "Fighting Fund." But the small-time operator, with access to Photoshop software and a Xerox machine doesn't necessarily have less of an agenda than the man with access to a broadcasting satellite and million-dollar advertising campaign.

The Political

When that agenda is political, it boils down to a straight fight, not between right and might, but between left and right. Radio broadcaster, Dave Emory, for example, has always been keen to establish his credentials as a politically motivated animal. He takes his cue from his mentor, Mae Brussell, in propagating the theory that so many German fascists were assimilated into the American power structure that they ended up running the country. Emory's a left-winger. He doesn't like the right, and he has an axe to grind. So he takes every opportunity to tell us that the right is up to all sorts of conspiratorial nonsense that should make you worry about the future of the world.

Nesta Webster was the godmother of political conspiracy theory. She was right-wing, verging on being one of the Nazis that Dave Emory tells us are now in charge of the world. She set out to sell us a world that was actually run by a conspiracy of socialists. She demonized them, literally, by dredging up research that proved they were actually satanists, and then she added a nasty anti-semitic slant. But once again, it was done via pseudo-rational argument and intensive, seemingly authentic research. The level of debate between the politically incompatible frequently descends to that of the playground: "You're just an evil neo-nazi cult masquerading as a politician, peddling lies about how the Jews really run the world so you can obfuscate the fact that you're planning to install a new order," is one side of the argument; "You're just saying that because you're a communist cadre in league with international bankers, manipulating events and the media to prevent people from discovering that you're going around eliminating anyone who stands in the way of *your* hidden central government," could well be the other.

As a result of combative political posturing, the real issues are often obscured by mud slinging. Meanwhile, the "corrupt" corporation or "devious" politicians who cynically conspire to cheat or hoodwink us become increasingly adroit at counteracting the conspiracy theorist. They may do it by highlighting the political agenda or discrediting the sources, but if powerful enough, they will have recourse to more extreme and sinister measures. Spurious legal charges, character assassinations, ruined careers, mysterious disappearances and dubious suicides

Niccoló Machiavelli, the founder of political manipulation.

are potential consequences for any person altruistic, professional, political or oddball enough to take them on.

Unless of course the theorist has the most devastating evidence imaginable. The conclusive proof of which sinister element it is that holds ultimate power over all our lives. If you have access to that information, and make it known, it appears that the nominated secret rulers of the world pursue one of the most Machiavellian tactics of all. They simply ignore you. And in that way:

Everyone sees what you seem to be, but few
discover what you are; and those few will not dare
to oppose the voice of the many.

The Prince, Machiavelli

NICCOLO MACHIAVELLI
b. 1489, Florence, Italy
d. 1527, Florence, Italy
Philosopher

Machiavelli was raised in Florence when the city was a significant power under the Medici family. He embarked on a diplomatic career that took him around Europe, allowing him to witness the machinations of the powerful. They were turbulent times and Niccoló, after backing the wrong side in a power struggle, ended up being tortured for conspiring against the Medici. He was banished from political life.

He spent that time writing and in 1513 produced *The Prince*, essentially a handbook for would-be rulers and a powerful influence on politicians ever since. Machiavelli was probably the progenitor of realpolitik, more recently referred to as the "spin doctor." While there is a pragmatic ruthlessness inherent in Machiavelli's work, it will probably come as a shock to most conspiricists that in *The Discourses* he advised his pupils against engaging in conspiracy on the grounds that the more people were involved, the more likely the plot was to come unglued. However, as with any great writer, the disciples will read what they want and there's no doubt that for centuries students of Machiavelli have applied his principles in their conspiring.

There is one other bizarre place that Niccoló slots into conspiracy history. In 1864, a French satirist penned *Dialogues in Hell Between Machiavelli and Montesquieu* as an attack on Napoleon III. By a convoluted process, that work came to be used as the basis for the controversial *Protocols of the Elders of Zion,* the 1920s book on which much anti-Semitism has been based ever since.

See also: *The Protocols of the Elders of Zion p.249*

NESTA WEBSTER
b. 1876, Hertfordshire, England
d. 1960, location unknown
Author and political activist

Nesta Bevan was the daughter of a prosperous Hertfordshire banker. In 1902, a psychic gave her a description of the man she would marry. Two years later, while on a trip to India, she met district police official Arthur Webster. He fitted the psychic's description and they married. They settled quietly in Surrey where Nesta started reading about the trials of the nobility during the French Revolution and became convinced that she was the Comtesse de Sabran – a member of the

French aristocracy – reincarnated. Gripped by this revelation, she wrote two novels based on her "experiences." Encouraged by critical reaction, and particularly delighted by the comments of the grandson of a guillotined French nobleman who said: "No-one could have written that book who had not lived at the court of Marie Antoinette," she plunged into further research. She concluded that the French Revolution was the result of a conspiracy orchestrated by the Illuminati and the Jews. In 1920 she published her findings in a book, *The French Revolution, A Study In Democracy.*

Although Nesta was convinced that that book, and subsequent ones, were being suppressed by a left-wing conspiracy, her works were actually well received in the upper echelons of the establishment and she was invited to give lectures to high-ranking military and secret service officers. By all accounts she was articulate and exotic enough to win a lot of influential friends in those circles. Lord Kitchener was moved enough to describe Nesta as the: "foremost opponent of subversion."

During the run-up to World War II, Nesta started issuing warnings that dark forces were amassing in order to promulgate a new despotic regime that would plunge the planet into an era of evil. No, not Nazism. She thought that was a good thing. She joined the British Fascist Party and became friendly with the likes of their leader Oswald Mosely and William Joyce (Lord Haw Haw). The dark forces that Webster prophesied were Jewish and communist. Naturally she became a Hitler apologist. In 1933 she wrote in the right-wing *Patriot* magazine:

> That Hitler is doing the best thing for Germany seems at present undeniable … in Germany, as everywhere else in the east of Europe, the communists being predominantly Jewish, suppressing communism necessarily involves taking action against a number of Jews … He has done what no other statesman of his day has dared to do – set out to grapple fearlessly with the Jewish problem …

Imagine her disillusionment when Hitler subsequently signed a pact with Stalin. She pretty much gave up the fight after that. There was the occasional foray into print and debate, but she felt that she'd done her best to alert the world and they'd ignored her. She also believed that someone was coming to get her. Even as a grand old lady in her 70s she would open the front door with a loaded pistol in her hand.

Nesta Webster's legacy is of a truly disparate nature.

Clearly she is adored by right-wing organizations around the world. Yet she also held strong and trenchant views on the role of women in politics which has led to many of her ideas being absorbed into modern feminist ideologies. Even the UFOlogists get in on the act, claiming that, during World War I, Nesta spent her time spotting alien spacecraft while ostensibly looking for enemy spy signals in the night.

However, the right-wing shenanigans have resulted in her being overlooked as a genuinely interesting writer who conducted phenomenal research and presented her work with clarity. Her 1924 book *Secret Societies and Subversive Movements* is seminal in the purest form of the word, outlining in detail the origins of the Knights Templars, Masons, Cabalists, Satanists, Occultists, Rosicrucians, Zoroastrians, and Muslim fundamentalists.

In 1972, 12 years after her death, a right-wing publisher finally agreed to publish Nesta memoirs *Crowded Hours*. It never happened. The last remaining manuscript was stolen from the office by a "mysterious American visitor."

See also: *Knights Templar p.243; The French Revolution p.247; Rosicrucians p.283; Freemasons p.284; The Bavarian Illuminati p.285*

CARROLL QUIGLEY

b. 1910, Boston, Massachusetts
d. 1977, Washington DC
Author and academic

In 1966, Quigley published a thorough history of the 20th century entitled, *Tragedy and Hope*. The bit that got conspiracy theorists excited, and continues to do so, started:

> There does exist, and has existed for a generation, an international Anglophile network ... I have studied it for 20 years and was permitted ... to examine its papers and secret records.

The passage has been referred to ever since as "The Smoking Gun." Quigley went on to recount that this "network" was conceived by British diamond magnate Cecil Rhodes as part of his plan to amalgamate all English-speaking nations. Through his "Round Table" organization it became intent on administering world affairs via various bankers and trade organizations. The book seemed to disappear quickly from the bookshops. Maybe it was very popular. Or perhaps the ruling elite had it quashed for revealing far too much about their power base. Some have attributed quotes to Quigley

which indicate that he thought so. On the other hand he suggested in private to students that he was embarrassed by the kerfuffle and distanced himself from those, such as the right wing John Birch Group, who were convinced that he'd provided evidence of a hidden world government. Controversy surrounded Quigley again in 1992 when an ex-student from Georgetown University, soon-to-be-president, William Clinton, in his acceptance speech at the Democratic convention, cited Professor Quigley and John F. Kennedy as major influences. As far as the conspiracy community was concerned, this proved that the gun was still smoking.

See also: *Council for Foreign Relations p.104; Cecil Rhodes' Round Table p.290*

HAROLD WEISBERG

b. 1913, Wilmington, Delaware
d. 2002, Frederick, Maryland
Author and farmer

In 1963, Weisberg was tending his chickens when he heard the news about President John F. Kennedy's assassination. By 1965 he was one of the first to criticize the official line with his book *Whitewash: The Report on the Warren Report*. At first no publisher would touch it, so he raised the money himself and quickly sold 30,000 copies.

Weisberg wasn't just an award-winning poultry farmer; his career included spells as a soldier, journalist and State Department intelligence analyst. But he eventually became a full-time conspiracy theorist, publishing seven books on the Kennedy assassination alone. In 1968 he entered into the controversy over murdered civil rights leader Martin Luther King, even working for alleged assassin James Earl Ray as an independent investigator. Throughout the 1970s he fought a number of actions against the US Government to have documents on both assassinations released under the Freedom of Information Act. One of Weisberg's legacies is that he was responsible for significant changes in laws governing classification of information.

Weisberg believed the 1964 *President's Commission on the Assassination of President Kennedy* was shoddily put together, calling it "superficial and immature." He also had little time for the often haphazard methods used by other conspiracy theorists. His own research into everything was meticulous and diligent. He left behind a Kennedy Archive of 25,000 original documents along with 85,000 on Luther King. They are housed at Hood College in Frederick and, in accordance with his wishes, available for anyone to view.

CLAIRE STERLING
b. 1919, Queens, New York
d. 1995, Arezzo, Italy
Journalist and author

Sterling was a largely politically motivated journalist, beloved of the administration of ex-President Ronald Reagan, who worked in Italy for most of her career. There are many who would say that she was a CIA stooge.

She was a lifelong, committed anti-communist, and in 1984 she and Paul Henze (another CIA-friendly scribe) wrote *The Time of the Assassins*. The gist of the book was that the Turkish terrorist Mehmet Ali Agca, who attempted to kill Pope John Paul II in 1981, was working for Bulgarian spies under the aegis of the USSR. There is a massive body of evidence to suggest that this was nonsense. Sterling's 1981 book *The Terror Network* reckoned that virtually every terrorist group in the world was backed by the Russians. Apparently, such were the magnitude of her discoveries, she had to write the book under armed guard. William Casey, the CIA director at the time, was reported to have told senior staff who had failed to come up with evidence of such a conspiracy: "Forget this mush ... I paid $13.95 for this (Sterling's book) and it told me more than you bastards whom I pay $50,000 a year." It has been pointed out that Casey should perhaps have consulted the less well paid CIA agents who, off the record, had informed much of Sterling's investigations. While Sterling was no doubt influenced by her political agenda, she was clearly capable of valid research, as her authoritative books on the origins and activities of the Mafia testify.

See also: *Pope John Paul I p.63; The Mafia p.281*

EARLING CAROTHERS GARRISON
b. 1921, Knoxville, Iowa
d. 1995, New Orleans, Louisiana
District attorney and writer

In 1963, at the time of the assassination of President John F. Kennedy, Earling (Jim to his friends) Garrison was a highly successful New Orleans district attorney. He boasted, in fact, that he had never lost a case. Garrison's record was severely blemished in 1967, however, when he prosecuted prominent local businessman Clay Shaw for conspiring to kill President Kennedy.

His case rested on the fact that alleged assassin Lee Harvey Oswald had spent time in New Orleans shortly before the assassination. Unfortunately for Garrison, the rest of the picture was painted for him by a collection of local junkies, drunks, and petty crooks looking for money. Nevertheless, Garrison took much of what they said at face value and came to believe that the conspiracy was down to an alliance between the CIA, anti-Castro Cubans, a "Military-Industrial Complex," and a gaggle of homosexual thrill seekers who thought that killing Kennedy would give them a kick. He confidently issued an announcement long before the trial stating: "My staff and I solved the case weeks ago. I wouldn't say this if we didn't have evidence beyond a shadow of a doubt."

The case was thrown out of court, mainly due to the bizarre array of unreliable and unstable witnesses. One of them admitted in court that he fingerprinted his young daughter every day to ensure that she hadn't been replaced in the night. The foreman of the jury reckoned that he had more faith in the 1964 *President's Commission on the Assassination of President Kennedy* after Garrison's evidence than he had before the trial. Garrison was subsequently lampooned and vilified by virtually everyone who had an

Claire Sterling's *Time of the Assassins* recounted the attempted assassination of Pope John Paul II.

opinion on the subject. His detractors pointed out that he was busted out of the Texas National Guard, his doctor writing that Garrison had: "severe and disabling psychoneurosis, which interfered with his social and professional adjustment to a marked degree ... he is considered totally incapacitated from the standpoint of military duty and moderately incapacitated in civilian adaptability."

It was also claimed that Garrison had violated all manner of procedure in the pursuit of his suspects; that he was inconsistent in his accusations and that he had both falsified and destroyed evidence that would have exonerated Shaw. Most damning were the testimonies of those on his team who had walked out on Garrison during the Shaw investigation. Apparently they were appalled at the district attorney's obsessions and the lengths he went to in order to "prove" his case. One of them, David Lifton, called his colleague: "intellectually dishonest, a reckless prosecutor, and a total charlatan."

Garrison was to claim that he was the victim of a concerted effort by the CIA to shut him up, and that his former staffers were part of the intelligence team employed to discredit his endeavours.

The vilification of Jim Garrison was largely maintained – even by the conspiracy theory community – and although in his defence he wrote three books on the subject, he was ostracized for the rest of his life. Significantly, though, he never lost his job as district attorney and was ultimately promoted to the Louisiana Supreme Court.

Then in 1991 Oliver Stone released the movie *JFK* in which Hollywood star, Kevin Costner, played Garrison as a steel-jawed, singular man of honour flying in the face of all the elements that were conspiring to keep him from the truth. It was something of a rehabilitation for Garrison and it is more than likely the movie image that the public will remember him by.

Not the conspiracy theorists though, who take a different perspective. There have been prolonged howls of outrage over Stone's redemption of Garrison. One of the most vitriolic from the respected writer and researcher, Harold Weisberg. In a letter to the director he wrote: "You have every right to play Mack Sennett in a Keystone Kops Pink Panther, but as an investigator, Jim Garrison could not find a pubic hair in a whorehouse at rush hour."

See also: *John Fitzgerald Kennedy p.54 Harold Weisberg p.179*

MARY FERRELL
b. 1922, Memphis, Tennessee
d. 2004, Dallas, Texas
   Researcher and archivist

Ferrell was working as a legal secretary in Dallas when John F. Kennedy was assassinated in 1963. She remembers hearing a radio bulletin which said that the suspect was around 30, 6 ft tall and 165 lbs, wearing a white shirt and khaki trousers. She got suspicious when police arrested a 23-year-old wearing a red-brown shirt and brown trousers.

She immediately started to compile information which was collated onto cards, detailing information on 8,200 people involved in the case. She'd amassed 40,000 cards by 1986 when researcher Daniel Brandt helped her to transfer the data onto computer. She'd also produced a four-volume chronology of key events and figures, including an almost minute-by-minute timeline of suspect Lee Harvey Oswald's movements. One of her skills was her photographic memory. It meant that when she was shown documents she wasn't allowed to photocopy or take away, she could go home and type the whole thing up from memory.

Ferrell never wrote a book, preferring instead to act as a resource centre for other writers who wanted to go down that route. She was generous with information and time. Writers tell of spending 12-hour shifts at her home while she went through the minutiae of the assassination in exhausting detail. "She is the hub of the JFK research community," said one of her colleagues, "No one writes a paper without Mary. No one publishes a book without Mary."

Ferrell was also a prime mover in the JFK Lancer organization which holds an annual "November in Dallas" conference to discuss new findings. In 2001 her archives were donated to the Mary Ferrell Foundation in Boston.

See also: *John Fitzgerald Kennedy p.54; Daniel Brandt p.187*

MAE BRUSSELL
b. 1922, Beverley Hills
d. 1988, Carmel, California
   Broadcaster and researcher

The daughter of a prominent Beverley Hills rabbi, Mae was an ordinary wife and mother until 1963 when she saw alleged John F. Kennedy assassin, Lee Harvey Oswald, murdered live on TV by Jack Ruby. The research she started would consume her for the rest of her life.

US presidential hopeful Lyndon LaRouche, September 1987.

When the official *President's Commission on the Assassination of President Kennedy* came out in 1964, Mae Brussell proceeded to spend 8 years studying the entire 26 volumes, cross-referencing it with other material and archiving an extraordinary 27,000 pages of analysis. What she discoverd, or what she believed she discovered, became an all-consuming obsession for her. Every person, every event, every media report initiated a whole new world of research into how America was controlled. It would be fair to say that Brussell was one of the most prolific sources of conspiracy theory ever. The central tenet for all of them was that the US was in grave danger of being run by Nazis. These comprised mainly German aerospace and weapons experts, but also quite a few military figures, who had been assimilated into government and intelligence services after World War II.

In 1971, Brussell started broadcasting on her local radio station, KLRB, a weekly show initially called *Dialogue Conspiracy*. She later changed the name to *World Watchers International*, hoping that the format would take off in the way Weight Watchers had done.

Brussell did indeed build up an impressive worldwide mailing list of "members" to whom she sent tapes of the show each week and who, in return, furnished her with fur-

ther information to fuel her research and investigation. Apparently they preferred to refer to themselves as her "Brussell's Sprouts."

The shows were both breathless in delivery – as she sometimes struggled to pour out all she had learnt – and breathtaking, as she encompassed everything from the fact that Hitler was living in a clinic in Switzerland to Patty Hearst as a CIA puppet. Occasionally death threats would drive her off the air back to her file-crammed house where the broadcasts were taped and posted to radio stations.

Mae also analyzed the information she studied to make predictions. Sometimes she was widely off the mark, as she told an interviewer in 1971:

> Russia and China will give (ex-disgraced president) Nixon Vietnam in exchange for opening up world trade, in return for wheat for Russia, and Boeing airplanes for China."

Other times she was spot on. It appears that she had the real story on the Watergate scandal while everyone else was still swallowing the White House lines. In 1972 she was asked to contribute her findings on the scandal to satirical underground magazine, *The Realist*. Publisher Paul Krassner said his printer wouldn't touch the issue without a $5,000 cash payment upfront. John Lennon came up with the money.

Which is somehow fitting, as she later revealed that Lennon was assassinated by the Nazis – as was every other rock star who died in the 1960s and 1970s. She believed that the Nazis were as keen to get rid of the social revolutionaries as they were the politicos. She claimed that: "Only people like Sonny and Cher, the Osmonds, John Denver, and Captain and Tennille make it as role models. They either have to tame you or kill you."

The fact that many of the celebrities that Mae Brussell identified as targets were also partial to pharmaceuticals merely confirmed that the Nazis were using, variously, drugs and mind-control techniques in order to manipulate assassins and criminals.

Mae died of cancer in 1988. She was 66. At the time she had been engaged in research on a Nazi war criminal working high up in the Pentagon, and a senior officer in army intelligence who ran a Satanic pedophile ring.

Included in her legacy were 39 filing cabinets full of raw data and more than 8,000 books. It took two lorries to move her boxes of files and newspaper clippings. Among the archive were extensive notes on the use of "Rapid Cancer" as a CIA assassination method.

See also: *John Fitzgerald Kennedy p.54; The Realist p.86; Conspiracy Radio p.93; Watergate p.148; Daniel Brandt p.187; Project PAPERCLIP p.220*

LYNDON LAROUCHE
b. 1922, Rochester, New Hampshire
Businessman and politician

A wealthy man with business interests in publishing and information technology, Lyndon LaRouche was so successful that he was able to run as the Democratic nominated candidate for presidency in 1980, 1984, 1988, 1992, 1996, and 2000. Unfortunately, it appears that, in 1989, LaRouche resorted to crime to finance his campaign and he was prosecuted for fraud and conspiracy to obstruct justice. He beat that case but was later sentenced to 15 years for postal fraud, illegal fund-raising and tax evasion. He got out in 1994, but some of his associates are still incarcerated and LaRouche continues to campaign for their freedom.

LaRouche is adamant that he is the victim of a conspiracy headed by the FBI and politician Henry Kissinger. He believes that it would be in their interests to have him silenced because of what he knows about who really runs the world; namely Queen Elizabeth II who supports her regime by running an international drug dealing cartel. According to his book, *Why Your Child Became a Drug Addict*, she had British secret service agency MI5 manufacture 1960s rock 'n' roll band, the Beatles, specifically so that they could introduce Americans to: "the rock-drug-sex counterculture."

Because of this moral threat to the young, they are the ones the LaRouche group actively targets for membership. Colleges across the US report branches ardently seeking out recruits, a high proportion of whom subsequently drop out of their studies. This has led to allegations of the LaRouche organization being a sinister cult, which engages in intimidation, fraud and mind-control.

NORMAN KINGLSEY MAILER
b. 1923, New Jersey, USA
Author

Norman Mailer was raised in New York and educated at Harvard University. He served in the army during World War II, and in 1948 wrote his epic novel, *The Naked And The Dead*, still considered by many as one of the greatest works to deal with the realities of war.

In the 1960s Mailer became involved in the anti-Vietnam War movement, and in 1967 was arrested during a demonstration at the Pentagon. His account of these events in his factual novel, *Armies of the Night (*1969), won him the first of two Pulitzer Prizes. In 1969 Mailer ran as candidate for Mayor of New York as an independent, campaigning for New York City to become the 51st State. He lost, attracting 5 percent of the final vote.

In 1973, the author delved for the first time into the world of archetypal conspiracy theory when he published *Marilyn: A Biography*, in which he speculated that Monroe was murdered in an attempt to frame Robert Kennedy. In 1991 he published the 1,300-page *Harlot's Ghost*, which mixed fictional characters with factual, against a background of real events concerning the CIA's involvement in the unsuccessful 1961 invasion of Cuba, the 1963 assassination of President John F. Kennedy and the 1972 Watergate scandal.

During research for *Harlot's Ghost* Mailer unearthed new material from USSR archives relating to JFK assassin Lee Harvey Oswald. His 1995 book, *Oswald's Tale,* proposes that Oswald was a revolutionary altruist who killed the president in order to make a name for himself.

See also: *Marilyn Monroe p.53; John Fitzgerald Kennedy p.54; Watergate p.148*

RODNEY STICH

b. 1923, New Jersey
Federal Aviation Authority (FAA) investigator
and author

Stich's impressive aviation career dates back to 1941 when he was a World War II naval pilot and instructor. He later spent time as a commercial pilot, then worked as a Federal Aviation Administration investigator from 1962 to 1968. His work there led him to believe that there was major corruption at the heart of the aviation business.

Stich started a 30-year whistle-blowing campaign that entailed filing his own federal actions in courts throughout the US. In 1968 he wrote *Unfriendly Skies* – disconcerting reading for anyone about to get on a plane. There ensued a tale of Job-like proportions in which Stich doggedly filed private lawsuits against the FAA and eventually lost his business, money, home, and ultimately his liberty. He was jailed in 1986 for six months for contempt of court.

Stich claims that while he was still in prison, he was approached by a CIA operative who confirmed all of his suspicions and more besides. It led him to start writing books such as *Defrauding America* (1995), which alleges endemic federal corruption among: "agents of the FBI, DEA, Customs, Secret Service, CIA, including the former heads of secret CIA airlines and secret CIA financial operations."

Stich writes: "I was fortunate in having dozens of insiders provide me with information over the years. I avoid the word, "conspiracy," as it raises thinking in many people's minds of things far out, even though conspiracies are everywhere … one of the issues was my attempt to report the federal offences in the government's aviation safety offices, where the *primary* blame for the successful hijackings of 9/11 really belongs. That is a very sensitive area."

See also: *World Trade Center p.262*

EUGENE LUTHER GORE VIDAL

b. 1925, New York
Author

Gore Vidal was born at the United States Military Academy at West Point, where his father was a military instructor. He was brought up in Washington DC where his blind grandfather was a Democrat senator. The young Vidal's duties included reading political documents to him and acting as his guide at political meetings, which gave him a precocious insight into the machinations of government.

Gore Vidal, half brother of Jacqueline Kennedy, was close to the first family in the 1960s but has been a constant critic of many US political and military institutions for over 40 years.

Vidal joined the US Army Reserves in 1934 and, at the age of 21, wrote his first novel *Williwaw*, which detailed his military experiences. He went on to become one of the most prolific, respected and contentious writers of the 20th and 21st centuries.

Vidal has always been concerned with the political arena – he twice stood unsuccessfully as Democratic candidate for Congress – and is one of the most vocal, and erudite, critics of contemporary government. The author is the half brother of Jacqueline Kennedy Onassis, and in the 1960s became close to the incumbent President John F. Kennedy. He enjoyed less cordial relations with the president's brother. In 1961 Vidal wrote to Robert Kennedy, at the Justice Department, complaining about the FBI. He accused the agency of having a cavalier approach to civil liberties and of fostering relationships with the Ku Klux Klan. Vidal felt that he was fobbed off, and at a 1961 White House dinner a famous confrontation ensued in which words were exchanged between the two, many of them obscene.

Vidal has continued to attack the FBI, the CIA, most ruling administrations and the news media, which he believes accept the official version of events with docility. Following the 1993 siege of Waco, in which the Bureau of Alcohol, Tobacco and Firearms, and FBI agents, killed 86 members of the Branch Davidian cult, Vidal accused both agencies of heavy-handed tactics, and of then lying in order to cover up their actions.

In the late 1990s, Vidal entered into correspondence with Timothy McVeigh, the man accused and convicted of the 1995 bombing of a Federal building in Oklahoma, which resulted in the deaths of 169 people. A relationship developed to the point where McVeigh invited Vidal to be a witness at his execution in 2001. Vidal was unable to attend, but has since written extensively about the events at Oklahoma. He has proposed that McVeigh may have been acting in conjunction with government-infiltrated extremists, and decided to take the blame himself as a "Good Soldier." He has also theorized that McVeigh may have been entirely innocent but accepted responsibility for the atrocity, partly as a gesture in support of the victims of the Waco siege. Speaking at the Edinburgh Book Festival in 2001, Vidal alleged that the FBI were directly involved in the bombing and said:

> I have been working with a researcher who knows at least five of the people involved in the making of the bomb and its detonation. It may well be that McVeigh did not do it. In fact, I am sure he didn't do

it. But when he found out he was going to be the patsy, he did something psychologically very strange. He decided to grab all credit for it himself, because he had no fear of death."

In a 2001 *Vanity Fair* article on the Oklahoma bombing, Vidal lamented the way he had been treated by the media, claiming that during interviews he was cut short whenever he dealt with conspiracies, or that he was derided. In other interviews he has reiterated his concern that anyone who advocates a conspiracy theory is automatically ridiculed.

Vidal has also been at the forefront of proposing the theory that President Bush's administration had advance knowledge of the 2001 terrorist attacks on the New York World Trade Center. In his 2002 work *The Enemy Within* he alleges that the government's agenda was to justify a pre-planned invasion of Afghanistan, in order to secure oil fields, and to initiate a clamp-down on civil liberties within the United States.

See also: *John Fitzgerald Kennedy. p54; Robert Francis Kennedy p.54; Oklahoma City Bombing p.163; World Trade Centre p.262; Ku Klux Klan p.287*

NOAM CHOMSKY
b. 1928, Philadelphia, Pennsylvania
Linguist and political commentator

The man often described as "the most intelligent alive" has said that he doesn't believe in conspiracy theories.

Notwithstanding, self-proclaimed anarchist Chomsky has maintained a radical stance for more than 50 years, speaking out over the corruption of the US media who he believes are committed to controlling minds through censorship. "A disproportionately high coverage of professional sport," he says, for example, "is not only a major distraction against things that really matter ... but also a contributor to political complacency."

Chomsky is a fierce challenger of hierarchy, highlighting "the double speak" and: "strategic lies of the government that have manufactured the consent of a nation towards global dominance." In his book *9-11* He argues that: "The US is the *actual* leading terrorist state."

Opinions like those have not endeared him to the authorities. In 1973, 10,000 copies of Chomsky's book *Counter–revolutionary Violence* rolled off the presses and were immediately withdrawn by the publishers because of their exposure of cover-ups over US involvement in Vietnam.

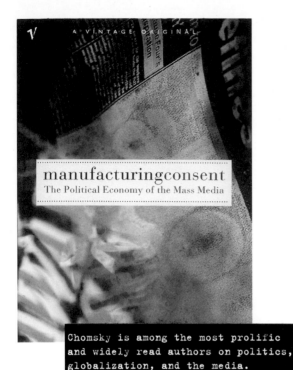

manufacturingconsent
The Political Economy of the Mass Media

Chomsky is among the most prolific and widely read authors on politics, globalization, and the media.

His early and outspoken criticism of the war lead to his inclusion on President Nixon's "enemies list", while his involvement in peace protests resulted in several arrests on charges of civil disobedience. Since then Chomsky has written dozens of books, including perhaps his most famous, *Manufacturing Consent – The Political Economy of the Mass Media* (1992), which examines the supportive relationship between the media, corporations and the political status quo. He also remains at the centre of controversial activism.

Despite being Jewish, his views on Zionism and criticism of Israeli policies have led to strident accusations from some commentators of anti-Semitism.

See also: *Anti-Defamation League p.249; World Trade Center p.262*

PETER DALE SCOTT
b. 1929, Montreal, Canada
Professor, author and diplomat

Dale Scott graduated from McGill University, Montreal, in 1949 and after studying in Paris and at Oxford, was awarded his doctorate in political science by McGill in 1955; he went on to serve in the Canadian Department of External Affairs

as a Foreign Service Officer. From 1966 he taught in the Department of English at the University of California, Berkeley. In the 1960s he became involved in the anti-Vietnam-War movement. When he later used the Freedom of Information Act to obtain his FBI files, he found that the organization had amassed 985 pages of information on him.

In 1972, he wrote *The War Conspiracy* which detailed his theories on why the US really went to war in Vietnam. During the course of his research he came up with the premise for his second book, *The Assassinations: Dallas and Beyond,* in which he coined the phrase "Deep Politics" to describe political conspirators not directly involved with government.

In 1987, his research into government involvement in drug peddling led to his appointment as a consultant to the Center for International Development Policy, which entailed presenting his evidence to 2004 presidential candidate, Senator John Kerry. In 1991, he wrote *Cocaine Politics: Drugs, Armies, and the CIA in Central America,* a book detailing CIA involvement in drug trafficking. Scott followed with further titles on the Iran-Contra affair, the assassination of President John F. Kennedy, war and drug conspiracies, along with three volumes of poetry. He is also a co-founder of the Peace and Conflict Studies Program at Berkeley and of the Coalition on Political Assassinations.

See also: *John Fitzgerald Kennedy p.54; Iran-Contra p.228*

SHERMAN SKOLNICK
b. 1930, Chicago
Broadcaster and activist

A polio sufferer confined to a wheelchair all his life, Skolnick is a one-man conspiracy generator.

In 1963, he founded the "Citizen's Committee to Clean Up the Courts" as a self-appointed legal watchdog. In 1969 he was thrown into jail for contempt of court, after accusing a number of judges of bribery and refusing to name his sources. He was subsequently vindicated after a public outcry, and an official investigation was followed by resignations and convictions.

In November 1972, Skolnick filed a lawsuit against the National Transportation Board, arguing that they should be disqualified from investigating a December plane crash, which killed 43 people. Skolnick alleged that the NTB had links with United Airlines, who were also largely owned by the Rockefeller banking family. He lost that one, so in 1973 he wrote his only book, *The Secret History of Airplane*

Sabotage, claiming that the plane was full of key Watergate figures, one of whom was carrying vast sums of money made from blackmailing President Richard Nixon for conspiring to have President John F. Kennedy killed in 1963. There ensued a furious legal battle with Rockefeller lawyers, resulting in the book being pulped as it left the presses.

Since 1995 Skolnick, has broadcast his *Broadside* programme on cable TV, and continued to use the courts to pursue major figures he believes are guilty of major crimes. But it was the internet that really opened the floodgates of Skolnick's relentless conspiratorial deluge. The bulk of it too litigiously risky to be detailed here. Search him and see.

See also: *John Fitzgerald Kennedy p.54; Watergate p.148*

ACE HAYES

b. 1940, Portland, Oregon
d. 1998, Portland, Oregon
  Activist and publisher

Hayes was a wild-eyed ex-logger with a big appetite for life, and an even bigger appetite for researching the facts behind the news.

In the 1950s, he served in the US navy but by the late 1960s was leading anti-Vietnam War demonstrations and organizing local farm workers into trade unions. He was apparently asked to join the Communist Party, but declined on the grounds that they were "too conservative."

The 1970s saw him take off for Nicaragua to work for the marxist Sandinistas. What Hayes's role was there is not entirely clear, but it seems he never denied the accusations of gun-running reported in some newspapers.

Ace moved back to Oregon during the 1980s where he lectured at a local college in "radical research" and "secret government in America". He also started monthly seminars, which were broadcast on cable channels in Oregon. His local paper, *The Oregonian*, reported that he attracted: "a bizarre following of tax resistors, mutant hippies and gun-totin' computer geeks." In 1993, he established the *Portland Free Press* so that he could publish his findings to a wider audience. The magazine's slogan was: "read and quoted by the CIA, among others – not, of course, with any great pleasure."

Like all the best conspiracy researchers, Hayes was obsessive about accuracy and scathing about those who didn't put in the legwork. He once said: "I'm a hard ass on truth and facts because I know that credibility is like virginity – a hell of a lot easier to retain than it is to recover."

DANIEL BRANDT

b. 1948
  Researcher and webmaster

Brandt has been at the forefront of conspiracy research for decades and for the last 30 years has been compiling the huge conspiracy database, *Namebase*. It has been online since 1995, and is the most comprehensive resource imaginable, with detailed information on over 125,000 people. He also writes articles and essays at a prodigious rate.

His fields of expertise are legion, but in the area of CIA and intelligence organizations he is arguably one of the leading experts in the world. There have even been rumours that had Ralph Nader been elected president in 2000, he would have appointed Brandt head of the CIA, such is the breadth of his knowledge on the espionage community.

In latter years Brandt has become well known for his activities as an anti-Google campaigner. He asserts that the popular search engine is invidious in the way it collates information on searchers and how it ranks results. In a 2003 interview he said: "They don't know what the word: 'public interest' means; it's completely outside their frame of reference. Most of those PhDs at Google wouldn't recognize a philosophical principle if they ran over one in their SUVs."

Sceptics suggest that this may be resentment at not having his pages ranked as highly as he would like. Nevertheless Brandt has set up a website, Google Watch, and amassed a staggering amount of data on the company. He has similar issues with on-line bookseller Amazon.com.

See also: *The Internet p.88*

JIM KEITH

b. 1949, Los Angeles, California
d. 1999, Reno, Nevada
  Author

Jim Keith started writing on conspiracy theories in the early 1970s. Over the next 30 years he published books on flying saucers, the Gemstone Files, the Oklahoma bombing, "Black Helicopters", and mind control. He also wrote countless articles and contributed to broadcasts on every other conspiracy in the canon. In 1999 he fell off a stage at the infamous Nevada alternative arts "Burning Man" Festival, breaking a leg. He later died in hospital. The coroner's report indicated that he suffered a fatal blood clot, due to related kidney problems, while undergoing surgery. His nephew claims that Keith was adamant that he should not be anaesthetized. He had apparently told friends that he believed if he "went under" he wouldn't "come back up."

Shortly before his death Keith was engaged in two contentious pieces of research. The first was the book he wrote, with *Steamshovel* publisher Kenn Thomas, called *Octopus*. It concerned the case of researcher Danny Casolaro who died in 1991 while investigating a conspiracy to steal surveillance software which, he believed, embroiled the Justice Department with a secret organization called the "Octopus." The death was officially suicide. But Jim Keith doubted that. The second piece of research became an article on the now defunct British website *Nitronews*. It was entitled: "Princess Diana Was Pregnant; Fayed's Physician Examined Her."

Apparently he once told a colleague that he had a law – Keith's Law: "all conspiracy authors must die in mysterious circumstances." His friend and co-publisher, Kenn Thomas, is currently investigating the circumstances of Keith's death.

See also: *Danny Casolaro p.70; Steamshovel p.92; The Gemstone File p.116; Prince Philip Ordered Diana's Murder p.274*

DANIEL PIPES
b. 1949, Boston, Massachusetts
Author and political analyst

A neo-conservative expert in Middle Eastern affairs with a dozen books on the region under his belt, Pipes is a dichotomy of conspiracy theory.

In 1997, he wrote *Conspiracy: How the Paranoid Style Flourishes and Where It Comes From*, which largely debunked the whole genre. While clearly setting out the difference between actual conspiracy, and the muddled thinking that can surround a "conspiracy theory", he takes the Machiavellian perspective on the likelihood of conspiratorial success: "For the conspiracy is discovered before the deed happens, which is done without much difficulty." He takes the elevated sceptic's line on most of the theory. On the other hand, he is the progenitor of a massive theory of his own; that Muslims are conspiring to overthrow the United States in order to turn it into an Islamic State.

Since the early 1990s Pipes has been warning of this threat, stating that: "Islamism is fascism." Many of Pipes' advocates believe that, had he been heeded, the 2001 terrorist attack on the World Trade Center could have been prevented. In his spare time Pipes also runs *Campus Watch*, a website that monitors and criticizes academics who take a pro-Muslim/anti-Israel line.

Compounding the controversy surrounding his views was his appointment, by President George Bush, to the board of the United States Institute of Peace, a group apparently established with a mission to find solutions to conflicts between the East and the West. His appointment has been lambasted by members of all faiths, who believe that Pipes has spent his career demonizing Islam. He also works for the Department of Defense with their "Special Task Force on Terrorism and Technology."

See also: *World Trade Center p.262*

DAVID ICKE
b. 1952, Leicester, England
Author and broadcaster

Icke was a well-known British footballer and respected sports commentator until 1991, when he appeared on the Terry Wogan BBC TV talk show, announced that he was the son of God, predicted apocalyptic world events, and hinted at dark forces at work in the world. The whole country laughed at him.

The theory that has attracted most attention is that the world is run by giant, shape-shifting, blood-drinking, sexually deviant lizards. Icke claims that these creatures are extraterrestial in origin, and are determined to enslave the human race. He often refers to the lizard people as "The Illuminati" and "A New World Order." Because he also launches vituperative attacks on organized religion – including the Jewish faith – he has been accused with extreme vehemence of being anti-Semitic. Something he denies with equal vehemence.

Icke is a prolific and successful man. His books sell well and his speaking tours are full. Paradoxically a lot of his research into a variety of important conspiracies is enlightened and stands up to scrutiny. Yet most find it hard to see past the shape-shifting lizards, which include the British Royal Family and most world leaders, along with country singers Kris Kristofferson and Boxcar Willie. All of whom have had their "lizard genealogy" studied by Icke and come up green and scaly. But then, as Icke is quick to point out, not one of the long list of rich and powerful people he identifies as reptilian villains have ever taken the trouble to sue him.

See also: *Jon Ronson p.191; The Anti-Defamation League p.249; The Bavarian Illuminati p.285*

RON BONDS
b. 1953
d. 2001
Author and publisher

From the founding of his book imprint IllumiNet in 1992, until his death in 2001, Ron Bonds made a phenomenal impact in the world of marginal publishing, providing a mainstream offshoot that caters to an underground with interests in alternative ideas and obscure information.

The earliest works published by Bonds include the first publication of *The Idle Warriors*, a novel about Lee Harvey Oswald, which was written a year before the JFK assassination by Oswald's Marine Corps friend, Kerry Thornley. Bonds knew Thornley as a marginals denizen in his hometown of Atlanta, Georgia.

Other early titles include *Zenarchy*, on Thornley's personal philosophy, and the first book version of *Principia Discordia*, a graphics-laden samizdat on the worship of the chaos deity, Eris. The next major IllumiNet title was a reprint of *The Mothman Prophecies*, by paranormalist writer John Keel. *The Mothman Prophecies* became a major motion picture starring Richard Gere, and released shortly after Bonds died.

IllumiNet's biggest star was conspiracy author Jim Keith, a marginals magazine writer, internet columnist and personality, celebrated for uncovering strange research and conspiratorial connections. IllumiNet published his best-known works, including *Black Helicopters Over America*, *OKBomb!* and *Casebook on the Men in Black*, and Bonds considered him a partner in the publishing concern. Bonds became disheartened when Keith died under unusual circumstances in 1999 but continued to publish IllumiNet's unusual fare.

Bonds died two years later, on April 8th, 2001, after eating food tainted with clostridium at a Mexican restaurant in Atlanta. Strangely, Keith previously had written about stockpiles of that particular bacteria kept by the CIA as a potential bioweapon.

MICHAEL MOORE
b. 1954, Davison, Michigan
Author and film-maker

Moore's home town of Davison, a suburb of Flint, Michigan was dependent on car manufacturer General Motors until 1989 when they closed the factory, and moved their operation to Mexico to take advantage of lower labour costs. Moore's first film *Roger & Me* (1989) detailed the effect of the move on his community. Since then he has made films, written books and presented TV shows on all manner of

Filmmaker and author, Michael Moore, has brought global conspiracies to the masses though, increasingly, he has his detractors.

injustices, corruption and political scandal. There are two actual "conspiracies" synonymous with Michael Moore. The first is the allegation in his 2001 book, *Stupid White Men,* that President George Bush perpetrated electoral fraud to win the 2000 elections. The second – as detailed in the 2004 film, *Fahrenheit 9/11* – concerns the strong, and injurious ties between the Bush and Saudi Arabian Bin Laden families.

It is difficult to examine Moore's output without being acutely aware that he has a finely tuned comedic gift. Some feel that faced with the choice between making a well-researched, cogent, political point and going for the cheap laugh, he favours the latter.

Critics point out that for a man so virulently opposed to corporate greed and personal cupidity, he seems bent on amassing a fortune. Anti-Moore websites, of which there are many, brand him a lying, dilettante, anti-American hypocrite. Which doesn't deter from the fact that Moore has managed to bring a radical agenda right to the heart of American mainstream culture. When his 2002 film on gun culture, *Bowling for Columbine,* won an Oscar in 2003, he took the opportunity to use his acceptance speech to attack President Bush and the war in Iraq.

See also: *World Trade Center p.262*

'Savage, brilliant, funny, tremendously intelligent.'
John Cleese

LOVE ALL THE PEOPLE
Letters, Lyrics, Routines
BILL HICKS

Bill Hicks self-combusted at the age of just 32, leaving behind a legacy of vituperative work.

GERALD POSNER
b. 1954, San Francisco
Author and lawyer

In 1994, Posner wrote, *Case Closed: Lee Harvey Oswald and the Assassination of JFK,* in which he posited one of the most contentious theories imaginable: that Lee Harvey Oswald assassinated President John F. Kennedy in 1963 because Kennedy was a mentally unstable left-winger.

It caused a furor among conspiricists who have been queuing up to attack Mr Posner ever since. Much has been made of the opening gambit, where he states that more than 2,000 books have been written on the Kennedy assassination. And that they were all written to cash in on the Kennedy legacy. Other Kennedy experts point out that there have actually been fewer than 400 books written on the subject, and they also claim that the genre is far from lucrative. Perhaps because of this slight on their integrity, Posner's research has come under intense scrutiny and subsequent criticism.

In 1999, he published a book called, *Killing the Dream: James Earl Ray and the Assassination of Martin Luther King,* in which he claimed that James Earl Ray killed the civil rights leader of his own volition.

Cue howls of outrage from everyone. Especially the Coalition on Political Assassinations who, along with Earl Ray's brother Jerry, harangued the author at a Memphis book signing until they were arrested.

In 2003, he further irritated conspiracy theorists by writing a book called *Why America Slept: The Failure to Prevent 9/11*. His argument was that Arab terrorists were solely responsible for the terrorist outrages.

See also: *John Fitzgerald Kennedy p.54; Martin Luther King p.58; World Trade Center p.262; The Ku Klux Klan p.287*

WILLIAM MELVIN HICKS
b. 1961, Valdosta, Georgia
d. 1994, Little Rock, Arkansas
Stand-up comic

Bill Hicks was a comedian in the same way that Woody Guthrie was a folk singer. He was outstanding at what he did, he loved his country enough to keep on criticizing it, and he knew what he was talking about. For many younger Americans in the 1990s, his act was their first introduction to the machinations of political conspiracy.

Hicks started his career in 1978 in Houston and within a short time was performing up to 300 shows a year around the world. For most of that time the comic appeared to be on a self-destructive path hinged around the ingestion of drugs and alcohol to excess. It never seemed to dull his edge, though, or his capacity for researching and then pointing out the anomalies in the official line on such topics as the assassination of John F. Kennedy; arms to Iraq; the first Gulf War; the conspiracies that elected Presidents Reagan and Bush senior or the massacre/mass suicides at the siege of Waco.

In the summer of 1993, having quit drugs and drinking, Hicks was diagnosed with pancreatic cancer.

He continued to tour, and in the October made a record 12th appearance on the Letterman TV talk show. His segment included a typically robust attack on anti-abortionists, and he was subsequently dropped from the show. The advertisement breaks had been booked up by a Pro-Life group.

Hicks played his final show in January 1994, six weeks before he died.

JON RONSON
b. 1967, Cardiff, Wales
Author and film-maker

After spending time as a rock band manager and local radio DJ, Ronson found a niche writing for London listings magazine, *Time Out*. He would gently send up those with eccentric views by befriending them and getting them to open up without appearing – either to the subject or the reader – to be making fun.

He hit his stride in 2001 with the UK's Channel Four TV show, *Secret Rulers of the World,* which went on to form the basis of his 2001 book, *Them: Adventures with Extremists.* Ronson's modus operandi was to hang out with a variety of oddities, some of them conspiracy theorists, and via the gentlest of innocuous probing, allow them to express themselves freely – with fascinating consequences. His efforts brought many lesser known conspiracies to a much wider consciousness. His shadowing of David Icke on a Canadian tour brought them both into conflict with the Anti-Defamation League. Ronson who is Jewish, was as bewildered as Icke to learn that they believe "lizards" is a code name for "Jew."

While covering territory that had been dealt with by many before him, Ronson did manage to come up with fascinating new footage and facts on secret societies, the Bohemian Club and the Bilderberg Group. His adventures with the latter almost led to his arrest in the company of Jim Tucker, the editor of the right-wing conspiracy tabloid, *Spotlight*.

Ronson's 2005 book, *The Men Who Stare at Goats,* was another gently sardonic look at the US military's more unorthodox research into mind control techniques and psychic operations.

See also: *Liberty Lobby p.86; The Bilderberg Group p.108; David Icke p.188; Anti-Defamation League p.249; Bohemian Club p.289*

ROB STERLING
b. 1969, Silver Spring, Maryland
Author and researcher

Rob Sterling founded *The Konformist* website in 1996 for the explicit purpose of: "rebellion, konspiracy and subversion." It became popular with the parapolitical internet-browsing public, primarily due to the ontological guerrilla style of the editor.

Sterling shaped *The Konformist* by selecting reports and editorials that examined trends in conspiracy and cover-up, as well as rumours that often later became items in the mainstream news. Humorist Paul Krassner said of Sterling: "One of the main reasons I ceased publication of *The Realist* (the famed underground newspaper) after 40 years is because *The Konformist* carries on its tradition in cyberspace." Although it gathers stories from obscure and wide-ranging sources, *The Konformist* is at its best when Sterling produces original writing. He regularly skewers secret masters and hidden mechanisms of control with a "Beast of the Month" column, highlighting the most egregious examples of corporate and cultural crime. Recipients have included neoconservative Paul Wolfowitz, considered by many to be the architect of the Iraq War, and the sons of Saddam Hussein.

Sterling has appeared on the Fox TV network in the US denouncing media censorship conspiracy, at lectures he exhorts crowds to go and rob banks, all aimed as nose-thumbings towards implacable power. While much of Sterling's writing reflects a preoccupation with the sex industry, he has also published a political book, *50 Reasons Not to Vote for Bush*. True to form, it was a brilliant satire and was utterly ineffectual in the American election results of 2004.

See also: *The Realist p.86*

medical conspiracies

If we are to remain alive we have to be able to trust the air we breathe, the water we drink, and the food we eat. And if we get sick, we absolutely have to trust the medicines we are given, and the doctors who administer them.

But we don't have to worry about that do we? There are checks and balances in place for all of those things, carefully considered legislation passed by elected officials who canvassed honestly for our votes. Regulatory bodies comprised of unbiased experts appointed by those legislators. There are even voluntary codes of conduct and formal agreements in place, to ensure that nothing can jeopardize those basic life-giving elements: air, food, water, and the best medical care available.

Take a deep breath. A good lung-full of life-giving oxygen. And hold it until you've read to the end of this chapter. It might be safer. You might be out there in the mountains surrounded by invigorating ozone, but for all you know someone has slipped something really nasty into the atmosphere. And they may have done it just to see what happened to you.

Dispensing bacteria
In 1977, after a series of press reports on secret biochemical weapon testing, the US government initiated the "Hearings Before the Subcommittee on Health and Scientific Research of the Committee on Human Resources on the Examination of Serious Deficiencies in the Defense Department's Efforts to Protect the Human Subjects." At those hearings the army *admitted* to having tested biological weapons in the open air a total of 239 times between 1949 and 1969. Among the various experiments they carried was one that involved dispersing bacteria around the airport and Greyhound station in Washington DC, to determine how far and fast people carried infections while travelling. In 1968 the military also dropped light bulbs full of Niger, a bacillus related to anthrax, onto subway tracks in Manhattan to "monitor the spread of the agent through the tunnels."

Their official report said: "Similar covert attacks with a pathogenic agent during peak traffic periods could be expected to expose large numbers of people to infection and subsequent illness or death." But these experiments took place a long time ago, didn't they? And, as a consequence of the Senate Commission, didn't President Nixon order the Pentagon to destroy their biological weapons and end their research? Indeed he did. And there was a plethora of positive press opportunities, with photos of scientists destroying viruses, dismantling equipment, and demolishing facilities.

Fort Detrick – the remote Arkansas base where the majority of chemical weapons research had been carried out since the 1950s – was handed over to the National Cancer Institute. The Pentagon continued to maintain a small unit there, however: The Army Medical Research Institute Of Infectious Diseases. In 1982 a Pentagon spokesman told British journalists Jeremy Paxman and Robert Harris that the facility was for researching "those diseases which continue to plague mankind."

During the Cold War, the army argued that they had increasing evidence that the USSR was still developing its biological weapons. On that basis that US scientists had to understand the potential threat, so the research had to continue for defensive purposes. Part of Nixon's grand gesture towards guaranteeing us safer air was to hand the majority of that research over to universities.

Lethal viruses
By 1986 the government was distributing over $42 million a year to 24 separate academic institutes to be used for research into infectious diseases. When the biology department at Massachusetts Institute Of Technology decided that they didn't want their $2 million if it entailed producing potentially lethal viruses, they were forced to back down. It was made clear that other vital funding would be denied them unless they took the money and got on with the business of developing new strains of nasty bugs.

So can we all breathe such a big sigh of relief, safe in the knowledge that sensible, learnt, impartial academics are currently in charge of finding out how best we can protect ourselves from a biochemical attack? Certainly there is to evidence that university professors are dropping light bulbs full of deadly germs into subways. And obviously we all breathe easier for knowing that medical academic research has produced vaccines to protect us against many viruses that could otherwise kill us.

Yet perhaps we should hold our breath a little longer. In 1918 the world faced an international epidemic of a mysterious disease. "Spanish Flu" infected and killed millions. There was no known cure, and the Federal Bureau of Health stated that more servicemen died from the disease than were killed in battle during World War I. And then the disease simply vanished, never to be seen again. Until 2002 when the Armed Forces Institute of Pathology tried to recreate it for us "under high biosafety conditions" at the Department of Agriculture in Athens, Georgia. They used frozen 1918 genetic material, created a similar virus to Spanish Flu, and established that it was deadlier to mice than normal influenza.

Disease tinkering

In 2004 the British Medical Association published a report, *Biotechnology, Weapons and Humanity,* in which it raised the alarm over the tinkering with diseases that goes on in laboratories around the world. Not just the recreation of dormant ones such as Spanish Flu and Black Death, but the genetic modification of existing viruses such as Anthrax. Some believe that the diseases we already fear are being manipulated so that they can be used to target specific ethnic groups. Vivienne Nathanson, the BMA's head of science and ethics said: "The very existence of international laws to protect us is being questioned ... most worryingly of all, it's never been easier to develop biological weapons."

Another area of concern for the BMA's report was "Crop Control Viruses," the manufacturing of biological agents which specifically target agriculture. The concept of using a biological weapon to hit vegetation is not entirely new. During the Vietnam war the US air force sprayed millions of gallons of "Agent Orange," a herbicide designed to defoliate the jungle, thus denying the enemy of cover. Of course it also destroyed crops, and wasn't too healthy for the people who ingested the chemical. American servicemen

and Vietnamese civilians have been suffering from disease believed to be related to Agent Orange as the military stopped using it in 1975. In 2004, lawsuits were launched by the "Vietnam Victims of Agent Orange Association" against the manufacturers of the herbicide over long-term effects, which include birth defects amongst those whose parents were exposed. One of those manufacturers is the Monsanto corporation.

Genetic modification

Monsanto, sometimes referred to as "Monsatan" by its detractors, is a multinational agricultural and biotechnology company at the forefront of both growing vegetation, and providing the means to destroy it. For example, they produce a powerful herbicide called "Roundup." They also produce a genetically modified soya plant called "Roundup Ready." It's a stroke of symbiotic commercial genius. If you grow the soya, you need the weed killer. If you use the weed killer, because it kills everything else, the only thing that you will be able to grow is the soya. Monsanto are also pioneers of genetically modified food – they made the first commercially available food, a tomato called "FlavrSavr." Today, more than 70 percent of the food consumed in the US has GM ingredients. The remaining 30 percent is difficult to identify for the simple reason that the Food and Drug Administration also ruled that there was no need to separately label GM foods.

In due course, scientists working independently of the food corporations started to do their own research on GM products. Some of them came up with less than positive results. Rats which had eaten GM products were developing cancers and people were developing stomach complaints. There were allegations that the food companies had either tested incompletely or were deliberately suppressing the results of negative tests. We are eating food that we trust the FDA to regulate, but is our trust misplaced?

Anti-GM food campaigner Jeffrey Smith believes so. His 2003 book *Seeds of Deception: Exposing Industry and Government Lies About the Safety of the Genetically Engineered Foods You're Eating* couldn't have a more explicit title. Smith believes that there were advisers at the FD who warned against the alleged dangers of GM foods, but that the manufacturers had so much political influence that the detractors were shouted down. He says:

> How could the agency put such a dangerous industry-friendly policy in place, when their own scientists had insisted that each GM variety should be subjected to long-term safety tests before being allowed on the market? One hint was that a former attorney to the biotech giant Monsanto was in charge of FDA policy-making. Another hint comes from a memo by former FDA Commissioner David Kessler, who described the agency's policy as "consistent with the general biotechnology policy established by the Office of the President."

Passing the medical test

It's not just in the area of new foods that people have raised concerns about the effectiveness and impartiality of the FDA. The testing of medicines is also on the agenda.

In June 2000, a Senate Committee on Government Reform Hearing took place which was entitled "Conflicts of interest and vaccine development – preserving the integrity of the process." The purpose of the hearing was to determine whether the drug companies have too much influence over the processes involved in determining if vaccines are safe. The conclusion was that they do. Taking the example of the "Rotavirus Vaccine" – approved in 1999 and then withdrawn after children who took it developed serious bowel obstructions – Senator Dan Burton said:

> How confident in the safety and need of specific vaccines would doctors and parents be if they learnt the following: one, that members, including the chair of the FDA and CDC advisory committees who make these decisions own stock in drug companies that make the vaccines. Two, that individuals on both advisory committees own patents for vaccines under consideration, or are affected by the decisions of the committees?

In 2004, FDA Drug Safety Reviewer David Graham told a Senate Finance Committee that, while the common arthritis treatment, Vioxx, had been taken off the market (after it was found to cause serious heart problems), there were at least five other drugs being routinely prescribed that he believed were dangerous: "I wouldn't," he said, "even give them to my mother-in-law." Graham also alleged that, on discovering the dangers of Vioxx, he had been coerced by senior FDA members into dropping publication of his findings. When he refused to back down, his research was systematically rubbished in a high-profile campaign. In his testimony to the Senate he said:

> Today, you, we, are faced with what may be the single greatest drug safety catastrophe in the history of the world. We are talking about a catastrophe that I strongly believe could have, should have been largely or completely avoided. But it wasn't, and over 100,000 Americans have paid dearly for this failure. In my opinion, the FDA has let the American people down, and sadly, betrayed a public trust.

Drink for health

So it appears that we can't wholly trust the air that we breathe, the food we eat, or the medication we've been prescribed. But can we at least trust the water with which we wash down our questionable food and medicine? The people who treat our drinking water clearly work hard to ensure that it's in premium condition for human consumption. So long as no-one has dropped one of those nasty viruses in it, we can at least breathe easy as we drink deep. In fact a lot of water authorities are so concerned for our health, they go the extra mile. To ensure that we all have healthy teeth and good strong bones, they add fluoride to our water.

In 2004, the American Dental Association's website told us: "For over five decades, the American Dental Association has continuously endorsed the fluoridation of community water supplies and the use of fluoride-containing products as safe and effective measures for preventing tooth decay." Back in 1944, however, their October journal carried an editorial which said: "We do know the use of drinking water containing as little as 1.2 to 3.0 parts per million of fluorine will cause such

A flight of four US Air Force Ranch Hand C-123s spray a Viet Cong jungle with a defoliating liquid (presumed to be Agent Orange). The aircraft cover a swathe of more than 1,000 feet on each pass over the dense jungle.

developmental disturbances in bones as osteosclerosis, spondylosis, and osteoporosis, as well as goiter, and we cannot afford to run the risk of producing such serious systemic disturbances in applying what is at present a doubtful procedure intended to prevent development of dental disfigurements among children." It would obviously be churlish to pull the ADA up over a discrepancy in their policy over 60 years ago. Times have changed, research is more effective, fluoride administration methods more sophisticated, and the controls over adding dangerous chemicals to things, we hope, are stringent.

Except that half a century later there were a number of experts still taking the original, sceptical standpoint. In fact, some of them were telling us that fluoridation was more dangerous now than it was in 1944. Prior to 1998, Canadian Dentist Dr Hardy Limeback was an enthusiastic advocate of fluoridation. The head of the Department of Preventive Dentistry for the University of Toronto, and president of the Canadian Association for Dental Research, Limeback is regarded as Canada's leading authority on fluoridation. In April 1998, he started to give interviews denouncing the adding of fluoride to drinking water. He also said that children under three should never use fluoridated toothpaste or drink baby formula made with fluoridated water. In an interview he said:

The vast majority of all fluoride additives come from Tampa Bay, Florida smokestack scrubbers. The additives are a toxic by-product of the super-phosphate fertilizer industry ... We're also exposing innocent, unsuspecting people to deadly elements of lead, arsenic, and radium, all of them carcinogenic ... your well-intentioned dentist is simply following 50 years of misinformation from public health and the dental association. Me, too. Unfortunately, we were wrong.

For those of us happy to just turn on the tap and hope that what comes out will be good for us, there is no way of knowing which school of thought is the correct one. We would have hoped we could have trusted our dentist, at least. And if not him or her, the regulatory body the dentist belongs to and that governs his or her conduct. The one that abides by the laws that our government put in place, to protect us from harmful substances in the air, food, water, and medicines on which our very lives depend.

Take another deep breath and read on.

1883
EUGENICS

The US and other western nations have forcibly performed sterilization on "unfit" citizens

The Greek philosopher Plato (c. 427–327 BC) was the first to suggest that procreation should be controlled by the government, with a view to breeding a stronger race. The ancient Greek race of Spartans were also believed to practice a form of unnatural selection, which included leaving weakling infants to die outside their city walls.

It wasn't until 1883, however, that British scientist Sir Francis Galton came up with the term "eugenics," from the Greek for "well born." Galton was a cousin of Charles Darwin, renowned evolutionist and father of the theory of natural selection. Galton believed that the majority of a person's traits, good and bad, were hereditary. Therefore, if there could be some control over those allowed to give birth, the human race would be improved. In 1873 he wrote:

> I do not see why any insolence of caste should prevent the gifted class, when they had the power, from treating their compatriots with all kindness, so long as they maintained celibacy. But if these continued to procreate children inferior in moral, intellectual and physical qualities, it is easy to believe the time may come when such persons would be considered as enemies to the state.

Galton also drew the distinction between "positive" and "negative" eugenics. The former concerns encouraging the "right" people to breed, and the latter is about discouraging, or even preventing, the "wrong" people from breeding.

In the US, in particular, eugenics became an extraordinarily popular science. The inventor of the telephone, Alexander Graham Bell, worked with deaf people, and in 1881 he published *Memoir upon the Formation of a Deaf Variety of the Human Race*, in which he advocated that deaf people should not be allowed to marry as they were likely to produce deaf offspring.

The research and development that went into the science attracted funding from a number of well-known wealthy men, including the banking tycoon John D. Rockefeller and breakfast cereal mogul John Harvey Kellogg.

The conspiracy theory

Various states, specifically the United States, Nazi Germany, Canada, Australia, Norway, Finland, Estonia, Switzerland, and Iceland, practiced eugenics on unwilling, and often unwitting, groups of their own citizens.

In some cases there was a supposedly altruistic motive. It was argued, for example, that women who were severely mentally ill were too vulnerable to risk any chance of falling pregnant. In more extreme cases in the US, and specifically Nazi Germany, eugenics was also practiced as a means to control racial "purity."

The evidence

The proof that the "science" of eugenics was used to justify sterilization is incontrovertible. In 1855, the state of Kansas was the first to enact a law making castration a punishment for any black man raping, or attempting to rape, a white woman. In 1907, Texas passed a law allowing castration for rapists, and those who committed incest.

By the 1920s, the practice had rolled out across the United States and, in many of them, laws were broadened to include the sterilization of the mentally ill, although the definitions of mental illness were less than specific. Included in legislation of the time are such terms as "feeble-minded," "idiots," "morons," "moral degenerates," "imbeciles," "epileptics," "alcoholics," and "retards." Those responsible for diagnosing conditions which warranted sterilization were frequently unqualified to do so. Sometimes all that was required was a rudimentary IQ test, administered by court officials or hospital staff.

In his 1991 book *The Surgical Solution*, doctor and lawyer Philip Reilly estimates that up to 10,000 American men and women a year were sterilized, without their consent, between 1907 and 1963.

One of the first laws Adolf Hitler passed on coming to power in 1933 was the *Gesetz zur Verhütung erbkranken Nachwuchses* (Law for the Prevention of Hereditarily Diseased Offspring). He created over 200 "eugenics courts" across Germany to hear evidence against those who should be sterilized, or, in extreme cases, exterminated.

The remit of the courts put the onus on physicians to report all patients with mental illnesses, epilepsy, and physical deformities, which included the disabled, the blind, and the deaf. Doctors faced prosecution themselves for failing to make the reports, and hundreds of thousands of people were duly turned over to eugenics courts. Many ended up in the hands of doctors and scientists who performed horrific experiments in the pursuit of their "science."

At the postwar Nuremberg Trials, senior Nazi personnel involved in eugenics projects cited America's precedent history as part of their defence.

The verdict

Thousands of people were forcibly sterilized in the West, not just in Nazi Germany but even in the US, where the last forcible sterilization occurred as recently as 1963. Today, because of its association in most people's minds with Nazism, eugenics has been forced to rebrand. There are still Galton Institutes in Britain and America, but they like to refer to their field of study as "crypto-eugenics." The scientists accentuate the "positive" side of their work, stressing the value of their research into artificial insemination, in-vitro fertilization, and cryo-preservation of sperm, eggs, and embryos.

1915

BIOCHEMICAL WEAPONS

Deadly chemicals and viruses were used in warfare and terrorism

It is difficult to pinpoint the exact date that modern biochemical weapons were first developed, although, as early as 1899, there was a fear that they were about to be used. That same year several countries signed the Hague Declaration, in which they agreed "to abstain from the use of projectiles the object of which is the diffusion of asphyxiating or deleterious gases."

Notwithstanding, in 1915 German troops launched a chlorine gas attack against British, French, and Canadian troops near Ypres in France which killed 10,000 men in two days and left thousands more permanently disabled. The Germans argued they had complied with the Hague Declaration by releasing the gas via *cylinders* as opposed to outlawed projectiles.

The initiative to use poison gas in the trenches of World War I was spearheaded by Nobel Prize-winning chemist Fritz Haber. On receiving the award in 1919, he prophesied: "In no future war will the military be able to ignore poison gas. It is a higher form of killing." By the end of World War I, 1.3 million men had been poisoned by gas. Almost 100,000 had been killed, and military scientists around the world were rushing to research this "higher form of killing."

In 1916, the UK military bought land at Porton Down in Wiltshire, and established what was to become, at 7,000 acres, the biggest chemical and biological weapons facility in the world. Testing of the effects of chemicals at Porton Down was initially limited to animal subjects, along with the examination of cadavers of soldiers who had died from inhaling mustard gas. But, by the early 1920s, scientists were conducting experiments on themselves, and then on volunteers from the army. Experiments involving soldiers continued at the research centre right up until the 1980s.

An early proponent of chemical warfare was Winston Churchill. In 1920, while he was Minister of War, he advocated deploying chemical weapons against Iraqi insurgents, saying: "I am strongly in favour of using poisoned gas against uncivilized tribes to spread a lively terror." Although historians differ on whether or not the weapons were actually used in Iraq, there is evidence that, during his tenure, poison gases were used on Afghani and Turkish rebels.

In 1925, 38 countries signed the Geneva Protocol, prohibiting "… the use of bacteriological methods of warfare." Under pressure from the chemicals industry, the US never ratified the Protocol. The Japanese also refused to participate, and during their war with China from 1937 to 1945 established "Unit 731" to develop chemical and biological weapons, where they conducted experiments on thousands of Chinese soldiers. After World War II, the US military offered the Unit 731 scientists immunity from prosecution for war crimes in exchange for their research. During the Cold War, both the USSR and the US spent billions of dollars on developing chemical and biological weapons.

The availability of chemical weapons means that most regimes, governments, and even terrorist organizations are now in possession of these highly effective weapons. In March 1988, the world was shocked by images of up to 5,000

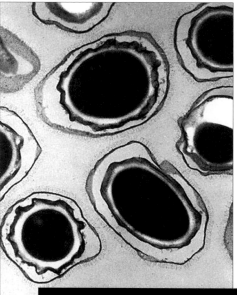

Bacillus anthracis spores. A photomicrograph from the website for the US military's anthrax vaccine programme.

Kurdish civilians gassed to death by Iraqi dictator Saddam Hussein (although there are also intelligence reports indicating that Iran, with whom the Iraqis were at war, may have been responsible for that atrocity).

In 2001, five people died and 19 more were seriously infected with the deadly virus after samples were sent through the US Mail. Initially, it was believed that this was a terrorist act, but the FBI have discounted that theory. There is a strong possibility that the virus was actually distributed by a disgruntled employee at an American bio-defence laboratory.

The subsequent panic over the anthrax incidents, and the very real concerns over terrorists arming themselves with chemical weapons, has led to a massive investment in defending the US against such an attack. In 2004, President George W. Bush launched the $5.6 billion Project Bio-Shield to research and develop responses to bio-terrorism. He said: "We know that the terrorists seek an even deadlier technology, and if they acquire chemical, biological, or nuclear weapons we have no doubt they will use them to cause even greater harm."

The conspiracies

The two questions which exercise the most debate are: 1. Have those weapons been used by the US – who have a stated policy of never using biochemical weapons – as a weapon of war? 2. Have there been any tests on individuals, specifically military personnel and unwitting members of the public?

The evidence

During the Korean War of the early 1950s, the Chinese and Koreans claimed that US planes dropped infected voles, clams, and "flea bombs" carrying anthrax and yellow fever. They said they had statements from captured US pilots which supported those allegations. The American military counter with the accusation that the US pilots were the victims of brainwashing techniques.

In 1952, the International Scientific Commission produced a 700-page report in which they supported the Chinese and Korean claims. Dr Joseph Needham, the British scientist who served on the commission, said: "Mostly it was experimental work as far as we could see...The experiments didn't seem to be very successful, but we were unanimous in our conclusions."

Throughout the early 1950s, the US military conducted an alarming number of similar secret experimental tests on American cities. In 1950, for example, the navy sprayed

bacteria, Serratiamarcescens, over San Francisco Bay. The clouds drifted across the city and infected eleven people, one of whom died. There are those who believe that the virus is prevalent in San Francisco to this day.

Media investigation into the San Francisco "attack" and similar cases in Washington and New York finally led to a Senate Committee hearing in 1977. In their testimony the Army admitted to 239 open-air tests of biological weapons between 1949 and 1969. A Congressional hearing in 1994 revealed that up to 500,000 Americans were endangered by secret tests between 1940 and 1974.

Successful lawsuits in the UK and the US by ex-soldiers against their former employers continue to uncover systematic testing on soldiers who had no idea of what was being administered to them. By 2000 it was estimated that over 20,000 people were engaged in legal action against the US government over biochemical experiments.

At Porton Down, recent enquiries into the deaths of soldiers revealed that over 3,000 men had been exposed to sarin gas during experiments. Those men who died had a verdict of "death by misadventure" recorded by the coroner.

The verdict

There is incontrovertible evidence that despite avowedly renouncing chemical weapons development, many governments, including the US, have continued research and testing. Many of them argue that their activities are purely in the interest of defence, on the grounds that they need to be able to combat the weapons that their enemies may have access to.

See also: *MKULTRA p.143; Biochemical Weapons p.197; Aids p.200; SARS p.205; Project Coast and Dr Death p.227; Gulf War Syndrome p.231; Aum Shinryko/Aleph p.295*

1932
CURE FOR CANCER

A cure for cancer has been suppressed

Cancer is one of the most feared and dangerous diseases of the 21st century. It comes in many forms, some of which are treatable, but after decades of research it remains the second most common cause of death in the western world.

Billions of dollars are spent on research, and the palliative treatments for terminal cancer are expensive, involving large quantities of drugs and sophisticated equipment. So the theory revolves around an industrial/medical/pharmaceutical cartel that suppresses any successful cure.

In the 1930s, Dr Royal Raymond Rife was working as an optics engineer in San Diego where he developed a machine which, he claimed, destroyed any virus by bombarding it with oscillating electromagnetic waves. He said he had used it to cure 15 terminally ill cancer patients, and was preparing for major production of his machine when the American Medical Association ordered a total ban on its use. Over the next five years, Rife was systematically discredited, the prototype of the machine was stolen, and a fire destroyed all his notes and plans.

Rife died in 1971 and would probably have been forgotten if author Barry Lynes hadn't written a series of books investigating the "conspiracy" against his machine. In his 1990 volume, *The Healing of Cancer, the Cures, the Cover-ups and the Solution Now!*, he says: "Neither Congress nor the media desire to lift the manhole cover on this sewer of corruption ... The vested interests are very powerful." There is no hard evidence to suggest that Rife's machine actually worked, although a number of people claim to have rebuilt it. Some of these even offer the machine for sale over the internet. However, "authentic" cures for cancer, and other terminal illnesses, are also widely recognized as one of the most popular confidence tricks on the World Wide Web.

1932–72
THE TUSKEGEE SYPHILIS STUDY

The US Public Health Service allowed African-American syphilis sufferers to go untreated

Syphilis is a sexually transmitted disease that, if not detected and treated, leads to serious internal damage and a painful death.

In 1932, a medical experiment was conducted by the Public Health Service on 400 poor, black, syphilitic farmers in Tuskegee, Alabama. The men were recruited to participate in a research programme, which entitled them to free meals, a "Thank You" certificate from the Surgeon General's office and a $50 insurance payment when they died to help pay for their burial. The last benefit was important because the research entailed performing autopsies on syphilitic fatalities. The men were not told they had syphilis; doctors told them they were receiving treatment for "bad blood."

In the mid-1940s, it became clear that penicillin was highly effective in treating the disease. None of the men was offered the drug, and there is evidence to suggest that the hospital contacted their personal physicians to ensure they were never treated with penicillin. In 1972, health workers blew the whistle, and a front-page article in the *New York Times* ensured that the research ceased and, eventually, that laws governing medical experiments were changed. There were 74 Tuskegee survivors; 128 men had died of syphilis, or related conditions; 40 of their wives were infected; and 19 children had been born with congenital syphilis. Eventually, between them, they were awarded $9 million in compensation, and in 1997 President Bill Clinton travelled to Tuskegee to personally apologize on behalf of the government.

1940
FLUORIDATION

A dangerous chemical is added to drinking water as method of mind control

Fluoride is a chemical added by many municipal authorities to drinking water at source, specifically to protect against tooth decay. At least 60 percent of Americans have fluoride in their water. There has been inconclusive research from proponents and detractors raging for decades about whether or not the chemical has any real benefit. On the detractors' side there are also medical professionals who believe that fluoride is actually detrimental to health. Ever since its emergence it has been the subject of thousands of lawsuits, usually brought by individuals against their local water authorities.

Fluoride was one of the many chemicals that the Nazis experimented with during World War II, and some researchers claim they were planning to use sodium fluoride as a form of mass mind control. At the end of the war, a chemist by the name of Charles Perkins was sent to Germany to investigate the notorious Farben chemical works.

In 1954, he wrote a famous letter to the Lee Foundation for Nutritional Research, in which he said:

> Repeated doses of infinitesimal amounts of fluoride will in time reduce an individual's power to resist domination, by slowly poisoning and narcotizing a certain area of the brain, thus making him submissive to the will of those who wish to govern him.

More recently, it has been pointed out that the fluoride added to water supplies is frequently a by-product of steel, uranium, and aluminium manufacture. Could those powerful lobbies be manipulating research to "prove" that their contaminated waste is actually good for us?

AIDS protesters camp out on a New York street, December 9th, 1990.

1981
AIDS

The Aids virus was deliberately developed to eradicate certain sections of society

Acquired immune deficiency syndrome (Aids) is one of the most virulent and feared diseases facing us today. Very little is known about where it came from and, more crucially, there is no known cure. What we do know is that millions around the world are infected with the highly infectious HIV (human immunodeficiency virus) which triggers the disease.

Even the disease's discovery is blighted by contention, with two doctors apparently discovering and naming the virus at the same time. The American Professor Robert Gallo and Professor Luc Montagnier of Paris agreed to share the "honours." It was Gallo who came up with the research that HIV came from African monkeys, suggesting that a hunter with an open sore perhaps ate one of them.

While the virus may arguably have been dormant since the 1950s, the first recorded cases of people dying from Aids were four young homosexual men from Los Angeles in 1981. The men appeared to be suffering from a form of pneumonia, but had multiple symptoms indicating low immunity systems. They also had Kaposi's sarcoma which is a rare form of cancer in young men.

The conspiracy theory

Aids has attracted dozens of theories. It came from outer space in the wake of a comet, or is the result of voodoo spells from Haitian witch doctors, to name but two. The unprovable, but nevertheless highly popular, theory among religious people is that God sent a plague to punish those members of society – homosexuals, the promiscuous, and the junkies – with whom he was displeased. Secularly speaking, however, the most prevalent theory is that some agency in the US decided to unleash the virus as a biological weapon, perhaps to eliminate so-called "useless eaters" or maybe just as an experiment that went catastrophically wrong. "How come," the theorists ask, "if the disease came from a man with an open sore eating a monkey in Africa some time in the 1950s, the next time it turned up was among previously healthy, white gay men in California?"

The evidence

The trail starts in 1969 when army biological expert Dr Donald McArthur attended a Senate Committee meeting devoted to the subject of "synthetic biological agents." He asked the committee for $10 million for research, writing in his report:

Within the next five to ten years, it would probably be possible to make a new infective microorganism which could differ in certain important aspects from any known disease-causing organisms. Most important of these is that it might be refractory to the immunological and therapeutic processes upon which we depend to maintain our relative freedom from infectious disease.

While there is no evidence that Dr McArthur actually got the money, this is considered to be the "smoking gun" which proves the military were definitely interested in developing an Aids-style virus.

Ten years later, we come to the medical trials that ran at the New York City Blood Center between 1978 and 1981. A thousand healthy homosexual men volunteered to be injected with an experimental vaccine, apparently developed to combat hepatitis B. By August 1981, the first case of Aids was reported in Manhattan. Out of the first 26 recorded cases of HIV infection in the US, 20 were in the New York area, and they all fitted the criteria required of the volunteers. Were they really part of Dr McArthur's $10 million dollar research programme?

In 1983, Dr Robert Strecker was conducting research, for a medical insurance company, into the risks involved in offering health cover to those who were HIV-positive. Together with his lawyer brother Tom, he claimed to have uncovered thousands of documents which proved Aids was a man-made virus. After sending their findings to everyone they could think of, and being almost totally ignored, they released a video, *The Strecker Memorandum*. The allegations within it are outrageous, and it has caused enormous controversy. The lack of visible documentation, however, makes it a difficult medium to analyze with any real authority. In 1988, Ted Strecker was found shot dead at his home. The verdict was suicide. There was no note, and his brother said: "I don't think my brother died from a self-inflicted gunshot wound."

By the mid-1980s, with the Cold War at its height, the USSR was planting stories throughout the world that the Americans developed Aids as a biochemical weapon. Although the Russian claims ceased, as relations improved between the two states, there are many who still believe that to be the case. Specifically, those who believe that the target was the black community.

In 1987, the London *Times* printed a front-page report on a smallpox vaccination programme across Africa during the 1970s. It presented new findings showing that the smallpox shots could have triggered the dormant HIV virus. The conspiracists believe that was no tragic accident.

The verdict

As yet there is no hard, incontrovertible evidence that the Aids virus was deliberately engineered and released; but it is also clear that not all the crucial information is in the public domain.

See also: *Biochemical Weapons p.197*

1985

MERCURY AMALGAM FILLINGS
Dentists use a poison to fill tooth cavities

The "silver" fillings used by dentists are an amalgam of mercury, silver, and base metals. Mercury is a toxic substance, particularly in vapor form.

In 1985, Colorado dentist Hal Huggins wrote, *It's All in Your Head,* in which he warned of the dangers of mercury's poisonous properties. Huggins was one of the first dentists to fill teeth without using mercury, and he made extraordinary claims about the improved health of patients who had their fillings replaced. Conditions alleviated included multiple sclerosis, Alzheimer's disease, and rheumatoid arthritis. In 1996, Huggins lost his licence and was castigated by the judge presiding over his case: "He has taken advantage of the hope of his patients for an easy fix to their medical problems and has used this to develop a lucrative business for himself."

Huggins continues to write and work as a "consultant" but vows that he will never reapply for a licence: "I would just be back to wearing a bullet-proof vest," he says. "They [the American Dental Association] almost killed me." As Huggins's book appeared a number of dentists have renounced mercury fillings, and lawsuits are being filed against individual dentists and the ADA. Anti-amalgam campaigner Dr Boyd Haley says that the ADA make good money from the mercury manufacturers, and that dentists get a higher profit on the fillings. He says, "The ADA right now is lying to Congress, telling them that this [his research] is just junk science."

1987
FLUOXETINE HYDROCHLORIDE
(PROZAC)

Test results on a drug that causes suicidal tendencies were supressed

Brand names for fluoxetine hydrochloride include Prozac, which, throughout the 1990s, was a lucrative, but controversial, treatment for depression and related conditions. In 1998, pharmaceutical company Eli Lilly made $2.8 billion from Prozac sales.

In 1999 psychiatrist David Healey criticized the drug in a lecture at Toronto University: "These drugs may have been responsible for one death for every day that Prozac has been on the market." Dr Healey was due to start a professorship at the university in 2000, but in December 1999 received an email withdrawing the offer: "We do not feel your approach is compatible with the goals for development of the academic and clinical resource that we have." It transpired that Eli Lilly provided funding for the university. Healey sued, settled out of court, and continued to criticize the drug.

As other medical experts started expressing disquiet, drug companies faced lawsuits from relatives of suicides prescribed fluoxetine. They also started to run into trouble with the Food and Drug Administration (FDA), the body responsible for regulating their products, who voted to enforce a ruling that fluoxetine packaging should carry a "black box" warning of the increased risk of suicide.

In 2004, the New York Attorney General launched a lawsuit against GlaxoSmithKline over claims they suppressed tests proving that fluoxetine users developed suicidal tendencies. The company settled out of court, for $2.5 million, and agreed to make public results of future tests.

See also: *Methylphenidate (Ritalin) p.202*

1990
METHYLPHENIDATE
(RITALIN)

Children are prescribed dangerous and addictive drug

Methylphenidate, brand name Ritalin, is used to treat attention deficit disorder (ADD) and attention deficit hyperactivity disorder (ADHD), sometimes known as "hyperactivity." The condition affects the emotional stability of children, and Ritalin is effective in helping them concentrate and stay calm. According to a United Nations study 12 percent of adolescent boys in the US are taking Ritalin.

Some experts consider the drug too dangerous to be administered to children; side effects can include heart disease and psychotic conditions. Ritalin is also a potentially addictive from of amphetamine, which may serve as a "gateway" drug – that is, users will progress to harder drugs. Ritalin is popular among some habitual drug users, who refer to it as "kiddy cocaine." There is anecdotal evidence suggesting that children are trading it for recreational use. There is also an (unproven) argument that Ritalin is used by parents and schools as a "liquid cosh" to control healthy children who are merely badly behaved.

Some doctors even feel the relatively recent diagnoses of ADD and ADHD are not legitimate medical conditions, but an invention of the drug companies. In 2000, lawsuits were filed against the Novartis Pharmaceutical Corporation on behalf of groups of parents alleging that they "conspired, and colluded to create, develop, and promote the diagnosis of attention deficit disorder (ADD) and attention deficit hyperactivity disorder (ADHD) in a highly successful effort to increase the market for its product Ritalin."

See also: *Fluoxetine Hydrochloride p.202*

1992
GENETICALLY MODIFIED
FOOD

GM foods are dangerous to human health but they are still being marketed worldwide

The late 20th century saw scientists finally discovering some of the keys that unlock the complex genetic codes which make up all living things. By 1992 they had come up with the first commercially grown, genetically modified tomato. The food manufacturer Calgene presented the US Food and Drug Administration with the "FlavrSavr." The FDA ruled that the tomato was a bona fide food, that it posed no health risks, and that it didn't need to be labelled to show that it had been modified.

Within months, Calgene and their competitors had rolled out dozens of modified fruits, vegetables, cereals, and milk. By 1997, four million hectares were dedicated to the cultivation of GM crops. It is now estimated that 70 percent of food sold in the US includes modified ingredients.

The manufacturers' claims for the new technology are impressive. GM foods can be made resistant to insects, diseases, adverse weather conditions, and pesticides. Growing times are reduced, yields are higher, and crops can be grown outside of their traditional environment. GM foods can have additional built-in vitamins to combat malnutrition, and vaccines to protect against disease. There is even talk of plants which can produce new kinds of plastic compounds. And, of course, the big argument is that famine could soon be eradicated. Or it would be if the international backlash against GM foods didn't include many of the African states it should be helping. Many of them have refused to accept the new products until there is more conclusive testing on the long-term effects on humans and their environment. Even taking aside ethical issues arising from what many see as tampering with nature, there are a myriad concerns over GM foods, the main thrust being that they are far too new and under-researched for us to ascertain their long-term safety.

The conspiracy theories

The Monsanto food manufacturer is a massive corporation, and consequently falls under the most suspicion from conspiracy theorists, particularly as the research and development of all their products is protected by patent and copyright laws, making it virtually impossible to elicit information. They are accused of presenting only findings from research that present their products favourably. Rumours abound of suppressed negative tests on animals.

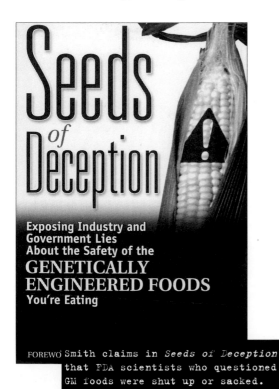

FOREWO Smith claims in *Seeds of Deception* that FDA scientists who questioned GM foods were shut up or sacked.

The company has spent fortunes on research and development, so it needs the world to buy GM foods as quickly as possible, without quibbling about laboratory reports.

The evidence

One of the very few negative studies into the new food technology was performed by Hungarian scientist Dr Arpad Pusztai, who fed rats a diet of GM potatoes. He claimed his subjects developed smaller brains, livers, and testicles, that their immune systems were damaged, and that they developed pre-cancerous cells. Two days after publishing his findings, he was sacked from his post at Aberdeen University. His team was disbanded and lawsuits arrived to stop any further findings being released – none of which would surprise anti-GM food campaigner Jeffrey Smith. In his 2003 book *Seeds of Deception: Exposing Industry and Government Lies About the Safety of the Genetically Engineered Foods You're Eating*, he claims that FDA scientists who voiced concerns over GM foods were "kicked out, muzzled, fired, or silenced on the issue."

In an interview to promote the book, Smith said: "We're feeding the products of an infant science to millions of people and releasing them into the environment where they can never be recalled. The pro-biotech people call me anti-science. I say, "Look at the science." An independent person looking at the science would never allow these foods to be fed to humans or animals." Perhaps most ominously, in 1999 Monsanto banned some GM foods from the staff canteen at their UK headquarters. A statement from their caterer said: "In response to concern raised by our customers over the use of GMFs [genetically modified foods], and to comply with government legislation, we have taken the decision to remove, as far as is practicable, GM soya and maize from all food products served in our restaurant."

The verdict

As campaigner Jeffrey Smith said, genetic modification is an "infant science" and the side-effects of GM foods, if any, may not be known for very many years; in the circumstances, some say that GM foods have been released on to world markets with indecent haste. However, there is no evidence that Monsanto or other corporations have knowingly sold potentially dangerous GM products without proper testing.

See also: *Soya Production p.204*

1996
SOYA PRODUCTION
Consumers are unable to determine safety of
genetically modified food

The soya plant, one of the world's oldest cultivated crops,
reached the US in the 1800s and remained a staple food because of its versatility. It is estimated that 75 percent of
all manufactured foods contain soya, or soya-based derivatives, including margarine, bread, and cereals.

In 1996, food conglomerate Monsanto introduced their
genetically modified "RoundUp Ready" soya. "RoundUp" is
a powerful herbicide manufactured by the company's chemical division. The plants had been manipulated to withstand
increasingly heavy doses of the chemical.

When the new GM soya reached Europe, concerns were
raised by health experts over the effects of the herbicide
on the consumer. Some researchers went so far as to link
the product with male infertility and cancer.

Adverse publicity led to many European supermarkets
bowing to consumer pressure and announcing a ban on GM
foods. However, in the US, modified soya is mixed with the
natural plant. The Food and Drug Administration has accepted the manufacturers' claim that there is no difference
between the two, and no need to separately label them.
Consequently, those supermarkets, and their customers,
are unable to make choices over which variety they buy.

"RoundUp" herbicide and soya are also sold to develop-
ing-world farmers, leading to allegations that Monsanto
have ensured they can grow nothing else. The herbicide
kills everything except the modified soya; so they can only
grow one crop, available from only one source. There is no
doubt that the world's industrial food manufacturers are
aggressively marketing and distributing their new GM products. Opinion is still divided as to how much long-term
damage these foods will do to our health and environment.

See also: *Genetically Modified Food p.202*

1998
MEASLES, MUMPS, RUBELLA VACCINE
Triple vaccination for children causes autism

Measles, mumps, and rubella were common childhood illnesses until the 1970s when inoculations became widely
available. In the 1980s, the vaccines were combined into a
single "MMR vaccine."

In 1998 in the UK, Dr Andrew Wakefield published an
article in medical journal *The Lancet* which made the link
between the MMR jab to bowel diseases and autism, a
neurological condition affecting the development of communication. Wakefield's findings created a press furore, and
subsequently led to his vilification. In *MMR: Science &
Fiction*, Richard Horton, editor of *The Lancet*, tells of senior
doctors gloating over their part in destroying Wakefield's
career. Wakefield himself believes his phone is tapped and
his home bugged.

In the US, Rick Rollens, of Defeat Autism Now, claims
that as the state of California introduced compulsory MMR
jabs in 1979, there has been an 800 percent increase in
autism. He believes that research supporting the vaccine
is funded by pharmaceutical companies. They are also accused of heavy-handed tactics when dealing with families
pursuing legal action against them, in one instance having
lawyers, with injunctions, waiting at hospitals to prevent
autistic children receiving independent tests.

The vaccine's opponents certainly remain vocal across
the world – and convinced of their case. However, the
overwhelming majority of medical experts and health professionals do believe that the MMR vaccine is on balance
the safest method of guarding against measles, mumps,
and rubella.

1998
STEM CELL RESEARCH
Scientists are creating cloned humans

Stem cells are mainly found in fetal tissue and brand-new
embryos. At that stage they are "unspecialized," which
means they have yet to develop into cells that perform a
distinct function. Scientists have found a way to extract
and grow those cells, and are endeavouring to find a way to
form specific tissues, which can be used to repair the
relevant damaged organs.

Since 1988, cells have been taken from placenta or um-
bilical cords and used, with some success, in the treatment
of Gunther's disease, Hunter syndrome, Hurler syndrome,
and acute lymphocytic leukemia. Then, in 1998, biologists
from Wisconsin University developed a system for extract-
ing cells from human embryos.

The medical profession is excited by the healing potential of embryonic stem cells, and many governments are
pouring funds into research. In the US, however, President
Bush has stated that he is opposed to stem cell research on
moral and ethical grounds. Since 2001, research has been

Policemen wear masks to ward off the SARS virus as they patrol an empty Forbidden City in China's capital on May 16th, 2003.

strictly controlled, and funds limited mainly to developing adult stem cells.

Some fringe conspiracy theorists believe the agenda is to grow new, cloned human beings for nefarious purposes. British author David Icke, for example, believes that the world is run by shape-shifting lizards who prey on the human race. He argues that stem cell researchers are actually creating a new food technology. The theory is problematic because Icke also believes that Bush is one of the key figures in the alien "Illuminati."

See also: *David Icke p.188; the Bavarian Illuminati p.285*

2002
SEVERE ACUTE RESPIRATORY SYNDROME (SARS)

Mystery disease was covered up by Chinese government

In February 2003, an American businessman flying from China became ill, with what appeared to be pneumonia. His condition was so bad that the plane stopped in Vietnam so he could receive treatment. He subsequently died, as did several of the hospital staff who had been in contact with him. The hospital realized they were dealing with a new virus and contacted the World Health Organization (WHO). On March 12th 2003, the WHO issued a global alert. They had found a mysterious and highly infectious new virus: severe acute respiratory syndrome (SARS).

In April 2003, Chinese military doctor Jiang Yanyong told the media that the disease had become known to his department in November 2002. He also claimed that senior health officials had been conspiring to keep a lid on the news. Jiang became a national hero and senior government ministers lost their jobs over the scandal. But there are some who see Jiang as a pawn in an internal political struggle. In July 2004, he was arrested and detained for seven weeks of "political re-education" after criticizing the government.

Teams of Dutch, Russian, and US scientists have all done tests on the virus, confirming that it could be manmade. The WHO's own research tracked the origin of the disease to the Guangdong Province in southern China. The first cases appear to have originated in army hospitals, and Guangdong is allegedly the location for one of China's biggest bioweapon research centres. The actual source of SARS is still considered by most credible experts to be a mystery.

See also: *Biochemical Weapons p.197*

> Military conspiracies are usually viewed
> as right-wing attempts to establish fascist
> control over democratically elected
> governments. These are not necessarily
> coups d'état where the generals form
> juntas, as has been the case in several
> Latin American countries, but may be an
> attempt to install a suitably acquiescent
> political puppet.

Although coup attempts are normally associated with unstable nations, modern generations of Americans are often unaware that such an attempt was made in their own country in the decade leading up to World War II. Fascist sympathizers on Wall Street plotted to install a popular US army general in the White House, using Remington weapons to force aside Roosevelt. Incredible as it may seem, this was no conspiracy theory, but a real conspiracy between some of the biggest names on Wall Street.

Military records

The developing world is well known for producing its leadership from the ranks of its armed forces, but figures in the western world have also risen to prominence via this route. General Eisenhower is the prime example, though less glorious military service records do feature in modern political campaigns. President George W. Bush served in the Alabama National Guard ... or did he? It became a key issue in the 2000 presidential race, just as John Kerry's military record in Vietnam became one in the 2004 campaign. On May 24th, 1972 George Bush Jr requested a six-month transfer from the Texas National Guard to a reserve unit in Alabama so that he would be able to work on Winton Blount's US Senate campaign. The desire to assist in the political career of a family friend was denied, but Bush had already set off for Alabama. Another official request was made on September 5th, 1972 to serve in a different Alabama unit, which was accepted by his commanding officer in Texas, Colonel William Harris. This was the 187th Tac Recon Group at Danelly ANG Base. Conspiracy theories arose after the commanding officer at Danelly, Lieutenant Colonel William

Turnipseed, went on record as saying that he never saw Bush at the base. Researcher Marty Heldt subpoenaed Bush's military records through a Freedom of Information Act request and found that the corner of one page of the file had been ripped off. This happened to cover the period November 1972 to May 1973. Despite Bush's denials made via his spokesman, Dan Bartlett, in *George* magazine, conspiracy theorists believe that the president was lying about his military service. Alabama Vietnam veterans were even offering a reward for proof that Bush had actually reported for duty at the base.

As is strangely common in military cover-ups, dental records are used to prove or disprove a theory. Military records of a dental examination carried out on January 6th 1973 were released by the White House on February 11th 2004 as proof that Bush was at the base during the period.

Dead Nazis

Dental records were also used to confirm the identities of dead Nazis at the end of World War II when conspiracy theorists insisted that they be named. To paraphrase General MacArthur, old soldiers never die, they fade away into the jungles of South America. Take, for example, Adolf Hitler. When the Soviet leader Joseph Stalin was asked by President Harry Truman at the Potsdam conference if Hitler had died in the Berlin bunker, he replied, "No." When the same question was asked by US Secretary of State Jimmy Byrnes, Stalin replied that Hitler had fled Berlin and gone to Argentina. Yet years later the KGB admitted to possessing Hitler's lower jaw and to having flushed his cremated ashes down the sewers of Berlin. The general responsible for this was also at one point the head of the KGB Disinformation Department, so what is one to make of the story? Dental records were used to identify Martin Bormann and Heinrich Himmler, both of whom have conspiracy theories surrounding their deaths. Even the dental records themselves become part of conspiracy theories as stories circulate about Hitler's collection and hiding of all top Nazi files. The dental records of the Nazi elite held at the National Archives in Washington are drawn from memory by Professor Hugo Blaschke. Forensic investigations of corpses aimed to establish the existence of physical doubles, the doppelgangers, who were willing to take their masters' places and sacrifice their own lives to provide a second chance for the Nazi elite to secretly rebuild the Reich somewhere else. Whether it was in Argentina, Paraguay, Brazil or the frozen continent of Antarctica, military organizations would continue to promote the right-wing, anti-communist ideals of the Nazis. As the Cold War developed and the Soviet Union became the number one enemy of the West, these paramilitary organizations started to be recruited by the United States in sabotage operations worldwide which invariably backfired when they became indistinguishable from terrorism.

The big three

After many years of silence, declassified documents heralding the secret successes of military intelligence operations during World War II started to appear in the 1970s. The single biggest disclosure was the revelation that the Allies had been reading the German coded signals for most of the war. The various German military ciphers had been broken by the cryptologists at Bletchley Park in England, and this fact alone had become the biggest secret of the war. It was to be protected at all costs, even if that meant deliberately ignoring attack warnings if military preparations obviously alerted the enemy to the possibility that their secret tactical and strategic communications were being read. Conspiracy theories sprang up over the German bombing of Coventry in 1940 and the German paratrooper invasion of Crete in 1941 where the so-called ENIGMA decrypts were supposed to clearly identify the targets ahead of time. Prime Minister Winston Churchill was accused of sacrificing both Coventry and Crete in order to maintain security for future, more important, uses of the ENIGMA traffic.

It was not just the German codes which had been broken, but also those of the other Axis power, Japan. Its diplomatic and naval codes were allegedly being read on the build-up to Pearl Harbor, and that disaster was allowed to happen as the justifiable reason for the US to enter the war. This was planned either by Churchill, who desperately needed the US to get involved, or by Roosevelt, or by both of them working together in a conspiracy. Stalin would later

see them definitely conspiring against him during the siege of Stalingrad, as they refused to open up another front in Europe, preferring to concentrate on North Africa.

Stalin's paranoia, which had caused widespread purges of Soviet society during the 1930s, had reached the Red Army in 1937. Seeing the influence of German agents everywhere, Stalin and his NKVD chief Yezhov – from whose name the whole murderous bloody period took its name, the Yezhovshchina – picked on its best general, Mikhail Nikolayevich Tukhachevsky, and initiated a purge which decimated the Red Army. Most of the top military elite, with all their experience, were either imprisoned or executed in the crucial years leading up to World War II. Stalin's initial Non-Aggression Treaty with Hitler bought him some time to rebuild, but the shock of the German invasion of Russia in Operation BARBAROSSA in 1941 was partially down to the self-inflicted weakness of the Red Army following the purges. Another reason for the shock was Stalin's inherent disbelief in all intelligence that warned him of the impending attack. This refusal to believe intelligence was a symptom of his paranoia.

The fog of war

Conspiracy theorists are firm believers in the inability of the US to declare war first on anybody. If the US wants to go to war with whatever-sized enemy – a nation state or, more recently, terrorist organizations – it has to arrange an "unprovoked" attack upon itself so that it can have the moral high ground in seeking retaliation. An example is the Gulf of Tonkin in 1964, at the beginning of the Vietnam War, when the US is alleged to have deliberately provoked North Vietnamese forces into attacking US ships in order to justify an escalation of the conflict. A slight variant is the Pearl Harbor scenario already mentioned, where an enemy attack is allowed to happen without adequate defence in order to magnify the horror felt by the US politicians and population, thus allowing a rapid uncontested declaration of war in retaliation. Another example is the Northwoods plan of 1962. This idea, which was never followed through, was to stage-manage a terrorist attack on the US; the attack would be blamed on Cuba and used as a justification for invading that nation. The Northwoods plan was only a plan, yet it would later be seized as a template for some of the crazier 9/11 conspiracies.

Each military disaster is also a military success for the other side in the conflict and this must never be overlooked. Similarly, intelligence failures are also examples of successful deception operations perpetrated by the enemy. When a lesser foe inflicts a defeat upon a mighty nation, conspiracy theorists will see only the hidden signs of a traitor or saboteur. War, despite its planning, is chaotic as soon as the first round is fired. The great military theorist, Carl von Clausewitz, was fully aware of this, and described the conditions which enable errors to be made as the "fog of war." Human error contributes to the great uncertainty of war and, by extension, to the great uncertainty of history. Historians subscribe to the "cock-up theory", where the apparent human infallibility factor that exists within conspiracy theories does not exist in reality. People make mistakes, and strange, unexpected outcomes of military operations occur. Defeat in combat does happen, not because there is some sinister deliberate reason for losing a battle in order to win the war, but because the enemy was superior on that occasion.

Dirty fighting

There is also a conspiracy theory that takes the most evil practices of warfare, those which are banned by the Geneva Conventions, and claims that the "clean" fighters, the civilized armies of the West, resort to them when faced with the "dirty" fighters, the uncivilized armies of the developing world. One example is the use of chemical and bacteriological weapons during the first Gulf War by the US, when Saddam Hussein's previous deployment of gas attacks on the Kurds raised the threat of its probable use against the US and coalition troops. Following the paper trail of how Iraq came into possession of such weapons would ultimately lead to the United States. Times change in international conflict and allies become enemies and vice versa. Conspiracy theorists tend to ignore these sea changes in international relations and assume that arms agreements are always secret and sinister, run by immoral cabals with no allegiance to anything other than money and world power. Within conflicts they will always search for examples where the side fighting for good lapses into acts of atypical barbarism, sometimes on its own kind, in order to blame the enemy for the atrocity.

Chemical attacks, by their very nature, can blow back on the perpetrators. An example is Agent Orange, used as a defoliant in Vietnam. Likewise, pharmaceuticals supplied to troops to protect them against chemical and biological weapons are claimed to produce dangerous side effects. Controversy still exists about whether Gulf War syndrome is an actual disease or a psychological state similar to that of shellshock, a condition of the mind which pre-dates the administering of drug-cocktails to the modern soldier. There is an instance where an individual war veteran comes to terms with a nervous debility by blaming it on some secret nerve agent attack by his own forces during the Vietnam War, then manages to sell the conspiracy theory as reality to a CNN reporter. The public desire for dirty tricks to be exposed can encourage fantasists to create new conspiracies.

Militia

As Hollywood developed the role of Special Forces in the mind of the public, with films such as *Delta Force* (1986), with Chuck Norris and Lee Marvin, and *Navy Seals* (1990) with Charlie Sheen, the idea of clandestine military operations soon dominated all concepts of war. Secret missions behind enemy lines with the attendant deniability would allow theorists to imagine the same techniques being used against their own citizens. Senate investigations during the 1970s revealed the CIA and military surveillance of domestic targets, and this would seem to reinforce the suspicions held by some that the government was about to declare war on its people. In a response to this perceived threat, the Militia Movement in the US exercised its constitutional right to "keep and bear arms" to maintain the "security of a free state." Any attempts on gun control were seen as an infringement of the Second Amendment of the Bill of Rights, and could originate only from sources external to the US. The militia's favourite villain was the United Nations, which would use foreign troops to occupy the US once stringent gun-control policies were enacted. As proof of the planning already underway, international road signs were appearing on normal American signs to assist the foreign UN troops once the occupation occurred. These tactical markers (TACMARS) identified strategic and tactical locations, and foreign troops in foreign vehicles were sometimes seen infiltrating into rural areas. In reality, these sightings were nothing more than NATO manoeuvres.

Stealth

When military techniques were introduced into the fight against drug production in Latin America, other stages of the distribution came under a similar treatment. The Drug Enforcement Agency would employ military helicopters for stealth-like surveillance operations within the US. As night-vision capabilities improved for the pilots, the need for external lights diminished and the so-called "black helicopter" entered conspiracy theories. Stealth technology in aircraft had taken several decades to produce and was usually carried out on top-secret military bases such as Area 51 at Groom Lake, Nevada. Retrospectively, once the F-117 Stealth Fighter was first seen in public, earlier sightings previously attributed to UFOs were now explained. As would be expected in such circumstances, research and development had been kept under strict security, feeding the conspiracy theories. Over-inquisitive American citizens were as much a risk to national security as Soviet spies.

Deception

The desire to keep military operations secret in both war and peacetime is a standard requirement for the safety of the armed forces personnel involved. It is imperative that the enemy does not know the correct intention, and this usually involves the dissemination of disinformation. Conspiracy theorists are likely to be picking up the same partial intelligence as the enemy and forming conclusions just as wrong. If this is the case, then the military's deception operations have been a success. World War II provided a classic example of military deception in the use of the Double Cross System by the British to fool the Germans into believing that their spies were reporting the truth when in fact the whole network was under British control. Dummy aircraft on runways of fake airfields wasted German bombing raids, and dummy tanks concentrated enemy forces in the wrong position. This technique of deceiving the enemy is used as much today as it was during previous wars. Just as fog machines were used to conceal the exact location of targets from

As with many US presidents, George W. Bush's military past is murky.

overhead aircraft, other methods are used to deliberately create a "fog of war" over past missions. Conspiracy theorists create their alternative explanations of historical events based on declassified documents, which are usually incomplete but are taken to be accurate accounts. Some of the World War II documents have been kept secret for so long for reasons of national security; some are still under classified status because their military significance is ongoing.

Former members of the armed forces make the most persuasive cases for conspiracies because they are able to blend in truthful facts of their own military experiences with speculations as to motives that usually lie outside their knowledge. Military conspiracy theories tend to have sufficient military jargon and weapon designations to appear well researched, but many fall down on the basic implausibility of the operations. Also the willingness to needlessly sacrifice one's own forces for a short-term tactical gain is not as widespread a quality in military leaders as theorists seem to believe.

1930–40
NAZIS AND GENERAL MOTORS

US car giant aided the German war effort through its overseas subsidiaries

In the lead-up to World War II and during it, the US automotive giant General Motors was involved in the production of enemy trucks and fuel conversions in Nazi Germany.

In 1935, General Motors' subsidiary Adam Opel AG, the largest automobile company in Germany, established a heavy-truck production line at Brandenburg. From that location, specially picked to make it less vulnerable to air attacks in future wars, GM supplied Opel "Blitz" trucks to the Wehrmacht. As a reward for his contributions to the Nazi military preparations, GM's chief executive for overseas operations, James Mooney, was awarded the Order of the German Eagle (First Class) by Adolf Hitler. In April 1943, according to Charles Higham's *Trading with the Enemy*, GM in Stockholm was continuing to supply the Nazis with equipment and spare parts. In neutral Switzerland, GM handled conversions from gasoline to wood-gasoline for the Nazis.

In February 1974, Bradford Snell presented evidence to the US Senate Subcommittee on Antitrust and Monopoly detailing GM's involvement in the production of synthetic tetraethyl fuel for the German army. GM assisted the Nazi cartel IG Farben and the US's own Standard Oil of New Jersey in the supply of an alternative to Germany's scarce petroleum reserves on the lead-up to war.

Senate investigations found that General Motors, acting as a subsidiary of the Du Pont corporation run by fascist-sympathizer Irenne Du Pont, did contribute to the Nazi war effort through Opel, and its alliance with IG Farben.

1934

GENERAL SMEDLEY BUTLER
AND THE PLANNED US COUP

Wall Street tried to finance a right-wing coup against President Roosevelt

In 1934, communist journalist, John L. Spivak, claimed that Wall Street financiers and industrialists plotted to overthrow President Franklin D. Roosevelt and replace him with a fascist dictatorship under General Smedley Butler. Conspiracy theories about a fascist coup had been circulating the previous year after the assassination attempt on FDR, from which he escaped unscathed but which mortally wounded Chicago mayor Anton Cermak. The assassin, Giuseppe Zangara, was captured and, like Lee Harvey Oswald

some years later, was determined to be a "lone nut." Rumours spread that he was really in the employ of either a cabal of Wall Street financiers or the Mafia. The 1934 coup d'état plot was viewed as a second attempt to remove FDR from power. Spivak's story, in true conspiracy style, blamed the attempt on Jewish financial institutions, which he claimed were also financing Hitler's rise in Germany. This anti-Semitic core to his theory only raised doubts about the veracity of the other details of the coup plot.

The conspiracy theory

General Smedley Butler was one of the most popular soldiers in the US, and among the most loyal to his commander-in-chief, President Roosevelt. When Butler was approached by fascist-sympathizing attorney, Gerald MacGuire, and given the chance to lead the coup d'état, he played along, with the aim of gathering more information on who the plotters were. A massive $3 million war chest was available for the funding of a terrorist army; and the shadowy cabal behind the plot were the Du Pont corporation, its subsidiary General Motors, and Morgan Bank of Wall Street. General Butler learnt that over a million supporters were guaranteed to join in the coup and that the arms and ammunition would be supplied by Remington, another Du Pont subsidiary. With the grand scale of the plot revealed to him, he then dutifully reported it all to the White House.

The evidence

President Roosevelt's first reaction was to arrest the leaders of Morgan Bank and Du Pont, but there were economic factors to take into account. Following the great stock market crash of 1929, the American economy had fallen into the severest of depressions: 1934 was not the time to rock the fragile confidence of Wall Street by destroying one of its leading financial institutions, and FDR was not going to be held responsible for possibly triggering another stock market crash. So Roosevelt had to take a different route to defuse the plot. He used the press. By leaking the story and letting the newspapers bounce around the idea of a fascist coup originating from Wall Street, the president hoped the pressures for a coup would subside. The press generally found the whole idea absurd. Yet later in 1934, an investigation of the whole affair was instigated by the Congressional Committee on Un-American Activities. Butler testified to the accuracy of the claims made in the press, and representatives of the conspiracy were also summoned to testify. Naturally they denied any knowledge of the plot to replace the president.

The verdict

It took four years for the House of Representatives committee to release its report on the coup d'état plot, deeming it a safer time as Wall Street had recovered from its economic depression. Nevertheless, the report was marked for "restricted circulation" and showed that the committee had managed to verify all of the statements made by General Butler in his testimony: "Certain persons made an attempt to establish a fascist organization in this country."

Despite the extreme seriousness of the threat to the constitution of the US and the position of its president, no charges were made against the perpetrators. Captains of industry and finance were allowed to continue with their businesses as usual, suffering only the knowledge that they had been found out and their affiliations with Nazi Germany were now exposed. The fact that nobody was imprisoned would fuel further conspiracy theories.

See also: *Nazis and General Motors p.210*

1936–7
CONSPIRACIES DUPE SOVIET LEADER STALIN
The Nazis fooled Stalin into purging his Red Army

On June 1st, 1937 Stalin announced to a large group of military commanders in the Kremlin that their high command consisted overwhelmingly of German agents. Eleven days later, Marshal Mikhail Nikolayevich Tukhachevsky, and seven other generals accused of leading this "counter-revolutionary conspiracy fascist organization," were executed in a move which would spark off a massive purge of the Red Army. This claimed the lives of three out of five marshals, 15 out of 16 commanders, 60 out of 67 corps commanders and all 17 commissars; 13,000 officers were permanently removed from the Red Army, their exact fate is unknown, though the options were either execution or the gulags.

The conspiracy theories

It is claimed by some historians that the whole affair was a deliberate act of concealing a dark secret from Stalin's past, while others believe that it was part of a clever disinformation operation emanating from Himmler's SS.

So far as the "dark secret" theory goes, the starting point is that the Soviet generals knew about Stalin's secret Okhrana file, identifying him as a double agent of the Czar's secret police. Back in February 1913, Stalin was arrested as a Marxist but received a suspiciously light sentence. Roman

Brackman's *Secret File of Joseph Stalin* (2001) claims that the Great Purges were Stalin's attempt to kill anyone who had knowledge of his being a double agent.

The Nazi disinformation plot theory, meanwhile, was suggested by Robert Conquest in his book, *The Great Terror* (1968). Here, Conquest suggests that the generals were executed as a direct result of a Nazi disinformation operation, created by SS Reichsführer Heinrich Himmler and Obergruppenführer Reinhard Heydrich, to take advantage of Stalin's increased paranoia and personal hatred of Tukhachevsky. Heydrich, together with two subordinates from his security service, Sicherheits Dienst (SD), Alfred Naujocks, and Dr Herman Behrends, obtained signatures of several Soviet generals and forged letters that reported Marshal Tukhachevsky's intention of overthrowing Stalin in a military coup. Behrends was tasked to deliver the forgeries to Prague, where the president of Czechoslovakia, Edvard Benes, passed them on to Stalin in good faith. Professor Pawel Wieczorkiewicz from Warsaw University, after reading through the Russian Archives of the NKVD (the Soviet secret police and forerunner of the KGB), concluded that Stalin had indicated by proxy to the Nazis that he was interested in sleaze on Tukhachevsky. He therefore claimed that Stalin had initiated the plot, not Heydrich.

Stalin had accused Tukhachevsky once before, in 1930, three years before Hitler had even come to power. The OGPU (forerunner of the NKVD) interrogations of two officers had revealed the Chief of Staff was planning a coup against the Politburo, but these were not believed by Stalin's ally Sergo Ordzhonikidze, president of the Central Control Commission, so the case was dropped. Stalin's hatred of Tukhachevsky stemmed from the Polish–Soviet War of 1920, when the military commander failed to capture Warsaw. Polish cryptologists were reading Soviet Army radio messages, which gave Stalin added reasons to suspect treachery.

The verdicts

So far as Brackman's Okhrana theory is concerned, it must be borne in mind that many of the people who knew Stalin from that period were allowed to survive the purges, while over a million who didn't know him died. Also, in 1936, Tukhachevsky had criticized the People's Commissar for Defence, Voroshilov, for military incompetence. From that time on, Voroshilov, with the NKVD's Yezhov, were out for revenge, advising Stalin to purge the army. Under torture Tukhachevsky subsequently confessed to being a German agent. Although Stalin linked his recruitment in with a German seductress by the name of Josephine

Pope Pius XII leaves the presidential palace in Berlin.

Heinze, no German evidence was presented at the trial.

If Heydrich's forged documents were as important as Robert Conquest maintains, meanwhile, how come they were never produced in the military court? Stalin had all the proof he needed to execute Tukhachevsky – his bloodstained confession, which is apparently still in the NKVD archives. In 1957, four years after Stalin's death, Nikita Khrushchev declared that the charges made against Marshal Tukhachevsky and the seven other generals had been fabricated. Their public reputations were restored, but some skeptical historians view Khrushchev's comments as Cold War propaganda, desperate to rule out the belief that a military conspiracy against Stalin could have been possible.

1940s
NAZIS AND THE VATICAN
Pope Pius XII refused to criticize the Holocaust because he was secretly pro-Nazi and anti-Semitic

Supposed revelations about the early career of the wartime Pope have led conspiracy theorists to seek fascist policies within the Vatican. Eugenio Pacelli was previously the papal nuncio in Munich, when, according to the eyewitness account of his housekeeper, Sister Pascalina, he received Hitler late one evening and gave the Führer a large amount of money to invest in the rising German economy.

This account has to be measured against the very public stance that Pacelli took against the Nazis in 1937, when he was the Vatican's secretary of state and drafted Pope Pius

XI's encyclical, condemning Nazism as un-Christian. That document was smuggled into Germany and caused the confiscation of presses and imprisonment of many Catholics. Once Pacelli became Pope Pius XII, his 1942 speech criticizing the persecutions only led to more persecutions and that is why he stopped making public protests. Persecuted groups had pleaded with him to not stir up the Nazis. When the Allies eventually issued a condemnation of Nazi atrocities against the Jews, he refused to sign unless he could also condemn the slaughter of Jews by Stalin.

As for being anti-Semitic, Pope Pius XII saved an estimated 700,000 Jews from the concentration camps by issuing false Christian baptismal certificates and hiding many in the sanctuaries of monasteries and convents. His choice of diplomacy over protest prevented widescale martyrdom, and this has promoted a recent rethink among Church historians and calls for his canonization.

See also: *Nazis Escape "Ratlines" and the Vatican p.218*

1940–5
ACTIVITIES OF UNIT 731
COVERED UP
US masked Japanese use of plague weapons against the Chinese

The US was willing to cover up the war crimes of Japanese biological warfare Unit 731 in return for acquiring the research and expertise of the scientists involved.

In November 1941, American and British intelligence services became aware of an outbreak of bubonic plague at Changte in Hunan province of China, spread by an aeroplane from Unit 731, based in Pingfang, Manchuria. John W. Powell's article, "Japan's Biological Weapons 1930–1945", in the October 1981 issue of the *Bulletin of Atomic Scientists* was the first to claim that the US had covered up the war crimes. Colonel Murray Sanders, from the US biological warfare centre at Fort Detrick in Maryland, was in charge of hunting down the BW stocks and personnel. General Douglas MacArthur agreed to promise the scientists immunity in return for their secrets.

A similar situation existed in Germany, but there BW scientists were being condemned as war criminals by the International Military Tribunal at Nuremberg. In the case of the Japanese Unit 731, no charges were ever made by the chief prosecutor of the Tokyo trial, Joseph Keenan. This must be contrasted with the Soviet 1949 Khabarovsk trial of Japanese war criminals for bacteriological warfare.

MacArthur was given authorization by the State-War-Navy Coordinating Committee to offer the fugitive leader of Unit 731, Ishii Shiro, and his scientists, immunity from prosecution for war crimes in return for research data. The US policy of denying the Soviets access to the experts of Unit 731 overruled any legal action similar to Nuremberg.

See also: *Project COAST and Dr Death p.227*

1941
ROOSEVELT AND CHURCHILL LET PEARL HARBOR HAPPEN

The two leaders conspired to withhold intelligence to bring the US into World War II

On Sunday December 7th, 1941, at 7.55am, the Japanese Imperial Navy launched a surprise air attack on the American Pacific fleet located at Pearl Harbor in Hawaii. Eighteen ships were sunk or badly damaged, 188 aircraft were destroyed, mainly on the ground, and 2,403 people were killed in an act that brought the US into the war. The next day, President Roosevelt signed a declaration of war against Japan and this was followed on December 11th by Hitler's declaration of war against the US.

The conspiracy theories

This sequence of events has convinced some conspiracy theorists that Pearl Harbor was allowed to happen in order for the US to have a justified reason for entering World War II. They claim that advance warning of the Japanese attack was deliberately ignored so that the US could be seen as responding to the unprovoked attack of an aggressor. Because of the Axis alliance, it was assumed that Germany would come to the defence of Japan once the US had declared war, and that this was the ultimate aim. Roosevelt's decision to declare war was actually announced prematurely by Winston Churchill in the House of Commons, two hours before his own formal statement. The British prime minister's obvious jubilation at the entry of the US also raised suspicions that he had orchestrated the whole thing. Various theories abound concerning Churchill's advance knowledge and how he withheld that from Roosevelt, in order to draw his reluctant ally into the war. Other theories charge that both Roosevelt and Churchill conspired to withhold critical intelligence. As with all conspiracy theories concerning military disasters, they have to be weighed up against the "cock-up" theory of history, which assumes that human error is responsible.

The evidence

On December 7th, just minutes after FDR heard of the attack and before any damage reports were in, he phoned Lord Halifax at the British Embassy in Washington and told him that most of the fleet had been at sea and that none of the newer ships were in Pearl Harbor. This fortunate disposition of the Pacific fleet raised suspicions that the older battleships had been sacrificed and that the important aircraft carriers were deliberately kept out of the area. American Admiral Bloch even callously testified later that the Japanese "only destroyed a lot of old hardware. In a sense they did us a favour."

With the declassification of wartime intelligence files on both sides of the Atlantic, investigators have sifted through the decrypts for evidence of advance knowledge of the attack. Both the Americans and the British had broken the Japanese diplomatic code, PURPLE, so were able to read the messages ordering the shut-down of embassies and destruction of documents, preset for 1pm December 7th, 1941, and 7.30am in Hawaii. For years, both countries had kept classified the fact that they had also cracked the JN-25 Japanese naval operational cipher. Conspiracy theorists believe that this allowed the Japanese movements towards Pearl Harbor to be tracked.

It is true that the Pacific fleet aircraft carriers were not in Pearl Harbor, but their reasons for being elsewhere are pretty well accounted for. For example, the *USS Enterprise* was scheduled to return from Wake Island around 7am on the fateful day but had been held back by bad weather. Nevertheless, it was close enough to engage Japanese aircraft in aerial combat and, therefore, could not have been deemed to be in safe waters. The *USS Lexington* was on its way to Midway Island to reinforce the forward base, and the *USS Saratoga* was in the naval dockyard at San Diego. As for the PURPLE decrypts during the 24 hours before the attack, General Marshall did alert Hawaii and had made several attempts to confirm whether his warning had been delivered, but to no avail. Atmospheric conditions conspired to force the message to be telegraphed instead.

While it is also true that the US and the UK had broken the naval code JN-25, the Japanese fleet had adopted very strict radio silence during the operation. Other intelligence had pointed to the target being Singapore, not Hawaii. Even so, the naval codes had been recently superseded by the, as then, unbroken codes JN-25B7 and JN-25B8.

The verdict
Both Roosevelt and Churchill had strong ties to the navy, which rules out any deliberate sacrifice of ships and sailors' lives. Theorists who claim that intelligence was available fail to understand the nature of the intelligence process. Intelligence failures are very seldom the fault of intelligence gathering, but the way the intelligence is interpreted by the decision makers. Detailed searching of archives, after the event, is always bound to find something that was overlooked during the real-time pressures. This is a prime example of the "cock-up" theory at work, delaying crucial messages. Nothing must be taken away from the stealth of the Japanese navy in carrying out this major operation.

See also: *Churchill, Coventry, and the ENIGMA Secret p.225*

1941
RUDOLF HESS AND THE FLIGHT TO BRITAIN
b. April 26th, 1894, Alexandria, Egypt
d. August 17th, 1987, Spandau Prison, Berlin?
   Hess's flight to Scotland was part of an MI5 plot

There are several Rudolf Hess conspiracies involving the existence of doppelgangers and the confinement in Spandau prison of the wrong man. They seem to be based on a common belief that Nazi leaders never die when they're supposed to and have willing doubles to take the punishment. Doppelgangers aside, there are elements of Hess's myste-

rious flight to Scotland which open themselves to conspiracy theories. The deputy, who wrote down Hitler's *Mein Kampf* in dictation, chose to abandon his leader and make peace overtures with the Duke of Hamilton by flying his Messerschmidt to Scotland on May 10th, 1941, and parachuting into a field near the duke's country estate. Hess wrongfully believed his intended host to be an influential member of a British peace party. Records show that MI5 had intercepted a letter from Hess suggesting peace talks, but the message was never forwarded to Hamilton. When Hess duly arrived, there appears to be confusion over exactly what Britain was going to do with him. Churchill was in favour of parading him around as a very obvious sign that the Nazi leadership was divided, but the Cabinet overruled him, preferring to use him in a disinformation campaign. Instead of being seen to have acted on his own initiative, they wanted Hess to appear as an official peace emissary from Hitler, in the eyes of Stalin, hoping that the latter's inherent paranoia would make him believe that Hitler wanted to concentrate just on the eastern front. This is a case where official disinformation breeds conspiracy theories.

1941–8
ALLIED MISTREATMENT OF PRISONERS OF WAR
   Eisenhower sanctioned the death of a million German prisoners

The Allies, under General Eisenhower, were responsible for the deaths of a million German prisoners of war, caused by willful mistreatment, both during and after the war.

In 1989, Canadian novelist James Bacque's *Other Losses: An Investigation into the Mass Deaths of German Prisoners of War at the Hands of the French and Americans After World War II* alleged that Eisenhower's mistreatment of POWs was due to his intense hatred of the Germans. This controversial fact had to be covered up as it negated the outrage against the Nazi's Holocaust atrocities. The claims were dealt with effectively in 1992 by Gunter Bischof and Stephen Ambrose's *Eisenhower and the German POWs: Facts Against Falsehood*, in which West German-produced mortality statistics showed that only one percent of German POWs died annually during US internment, a figure comparable with that of US POWs dying in German camps. American treatment of German POWs and vice versa conformed to the Geneva Conventions, unlike that of the Soviet Union, a non-signatory nation. Statistics show that up to 50 per cent of German POWs died in Soviet hands, compared with up to 80 percent of Soviet

POWs in German hands. One can easily see that the claims of US mistreatment of enemy POWs, though bound to happen, never happened on the extreme scale of other nations. Bacque's attempt to blame the deaths of a million POWs on Eisenhower was based on false figures and ignorance of the official West German Maschke Commission study.

1942
PHILADELPHIA EXPERIMENT COVER-UP

A top-secret US navy invisibility experiment, which ended in disaster, was covered up

The theory originates from a drifter, named Carl Allen, who claimed in 1955 to have been a merchant seaman on board the *USS Andrew Furuseth* during World War II. His alleged eyewitness account described invisibility experiments carried out on the *USS Eldridge*, which caused the destroyer to disappear from its berth at the Philadelphia Navy Yard, appear in Norfolk, Virginia, hundreds of miles away, then reappear back in Philadelphia. Claiming that the experiment used high energy force fields which caused burns, madness and deaths, Allen's story convinced authors William Moore and Charles Berlitz to investigate further. Failing to locate the *USS Eldridge* in Philadelphia did not prevent them from writing a bestseller.

Carl Allen is rumoured to have confessed that the whole story was a hoax, but later denied the confession. Moore and Berlitz used Allen's real-life service on the *USS Andrew Furuseth,* during 1943 and 1944, as an anchor on which to pin the second fact that Albert Einstein was a US navy scientific consultant in 1943. By attributing Einstein's unified field theory to the speculative experiments on altering a ship's magnetic attraction of enemy mines, the authors pushed credibility too far by seriously considering Allen's claims of actual physical invisibility and teleportation.

The story belongs in the realm of science fiction, reinforced by the film *1984*, which adds time travel to the theme.

1942–3
ALLIED FORCES FAIL TO RELIEVE STALINGRAD

Churchill and Roosevelt were conspiring against Stalin by not opening a second front in Europe

Stalin was the ultimate conspiracy theorist, seeing enemies everywhere within the Soviet Union and trusting no-one. The word "Allies" was a misnomer, as Stalin did very little in the way of providing information to encourage the other two leaders to offer help. Churchill convinced Roosevelt to move the campaign to North Africa instead, and this even ruled out the opening of a second front through an invasion of France during 1943. When the German Sixth Army laid siege to Stalingrad, Hitler had overruled any misgivings from the German High Command and completely underestimated the enemy forces. Stalin had managed to conceal large numbers of reserve units, which enabled the Russian Army to launch a counteroffensive, encircle the Sixth Army and mark the turning point of the war on the eastern front. Stalin's continued distrust of the Allies led to blatantly false reports being sent to Roosevelt and Churchill, claiming that the situation in Stalingrad was getting worse, just as it was actually improving for the Soviet forces. Hitler issued the famous order to General Paulus and the Sixth Army, refusing to allow them to retreat. That resulted in their eventual destruction.

Stalin was correct to believe that Roosevelt and Churchill were conspiring. Hitler's recent launching of Operation BARBAROSSA, the invasion of the Soviet Union, had broken the long-standing controversial German–Soviet Non-Aggression Treaty and that was still fresh in their distrustful minds.

See also: *Conspiracies Dupe Soviet Leader Stalin p.211*

1943
OPERATION MARKET GARDEN

OMG was a devious plan to delay the end of World War II

Was the massive Allied airborne attack on Arnhem in 1944 allowed to fail as part of a complicated Allied deception plan to prolong the war, or was it a military cock-up?

On September 17th, 1944, Allied paratroopers took part in a secret attack on Arnhem, code-named Operation MARKET GARDEN. As soon as they hit the ground they were met by two SS Panzer divisions in and around the target drop zone. Six weeks afterwards, a self-confessed Abwehr agent, named Cornelis Verloop, identified the Dutch resistance leader Christiaan Lindemans as a fellow Abwehr agent. From his interrogation it was revealed that he had crossed the enemy lines four days before Operation MARKET GARDEN, supposedly to rendezvous with Allied troops being hidden by Dutch resistance near Eindhoven. In fact he had rendezvoused with Colonel Kiesewetter of the Abwehr at its Driebergen headquarters, passing on to him details of the operation a full two days before the planned attack.

Anne Laurens, in her 1971 book, *The Lindemans Affair*, proposed the conspiracy theory that Lindemans was in fact a British double agent, deliberately feeding the Abwehr with information which would prolong the war. The theory ignores the fact that no military commander would deliberately sacrifice such a large operation as MARKET GARDEN to achieve a minor deception. As it turned out, according to Abwehr sources, Lindemans was believed to be a British deception agent and the presence of the two SS Panzer divisions at Arnhem was purely coincidental, as Lindemans had not known the exact details of the drop.

1944
MARTIN BORMANN WAS A KGB SPY

b. June 17th, 1900, Halberstadt, Germany

d. May 2nd, 1945, Berlin, Germany

Bormann was really the highest-level soviet spy within the German high command

The theory suggests that Martin Bormann was really the Soviet spy code-named WERTHER, who provided inside information on Hitler's plans, which allowed Stalin to anticipate most of the German military campaigns.

The conspiracy theory

The identity of the famous WERTHER has been the subject of many speculative histories of the "Red Orchestra" (Rote Kapelle), the Soviet spy ring which operated out of Switzerland during World War II. The theory that it was Martin Bormann was renewed by double-Pulitzer prizewinner Louis Kilzer in his book *Hitler's Traitor: Martin Bormann and the Defeat of the Reich, in* 2000. The theory is based on the extremely rapid, almost simultaneous, transmission of intelligence, which could only have come from Hitler's inner circle. It is claimed that WERTHER was able to pass on battle orders before the front-line commanders had even received them. German military reverses at Stalingrad and Kursk suddenly become explainable due to Stalin's access to what the Germans were planning to do next.

The evidence

Kilzer stresses the fact that Bormann had unrestricted access to the minutes of Hitler's military planning session from 1942 onwards, the period when his personal stenographers were employed. In books of this sort, important spies are always major, famous characters, whereas in reality, it's the very minor, insignificant ones who are generally responsible for the collection and passing on of intelligence. It is more likely to be the stenographers themselves than Martin Bormann.

Keitel, Goering, Hitler, and Bormann at Fuehrer Headquarters, July 20th, 1944, an hour after an attempted bomb plot on Hitler's life.

Previous investigations of the WERTHER case have pointed to it not being an individual agent, but a group of agents collectively code-named. Bernd Ruland, in his 1973 book *Moscow's Eyes*, claimed that WERTHER was two teleprinter operators at the German High Command (OKW) radio centre at Zossen. These girls, whose identities Ruland promised to conceal until after their deaths, were able to obtain carbon copies of the OKW teleprinter messages after they had been decrypted by the Geheimschreiber cipher machines. Ruland was their supervisor and, having discovered their treachery, he was also recruited into the anti-Nazi conspiracy. Unfortunately, Ruland died before the deaths of the women, and their identities are still unrevealed. What gives Ruland's book some credence is the fact that it was recommended by Alexander Rado, the leader of the Red Orchestra's spy ring in Switzerland.

Bormann's stenographers were used to secretly record Hitler's conversations for posterity. One of them omitted sensitive military material, but the other obeyed Bormann's orders for full uncensored reporting. British intelligence officer and historian Hugh Trevor-Roper used these same records to publish *Hitler's Table Talk* after the war.

In the fall of 1971, Major General Reinhard Gehlen, the former chief of the Foreign Armies East section of the General Staff, published his memoirs in which he shocked the world by claiming Bormann had died in the Soviet Union only two years before. Basing this on reliable reports of Bormann appearing in a film watching a sports event with high-ranking Soviet officials, Gehlen further revealed in a sworn testimony that during the war both he and his superior, Abwehr chief Admiral Canaris, had suspected Bormann of being a spy. The reason for this was the search for an apparent security leak in the top echelon of the military command, which was responsible for the rapid passing of German commands to the enemy. Gehlen's "reliable source" on Bormann's survival and later death was never named, and the evidence has to be weighed up against the dental record identification of Bormann's skull in 1971, and the DNA testing in 1990.

The verdict

Bormann appears to have committed joint suicide with Hitler's physician, Dr Ludwig Stumpfegger, in the early hours of May 2nd, 1945 on the bridge at Invalidenstrasse in Berlin, rather than face the Russian troops. Why would he have used the poison capsule if he really was WERTHER? Surely a Soviet agent would have stayed put in the Berlin bunker or have had a plan to safely make contact with his employers. Stalin would have been eager to shake the hand of WERTHER.

1945
HEINRICH HIMMLER FAKED HIS OWN DEATH

b. October 7th, 1900, Munich, Germany
d. May 23rd, 1945, near Luneberg, Germany?

The man claiming to be SS Reichsfuhrer Heinrich Himmler was really a double named Heinrich Hitzinger

This is yet another Nazi doppelganger theory where an ultra-loyal physical double pretends to be the real character and dies in custody. On May 21st, 1945, Himmler, having shaved off his moustache and wearing an eyepatch, was arrested at a security point on the Oste River, near Bremervoerde. The Black Watch guards inspected his eye and found it to be undamaged. Together with his two SS travelling companions, Himmler was taken to an interrogation centre where he claimed to be Heinrich Hitzinger, a man who, allegedly, did bear a strong resemblance to him. After two days of deception, he finally admitted his real identity. When searched by a British doctor for the presence of a poisonous potassium cyanide vial, Himmler bit down on the one he had successfully hidden and died soon after.

British surgeon and forensics expert Hugh Thomas, in his 2001 book *The Unlikely Death of Heinrich Himmler*, points out some alleged post-mortem inconsistencies, such as the absence of a duelling scar on the corpse's left cheek, and the bullet wound sustained in an attempt on Hitler's life in 1943. He proposes the theory that the suicide was really Heinrich Hitzinger. Conspiracy surrounds the case as Himmler's files are still sealed by the British government until 2045. They are likely to reveal the confessions made by Himmler's two travelling companions.

See also: *Hitler Survived the End of World War II p.218*

1945
HIROSHIMA WAS BOMBED USING NAZI URANIUM

Radioactive raw material seized en route to Japan was used in Manhattan Project

A German U-boat carrying uranium oxide to Tokyo for use in the Japanese atomic bomb project surrendered to the US navy and its cargo disappeared.

After the suicide of Hitler, German submarine U-234 surrendered in the north Atlantic and was taken to the US naval base at Portsmouth, New Hampshire, arriving on May 19th, 1945. The uranium oxide was carried off the U-boat in ten cases, each weighing 560kg (1,235lb), and inventoried along with the rest of the cargo. From there, the paper trail runs cold. The uranium oxide would be enough to produce about 3.5kg (9lb) of the isotope U-235, enough to make up one-fifth of the atomic bomb that was dropped on Hiroshima. Yet government security surrounds the destination of the material. Did it make its way into the mix for the bomb that demonstrated to the Japanese that the American atomic bomb project had finished the race?

Robert Wilcox, author of *Japan's Secret War*, checked through the Manhattan Project papers in the National Archives and found no records of the U-234 or its cargo of U-235. A former official of the Manhattan Project, John Lansdale, claims that it made its way into the general supply. From when the cargo was unloaded until the bombing of Hiroshima on August 6th and Nagasaki on August 9th 1945, may have been too short a period of time in which to extract the U-235 from the oxide ore. The Manhattan Project transportation documentation is either lost or being withheld for some unknown reason.

1945
HITLER SURVIVED THE END OF WORLD WAR II
b. April 20th, 1889, Braunau-am-Inn, Austria
d. April 30th, 1945, Berlin

After the end of the war, Soviet leaders denied that they had proof of Hitler's death

Hitler's suicide in the Berlin bunker underneath the Reich Chancellery on the last day of April 1945, in an area under Soviet military control, was devoid of evidence for Allied investigators so it was only natural that his death would be questioned. The Soviet claims that his body had been cremated did not alleviate concerns. The lower jaw was removed so that dental records could be checked later, though some theorists believe that Hitler had ordered the secret evacuation of all dental records of Reich leaders.

As the Russians later removed the corpse, reduced it to ashes and flushed it down the Berlin sewers to eliminate a future cult shrine developing, all that we have to go on are the immediate postwar comments of some of the leaders who would have access to proof if it did exist.

When President Truman asked Joseph Stalin at the Potsdam conference if Hitler was dead, the Soviet leader replied: "No." Marshal Zhukov, whose troops were the ones who occupied Berlin, was reported as saying: "We have found no corpse that could be Hitler's." This does not cor-

respond with later claims. Colonel Heimlich, former chief of US intelligence in Berlin, who was put in charge of investigating Hitler's suicide, concluded: "No insurance company in America would pay a claim on Adolf Hitler."

If Hitler did survive the war, where would he have gone? Stalin told US secretary of state Jimmy Byrnes: "He is not dead. He escaped either to Spain or Argentina." This is a prime example of Stalin playing with the minds of his new enemies, knowing full well that Hitler was dead.

See also: *Heinrich Himmler Faked his Own Death p.217*

1945
NAZIS ESCAPE "RATLINES" AND THE VATICAN
The Vatican helped Nazi war criminals escape from Europe

After World War II, there were two main escape routes, termed "ratlines," for Nazis guilty of war crimes, both of them through Italy, and both involving the Vatican.

The main one, the Intermarium, was run by American Intelligence with the help of Monsignor Krunoslav Draganovic in Genoa; the other was run by Bishop Alois Hudal, rector of the German College of Santa Maria dell'Anima in Rome. A blind eye was turned to the activities of the latter, because the Americans and British were deeply involved in the Intermarium, assisting the former Nazis become intelligence agents in the West and important assets in the new Cold War ahead. At one point in 1946 the ratline was able to save an entire Ukrainian Waffen SS division of 11,000 men with their families.

The Organisation der Ehemaligen SS Angehorigen (ODESSA), made famous by novelist Frederick Forsyth and his source, Jewish Nazi hunter Simon Wiesenthal, may be a figment of the imagination as an SS ratline organization.

Bishop Hudal was a well-known pro-Nazi prelate in Rome (and an informant for the Abwehr during the war) who provided Red Cross passports, tickets and visas to Latin America for Nazis on the run. Exposed in 1949, his network was eventually closed down because of Vatican pressure. At the beginning of 1950, the German press charged Hudal with having hidden Nuremberg escapee Otto Skorzeny in Rome, whereas another top Nazi, Klaus Barbie, had been spirited out of Europe by Monsignor Draganovic.

See also: *Nazis and the Vatican p.212; Nazi and Golden Lily Gold p.219*

1945
NAZIS AND GOLDEN LILY
GOLD

Both German and Japanese armies plundered enemy lands only to lose treasures to American forces

As war raged across Europe and the Far East, the treasures of once-independent cultures were systematically looted by the armies of occupation. As the war came to an end, there would be frantic attempts to preserve these massively wealthy hoards in the hands of the defeated Axis powers, with the victors joining in the hunt as well. National treasures would not necessarily be returned to their original owners and the wealth stolen in the form of gold or other precious metals would be forever lost into the heavily secure world of international banking.

The conspiracy theories

Conspiracy theories concentrate on the role of these looted treasures in the financing of American secret operations around the world and the supposed existence of unbelievably large secret bank accounts in the names of some very familiar characters from World War II.

European treasures: the evidence

As the Germans overran France, the SS set up a special unit to exploit the looting opportunities that regularly arose. The Devisenschutzkommando employed local talent in the form of French bankers who knew exactly where to search for stashed gold and currency. Their treasure-hunting skills were rewarded by the SS allowing them a ten percent finder's fee. Needless to say, in such looting operations, the Frenchmen would have to consider whether they needed to part with any of the treasure at all. Only individuals of a criminal persuasion would be attracted to the SS contracts in the first place, and the amount of extra looting that was never acknowledged would be siphoned off into private accounts for postwar fortunes.

An example can be found in the famous case of the Reichsbank treasure, estimated at $2.5 billion, which is still listed in the *Guinness Book of Records* as the largest unsolved bank robbery in history. It is claimed by some that the treasure was transported secretly across Austria, through the Brenner Pass into Italy and then on down into the Vatican Bank. As the US Third Army made its way across Germany, OSS officer Allen Dulles tipped off General Patton on the whereabouts of some more of the hidden Nazi treasure, $315 million worth in the Kaiseroda mine at Merkers.

This was then transferred to the Reichsbank in Frankfurt under heavy security.

Golden Lily: the evidence

As the Japanese overran China and Southeast Asia, they too set about looting the wealth of their occupied countries. Prince Chichibu was the royal head of the GOLDEN LILY operation, which involved the large-scale plundering of Chinese treasures and their transportation back to Japan aboard hospital ships. When the American navy achieved a submarine blockade of the Japanese islands, Prince Chichibu transferred the operation to the Philippines. It was later estimated that treasure worth over $100 billion was hidden there, as they could make use of the extensive system of natural caves. In a particularly ruthless set of operations, gold was hidden at sea by the simple process of torpedoing Japanese ships and killing all the crew to maintain the secrecy of the location.

At the end of the war, Filipino guerrillas who were following a party of Japanese soldiers to a secret location in the Philippines discovered that they were depositing treasure. Accompanying the guerrillas was an OSS major who observed the dynamiting of the cave and the exit of the Japanese. When the cave was reopened, the contents included heavy bronze cases packed with gold. The treasure was kept in situ until OSS officers "Wild Bill" Donovan and Edward Langsdale supervised the extraction.

The gold was removed from the Philippines and deposited in 176 bank accounts in 42 different countries, making up the basis of the newly created CIA's off-book financing, allowing covert operations to be carried out without Senate knowledge or approval. One account, in the name of Langsdale in the Geneva branch of the Union Banque Suisse held 20,000 tonnes (19.685 tons) of gold, and others elsewhere held hundreds of millions of dollars of bullion in the names of Herbert Hoover and General MacArthur.

The verdicts

The Nazi gold is well documented by Jewish attempts to reclaim it from Swiss banks. The Golden Lily hoard in the Philippines is also confirmed, but the involvement of famous Americans is based on the controversial research carried out for Sterling and Peggy Seagrave's book, *Gold Warriors: America's Secret Recovery of Yamashita's Gold*, and must therefore be treated with caution.

See also: *Nazis escape "ratlines" and the Vatican p.218*

1946
PROJECT PAPERCLIP – NAZIS WERE HELPED TO ENTER US

Nazi scientists guilty of war crimes were given false records to facilitate their entry into the US

As the US army advanced across Europe and overran German military sites, it became increasingly obvious that the level of German technology was far in advance of their own. The scientific specialists in rocket design and aeronautics were eagerly sought by all the Allied powers. In order to gain from their expertise and also deny their use to the Soviet Union, contracts were offered for some of these specialists to work in the US. In certain cases, the scientists also had undesirable SS memberships which legally denied them the right to enter the US. Others were directly involved in war crimes, yet they were accepted because it was believed that their contributions could shorten the war against Japan. Project PAPERCLIP, named after the technique of identifying the wanted personnel with a simple paperclip on their files, was eventually responsible for the controversial hiring of more than 1,600 scientists and technicians. The whole period when PAPERCLIP was in operation was not as covert as desired by the State-War-Navy Coordinating Committee when it first set it up, and the main critic of the recruitment programme was the State Department whose visa regulations were being circumvented.

Original disqualifying report cards from SS records provided evidence for the first stage of the vetting process by the Joint Intelligence Objectives Agency (JIOA), but these were later altered to allow SS officers such as Wernher von Braun to enter the US.

1946–7
ADMIRAL BYRD AND OPERATION HIGH JUMP

US Navy military expedition to Antarctica lost battle against Nazi flying saucers

With the discovery of hitherto secret aeronautical research establishments by the Allied troops as they advanced across Germany at the tail end of World War II in Europe, the scale by which Nazi technology had outstripped anything elsewhere shocked scientists in the US. Reports of unusual anti-aircraft devices which shadowed the flight of Allied bombers, known as "Foo Fighters", and delta-wing prototypes created a later UFO culture which has survived up to the present day.

The conspiracy theory

The question of where the defeated Third Reich would seek sanctuary to develop this technology further was answered cryptically by Admiral Dönitz in 1943: "The German U-boat fleet is proud to have made an earthly paradise, an impregnable fortress for the Führer, somewhere in the world." This answer promoted conspiracy theories about the existence of a secret Nazi flying saucer base in Antarctica, not least because the theorists knew that the concept of a Shangri-La tied in with Hitler's own occult beliefs. Rumours of Hitler's escape to Argentina also seemed to point to an eventual destination a couple of thousand miles further south: that is, Antarctica. And, of course, Nazi interest in the frozen continent was well known – in 1938, they had seized the territory, formerly claimed by Norway, and renamed it Neuschwabenland.

The threat from a Nazi base in Antarctica, utilizing advanced aircraft capable of flying in such inhospitable conditions, caused the setting up of an American task-force code-named Operation HIGH JUMP. Led by the famous polar explorer, Admiral Byrd, the expedition consisted of nearly 5,000 military personnel, numerous ships and an aircraft carrier. The military campaign was a disastrous defeat for the US navy as the Nazi aircraft easily fought off the invasion. More extreme conspiracies put the success down to technology, not of Nazi origin, but extraterrestrial origin. Diaries purporting to belong to Admiral Byrd supposedly detail secret meetings with an advanced subterranean race.

The evidence

Admiral Byrd did indeed lead an expedition to Antarctica, code-named Operation HIGH JUMP. It comprised 4,700 personnel, six helicopters, six Martin PBM flying boats, two seaplane tenders, 15 other aircraft, 13 US navy support ships and one aircraft carrier, the *USS Philippine Sea*. His orders from Admiral Chester Nimitz, commander of the US navy, were to test military capabilities in severe conditions and to consolidate and extend American sovereignty over as much of Antarctica as he could. It was originally planned as a six-month operation, but Admiral Byrd had to abandon the mission after only eight weeks. Far from being advanced Nazi aircraft or alien flying saucers that beat back the US navy, it was the extreme weather conditions. Documentary film footage was taken of the expedition and this shows helicopters and aircraft being blown off the aircraft carrier by high winds and violent seas. There is even footage of a US navy submarine frozen half out of the water with its crew being evacuated.

The failure of the operation demonstrated a very clear hole in the defence of the US. Its armed forces were totally ill-equipped for fighting in polar terrain. The emergent threat from the Soviet Union crossing over the North Pole was the strategic reason for sending HIGH JUMP to the other end of the globe. The American sector of Antarctica would provide the ideal training ground for the development of Arctic warfare.

The verdict

Antarctica presented as alien an environment to the US navy in 1946–7 as it does today, but that does not mean that there were real alien bases hidden underground. The Nazis had shown an interest in the development of Neuschwabenland in the immediate prewar years, and the U-boat capability to reach the icy continent, combined with Admiral Dönitz's cryptic comments, fed stories that Hitler had escaped there after the war. It is intriguing that Admiral Byrd was in contact with the original Nazi expedition led by Captain Ritscher, but there are no theories that the admiral deliberately sabotaged the US navy effort, just ones about him meeting with a subterranean race, obviously influenced by the Nazi mythos. Operation HIGH JUMP was defeated by something far more powerful than renegade Nazis and flying saucers: the fierce inhospitable environment of Antarctica and its surrounding seas.

1948
OPERATIONS "STAY BEHIND" AND "GLADIO"

The US established secret guerrilla armies to prevent communist influence in Italy after World War II

Operation STAY BEHIND, as its name suggests, involved the plan for anti-communist guerrilla forces to stay behind if conventional armies were forced to retreat from a Soviet invasion. The National Security Council created the Office of Policy Coordination in 1948 to carry out such covert actions in the target countries. The operations took on a more military command structure during the period 1949 to 1952, with the eventual setting up of a Clandestine Coordinating Committee within the Supreme Headquarters Allied Powers Europe (SHAPE).

US documents declassified in the 1970s revealed the secret agreement between the CIA and General Giovanni de Lorenzo, the chief of SIFAR (Italian Military Intelligence), dated November 1956, code-named GLADIO, in which a guerrilla force of 1,000 men was set up in Sardinia. At the Capo Marragui base, they were trained by US and British agents in espionage, sabotage and subversion. Over a hundred weapons and ammunition dumps were established in Northern Italy in preparation for a Soviet invasion, which would probably occur through the Gorizia gap.

The GLADIO network was organized into 40 independent cells, 12 responsible for guerrilla warfare, 10 for sabotage operations, 6 for intelligence-gathering, 6 for codes and radio communications, and 6 for running escape routes.

The conspiracy theory

The clandestine SHAPE military organization, which was set up to carry out the anti-Soviet guerrilla campaign if the Soviets succeeded in overrunning Europe during a future war, was actually used to carry out right-wing terrorist outrages in Italy.

The evidence

When the Communists gained 25 percent of the vote in the 1963 elections, General de Lorenzo, by then the commander of the paramilitary *carabinieri* as well as head of SIFAR, led a group of right-wing Christian Democrats, with the apparent sanction of President Antonio Segni, in a coup attempt against the premier, Aldo Moro. Operation SOLO was to have included the assassination of Moro, but the coup was called off at the last minute. Another coup attempt was made in December 1970, this time by Prince Julio Valerio Borghese, an ex-commander of Mussolini's Decima MAS (Tenth Light Flotilla). This too was called off at the last minute. However, at the subsequent trial, Colonel Amos Spiazzi proudly announced his membership of GLADIO after his acquittal.

CIA efforts to shut down GLADIO from the late 1960s were hampered by its continuing use to the US as a channel of communication with the Italian security establishment. As Italy experienced a wave of unexplained terrorist bombings between 1969 and 1984, the Communist Party blamed GLADIO. The 1972 Peteano car bomb attack that killed three *carabinieri* involved explosives which had been reported missing two months before from a GLADIO arms dump at Aurisina, near Trieste. General Geraldo Serraville of SIFAR, and head of GLADIO from 1971 to 1974, also blamed renegade GLADIO operatives for the bombing of Argo 16, a plane carrying Arabs expelled from Italy for trying to blow up an Israeli airliner, in 1973.

Giulio Andreotti, the Italian Minister of Defence, denied the existence of GLADIO in 1974, and again when he became prime minister, claiming that it had been disbanded

Stato Maggiore della Difesa
VIETATA DIVULGAZIONE
SERVIZIO INFORMAZIONI DELLE FORZE ARMATE
- Ufficio "R" - Sezione "SAD" -

Roma, li 1 Giugno 1959

LE "FORZE SPECIALI" DEL SIFAR E L'OPERAZIONE "GLADIO"

Declassified Report by the Italian Military Secret Service (SIFAR) on Operation "Gladio," June 1959.

in 1972. The 1980 Bologna railway station bombing, which killed 85 people, was sourced back to GLADIO explosives.

Following a call from the European Parliament in November 1990 to investigate GLADIO, General Paolo Inzerilli, chief of staff of the Italian security service SISMI, told a parliamentary commission on terrorism that the prime minister had now officially dismantled GLADIO, 18 years after Andreotti had claimed it disbanded.

The verdict

With its two-fold mission of preparing for guerrilla warfare against an anticipated Soviet invasion and a more likely case of communist subversion within Italy, GLADIO amassed a large number of weapons dumps. Communist election successes forced renegade elements to consider taking independent action which, with the ready availability of explosives and trained personnel, led to terrorist outrages. Events such as the Bologna station bombing would be unsuccessfully blamed on left-wing terrorists and resultant trials exposed links to the Italian secret service.

1950
RED CONSPIRACY – WHO STARTED THE KOREAN WAR?
Communist archive documents confirm conspiracy between China, Soviet Union and North Korea

The Korean War was started at 4am on June 25th, 1950, when North Korean troops crossed the 38th parallel and invaded South Korea. That is the generally accepted view. The claim of the North Korean leader, Kim Il-sung, that his troops were reacting to a provocation from South Korea is considered a lie, seeking justification for what was in reality a cold-blooded offensive move. According to the "Reluctant Dragon" theory, China's delayed entry into the war was also viewed as a defensive measure when the United Nations forces under the command of General MacArthur threatened the northern border with China. The Soviet Union's absence from the conflict, except for its provision of military hardware, was interpreted as a signal that it did not want to escalate the war.

Since the release of declassified documents from the archives of Russia, China, and even North Korea, the previously suspected belief that all three had conspired to start the Korean War has been shown to be accurate. This "Red Conspiracy" turned from theory into fact with the evidence of private meetings between Kim Il-sung, Joseph Stalin, and Mao Zedong in the months before the invasion. The North Koreans asked for and received the repatriation of Korean units from the Chinese People's Liberation Army, plus Mao's promise of Chinese reinforcements which were then amassing on the Yalu river border. Stalin promised material support for the invasion, which he saw as the start of a war in the East when the conditions in Europe looked to be stalemated.

1951
OTTO SKORZENY AND THE PALADIN MERCENARIES
Western intelligence agencies used fascist murderers as contract killers during the Cold War

In 1952, former SS commando leader Colonel Otto Skorzeny set up a right-wing terrorist organization, known as the International Fascista, which was used by both the CIA and the West German Gehlen network to wage covert war against communist groups all over the world. There were links made with Spain's Fuerza Nueva and the Guerrillas of Christ the King, France's Aginter Presse, Italy's Ordine Nuovo and

Argentina's Alianza Anticomunista Apostolica. Former agents from the SS, the French OAS and Portugal's PIDE became members of Skorzeny's offshoot mercenary organization, Paladin, which was responsible for the 1973 bombing of Rome's Fiumicino airport that claimed 32 lives. Paladin then attempted to blame the communists.

Although headquartered in Albufera, Spain, Paladin operated out of Skorzeny's export–import offices and cover firm MC Inc, which was located at the same Madrid address as a front organization of the Spanish intelligence agency SCOE. Also present in that same building was an office of the CIA. Paladin mercenaries were used to kidnap and execute leaders of the Basque ETA terrorist organization as well as carry out reciprocal bombing campaigns in Basque country during the period 1974–6.

The Skorzeny-controlled weapons supplier World Armco, with its headquarters in Paris, was registered in the name of Paladin's manager, Dr Gerhard Hartmut von Schubert. He had previously been a member of Joseph Goebbels' propaganda ministry, and upon Skorzeny's death in 1975 took over control of Paladin.

As the fight against communist-backed terrorism became increasingly more violent, the intelligence agencies found a suitably hard-core counter-force in Paladin.

See also: *Operations STAY BEHIND and GLADIO p.221*

1959
THE MANCHURIAN CANDIDATE
Unwitting assassins can be brainwashed or hypnotically programmed to kill political targets

The term "Manchurian Candidate" originates from the 1959 bestselling novel of the same name, written by Richard Condon, and made popular by the movie, starring Frank Sinatra and Laurence Harvey in 1962, and the remake, starring Denzel Washington and Meryl Streep in 2004. The story involves the creation of a remote-controlled assassin by Soviet and Chinese brainwashers located in Manchuria during the Korean War. The assassin is an American POW who returns to the US programmed to kill the president. Conspiracists have found this book ahead of its time, and the belief in mind-controlled killers figured significantly in the plots of real-life political assassinations of the 1960s. But is it possible to programme people to kill against their will?

The "Manchurian" element is derived from the Chinese propaganda use of public confessions from captured US pilots during the Korean War. By the end of the war, 70 percent of US prisoners were said to have confessed to various war crimes and a significant number continued to stick by their confessions after they had been repatriated. In 1953, Drs Harold Wolff and Lawrence Hinkle of Cornell University Medical College carried out an official CIA study on communist brainwashing techniques and concluded that not only normal, but also brutal, police methods were being applied for confessions. Chinese political re-education was achieved with no apparent use of drugs or hypnosis. This did not prevent the CIA attempting to use hypnosis in their own ARTICHOKE and MKULTRA programs to create a programmed assassin, but their eventual conclusions were that it was unreliable in operational conditions.

The concept of brainwashing and hypnotic programing as tools in the creation of a perfect assassin is unrealistic.

1962
OPERATION NORTHWOODS
The US considered fake terrorist attacks on its own citizens to provoke a popular war against Cuba

Operation NORTHWOODS was the code-name for a collection of plans involving the deliberate sacrifice of American and other friendly nationals in covert actions aimed at blaming the regime of Fidel Castro. These actions would involve terrorist attacks on mainland civilian targets and offshore military bases. Innocent human casualties and fatalities would be considered as important for the perceived greater good. For example, there were plans to carry out bombing campaigns among the Cuban exile community in Florida as well as direct attacks on the US naval base at Guantánamo Bay. General Lemnitzer, chairman of the Joint Chiefs of Staff, even considered the possibility of using astronaut John Glenn's extremely risky first space flight as a pretext for war, if Glenn should unfortunately die.

Evidence of electronic interference with the spacecraft, emanating from Cuba, would be fabricated if required. Elaborate ruses involving civilian airliners to be shot down by imaginary Cuban fighters were mixed with the deliberate sinking of US ships in the waters around Cuba, to produce a whole myriad of provocations, of which some would bring in other countries. These are not conspiracy theories: they are official plots in the planning stage recorded in an Operation NORTHWOODS memo sent to Defense Secretary Robert McNamara, with the full backing of Lemnitzer and the joint chiefs of staff. President Kennedy vetoed the ideas.

See also: *Tonkin Gulf Incidents p.224*

1964
TONKIN GULF INCIDENTS

President Johnson allowed provocative raids on North Vietnam to encourage the justifiable escalation of war

Did the Johnson administration deliberately provoke North Vietnamese forces into an attack on US ships in the Gulf of Tonkin, in order to justify an escalation in the conflict?

On the evening of August 4th, 1964, two US navy destroyers, the *Maddox* and the *C. Turner Joy*, were patrolling the Gulf of Tonkin off the North Vietnamese coast when they came under apparent attack from Democratic Republic of Vietnam (DRV) torpedo boats. The *Maddox* picked up sonar but no radar targets and the *C. Turner Joy* the reverse. Captain John Herrick, patrol commander of the US forces in the Gulf of Tonkin, expressed doubts about the reality of the attack. Despite this, President Lyndon Johnson, acting on DRV communications intercepts and the advice of Admiral Ulysses S. Grant Sharp, ordered retaliatory air strikes against the North Vietnamese coastline and mainland. Conspiracy theorists believe that the decrypts referred not to this incident, but an earlier blatant provocation by the *Maddox* on August 2nd, 1964. Operating illegally in North Vietnamese territorial waters, the destroyer was part of a covert campaign OPLAN-34A to support shelling of coastal islands by the Republic of Vietnam (RVN). Three DRV patrol boats attacked the *Maddox* but, when the destroyer returned fire, one was sunk. The *Maddox* was outside North Vietnamese territorial waters on August 4th but inside on August 2nd.

This may be a case of fog of war: everything rests on the accuracy of the intercepts which, it is claimed, prove the attack had been launched by the DRV.

See also: *Operation NORTHWOODS p.223*

1967
USS LIBERTY ATTACKED BY ISRAELI JETS

The US spy ship was mistaken for an Egyptian vessel in international waters

On June 8th, 1967, during the Six Day War between Israel and the Arab States, the American intelligence ship *USS Liberty* was attacked for a period of 75 minutes by Israeli jets and motor torpedo boats. On a ship which was clearly flying the American flag and sailing in international waters, 34 men died and 172 were wounded. Israel claimed that the unfortunate accident was a case of mistaken identity, with the *USS Liberty* believed to be the out-of-service Egyptian horse carrier *El Queseir*.

The Israeli Defence Forces History Department, Research and Instruction Branch, in its defence, eventually issued a report on the attacks in 1982. Two gun camera photographs, of extremely poor quality, were provided as proof that the target ship was not flying an American flag. In 1987, better quality photographs were shown on the UK's Thames TV documentary, *Attack on the* Liberty, which had a sufficient number of discrepancies, when compared with real photographs of the *USS Liberty,* to expose the IDF copies as fakes. Conspiracy theorists ask why would Israel attempt to cover up what should have been a simple case of mistaken identification, if they weren't guilty? The US navy claim that two Israeli Mirage jets had circled the *USS Liberty* three times approximately one hour before the attack. American Secretary of State Dean Rusk denied that it was an accident, but the question to be asked is what possible reason could the IDF have had in attacking a ship belonging to its major ally?

See also: *Tonkin Gulf Incidents p.224*

1970
KISS THE BOYS GOODBYE – US SOLDIERS LOST IN VIETNAM

The US reneged on a deal to ransom the MIAs and POWs for $4 billion

The reason so many POWs were left behind in Vietnam, according to the 1990 book *Kiss the Boys Goodbye,* by husband and wife team William and Monika Stevenson, was because there had been a secret clause in the Paris Peace Accord negotiated by Kissinger on behalf of President Nixon. It involved a $4 billion reparation agreement by the US to North Vietnam, which was immediately reneged upon.

Support for this theory seemed to appear in 1992 with the testimony of Richard Allen, former National Security Advisor to President Reagan, before a US Senate Select Committee on the POW/MIA (Missing in Action) issue. He revealed an offer made by Vietnam in 1981 through a third country to free all remaining POWs in return for the $4 billion which the US had originally promised. An apparent eyewitness to the White House discussion, a Secret Service agent on duty at the time, was unsuccessfully subpoenaed to corroborate Allen's testimony. When Allen then retracted his own testimony, the whole affair became once again a conspiracy theory. The *Washington Times* reported that Vice-President Bush had said the whole affair was a lost cause and CIA Director, Casey, classified the Vietnamese suggestion as blackmail. The number of POWs involved in the apparent offer was described by Allen as dozens or hundreds, which, when exchanged for the suspected $4 billion, would put a very high price on their freedom, one which the US government was, understandably, not willing to pay.

Director Casey's comments indicate that the conspiracy theory is probably true.

1970
OPERATION TAILWIND
The US Air Force used nerve gas on US Army deserters in Laos

According to a 1998 article in *Time* magazine, written by Peter Arnett and April Oliver, the US air force dropped a nerve gas known as GB on non-combatants and US army deserters in Laos on September 11th, 1970.

Arnett and Oliver's article is based on interviews with ex-Sergeant Mike Hagen and ex-Lieutenant Robert Van Buskirk of the US Army Studies and Observation Group (SOG), which had been inserted into the area along with 140 Montagnard tribesmen. The targeted base camp, a town called Chavan, was found to have the dead bodies of 20 American defectors among the Pathet Lao, North Vietnamese army and civilian corpses. The presence of the defectors had been known before the raid and their killing was the main aim of the mission involving the nerve gas attack, even though no effort was made to identify them.

John Plaster's book *SOG: The Secret Wars of America's Commandos in Vietnam* (1997) describes TAILWIND as a diversionary operation to draw NVA forces away from a major operation being conducted by the Hmong tribesmen in southern Laos. A-1 Skyraiders dropped CBU-19 cluster bombs on the NVA, filled with CS riot-control tear gas, not the nerve gas canisters as mentioned in the Arnett article. The aim of the bombing was to impair the vision of the NVA anti-aircraft gunners. GB, otherwise known as sarin, is not a gas, nor does it attack the nerves. Hagen and Buskirk are accused of giving inaccurate testimonies due to a service-related disability claim and mischievous fantasy respectively.

See also: *Operation BLACK DOG p.231*

1974
CHURCHILL, COVENTRY, AND THE ENIGMA SECRET
Churchill let Coventry be bombed by the Luftwaffe despite knowing about it in advance

The conspiracy of silence surrounding the fact that Britain had broken the German ENIGMA codes and had been reading the enemy's secret communications during World War II was maintained until the 1974 publication of F.W. Winterbotham's *The Ultra Secret*. Readers were shocked to learn that the devastating Luftwaffe bombing raid on Coventry during the night of November 14th, 1940, was known about in advance, through the appearance of the city's name in one of the ENIGMA decrypts. Winterbotham claimed that Prime Minister Winston Churchill had had to make the extremely difficult decision to sacrifice Coventry in order to ensure that the Germans did not suspect that their coded messages were being read. However, F.H. Hinsley's later official history *British Intelligence in the Second World War* categorically stated that Coventry was never mentioned in the ENIGMA decrypts.

Could Winterbotham have been mistaken? Air Ministry papers released into the public domain show that he was. At 1pm on November 14th, the RAF intercepted the Luftwaffe's X-Gerät directional radio beams, which were being tested in preparation for that night's raid. By 3pm, the RAF had calculated that these directional beams intersected over Coventry. This was reported to Churchill who took no action to evacuate the city as electronic countermeasures were planned to take place. Unfortunately, the incorrect frequencies were given to the jamming stations, and the operation to prevent the Coventry raid failed.

So, Churchill did know about Coventry being targeted by the Luftwaffe, but not through any ENIGMA decrypts.

See also: *Roosevelt and Churchill let Pearl Harbor Attack Happen p.213*

1979
US AND UK INVOLVEMENT IN THE AFGHANISTAN WAR
Both governments were supplying advanced technological weapons to the Mujahideen

The Soviets invaded Afghanistan in 1979 and remained there until 1989. The CIA relished the idea of turning Afghanistan into the USSR's Vietnam, but was wary of it looking like a US–Soviet war. However, the appearance of advanced technological weapons systems being used by the Afghan tribesmen soon revealed American and British involvement in the war. The original CIA budget for covert operations in Afghanistan was set at $30 million. By 1984 it shot up to $120 million. This was followed by a mushrooming to $250 million in 1985, $470 million in 1986 and $630 million in 1987. Each of these amounts was matched by the oil-rich Saudis.

The conspiracy theory

The Mujahideen forces were covertly supported by the US and the UK. Using the Pakistani secret service, the Interservices Intelligence Directorate (ISI), as a conduit, huge amounts of arms were supplied to the freedom fighters – who would go on to become the terrorists of today.

The evidence

With the introduction of the Soviet special forces, the Spetnaz, in 1984, the counter-insurgency techniques improved. Helicopter gunships, especially the awesome MI-24 "Hind," penetrated deep into Mujahideen country in Vietnam-style "seek and destroy" assault missions. To deal with the success of the gunships, the CIA decided to arm the rebels with an anti-aircraft weapons system. Hoping to maintain "plausible deniability" for the US, the CIA provided a British-made system named the Blowpipe. It had been a disappointment in the Falklands War and had become obsolescent in the British armed forces, having been replaced by the Javelin. As a weapon, it had to be fired at either a head-on approaching or tail-on disappearing target. The missile continued to be guided optically with a thumb control, which meant that the firer had to stay standing up. This, together with its lengthy training period, high firing-failure rate and unsuitability for transporting across the rough Afghan terrain, meant that an alternative was soon needed. As a result, pressure mounted for Congress to approve the sending of Stinger missiles. President Reagan signed the National Security Decision Directive 166 in March 1985, paving the way for the Stinger deployment.

In order to prevent the high-tech weapons falling into the hands of terrorists, special firing procedures and return/replacement deals were worked out with the rebels. They could get another Stinger only by returning the empty firing tube of the one used in an attack.

Each MiG aircraft cost an average of $20 million or more, and this had to be contrasted with $60,000–70,000 each for a Stinger. With a CIA estimated hit rate of 70 percent, that provided a very good return on the investment. There is much debate over the effect of the Stinger on the Soviet withdrawal from Afghanistan. The commander of Soviet forces in Afghanistan, General Valentin Varennikov, claimed that a total of 114 planes and 332 helicopters were destroyed from 1979 to 1989. The Stingers were introduced in 1986 and he claimed that there was no appreciable increase in the numbers of Soviet aircraft lost, only Afghan ones. The Soviet military also claimed that more aircraft were shot down using the Chinese-supplied Dashika 12.7mm heavy machine guns than the Stingers. CIA reports also tended to stress the fear of the Stinger, rather than its performance, making the Soviet gunship pilots avoid the Mujahideen country which had now become known as "Stinger Country." This withdrawal of helicopter operations from certain parts of Afghanistan allowed the further unrestricted flow of US arms from across the Pakistani border.

The verdict

During the war, a total of 80,000 Mujahideen resistance fighters were trained in seven ISI camps in Pakistan, fully financed by the CIA. With the success of the covert war and subsequent collapse of the Soviet Union, both the CIA and the ISI have revealed details of the war in several books by former intelligence officers involved. Recently interest has been rekindled in the Mujahideen struggle because of the involvement of the al-Qaeda terrorist Osama bin Laden.

1979

AGENT ORANGE

US government attempted to cover up the dangerous side effects of its military defoliant

During the period 1962–70, in the Vietnam War, a herbicide named Agent Orange was used by the US Military Assistance Command, Vietnam (MACV), in a defoliation campaign aimed at reducing enemy cover from aircraft and destroying food crops used to feed communist forces. Vietnam veterans accused the US government, and the private pharmaceutical companies that manufactured the chemical, of using US military personnel as unwitting guinea pigs. As the problem became more widely known, the government was also accused of covering up the extent of the disabilities.

Agent Orange contained n-butyl esters of 2,4 dichlorophenoxyacetic acid (2,4-D), 2,4,5- trichlorophenoxyacetic acid (2,4,5-T) and 2,3,7,8-tetrachlorodibenzo-p-dioxin (TCDD). The latter is one of the most toxic chemicals known to man. Agent Orange was mainly sprayed from specially equipped C-123 aircraft, with smaller amounts coming from back-pack units carried by soldiers. It was not just enemy territory that was sprayed; US camp perimeters were similarly cleared.

Medical studies have shown that there is a link between exposure to Agent Orange and chloracne, non-Hodgkin's lymphoma, Hodgkin's disease, and soft-tissue sarcoma. Suggestive evidence also exists for a link between the defoliant and various kinds of respiratory cancers, prostate cancer, and multiple myeloma. Epidemiological studies suggested that there was a significantly greater risk for Vietnam veterans' offspring to be born with spina bifida. As a result of a class-action lawsuit against several manufacturers of Agent Orange, a massive compensation fund was established as an out-of-court settlement to help the veterans and their families deal with the disabilities.

See also: *Gulf War Syndrome p.231*

1980s
US AND UK ARMED SADDAM
IN HIS WAR WITH IRAN
During the Iran–Iraq war both nations armed Saddam Hussein despite their supposed neutral stance

Following the overthrow of the Shah of Iran by Islamic fundamentalists and the taking of hostages in Tehran, the US supported neighbouring Iraq in its eight-year war. British reasons for backing Iraq were related to the loss of the lucrative Iran market, and the relaxing of the Iraqi-imposed trade embargo with the UK following the expulsion of Iraqi diplomats in 1978. For example, British Aerospace's munitions subsidiary, Royal Ordnance, "unwittingly" sold Iraq 900 strips of explosive retardant via an intermediary. The material was used to propel large rockets.

During the first half of the decade, Iraq was the world's largest importer of major weapons systems, spending over a quarter of its gross domestic product. British arms sales policy was one of neutrality but at the same time there was a willingness to supply "non-lethal" defence-related equipment to either side, while simultaneously seeking a peaceful resolution to the conflict.

In 1983 Donald Rumsfeld, then acting as a special presidential envoy, visited Saddam Hussein in Baghdad and agreed to supply weapons and arrange the financing of the purchase. However, to put it all into perspective, according to the 1989 *SIPRI Yearbook* data, 75 percent of the weapons used during the war were supplied by the Soviet Union and France. Many countries, including the US and the UK, had actually continued to trade with Iran as well, despite official policy statements to the contrary.

See also: *Iraq WMD Conspiracy p.234*

1980
PROJECT COAST AND DR
DEATH (WOUTER BASSON)
South African chemical and biological warfare weapons were tested on ANC rebels

The South African Defence Force used chemical and biological weapons (CBW) on members of the Marxist African National Congress (ANC) during the apartheid era. This was in contravention of the 1925 Geneva Convention and 1975 Convention on the Prohibition of the Development, Production, and Stockpiling of Bacteriological and Toxic Weapons and on their Destruction.

According to Gould and Folb's *The South African Chemical and Biological Warfare Program*, South Africa's Prime Minister P.W. Botha ordered the setting up of a top-secret CBW program in April 1981, code-named Project COAST. The head of the program was a 30-year-old cardiologist and Botha's personal physician, Wouter Basson. Working for the SADF's medical military unit, the 7th SAMS Battalion, he gained experience of Western CBW through fact-finding tours and realized how far South Africa was behind in its research and development. Given an annual budget of $10 million and a research staff of approximately 200 scientists, Basson carried out experiments on captured prisoners during the ANC guerrilla campaign.

In 1997, Basson was tried by the Truth and Reconciliation Commission for his role in the CBW program. Nicknamed "Dr Death" by the media, Basson was charged with 64 counts including the invention of race-specific poisons. Many of the charges against him were for the chemical killing of ANC guerrillas in neighbouring countries such as Mozambique, Swaziland, and Namibia, all of which were outside the jurisdiction of South Africa. By 2000, he was free on bail and working at the South African army's hospital in Pretoria.

See also: *Activities in Unit 731 Covered Up p.212*

1981
SINKING OF THE *BELGRANO*
BY BRITISH ROYAL NAVY

UK Government covered up the fact that the *Belgrano* was sailing away from the war zone when it was sunk

On May 2nd, 1982, during the Falklands War, the Argentinean cruiser *General Belgrano* was sunk by the British submarine *HMS Conqueror* even though it was sailing away from the main UK carrier fleet and was outside the 200-mile exclusion zone established by the British. This fact was covered up by the British government until exposed by a senior Ministry of Defence civil servant.

The civil servant, Clive Ponting, handed over documents to Labour Party back-bencher Tam Dayell, who wrongly suspected that the sinking was carried out to scupper a peace plan being brokered by Peru. Ponting was subsequently charged with breaking the Official Secrets Act, but the trial produced an acquittal based on the defence that the information was in the public interest.

The *General Belgrano* had belonged to only one of several battle groups which threatened the security of Rear Admiral Sandy Woodward's Task Force 317 in the south Atlantic. To counter the threat to the surface fleet, another British task force was present, designated TF 324, consisting of nuclear-powered submarines which were completely outside the control of Woodward. The rules of engagement for the two task forces were different and TF 324's needed to be altered to deal with the *Belgrano*. By the time permission was received from Prime Minister Thatcher, the cruiser had altered course, but was still sunk.

In 1994, the Buenos Aires government agreed with the original Thatcher government's view that the sinking of the *General Belgrano* had been a legal act of war.

1982
IRAN CONTRA

US ransomed hostages by illegally selling missiles to Iran, then used the profits to fund Nicaraguan rebels

After the overthrow of the pro-western Shah of Iran in 1979 the Islamic revolution led by the Ayatollah Khomeini took a very anti-American stance. Militant students invaded the US embassy in Tehran and held the staff hostage for over a year. When they were finally released, the apparent US impotence, aggravated by the failed Delta Force rescue attempt, cost President Carter a second term. Though there are conspiracy theories which claim that the release of the Tehran hostages was negotiated to coincide with Ronald Reagan's inauguration, the new president would also find himself having to deal with middle eastern kidnappings. A prominent example was the CIA Beirut station chief, William Buckley, who was held hostage in Lebanon by Hezbollah, a fundamentalist Islamic group with links to Iran.

The conspiracy theory

Despite US Congressional refusal to recognize the Contra rebels fighting the leftist government of Nicaragua, and the existence of an arms embargo against Iran, a powerful cabal within the White House was running a foreign policy independently of Congress, supplying military support where it was officially, and therefore legally, denied. The two different spheres of operation were connected by a myriad financial links commonly found within conspiracy theories, yet this was no theory. It was a real conspiracy, involving members of the Washington elite who were acting on their own, against the wishes of the American public, abusing the power entrusted to them through the democratic process. In fact, they were accused of acting in a way more befitting a junta.

The Iran conspiracy: theory and evidence

Despite the US secretary of state declaring that Iran was a sponsor of international terrorism and the launch of Operation STAUNCH – an arms embargo against the Khomeini regime – there were elements of the administration who were pursuing a path of negotiation with Iranian moderates. An exiled Iranian merchant, Manucher Ghorbanifar, had approached Israeli foreign minister David Kimche with the moderates' offer to release Buckley in return for a small shipment of US arms to Iran for use in its war with Iraq. Kimche passed the suggestion on to Robert McFarlane, the then US national security advisor who discussed it with President Reagan and the chief of staff Donald Regan, on July 18th, 1985. The deal was approved on August 6th, despite opposition from the secretaries of state and defence, and involved 100 TOW (Tube-launched, Optically-tracked, Wire-guided) missiles being shipped to Israel to replace the 96 that it had sent to Iran. When the Iranian moderates failed to release Buckley or any of the other hostages held by Hezbollah, but asked for 400 more missiles, Reagan agreed. This resulted in the release of only one hostage, the Reverend Benjamin Weir. Lieutenant Oliver North, a National Security Council staffer, was sent to the Middle East to negotiate better terms, but even an arms deal of 3,504 TOWs failed to release the hostages. After only part of the shipment was carried out, the scandal hit the press headlines.

A Lebanese magazine described a secret visit made in May 1986, to Iran, by North and McFarlane. Not only were the men breaching the arms embargo against Iran, but they were also acting against the much-publicized Reagan maxim that "America will never make concessions to terrorists."

In an attempt to distance himself from the scandal, Reagan appointed an investigative commission under the chairmanship of former Republican senator John Tower, but then confused matters somewhat by giving contradictory testimonies as to his knowledge of the affair. The Tower board managed to find hundreds of documents, previously thought to have been destroyed by North, still on his computer, detailing both the Iranian arms-for-hostages deals and another controversial operation being carried out in Central America. This was the Contra side of what would become known as the Iran Contra scandal.

The Contra conspiracy: theory and evidence

The Sandanista government took power in Nicaragua in 1979, and two years later Reagan authorized the CIA to support the Contra rebels in their fight against communism. Nearly $20 million was allocated to the setting up of a 500-man paramilitary and political "action team" of exiles that would operate inside Nicaragua. CIA director, William Casey, misled the congressional intelligence committees into believing that the covert operations were aimed at the interdiction of arms traffic flowing from Nicaragua to El Salvadoran communist rebels. When the true reason became known, Congress responded adversely by passing the Boland Amendment in 1982 that outlawed the funding of attempts to overthrow the legitimate Sandanista government. When Reagan ignored this and authorized the CIA to mine the Nicaraguan harbours, Congress responded again by passing a second Boland Amendment in June 1984 that banned all further CIA operations against the Sandanistas.

On October 5th, 1986, mercenary pilot Eugene Hasenfus was shot down over Nicaragua while flying an arms supply mission to Contra rebels. Within days he was on TV revealing the extent of the Reagan administration's involvement. On November 25th, Reagan and Attorney General Edwin Meese announced to the American nation that there was a connection between the Contra scandal and the recently revealed Iran arms deal. North had diverted profits from the Iranian missile sales to finance the Contra operations. CIA

President Reagan admits in a TV address, March 4th, 1987, that he traded arms for hostages with Iran and funnelled profits to the Contras.

director Casey died of a brain hemorrhage on the morning he was due to testify before the congressional committee investigating the Iran Contra affair.

The verdict

As is the case in US political conspiracies, the question of how far up the responsibility goes before it threatens the reputation of the president himself is usually answered by he who falls on his sword or he who is pushed onto his sword. In the case of the Iran Contra scandal, it was Admiral John Poindexter, President Reagan's national security advisor. Reagan's actual complicity in the full plot is still suspect, as it was always the duty of the other plotters to protect their commander-in-chief by maintaining a firm degree of "plausible deniability." Poindexter's and North's testimonies at the congressional hearings in 1987 were given under immunity and this ensured that their convictions were later overturned by a court of appeals. No-one involved in the conspiracy went to prison, thanks to presidential pardons.

See also: *Overthrow of Panama's General Manuel Noriega p.230*

1987
KLAUS BARBIE, THE
BUTCHER OF LYON

b. October 25th, 1913, Bad Godesberg, Germany

d. September 25th, 1991, Lyon, France

Former SS officer revealed his secret American employment during a war crimes trial

Klaus Barbie, the infamous SS officer known as the Butcher of Lyon, who was extradited from Bolivia to face trial in France in May 1987, had spent most of his postwar years on the run as an American intelligence agent. Immediately following Germany's surrender, Barbie had become a leading member of an underground SS organization, which hoped to contract itself out to the Americans when the Cold War started. As fiercely anti-communist as they come, the former SS group became an attractive proposition, but not before the American Counter-Intelligence Corps (CIC) decided to negotiate with them from a position of strength. First the CIC infiltrated the group, then arrested all but one of the leaders and offered them work in return for their freedom. Barbie had escaped by climbing out of his bathroom window, but the CIC eventually managed to recruit him by offering him more money than he could refuse. He surrendered himself in June 1947 and for the next two years acted as an American agent in West Germany, countering the threat from Soviet agents.

American State Department investigator Allan Ryan has shown that the CIC was also responsible for Barbie's disappearance from Germany in 1949, when he was relocated to Bolivia. Living under the assumed name of Klaus Altmann, he continued to carry out operations against the communists. He even became a Bolivian government advisor on internment camps. Despite no longer being legally accountable for his crimes against the French Resistance, the Lyon court charged him with crimes against humanity. He was found guilty and sentenced to life imprisonment. He died in September 1991.

1988
OVERTHROW OF PANAMA'S
GENERAL MANUEL NORIEGA

Former CIA asset is indicted for drug smuggling and money laundering

The US invaded Panama in December 1989 to prevent it having to return the leasehold of the Panama Canal Zone on January 1st, 1990. It overthrew the Panamanian de facto leader, Manuel Noriega, who had changed from being a CIA asset to a political liability on several separate occasions.

Newsweek reported in 1990 that Noriega had been in the pay of the CIA and the Pentagon during the first period of 1970–6 at a rate of more than $100,000 per year. President Carter removed him from the payroll in 1977 for the rest of his term in the White House. The CIA put him back on with the same salary during the Reagan–Bush period. There were charges of money laundering and drug smuggling during his time as a member of the ruling military junta.

Noriega became an important conduit for the supply of arms to the Contras in their CIA-sponsored fight against the Sandinista government of Nicaragua.

As the decade wore on, Noriega's criminal past came under scrutiny from the Drug Enforcement Agency and the US press. His indictment on federal drug charges in 1988 prompted the CIA to fund political opposition to Noriega. This led to his abandonment of the electoral process and widespread violence.

After the US invasion of Panama in 1989, its forces confiscated thousands of boxes of government documents relating to the Noriega era, refusing to hand them over to the new government's criminal investigators. It is assumed that they revealed the true extent of the CIA's involvement. Noriega was convicted in April 1992 on charges of drug smuggling, racketeering and money laundering. He is currently serving a 40-year prison sentence.

See also: *Iran Contra p.228*

1989
BLACK HELICOPTERS

US government uses military aircraft in the illegal surveillance of militia groups

The American government uses sinister black helicopters to carry out the illegal surveillance of its own citizens, as part of a plot to facilitate the takeover of the country by the United Nations.

From their initial sightings in the 1970s, when they were associated with UFO events and cattle mutilations, the black helicopters have entered mainstream conspiracy theories as agents of the New World Order. Jim Keith's *Black Helicopters Over America* (1994) links them in with the surveillance of the US militia movement by federal government agencies bent on allowing foreign forces to invade the US. Thinking that they were under surveillance by black helicopters, the militia of Montana once tried to shoot down an Idaho National Guard AH-64 Apache as it flew over a ranch owned by fugitive militia leader Calvin Greenup.

Black helicopters have been developed by the US militia movement as transporters for covert operations, and their deployment by domestic law enforcement agencies raises questions under the Posse Comitatus Act, which prohibits American military personnel from direct participation in law enforcement activities. Following the Iranian hostage rescue fiasco where US Marine helicopters failed in the desert, Delta Force founder Charlie Beckwith established a helicopter unit just for special covert operations. This became the American Army's 106th Special Operations Aviation Regiment (Airborne) based at Fort Campbell, Kentucky. The "black helicopter" found its perfect manifestation in the stealth-like UH-60 Black Hawk.

Far from being a United Nations surveillance aircraft, the militia's black helicopter is more likely to be an unmarked Drug Enforcement Agency chopper on a drug smuggling interdiction mission.

1990
OPERATION BLACK DOG
The US used biological weapons in the Gulf War

The internet conspiracy theorist David Guyatt, on his DeepBlackLies website, claims to have investigated a case that involved the US using biological weapons during the first Gulf War.

Operation BLACK DOG involved a CIA aircraft launched from an American carrier in the Red Sea targeted on an Iraqi chemical and biological warfare weapons plant. Guyatt's source was unable to identify the carrier, but speculates that it was either the USS Saratoga or the USS Kennedy. The aircraft crashed in Iraq, accidentally releasing its deadly bacteriological agent, but again, the source was unable to identify the agent, claiming it had no name, only a batch number. It was a bacterium which caused those contaminated to drown in their own fluids.

Guyatt's source claims to have been involved in the recovery of the aircraft wreckage and its munitions, and been so appalled by the use of bacteriological warfare that he took photographic evidence and subsequently passed it on to the United Nations.

This has all the elements of a conspiracy theory: the CIA using bacteriological weapons illegally, in an unmarked aircraft, launched from an unidentified aircraft carrier in the Red Sea. Even the weapon itself is unidentified. The secrecy surrounding real special ops allows fake ones to be equally unsatisfactorily described. One has to ask why was the greatest threat of exposure brushed aside for a single pre-war mission? It appears to be nothing more than an attempt to tar the US special forces and CIA with the same evil brush as Saddam Hussein.

See also: *Operation TAILWIND p.225*

1991
GULF WAR SYNDROME
Coalition governments used dangerous anti-nerve gas drugs to "protect" their own troops

Veterans of the first Gulf War of 1990–1991 have accused their governments of subjecting them to untested chemical weapons and anti-nerve gas drugs and then covering this up, in the same way as the US government dealt with the Agent Orange issue after Vietnam.

Symptoms include short-term memory loss, breathing difficulties, headaches, rashes and birth defects of their offspring. These ailments are reported by veterans from the various Coalition forces and are related to the prophylactic vaccines and medications used in anticipation of the Iraqi deployment of biological and chemical warfare agents. Some soldiers were exposed to depleted uranium shells used to penetrate tank armour.

According to Pentagon research, only 1 percent of all Gulf war veterans have claimed to suffer from unknown diseases. In November 1996, the *New England Journal of Medicine* disputed the existence of Gulf War syndrome. Some of the cases could be explained away by the symptoms of leichmaniasis, a parasitic disease spread by sand flies in the Iraqi and Kuwaiti deserts. Medical historians have shown how many previous wars have produced undiagnosable diseases similar in symptoms to those claimed to be Gulf War syndrome. A frequently cited case is that of shell-shock, which occurred in the days before medical cocktails were administered to soldiers going into battle. Exactly the same cocktails were given to those NATO soldiers serving in Bosnia, with no great occurrence of the syndrome.

One has to consider the lure of massive financial compensation resulting from possible successful litigation à la Agent Orange.

See also: *Agent Orange p.226*

1992
PROJECT HAARP

New forms of electronic warfare threaten to disrupt the earth's atmosphere

The US government is carrying out secret experiments on the Earth's ionosphere which could pave the way for radically different kinds of warfare in the future. The nature of the research is also a threat to the natural safety afforded the planet by the upper atmosphere.

High-frequency Active Auroral Research Project (HAARP) was first publicized to the world of conspiracy theorists in the 1995 publication of Nick Begich and Jeanne Manning's *Angels Don't Play This HAARP*, and conspiracy themes were further investigated in Jerry Smith's *HAARP: The Ultimate Weapon of the Conspiracy* (1998). Developing the technology first invented by Nikola Tesla, HAARP alters the Earth's atmospheric, ionospheric and magnetospheric regions to enable electromagnetic warfare between the US and Russia and, more sinisterly, surveillance of its own population.

The ionosphere is used to bounce radio waves over the horizon and around the Earth, thus making worldwide communications possible, but any disruption to the ionosphere may not be as selective as theorists believe, thus questioning its tactical use. HAARP was set up near Gakona, Alaska, by the US Department of Defense to build a transmitter capable of turning the aurora (Northern Lights) into a virtual antenna. The extremely low frequency (ELF) waves produced could be used to penetrate deep under the sea, thus allowing communication with the American navy's submarine fleet. Experimentation on the ionosphere creates fears of a hole being burnt in the planet's protective layer, as ELF also raises fears of scrambling the human mind. Both are officially denied.

See also: *Tesla Weapons of Doom p.232*

1993
CRASHING OF FLIGHT ZULU DELTA

RAF helicopter crash on Mull of Kintyre was wrongly blamed on pilot error

At about 5.30pm on June 2nd, 1994, a British army Chinook helicopter, bearing the designation Zulu Delta 576, took off from RAF Aldergrove, Northern Ireland, carrying 25 passengers on a short trip across to Inverness, Scotland, to attend a security conference. On board were leading members of Britain's intelligence community including officers from MI5, army intelligence, SAS and the RUC's Special Branch. At about 6pm the helicopter crashed into the Mull of Kintyre, killing all on board. The subsequent RAF Board of Inquiry found the two pilots guilty of gross negligence rather than admit the real reason for the crash.

Under Scottish law, the families of the pilots were able to cross-examine the RAF through the establishment of a Fatal Accident Inquiry. Sheriff Sir Stephen Young ruled that the cause of the crash was unknown but he disagreed with the conclusions of the RAF board.

Paladin Pictures, in their 1998 documentary *The Last Flight of Zulu Delta 576*, provided evidence of a problem commonly found with the Chinook helicopters which was withheld from both inquiries. This was the faulty on-board computer software system called FADEQ that controlled the Chinook engines. Three weeks before the crash, Zulu Delta 576 had suffered a serious failing of the control system, involving sudden engine run-ups and shutdowns. This was repeated in other Chinooks and the Ministry of Defence sued the manufacturer Boeing and the software supplier Textron Lycoming. Boeing settled out of court, and Textron Lycoming was ordered to pay $3 million in damages.

As of 2005, Prime Minister Tony Blair has continued to blame the crash on pilot error.

1995
TESLA WEAPONS OF DOOM

A Japanese cult's obsession with earthquake-inducing weapons of science fiction

A new generation of weapons are being developed which utilize natural forces of destruction such as hurricanes and earthquakes. These are based on research carried out by the extraordinary inventor Nikola Tesla and have attracted the interest of sinister apocalyptic cults involved in terrorism.

On January 8th, 1995, Shoko Asahara, leader of the Japanese cult, Aum Shinrikyo, announced in a radio broadcast that: "Japan will be attacked by an earthquake in 1995. The most likely place is Kobe." Nine days after this prophecy, the city of Kobe was hit by a powerful earthquake. This statement was either precognition or advertising the possession of a new terrorist weapon.

Following the sarin attack on the Tokyo underground, which was allegedly committed by Aum, the US Senate Permanent Subcommittee on Investigations, under the chairmanship of Senator Sam Nunn, carried out a study of the cult's finances and obsession with doomsday machines.

Aum Shinrikyo cult members parade in Tokyo wearing masks in the likeness of their leader Asahara Shoko.

Representatives of Aum had visited the headquarters of the International Tesla Society in New York looking for patents and documents, but such research notes were seized by the US government on Tesla's death in 1943 and have remained under national security status ever since.

Tesla's inventions, especially the HAARP use of extremely low frequency (ELF) waves for Earth-penetrating tomography (EPT), allow the possible prediction of earthquakes and volcanic eruptions. Its subterranean surveying capabilities suggest in the minds of some that what can be used to detect fault-lines can also be used to affect them. This deduction does not, however, reveal a realistic grasp of the principles of geology.

See also: *Project HAARP p.232*

1996
FLIGHT TWA 800 SHOT DOWN BY US MILITARY

Crash debris indicated that passenger plane was hit by a missile

At 8.31pm on July 17th, 1996, a Boeing 747-131 exploded in mid-air en route from JFK International Airport in New York to Charles de Gaulle International Airport in Paris. All 230 passengers and 18 crew on board the TWA 800 flight were killed. Thirty-four independent eyewitnesses claimed to have seen missile-like trails in the sky and objects streaking towards the plane. James Sanders, in his book *The Downing of TWA Flight 800*, claims that the Boeing was shot down by an errant missile fired from a nearby Aegis cruiser on American naval exercises.

Sanders specifically cites a bullet-like entrance and exit wound in the aircraft cabin, combined with a red residue on some of the passenger seats, as an indication that an exhaust motor passed through. He claims that the FBI tried to suppress Federal Aviation Administration radar reports that had indicated an "unidentified object" approaching the TWA flight.

This object was an anti-missile missile originally fired to bring down a US navy BQM-74E drone missile, but it failed to lock on to the target and locked on instead to the TWA flight. It passed through the Boeing and must have caused the ignition as it lacked a warhead itself.

The National Transportation Safety Board investigators concluded that the probable cause of the crash was an explosion in the central fuel tank but could not determine the source of the ignition of the fuel air mixture. The NTSB tested Stinger anti-aircraft missiles and concluded that they did not have the range to hit the TWA flight.

2002
AFGHAN WAR FOR OIL
The war in Afghanistan was part of a US plan to dominate oil and gas resources in Central Asia

With the 1991 dissolution of the Soviet Union, American oil companies acquired rights to as much as 75 percent of the output of the new oil and gas fields in the former republics of Turkmenistan and Kazakhstan, hailing them as a potential alternative to the unstable Persian Gulf supplies. The major problem was how to get the oil and gas out of the landlocked region and delivered to the world markets. The dominant route was north through the Russian pipeline system, but the American desire to break the Russian monopoly led to the planning of a pipeline south through Afghanistan and Pakistan to the Indian Ocean. The US-based Unocal oil company began negotiations with the Taliban regime in Kabul but the talks broke down after the 1998 bombings of the US embassies in Kenya and Tanzania. The Clinton administration retaliated with cruise missile strikes on al-Qaeda training camps in Afghanistan.

Yet neither the Clinton nor Bush administrations put Afghanistan on the official State Department list of states charged with sponsoring terrorism, an act which would have outlawed trading with the Taliban. This American willingness to involve the Taliban in the pipeline project must be noted. It was the refusal of the Taliban to hand over Osama bin Laden that initiated the military planning before 9/11.

See also: *Iraqi War for Oil p.234*

2003
IRAQI WAR FOR OIL
US waged war in Iraq to secure long-term oil supplies

The war on Iraq was primarily to allow the US to control the second largest oil producer in a strategic attempt to weaken Saudi Arabia's domination of the oil markets.

Iraq's oil reserves are estimated to be at least 115 billion barrels. American oil companies had been banished from Iraq as the United Nations sanctions were imposed before the first Gulf War and their place had been willfully taken by Russian and French companies. Any American action against Iraq was bound to involve the renegotiation of oil contracts in the post-Saddam period with the Russians and French the obvious losers. For its role in supporting the American military operation, Britain would also gain in the allocation of contracts.

The Bush White House was well known for its deep ties with the oil business. The president was a former director of Harken Energy Corp, vice-president Dick Cheney was a chief executive officer of Halliburton Energy Services Corp, and national security advisor Condoleezza Rice was on the board of directors at Chevron. Such knowledge of the oil business would have prepared these leaders for the problems of achieving the ultimate "strategic petroleum reserve" (compared with its current 600 million barrels). The Iraqi oil infrastructure is in need of years of rebuilding and billions of dollars of investment. Freeing up Iraqi oil for export would flood the market, drive down prices and damage corporate profits in the US. But the Bush administration's stated aim to make energy security a priority of American trade and foreign policy cannot be ignored.

See also: *Afghan War for Oil p.234*

2004
IRAQ WMD CONSPIRACY
Iraqi scientists deliberately misled Saddam Hussein into believing he still had WMDs

Accusations against Saddam Hussein and his regime over the whole question of possession of weapons of mass destruction were never convincingly refuted. If Saddam no longer possessed these weapons, why did he allow the US and its Allies to believe that he did? He must have known that the WMDs were being used as an excuse for invasion.

Theories to explain the subsequent failure to locate any WMDs in Iraq after the war centre around Saddam's successful exporting of the incriminating weapons to a friendly neighbour such as Syria, or their transfer to ships on the high seas. The sheer size of Iraq and the previous unsuccessful attempts to find weapons dumps after the first Gulf War, until they were later revealed by Iraqi defectors, point to the difficulties of locating secret caches.

The conspiracy theory
The failure to find WMDs inspired the creation of a new conspiracy theory. This was an internal Iraqi one involving the scientists employed in the illegal manufacture of chemical and biological weapons. Did they lie to Saddam Hussein about their development of WMDs?

In his January 20th, 2004 State of the Union Address, President Bush said: "The Kay Report identified dozens of WMD-related program activities and significant amounts of equipment that Iraq concealed from the UN." Three days later, the head of the 1,400-member Iraq Survey Group (ISG), Dr David Kay, resigned from his position as special advisor to CIA director George Tenet, and refuted what his president had said in the speech. "I don't think they existed. What everyone was thinking about is stockpiles produced after the end of the Gulf War, and I don't think there was a large-scale production program in the 90s." In his report, Kay had said that his team had found that the Iraqi senior leadership "had an intention to continue to pursue their WMD activities. That they, in fact, had a large number of WMD-related activities." Iraqi scientists were "working on developing weapons or weapons concepts" but had not entered the production phase. Kay's contribution to conspiracy theory comes in his suggestion that the Iraqi scientists had actually fooled Saddam into believing that he possessed a WMD program. This would explain his resistance to providing evidence of the claimed destruction of WMD stockpiles from the previous Gulf War. Saddam was thus willing to risk his own life and that of his regime over non-existent weapons.

The evidence

Whatever arguments exist over the intelligence reports of WMDs in Iraq and their justification for the toppling of Saddam Hussein and his regime, it must not be forgotten that WMDs did exist at one point in recent history.

In 1995, thanks to the defection of several high-ranking Iraqi officials, the UN was informed that Iraq had manufactured at least 3.9 tons of VX nerve gas and acquired 805 tons of precursor ingredients for the production of more VX. Iraq had also produced 8,500 litres (2,244 gallons) of anthrax, 550 artillery shells filled with mustard gas, at least 157 aerial bombs filled with germ agents, and 25 missile warheads containing anthrax, aflatoxin, and botulinum.

The Iraqi government repeatedly insisted that these weapons had been destroyed "secretly" but failed to provide convincing proof. The cat-and-mouse game between the Iraqi regime and the UN weapons inspectors continued for the next few years, during which Saddam even threatened to shoot down U-2 flights over Iraq. The evasive nature of the Iraqi authorities could not be interpreted as anything other than guilt.

The verdict

Kay's theory portrays Iraqi scientists in a completely different light from that experienced by the UN weapons inspectors before the war. The scientific community refused to help the investigators because of threats to themselves and their families from the Ba'ath Party, the Iraqi intelligence service, and the Republican Guard. Kay's belief in their ability to successfully hoodwink Saddam and all the organizations just mentioned is too far-fetched, even for conspiracy theorists.

See also: *US and UK Armed Saddam Hussein in his War with Iran p.227*

2005
GUANTANAMO AND ABU GHRAIB CONSPIRACIES
US prison torture photographs inspired fake execution videos of US hostages

The videotaped execution of US citizen Nick Berg in Iraq in May 2004 was allegedly carried out by Muslim militant Abu Musab al-Zarqawi and broadcast via the Muntada al-Ansar website. The Arabic satellite news channel Al-Jazeera supported the claim that the video pictures of the beheading were fake and that the whole episode was a psychological warfare operation perpetrated by the CIA to take attention off the prison abuses at Guantánamo Bay in Cuba and at Abu Ghraib, Iraq.

The video contained discontinuities in the time-stamp on the screen with obvious editing jumps. The orange jump suit worn by the person claimed to be Berg was available only in Guantánamo Bay prison in Cuba, where Islamic terrorists are held, and the background video scene resembles the cells and furniture at Abu Ghraib. The man claiming to be Al-Zarqawi has neither the tattoos nor the prosthetic leg known to be his.

Shortly after the Berg video was released, a deliberate fake was made by Benjamin Vanderford which was so realistic that it was broadcast on Arab TV.

Subsequent confirmed decapitations have raised doubts about the original Berg conspiracy theories. On June 18th, 2004, the TV station Al-Arabiya showed photographs of the kidnapped hostage, Paul Johnson, being beheaded under similar conditions to Nick Berg. He was also wearing the orange prison overalls believed by conspiracy theorists to have only been available in Guantánamo Bay. Several days later, another beheading, this time of a South Korean, was shown by Al-Jazeera, with similar details.

The terrorist videos are unprofessionally produced but deliberately styled on American prison photographs as a psychological weapon in the war of minds.

religious conspiracies

Between them, religious conspiracy theories contain all the main ingredients for a rattling good yarn: power, politics, faith, greed, money, control, passion, secrecy, mystery, and some shady "they" who want to withhold information.

No wonder, then, that Dan Brown's *The Da Vinci Code* was a runaway bestseller concerning, as it does, all those elements woven into a story which involves the order of the Priory of Sion, the Catholic sect Opus Dei, the Catholic Church, the assumption that the Holy Grail is Christ's bloodline, and a truth-seeking heroine descended from Jesus. Mystery upon mystery is revealed in a work of fiction that concerns itself with religion and conspiracy theories – based, Brown claims boldly, on fact.

Common elements
The conspiracies that follow have other elements in common. The story of Roberto Calvi, who had dealings with the Vatican bank and was found hanging under Blackfriars Bridge in London in 1982, and perhaps the Vatican Nazi gold scandal, stand alone in being regular news stories. Both these have definitely occurred and, in addition, grow more complex and involved over time. Beyond these, there are three types of theory here, often overlapping and all concerned with control. The first is the "forces too mystical and powerful for us to understand have it all under control" theory. Second is the "large, shadowy sinister organization is manipulating the world" theory. Finally there's the revisionist or "the history you were taught is wrong and this is what 'they' have to gain from it" theory.

To a sceptic's eye, the first kind – Scientology, Nostradamus, The Bible Code – preys on the vulnerable. In *Being and Nothingness*, Jean-Paul Sartre said, "Man is condemned to be free; because once thrown into the world, he is responsible for everything he does." When the world feels large, frightening and inexplicable, some feel the need to appeal to an equally large, inexplicable force for good, or at least one that seems to have a handle on things. Hence the huge sales of books containing Nostradamus's writings

after the 9/11 attacks. Those who subscribe to Scientology, or the predictions of Nostradamus, or the Bible Codes are handing themselves over to a more powerful other. It might be said that anyone who subscribes to a religion is doing the same. A Freudian would say such people needed a parent. Religious faith itself can make individuals vulnerable too – hence the number of eminent minds that support the Bible Code.

The "shadowy organization" in the context of religious conspiracy theories is usually the Catholic Church. Conspiracy theories linked to the Catholic church include Avro Manhattan, Opus Dei, Knights of Malta, Knights Templar, Priory of Sion, arguably Roberto Calvi – and the Jesuits do not go unremembered – see the entry on the Black Pope. It has to be said they tend to have a post-rationalist feel, in that conspiracy theorists have made up their mind that the Catholic Church is up to no good and so they contrive support for their view in everything they see. The "evidence" is not always watertight. "He looks like just a very evil individual," says author Eric Jon Phelps of the Jesuit General, who he says is also controlling the actual "white" Pope. It is also often the same whichever group is the accused so that, depending on who you ask, either the Catholics or the Jesuits were responsible for World War II.

When one thinks of conspiracy theories, though, one thinks of the revisionist theory, which often features the shadowy organization lurking in the background. The subjects of these range from those which are hotly debated by serious scholars the world over (the Dead Sea Scrolls, the Turin Shroud, the Vatican's Nazi gold); through the vaguely plausible (Knights Templar, the Priory of Sion, Moses was Egyptian); to the wacky theory held by a single source (Ron Wyatt, "God's archaeologist"; Erich von Daniken and his theory that ancient engineering was carried out with help from extraterrestrial forces.)

Inside the mind of the conspiracy theorist
So how trustworthy is the average conspiracy theorist as a source? Is there even such a thing as "the average conspiracy theorist"? For a number of reasons the answers are

generally. probably not very and no . One of the most interesting aspects of conspiracies in general is the inner life of those who create or defend them. Where the theories are concerned with something that is by its nature so irrational and heartfelt as religion, this becomes more complex still, as faith makes individuals believe more unquestioningly, and makes more plausible people claim more extraordinary things.

When there is no solid evidence to support a theory, and whether one believes it or not, one cannot help but speculate on whether the individuals concerned are cynical or in earnest. What kind of relationship do they have with the truth? Often they are authors too, so is there a book-sales aspect? Which are the plausible, charismatic fantasists, which are the lone pioneers, and which are the con men? It is hard to tell whether Erich von Daniken really believed Mayan statues to represent astronauts – harder still when one reads the sleights of hand and factual errors in his book and learns he had a conviction for fraud. But the deathbed affirmation of Ron Wyatt suggests he really did think he was God's archaeologist. Martin Frankel, however, was without doubt a con man.

And what of those who are attracted to conspiracy theories? Is there a type? Should they be pitied or dismissed for their gullibility, or respected for their open-mindedness and pioneering spirit? Again solid answers, as with conspiracy theories themselves, are elusive. And where there is no solid evidence it is difficult to conclude superior minds are at work. The Scientologist's personality test seems to pre-empt a degree of emotional if not mental vulnerability in those who take it which exceeds that of the man on the street. But some of those who believe the Catholic Church is behind a conspiracy to withhold information found within the Dead Sea Scrolls are academics who say they are merely calling for increased intellectual rigor.

Sometimes, however, it seems as though the followers of conspiracy theories are merely engaged in a kind of game of fitting the world into their chosen way of seeing. Sometimes one wonders whether it is almost an entertaining diversion – a fun means of interpreting events which runs contrary to the real, mundane truth of them. This is a particularly tempting conclusion where conspiracists attempt to weave all the main theories into one.

The grand unifying theory

This is another baffling aspect of religious conspiracy theories: the way in which those who create and defend them sometimes make them interlink. It is not surprising that many theories concern the Catholic Church, nor that elements of the stories are similar, but they become most confounding when a certain type of conspiracy theorist effortlessly joins them all up into a kind of meta conspiracy theory. For example: the *Templars* – who were closely allied with the Knights of Malta – and the Priory of Sion looked after information which suggested that Christ did not die on the cross or at least that his bloodline survived. Ron Wyatt found some sites which contained this kind of information; the Dead Sea Scrolls also contain these kind of documents as well as ones which suggest Jesus was an Essene; the Essenes used cloths like the Turin Shroud during burials ... and so it goes on.

Well possibly. It is as though a whole underground history exists which only refers to itself, taking no information from outside or orthodox sources. Clearly this is as narrow an approach in its way as believing the received view of history unquestioningly. Scholars who have devoted their lives to researching periods in history are ignored in favour of conspiracy theorists who put forward theories which are sexier in a sense – there is a lot of talk about Christ's blood line, treasure, protection by mystical age-old orders, Mary Magdalene. But these conspiracy theorists offer less in the way of hard evidence to back them up. What certainly exists is a certain type of mind which thinks it is possible to wrap up everything that is mysterious in one box and mentally put it away. Perhaps these minds are not as subversive as they think; perhaps their concern is with feeling safe and "on top" of the big, wide world. Grand unifying theories are suspect and counter-intuitive to many who have experienced normal life in all its chaotic, random glory.

But before dismissing conspiracy theories and those who enjoy them with an airy, sceptical wave of the hand, it is worth noting that they do not exist in a vacuum or solely among the insane. Conspiracy theories are both an extension of what human beings do every day and a continuation of what they have done throughout history. To some extent, even the archest of sceptics rearranges the world to make it fit their belief system or way of seeing. This kind of reordering is as natural as it is difficult to spot in oneself. People who adhere to conspiracy theories are engaged in what all human beings do – only more so. They may have lost their way; they may be mad; they may be incapable of taking responsibility for their own lives; they may have too much time on their hands; or then again, they may even be right.

Conspiracy theories are also a continuation of a storytelling tradition that is as old as civilization itself. In particular they are closest to the oral tradition whereby the teller feels free to place emphasis on whichever aspect of the story they choose, and the story is thus reshaped over time. Since before Ancient Greece, with its numerous gods displaying various human traits and indulging in whimsical but earth-shattering behaviour, people have told each other stories incorporating good and evil. Tales of big bad forces beyond the normal man's control serve to entertain their audience and reassure it that the universe is unfolding without them.

Lessons for the study of history

However unreliable one feels the sources of at least some conspiracy theories to be, there are important lessons to be learnt from them for the study of history. Clearly, too slavish an adherence to simplifying, unifying theories shows a lack of intellectual rigor or capacity, but so too does unquestioning adherence to traditional doctrines, whether they be Christian, Jewish or Jesuit. The mindset of the conspiracy theorist is in a sense closed, in that often it will not entertain orthodox teaching. Still, researching conspiracy theories soon opens one up to the notion of not believing everything one reads, whether it be written by an undergraduate with their own website or an eminent academic. Anything that encourages the mind to question and quest has to be a worthwhile exercise.

There is currently a great deal of interest in the way in which history is told. Religious conspiracy theories remind us at every turn that any historical account is no more than a version of events. Quite apart from any religious or other real agenda an author might have, human beings make mistakes all the time both factually and in their judgments. In *The Da Vinci Code*, Dan Brown is fond of saying that history is always written by the winners, but of course life is really a lot more arbitrary than that. True, we are now discovering that the Dark Ages was not simply a vacuum followed by Catholicism, that the Victorians wanted the world to believe everything stops when a great empire crumbles – we have learnt from nature that when one species becomes extinct, another invariably takes its place. And true, individuals and organizations invent or borrow their history in order to give themselves credibility: possibly the Freemasons are among them; certainly the US history of the cowboy website that omits to mention Spanish immigrants is one.

As the UK's Channel 4 documentary "Who Wrote the Bible?" presented by theologian Robert Beckford on Christmas day 2004

The Number One *New York Times* Bestseller

DAN BROWN THE DA VINCI CODE

'Fascinating and absorbing... A great, riveting read. I loved this book'

An entire industry has grown up around the theories put forward in Dan Brown's *The Da Vinci Code*.

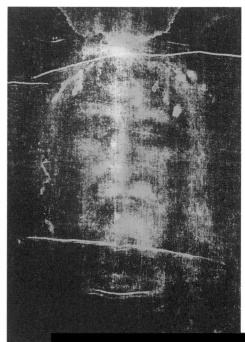

The Turin Shroud in the Cathedral of Turin, Italy, has been venerated by many as the burial cloth of Jesus.

sought to know the truth about his faith. He is an example to theorists, Christians, and scholars alike.

So could the detail contained in conspiracy theories such as Jesus Didn't Die on the Cross, the Priory of Sion and Knights Templar be telling a new, more accurate version of the story of Jesus? Of course it is possible, but what serious scholarship tends to avoid and conspiracists include is a kind of evil intent behind their theories which makes it more than simply another version of history. It is easier to trust a commentator whose priority is objectivity rather than to produce a rattling good yarn or prove that "they" are out to get us. The kinds of people who dedicate their lives to theology do not conclude that the Catholics or the Jesuits or the Jews are behind all major world events.

But if the study of history had become too polarized, with history books covering the received view and the wilder theories being accessible only via the internet or page-turning popular fiction, there are signs of a change. Documentaries which offer an alternative view of history are no longer sneeringly dismissed as "Revisionist" by historians, or if they are no-one is listening.

Whether it is by conspiracy theorists or respectable historians or the passage of time, it is most important to bear in mind that history gets skewed. Serious scholars such as Beckford show us that even in the Bible authors with agendas are sometimes responsible for warping a narrative. Mistakes are made, too. Over two or three thousand years, important texts get lost and rewritten. Languages become extinct and all that survive are bad translations. Gaps in knowledge are plugged and educated guesses turn out to be wrong, allowing scholars to correct their own work and that of others. We must always guard against intellectual laziness. We must keep disagreeing with each other in a way conspiracy theorists seem loathe to. We must be wary when we observe and seek to understand the world, as the bogeymen may not be the ones that conspiracy theorists think.

testified, few biblical scholars now believe either that the Bible – including the New Testament – should be taken literally, or that the authors of its books correspond rigidly to the names they are given. It is generally acknowledged, for instance, that the book of Moses has four different authors, all with very different writing styles and different agendas. Similarly, the gospels of Matthew, Mark, Luke, and John not only concern themselves with different aspects of Jesus's story but also might choose to emphasize his Jewishness (Matthew) or his divinity (John).

The Catholic Church conspiracies section well illustrates how history and conspiracies are born and get written and rewritten according to the agendas of their respective authors. But clearly enquiry should not merely be the domain of sceptics or those who seek to knock powerful religions. Robert Beckford's approach was all the more forceful because he

10BC
MOSES WAS EGYPTIAN

Moses and the pharaoh Akhenaten were one and the same

The suggestion that Moses might be Egyptian not Hebrew is as old as the Old Testament: Exodus describes him as such. The similarities between the Ten Commandments and the Egyptian Book of the Dead have often been noted. Some, including controversial author Laurence Gardner in *Genesis of the Grail Kings*, claim Moses was the pharaoh Akhenaten, who angered Egyptian religious authorities by closing down temples and building new ones devoted to a vague, faceless, omniscient god called Aten.

Many similarities exist between the childhoods of Akhenaten and Moses. It was decreed that if Akhenaten was a son and potential heir to the throne of Amenhotep III he should be killed. According to Gardner the first son died prematurely but the second was saved by midwives, who floated him downstream in a basket to the house of his grandfather's half-brother, Levi. As with so many religious conspiracy theories, such an interpretation does not fit in with orthodox teaching. If proven, it would unseat the whole of Christian tradition.

There are more parallels: Akhenaten led his people through Sinai to marshy Lake Timash, and his followers called him *Mose*, *Meses* or *Mosis* meaning "heir" or "born of". The tablets must have been written in hieroglyphs, say authors Knight and Lomas, because there was no written Hebrew then and it would have been the only script Moses could understand. *Moses and Akhenaten: The Secret History of Egypt at the Time of the Exodus* by Ahmed Osman contains more detail concerning this compelling theory.

AD1
JESUS DIDN'T DIE ON THE CROSS

The Holy Grail is Christ's bloodline and powerful orders exist partly to protect it

This theory concerns itself with the precise nature of the Holy Grail. Traditionally, this was the cup or platter used by Jesus at the Last Supper into which Joseph of Arimathea received Christ's blood at the Cross. Arthurian legend has it that medieval knights went on quests for the Grail. For some, the Grail was the bloodline not the goblet. Among others, Henry Lincoln, Michael Baigent and Richard Leigh, authors of the 1982 bestseller *Holy Blood, Holy Grail*,

developed a theory from the bare bones of Hugh J. Schonfield's book *The Passover Plot*. One version of the theory claims that Jesus had "begat" offspring with Mary Magdalene before his crucifixion. An even more subversive version suggests not only that Jesus was conceived in the normal manner – as opposed to being the result of an "immaculate conception" – but also that his friends rescued him from the Cross and he went on to marry Mary Magdalene. Together they had three children – a daughter and two sons. The family then moved to the south of France. Here they intermarried with the royal Franks. Eventually, their progeny became the mystical Merovingian dynasty. The Priory of Sion, conspiracists maintain, possessed proof of this. For them, the main mission of both the Templars and the Priory of Sion was to protect this Grail. In medieval texts this appeared as "Sangraal" or "Sangreal" which they read as *sang réal* or "royal blood". Others, including BBC documentary director Richard Denton believe that having survived the crucifixion, Jesus travelled east to Kashmir, India, where he had a family and lived to the age of 120.

The conspiracy theory

The idea is that the term "Holy Grail" is a deliberate misinterpretation by the Catholic Church of "Sangreal" – which became "Saint Grail" rather than the correct "sang real". According to this theory, King Arthur, his knights, and the chalice are at best colourful legends with no foundation in truth and at worst a smokescreen. The real Arthur, it is suggested by those who favour the French theory, was a Merovingian warlord whose nickname was "Artos" or "the bear". Over the centuries, it is claimed, the blood of Christ was passed down through the generations, even reaching the Scottish Sinclairs and Greek and Italian nobility.

Clearly such a bloodline would be immensely threatening to orthodox Catholicism and its version of the early days of Christianity. Fundamental tenets about Jesus would be overthrown if it were proved true, and the Catholics' divine right to authority would be challenged. Much better, goes the conspiracy, to maintain the myth – however implausible – that the circumstances surrounding Jesus's birth and death were miraculous in nature. It is preferable that cosy legends about Arthur and his knights exist than the true story of power-hungry priests muscling in on and taking over the authority of Hebrew royals.

The evidence

There is something persuasive about the idea of Jesus being born in the normal way, without the leap of logic that

A Byzantine enamel depicting the moment of Christ's announcement of betrayal at the Last Supper. John can be seen resting his head in Christ's lap while Judas is seated at the opposite side of the table.

"immaculate conception" demands. Joseph, Mary's husband, was certainly of royal lineage, being a descendent of King David. One legend has it that when Joseph of Arimathea visited England, he did so with the Grail. Although there was no mention of a chalice, he did bring Justus, his nephew – and Jesus's oldest son. For those who like their conspiracy theories modernized, apparently Princess Diana was a descendent of the House of French Stuarts, who, unlike her husband's family, were a part of Jesus's royal bloodline. Some speculate that the English version of the Priory of Sion, a secret order called the Meonia which protects the fate of the British Isles – and with which, they say, Diana had links – was involved in Diana joining the Windsor clan.

The verdict

The "Blood Royal" or "Holy Grail" story is that rare thing: a conspiracy that has more common sense about it than the official version. That is, if you believe in the existence and life of Christ in the first place.

See also: *Catholic Church Conspiracies p.242; Knights Templar p.243; The Priory of Sion p.246*

c 200
CABBALA

Ancient Jewish writings are a blueprint for world domination

The Hebrew word *cabbala* literally means "received or traditional lore." Referring to a system of beliefs handed down orally by rabbinical scholars for thousands of years, it includes looking at the Old Testament and using hidden matrices of numbers and words to determine the nature of God. Many believe that the cabbala has great occult power. When these teachings were first committed to writing is shrouded in mystery. The *Sepher Yetzirah* or *Book of Formation* has perhaps been available in written form since around AD 200. The first appearance of the *Sepher ha Zohar* or *Book of Light* was towards the end of the 13th century.

In 1869, the French writer Gougenot des Mousseaux published *The Jew, Jewry, and the Judafication of the Christian Peoples*, in which he made the connection between Freemasons and the cabbala. He claimed that Jews had infiltrated the secret society and that their agenda was to take over the world and destroy Christianity. He also detailed "satanic rituals," including human sacrifices. Mousseaux was poisoned in 1876, while taking holy communion. He had allegedly received a note earlier in the day telling him to test all his food on his dog, as he had been condemned to death at a secret meeting of Jews.

There are those who still believe in a Jewish/Freemasonry conspiracy to establish a new world order based on mystical cabbalistic rituals.

See also: *Freemasons p.284*

1099
SOVEREIGN MILITARY ORDER OF MALTA
The 900-year-old order wields huge influence today

After crusaders took Jerusalem in 1099, a group of Italian merchants who had created a hospital there dedicated to St John organized themselves into an order – the Hospitallers. When the Holy Land was lost, they and the Templars moved to Cyprus. After the Templars were crushed, it is said that the Hospitallers gained much of their property and suddenly became hugely prosperous and influential. There was another move, to Rhodes, but in 1522 when the Turks took the island, the Hospitallers relocated to Malta, where they became known as the Sovereign and Military Order of Malta or the Knights of Malta.

The order splintered into smaller groups throughout Europe from the turn of the 18th century, but the highest profile is based in Rome where, officially, it is involved in humanitarian work. There are those who maintain, however, that the organization wields an alarming amount of power, not always of a charitable kind.

According to authors Baigent, Leigh and Lincoln in *Holy Blood, Holy Grail*, the Order of Malta acts as a conduit between US government agencies and the Vatican. Conspiracy theorist David Icke claims the Catholic and Protestant churches are as one. Many powerful men have been connected with the order by conspiracists, including CIA directors William Casey and John McCone, Chrysler chairman Lee Iacocca, US ambassador to the Vatican William Wilson and Dr Luigi Gedda, the head of Catholic Action. None have confirmed that they were ever in the Order.

See also: *Knights Templar p.243*

1200
CATHOLIC CHURCH CONSPIRACIES
Did the Catholic Church crush the Cathars by sheer force, and why?

In 1200, the Roman Catholic Church had dominated Europe without serious challenge for 800 years. "Heresy" had occasionally been invoked in order for the religion to retain control but only against individual dissenting preachers or small pagan sects. Then along came the Cathars or Albigensians. Even now there are two entirely diverging views about this religious sect, but what is certain is that they were the first mass movement to resist the authority of the Catholic Church.

Based mainly in the Languedoc region of southern France, the Cathars were protected by disillusioned bishops and southern French nobility. In the 1100s, southern France was urbanizing, advanced and independent in its outlook and much of the region was in the process of converting to Catharism. The appeal of the religion then was its asceticism. The word "cathar" means "pure ones". Malcolm Lambert, author of *The Cathars*, points out that they grew out of a new climate in which people were demanding more of their Church. There was a feeling that the existing Church was rotten and people wanted their holy men to be holier. Catharism took the same texts as Catholicism but reached different conclusions and those were unequivocal: there was good (light, God) and there was evil (dark, Satan).

Then in 1198, Pope Innocent III came to power and made it his business to suppress the Cathars. At first his attempts were peaceful. He sent priests to convert Cathars, but they failed. He then suspended the authority of the bishops in the south and sought the support of the nobles there. Those who refused to support him, among them Count Raymond VI of Toulouse, brother-in-law of the King of England and cousin of the King of France, were excommunicated.

Count Raymond went to see one of the Pope's men, Pierre de Castelnau, and an argument ensued. The next day, Castelnau was killed. The Pope's reaction was to blame Raymond and declare a crusade against the Cathars – the first of the Albigensian crusades. In order to win support for his cause he offered the land of the "heretics" to anyone who would fight. This attracted nobility from the north of France. War against the Cathars began in earnest and by the late 1220s the infamous Inquisition were carrying out raids and burning "heretics" all over southern France. Eventually the entire Cathar movement was obliterated.

The conspiracy theory

This conspiracy theory is a debate that rages more hotly between historians today than ever before, and it is multi faceted. The traditional view of the Inquisition is of an all-consuming, ruthless, power-crazed machine that knocked down anyone in its way, trumping up charges of heresy where necessary. Sometimes these commentators portray the Cathars as a peace-loving sect, with women and nature at the centre of their doctrine. However, recently there has been a reaction against this view. Some historians are beginning to say that the damage done by the Inquisition has been vastly exaggerated by the Vatican's enemies and that the Cathars were a more warlike movement. True conspiracy theorists believe the Cathars were suppressed because they had information that would damage the Catholic Church, perhaps relating to Jesus's bloodline. Some would have it that the Cathars buried these secrets and/or their treasure and that the Templars – who may or may not have given the knowledge in the first place – went on to take care of them. It is said that Templars maintained close relations with Cathars and often protected them.

The evidence

It is difficult to prove conclusively that there were links between the Cathars and the Templars, and evidence of secrets held by the Cathars is non-existent. It is also impossible to determine both the true extent to which the Inquisition used force to crush the Cathars and the Cathars' level of aggression in response to it. As with so much of history and with so many religious conspiracy theories, the views of commentators often seem to reflect their religious allegiance or fondness for a good conspiracy. For instance, author Jim Marrs maintains that not much was known about the Cathars until recently because the only available information had been filtered through the Catholic Church.

The verdict

Although history is capable of exaggerating events, what is certain is that a whole powerful movement was wiped out, which suggests a high level of aggression. Where that aggression originated is unproven.

See also: *Jesus Didn't Die on the Cross p.240; Knights Templar p.243; The Priory of Sion p.246*

1314
KNIGHTS TEMPLAR

An ancient order of warrior knights became powerful possibly through protecting the Holy Grail

In 1118, nine French crusaders asked King Baldwin II of Jerusalem for permission to stay in the ruins of Solomon's Temple in order, they said, to protect pilgrims travelling to the Holy Land. Permission was granted, and the Order of the Poor Knights of Christ and of the Temple of Solomon was formed. Soon the knights had gained immense wealth, power, and influence.

But they held too much power for some. For, on Friday October 13th, 1307, all the Knights Templar were simultaneously arrested by the King of France, Philip the Fair, and Pope Clement using heresy laws which allowed them to seize the knights' wealth. But why precisely? Some say they were threatened by their potency and immunity; others allege that Philip needed their money to support his war against England's Edward I. Conspiracy theorists maintain that King Philip and the Pope were fearful of mysterious secrets held by the knights. By March 19th, 1314, Jacques de Molay, the last Grand Master, was burned at the stake. It is said that, as he burned, he cursed the king and Pope, saying that they would join him within a year. Just one month later Clement died and seven months after that Philip, too, met his end.

Argument still rages over whether the Knights Templar were antecedents of the Freemasons or even the Illuminati. Some believe the Templars went underground after Molay's death and were reincarnated in the 17th century as the Masons, others that the Masons used this story to give their society an illustrious pedigree. The structure of the Freemasons owes much to that of the Knights Templar.

The conspiracy theory

Theories regarding the Knights Templar and their alleged secrets abound. One of the most intriguing casts them as the first guardians of documentation showing that Christian history had been rewritten at an early stage, and that Jesus's wife – Mary Magdalene – and progeny moved to France, where their descendents still live to this day.

The evidence

Certainly the order amassed a huge amount of wealth in a short space of time. For some researchers King Baldwin's compliance, and alleged payment of a small stipend to the knights, points towards an ulterior motive on his part. All nine of the original knights were noblemen who were closely related either by family ties or by connections to the Cistercian monks and Flemish royalty. For the first nine years of their existence they recruited no new members. Once installed in the temple, the knights made extensive excavations. According to some accounts, these led to the Templars acquiring scrolls of hidden knowledge and other artefacts – possibly even the Ark of the Covenant.

No-one can agree on precisely what the Templars were looking for under the Temple of Solomon or whether they found it. The more committed conspiracy theorists say they found that important and potentially inflammatory documentation and went on to bury it in Sion; others argue that a find of such magnitude would have been heralded and carried back to Europe with much ceremony.

Perhaps the original nine knights searched in vain for nine years and then began applying their considerable energy and influence to recruitment and other projects. At its peak, the order had a membership of around 20,000 knights. Their power was immense, which raises unanswerable questions about their apparent willingness to submit to the king and the Pope. Jim Marrs' *Rule By Secrecy* equates their rise with that of a present-day multinational. It has even been suggested that they discovered America before Columbus, who flew the red cross of the Templars on his sails. What is undisputed about their legacy is their contribution to the world of finance. Members acted as early tax collectors, debt collectors, trustees, brokers, and property developers.

See also: *The Priory of Sion p.246; Dead Sea Scrolls Deception p.257; Freemasons p.284; The Bavarian Illuminati p.285*

1350
THE TURIN SHROUD
A piece of cloth is the burial shroud of Jesus

The Turin Shroud is a large piece of linen that carries the faint image of a long-haired man with a beard. He appears to have wounds consistent with crucifixion and laceration, and a wound on the right side of his chest where Jesus is supposed to have been lanced as he hung on the cross. There are marks along his forehead consistent with the wearing of a crown of thorns. The Turin Shroud has been controversial since its "discovery" in 1389 by Bishop Pierre d'Arcis. The bishop himself was unconvinced of its authenticity. Yet there are those who maintain that this is the shroud in which Jesus was buried and that his image was transferred onto the cloth.

The conspiracy theory
There are many theories surrounding the shroud, but several main questions. Is this the shroud of Jesus? If not, was it a mid-14th-century fake? If not, whose shroud is it?

The evidence
To begin with the most recent scientific evidence, in 1988 three independent teams of researchers used carbon-14 dating techniques to establish the age of the fabric. They concluded that the shroud was created between 1260 and 1390. Another scientific experiment carried out ten years earlier concluded that the image was a painting. Undeterred, scientists maintaining that the shroud was that of Jesus claimed that the carbon-dating process had been corrupted by the use of a bioplastic coating which threw off the results by a neat 1300 years. And the idea of it being a painting? No problem: paint flecks from other paintings had been transferred on to the shroud when the owners of the works had pressed them against it to sanctify them.

If it dates from further back than 1389, say the sceptics, where are the references to it? It is the Edessan icon, says writer Ian Wilson (author of *The Blood and the Shroud: New Evidence That the World's Most Sacred Relic Is Real*) or at least, a piece of cloth with the image of Jesus's head on it that is referred to from the 4th century onwards. And it was folded, which was why only the head was mentioned.

There are always those keen to merge conspiracy theories, and the case of the Turin Shroud is no exception. In the 1960s a UK researcher pointed to the similarity between this type of burial and the burial rituals of the small sect of ancient Israelites responsible for creating the Dead Sea Scrolls. Others claim it was in the possession of the Knights Templar for 150 years from 1204. It has even been claimed that the image is that of Jacques de Molay, the last Templar Grand Master, burned at the stake in 1314. Some go as far as to speculate that it is the Holy Grail.

There is conjecture on the part of shroud defenders certainly, but there is also enough science for it to remain a knotty problem. For every pro-shrouder asking why, if it is a fake, more relics were not made and profited from, there is a chemist who has done some real research. Like Alan Adler who claimed in *Time* magazine that the blood was not only real but that – and here was the rub for him – long before such processes were understood, it was clotted.

The verdict
Whatever its real origin, the Turin Shroud is a complex riddle. Even if it was forged in the mid-14th century, it is

still intriguing, because the forger's sophisticated creation continues to confound us today. The image looks like a negative, but clearly there were no cameras then. Although science is able to provide persuasive evidence that the shroud is a mere seven centuries old, no clues about motivation, method, or identity were left by its creator.

See also: *Knights Templar p.243; The Priory of Sion p.246; Dead Sea Scrolls Deception p.257*

1555
NOSTRADAMUS
b. 1503, Saint Remy, France
d. 1566, Salon, France
   The mid-16th-century "seer" believed he was able to predict future world events

Michel de Nostredame was born in southern France in 1503 to a relatively prosperous family of corn traders and educated in several academic subjects while he was still young, including science, maths, languages (Latin, Greek, and Hebrew), and astrology. He also received a broad religious education. His father had been Jewish but converted to Roman Catholicism. This may have led Nostradamus to study Jewish scriptures as well as the New Testament. Throughout his life he is said to have been particularly interested in Cabbala, a mystic branch of Judaism, and the apocalyptic prophesies in the book of Revelation.

Nostradamus left home in 1522 to study medicine at Montpellier. After this he worked briefly as a professor of medicine and then began applying his skills to treating bubonic plague victims throughout southern France. He gained something of a reputation while practicing – encouraging proper sanitation and the use of new medicines – but it was sadly not enough to save his first wife and children from the disease. In the late 1540s he remarried and moved to Salon near the Mediterranean coast where he began to concentrate on formulating prophesies. This he did late at night through meditation, focusing on fire and water, aided by his knowledge of astrology and an "angelic spirit". He may well have also enlisted the help of a mild hallucinogen such as nutmeg.

The results were often ominous, claiming to foresee battles and disaster, and were greeted by a mixed reception. Some thought him evil, insane, or a fraud; many of the elite believed him to be spiritually inspired. Soon he had gained a reputation throughout Europe again, but now as a seer.

The conspiracy theory
His prophesying career was extremely prolific. The work now known as "The Centuries" consisted of around a thousand "quatrains" – four-line works couched deliberately, he said to his son Cesar, in mystifying terms to prevent them from being destroyed by the authorities. He insisted enlightened people would better understand them in the future. Several examples of his quatrains are referred to again and again. One favourite is the following:

Century 2 Quatrain 24
Beasts ferocious with hunger will cross the rivers
The greater part of the battlefield will be against Hister.
Into a cage of iron will the great one be drawn,
When the child of Germany observes nothing.

The evidence
Clearly this quatrain predicts Hitler's Nazi regime, Nostradamus's followers insist. Not only that, but there was a resurgence of interest in him when it was alleged that he had predicted the World Trade Centre attacks in several quatrains. Actually the one that follows, which was widely circulated via email, was made up before the attack by a Nostradamus sceptic trying to demonstrate how general and vague his predictions were:

In the City of God there will be a great thunder,
Two Brothers torn apart by Chaos,
While the fortress endures, the great leader will succumb.
The third big war will begin when the big city is burning.

Other genuine quatrains applied at the time were obscure at best and inaccurate at worst:

Century 10, Quatrain 72
The year 1999 seven months
From the sky will come the great King of Terror.
To resuscitate the great King of the Mongols.
Before and after, Mars reigns by good luck.

Century 6, Quatrain 97
At forty-five degrees the sky will burn,
Fire to approach the great new city:
In an instant a great scattered flame will leap up,
When one will want to demand proof of the Normans.

The verdict

The prophesies of Nostradamus are applied too readily. In common with many conspiracy theories, when the actions of human beings seem to be simply too terrible to fathom, people appeal to some kind of grander scheme for comfort. Any accuracy is the result of our making it so. A scrutiny of his work shows his prophesies appear to contain truth because in both nature and number they cover so many bases in such ambiguous terms. It is true that the word "Hister" resembles "Hitler," especially in a quatrain that mentions Germany – but Hister was then a geographical region.

Some commentators despair of our susceptibility. "I can't have been alone in shuddering, last autumn, when it turned out that the Renaissance seer Nostradamus had correctly prophesied the destruction of the World Trade Centre in New York," began Robert Winder in the British magazine *New Statesman* on May 27, 2002. "All at once it came to me, with terrible certainty, that this was a reference to Peter Schmeichel, the "towering" new goalkeeper for Manchester City, a British football club, doomed to take a knock this season. Or was it?"

1694
THE BANK OF ENGLAND
Jewish cabal secretly controls English government

In 1694, England was practically bankrupt. A civil war, followed by wars in Ireland and France, had proved financially disastrous. A Scottish banker by the name of William Paterson came up with a plan which entailed a consortium of financiers each contributing funds to form a bank which would loan the government money. The financiers duly came up with £1.2 million, established the Bank of England, and invented the notion of a "national debt" recoupable through taxation.

One of the terms of their charter was that the identity of the moneylenders should remain secret. It was rumoured, however, that they were Jewish bankers, probably the same ones who founded the Bank of Holland. Paterson was considered to be a mere front for the group.

The conspiracy is supposed to have been started in 1647 during the Civil War by anti-Royalist leader Oliver Cromwell. The Jews had been thrown out of England in 1290, but Cromwell wrote a letter to a Dutch financier in which he said: "In return for financial support will advocate admission of Jews to England."

Jews were readmitted to England during Cromwell's brief rule, but the theorists believe that he was double-crossed by the Jewish bankers, who supported the monarchy because they knew they could persuade a king to grant them a charter for their central bank. There are also people who believe that the bankers engineered the wars with France in order to drain the English finances.

See also: *Amschel Rothschild p.74*

1780
THE PRIORY OF SION
The mysterious organization is alleged by some to be guardians of the Holy Grail

In 1885, it is said that a young, charismatic, well-educated priest named Bérenger Saunière took over the parish of Rennes-le-Château deep in the Pyrenees. One of the first tasks he set himself was to renovate the town's small church which was situated on top of a sacred 6th-century site. According to authors Henry Lincoln, Michael Baigent, and Richard Leigh in their 1982 bestseller *Holy Blood, Holy Grail*, while doing so the priest found several parchments under

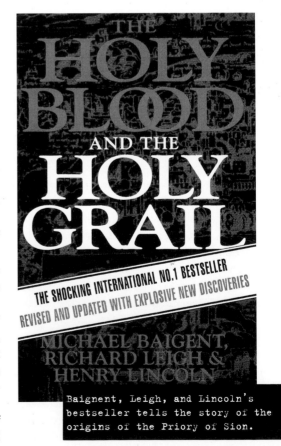

Baigent, Leigh, and Lincoln's bestseller tells the story of the origins of the Priory of Sion.

the church's altar stone in a hollowed out Visigothic pillar. Two were from 1244 and 1644; the remainder were more recent. According to Lincoln et al, the latter were created in 1780 and contained ciphers and codes which were so complicated that a computer couldn't crack them. By their account, Saunière then travelled to nearby Carcassone to show his discoveries to the bishop there. The bishop sent him to Paris so that the parchments could be examined by scholars. They translated one of the ciphers which said, "To Dagobert II King and to Sion belongs this treasure and he is there dead."

Before long, Saunière was mixing with the Parisian elite, many of whom dabbled in the occult. Returning to Rennes-le-Château, he discovered a crypt in the church which contained skeletons. He then began decorating the church with bizarre images such as a wall relief of Jesus on top of a hill with an object resembling a stack of money at its base. He also depicted Jesus either being carried into a tomb or out of it. Not only that, but the story had it that Saunière had amassed enormous wealth and spent a fortune on renovating Rennes-le-Château and collecting expensive artefacts including rare china and antiques. He died penniless in 1917. However, before his former housekeeper died, she mentioned a secret that would make its owner rich and powerful.

The conspiracy theory

Some conspiracy theorists who subscribe to the story speculate that Saunière had unearthed riches, others that he had uncovered information, possibly relating to Christ's bloodline, which enabled him to blackmail the Church.

One view mooted was that the priest had discovered secrets that belonged to the Priory of Sion, an organization that is often linked to the Knights Templar, which had existed for 900 years to protect the Holy Grail. Dan Brown's 2003 bestseller, *The Da Vinci Code*, is a fictional work but the author claims to have got the essentials about the organizations which he includes within it right. Brown boldly proclaims at the front of his book that it is a fact that the Priory of Sion is a secret European society founded in 1099. He goes on to say that the National Library of Paris discovered parchments in 1975 which identified several eminent former members of the society, among them Sir Isaac Newton, Sandro Botticelli, Victor Hugo, and, unsurprisingly, Leonardo da Vinci.

In the novel, Brown writes that after the Knights Templar were officially obliterated in 1307, "the Templars' shadowy architects" smuggled their documents from Paris on to Templar ships in La Rochelle in western France, at which point no-one knows where they went. This fits in neatly with Lincoln et al.'s story. For Brown, the documents included the Holy Grail which was in fact a document revealing Christ's bloodline. They had to be kept secret because otherwise they would be seized and destroyed by a Catholic Church unwilling to have the official history of their origins disproved. Conspiracy theorists claim that descendants of Christ are alive and well and living in France and/or England. But there are also those who say that the society itself was a hoax formed no earlier than the 18th century and possibly as late as the 20th.

The evidence

Dan Brown is not the only investigator to have claimed that the modern organization calling itself the Priory of Sion is the same one that was founded in 1099. Lincoln et al claimed to have discovered that an enigmatic character called Pierre Plantard de Saint-Clair is its secretary general. Lincoln et al also claim to have established through their investigations that Plantard was linked to King Dagobert II and the Merovingian dynasty. For supporters of the Grail-as-Christ's-bloodline theory, this would make him a descendent of Jesus.

The verdict

It is difficult to give a verdict on an organization which is so shadowy and secretive by nature. The aspect of this story which makes it most incredible is that it can be traced back to so few people: Henry Lincoln, Michael Baigent, and Richard Leigh, and a man who Vankin and Whalen describe as the "wily old aristocrat" Pierre Plantard de Saint-Clair. (Incidentally, in September 2004, Brown was charged with plagiarism by Michael Baigent and Richard Leigh who said that *The Da Vinci Code* was substantially based upon their book *Holy Blood, Holy Grail*.)

See also: *Jesus Didn't Die on the Cross p.240; Catholic Church Conspiracies p.242; Knights Templar p.243; The Priory of Sion p.246*

1789
THE FRENCH REVOLUTION

The Revolution was a Jewish conspiracy to control

In 1798, with the French at war with each other, priest Augustin de Barruel, wrote *Mémoire pour servir à l'histoire du Jacobinisme* claiming that the revolution was being orchestrated by a secret society founded by a group known as the Illuminati and spearheaded by Freemasons. In 1806, he received a letter from a mysterious Italian officer called Simonini, concurring with his conclusion but also offering "proof" that Jews were the real guiding force behind the Illuminati. In 1882, French clergyman Abbé Chabauty claimed to have found two letters that had been written in 1489. The first, from a Rabbi Chamor in Arles, complained that the king of France had ordered all Jews to "become Christians or leave his territory." The letter went on to detail persecutions and asked the "Prince of the Jews in Constantinople" for advice. The reply advised the Jews of Arles to pretend to be Christians while subverting the state that was oppressing them: "See to it that your children become advocates and notaries ... get the Christians under your yoke, you will dominate the world."

Chabauty believed that he had found evidence that Jews had been plotting to overturn the French monarchy for centuries. The notion was revived in the 1920s when theorist Nesta Webster published *The French Revolution: A Study in Democracy*, in which she claimed she was a reincarnated French noblewoman with firsthand evidence of a Jewish Illuminati conspiracy.

See also: *Nesta Webster p.178; Freemasons p.284; The Bavarian Illuminati p.285*

1850–present day
CONTROL OF THE MEDIA
Jewish media barons control the news

If Jews really are behind a hidden world government, control of the media enables them to manipulate the news. Those right-wing Christians who believe that hidden government is satanic also believe the Jewish media undermine Christian values by promoting secular theories and a lax moral code.

The favourite quote of such theorists is ex-Vice-President Spiro Agnew's: "The people who own and manage national impact media are Jewish and, with other influential Jews, helped create a disastrous US Mideast policy. All you have to do is check the real policymakers and owners and you find a much higher concentration of Jewish people than you're going to find in the population."

Agnew went on to mention leading Jewish media figures of the time. A number of predominantly anti-Semitic sources also give long lists of the names of people currently involved in the media who are apparently Jewish.

To argue against this, just because a person's name appears to be Jewish, it doesn't necessarily mean they are. And just because a person works in the media, it doesn't mean they control the news. It is also pointed out that two of the most powerful media empires of the 20th century were built by gentiles, namely Ted Turner and Rupert Murdoch. To which the conspiracy theorists retaliate that Murdoch's mother was Jewish and that Turner was "forced" to sell his controlling interest to Jewish moguls.

See also: *Hollywood p.249*

1894
THE DREYFUS AFFAIR
A French army officer was framed by anti-Semites

Alfred Dreyfus, who was Jewish, was a captain in the French army. In 1894, he was charged with passing military secrets to the Germans and convicted when handwriting experts testified that his writing was the same as that on documents found in the rubbish of a German military attaché. Dreyfus was not allowed to examine the evidence and was sentenced to life imprisonment on the notorious Devil's Island.

In 1898, the case was reopened by Lt-Col Georges Picquart, who uncovered overwhelming evidence that the culprit was a Major Walsin Esterhazy. Picquart was trans-

Alfred Dreyfus in his prison cell
(*Le Petit Journal*, 1895.)

ferred to Tunisia before he could present his findings. An unknown officer, who had supplied damning evidence that senior officers forged documents, was interrogated and immediately committed suicide. The army subsequently found Esterhazy innocent. In the same year, the novelist Emile Zola wrote an article defending Dreyfus and stridently criticizing the army. "J'accuse" has been hailed as the "greatest newspaper article of all time." The army sued for libel, the trial provoked riots in the streets, and Zola was convicted and fled to England. Picquart, meanwhile, was arrested for forging the Esterhazy documents and dismissed from the army. In 1902, Zola was asphyxiated by fumes from his blocked-up chimney (it is not known whether this was a genuine accident or the chimney was blocked deliberately).

Finally, in 1906, Dreyfus was pardoned and rejoined the army. In 1908, while attending a memorial service for Zola, he was shot and wounded by a right-wing journalist. The journalist was subsequently acquitted of attempted murder.

1903
THE PROTOCOLS OF THE ELDERS OF ZION
Book revealed secret plans to establish Jewish world supremacy

The Protocols of the Elders of Zion is a book comprising a series of short essays in which anonymous, but apparently powerful, Jews outline strategies for ruling the world and enslaving Christians. It was preceded by a raft of 19th-century literature from around Europe perpetrating the theory that Jews were secretly plotting to take over the world.

The origin of the title is obscure, but the book's first appearance in complete form was probably in 1903, when the anti-Semitic Russian newspaper Znamya (The Banner) serialized the document. The release of The Protocols gave rise to widespread persecution of Jews throughout Russia.

In the US, vehicle manufacturer Henry Ford was so convinced of their contents that in 1920 he paid for their publication in English. Meanwhile in London, The Times newspaper expressed its concern with an editorial demanding investigation into The Protocols: "What malevolent assembly concocted these plans, and gloated over their exposition?" A year later, they published a full retraction on the grounds that a mysterious Russian, Mr X, had given them conclusive proof that The Protocols was a forgery. Ford also withdrew his support and issued an apology.

In the early 1930s, Hitler used The Protocols as a central argument for the extermination of Jews in Nazi Germany.

To this day a significant number of people believe they are authentic and that their principles are still being applied.

See also: Machiavelli p.178; Henry Ford p.251

1903
HOLLYWOOD
Jews control the motion picture business

At the turn of the 20th century, America saw an influx of European Jewish entrepreneurs who found the fledgling movie business an attractive proposition. Within 20 years a string of successful studios – Fox, Paramount, MGM, Universal Pictures, Warner Brothers – were all started by innovative Jewish businessmen.

In 1919, industrialist Henry Ford bought a newspaper, the Dearborn Independent, so he could fulminate against the conspiracy of "international Jews." In 1921, he wrote: "As soon as the Jews gained control of the 'movies,' we had a movie problem…It is the genius of that race to create problems of a moral character in whatever business they achieve a majority." In 1938, the House Committee on Un-American Activities was formed, essentially to root out communism. The HUAC considered Hollywood to be full of "Reds," and a lengthy investigation was launched, apparently motivated in part by anti-Semitism. One HUAC investigator said: "The Jews in Germany stuck their necks out too far and Hitler took care of them and the same thing will happen here unless they watch their steps."

In reality, the Jewish moguls who controlled the motion picture business were desperate not to allow a Jewish influence into their movies. They recognized the dangers posed by anti-Semitism. Jewish writers and actors were often encouraged to play down their cultural influences.

There are those who believe Hollywood is still controlled by Jews and that their agenda is to undermine Christian values while disseminating pro-Zionist propaganda.

See also: Control of the Media p.248; Henry Ford p.251

1913
THE ANTI-DEFAMATION LEAGUE
Civil rights group broke the law to intimidate opponents and gather intelligence

The Anti-Defamation League (ADL) was established in 1913 by Sigmund Livingston, a Chicago lawyer and member of the Independent Order of B'nai B'rith (Sons of the Covenant). The B'nai B'rith is an organization dedicated to Jewish welfare, engaging in community work, disaster relief, and human rights activities.

The ADL was set up specifically to address anti-Semitism and combat prejudice against the Jewish community. Its charter clearly states: "The immediate object of the League is to stop, by appeals to reason and conscience and, if necessary, by appeals to law, the defamation of the Jewish people. Its ultimate purpose is to secure justice and fair treatment to all citizens alike and to put an end forever to unjust and unfair discrimination against and ridicule of any sect or body of citizens."

Since its inception, the ADL has become a high-profile organization, wielding power and influence through lobbying, press, and information-gathering services. It is also rich, with an estimated income of over $40 million a year.

The ADL spends these resources identifying, exposing, and publicizing the activities of those it believes to be anti-Semitic. However, some detractors express concern that the ADL has become more of a propaganda machine for the state of Israel. The Jewish writer Noam Chomsky said in his 1989 book *Necessary Illusions*: "The ADL has virtually abandoned its earlier role as a civil rights organization, becoming 'one of the main pillars' of Israeli propaganda...engaged in surveillance, blacklisting, compilation of FBI-style files circulated to adherents for the purpose of defamation, angry public responses to criticism of Israeli actions, and so on."

Chomsky's attack led to the ADL putting the writer on its list of known anti-Semites.

The conspiracy theory

The two most common accusations against the ADL are that it is heavy-handed when dealing with those who criticize its methods and that it gathers intelligence illegally. The first of these has even resulted in allegations of associations with organized crime. There are those who claim that the ADL promises gangsters that, if they donate funds, the organization will level accusations of anti-Semitism against any media groups or lawmen who target the criminals. There was a minor scandal in 1985 when Cleveland mobster Moe Dalitz was featured on the cover of the ADL journal *Bulletin*, lauded as a generous donor.

The evidence

The ADL has one of the most comprehensive archives in the world, detailing activities and personnel involved in right-wing groups, anti-Semites, and fringe organizations. For 40 years one of the people involved in the collection of that data was investigator Roy Bullock. In 1992, he was arrested and over 10,000 files were seized from his offices and those of the ADL headquarters in San Francisco and Los Angeles. Also arrested was San Francisco police inspector Tom Gerard, who was eventually convicted of supplying Bullock with illegally accessed government information.

Bullock had been illegally collecting information on a range of groups and individuals, including pro-Palestinians, Jewish dissidents, and anti-apartheid activists. The Israeli government was at the time a supporter of the white South African regime, and Bullock later admitted that he was working for the South Africans.

Although the ADL distanced itself from Bullock, maintaining he was a freelance operative hired on a casual basis, many believed that here was the evidence to prove that the ADL was collecting information for both the South African and the Israeli secret services. In 2002, the ADL settled out of court for $168,000 with 19 plaintiffs who had launched lawsuits against it as a result of Bullock's activities. It was the third out-of-court settlement arising from the affair. The suits were initiated mainly by Republican Senator Pete McCloskey, who claimed that the information the ADL had on him, and others, amounted to an invasion of privacy.

The verdict

Noam Chomsky is one of the most respected critics of the American establishment. That his book argues that the charges against the ADL are valid is noteworthy.

See also: *Noam Chomsky p.185*

1917
THE RUSSIAN REVOLUTION
The Revolution was a Jewish conspiracy to establish a superpower

In 1848, the political philosopher Karl Marx wrote his *Communist Manifesto*, which became the blueprint for the leaders of the Russian Revolution. The mere fact that Marx was Jewish is the main argument in favour of this conspiracy. Although some go so far as to claim that Marx was hired to write his manifesto by Adam Weishaupt, the founder of the Illuminati.

In 1918, David Francis, US ambassador to Russia, wrote in a letter to Washington: "The Bolshevik leaders here, most of whom are Jews ... are trying to start a worldwide social revolution." And in 1920, Winston Churchill, the future

Henry Ford in his first car and pride and joy, the 1896 Quadricycle.

British prime minister, made reference in an article to the "international Jew," maintaining that Jews played a "great role" in the Bolshevik revolution. It was shortly before the revolution that *The Protocols of the Elders of Zion* were discovered in Russia and then disseminated throughout the world. *The Protocols* are supposed to have the ultimate proof that Jews are engaged in a conspiracy to enslave the world and destroy Christianity. There are those who believe that they were a propaganda ploy by the tsar, who was desperate to discredit the increasingly popular Bolsheviks.

If there was an international Jewish conspiracy to establish a new world order in Russia, it backfired horribly. Under Lenin and then Stalin, anti-Semitic persecution claimed the lives and liberty of millions of Jews.

See also: *The Protocols of the Elders of Zion p.249*

1919
HENRY FORD
Industrialist published anti-Semitic propaganda

Henry Ford was the industrialist who invented the assembly-line method of mass production. This meant he could manufacture reliable cars cheaply, and in the process he made himself a fortune. In 1919, he spent some of that money on a newspaper called the *Dearborn Independent*. He also hired journalist William Cameron to write "Mr Ford's Page," in which his views were made public. They included his opinion that Jewish bankers had started World War I and that Jewish automobile traders were sabotaging his business. When he ran out of ideas for the column, Ford hired intelligence experts to unearth proof of a Jewish world conspiracy. In 1920, he was shown a copy of the infamous *Protocols of the Elders of Zion*, which allegedly proved that Jews were conspiring to rule the world. Ford was so impressed that he had *The Protocols* serialized in his paper and subsequently published as a book, *The International Jew*.

Lawsuits soon started to arrive from libelled Jewish businessmen, a boycott of his cars was threatened, and Ford started to backpedal. He issued retractions, accepted that *The Protocols* were a fraud, and claimed Cameron had been acting of his own volition.

By this time, however, *The International Jew* had been read by Adolf Hitler. The Nazi dictator was so impressed with Ford that he kept a photograph of him on his desk and frequently expressed his support for the idea that Ford should run for president.

See also: *The Protocols of the Elders of Zion p.249*

1928
OPUS DEI

A branch of the catholic church is unnecessarily elitist and secretive

In 2002, a new saint was created. His name was Josemaría Escrivá de Balaguer, and he had been the founder of Opus Dei – meaning "work of god" – an organization based on the principle that Catholics could achieve holiness and spread the word of God in their everyday lives. Escrivá – who claimed God made him see Opus Dei on a retreat in Madrid – had died in 1975. There were several remarkable aspects of his canonization. Not only had it occurred at unprecedented speed, but he was a controversial figure. Before he was sainted, former members of the organization wrote to the Pope attacking Escrivá for his "arrogance and malevolent temper … his indifference to the poor, his love of luxury and ostentation." Not only that, but it was also alleged that he was connected with the Franco dictatorship and was quoted as saying that Hitler would save Christianity from communism.

The conspiracy theory
As BBC journalist Jan Repa has pointed out, "personal failings have never been a bar to Christian sainthood," but it was the behaviour of the Vatican towards both the man and his

organization that were striking. Even before the fast-track canonization, Opus Dei had been given special treatment by the Pope. Not only that, but it appeared to some to be unnecessarily secretive and hierarchical, and recruits had to be invited to join. This led critics to describe it as a sort of Catholic Freemasonry, and to speculate that it used its power beyond the spheres of religion and charity.

The evidence
There are more than 80,000 members of Opus Dei in 80 countries worldwide. The official Opus Dei website, describes it as a "personal prelature" which focuses on helping the faith of individuals to grow and be at one with their day-to-day activities.

This "personal prelature" was granted in 1982 by Pope John Paul II and is the only organization of its type, which shows the high regard in which the Pope held it. Granting it such status gives members freedom from the geographical jurisdiction of individual countries. It is the favour that it is felt to have with the Vatican that worries the critics. Some ask not only why it was given such freedom, but also what the Pope was expecting them to do with it. The same former members who wrote to John Paul about Escrivá expressed concern that Opus Dei was causing "moral damage" as a result of its culture of secrecy. This is ironic when it has been suggested that part of the Vatican's favouritism for the organization is due to its concern with maintaining traditional moral standards seen as under threat in the modern world.

The verdict
If the organization essentially concerns itself with modern-day missionary work, it is difficult to fathom why Opus Dei need employ such "discretion" and why it was awarded special status by the Vatican. Its combination of secrecy and religious piety, and claims that some of its members practice "self-mortification" including flagellation and fasting, have both attracted attention and assured it a starring role in Dan Brown's blockbuster *The Da Vinci Code*. Whatever the real nature of the organization, it is doubtful whether its purposes are best served by devoting most of its website to dismissing aspects of Brown's book.

See also: *Jesus Didn't Die on the Cross p.240; Catholic Church Conspiracies p.242; Knights Templar p.243; The Priory of Sion p.246*

Opus Dei founder Josemaría Escrivá.

1933
NAZI-ZIONIST
COLLABORATION
Jewish groups supported Nazi policies

Prior to World War II, Palestine was occupied by the British, who were contending with a variety of militant Zionist liberation organizations, some of whom deployed terror tactics. One of them, the notorious Stern Gang, sent a communiqué to the German government offering their support for National Socialism, recognizing that Germany had a "Jewish Problem," and suggesting that repatriation to Palestine might be a mutually beneficial solution.

For a while the Nazis did take the repatriation option seriously. In 1933, they made an agreement with the German Zionist Federation and the Anglo-Palestine Bank, which allocated Jewish money to buy German goods which were sold in Palestine. The proceeds were used to fund the emigration of 60,000 German Jews to Palestine.

In 1937, top Gestapo officer Adolf Eichmann was formally invited to Palestine for discussions with Zionist groups, but was almost immediately deported to Egypt by the British, who also put an immediate stop to the repatriation scheme.

By this time, however, the Germans were already developing the idea that extermination was a better solution to their "Jewish Problem." Eichmann was the officer put in charge of the programme, but, perversely, while implementing horrific policies of genocide, he always proclaimed great admiration for Zionism. Accusations of corroboration by Jewish leaders, allowing prominent Jews to escape while betraying thousands of their fellows, were ubiquitous wherever Eichmann perpetrated his crimes.

See also: *Holocaust Denial p.253*

January 20th, 1942
WANNSEE PROTOCOL
High-ranking Nazis discussed extermination of Jews

On January 20th, 1942, 15 leading members of the Nazi administration met at Wannsee Haus, a country retreat just outside Berlin. The purpose of the meeting was to discuss ways forward in dealing with the "Jewish Problem." The mass slaughter of Jews was well under way and an operation of that size clearly needed careful planning. The Wannsee Protocol gives an insight into the efficiency of those plans.

It was standard practice to destroy all documents linking the German high command to the extermination of the Jews, but a copy of the Wannsee Haus minutes was discovered at the German Foreign Office in 1947. It makes chilling reading, as the officers dispassionately report on their attempts to rid Europe of Jews, recommend sterilization for those of mixed race, and make specific reference to the "Final Solution."

Those who deny that the Holocaust happened point out that the minutes never explicitly refer to the execution of Jews. But the Gestapo officer in charge of implementing the plans for the Final Solution, Adolf Eichmann, testified after the war that he had been through the minutes and sanitized them. He also recalled the occasion as being highly civilized, with an excellent dinner, fine wines, and cigars: "After this Wannsee conference we were sitting together peacefully, and not in order to talk shop, but in order to relax after the long hours of strain."

See also: *Holocaust Denial p.253*

1950s to present day
HOLOCAUST DENIAL
Mass extermination of the Jews was a Zionist fabrication

The Holocaust is the term given to the Nazi policy of mass extermination, in the 1930s and 1940s, of millions of people they deemed undesirable. While those exterminated included gypsies, Jehovah's Witnesses, homosexuals, dissidents, the mentally ill, and the disabled, by far the greatest number to die were Jewish.

Death camps were built all over Nazi-occupied Europe to house Jews, many of whom were eventually executed in gas chambers. Millions more were starved or worked to death in the camps. There was also a specific army unit, Einsatzgruppen, responsible for wiping out entire communities in occupied countries.

The scale of the slaughter was such that it is impossible to say with accuracy how many were killed. Adolf Eichmann, the administrator of the genocide, testified that he believed it was 6 million and that is the figure that is now embedded in our consciousness. Even the most conservative of researchers put the figure at a little over 5 million and it may be as high as 11 million.

A significant number of people around the world believe that the Holocaust never happened. Others are prepared to accept that the Germans did persecute the Jews but that the scale has been exaggerated. And there are some apologists for Hitler, like British revisionist "historian" David

Irving, who believe that whatever atrocities occurred did so without the knowledge or approval of the Führer. They are known as "Holocaust deniers."

The conspiracy theory

Among far-right-wing groups and neo-Nazi extremists, it is popular to believe that the Holocaust is a myth concocted by a Jewish-owned media as propaganda to garner support for the state of Israel. Many also say that the reason the figure is given as 6 million is for financial gain. After the war, the German nation was ordered to make reparations based on the number of people killed. Deniers state that it is clearly in the interests of Jews to exaggerate the numbers, in order to inflate the amount of compensation. In reality, reparations were based on the cost of relocating survivors. It would surely have been more profitable to say that there were more of *them*.

The evidence

There is massive, incontrovertible evidence that the Holocaust happened and that it was on a colossal scale. The German army kept meticulous records of everything they did. Numbers were recorded – dates, times, and even the amounts of gas used. The individual testimonies of both camp survivors and those Germans who followed orders to kill Jews run into tens of thousands. And then there is the harrowing footage of traumatized Allied soldiers arriving at death camps to discover mass graves, working gas chambers, and emaciated, brutalized survivors.

Much of the evidence supplied by the deniers seems to hinge on a distorted view of obscure documents of spurious origin. In Deborah Lipstadt's *Denying the Holocaust* (1993) and Richard J. Evans's *Telling Lies about Hitler* (2002), the authors examine documents that deniers say support their theories. Both are able to clearly demonstrate that in every case the deniers either lied about their content or took passages out of context.

Notwithstanding, in 1979 an organization called the Institute for Historical Review was so convinced of its evidence that it offered $50,000 to anyone who "could prove that the Nazis operated gas chambers to terminate Jews."

Mel Mermelstein, a survivor of the death camp at Auschwitz, duly compiled extensive evidence and applied for his money. When the IHR ignored him, he sued, and was awarded the $50,000 plus an extra $40,000 for pain and suffering.

The only "scientific" evidence offered in support of the deniers was in 1985, when Ernst Zundel, a German émigré

to Canada, was prosecuted for "disseminating and publishing literature denying the Holocaust." As an expert witness he called "execution specialist" Fred Leuchter. Leuchter visited the sites of death camps, surreptitiously removed stone samples, tested them, and concluded that there was no evidence of cyanide within them.

Zundel was sentenced to imprisonment, while Leuchter was discredited, and prosecuted for presenting himself as an engineer without a licence. Other experts pointed out that even if the stone had been in a fit state to analyze, the gas would only have penetrated it to the depth of a human hair.

As far as Hitler's role is concerned, it would seem that, despite attempts by the likes of Irving to portray him as a benign leader, ignorant of any atrocities, his own words betray his real agenda. In a 1939 speech he said: "If international Jewish financiers inside and outside Europe again succeed in plunging the nations into a world war, the result will not be the...victory of Jewry, but the annihilation of the Jewish race in Europe."

The verdict

No credible evidence has ever been offered to prove that the mass extermination of the Jews was a Zionist fabrication. On the other hand, there is incontrovertible evidence proving that the Holocaust was meticulously planned and executed by the Nazis.

See also: *Wannsee Protocol p.253*

1954
SCIENTOLOGY

Controversial "applied religious philosophy" aims for "a civilization without insanity"

Scientology evolved from a movement called Dianetics. Both maintain that people can be freed from painful memories ("engrams") by a process known as "auditing." Scientology, which promises immortality to its followers – it claims to have 8 million worldwide – engages in charity and social reform. It was founded by L. Ron Hubbard from an eclectic mix of psychoanalysis, religion, and science. He died in 1986 aged 74.

Sceptics raise several questions about Scientology: some say it is a cult, concerned with mind control and money. Others say that Hubbard was unhinged or made up much of the life story which he presented as the foundation for his "philosophy."

While there is a slickness and surface plausibility to Scientology, it is vague: scientists point out that real science invites scrutiny from outsiders; philosophers point to Hubbard's misuse of terms such as "axiom."

Critics of the church claim that the Scientology personality test anticipates problems in the minds of its respondents, which is offered as proof for those who see it as a cult. However the Church of Scientology continues to play a large and important part in lives of many millions of people the world over. It numbers among its supporters Hollywood luminaries such as John Travolta, Tom Cruise, and Kirstie Alley. When asked by a national TV news programme whether they felt the need to defend Scientology, both Travolta and Allie replied, emphatically, "No."

1965
AVRO MANHATTAN AND THE VATICAN
Writer against the Catholic Church
b. 1914, Milan, Italy
d. 1990 (place not known)
   The Catholic church is a threatening force influencing all major world events

Baron Avro Manhattan, descendant of the House of Savoy, was born in Italy but educated at the Sorbonne and the London School of Economics, and was friends with H. G. Wells, Marie Stopes, Pablo Picasso, and George Bernard Shaw. During World War II, he ran a radio station called "Radio Freedom" from London, which broadcast to the occupied countries of Europe. Best-known among the scores of books he wrote during his lifetime were *The Vatican in World Politics* (1949), which ran to 57 editions and was translated into most major languages including Chinese, Russian, and most recently Korean, and *Vatican Imperialism in the 20th Century* (Zondervan, Michigan, 1965). He was a member of several societies including the Royal Society of Literature, Society of Authors, Ethical Union, P.E.N., and the British Interplanetary Society.

The conspiracy theory
Both of his major books concern themselves with the same issue: the vast scope of the Catholic Church's influence throughout history. In *The Vatican and World Politics*, he claims that the Vatican's role must be taken into account when considering any political or world event. There is no such thing, he says, as an important world situation free of its influence. By 1965, in *Vatican Imperialism in the 20th Century*, he was expressing himself in stronger terms still, referring to the Catholic Church as the greatest giant alive and saying that, because of this, its actions are of a type and scale which are to be expected of such a colossus. There has never before been such a monster, so determined to take over the human race, Manhattan continues. She is a monster who will fight any competition or enemy.

Still, there is one ancient enemy of the Vatican which has not allowed itself to be obliterated by it, he goes on. According to the book, Catholicism's arch enemy is the Orthodox Church to the extent that the entire purpose of the Thousand-Year War was to destroy and subjugate it or force it to be absorbed into Catholic Church. Manhattan was convinced that the religion does not mind how it achieves this – to what lengths it has to go. He believes the Vatican capable of efforts of a terrible, unscrupulous nature. They produce masterpieces of cunning, he says, and double dealing. Every type of secret negotiation has been employed by them in order to overcome Orthodoxy, according to Manhattan.

The evidence
There are many events in history which are interpreted by Avro as backing up his theory, among them the Russian Revolution which "by sweeping away czarism, swept away also the established Orthodox Church." He also garners both world wars in support of his case.

The verdict
By likening the Catholic Church to a monster at the beginning of *Vatican Imperialism*, Avro in a sense answers the most obvious question: what is the purpose of chasing such growth so obsessively? The purpose, he is saying, is growth itself. For those who agree with him, the actions of the Bush administration post-9/11 must appear to bear it out. But observed through different eyes, with an interpretation of events that does not assume malignant intention on the part of major organizations and without the assumption that the Catholic Church is carrying out a grand, sinister plan for world domination, Catholicism may be seen merely as a successful religion. To use Avro's own monsters example, in nature species that thrive, often at the expense of others, are seen merely as successful. Avro's is a conspiracy theory that relies on a particular way of seeing on the part of the individual; such reliance removes much of its force.

See also: *Catholic Church Conspiracies p.242*

1968

WAS GOD AN ASTRONAUT?

In ancient times sophisticated engineering was the result of extraterrestrial forces

Erich von Daniken put forward this idea in his 1968 book *Chariots of the Gods: Was God and Astronaut?* In what turned out to be a bestseller, he claimed that extraterrestrials visited ancient civilizations, and were responsible for engineering some of the great, enigmatic structures of South America, most famously the Nazca lines. As evidence he used existing artefacts, noting that a stone in a Mexican temple resembled a space rocket, for instance. It is a representation of an astronaut made by the indigenous peoples, he claimed.

This was typical of the "evidence" that Von Daniken used in support of his theories. In this instance the figure was actually a Palenque ruler named Pakal. Mayan experts and scientists alike dismiss his theories on the basis that he does not give ancient civilizations any credit for technological innovation: the fact that it is hard to work out exactly how the Egyptians created the pyramids in no sense suggests that they could not have done so.

1982

CALVI AND THE VATICAN BANK

b. 1920, Milan, Italy

d. 1982, London

"God's banker" found hanging under London's Blackfriars Bridge in 1982

On June 19th, 1982, the body of Italian banker Roberto Calvi was found hanging from Blackfriars Bridge in London. He had bricks in his underpants and trouser pockets and around $15,000 in three different currencies. Known as "God's Banker" for his links with the Vatican, Calvi was chairman of Banco Ambrosiano, Italy's largest private bank, in Milan. He had also been arrested in May 1981 for being involved in the illegal export of several billion lire, and sentenced to four years' imprisonment. He was released pending an appeal which was due the following week. While in prison he attempted suicide, and police at first treated his death as such.

Calvi was linked to the Vatican via archbishop Paul Marcinkus, the Pope's bodyguard and head of the Vatican bank, which had a substantial shareholding in Ambrosiano. The day before Calvi was found dead, his secretary had committed suicide by jumping off the fourth floor of Ambrosiano's headquarters in Milan. She left a note blaming her boss for the damage done to the bank – which was by now close to collapse – and its employees.

The conspiracy theory

In 1983, the verdict of suicide was overturned by a second inquest in favour of an open verdict. In October 2002, forensic experts said that Calvi had been murdered. In July 2003, Italian prosecutors revealed that Calvi had been a member of Propaganda 2, the infamous Masonic lodge to which key members of the Italian establishment, including members of the Mafia, belonged. They concluded that he had been murdered by the Mafia. Calvi's son, Carlo, claimed that the Mafia murdered his father for failing to honour debts and because he knew too much about alleged links between the Mafia and the Vatican's finances. Politicians were involved too, he felt, because Ambrosiano was also the finance house through which unlawful payments to leading politicians were made by large corporations.

The evidence

Renato Borzone, the lawyer of Flavio Carboni, one of the accused, claimed there was no proof that Calvi was murdered, adding, "prosecutors are relying on a phoney testimony by Mafia turncoats." But forensic experts claimed that Calvi's neck showed no signs of the usual injuries associated with death by hanging and that his hands had not touched the stones in his pockets. The marks on his neck, they said, were consistent with death by strangulation.

The verdict

At the time of writing, there is no official verdict. In May 2004, three Italian men and an Austrian woman were to stand trial accused of Calvi's murder. They are: Flavio Carboni, a Sardinian businessman; Manuela Kleinszig, Carboni's Austrian girlfriend; Ernesto Diotallevi, a leading figure in the Rome's underworld; and Mafia boss Pippo Calo. All deny involvement in the murder.

For the City of London police and Italian authorities, the story is becoming ever more fleshed out. They now claim Calvi was lured on to a boat on the Thames by the Mafia and then garrotted from behind. The money and concrete bricks were then put in his pockets; the rope was made into a noose; and his body was hung on scaffolding by the bridge.

The boat was hired by Italian drugs dealer and playboy Sergio Vaccari, who was found murdered in his flat in Holland Park three months after Calvi's murder. He had been stabbed 15 times in the face and neck. It is believed that Vaccari, who helped Calvi find a flat in London, was killed by the Mafia because he threatened to reveal details of Calvi's killer to the authorities unless his drug debts were written off. This theory's advantage as a conspiracy theory is its disadvantage as far as finding out the truth goes: it takes place in Italy. For once the wilder claims may be true but the full truth of the matter may never be established. Italy's legal system is notoriously slow, so it is doubtful whether all the answers will be found any time soon.

1993
DEAD SEA SCROLLS
DECEPTION
Ancient scrolls found near Jerusalem between 1947 and 1956 revealed that Christianity predated Christ

The Dead Sea Scrolls were found in 11 caves near the ruins at Qumran, along the northwest shore of the Dead Sea, 13 miles east of Jerusalem, between 1947 and 1956. There are 825–870 scrolls in all, though many exist as fragments. They include all but one book of the Old Testament: 25 copies of Deuteronomy, 30 copies of the Psalms, and 19 copies of Isaiah. The Isaiah scroll is 1,000 years older than any previously known copy. The non-Biblical texts include laws, rules, and war conduct and Biblical commentaries. Most are written in Hebrew or Aramaic – a few are in Greek.

The conspiracy theory
When the scrolls were discovered the mainly Catholic "international team" that took charge seemed to many to take a long time with and be overprotective of them. Because the scrolls appeared to be those of a Jewish sect – possibly the Essenes: fundamental, apocalyptic Baptists opposed by the establishment priesthood in Jerusalem – some speculated that the team had something to hide. Among other remarkable things, said Michael Baigent and Richard Leigh in their book *The Dead Sea Scrolls Deception*, the scrolls revised the whole of orthodox Christian teaching. Not only did they infer from the scrolls that Christianity had predated Christ but that he was influenced by, or was even part of, that Jewish breakaway group. For those who like their conspiracy theories combined, the Turin Shroud suggests a method of burial practiced by this same sect.

The evidence
The general consensus about the origins of the scrolls keeps changing. In 1963, Karl Heinrich Rengstorf of the University

of Münster put forward the idea that they came from the library of the Jewish temple in Jerusalem, having been removed for safekeeping during the siege between AD67 and 70. This was rejected at the time but revived during the 1990s by scholars such as Norman Golb who added that the divergence of writing styles suggested that they came from several libraries.

Among the evidence cited for the scrolls having been created away from Qumran is the fact that no parchments or writing implements have been found there. Despite this, once the scrolls were "freed" and exhibited in the US, first in Chicago in 1991, the exhibition's literature concluded that one of the rooms at the ruins was a "scriptorium." As well as Golb, Ludwig Rosenberger, Professor in Jewish History and Civilization at Chicago University feels that the evidence at the exhibition was wrongly skewed in favour of the Essene theory. "In sum," asks a paper written by Golb and Rosenberger outlining several controversial aspects, "is the exhibition intellectually honest?" In 1993, the scrolls were exhibited at the Library of Congress in Washington DC.

Whether the content of the scrolls has the shattering implications for the Christian Church that Baigent and Leigh claim – such as that Paul was planted by the Romans to disrupt this new religious movement – the handling of the scrolls has been problematic. One of the omissions from the exhibition that most enraged academics and conspiracy theorists alike was that of the Copper Scroll, which appears to mention holy places where treasures are buried and which, for many, conflicts with the Essene theory.

The verdict
Temperatures still run high on the Dead Sea Scrolls question and eminent minds continue to apply themselves to it. In August 2004, separate archeological discoveries were being made at Qumran which pro- and anti-Essene theorists both believed supported their cause. But were Catholics deliberately withholding information due to the potentially catastrophic consequences for their faith if the content was to get out? Unlikely. The reason may be more mundane and in a sense disappointing: naked ambition. Perhaps if the team held the documents for longer than they needed to it was to ensure that the scrolls were "theirs" in the eyes of the academic community.

See also: *Jesus Didn't Die on the Cross p.240; Catholic Church Conspiracies p.242; The Priory of Sion p.246*

November 5th, 1991
MOSSAD KILLED ROBERT MAXWELL

British media tycoon was killed by the Israeli secret services

The body of publishing mogul Robert Maxwell was found floating in the sea near his yacht, the *Lady Ghislaine*, off the Canary Islands on November 5th, 1991. He had not been seen for hours before his death.

Rumours of connections with Mossad and other international spy groups had long circulated about Maxwell and his publishing empire's finances had been under official scrutiny. Nevertheless, the Spanish authorities concluded that Maxwell had died of a heart attack, although there was no history of heart disease. His daughter Ghislaine said the family was satisfied with the investigation, and his widow, sons, and their lawyers insisted that the death was accidental, perhaps with an eye towards Maxwell's $35.8 million insurance against accidental death. A forensic specialist who worked on the autopsy later noted that a perforation under Maxwell's left ear could have been caused by an injection of a lethal substance. Labour Party MP George Galloway openly speculated in the House of Commons that Maxwell was murdered because "dead men tell no tales."

Publishing magnate Robert Maxwell visiting Paris in November 1987. Was Mossad involved in his death?

Former prime minister John Major publicly denied that British intelligence was investigating Maxwell's finances after his death. By 1995, however, the Serious Fraud Office had spent $13.9 million tracing Maxwell's financial holdings. This resulted in charges against his financial advisors and his two sons for defrauding the pension fund of his newspaper chain, Mirror Group.

One charge claimed that, months before his death, Maxwell had used pension assets and shares in Scitex Corporation illegally to raise money for other Maxwell companies. The collapse of Maxwell's empire had begun well before he died, lending credence to the suicide theory.

1994
FRANKLIN COVER-UP

Wild accusations of satanism and child abuse by America's ruling elite

This conspiracy theory could not be more ambitious in its scope. It alleges that on May 3rd, 1994, a documentary called *Conspiracy of Silence* (made by a British company) was due to air on the Discovery Channel but was withdrawn as a result of congressmen threatening "the TV Cable industry" with restrictive legislation if it was aired. And it was no wonder: the documentary, claimed John Decamp, former republican senator and author of *The Franklin Cover-up: Child Abuse, Satanism and Murder in Nebraska*, was about to expose a network of religious leaders and Washington politicians who flew children to Washington DC for Satanic sex orgies. Allegedly the sex-ring story was unearthed during investigations into the reasons for the collapse of the Omaha, Nebraska Franklin Community Federal Credit Union in 1988; since when the story has been referred to as the Franklin cover-up.

It has spawned a host of websites that repeat Franklin's claims but add no new evidence or real support to the original claim.

1997
THE BIBLE CODE

The Bible Code claims the good book predicted world events thousands of years in advance

In 1997, *The Bible Code* was published. It became a best-seller. In it author Michael Drosnin, by his own account "a sceptical secular reporter" begins by describing how he sent a letter to Yitzhak Rabin warning the Israeli Prime Minister he was going to be assassinated. The letter explained that there was a code hidden within the Bible that predicted events thousands of years before they occurred. The name "Yitzhak Rabin" appeared in the text, claimed Drosnin, and across it the words "assassin that will assassinate." For defenders of the code this was just the latest in a series of accurate assassination predictions contained in the Bible which included Anwar Saddat and John and Robert Kennedy.

The conspiracy theory

The man who introduced Drosnin to the code was Dr Eliyahu Rips, an eminent mathematician based in Jerusalem. According to him the code had first been discovered by Rabbi H.M.D. Weissmandel in Prague, 50 years before. The rabbi applied a "skip code" to the Bible. He took a letter from the beginning of Genesis, skipped 50 letters and took the next letter, skipped another 50 and so on, and the word "Torah" meaning "teaching" or "divine teaching" was spelt out. The same thing happened in the books of Exodus, Numbers, and Deuteronomy.

Using this same principal, Rips found, among other things, the date January 18, 1991 – the date on which the Gulf War began. That day was Rips' real epiphany, just as Drosnin's was the day that Rabin was assassinated.

So what else does the Bible code predict? Nothing less than the end of the world – with the qualification that we can save ourselves with the help of the code. The words "atomic holocaust", "end of days" and "code will save" appear near each other, he claims. When does the code say this might happen? 2006.

The evidence

In November 2003, *Horizon* on BBC2 decided to investigate. Drosnin issued the challenge to his detractors that if they found in advance a message about the assassination of a prime minister within *Moby Dick*, he would believe them. Brendan McKay, an expert in advance probability theory, took up the challenge. Sure enough, he found Kennedy and underneath "he shall be killed" in the novel. There were also "references" to more recent events, including the death of Diana. Drosnin claimed that McKay was playing word games. McKay insisted that for statisticians – and although Rips was a brilliant mathematician, he was not a statistician – results are only significant when exactly what is being looked for is specified in advance. Code defenders had looked for a name like Rabin's but not specified any phrases they would find significant. This, McKay maintained, vastly increased the chances of finding something that appeared to be significant.

Eventually, defenders of the code and sceptics agreed on a procedure and the material was run through a computer program to look for statistical significance. The conclusion reached was that there was no evidence for the existence of a Bible code. Rips remained steadfast in his conviction, however, claiming that the programme makers made many mistakes in their processing. Yet McKay says that even the number of errors they claim could not explain away such a negative conclusion.

The verdict

Distinguished scholars on both sides continue to defend their thinking passionately. Nobody has yet devised a scientific and universally acceptable way of investigating such codes. Until they do, the individual is left with only their instincts to guide them.

1997

VATICAN GOLD

Wartime documents allege that the Vatican handled Nazi gold

In July 1997, a newly declassified US document dated October 1946 was uncovered alleging that the Vatican was holding Nazi-era gold valued at about $170 million. The gold had supposedly been looted by the Nazi-installed Ustasha government in Yugoslavia from hundreds of thousands of Serbs, Jews, and Gypsies it had exterminated during the war. A memo from Treasury agent Emerson Bigelow to his superior said that approximately 200 million Swiss francs were originally "held in the Vatican for safekeeping." The Vatican denies handling the looted money.

The plot soon thickened. Before long, Holocaust experts were accusing the Vatican of having used the gold to smuggle Nazi war criminals into Latin America and the Middle East after the fall of Nazi Germany. According to Shimon Samuels, director of the Simon Wiesenthal Centre, leaders of the enquiry into Nazi gold, the "gold-line" or channel used to smuggle gold was linked to the "rat line" by which criminals were helped out of Europe.

This controversy arose amid allegations that Swiss banks lacked transparency over the presence of Nazi gold in Swiss bank vaults. The Vatican, keen to avoid such publicity, reviewed the existing plan, which was to make the archive public in many years' time. After some initial reluctance, it decided that the World War II archive should be made available to historians from the beginning of 2003. Although the archive does not preclude the Vatican's involvement in the

Nazi gold scandal, there is evidence that the Vatican intervened on behalf of the Jews during that period.

1999
MARTIN FRANKEL AFFAIR
Frankel, Martin
b. 1954, Toledo, Ohio
  A swindler who used the Catholic Church as a front

In September 1999, after an international manhunt, a financier who had amassed a total of $200 million over a decade was arrested by German police. He was carrying nine passports and 547 diamonds. From 1998 he had posed as the head of a new Catholic charity, a bogus organization which he called the St Francis of Assisi Foundation. This brought the support of those close to the Vatican and, it was claimed, the legitimate Vatican charity Monitor Ecclesiasticus. His plan was to set up a Vatican foundation that he would secretly control. The Vatican denied any link with Frankel.

Frankel's was a colourful story involving an unlikely gawky misfit with a passion for S&M sex, fine wine, and fast cars. Eventually he had women fighting over him. Although he was described by some as "bumbling," he managed to swindle insurance companies in five states out of vast sums of money and pleaded guilty to 24 federal charges including racketeering, securities fraud, and conspiracy. It was when he tried to go global that his world began to fall apart. In December 2004 he was jailed for 16 years and eight months.

The extent to which high-ranking Catholic officials had knowledge of Frankel is unclear, but certainly some close to the Vatican were involved. In 2002, Msgr. Emilio Colagiovanni, 84, an Italian priest pleaded guilty to federal counts of conspiracy to commit wire fraud and money laundering. He was fined $15,000 and placed on five years' probation for his minor role in Frankel's massive swindling scheme. At his sentencing he said he was "very sorry if anybody had been hurt" by his actions.

1999
"GOD'S ARCHEOLOGIST"
RON WYATT
b. Kentucky, 1933
d. Memphis, TN, 1999
  An individual who believed that, guided by God, he had found many significant Christian sites

On August 4th, 1999, Ron Wyatt, "God's archeologist," died of cancer. Before he passed away, surrounded by family and friends in a hospital in Memphis, Tennessee, he was given a last chance to reaffirm or recant the astonishing claims he had made about his discoveries for almost 40 years. Without hesitation he reaffirmed them.

His quest had begun in 1960, when he was 27 years old. Having been brought up a Seventh Day Adventist and believing the Bible to be factually correct, he was particularly struck by an article in *Life* magazine telling of how a Turkish military plane had photographed a shape on Mount Ararat that resembled a boat. Over the following 15 years he became fixated with the story and convinced that it was Noah's Ark. He then visited the site several times, undertook archaeological work and steadfastly maintained that his critics were wrong and he had found the ark.

And there were to be further amazing "discoveries". He set out to find the route the Israelites had taken on their way to the Promised Land. Focusing his efforts on the Red Sea, within days he found "evidence" to support his conclusions. Not only did he discover a broad ridge where the water was shallow but he said he had found chariot remains at the bottom of the sea. The breathtaking claims did not stop there: he found Mount Sinai and the precise place where Moses had received the Ten Commandments; most impressive of all he found the site of Jesus's crucifixion and below it the final destination of the Ark of the Covenant.

The conspiracy theory
For Wyatt, any questioning of his "discoveries" was the work of the Devil. If he was accused of being secretive or of covering his tracks too readily, he claimed that he had been asked to restore sites by the authorities who, depending on the site in question, feared religious war or large-scale conversion to Judaism. Wyatt's critics included scientists and religious commentators alike, some of whom called his work "The great Christian scam". The Seventh Day Adventists who he had abandoned were among his harshest critics.

The evidence
As it was a question of faith, "proof" for Wyatt and his supporters came in a form unrecognizable to many. How did he make such a number of extraordinary discoveries? Simple, said Wyatt – he was guided by God. Sceptics criticized his loose language and use of unclear photographs and footage, saying such roughness was supposed to give his claims an authenticity they lacked. "The implication," wrote *Fortean Times* writer Jack Romano, "is that naivety was synonymous with honesty." But criticism of the style of an enquiry does not help to prove or disprove its conclusions.

Could Wyatt have discovered the Ark? Gustave Doré's engraving depicts the Ark coming to rest on Mount Ararat.

In a sense just as unhelpfully, the pro-Wyatt side garnered the degree of luck he had experienced throughout his life in support of their cause. Red tape had disappeared, said Wyatt, visas were granted and, just as it was looking as though work might have to cease, financial backing was supplied. Not only that but he claimed, said Romano, that there was divine intervention, "including the death of enemies, angelic visitations, localized earthquakes – even governments falling. Ron pointed out that this was, of course, none of his doing and he was merely the tool of a greater authority." There were attacks, arrests, kidnaps, deportations, "but," Romano continued, "in a career that spanned 22 years and over 100 trips, he providentially survived everything that was thrown at him."

Still, this did not rid him of the problem of very detailed criticism from scholars such as geologist Dr Salih Bayraktutan, who visited the "ark site" many times and dismissed Wyatt's claims that there were "trainloads of petrified wood" there. Detailed geological work has also led several specialists to conclude that "the ark" is a natural phenomenon which also occurs elsewhere.

The verdict

Claim and counter claim continue to be made. Since Wyatt's "discovery" of the ark in 1960, which was certainly of the dimensions laid down in the Bible, firm scientific data has been hard to come by. Scientists and archeologists continue to criticize his methods and dispute his findings. As with so many individuals who make wild, unorthodox claims which are difficult to confirm or deny, the focus has shifted to his motivation and mind. Given that his "evidence" is shaky if not actually fabricated, in a sense the most interesting aspect of this enquiry is whether Ron Wyatt was in earnest. There seems little doubt about that. As a committed Christian, it would be extremely serious for Wyatt to lie about such matters. At the very least, if Ron Wyatt made up his claims, he felt that he had been granted permission to do so by the highest authority of all.

2000
THE "BLACK" POPE
The head of the Jesuits gives orders to the "white" Pope

This theory was mentioned in passing in the Preface of M.F. Cusack's 1896 book *The Black Pope*, where the author says: "Those Romanists who do not greatly love the Jesuits, and their number is not limited, use the term as indicating that the Black Pope rules the White Pope." In recent years it was resurrected in the "alternative" newspaper *Spectrum*, by *Vatican Assassins* author Eric Jon Phelps, who was interviewed in the May 2000 issue. In the interview, Phelps shows himself to be a proponent of the single unifying conspiracy theory, bringing together the Jesuits, the Knights of Malta, the Freemasons, the Mafia, even President Kennedy, in a way which, as far as both interviewer and interviewee are concerned, is seamless. In his introduction to the piece, interviewer Rick Martin is ambitious and grand in his scope. "Let's call this story the 'Jesuit-Vatican connection' to the unfolding New World Order agenda," he says.

According to Phelps, the Jesuits or Society of Jesus has a Supreme Jesuit General, and other high Jesuit Generals who, unbeknown to those lower down in the hierarchy, are sorcerers. Not only that, he says, but they worship Lucifer who, for Phelps, is distinct from Satan. The ultimate goal of the Jesuits, Phelps believes, is to rule the world with a Pope of their making in Solomon's rebuilt temple in Jerusalem.

The conspiracy theory

The Supreme Jesuit General is generally known as "the Black Pope". Martin states that "black here refers to hidden, evil activities, not to race or colour." According to Phelps, the Black Pope gives orders to the actual Pope. This alone is a bewildering notion, but the author does not stop there – Phelps can name the evil manipulator. He is apparently a

Dutchman, Count Hans Kolvenbach (who has sensibly been silent on these preposterous claims against him). His predecessors were Pedro Arrupe, who died in 1988, and before him, Jean-Baptist Janssens, who passed away in 1964.

One of the wilder claims on the internet concerning the Black Pope is that he ordered the 9/11 attacks on the World Trade Centre and the Pentagon.

The evidence

Phelps uses the testimony of a controversial figure, Alberto Rivera, to support his case. Rivera claimed to have been a top Jesuit and hence invited to a "Black Mass" in Spain in the late 1960s. There, apparently, you are involved in the worship of Lucifer, dressed entirely in black clothes.

Phelps also mentions a photograph of the existing Black Pope (supposedly Hans von Kolvenbach), from Jean Lacoutre's *Jesuits: A Multi-Biography* as a kind of evidence, saying to *Spectrum*: "He's the Jesuit General, and he looks like just a very evil individual." Proof enough, presumably.

The verdict

Phelps is straightforward in his assessment of the influence of the Jesuits. Martin sums the author's position up by saying: "You, literally, link every major global conflict and political assassination to the hands of the Jesuit Order. The Jews, as with many other groups you mention, have been the unwitting pawns in this Jesuit Agenda." Such a grand scheme has a familiar ring; it is the anti-Jesuit version of the Catholic conspiracy theories. Just as Avro Manhattan and others saw the influence of Catholicism in all major world events, Phelps sees the Jesuits, thirsty for world domination. Indeed both work the same events into their apparently opposing schemes: Manhattan saw the Catholic Church as being behind World War II; Phelps maintains the Jesuits were responsible for the anti-Jewish fervor which led to Auschwitz. Neither views are founded on any concrete facts, both preferring conjecture and supposition.

See also: *Catholic Church Conspiracies p.242; Avro Manhattan and the Vatican p.255*

September 11th, 2001
WORLD TRADE CENTER
Jews were responsible for the attacks on the World Trade Center

Within hours of the two planes flying into New York's World Trade Center, the internet was full of rumours that Jews were responsible. Far-right anti-Semites and radical Muslim groups issued "reports" which "proved" a Zionist conspiracy. They claimed either that the state of Israel carried out the atrocity or that Mossad had known in advance but didn't disclose the information. It is generally believed that the motive was to provoke the US into a war against Islam.

The most persistent rumour is that, days before the attack, 4,000 Israeli citizens who worked at the World Trade Center were warned to stay away on September 11th. There is no evidence for this claim whatsoever.

Within hours of the attack five Israeli men were arrested in New York. They were allegedly filming the burning towers and appeared to be celebrating. The men were held for five weeks and then deported because their visas had expired. There were no charges brought against them.

While most of the information available on this Zionist conspiracy comes from extreme, fringe media, some mainstream sources have also published the theory that over 100 Israeli agents in America are posing as art students. An FBI report identified them as Mossad agents who were monitoring the activities of the hijackers but had been instructed not to alert the authorities. The FBI has denied all knowledge of such a spy ring.

See also: *World Trade Center p.262*

November 11th, 2004
YASSAR ARAFAT
Mystery surrounds death of Palestinian leader

Mohammed Abdel Rahman Abdel Raouf Arafat al-Qudua al-Husseini was born in Cairo, Egypt, in 1929, although he always claimed to have been born in Jerusalem. After graduating from Cairo University with a civil engineering degree, he became involved in radical politics, joining the Muslim Brotherhood and serving as president of the Union of Palestinian Students. In 1963, he founded Fatah, an organization dedicated to establishing an independent Palestinian state.

Fatah soon evolved into a terrorist organization operating against the state of Israel, involved in bombings, hijackings, and assassinations. In 1969, Arafat was appointed chairman of the Palestinian Liberation Organization, a position he held until his death. The PLO was initially also a terrorist organization, but, in 1974, Arafat instructed his members to withdraw from violence. As a result of his diplomatic endeavours he was awarded the Nobel Peace Prize in 1994. Terrorist attacks by extreme

Palestinian groups continued, however, and there is much evidence to suggest that Arafat was disingenuous in his condemnations of terror tactics.

Arafat was also phenomenally rich. Aside from donations by Arab leaders – among them Iraqi dictator Saddam Hussein – the PLO benefited directly from an extraordinary tax arrangement. The Israeli government handed over all taxes collected from Palestinians and Arafat had direct control over the money. Conservative estimates of the organization's wealth in 2004 were $2 billion.

Arafat's wife, Suha, created resentment in Palestine by living in Paris, where she drew an allowance of $100,000 a month. In 2003, an investigation into money laundering was launched after banks reported a transfer of over $1 million from PLO funds to Mrs Arafat's personal account. A subsequent audit of the PLO accounts revealed that $900 million were unaccounted for.

The conspiracy theory

Arafat seemed to die very quickly. He appeared to be healthy until admitted to hospital with a viral infection in October 2004. The PLO issued a statement saying that the condition was not life-threatening on October 31st. Then, 11 days later, he was dead.

French laws state that only members of a deceased's close family are allowed access to medical files, and for a period of time Mrs Arafat refused to let the PLO see the documentation concerning her husband's death. Meanwhile, two theories started to circulate: the first was that the Israelis had poisoned the PLO leader and the second that he had died of Aids (rumours of Arafat's bisexuality had been circulating for some years).

The evidence

The actual cause of Arafat's death remains a mystery, which has led to massive speculation. His nephew Nasser al-Kidwa told a press conference: "Examinations of X-rays and all imaginable tests...are still with the same results, the inability of reaching a clear diagnosis. That is precisely the reason why suspicions are there, because without a reason you cannot escape the other possibility ... that there is unnatural cause for the death."

The French authorities have ruled out poisoning, claiming that they would have investigated anything that appeared untoward. However, in April 2004 the Israeli prime minister, Ariel Sharon, made a direct threat to Arafat's life when he said: "I told the president [Bush] the following. In our first meeting about three years ago, I accepted your re-

Palestinians burn tyres in the streets after the news of Yasser Arafat's death spread in Gaza City.

quest not to harm Arafat physically. I told him I understand the problems surrounding the situation, but I am released from that pledge."

Certainly the Israeli army made no secret of their tactic of specifically targeting, with a high rate of success, Palestinians whom they saw as a threat. It is believed that they were reluctant to take out Arafat only because of concerns that killing him would create a powerful figure of martyrdom.

The Aids story first surfaced within a week of Arafat's death and received some mainstream attention. On November 19th, the *New York Post* reported Dr Ran Tur-Kaspa, an infectious disease expert, as having told journalists in Israel: "Yes, it could be Aids."

The verdict

The fact that the PLO issued a statement saying that Arafat's condition was not life-threatening on October 31st, but 11 days later he was dead, is suspicious. However, the truth will not be known until all the files have been released.

royal conspiracies

Royal families have always presented ample fodder for conspiracy theorists. Sometimes they are rumoured to have originated conspiracies themselves – against their people, their family, or other nations – and at other times have been the subject of such conspiracies. Even when they have little power, royals hold a position in society that others envy.

The fact that in the 21st century there are still "working" royal families who hold ostensibly powerful positions in democratic nations seems an oxymoron. Yet in the United Kingdom, Spain, Holland, and Sweden (to name a few) royal families enjoy lives of great privilege and favour. They do not, in general, lead quiet lives, however.

In previous centuries, including the last, various royals have found themselves at the centre of conspiracy-related speculation. This century is still young, and yet conspiracy theories are already forming around one or more of the royal families who continue to enjoy positions of prominence. While these families exist there will always be people who look to a long and bloody history of royal rule and misrule, concluding that every royal is as bad or mad as a previous generation. In the past, those closest to the throne had most to gain if the current monarch met an untimely end, so were not surprisingly implicated in the sudden death of the ruling king (or queen). It has also been proven that monarchs have frequently indulged in conspiracies to get rid of those who have either threatened them or thwarted their ambitions.

Early royal conspiracies

It has long been thought that Alexander the Great and his mother Olympias conspired to kill Alexander's father Philip II of Macedonia in 320 BC, when the ruler's new marriage threatened to produce a rival heir to the Macedonian throne. Philip's assassin was then killed on the spot – conspiracists claim that this was to prevent him disclosing the names of his fellow conspirators. Alexander took the crown and went

on to conquer most of the known world. And in 323 BC, when Alexander himself was taken ill at the age of 32 in Babylon after a prolonged drinking bout, there were rumours that he had been murdered, poisoned with strychnine. He died ten days later.

The man behind the conspiracy to murder the emperor was thought to be Antipater, the regent Alexander had left behind in Macedonia when he set off to conquer the Persian empire. Olympias had written to Alexander warning him of Antipater's ambition and Alexander had summoned Antipater to him in Babylon, certainly to strip him of his regency, if not to have him executed. Antipater was a close friend of Aristotle, who was appalled by Alexander's attempt to have himself deified. Aristotle's own nephew had been murdered by Alexander and Aristotle himself wrote of Alexander, his former pupil: "No free man willingly endures such rule."

Many historians believe that Aristotle supplied the poison. He certainly knew about strychnine, as his friend Theophrastus had described its use and dosage, and said that the best way to disguise its bitter taste was to administer it in undiluted wine. The poison was carried to Babylon by Antipater's son Cassander in a mule's hoof. It was administered, it was said, by a couple of Macedonian generals who were tired of Alexander's endless campaigning. Certainly there were few who mourned the passing of the man who had begun to behave as an increasingly unpredictable tyrant.

This conspiracy theory was widely believed for over 5,000 years. However, as recently as 2003, the case was "reopened" by ex-Scotland Yard deputy commissioner John Grieve. He concluded that Alexander had overdosed on white hellebore, which was widely used at the time as a medicine, in a desperate attempt to get himself fit for a planned campaign in the Arabian peninsula. When it comes to royals, there is no time limit on public interest, it seems.

Behind closed doors

Conspiracies against royalty grip us just as strongly as do conspiracies among royal families. The really clever anti-royal conspiracy theories are those that place a king, queen, or emperor at the centre of a conspiracy. There is a commonly held theory, for instance, that the idea of the "man in the iron mask" as the twin of Louis XIV was merely a convenient way to undermine the Bourbons. Voltaire, who had no time for his monarch, first popularized this theory during the Sun King's reign. In 1917 the Bolsheviks claimed that the Romanovs had smuggled Russia's gold out of the country, thus discrediting the Russian royal family who had already been executed by the revolutionaries.

Through history there have been many suggestions that royal families indulge in all manner of sexual perversions and Satanic worship. During the reign of Louis XIV a conspiracy known as *L'Affaire de la Chambre Ardente* came to light, named after the candlelit room in which the investigating officer carried out his interrogation. The conspiracy centred around a woman called Catherine Deshayes, a supplier of "succession powders" to the court (poisoning was a popular way to inherit wealth and title at the time). Under the threat of torture, Catherine admitted to being part of a Satanist cult that sacrificed babies at orgies where a naked woman's body was used as the altar table in a black mass performed by the notorious Abbé Guibourg. One of the worshippers was said to be the King's mistress, the Marquise de Montespan. Fearing that she was losing the King's favour to a younger rival, the Duchesse de Fontages, the Marquise had attended three of the "love masses" to try to win back the king's favour by acting as the nude altar table.

Catherine Deshayes and Abbé Guibourg admitted to murdering hundreds of children during a career in Satanism that spanned 13 years. Some 150 courtiers were arrested for poisoning and sentenced to death, slavery in the French galleys, or banishment. Madame Deshayes herself was burnt at the stake in 1680. However, the Marquise de Montespan returned, briefly, to favour at court.

The House of Windsor

Evidence for such a conspiracy seems almost laughable to modern ears, especially as the accused faced torture. But it was widely believed. Perhaps not so outlandish, either, when you consider that as recently as 1999, New Age guru David Icke claimed that the British royal family members

practise child sacrifice. But then the British royal family are at the centre of numerous conspiracy theories, even today. This is because under the British constitution, such as it is, The Queen appears to hold power. The British government is Her Majesty's government. At the beginning of each parliamentary session she sits in the House of Lords with her crown on and tells the assembled members of parliament what "my government" is going to do in the next session. On the face of it, she hires and fires prime ministers. She is also the head of state for Canada, Australia, New Zealand, and a number of other Commonwealth countries. The British navy and air force are the Royal Navy and Royal Air Force and the army swears fealty to her. In criminal courts, prosecutions are made in her name. She is also head of the Church of England, and the citizens of the United Kingdom – who consider themselves to be one of the freest people on Earth – are not citizens at all, but subjects of Her Britannic Majesty.

For most people in the world, the relationship between the House of Windsor and the British State is as arcane and impenetrable as the rules of cricket. If you were not brought up with it, you will never understand it – which is why so many conspiracists hold various anti-Windsor conspiracy theories to be true, all based on the idea that there is no smoke without fire, it seems. To the uninformed, the House of Windsor must be involved in some diabolical work in order to maintain its position of power and influence.

There is, of course, a conspiracy of sorts going on here. The royal family and the British people – and royal fans around the world – have entered into a tacit pact to keep what is essentially a fairytale alive. There is an appetite worldwide for the pomp and pageantry that the British royal family in particular provide. In 1981, over 700 million people watched the wedding of Prince Charles and Diana on TV and another million lined the streets of London. How can it be, ask the suspicious, that this family maintains its position, set so high above us with nothing to hold it up?

The Windsors themselves are not particularly clever, talented, or good-looking. Diana, Princess of Wales, was beautiful, but if she had not married into the royal family it is highly unlikely she could have achieved international acclaim. That means, to those who think in such a manner, that the Windsors are being kept in power by aliens from another dimension, or some Colombian drugs cartel.

That is not to say that all royals are true and good and above suspicion of performing any illegal act. In 1967, Prince Bernard of the Netherlands accepted £50,000 "commission" for trying to use his influence to persuade the Dutch government to buy fighter aircraft from the US firm Lockheed. But, so far, the British royal family have not been caught with their fingers in that kind of pie.

As the world sees it, when the President of the United States makes a state visit to Britain, he may well have private talks with the prime minister, but he very publicly dines with The Queen in Buckingham Palace. The President is, of course, an immensely powerful man. Thus, they are on a par. So, if the conspiracy theorists are to be believed, there must be something going on between them. At the very least, conspiracists will claim, there is some measure of tacit agreement concerning how the most powerful nation on Earth rules over so much of the planet; the Windsors must be helping the US in colonizing the globe.

Royals and the Press

The press is now far more inquisitive about the royal family than in the 1950s, when Queen Elizabeth came to the throne, yet there is no clear "proof" of nefarious dealings. As most of the family members are paid from the public purse, they are public property – why shouldn't we, the public, know more about them, their lives, and their business? The truth, of course, is that the Windsors' "professional" lives and business are dull and generally not worth reporting. There is little to find out about their professional duties as their only "job" is to appear at official functions. Everything is already known about these public events, which are usually rather innocuous and boring.

Aristotle teaching his young pupil Alexander the Great. Did the philosopher later supply the poison that killed the Emperor?

Telephoto lenses capture Diana and Dodi Fayed on their Mediterranean holiday, August 24th, 1997, seven days before their deaths in Paris.

This simply fuels the impression that there must be secret and mysterious dealings going on in private.

Of course we all do things we may be ashamed of in our private lives – whether it is being unfaithful to a spouse or dressing up as a Nazi for a fancy-dress party. So what are the deep, dark secrets of the royals? We know that Prince Philip and Princess Michael of Kent numbered among their close relatives many Nazis, as did Edward VIII and Wallis Simpson. The nature of what else they are covering up is a common and persistent subject of debate.

The dramatic death of Diana, Princess of Wales on August 31st, 1997 served to add a new layer of public speculation and wild conjecture about the Windsors. Although people now look back on her with affection, immediately before her death in 1997 she was not at her most popular – especially, it seems, because of her affair with Dodi Al-Fayed. But when she was killed in a hideous car accident she was almost immediately beatified. Psychologists have explained the extraordinary (and worldwide) outpouring of grief at her passing as a form of mass hysteria and even collective guilt – both of which have contributed to various conspiracy theories that have thrived in the years since Diana's death concerning how and why she died. Accidents have no part in conspiracy theories, ergo "someone" must have done it.

Diana had, shortly before her passing, gone through a very public falling out with the royal family – so, the laziest of the theories goes, they must have murdered her. The evil genius behind the conspiracy to do away with the poor innocent girl is currently favoured to be Prince Philip, who was known to dislike her. No matter how preposterous this idea may seem to anyone, there are a surprising number of people who "believe" it. Without proof, of course.

Curiously, the conspiracies surrounding the death of Diana have done little to undermine the long-term popularity or position of the British royal family. If anything, they have helped to keep them centre stage and sharply in the public eye – which obviously proves that they are so powerful that they can do anything and get away with it. If only all royal families had enjoyed such a powerful position, the course of history would have run very differently.

1586
WALSINGHAM AND MARY
QUEEN OF SCOTS

Sir Francis Walsingham conspired to execute Mary
Queen of Scots

After the Protestant Queen Elizabeth I came to the throne
of England in 1558, her position was threatened by her
cousin Mary Queen of Scots who was next in line and claimed
the allegiance of English Catholics. However, a conspiracy
in Scotland, sponsored by Elizabeth, led to her abdication
in 1567. She sought refuge in England, but was imprisoned
there for the next 18 years. However, she remained the focus
of hope for English Catholics.

In 1583, Elizabeth's principal minister, Sir Francis
Walsingham, uncovered a plot by the Catholic Francis
Throckmorton to depose her. French forces under Henri, duc
de Guise, were to invade England, free Mary, and restore
papal authority. Throckmorton was tried and executed.
Three years later, Walsingham uncovered another plot to
assassinate Elizabeth and put Mary on the throne, this time
with the backing of Philip II of Spain. The plot centred
around the Catholic Anthony Babington, though it has been
alleged that Babington was an agent provocateur in the pay
of Walsingham. He smuggled coded letters to Mary, via a
beer barrel, asking her for her approval of the plot. His letters and Mary's replies fell into Walsingham's hands and
they were almost certainly altered to strengthen the evidence indicating Mary's complicity in the conspiracy.

Throckmorton was executed. Mary was given a trial of dubious legality. She was not shown the evidence against her
and was not present when prosecution witnesses gave evidence. In any case, as queen of Scotland, the English courts
had no jurisdiction over her. Yet she was found guilty and
executed at Fortheringhay Castle on February 8th, 1587. The
following year Philip II sent the Armada in an attempt to invade England and return it to the Catholic fold. It, too, failed.

1669
THE MAN IN THE IRON MASK

b. Versailles, 1658?
d. Paris, 1703

A masked man held in French jails for 30 years was
the twin brother of Louis XIV

In 1669, a prisoner arrived at Pignerol – a fortress high in
the French Alps; 12 years later he was transferred to a prison
in nearby Exiles. In 1687, he was taken to a prison on the
island of Saint Marguerite; 11 years later he was moved to
the Bastille in Paris, where he died on November 19th, 1703.
The following day he was buried in the cemetery of Saint-
Paul under the name "Marchioly." His age was given as
"about 45." In the 34 years of his incarceration, no one had
seen his face.

During his move from Exiles to Saint Marguerite, he was
seen wearing an iron mask. It is not known who the masked
man was, but the secrecy surrounding his incarceration indicates some royal connection. Voltaire popularized the
theory that he was the twin of Louis XIV, and claimed that
king, though conceived first, had been born last. The prisoner was kept locked up to avoid problems with the
succession. Alexandre Dumas took up this idea in his novel
The Man in the Iron Mask, published in England in 1880.

Other theories claim variously that the prisoner was:
Louis's elder brother, the result of an extramarital affair of
his mother; a doctor who attended the post-mortem of Louis
XIII and discovered that he could not sire children; the real
father of Louis XIV; the playwright Molière who was
imprisoned by the Jesuits for having mocked religious big-
otry in his play *Tartuffe*; or Count Ercole Matthioli who had
double-crossed Louis XIV in a deal with the Duke of Mantua
and who wore a mask because it was very much the fashion
in Italy at the time.

1678
THE POPISH PLOT

Catholics conspired to kill Charles II and put his
brother James on the throne

After the Restoration of Charles II in 1660, British
Protestants were afraid that Catholics were trying to return
the Church of England to Rome. In 1673, parliament passed
the Test Acts. These forced public officials to swear an oath
to the king as head of the Church and take communion in a
Protestant service. As a Catholic, the King's brother James,
Duke of York, was unable to comply and was forced to resign
his position in the admiralty.

In 1678, a crooked Protestant priest named Titus Oates,
who had feigned conversion to Catholicism, claimed to have
unearthed a plot to assassinate Charles II and put the
Catholic James on the throne in his place. The plot was
given credence when Sir Edmund Berry Godfrey, the
Westminster magistrate in front of whom Oates had sworn
a deposition outlining the plot, was found murdered on
Primrose Hill. Then treasonable correspondence was discovered between Edward Coleman, secretary to the Duke of

York, and Louis XIV. Anti-Catholic feeling was running high as it was widely believed that French or Spanish Catholics had started the Great Fire of London in 1666. Some 35 innocent Catholics were summarily executed as a result of Oates's accusations.

Yet Charles himself examined Oates and found his testimony unconvincing. Inconsistencies in his story came to light and, in 1684, the Duke of York won a libel suit against Oates and was awarded £100,000 in damages. The following year Charles died and James came to the throne. Oates was convicted of perjury, flogged, pilloried, and imprisoned. However, James was deposed by the Glorious Revolution in 1688 and replaced by the Protestant William of Orange. Oates was released. He became a Baptist in 1693, but was expelled from the Church in 1701. He died in obscurity four years later.

1861

QUEEN VICTORIA HAD LOVERS

b. Kensington Palace, London, 1819
d. Osborne, Isle of Wight, 1901
The widowed Queen Victoria, the symbol of respectability, had secret lovers

Queen Victoria, the venerable ruler of the British empire throughout much of the 19th century, is the prime symbol of an age that is best remembered for its sexual repression. She was, for millions of her subjects, a symbol of motherhood and sexual continence. However, there are theories that, as a woman, she was not like that at all.

A Hanoverian, Victoria was brought up in a far less repressive sexual atmosphere than the one she ruled over. Her father had enjoyed a long-term affair with Madame St Laurent, who was referred to at court as "the French Lady," while her mother had indulged in a long intimate relationship with an Irishman, Sir John Conroy (who later impregnated one of Victoria's ladies of the bedchamber).

Aged just 20, Victoria fell in love with her cousin Prince Albert, declaring that "Albert's beauty is most striking." At their third meeting, she asked him to marry her. It is believed that it was Albert who was the champion of moral rectitude that so characterized the Victorian age. While the Queen dearly loved her husband she apparently enjoyed the physical side of their relationship rather more than he did. Despite having had nine children, Victoria is said to have hated pregnancy because Albert would use it as an excuse not to have sex with her for 18 months. When Albert died in 1861, Victoria was just 42 and still sexually active.

The conspiracy theory

The British royal family was extremely unpopular in Britain when Victoria came to the throne, largely because of the extravagant and licentious behaviour of George IV and his court. Inspired by the American Revolution, there had been several attempts to overthrow the monarchy in the UK by morally outraged and religious persons. To counteract this, the royal family became the very embodiment of bourgeois family life and Christian values.

Thus, when Albert died, Victoria had to be swathed in black and appear to all to be in mourning for the rest of her life. And yet she was a passionate woman in mid-life. She took lovers and, for the sake of political stability, this had to be hushed up. The court, media, and even Parliament were complicit in keeping her love affairs away from public scrutiny. The first of her lovers was her Scottish ghillie, John Brown (b. 1826). Despite being seven years her junior, Brown died in 1883. He was replaced in Victoria's affections by her Indian servant, Abdul Karim (b. 1863; d. 1909) who at the age of 24 had been sent as a "gift" to the empress from India.

The evidence

Within five years of Albert's death, Brown's salary had increased five-fold and he had been given a cottage at Balmoral. His status was raised to that of "Esquire," which placed him high in rank over her other servants. Victoria commissioned a portrait of Brown and had two special medals created in his honour.

Despite the efforts of the Crown and the Court, rumours that Victoria and Brown were secretly married became common, and certain newspapers openly referred to her as "Mrs Brown." Victoria called Abdul Karim "Munshi," gave him a cottage at Windsor, a carriage, and a staff of his own. She defended him against claims that he was a spy and refused to listen to those who said that it was inappropriate for her to be intimate with a "black man," a term she abhorred. She also had his portrait painted.

When Victoria died, her son Edward VII had the statue of John Brown in the hallway at Balmoral removed. It now stands in a wood nearby, overgrown with ivy. Other photographs and papers were destroyed. Similarly, when Munshi died, Edward had his papers burnt. In 2004, a letter written by Victoria at Brown's death came to light. In it, she said "that life for a second time is become [sic] most trying and sad to bear, deprived of all she so needs."

The verdict

We'll never know the whole truth about such intimate liaisons, but the story of Victoria and John Brown certainly made a good movie.

1917

WHAT HAPPENED TO THE ROMANOVS' GOLD?

Russia's gold reserves disappeared in mysterious circumstances during the Bolshevik Revolution

At the outbreak of World War I in 1914, Russia had the world's largest stock of gold – double that held in the Bank of England. By the time the Bolsheviks came to power in 1917, the country was almost bankrupt. Czar Nicholas II had shipped more than £68 million (£1.5 billion at today's prices) out of the country.

The gold was shipped both by British warship from Archangel to Liverpool or by Japanese warship from Vladivostok via Yokohama to Vancouver. From there it was carried on special trains to the Bank of England's depository in Ottawa. After the Russian royal family was massacred by the Bolsheviks in 1918, the new Soviet government in Moscow claimed that the money belonged to Russia and should therefore rightly be returned to them. However, the Bank of England maintained that the gold in fact belonged to Czar Nicholas personally and that when an heir turned up they would hand it over. However, when various women materialized claiming to the Grand Duchess Anastasia – Nicholas II's youngest daughter, who was thought to have survived the massacre – they were summarily dismissed.

Instead, the Bank of England employed the Czar's former finance minister, Peter Bark, on a healthy salary to manage the funds. He became a naturalized British subject and was knighted. To square the British royal family – who were cousins of the murdered Romanovs – Bark delivered a box of Russian imperial jewels that had once belonged to the Empress Marie. These have been handed down through generations of the royal family ever since and have been seen adorning The Queen, her late mother, Princess Margaret, Princess Anne, and Princess Michael of Kent.

1937

EDWARD AND MRS SIMPSON SPIED FOR THE NAZIS

Duke of Windsor: **b.** Surrey, 1894; **d.** Paris, 1972; Duchess of Windsor: **b.** Pennsylvania, 1896; **d.** Paris, 1986
Windsors conspired with the Nazis in World War II

Edward VIII abdicated the British throne in 1936 to marry the American Wallis Simpson because the British government maintained he could not marry a divorcee. However, FBI files released in 2003 show Mrs Simpson was in fact considered unsuitable because of her Nazi connections. She was thought to be passing secrets to her lover, Nazi Joachim von Ribbentrop, then German ambassador to Britain.

Edward VIII and Mrs Simpson – well known for their Nazi sympathies.

Edward himself was a Nazi sympathizer. After he acceded to the throne, a cable was sent to Adolf Hitler from the Germany embassy in London, which said: "An alliance between Germany and Britain is for him [the king] an urgent necessity." After the abdication, the Duke and Duchess of Windsor – as they now were – visited Nazi Germany, where the Duke told a cheering crowd in Leipzig: "What I have seen in Germany is a miracle." They met Hitler, dined with his deputy, Rudolf Hess, visited a concentration camp and signed a secret agreement, which would have returned Edward to the throne if Hitler had conquered Europe.

After the onset of World War II, the British government made Edward governor of the Bahamas to keep him out of harm's way. But his pro-Nazi views never wavered. In April 1941, he told a journalist: "It would be very ill-advised of America to enter the war against Germany as Europe is finished anyway." The Duchess added: "If the US entered the war, this country would go to history [sic] as the greatest sucker of all time." And he reportedly told a friend on the island: "After the war is over and Hitler will crush the Americans ... We'll take over ... They [the British] don't want me as their king, but I'll be back as their leader."

1943
THE MURDER OF SIR HARRY OAKES

The Duke of Windsor covered up the murder of a millionaire in the Bahamas

On July 8th, 1943, the half-charred body of Sir Harry Oakes, a multi-millionaire business associate of the Duke of Windsor, was found in his bed at home in Nassau in the Bahamas. Against all precedent, the Duke of Windsor took charge of the investigation. He side-stepped the local police department and called in two detectives from Miami to "investigate the suicide" of a prominent Bahamian citizen. Fingerprint evidence was destroyed. Photographs of the corpse at the crime scene were exposed to the light and the autopsy report said that Oakes had been killed with a blunt instrument, though a doctor who had examined the body said there were four bullet holes in the head.

Oakes' son-in-law Alfred de Marigny, who had been seen arguing with Oakes earlier that day, was charged with the murder. He was tried and found not guilty.

According to the conspiracy theory, Oakes and the duke were involved in laundering money through the Bahamas in defiance of currency regulations. Another cause for suspicion was the presence of Swedish businessman Axel

Wenner-Gren on the island. Wenner-Gren had been educated in Berlin and boasted that his close friendship with Hermann Goering had allowed Sweden to maintain its neutrality throughout World War II.

There is no doubt that the Duke of Windsor intervened in the case and his meddling had the effect of covering up the crime. Why he did that is not so clear. The duke was so steeped in wartime conspiracies that the cover-up of a murder was probably one of his lesser crimes.

1945
ANTHONY BLUNT'S REASON FOR GOING TO GERMANY

b. Bournemouth, 1907
d. London, 1983

Blunt stole papers for the royal family showing they had ties to Nazism

In 1945, Soviet spy Anthony Blunt, a double agent, was sent on a secret mission to Germany to repatriate papers which showed how various members of the British royal family were involved with the Nazis.

One of the Cambridge spy ring, Blunt had been recruited by the KGB at university in the 1930s. During World War II, he had joined MI5 and passed the names of British agents to Moscow. In 1945, though his loyalty was already suspect, he became Surveyor of the King's Pictures. Shortly afterwards, he and royal librarian Sir Owen Morshead travelled secretly to Germany to recover papers from Schloss Kronberg, ancestral home of the Hesse family. Prince Philip of Hesse had played intermediary between Adolf Hitler and the Duke of Windsor and it was thought that the secret agreement between the duke and Hitler might be there.

When Blunt and Morshead arrived at the castle they found it was being used as an US army club. In the nearby village they found Countess Margaret, head of the Hesse family. She wrote a letter to the officer in charge of the castle authorizing the papers' removal. But the officer refused to release the material without permission. So Blunt and Morshead sneaked into the attic where the papers were stored, grabbed two boxes, and made off with them. Other papers were thought to have concerned Prince Philip – suitor of the soon-to-be Queen Elizabeth – whose sisters had all married high-ranking Nazis. As a former member of MI5 and a member of the royal household, Blunt would be an ideal candidate for a mission to recover such incriminating papers.

See also: *Cambridge spies p.138*

1970
JACK THE RIPPER WAS
PRINCE EDDY

Queen Victoria's grandson went insane and
committed the Ripper murders

In 1970, Dr Thomas Stowell published an article in *The Criminologist* naming Prince Eddy, Duke of Clarence – the grandson of Queen Victoria, son of the Prince of Wales, and third in line to the throne – as Jack the Ripper. Stowell claimed to have used the private papers of the royal physician Sir William Withey Gull as his primary source material. The killer was referred to as "S," but there was enough internal evidence to identify Eddy as the culprit.

It seems that Eddy contracted syphilis which drove him insane. According to Stowell, the royal family knew that Eddy was the Ripper "definitely ... after the second murder, and possibly even after the first." But it was only after the third and fourth killings, which occurred on the same night, that Eddy was admitted to a private mental hospital. However, he escaped to murder Mary Kelly, the Ripper's final victim. After that he was incarcerated and died – not in the flu epidemic of 1892 as the palace maintained, but of

Queen Victoria's grandson Albert,
"Prince Eddy," the subject of one of
the many Jack the Ripper theories.

"softening of the brain" caused by syphilis. Ripperologists have pointed out that court records show Eddy was not in London on the dates of the murders. However, the accusation was repeated in 1978 in Frank Spiering's book *Prince Jack*. Spiering claimed to have found a copy of Gull's notes in the New York Academy of Medicine. He also said that the prime minister Lord Salisbury, possibly in collusion with the Prince of Wales, had Eddy killed with an overdose of morphine. However, another theory surfaced in Michael Harrison's biography of Eddy, *Clarence*. He claimed that the Ripper was in fact Eddy's tutor at Cambridge, James K. Stephen, who committed the murders to defame Eddy after the end of a homosexual relationship between them.

1976
JACK THE RIPPER WAS
ROYAL SURGEON SIR
WILLIAM WITHEY GULL

b. Colchester, 1816
d. London, 1890

Gull committed the Ripper murders to cover up the
secret marriage of Prince Eddy

Sir William Withey Gull was one of the leading doctors in 19th-century Britain, and was personal physician to Queen Victoria. In 1976, he became a surprise new suspect in the case of Jack the Ripper. In his book *Jack the Ripper: The Final Solution*, author Stephen Knight maintained that the Jack the Ripper murders were a royal conspiracy instigated to cover up the marriage of Prince Eddy to a commoner and Catholic named Alice Mary Crook. According to Knight, Eddy had met Crook while slumming in the East End of London with the impressionist painter Walter Sickert.

When Queen Victoria heard about the marriage she was furious. By this time Crook had given birth to a child. During much of Queen Victoria's reign, Britain was politically volatile and news that the heir to the throne had married a Catholic in violation of the 1701 Act of Settlement might have sparked a revolution. She ordered her prime minister Lord Salisbury to take care of the matter and Salisbury enlisted the aid of Sir William Gull.

The conspiracy theory
On Salisbury's orders, Eddy and Crook were seized from the apartment they shared in Cleveland Street, in London's West End. Eddy was put under Gull's care for the treatment of his syphilis and Gull had Crook confined to a mental asylum. She died insane in a workhouse in 1920. Eddy died too,

probably from syphilis, in 1892, before his father Bertie came to the throne as Edward VII.

However, when the Cleveland Street apartment had been raided, Eddy and Crook's daughter, Alice Margaret, was not there. She had been in the care of a girl named Mary Kelly, who had been introduced to the household by Sickert and became Alice's nanny. Sensing that she was in danger, Kelly lodged the baby with nuns and disappeared back into the East End, where she fell into a life of drink and prostitution. Unable to support herself – or to keep her mouth shut – Kelly was encouraged by her cronies to blackmail the government for hush money. Salisbury turned to Gull again for his help.

Gull and John Netley, the coachman who drove Prince Eddy on his nightly forays into the East End, devised a plan to get rid of Mary Kelly and those who knew about Eddy's indiscretion – or at least shut them up. They began killing Kelly's confidantes – who included known Ripper victims Polly Nichols, Annie Chapman, and Liz Stride – along with other women who they may have mistaken for Kelly. The Ripper's last known victim was Kelly herself.

The evidence

The doctors examining the corpse of the Ripper's first victim, Polly Nichols, concluded that the killer had some medical knowledge and was possibly a doctor himself. The second victim, Annie Chapman, had her intestines pulled out and thrown over her right shoulder; the flesh from her abdomen over her left. Her kidneys and ovaries were removed. The fourth victim also had her belly opened and her intestines thrown over her shoulder. And her left kidney was missing. All the victims had their throats slashed with a very sharp instrument, possibly a scalpel. In two cases, the head was almost severed completely in a single cut and the instantaneous severing of the vocal chords meant that they could not cry out.

The killer had more time to work on Mary Kelly as she was murdered in her room where he would not be disturbed until morning. She was dissected in a professional fashion. Both breasts were removed and laid on a table. Kelly's severed nose and flesh stripped from her legs were placed alongside. Her forehead was also stripped of flesh and her abdomen was opened. Her liver and intestines were removed. Gull was a specialist in physiology and anatomy. He was an advocate of vivisection and would have been skilled at dissecting corpses. Gull died fifteen months after the last murder. According to Knight, Netley later tried to run down Alice Margaret with his cab. Chased by an angry mob, he is

thought to have been drowned in the River Thames. Again according to Knight, Alice Margaret went on to marry Walter Sickert. Many of his paintings make reference to the Ripper and other murders.

The police never caught the Ripper. According to Knight's source – Joseph Sickert, son of Alice and the painter – it was because Assistant Commissioner of the Metropolitan Police Sir Robert Anderson was in on the conspiracy.

The verdict

A convincing case can be made that Gull was Jack the Ripper. However, Knight is on shaky ground as he fell out with his principal source, Joseph Sickert, when he named his father Walter Sickert as the third man alongside Gull and Netley instead of Sir Robert Anderson. Since then, Walter Sickert has been named as Jack the Ripper by crime writer Patricia Cornwell in her book *Portrait of a Killer: Jack the Ripper Case Closed*.

See also: *Prince Philip Ordered Diana's Murder p.273*

1997
PRINCE PHILIP ORDERED DIANA'S MURDER
Prince Philip: **b.** Corfu, 1921; Princess Diana:
b. Sandringham, Norfolk, 1961; **d.** Paris, 1997
Prince Philip ordered MI6 to kill Princess Diana to prevent her marrying a Muslim

The British royal family had every reason to murder Princess Diana. She was a loose cannon. Having spilt the beans on the heir to the throne, she upstaged the royal family at every opportunity. Her compassion towards Aids victims and her campaign against landmines made her a much-loved figure. The other royals seemed stiff and haughty by comparison. The revelations of her numerous lovers were an embarrassment and she was having a very public affair with playboy Dodi Al-Fayed, son of Harrods owner Mohammed Al-Fayed – a man so loathed by the British establishment that he was refused a UK passport.

Diana feared death in a car accident. Her one-time bodyguard and lover Barry Mannakee had died in a motorbike crash shortly after being dismissed from his post when their affair was discovered. She believed her fate would be the same.

The conspiracy theory
Mohammed Al-Fayed had claimed that Diana's planned assassination became urgent when it was discovered that the

mother of the heir to the throne was pregnant by his son Dodi – making a future British monarch half-brother to a Muslim. Al-Fayed believes that the crash was part of a conspiracy by elements of the UK establishment who were unhappy with the relationship between his son and Diana. He believes that the assassination was ordered by Prince Philip and carried out by Britain's secret service MI6.

MI6 certainly planned such operations, though there is no consensus on how it was carried out. A powerful hand-held strobe light could have been used to disorientate the driver. The car could have been forced into the wall of the tunnel by another car. The driver Henri Paul could have been killed by Trevor Rees-Jones, the Princess's bodyguard and member of the secret service who was sitting in the front seat next to him. It is noted that Rees-Jones was the only survivor of the crash who, it is said, buckled his seat-belt moments before impact. His injuries prevented him from speaking after the crash. An attempt was made on his life in hospital when he was administered a potentially fatal dose of sedative.

The possibility that he should be charged with manslaughter was raised by the French authorities, but charges were waived when it appeared he had no recollection of the crash.

The evidence

Diana told her voice coach Peter Settelen that she thought Barry Mannakee had been murdered. He filmed their conversations and the clip of her making the accusation was shown on NBC TV.

Then, ten months before her death, Diana wrote to her butler Paul Burrell claiming that "my husband is planning 'an accident' in my car, brake failure and serious head injury in order to make the path clear for him to marry." The letter was reproduced in Burrell's book *A Royal Duty*. Burrell said that she had written it as an "insurance policy" in case of her death. Dodi's father Mohammed Al-Fayed claims that, during a holiday in the South of France, Diana had told him that she had been threatened and was terrified of what might happen to her. "If anything happens to me," she said, "make sure those people are exposed. The person who is spearheading these threats is Prince Philip."

Former MI6 agent Richard Tomlinson revealed that British intelligence was planning a hit at the time of Diana's death. In a sworn deposition, he claimed MI6 officer Dr Nicholas Bernard Frank Fishwick, who was in charge of Balkan operations, showed him plans to assassinate the Serbian leader President Milosevic "by causing his personal limousine to crash." Fishwick proposed to arrange the crash in a tunnel, said Tomlinson, "because the proximity of concrete close to the road would ensure that the crash would be sufficiently violent to cause death or serious injury, and would also reduce the possibility that there might be independent, casual witnesses." Tomlinson noted that the scenario of the Milosevic plans bore "remarkable similarities to the circumstances and witness accounts of the crash that killed the Princess of Wales, Dodi Al-Fayed, and Henri Paul."

According to Tomlinson, Fishwick suggested that one way to cause the crash might be to disorientate the chauffeur using a strobe flash gun, a device which is occasionally deployed by special forces to, for example, disorientate helicopter pilots or terrorists, and about which MI6 officers are briefed during their training.

Diana's pregnancy was confirmed by a French police officer who spoke anonymously to the *Independent on Sunday*. The officer went on to confirm that he had papers to substantiate his claim and said the pregnancy was not revealed at the time because it had nothing to do with the investigation into the cause of the deaths after a car crash.

A 500-page report, based on 13 months of forensic tests on the crashed Mercedes 280-S, concluded that there was no evidence of any mechanical problems with the car. There had been reports that the Mercedes had been stolen several months before the crash and had to undergo extensive repairs. It was also said that it may have had water in the brake fluid and faulty air bags, which activated seconds before the crash. The report corroborated what several prominent crash experts had already concluded – that the Mercedes was travelling at approximately 62 mph at the time of the crash, not at the 120 mph initially claimed by French police. It also said that the Mercedes had collided with a white Fiat Uno just before it rammed, head-on, into the pillar. The Uno was tracked down to a garage in Tours by Pierre Ottavioli, a former police commissioner hired as a private investigator by the Al-Fayed family. But the French police said it was of no interest to their investigation.

The sole survivor of the crash was the secret service man, who had "no memory" of the crash.

The verdict

There is one problem with all the conspiracy theories surrounding the death of Diana – given the traditional antagonism between Britain and France, what motive could the French authorities have had to collude in the cover-up? Mohammed Al-Fayed's theory also falls down because he fails to make any connection between Prince Philip and MI6.

Former TV sports presenter David Icke. He claims the British royal family are descended from reptiles.

1999
ROYAL REPTILES RULE THE WORLD

The British royal family are shape-changing reptiles out to control the planet

New Age guru David Icke claims to have traced the blood line of the British royal family back through the emperors of Rome, Cleopatra, King Herod, Alexander the Great, and Philip of Macedonia, to Rameses II.

In ancient times, Icke says, a race of reptilians came to Earth, possibly from Mars, and interbred with humans so they could survive here. The clues are in the Bible and other ancient texts which say that the "sons of God" came down to mate with the "daughters of men." Since then, these hybrids – who are from the "lower fourth dimension" – have been controlling the world in a global conspiracy. Icke says he has met many eyewitnesses who have seen the royal family and other world leaders turn into reptiles. For some reason – possibly because they need human blood laced with adrenaline – the royal family regularly sacrifice children. Princess Diana found out about this. That was why they had to have her killed.

But the dead hand of Britain's reptilian royals is not confined to the United Kingdom. Their blood line is shared with all European royal families – and the presidents of the United States. Of the 43 presidents, Icke says 33 are related to Charlemagne and 20 to England's Edward III. Icke maintains that every presidential election since and including that of George Washington in 1789 has been won by the candidate with the most royal genes – so the "United States presidents are not chosen by ballot, they are chosen by blood."

2003
BRITISH ROYAL FAMILY RULE THE WORLD

The Queen of England is the head of a criminal cartel that controls the world

Queen Elizabeth II, as well as being head of state in the UK and of a number of Commonwealth countries including Australia and Canada, is also, covertly, head of state of the US, according to Sherman Skolnick of the website Conspiracy Planet. The British royal family, Skolnick explains, share a joint account at Coutts Bank and the Carlyle Group, containing $100 billion, with the Bush family. Another figure with a financial interest in that account is Saddam Hussein.

According to Skolnick, the bank account is used in order to launder illicit funds from gold smuggling and the sale of nuclear weapons via such companies as Donald Rumsfeld's Swiss firm, ABB, which supplied the North Koreans. It is also used to hide other weapons deals with known terrorists arranged by Hillary Rodham Clinton and her "lesbian business partner" Diane Lewis. The royal family is similarly head of a worldwide drug-smuggling cartel. And The Queen and Prince Philip have extensive interest in arms companies, particularly those that manufacture landmines. Naturally, when Princess Diana turned against landmines, she had to go.

Also complicit are Senator John Kerry, who is tied to the Bushes via the Skull and Bones secret society at Yale, and King Juan Carlos, whose position, Skolnick maintains, was strengthened by the 2004 bombings in Madrid. And who are the royals' enforcers? Well, there's MI6, the CIA, Mossad, the French secret service and, of course, the Jesuits.

This explains why, Skolnick says, "the subject matter of 'aristocracy' – who, what, why, and when – [is] seldom, if ever, taught in universities in North America." The British royal family have been, it seems, effectively hushed up.

```
If you come home to find your house has
been trashed, your first reaction will be
one of distress. But as soon as you have
assessed the damage, you'll want to know
who is responsible for the damage:
Burglars? Partying teenagers? A neighbour
with a grudge? Maybe your partner is just a
whole lot messier than you thought.
```

Suppose you never find out? There's no sign of a break in, your house looks like a disaster area, but no one made it that way. Do you have poltergeists? Are you the victim of a conspiracy? When something awful happens to us, we like to know who's responsible. We need closure and a solid entity to blame.

Someone to watch over you

We all know that our global home is in a lousy state. Would we feel better if we had a specific person, or group of people, to blame for the chaos?

Fundamentalists, specifically Christians, blame Satan. Not a person as such, but to them a very real entity hell-bent on spreading chaos and evil as he rampages through these "Last Days." The Devil is on a deadline. Any minute now, God is going to step in and put an end to his rule of evil. The downside for many of us is that God is going to assume that if you're not identifiably on his side, you must be playing for the black team. Better join up if you don't want to spend an eternity beating back the flames of Hades.

So who are you going to join to ensure protection? Even among the so-called "mainstream" religions there are a bewildering array of options, the vast majority of whom claim to have the one Real, Right, Definite, Divinely Authenticated, Get Out Of Hell Free card. The problem for a lot of people is that, as well as being expected to believe in a Devil they can't see, they're also going to be expected to have faith in a God they can't see. It takes a leap of faith that many just cannot make. So if someone you can physically see comes along, shares his divine revelations with you and gives you a moral code to keep you safe from the demons, you might go for that.

And on the whole there's a good chance you'll be a much better person for it. You'll have a moral structure on which to base decisions. You'll probably be welcomed into a nurturing and supportive community. And you will at last have an idea as to why bad things happen, and more importantly what you can do to prevent them. People who come into contact with members of "cults" for the first time are often shocked at how balanced, reasonable, and normal they are. Occupying the middle religious ground are a group of faiths – Jehovah's Witnesses, Mormons, Hare Krishna, for example – whose beliefs may not be conventional, but are not necessarily extreme. And they make perfect neighbours.

Protector turns enemy

Members of the Aum Shinrikyo, on the other hand, have proved themselves to be lousy neighbours. The people who lived near their various complexes in Japan had complained for months about strange smells, rotting plant life, stinging eyes and breathing difficulties. Little wonder. The Aum had built state-of-the-art chemical weapons plants, were murdering opponents by means of lethal injection, and testing out various means of mass delivery of poison gas. In 1995 a group of them wandered into the crowded Tokyo subway and released lethal clouds of sarin gas, killing and injuring thousands.

The Aum are an archetypal late-20th-century cult in every respect. In Shoko Asahara, they have the de rigueur, bearded weird leader. Like L. Ron Hubbard of the Scientologists, or the Unification Church's Sun Myung Moon, Asahara regularly made bizarre pronouncements and issued peculiar edicts. He could supposedly travel through time and his followers were instructed to scald their feet. Hubbard communed with the spirits of dead aliens and Scientologists engaged in staring competitions. Moon is the Messiah and insists on arranging the marriages of all his disciples, wedding them in mass ceremonies and dictating how they should have sex. Such charismatic, but conceivably crazy, cult leaders also need to provide the answers to the big questions; they have to give their followers something positive to believe in. Typically that would involve extraordinary personal development through following his, or her, tenets and rituals. It often also involves a big belief in a big answer to the big question. Who's going to sort this mess out?

Aum are principally an apocalyptic cult. In other words, they believe that Armageddon is coming and that only those who ally themselves to Asahara are going to survive. The official Aum website reported an urgent message from "His Holiness" sometime in the late 1990s:

> Towards the year 2000, there will be successive occurrences that are indescribably violent and full of terror. Japan will be turned into a devastated land by nuclear weapons. Those who will attack Japan will be allied forces with America at the core. In big cities, only one tenth of the population will survive ... Whether you can be the ones to be saved or not depends on how you equip yourselves ... I tell you, there is very little time left. I would like you to take as many initiations as possible and decrease your oxygen consumption, make alpha and theta brain waves appear and develop a resistance to outer shocks. I hope you will try your best.

If you make a confident pronouncement of that magnitude, you really are going to be praying for the end of the world. And if you're less than convinced by the power of your prayers, it may be a good idea to take more direct action. Which was the thinking behind the plan to make chemical weapons, and then send Aum members wandering around Tokyo releasing sarin into the crowded subway. That should decimate the population, precipitate Armageddon and create some demand for your "alpha and theta brainwaves."

The plants that the Aum built to manufacture their arms were colossal and equipped with state-of-the-art technology which must have cost a small fortune. Luckily they had a small fortune to spend. Which brings us to another factor that defines the modern "cult": the rapacious harvesting of funds required to feed those apocalyptic aspirations and a lifestyle appropriate for a globe-trotting guru.

A well-funded operation

L. Ron Hubbard's famous maxim that "if a man really wants to make a million dollars, the best way would be to start his own religion," is self-evident in the bank accounts of many of today's cults. Many of them have constructed labyrinthine corporate structures that make it difficult to make accurate estimates of actual wealth. But to take a relatively minor example, the comparatively small Japanesee Soka Gakkai group *officially* turns over one billion dollars a year.

It helps that in most countries in which Soka Gakkai operates it can, as a religious operation, claim exemption from paying taxes. It also helps swell the coffers if, as in the case of the Scientologists for example, members are prepared to work in the "Personality Testing" business on a voluntary basis.

Furthermore, if the products and services that the cult offers are also based on minimal capital expenditure, then you truly have a fabulous business model. Aum leader Asahara's used bath water must have cost next to nothing to produce, but sold as vials of "Miracle Pond" it was apparently worth two hundred dollars a time to his followers.

In this case, the cult has a business selling a virtually worthless waste product, often for cash, to people all over the world, who are also prepared to provide free labour to help that same society prosper. And, of course, the income is all tax-free. Whether or not you find the secret of eternal life and inner happiness may become a moot point as you open up your bank statements. And that's before you move into any of the murky areas that so many cults are believed to operate in, such as arms dealing, drug running, money laundering, extortion, and so on.

The relationship between a secret society and those followers who are prepared to pour money into it is a fairly complex one. Initially the recruit appears to receive some spiritual and even physical benefit. So enthusiastic are they about their new life, that they become almost pathologically generous. It is only when the mortgage company forecloses, or when their relatives see their inheritances disappearing, they may suddenly realize they are victims of mind-controlling charlatans.

If the cult plays it cleverly it will ensure that to become a full member one has to progress through different levels, each taking the recruit towards the goal of a "higher" level of spiritual consciousness – and with each level requiring a new financial commitment. They'll also prevent any troublesome family members from looking for the money, by surrounding their members with a supportive environment. All former ties are broken, and renewal discouraged due to potentially corrupting influences. Perhaps that environment remains the ideal one for one's personal growth and fulfillment of spiritual potential. Perhaps, as in so many tragic cases, it becomes the ideal environment for mass suicide or even genocide.

As popular as esoteric cults are, clearly the majority of us don't feel inclined to become members of one. Most of us are content either with mainstream religions or, increasingly, to dispense with religion altogether. We will still look around us and wonder who exactly is responsible for the mess, however. And if no one is going to tell us who that is, perhaps it's a secret. And perhaps the people who are keeping secrets from us know what's really going on.

Who's running the world?

The notion that there are secret rulers of the world has gripped the populace since the late 1770s when German Freemason Adam Weishaupt established a federation of bright sparks called the "Illuminati." When secret letters purportedly written by Weishaupt were accidentally revealed, the society was instantly disbanded and outlawed. Conspiracy theory has it that the Illuminati continued recruiting and that they run the world to this day. Obviously over time they transmogrified into something entirely different. Exactly what can be somewhat confusing. A cabal of Jewish bankers and businessmen is a popular view on the far right. British theorist David Icke would have us believe the Illuminati are in reality creatures from outer space masquerading as world leaders. While US businessman and quasi-cult leader Lyndon LaRouche believes the British Royal Family are in charge of the globe. The Freemasons still come under suspicion. As does virtually every organization whose stated policy is Not Telling Us Exactly What They Do.

In their infamous 1976 book *None Dare Call It Conspiracy*, Gary Allen and Larry Abraham claim that Karl Marx was approached by the Illuminati – calling themselves The League Of Just Men – who commissioned him to write his *Communist Manifesto*. They further claim that Marx's work was merely a rehash and update of Adam Weishaupt's earlier writings. Allen and Abraham would have us believe that the world is run by Communists in league with world bankers. They also suggest that the superbly wealthy British imperialist and businessman, Cecil Rhodes, was linked to the Illuminati. In the 1890s it seems that Rhodes had so much money he didn't know what to do with it. Among other things, he established his Round Table Organization in the UK, which the authors claim was a secret society dedicated to ruling the world: "The Round Table worked behind the scenes at the highest levels of British Government, influencing foreign policy and England's involvement and conduct of WW1."

Rhodes himself stated that one of his aims was: "the extension of British rule throughout the world ... the foundation of

Aum sect guru Shoko Ashara.

so great a power as to hereafter render wars impossible and promote the interests of humanity."

These aims sound reasonable on all counts (particularly if you are British), although clearly he failed to achieve every single one. Who wouldn't, given the financial resources, powerful contacts, and necessary resolve, want to make the world a better place? Perhaps those dastardly, clandestine manipulators are just trying to improve life for all of us. When journalist Jon Ronson was investigating the infamous Bilderberg Group he was only able to track down one of the powerful members prepared to talk to him about their activities: British politician Lord Denis Healey. Healey drew a distinction between "secret" and "private" and explained that the politicians and businessmen involved in the group were trying to change things for the better: "We couldn't go on forever fighting one another for nothing and killing people and rendering millions homeless. So we felt that a single community throughout the world would be a good thing."

When Ronson pointed out that many believed the Bilderberg Group were involved in a conspiracy, Healey said: "I've never heard such crap! That isn't a conspiracy! That is the *world*. It's the way things are done and quite rightly so."

Author Mark Twain had little time for conspiracy theories.

A big plot to do what?

Perhaps we have become so cynical about the pronouncements of politicians that we no longer believe anything they say. The internet, and the conspiracy publishing business, spew a relentless tide of "evidence" to link one secret group with another, that senior politician with those powerful bankers, which ties them all up in a big plot to ... do what?

Aside from promoting ideologies that another group may disagree with on political grounds, what harm have all these secret societies done to you and I? Founder of the respected conspiracy theory journal *Lobster,* Robin Ramsay wrote of the Skull & Bones Society: "The central problem here, as with all studies of elite groups, is that while it is possible to show that such groups have distinguished members, it is rarely possible to show that the fact of membership has had any particular impact. This gap is too often filled by conspiracy theorizing."

"A conspiracy is nothing but a secret agreement of a number of men for the pursuance of policies which they dare not admit in public," wrote Mark Twain. This book is full of proven examples of that very thing. People sitting down to think, and then enact, the unthinkable. Obviously The Ku Klux Klan must have held meetings in which they planned how best to burn churches and lynch black people. Clearly furtive deals are done between powerful men in secret that we may not approve of.

But the *world* is a big, unwieldy, unpredictable, and volatile planet. It is populated by capricious and erratic people. Who could possibly attempt to try to manage the whole lot and believe they could truly make a difference? How many have tried, from the Caesars down to Hitler, only to discover that they had bitten off more than they could chew? Surely as our planet appears to become even more chaotic and complex, there is no group out there, no matter how rich and well connected, that really believes it can secretly run the whole world? That is, of course, providing you're prepared to leave Satan out of the equation.

2000 BC
SATANISM
World is governed by ultimate evil entity

Humans have had a predilection for following evil ever since man first came up with the concept of a distinction between good and evil. There are a thousand interpretations of who, or what, the actual person/deity/concept/fallen angel constitutes. Every civilization, religion, and culture has different ideas of Satan.

The Judeo-Christian view is of a fallen angel who defied his creator, tempted man, and went on to wage war against goodness at every opportunity. The Islamic Satan, or Iblis, was the very Chief of Angels, expelled from heaven for his hubris in defying Allah by refusing to do obeisance to Adam. Both the Jewish and Islamic faiths broaden the concept of Satan to encompass anything which may be considered adversarial in an evil manner.

In the Middle Ages, European Christendom became obsessed with Satanism, witchcraft, and black magic to the extent that thousands of people were persecuted, tortured, and executed with ever-increasing brutality, all in the name of Jesus.

Most contemporary Satanic cults are likely to have evolved from the teachings of two men: Aleister Crowley (1875–1947) and Anton Szandor LaVey (1930–97). Crowley was a student of mysticism who developed his own brand of "high magick." In 1904 Crowley claimed to have seen a spirit in Cairo, Egypt, who instructed him to write *Liber Al vel Legis* (*The Book of the Law*) in which the magician outlined his creed: "Do what thou wilt shall be the whole of the law. Love is the law." Crowley also declared that he was the "Great Beast 666, Prophet of a New Aeon," a reference to the number on the head of Satan in St John's Revelation. In accordance with the biblical prophecy, Crowley believed this would lead to his overthrowing all religions and leading the world into a new era of chaos. Crowley's dissolute lifestyle and heretical pronouncements led to him being dubbed "the most wicked man in the world" by the British press. There is no doubt he was an exotic character, and that the rituals, spells, and emphasis he placed on the importance of sex even gave him an air of glamor, for some.

In a similar vein Anton LaVey, who was born in Cook County, Illinois, published his *Satanic Bible*, established himself as the High Priest of the Church of Satan, and started attracting followers from the world of show business. LaVey was also castigated by the media and, again, placed much emphasis on the importance of sex: he believed that the energy created by sexual congress was essential in summoning up dark forces. Confusingly, LaVey claimed not to believe in either Satan or Jesus as entities, claiming that: "Satan is a symbol, nothing more; [he] signifies our love of the worldly and our rejection of the pallid, ineffectual image of Christ on the cross."

It is from the teaching of those two that the disparate groups of "Satanists," that now practice in the western World, have based much of their philosophy. Most of them argue that they are simply normal people who have the right to worship in a different way. In 2004, for example, the British Royal Navy recognized the right of Leading Hand Seaman Chris Cranmer to do that very thing on board the ship HMS *Cumberland*.

Among fundamental Christian sects it is popular to believe that just about everyone and everything is Satanic. Even fellow Christians who don't observe the same strict creed are doomed to Hell. They quote St Paul's second letter to the Corinthians: "For Satan himself is transformed into an angel of light. Therefore it is no great thing if his ministers also be transformed as the ministers of righteousness; whose end shall be according to their works."

There are also those in our modern, secular, humanist, society who see Satan as merely a metaphor for anything bad that happens.

The conspiracy theory
The main theory is that the Devil is trying to run the world. Specifically, dear to the heart of the fundamentalist Christian is the belief that we live in the end of times, and the whole world is a battleground between God and Satan. Aware that the number 666 is up, Satan is determined to establish his rule over the affairs of men.

Then there is the horrible and evil irony of the Jewish people, who first gave us our traditional view of Satan, being so demonized as to be seen as "Satanic" conspirators. In large part, the right-wing commentator Nesta Webster laid the groundwork for the modern Satanization of the Jews. In her 1924 book *Secret Societies and Subversive Movements* she discourses at length on how the Jews have been practicing Satanic rituals since the Middle Ages.

Webster also promulgated the theory that the Masons were heavily involved in Satanic ritual and philosophy; that "by the power of association and the collective force they generate to influence public opinion and to float ideas in the outside world [they] may have far-reaching consquences." Webster perceived a Jewish/Masonic/Illuminati/communist cabal, with Satanic connections as a "danger to

Christian society." Her beliefs have reached down to the 21st century via a host of right-wing and anti-Semitic conspiracy theorists. For Webster it was, of course, godless Bolsheviks who were Satan's representatives on earth, a popular hypothesis right up until the end of the Cold War.

Today one can level the accusation of Satanism at anyone, accuse them of doing anything that isn't very nice, just because they're evil and want to rule the world. There is "evidence" that the Skull & Bones, Freemasons, the Bilderberg Group, George Bush and John Kerry, The British Royal Family, The CIA, al-Qaeda, Microsoft, Proctor & Gamble, and Janet and Michael Jackson are all Satanic.

Satanists have variously: invented the internet (WWW is equated with 666); killed Princess Diana; invented the popular Pokémon cartoons; conspired to coordinate the Manson Family, Son of Sam and Zodiac serial killings; and blown up the World Trade Center (one is apparently able to see Lucifer's face in the flames). Some even see Satan at work during the Superbowl: Janet Jackson deliberately exposed her breast at the 2004 Superbowl, revealing an occult symbol adorning her infamous nipple; that year's game was on the February 1st, a significant pagan day of the "Imboloc."

The evidence

Satan wants us to remain in ignorance of his grand design, so he has quietly insinuated himself into every aspect of modern life. It's up to individual Christians, or Muslims, to stay alert and look out for hidden clues. For those people who believe in him, the evidence is manifest in every act of nature or man that could be considered "evil." Those of a more sceptical nature will of course never see that evidence, thereby playing directly into the Devil's hands.

The verdict

Satanic cults undoubtedly exist; fundamentalist Christians also believe that Satan undoubtedly exists as an entity acting in the world. It is unlikely that self-proclaimed Satanists possess the power and influence that the fundamentalists believe them to wield, however. Secular thinkers, meanwhile, would say that humans appear to need no external supernatural help to encourage them to commit evil acts.

See also: *Nesta Webster p.178; Freemasons p.284; The Bavarian Illuminati p.285; Satanic Ritual Abuse p.294*

1282
THE MAFIA
Government agencies allowed criminal organization to manipulate world events

Sicily is an island with a long and bloody history of invasion, subversion, and revolution. In the late 1200s, while it was under French rule, there was a successful uprising by a group called the "Vespers." They evolved from a band of outlaws who terrorized invaders but offered protection to the indigenous people.

The word Mafia itself didn't appear until the 1860s, when Italian freedom fighter Garibaldi finally rid Sicily of all invaders and achieved unity with the Italian state. Some of his guerrillas had fought for years from caves in the hills called "Maha." Garibaldi apparently called them his "Squadri Della Mafia." They developed into a secret society with complex codes, initiation ceremonies, and an intricate system of social justice. Central to their system was the "Omerta," the inviolate code of silence.

During World War II, the Italian dictator Mussolini recognized the Mafia as such a threat to his position that he went to war with them. Hundreds were forced to flee, many to the US – where compatriots had been settling since the turn of the century, and where the Mafia found a suitable environment to continue their activities.

Organized and efficient, the Mafia developed a protective role in a community where immigrants were frequently victims of injustice and prejudice. Local police were often corrupt, so many victimized Italians were delighted to see the "Onorata Societa" arrive and provide them with the support and homage they required.

For a long time, the US was oblivious to the fact that humble Italian émigrés were industriously establishing the world's greatest crime cartel across the country. By the late 1920s, they had infiltrated practically every illegal activity, from prostitution and bootlegging illicit liquor to gambling and protection rackets. Furthermore, they were also putting their stamp on political life by donating campaign funds to malleable officials and potential mayoral candidates.

During World War II, the Mafia enthusiastically and pragmatically backed the Allied campaign to oust Mussolini both at home and abroad. Senior Mafia figures, among them, it is reported, Charles "Lucky" Luciano, provided intelligence and practical assistance to the Allies in the invasion of Sicily. One of the Mafia's major issues with the US government has always been that they felt they weren't treated

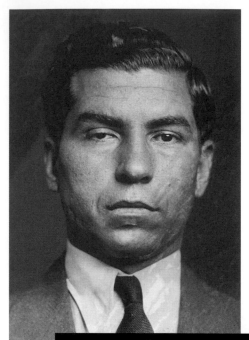

Charles "Lucky" Luciano allegedly gave the Allies information to help oust Mussolini.

The conspiracy theory

By the early 1960s, the Mafia was such a formidable force it managed to operate with seeming carte blanche. This led to accusations of involvement in fixing the election of President John F. Kennedy in 1960; the disastrous attempt to invade Cuba in 1962; assassinating John F. Kennedy in 1963 and his brother, Robert F. Kennedy, in 1968.

Both the FBI and the CIA share some responsibility for the growth of the Mafia throughout the 1950s. The latter by teaming up with mobsters for clandestine operations, specifically a series of ludicrous plots to assassinate Cuban President Fidel Castro.

The FBI under J. Edgar Hoover, meanwhile, was entirely ineffective in fighting the Mafia. This was largely because Hoover refused to accept that such a thing as organized crime even existed – though rumours abound that Hoover deliberately turned a blind eye to Mafia activities as he was being blackmailed by them.

The evidence

There is incontrovertible evidence that the CIA and the Mafia collaborated on a number of projects during the 1950s and 1960s. Testimony of ex-agency men, the mobsters themselves, and, latterly, surveillance by the FBI, all support those facts. It was John F. Kennedy who tried to put a stop to their alliance when he was elected president. In their 1980 book *High Treason: The Assassination of JFK & The Case For Conspiracy*, authors Harrison Livingstone and Robert Groden interviewed the chairman of the 1978 Assassination Committee, which had taken testimony from both CIA agents and gangsters. He said:

> We have nothing, we have no law, no government, no justice, no nothing as long as you have that intimate tie-in between the governmental law enforcement agencies at the highest level and the criminal element of our country. They're cheek by jowl and they continue to be. They're the same outfit now, the CIA and the Mafia.

with respect for their endeavours in the war. This may have been at the root of the problem that some key Mafia figures had with the US government after the war. The Mafia's very nomenclature for itself, "Cosa Nostra," meaning "our thing" or "our own affair," signifies that nosy law enforcing officers and governments should leave them to get on with policing their own business.

What happened instead was a war with authority that continues to this day, one in which the Mafia has shown itself to be a formidable opponent. Their power, both in Italy and the US, consolidated during the 1970s to the point where almost every major scandal in both countries could be linked to the Mafia.

Arguably, the 21st century has seen a decline in the organization's transatlantic grip on organized crime, as new groups and syndicates around the world have adopted their methods. But the ramifications of their complex and bloody legacy will be with us forever.

From Italian prime minister Giulio Andreotti – judicially accused of Mafia ties – to Watergate and CIA drug trafficking allegations, Cosa Nostra provides a rich vein of conspiracy theories to fascinate and appall us. Many of them have been demonstrably proven.

In Hoover's case, the evidence is less clear. He may well have recognized that the Mafia were just too powerful an organization for him to take on. However, we do know that the FBI director liked to bet on the horses. Staff who accompanied him to the track report that he always had good tips. Mafia staff report that they supplied him with those tips.

One of the FBI director's more notorious tactics was to obtain physical evidence of sexually compromised politicians and celebrities. Meyer Lansky claimed that he had hoisted Hoover with his own petard by commissioning pictures of him enjoying oral sex with his long-time boyfriend, and then used them to blackmail him.

Certainly individual FBI agents at the time report being reduced to sneaking around to US Narcotics Commissioner Harry Anslinger to surreptitiously Xerox his extensive files on the Mob. Anslinger is considered the number-one Mafia hunter of all time. The FBI agents had to sneak, because Hoover claimed Anslinger was a dangerous incompetent and any agent consorting with him faced the sack.

The verdict

The Mafia and CIA worked together on operations in the 1950s, 1960s, 1970s, and even the 1980s, and in the process were involved in world-changing events such as the assassination of President John F. Kennedy and the Iran/Contra scandal. They have allegedly played a major role in postwar Italian politics, including being involved with the P2 Masonic lodge (and the senior politicians who were members of it) and corruption at the Vatican bank.

See also: *The St Valentine's Day Massacre p.45; John Fitzgerald Kennedy p.54; Robert Francis Kennedy p.54; Jimmy Hoffa p.61; Pope John Paul I p.63; Paul Castellano p.66; Gemstone File p.116; J. Edgar Hoover Blackmailed by the Mob p.148; Calvi and the Vatican Bank p.256*

1407
ROSICRUCIANS
Mystical cult with Masonic connections

Some believe the German monk Christian Rosenkreuz started the "Croix Rose," or Red Cross, in 1402 after time spent studying with Eastern occultists. It is highly likely that he is a fictitious figure.

The movement was an esoteric Protestant group with beliefs drawn from diverse sources. These included the teachings of Greek philosopher Plato, and the mystical arts which Rosenkreuz allegedly learnt in Damascus.

The cult enjoyed a renaissance in the early 1600s when it was claimed that Rosenkreuz's body had been discovered, apparently in perfect condition. The anonymously written manifesto *Confessio Fraternitas* of 1615 took a militantly anti-papal line while advocating occult practices.

The Catholic establishment consequently branded the Rosicrucians heretics, and cult members were forced to move across Europe to escape persecution. Some ended up in

England where they allegedly forged links with Freemasons.

The first accusation of a conspiracy was in 1666 when the Marquise de Brinvilliers was discovered to have poisoned an indeterminate but significant number of people in Paris. It is alleged that she learnt her art from Rosicrucians.

Satanist Aleister Crowley belonged to the London Rosicrucian lodge, but grew disillusioned with them. He broke into their headquarters, stealing artifacts and documents which he later used in his "High Magick" ceremonies.

Robert Kennedy's assassin Sirhan Sirhan – who claims that he remembers nothing about his 1968 crime – was Rosicrucianist. Some believe he was hypnotized, and that the cult was behind the assassination.

Rosicrucians are sometimes cited as being part of the "New World Order" conspiracy, along with groups such as the Masons, Bilderberg, and Illuminati.

See also: *John Fitzgerald Kennedy p.54; Robert Francis Kennedy p.54; Freemasons p.284; The Bavarian Illuminati p.285*

1534
SOCIETY OF JESUS
Religious order controls world through "Black Pope"

The Society of Jesus, or Jesuits, was founded in Paris in 1534 by a group of students led by Spanish priest Inigo Lopez de Loyola. Their original charter was to: "Enter upon hospital and missionary work in Jerusalem, or to go without questioning wherever the pope might direct." Loyola expected a high standard of obedience from his priests, writing that they should be "well disciplined, like a corpse."

With papal approval they embarked on an international missionary campaign, but by the mid-1770s had caused consternation in virtually every country they visited. Radical challenges to tradition, zealous proselytizing, and a penchant for political interference all contributed to their downfall. By 1773 several countries had successfully lobbied the Pope to have the order suppressed. They were allowed to reform in the 19th century, and remain a force in the Catholic world today, with headquarters in the Vatican, and colleges and seminaries around the world.

Jesuits take "an extreme oath" in which they swear absolute fealty to an infallible pope, vowing to promote his cause by whatever means necessary. Loyola's blueprint philosophy was: "I will believe that the white that I see is black if the hierarchical Church so defines it." A small, but highly active group of theorists believe the Jesuits actually run the Catholic Church. They maintain that as the 1800s all popes have been figureheads. The Catholic Church is actually controlled by the head of the order, or "Black Pope," a reference to the "Black Arts" they claim the Jesuits practice. These include warmongering, political assassinations, and manipulation of events through their control of international banking and leading politicians. Whatever the truth of this particular allegation, the Jesuits remain a powerful, arch-conservative force within the Catholic Church today.

1600
THE YAKUZA
Japanese crime syndicate, similar to the Italian Mafia

The Yakuza is a complex organization which has probably been in existence in some form since the 1600s. Some Yakuza may be descended from honourable Robin Hood-style bandits who protected local people from ruthless overlords. Others, however, may be descended from murderous gamblers, pimps, and thieves who terrorized local people in the manner of ruthless overlords.

The Yakuza came into prominence following World War II. At that time, under the guidance of mysterious Japanese businessman, war criminal, and former CIA operative Yoshio Kodama, they seized control of Japan's black market. It is believed they were also responsible for one of the biggest systematic robberies of all time, taking advantage of the chaos in Japan to loot billions of dollars in bullion, much of which was hidden in the Philippines. Apparently, President Ferdinand Marcos found a third of it, and used Triads to sell it on the world gold markets.

Currently there are dozens of separate Yakuza gangs, the most powerful being the Yamaguchi-Gumi. They own over 2,000 "front" companies and specialize in money lending, property speculation, and narcotics.

Apart from dominating every single aspect of criminal activity in Japan, the Yakuza have also established themselves as forces in both the financial and political fabric of society, not just at home but all over the world. They are believed to be major shareholders in a significant number of banks, including the Bank of America.

Despite the passing of laws in Japan to try to restrict their activities, little is actually done, possibly because they own most police precincts, and possibly because of their links with, and funding of, the country's Liberal Democratic Party.

See also: *Aum Shinrikyo/Aleph p.295*

C1700
FREEMASONS
Secret society is involved in corruption and Satanic ritual

Freemasons are widely believed to be an offshoot of the order of Medieval religious warriors, the Knights Templar. The two are still associated today, but there is considerable confusion about when Masons first appeared as an individual, recognized body. The best estimate is around 1390, when the *Haliwell Script* or *Regius Poem* appeared. While this doesn't specifically mention Freemasonry, it appears to be an early form of Constitution, making reference to rituals and beliefs that later came to be associated with the movement.

While the name tells us that the organization started with English stone workers – probably as an innocuous trade federation – it seems that in the Middle Ages, an esoteric, anti-establishment movement attracted those on the fringes of the mainstream, and they started meeting in secret. This was essential, as was the use of code words, covert greetings, and rituals to weed out the infiltrator. It was a time when unorthodox behaviour could lead to accusations of witchcraft, followed by torture and a death.

Proper documentation of Masonic activity is not found until the early 1700s, when the Lodges felt sufficiently confident to admit their existence. By this time, the movement had appeared throughout Europe and had reached the American Colonies. George Washington was the first Masonic President, and is believed to be responsible for the significant amount of Masonic symbolism incorporated into American public buildings.

The group that arouses most suspicion among conspiracy theorists is the Bavarian Illuminati founded by Adam Weishaupt in 1776. There are many who believe that after his secret society was outlawed, Weishaupt infiltrated the Masons, bringing his plot to rule the world with him.

In 1738, Pope Clement XII issued a condemnation of Freemasons and banned all Catholics from joining Lodges; the ban remains in place to this day.

Masons remain an avowedly secret society. They operate levels of Brotherhood, so that more secrets are revealed the higher up a man (no women allowed) climbs. Their initiation rites and ceremonies are based around oaths of secrecy and anyone leaking the details will be expelled.

Nearly every small town in the western World has a local Lodge. Those who belong to it are either upstanding, frequently charitable, people – networking in the interests of their careers – or they are a Satanic cabal bent on establishing a New World Order via mendacious acts of diabolism; depending on which theory one believes.

The conspiracy theory

If you believe that Satan is responsible for all the evil in the world, and that the Freemasons are a Satanic organization, then clearly it is not difficult to see how they are at the bottom of every conspiracy in this book. Alternatively, if you believe that there is a Jewish/New World Order/Hidden Government/Illuminati scheme to enslave us all, then the Freemasons are clearly a part of that.

More prosaically perhaps, there is the accusation that Masonic groups conspire to promote the interests of fellow Masons, to the detriment of society at large. Men are promoted at work, awarded lucrative contracts, or extended leniency by the judicial system, on the basis of a secret handshake. Such patronage and protection can be on any level, from a local government official awarding contracts to fellow Lodge members, to horrific allegations of child abuse cover-ups that have implicated Lodges in the UK.

The evidence

There is masses of "proof" that Masons are Satanic/Semitic Planet Managers, if one cares to look for it. Websites and books attacking the organization have pages of graphic evidence that Masonic symbols pervade everything from the layout of the White House to the design of the dollar bill. Since 1935, the note has carried the Masonic legend: "Novus Ordo Seclorum". It was first used as part of the Great Seal of the United States in 1782 and actually means "New Order of the Ages." But it is easy to imagine how this might be translated to read as "New World Order." There are also reams of oral and written "evidence" drawn from leaked rituals and writings that support the same theories.

A considerable amount of evidence surrounding the multifarious conspiracies Masons are responsible for necessitates making the connection between arcane numerology, or symbolism, and the circumstances surrounding the event. So, for example, Dallas is at thirty-three degrees latitude. Thirty-three is the highest Masonic rank. Also, "dea" is Latin for goddess and "ley" is very similar to the Latin for "rule." In 1963, President John F. Kennedy was shot in Dealey Plaza, Dallas. A place "ruled" by the "goddess." The goddess is apparently Diana.

In 1997, Princess Diana died in a car crash at the Pont de l'Alma Tunnel, which used to be a site of significance to the Knights Templar. She was also wearing jewelry in the shape of a pentagram and had thirteen diamonds on her dress, significantly symbolic to those who believe that Masons were also responsible for her demise.

In the 1800s, British Prime Minister Disraeli warned against the grip Masons had on Victorian society; he was particularly concerned about the Royal Family's involvement. To this day, royal consort Prince Philip is one of the most senior figures in Freemasonry, a fact which gives grist to those who put the Windsor family at the centre of a great world conspiracy.

The verdict

Accusations that government and the legal profession are full of Masons, all protecting their own interests to the detriment of those they should be serving, have occasionally turned out to be founded in fact. Two well-researched books appeared in the 1980s which purported to lift the lid on small town and big business Masonic corruption in the UK. They were Stephen Knight's *The Brotherhood*, and *Inside The Brotherhood* by Martin Short.

The alternative view is that government and the judiciary will always have a significant proportion of practitioners who are corrupt. They are as likely to be Masons as members of the local chess club.

One of the most infamous Masonic-based conspiracies concerns the Italian P2 Lodge. It is well documented that, along with the Mafia, they were embroiled in the financial scandals that infested the Vatican bank, led to the murder of "God's Banker" Roberto Calvi, and quite conceivably were involved in the assassination of Pope John Paul 1.

See also: *Pope John Paul I p.63; John Stalker Affair p.155; Knights Templar p.243; Calvi and the Vatican Bank p.256; Prince Philip Ordered Diana's Murder p.273; The Bavarian Illuminati p.285; Satanic Ritual Abuse p.294*

1776

THE BAVARIAN ILLUMINATI

The "Enlightened Ones" were the secret rulers of the world

In 1785, an apostate Catholic priest by the name of Lanze was riding through the Bavarian town of Rogensburg in southern Germany. He was en route to Paris, France, from Frankfurt, and was carrying urgent documents sewn into the lining of his clothes. As Lanze reached the outskirts of Rogensburg a bolt of lightning blasted him and his horse into a charred cinder. When the police turned up they found the papers, mysteriously intact; the contents so alarming that they took them directly to the Bavarian government.

The authorities raided the offices of Adam Weishaupt, the man who had sent the documents, arrested him and outlawed his organization – The Bavarian Illuminati, or "Enlightened ones." They also sent word to France that they had seized letters addressed to the "Grand Master of the Grand Orient Masons" which showed that the Illuminati were plotting to overthrow the French monarchy and establish a republic.

Weishaupt is rumoured subsequently to have fled to Moscow, where he was able to continue orchestrating the French Revolution, before supposedly hiring Karl Marx to write a Communist manifesto, which led to the destruction of the Russian monarchy and founding of a Marxist republic. Others believe he joined the Freemasons, possibly in Scotland and, by stealth, effectively turned that movement into a carbon copy of his Illuminati. Other sources claim that he died quietly in Bavaria, after dedicating his life to refining the principles of Illuminatism.

The French, apparently, completely ignored the warnings from Bavaria about the letters to the "Jews of the Illuminati in France" which meant that, in 1789, the country was plunged into a bloody revolution that would last two years.

The act of God which had struck down the courier had brought the Illuminati to the attention of the world, although some researchers believe that the concept of the "enlightened ones" goes as far back as the warrior Knights Templars. Their mysterious rise to power across Europe in the Middle Ages is believed to have been based on an absorption of Middle Eastern occultism, and the complexity of the organization of their secret society.

Weishaupt, a university professor and former member of the Society of Jesus, is also alleged to have studied Eastern mysticism, and to have organized the Illuminati on a similar basis to the Knights Templar. His past as a Jesuit has also given rise to speculation that he actually based the Illuminati on their principles. The Jesuit founder, Ignatius Loyola, was suspected of being involved in a Spanish version of the "enlightened ones" and was interrogated, and then cleared, by Catholic officials in 1527.

Weishaupt established his version of the Illuminati as a political society in 1776, recruiting members from the brightest of his friends and students, among them according to some accounts, the composer Mozart and philosopher Goethe. Their stated aims included challenging Catholicism, disestablishing monarchies, abolition of private ownership, and the founding of a worldwide utopian society.

It should be borne in mind that there are a number of historians who believe that all of the forgoing is apocryphal, arguing that even Weishaupt himself is an allegorical character. His very name – Adam, the first man, coupled with the German for "wise head" – arouses suspicion.

Fictitious or not, the Bavarian Illuminati's mythical power is such that there are an extraordinary number who believe that the group gradually infiltrated all significant political groups and secret societies, right up until today. The Illuminati have become a catch-all label for any and every group that arouses suspicion of conspiracy. The Skull & Bones Society, the CIA, the Bilderberg Group, the Trilateral Commission, Bohemian Grove et al. are all implicated.

The conspiracy theory

If you believe that a secretive group is running the world, then you can claim that they are responsible for everything. From manipulating events throughout two world wars through to the spreading of Aids, the Illuminati have perpetrated a myriad of conspiracies.

The first major event they were supposedly involved with was the French Revolution, before moving on to organize the Russian Revolution. Political analysts have speculated over the similarity between early Weishaupt writings and those of Karl Marx.

Additionally, on the fringes, arch-conspiricist David Icke calls his shape-shifting lizard rulers "Illuminati." And researcher Jim Keith's 1993 book *Saucers of the Illuminati* details a conspiracy between aliens and the US government. Both men believe that the Illuminati are extraterrestrials, determined to enslave the human race.

The evidence

The theory of the Illuminati's all-pervading influence is largely based on the writings of Scottish mathematician John Robison. He claimed that he was a Mason, who had been asked to join the Illuminati, declined and became so convinced that the organization was evil that in 1798 he wrote *Proofs of Conspiracy* as a warning to the world. George Washington was sent a copy, and responded that he was well aware of the activities of the Illuminati and believed that they had "diabolical tenets."

At the same time a French priest, Augustin de Barruel wrote his book *Memoires pour servir à l'histoire du Jacobinisme* also warning of the Illuminati's perfidious influence, and distinguishing himself as the first to claim they had orchestrated the French Revolution. After publication, Barruel received a letter from a French army officer, J.B.

Simonini, professing that he had masqueraded as a Jew, been taken into the confidence of other Jews, and that they had revealed they were the real force behind the Illuminati. He claimed that the key action in their campaign was to install a Jewish pope. On such flimsy evidence was founded the notion, which continues to this day, that the Illuminati are a Jewish conspiracy to take over the world.

The doyenne of right-wing conspiracy theory, Nesta Webster, in her 1924 book *Secret Societies and Subversive Movements* produced extensive research to show that the Illuminati were, to all intents and purposes, communists. She suggests that they started both the French and the Russian Revolutions and that they posed a "real threat to modern society." She also gave credence to the notion that the Illuminati are a Jewish cabal.

The verdict

The Illuminati was indeed established as a secret society by Adam Weishaupt in 1776. Among its stated aims were to challenge the grip of the repressively conservative Bavarian Catholic Church of the day and to promote the work of new thinkers and writers, who were banned in Bavaria at the time. The society failed to flourish, however, and soon died out. But rumours of the Illuminati's continued existence

were taken up and fuelled by writers such as John Robison, as when the myth has apparently taken on a life of its own, despite the readily available evidence.

See also: *Skull & Bones p.99; The Bilderberg Group p.108; Nesta Webster p.178; Jim Keith p.187; David Icke p.188; Knights Templar p.243; Protocols of the Elders of Zion p.249; Society of Jesus p.283; Freemasons p.284; Bohemian Club p.289*

1865
THE KU KLUX KLAN
White supremacist extremists

The Ku Klux Klan was started in 1865 by Confederate General Nathan Bedford-Forrest in Pulaski, Tennessee. The name derives from *kyklos*, the Greek word for both circle and clan. It is also believed to be an onomatopoeic reference to the loading and cocking of a shotgun.

Initially the KKK had some altruistic basis as an organization dedicated to helping orphans and widows of the Civil War. However, they were also committed to anti-segregationist policies and were against the post-Civil War Reconstruction policies, and while there was an element of

Ku Klux Klan members at one of their ritualistic gatherings. The Klan, from the 1860s, was notorious for racial terrorism in the southern states.

legitimate political activity, the more reactionary elements were soon terrorizing the black community throughout the Southern states.

Bedford-Forrest grew so disturbed by the activities of Klansmen that he ordered them to disband in 1869. The rank and file ignored him, and stepped up their race-hate campaign. In 1871, President Ulysses Grant passed *The Klan Enforcement Act* which outlawed the organization and authorized the use of force in their suppression.

The trademark white hoods, flaming crosses, and brutal acts of violence have consolidated their image as one of the most notorious terrorist groups in the world. The present reality, however, is that as a unified group, the Klan is no longer the threat it once was. Riven by infighting and poor funding, it survives in the form of small isolated groups of white supremacist fanatics.

Even the Jewish Anti-Defamation League, which monitors race-hate groups around the world, says they are: "…a fragmented and amorphous collection of independent groups and individuals, constantly squabbling over diminishing memberships and limited resources. Passed over by most young white supremacists, who consider Klansmen to be ineffectual and faintly ridiculous old-timers, the group presents far less of a threat to public order than at any time in the past century."

That's not to say that Southern towns don't occasionally still suffer hate crimes from racists who claim to be operating under the auspices of the Ku Klux Klan.

The conspiracy theory

On a purely local basis, Klan members have undoubtedly over the years committed horrific crimes, including murders, for which they have not been brought to justice. Local law enforcement officers and members of the judiciary have been complicit in ensuring their immunity. Perhaps because of their quasi-Masonic structure, some of those senior members of the community have been involved in the Klan, and conspired to obstruct justice.

The Klan itself has a penchant for conspiracy theories. Its literature and websites are rich sources of "information" on plots to attack the white, Christian way of life. Jews have replaced African Americans as the real racial threat, and many Klan members propound theories that there is a One World Government, run by a Jewish elite, which controls law enforcement, banking, and the media.

The KKK are sporadically themselves victims of a conspiracy rumour that they own certain products popular with African Americans, and that their agenda is to attack the

black community through such products. Usually this is a popular food or beverage that is said to cause impotence only in black men. Kentucky Fried Chicken, Kool cigarettes, Tropical Fantasy, and Snapple are all products that have attracted the "Klan made" tag. Such conspiracy theories are groundless and should be reclassified as "urban myths."

The two major conspiracy theories involving the Klan are, first, that they were involved in the assassination of civil rights leader Martin Luther King in 1968; second, that Timothy McVeigh, who was convicted of blowing up a federal building in Oklahoma City in 1995, was acting as a member of the group.

The evidence

There is no doubt that the KKK, fellow white supremacists, and non-segregationists were overjoyed at the assassination of Martin Luther King, but there's little real evidence to suggest that they were involved in his murder.

However, according to an article in *The Memphis Commercial Appeal* in 1993, rogue army intelligence officers in the deep South who were nursing a racist agenda, recruited KKK members to conduct domestic intelligence operations. There were reports that both the officers, and their stooges in the Klan, were in Memphis on April 4th, 1968 – the day that King was shot.

James Earl Ray, a small-time crook and high-school dropout, was arrested in London in June 1968 for the shooting, having already spent some time globetrotting; he was carrying a large amount of cash when apprehended. Gerald Posner, the author of the 1998 book on King, *Killing the Dream*, speculates that "there was a conspiracy, but on a very low level. Someone, I'd guess part of a racist group, probably agreed to pay him [Ray] maybe $25,000 or $50,000." Although Ray at first confessed to committing the murder, he later retracted it. He was sentenced to 99 years in jail and in 1992 his book, *Who Killed Martin Luther King Jr?: The True Story by the Alleged Assassin* was published. In it, he said there had been a government cover-up.

As far as McVeigh is concerned, there is overwhelming evidence to suggest that he was a member of the Klan. FBI officers found such proof when they raided his house. But it also appears that at the time of the Oklahoma bombing, he was one of those disaffected young men who found the Klan "ineffectual and faintly ridiculous." A popular theory among the Klan is that the government carried out the atrocity, making McVeigh the patsy, in order to discredit them and other white supremacist groups.

The verdict

For many years a powerful, racist organization whose members committed many murders of African Americans, the KKK has little power today. So far as its involvement in the King assassination is concerned, in 1978 a congressional committee found that a "likelihood" existed that Ray had not acted alone. It is not suggested, however, that the KKK were involved as an organization. So far as McVeigh is concerned, several important questions remain unanswered about the Oklahoma bombing, but again it seems clear that the KKK as an organization were not involved.

See also: *Martin Luther King p.58; Oklahoma City Bombing p.163; Gerald Posner p.190; The Anti-Defamation League p.249*

1872
BOHEMIAN CLUB
World leaders belong to satanic society

The Bohemian Club was started in 1872 by a group of San Francisco journalists. At first they attracted true "bohemians" and writers like Jack London and Mark Twain, but the membership was soon extended to include businessmen and politicians.

They gradually became exclusive to the point of refusing entry to the members of their founding profession. Since 1923, it is believed that every Republican president, and some Democrat presidents, have been members, along with impressive numbers of influential figures in politics, industry and commerce.

Every July, the all-male members descend on Bohemia Grove, to camp in a 2,000-acre redwood forest. Eyewitness reports indicate they hold an arts festival, with elements of a middle-aged frat party, a level of important political debate, and some serious networking. There is also a ritualistic ceremony in which a "sacrifice" is made to "Moloch," manifest in an effigy of a giant owl.

It is the rituals that cause the most consternation among conspiracy theorists. Many see them as Satanic, and this has led to accusations of depraved, criminal behaviour. Among them, that the club is responsible for the hundreds of children who go missing from the area.

In the early 1990s, journalist Mark Philips "rescued" CIA mind-control "slave," Cathy O'Brien, from the club and in their 1995 book *Trance: Formation of America*, made lurid claims about the sexual proclivities of former Presidents Reagan, Bush, Clinton, and other Grove members. O'Brien

also claimed: "Slaves of advancing age or with failed programming were sacrificially murdered at random in the wooded grounds of Bohemia Grove and I felt it was only a matter of time until it would be me."

See also: *Skull & Bones p.99; Mkultra p.143; Satanism p.280; The Bavarian Illuminati p.285; Satanic Ritual Abuse p.294*

1875
THEOSOPHY
Esoteric cult of the "ascended masters"

The term Theosophy was coined by Ukrainian Helena Blavatsky after she had travelled extensively in the Far East, and been initiated into a secret doctrine by Tibetan monks whom she called "The White Brotherhood." They in turn received their knowledge from higher spiritual entities known as "Ascended Masters."

The fact that Blavatsky was the first European to receive this enlightenment endowed her with quasi-Messianic status. When she arrived in New York she attracted a following, in no small part due to her ability to physically manifest her occult powers, most of which were revealed to be a sham.

In 1875, Theosophy was established as a religion, and Blavatsky published her revelations. Theosophy assimilated elements of Buddhism and Hinduism into its creed, which aroused hostility among orthodox Christians. In her 1924

Helena Blavatsky, founder of the Theosophical Society.

book *Secret Societies and Subversive Movements,* conspiracy mistress Nesta Webster examined the religion and concluded it was: "Essentially a propagandist society which aims at substituting for the pure and simple teaching of Christianity the amazing compound of Eastern superstition, Cabalism, and 18th-century charlatanism."

There is some irony involved in the intrinsically anti-Semitic Webster attacking Blavatsky's cult as a "Cabalistic" – by which she meant Jewish – plot to undermine Christianity. Blavatsky herself, in the 1880s, defended Russian imperialist anti-Semitism at every opportunity.

Theosophy is considered to be the first "New Age" religion, and there are currently a number of cults who base their teachings on Blavatsky's writings. Some of them believe that the "Ascended Masters" she referred to were actually extraterrestrial beings.

See also: *Nesta Webster p.178; Cabbala p.241*

1882
KNIGHTS OF COLUMBUS

Charitable organization swears bloody oath against enemies

The Knights of Columbus were founded by Catholic priest Father Michael J. McGivney in Connecticut in the US in 1882. At the time Catholics were excluded from many unions and fraternal organizations, and McGinley envisioned a society that would provide a support network based on the teachings of the Church. He initiated an ethical insurance scheme, for example, which is still in operation today.

The KOC is usually associated with right-wing policies. In the 1950s, they threw their support behind Senator Joe McCarthy's anti-communist witch-hunts. It is also vocally anti-abortionist, and against same-sex marriages.

The organization is world-renowned for its charitable work, particularly in the fields of disaster relief, and assisting those who have been injured by land mines.

At the turn of the 20th century, allegations emerged that the KOC were part of a conspiracy to overthrow the Protestant faith. A booklet was circulated purporting to be the secret KOC "Bloody Oath," which included the promise:

"I will... wage relentless war secretly or openly against all heretics, Protestants and Liberals... I will hang, waste, boil, flay, strangle and bury alive these infamous heretics; rip up the stomachs and wombs of their women and crush their infants' heads

against the wall, in order to annihilate forever their execrable race."

KOC members brought successful libel actions against publishers of the oath, which they claimed was a forgery. Many courts found in their favour after hearing, in secret, the "real" KOC oath. For some theorists, particularly those who belong to Protestant extremist groups, it is "Rome's Bloody Oath" that remains the genuine article.

1902
CECIL RHODES' ROUND TABLE

b. 1853, Bishop's Stortford, Hertfordshire, UK
d. 1902, South Africa

British imperialist attempts to establish secret society to rule the world

Cecil Rhodes was the son of an English vicar who travelled to Africa as a young man and made a fortune from diamond mining. He became a serious force in African politics; Rhodesia – now known as Zimbabwe – was named after him.

In 1877, he wrote in his *Confession of Faith*: "Why should we not form a secret society with but one object: the furtherance of the British Empire and the bringing of the whole uncivilized world under British rule for the recovery of the United States for making the Anglo-Saxon race but one Empire." To this end it is believed that he subsequently established a Round Table organization and made overtures to influential Americans. Rhodes died in 1902, leaving seven wills, the first of which apparently committed funds to his empirical vision. The last will established The Rhodes Scholarship, which still provides funding for suitable Americans to study at Oxford University – the former president Bill Clinton being a well-known recipient. In 1919 Edward Mandel House met members of the Round Table in Paris. House was President Woodrow Wilson's right-hand man, and shared some of Rhodes' ideals. Apparently, House believed American politicians were unlikely to cooperate with an essentially British organization, so instead they constituted the Council on Foreign Relations in 1921.

The CFR still exists and many believe that far from being the "think tank on foreign policy" it claims to be, it is the embodiment of Rhodes' dream.

See also: *Council for Foreign Relations p.104*

1911
TRIADS
Secret society of Chinese criminals

In the 1760s, as the Chinese Hung clan fought to restore the Ming dynasty, they wore identifying triangles. They were the first to be known as "Triads." The Hungs were marginalized by the new dynasty they had supported and turned to crime. By the 1930s Civil War they were a formidable force, courted by both sides. When communist Mao Tse-Tung came to power in 1949, Triad members on the losing side of the Civil War fled to Hong Kong, Europe, and the US.

Triads were initially welcome among immigrant communities, offering protection from corrupt officials and indigenous gangsters. However, they also brought Mafia-style brutality, and even greater impenetrability in terms of law enforcement. There are now thousands of Triad groups operating throughout the world; there are also persistent rumours that, while appearing to be disparate, all are controlled by an omnipotent "Big Circle." Even if Triad gangs are merely localized groups of mobsters, they still cause major problems. Amid the usual rackets – prostitution, gambling, drugs – they are alleged to be involved in international weapons deals. In his 1999 book, *The Dragon Syndicates*, author Martin Booth claims they are behind the smuggling of nuclear weapons from the former USSR.

Triads have also exerted their grip on the lucrative Hong Kong movie business amid gruesome reports of shootings, beatings, and actors being forced to eat their own feces for not agreeing to Triad terms. There are many who believe that martial arts superstar Bruce Lee was assassinated for refusing to pay protection money to the Triads.

See also: *The Mafia p.281; The Yakuza p.284*

1918
THULE SOCIETY
Nazi occultists build flying saucers

Thule is a legendary island in the Far North, reputedly home to a great civilization who knew all the secrets of the universe. It was believed that members of the civilization were contactable through mystical rituals which would reveal their ancient secrets, endowing mental and physical superiority to the enlightened.

In 1918, Rudolf von Sebottendorff, a student of the occult, used the name to start a society initially for those interested in "German antiquity." In accordance with the political climate of the time, they began to disseminate anti-Semitic ideas; they also allied themselves with other groups who formed the mish-mash of societies that became the Nazi party. While denouncing Freemasonry as a Jewish plot, the society paradoxically adopted Masonic symbolism and hierarchal structure. They also engaged with those elements of Eastern mysticism and occult study that Hitler apparently found so fascinating.

After the war many top Nazis were found jobs in the US working for the military and in the government. Their scientific expertise in the fields of nuclear weapons and rocket technology was particularly invaluable.

There are those who theorize that the Nazis had already developed the technology to build flying saucers. Some take it a step further by claiming they developed this technology from their contacts with the Isle of Thule, whose inhabitants were actually extraterrestrials.

Some go further. UFO researcher Vladimir Terziski claims to have footage of secret underground bases in Antarctica. He says the Thule fled there en masse after the war and continue their interplanetary Nazi adventures today.

See also: *Admiral Byrd and Operation High Jump p.220; Project PAPERCLIP – Nazis Were Helped to Enter US p.220; Freemasons p.284; Odessa p.292; Nazi Flying Discs p.301*

1930
SOKA GAKKAI
Japanese cult wants to rule the world

Japanese educational reformer Tsunesaburo Makiguchi established Soka Gakkai, or "Value Creating Education Society" in 1930. In 1943 he was arrested after refusing to participate in patriotic rituals to support the Japanese war effort, and instructing his members to do likewise. He died in prison in 1944, without standing trial or being accused of specific crimes. Most sources refer to Makiguchi as being martyred as a "thought criminal." In 1960, current Chairman Daisaku Ikeda was appointed, and under his direction the sect has grown to an estimated ten million members worldwide.

Soka Gakkai is ostensibly a Buddhist organization which "promotes world peace and individual happiness." The sect attracts famous followers such as Tina Turner and Patrick Duffy. Ikeda has attracted the traditional accusations that befit his cult leader status, including rape, fraud, and keeping unsavoury company. He was supposedly great friends with Panamanian president Manuel Noriega, and Romanian tyrant Nicolae Ceausescu.

It is his political ambition, however, that worries conspiracy theorists. Ikeda's stated aim is that all of Japan, and subsequently the world, should follow him. He started by campaigning to win elections, at first covertly – so as not to affect the sect's charitable status – but recently more blatantly in conjunction with the "New Clean Government Party." They have made astute alliances and are currently part of the ruling coalition government.

Traditional Buddhists find his worldly ambitions distasteful, but Ikeda is undeterred, reportedly stating: "I learned... how to behave as a monarch. I shall be a man of the greatest power." It is also continually alleged that his power is achieved by strong-arm tactics. There are even those who believe that Soka Gakkai was responsible for the homicidal release of sarin gas into Tokyo subways in 1995.

See also: *Aum Shinrikyo/Aleph p.295*

1940
ODESSA
Organization set up to help Nazis escape after World War II

As World War II drew to a close, top Nazis, including Hitler's deputy Martin Bormann, met to discuss their future. It looked bleak. The Allies were advancing, they would be held to account for horrific crimes should they be captured, and there was a lot of looted money at stake.

It was decided all their resources should be diverted into protecting both themselves and the money. They set up the Odessa – Organization der ehemaligen SS-Angehörigen, (Organization of former SS members) – and an elaborate, underground escape route "Der Spiner" (The Spider).

They found many countries keen to exploit their skills. Middle Eastern states were eager to recruit the avidly anti-Semitic, especially those with military expertise. South American dictators were enamored of their experience in running totalitarian regimes. The USSR and the US vied for the services of espionage and hi-tech weapons specialists.

Taking advantage of postwar chaos, the efficiency of their advance planning, their stolen millions, and the help of senior Vatican officials, the Odessa found new homes all over the world. Many believe their legacy lives on in today's neo-Nazi and white supremacist groups who continue to be funded by Swiss bank accounts filled with the looted money.

Former director of the CIA Alan Dulles was especially keen to have German intelligence officers on board to fight the Cold War against the Soviet Bloc.

"We knew what we did. It was necessary that we used every son of a bitch as long as he was an anti-communist," says the CIA's Russian expert Harry Rositzke.

See also: *CIA and European Democracy p.107; Mae Brussell p.181; Nazis and the Vatican p.212; Hitler Survived the End of World War II p.218; Nazis and Golden Lily Gold p.219; Project PAPERCLIP – Nazis Were Helped to Enter US p.220*

1954
UNIFICATION CHURCH
Wealthy cult involved in crimes and political conspiracies

Sun Myung Moon was born Moon Yong-Myung in 1920 in North Korea. At 15, he claims Jesus told him he had been chosen to "purify the sex-corrupted lineage of mankind."

In 1954 Moon founded the Unification Church with his wife Hak Ja Han. The sect believes that Moon is Christ reborn and preaches sexual abstinence and world peace. He is not liked by either Christians or Jews. The former because of his belief that the cross should be eliminated from religion; the latter for claiming the Holocaust was a result of killing Christ. He has, however, formed an alliance with Louis Farrakhan, controversial leader of the Nation of Islam. The Church is wealthy with business interests which include *The Washington Post* and the United Press International Agency. It is said to own a third of the US fisheries industry, along with some gun factories trading as Kahr Arms.

Moon is famous for conducting mass arranged marriages in sports stadia around the globe and has strong dictates on marital sex. Apparently followers must only have sex when his picture is in the room; use certain positions in a proscribed order; and afterwards wipe their genitals with a cloth, supplied by the Church, which must never be washed. He is also outspoken on the subject of homosexuals, calling them "dung-eating dogs." Since 2003, the Church has been involved in government-funded sex education in US schools, advocating total sexual abstinence before marriage.

In 2004, Moon had himself crowned as a messianic "King of Peace" in a ceremony held at the US Senate. In front of an audience which included Members of Congress from both sides he said: "Leaders in the spirit world, including communist leaders such as Marx and Lenin, who committed all manner of barbarity, and dictators such as Hitler and Stalin, have found strength in my teachings, mended their ways and been reborn as new persons."

The conspiracy theory

Apart from the perhaps predictable theories circulating about the Church's use of mind-control techniques, there are also a wide-ranging number of theories involving money laundering, environmental crimes, immigration violations, and political conspiracies.

The fact that the Church owns powerful media outlets and clearly holds some influence with American politicians – ex-President George Bush Senior is a regular speaker at Unification events – leads many people to believe that Sun Myung Moon gets away with far more in the US than he does elsewhere.

The evidence

The Unification Church is known to have links with the South Korean CIA, and in 1976 Moon was investigated for being involved in the bribing of US officials to influence policy in South Korea; the scandal was known as "Koreagate." In 1982, Moon served 18 months in Danbury Federal Prison for tax fraud and conspiracy to obstruct justice. The Church claims the sentence was a case of religious persecution. In 1985, the Unification Church gave Oliver North – who masterminded the Iran-Contra scandal – $100,000 for his "Nicaraguan Freedom Fund" to help fight communist influences in South America. The Unification Church has been active throughout South America ever since.

In 1996, Uruguayan bank employees reported that more than 4,000 "Moonies" had deposited $25,000 in cash consecutively until they had amassed an $80 million credit. The investigation was dropped, but in 1998 Moon's former daughter-in-law, Nanssok Hong, wrote a book *Shadow of the Moons*. While it was a predominantly personal account of abuses suffered at the hands of the family, she also claimed to have been involved in money laundering.

The Unification Church is still fighting the Brazilian government in cases involving environmental crimes, illegal immigrants, and tax evasion. The Reverend Moon is banned from the UK; according to the government, his presence "would not be conducive to the public good." He is also not welcome in Germany or Japan, where he has alleged ties with the Yakuza.

The verdict

The fact that Moon served time in prison for tax fraud and conspiracy to obstruct justice, and that he provided funds to Oliver North, speaks volumes.

See also: *Iran Contra p.228; Yakuza p.284*

Over 4,000 Unification Church members are married by the Reverend Sun Myung Moon and his wife at a mass ceremony in Madison Square Garden in 1982.

1982
SATANIC RITUAL ABUSE
Satanists commit terrible crimes against children

Since medieval times, there have been sporadic outbursts of hysteria surrounding organized abuses by Satan and his followers. In 1334, 63 English women were accused of worshiping Satan, holding orgies, slaughtering babies, and feasting on their flesh. Some of the "witches" were burnt at the stake, and the practice of torturing people until they confessed they were in league with the Devil, continued across Europe for 400 years.

The more enlightened 20th century brought us the phenomenon of "Trial by media," and a subsequent international "Satanic panic." It may not have resulted in burnings at the stake, but still had horrific impact on the lives of ordinary families.

In 1980, Canadian Michelle Smith and her psychiatrist Lawrence Pazder wrote *Michelle Remembers*, in which she recounted tales of ritual abuse in the name of Satan. As a small child Michelle had witnessed human sacrifices, sexual abuse and seen actual demons. The book attracted intense media interest, with Smith and Pazder embarking on a chat show career.

Over the next decade, more highly publicized books appeared, written by "survivors" of SRA, in which they detailed the abuses. In 1987, talk show host Geraldo Rivera presented a series of primetime TV shows claiming that ritual abuse was practically an epidemic in the US. He said: "There are over one million Satanists in this country... The majority of them are linked in a highly organized, very secretive network. From small towns to large cities, they have attracted police and FBI attention to their Satanic ritual child abuse, child pornography, and grisly Satanic murders. The odds are that this is happening in your town."

The books, and subsequent media coverage, started a chain of events that resulted in mass accusations of Satanic ritual abuse around the world. Law enforcement officers, along with social and healthcare workers, were responsible for thousands of children being taken into state care. Hundreds of parents, teachers, and childcare professionals were arrested and imprisoned. Virtually all of them were finally exonerated.

The conspiracy theory
It is alleged that hundreds of thousands of children go missing every year, and end up as victims on the altars of an organized, international ring of practicing Satanists. The

Devil worshippers are able to get away with it because the ring has members at every level among police officers, politicians, and the judiciary. As virtually every world leader of the 20th and 21st century has been accused at some point of worshipping Satan, the protection of abusers is secured from the very top.

The evidence
All of the evidence comes from the alleged victims of Satanic ritual abuse, and it springs from two sources. The first is that of adults, like Michelle Smith, undergoing psychiatric care. Through the technique of "recovered memory therapy" they are able to recall events that happened to them when they were very young. The efficacy and ethical legitimacy of recovered memory therapy give cause for concern to the majority of credible mental health experts. Typically, adult victims of alleged Satanic ritual abuse undergoing RMT are suffering from mental illnesses like multiple personality disorder, schizophrenia or manic depression. The crux of the issue is whether they make the stories up because they're mentally ill, or whether the abuse they suppressed deep into their subconscious actually caused the mental illness.

The second body of oral evidence comes from children, and invariably makes for distressing reading, as they recount grisly scenes of extreme sex and violence. Those who believe in SRA believe it unlikely that so many children would lie about so much horror in explicit detail.

Sceptics claim the children are usually the victims of a rigorous interrogation, again based on flawed techniques, which in some cases actually guides their responses. Some of the graphically macabre descriptions were also easily traced to scenes in popular movies and literature.

Satanists claim the whole furor was invented by fundamentalist Christians as an attack on their faith. Unfortunately, there are horrible crimes committed where the perpetrator claims to have acted on the instructions of the Devil. Meanwhile, books, articles, and websites proliferate with personal testimony of victims. They argue that Satanists are so organized and pervasive they can eliminate any physical evidence.

The verdict
Despite extensive investigation by law enforcement agencies around the world, no physical evidence – photographs, film, forensics or human remains – have been produced to support the theory of SRA. This is unusual because the numbers of alleged conspirators involved are said

to be legion. There is, however, evidence that individual pedophiles have ritualized their abuse of children. During the "Satanic panic" of the 1990s, many law enforcers claimed the hysteria, and subsequent mass acquittals, meant they were unable to prosecute real child abusers.

See also: *Mae Brussell p.181; David Icke p.188; Satanism p.280; Bohemian Club p.289*

1984
AUM SHINRIKYO/ALEPH
Japanese cult releases poison gas into Tokyo subway

Japanese yoga instructor Shoko Asahara started Aum Shinrikyo (Supreme Truth) in 1984. He offered a creed based on Buddhism mixed with some radical apocalyptic Christianity. He also claimed supernatural powers, including the ability to walk through walls, become invisible, and cure the sick. The cult grew quickly and attracted some of the brightest scientific minds in Japan. In 1999, the British *Guardian* newspaper speculated that young people were drawn to the cult because it "exploited the spiritual vacuum left by Japan's economic boom years by offering what seemed like an alternative to Japan's straitjacket society."

Aum raised funds through legitimate technology-based enterprises and less legitimate ventures involving Russian weapons brokers. Asahara promised his followers that one day Aum would rule Japan and, in 1989, they fielded candidates in the Japanese general elections. After a disastrous showing, it appears that Asahara decided he would try a more direct approach: stepping up the arms dealing and starting to produce chemical weapons at several locations throughout Japan.

After a series of murders and low-level atrocities, Aum came to the attention of the world in 1995 when members released the deadly sarin gas into the Tokyo subway, killing 12 people, and leaving thousands more sick and injured. It was an attempt to precipitate the Armageddon that would bring them to power.

After an eight-year trial – in which it was revealed that Aum had contracts to supply computer software to the government – a number of the cult members were sentenced to death, among them Asahara.

The cult is still active, with thousands of members in Japan. They still see Asahara as the "Master" and, although they are outlawed in Russia, accept donations and membership fees through a Russian bank.

1997
HEAVEN'S GATE
Cult members commit mass suicide believing they are travelling into space

Marshall Applewhite was the son of an itinerant preacher, who lived a conventional life until he met nurse Bonnie Lu Nettles while he was a patient at a mental hospital. During his stay, Applewhite had decided that he was a messenger from an extraterrestrial whom he referred to as the "Older Member in the Evolutionary Level Above Human."

Somehow he convinced Nettles of his theories and they cut all ties with their families, changed their names to "Bo" and "Peep" and told everyone they were space aliens. In 1975 Bo, Peep, and 20 followers left their homes in Oregon and travelled to Colorado, expecting to be picked up by a spaceship.

Bo died in 1985, Peep changed his name again, to "Do," and turned up in San Diego, California, as leader of "Heaven's Gate" or "Total Overcomers Anonymous." He convinced his followers that their time spent on earth was a waiting period, and that soon they would be able to join the Older Member in the Evolutionary Level Above Human.

In 1997 an unusually bright comet, the Hale-Bopp, emerged. It was anticipated that it would be visible to the human eye as it passed. Radio presenter Art Bell took the lead from a group of "remote viewers" who reckoned the comet had a spaceship travelling alongside, and they had pictures to prove it. The pictures were subsequently proved to be fake, but by this time Bell and other theorists had given them immense publicity.

On March 26th 1997, Applewhite and 38 members of Heaven's Gate were discovered in their mansion. They had helped each other administer lethal doses of phenobarbital and washed it down with vodka. The male members of the cult had also castrated each other.

A statement on their website said: "... Hale-Bopp's approach is the "marker" we've been waiting for – the time for the arrival of the spacecraft from the Level Above Human to take us home."

See also: *Conspiracy Radio p.93*

> The idea that the Earth has been visited by creatures from beyond our world, from beyond our solar system, from different galaxies, has probably existed ever since man first gazed at the stars.

Up there in the sky, out there in space, there were clearly wonders beyond our understanding ... and there still are. It is in our nature to speculate about things we see as mysteries and our inquisitiveness has always fuelled the development of man's intelligence, gradually expanding our knowledge of everything that surrounds us. Through the ages, any anomaly that could not immediately be explained with reference to the sum total of man's wisdom and experience to that date was instead the subject of speculation. When speculation failed to produce a satisfactory answer, fanciful scenarios were drawn from the well of man's imagination. The ancient Egyptians believed that the stars were the souls of the dead, risen into the heavens to join the gods, while the Vikings explained the way that the sun travelled across the sky each day by saying that it was driven in a chariot by the goddess Sol to light the world. And if superior beings – gods – could be up there in the sky, then it is logical that they should want to visit their worshippers on Earth from time to time, especially those priests or leaders who claimed to be passing on their commands. Ancient illustrations exist from many cultures showing gods or angels descending from above.

Ancient roots of alien life

Now, we have to ask ourselves which came first, the concept of the stars as the realm of the gods or "gods" in the form of extraterrestrials who descended in great spaceships from the sky and instilled the notion in some early cultures? Were those ancient illustrations allegorical, drawn and carved from the imagination, or were they records of actual events? Writers such as Erich von Däniken believe that many ancient monuments, for instance the pyramids at Giza in Egypt and the Nasca Lines – carvings of geometric figures and animals, birds, and humans in the Nasca desert – in Peru, were beacons or landing areas for alien craft and that visitors from outer space have been arriving here for many thousands of years. As over 60 million copies of his books have been sold around the world, many people are clearly interested in his beliefs.

Belief is a key word when it comes to conspiracy theories, and never more so than when considering alien hypotheses. While the whole subject of UFOs and aliens may have originated with religious beliefs, it has now developed into something of a religion itself. And as with accepted forms of religion, you must have faith, because there is precious little indisputable evidence available. You can no more prove the existence of aliens than you can the existence of God. Religious cults play a hand too. For example, secret societies such as the Thule and Krill organizations in Nazi Germany claimed to have been in contact with aliens who delivered advanced technology to the Nazis, though this somehow failed to win them World War II. More recently, in 1997, 39 members of the Heaven's Gate cult committed suicide in San Diego, California, to set themselves free from their mortal bodies in order that they could be transported aboard a giant spaceship secretly approaching Earth in the shadow of the Hale-Bopp comet.

Links between religious beliefs and belief in aliens are legion. Many are convinced that alien bodies were discovered when one or more spacecraft crashed at Roswell, New Mexico, in 1947, and that there have been numerous other crashes, the Rendlesham Forest affair in Suffolk, England, in 1980 being another example. The theory goes that the existence of alien cadavers and UFOs was hushed up in order to stop the entire fabric of mainstream religion collapsing and thus causing worldwide panic.

Getting the facts right

Governments may, of course, have many other reasons for denying the existence of spacecraft piloted by aliens. Author Georgina Bruni conducted an in-depth investigation into the Rendlesham Forest mystery and, while in the process of so doing, attended a formal dinner at which British prime minister Margaret Thatcher was present. She could not resist asking Mrs Thatcher for her thoughts on

UFOs and received the reply: "You must get your facts right. You can't tell the people." No more was said on the matter, but Georgina's subsequent book about Rendlesham was entitled, *You Can't Tell the People*.

There are a number of points to note here about the way in which alien and UFO conspiracy theories develop. It may well have been Georgina's publisher who pounced on Mrs Thatcher's comment as an irresistibly sensational quote to use for the title of the book. Sensationalism sells, and publishers are in the business of making money, but promoting the more sensational aspects of UFO investigation can sometimes make the facts harder to see. In this instance, the prime minister's comment was used in a way that suggested she was endorsing the idea that UFOs and aliens are buzzing around the planet. However, it is far more likely that she meant something entirely different. "You must get your facts right" is very sensible advice that Mrs Thatcher was prone to offer regularly to her own staff and government ministers. She was a scientist by training – she liked hard facts and knew the dangers of dealing in half-truths. This, then, changes the import of the second part of her comment. "You can't tell the people" is an unfinished statement. "You can't tell the people" what, exactly? "You can't tell the people a load of old nonsense" might be a fairly accurate guess, but that wouldn't make a very good book title, would it?

This goes some way to illuminating another murky facet of alien conspiracy theories. Statements and evidence, unless entirely conclusive and indisputable, are open to interpretation. Just as ancient images of gods and angels can be taken to be astronauts and Mrs Thatcher's statement was used as "proof" of an official cover-up, so too was astronaut James Lovell's cheery message on Christmas Day 1968 given a more sinister meaning. With radio communication impossible when Apollo spacecraft were orbiting the "far side" of the moon, the astronauts had no communication with Earth and ground staff at Mission Control in Houston had no way of tracking them. Until the spacecraft emerged from the shadow of the moon, no one knew for sure if everything was OK – and this was the first time a manned flight had ever orbited the moon. Tensions were running high. Lovell's joke message as Apollo 8 came back into contact: "Please be informed that there is a Santa Claus," suggesting that the Apollo crew had spotted Father Christmas on his rounds, was meant to relieve the tension. It has, however, been interpreted by conspiracy enthusiasts as a coded message from Lovell to covertly let his controllers on Earth know that he and his crew had spotted alien bases on the dark side of the moon. Preposterous? Perhaps in this case, but people don't always mean exactly what they say, and this can be a major problem for investigators when questioning witnesses.

Interviewing someone about strange flying machines and lights in the sky spotted around Area 51 in Nevada needs to be done in a sensitive way. You should never ask questions that might suggest their own answers, especially when your interviewee has been in one of the most "suggestible" environments on the planet. On April 16th, 1996, Nevada's governor, Bob Miller, officially designated Nevada State Route 375, which skirts the Nellis Complex (home to the Groom Lake "Area 51" facility) Extraterrestrial Highway. After a drive along the Extraterrestrial Highway, you can stop in the town of Rachel, and pop into the roadside Little Ale'Inn and have an ET burger. Now, that silvery, cigar-shaped object you saw in the sky didn't have wings, did it? So it couldn't possibly have been a regular plane, could it?

People can, and do, become confused about what they have seen. Any police officer will tell you that three people standing in the same area of the same street at the same time can give entirely different versions of an incident without any one of them telling a lie; they are simply reporting what they remember seeing, which may not always tally with exactly what happened. In some cases, of course, witnesses claiming to have seen UFOs are not lying, confused or misremembering, they are simply wrong. Part of a report from the Flying Saucer Working Party set up by the British government in 1950 to investigate UFOs is an account from RAF Wing Commander Formby, who spotted a "circular shining disc moving on a regular flight path" in the distance. He observed it using a telescope on what he described as a day where "visibility was good, there being a cloudless sky and bright sunshine." Had he then lost sight of the object,

The F-117 Nighthawk was developed in total secrecy. Conspiracy theories inevitably grew up around it.

Breeding grounds

In building up a mystery surrounding UFOs and aliens and issuing statements that are then called into question, governments are breeding an environment in which speculation about the existence of alien UFOs can thrive. This might be to cover the deployment of secret aircraft. The F-117 Nighthawk stealth fighter was, after all, not known to the public until 1988, yet it entered service with the US Air Force in 1982. Prior to that it must have gone through a development and testing programme like any other aircraft. Authorization to begin production of the F-117 at the Lockheed Martin Advanced Developments Projects site, known as the "Skunk Works", in Burbank, California, was given in 1978. Did nobody notice any of these aircraft fly for ten years? If they did, they would have seen something unlike any other plane – a UFO.

Given that the Nighthawk and its technology are now 25 years out of date, what new secret aircraft have been tested over the last quarter of a century? It is not credible that there are no secret military projects currently in existence about which the general public, and a large part of our armed forces, know nothing. Were secret military aircraft flown over Belgium during the 1990 UFO wave? Test flights, manoeuvres, and operational sorties by such aircraft would almost certainly be classed as UFO sightings if they were spotted by anyone who had no inside knowledge. Maybe that is the way the authorities would like it to stay. If you can accept that, then it is not such a huge leap to accept that so-called "alien abductions" may also have something to do with our own security services.

This is not to say that aliens don't exist. While there is little or no concrete evidence to prove that they do, equally, as with God, there is no absolute proof that they don't. In fact, there is a mountain of statistical evidence to support the probability that there really are other forms of life in the universe beyond our planet. With so many billions of star systems from which to choose, the odds against life having developed out there, albeit perhaps not in the same way that it has here, seem pretty slim. However, although there is a strong likelihood that some form of life has evolved, the chances of its having developed to the extent that individuals could leave their own planet and travel through space are not so good. And the

this would have been a classic UFO experience, but he was able to keep it in view and "the attitude of the object changed so that it did not reflect the sunlight into the observer's eye ... it was identified as being a perfectly normal aircraft." An RAF officer is undoubtedly an expert witness when it comes to aircraft, but Wing Commander Formby could easily have been fooled by his own eyes. The Flying Saucer Working Party used such evidence to dismiss UFO reports as unworthy of further investigation, but this may well be an example of yet another element thrown in to complicate even further the alien conspiracy debates – misinformation.

Consider again the statement made by Mrs Thatcher to Georgina Bruni: "You must get your facts right. You can't tell the people." The prime minister was known for her forthright views on most subjects and it was her habit to be precise. Yet nothing about this statement is precise. It is entirely ambiguous. That does not, however, mean that what Mrs Thatcher said was not said deliberately. When asked a question by someone with whom she had been chatting, it would have been rude to ignore the question or brush it aside. Instead, she gave an answer that could be interpreted in different ways: either admitting to the existence of aliens was not in the interests of "the people" or you shouldn't go round stirring up nonsense. Some conspiracy theorists believe that the obfuscation created by people in authority is itself part of a conspiracy.

chances that they might, out of all the planets orbiting all the different star systems, have discovered us here on Earth then become quite remote. Even then, though, that doesn't mean it hasn't happened.

Do they know?

Some people believe that aliens officially made contact with the US government in the 1960s after landing at Holloman Air Force Base in New Mexico. Diplomatic relations were established and the aliens left an ambassador here, called KRLL, who

Report by the Flying Saucer Working Party, one of a flurry of reports on UFOs published by the British government in the early 1950s.

has since died. That the major powers know of the existence of aliens is the backbone of many conspiracy theories, but the misinformation that has been disseminated over the years is now thought to serve a different purpose. In encouraging the belief in aliens, our governments have been paving the way for an imminent announcement, possibly a staged "first contact," that we are not alone. Why would they do this?

On October 30th, 1938, Columbia Broadcasting System's radio dramatization of H.G. Wells's *The War of the Worlds*, starring Orson Welles, was aired as though an alien invasion were happening in real time. Despite the pre-programme announcement that the work was pure fiction, widespread panic ensued. People plagued the police and other emergency services for advice on how to evacuate their cities or protect themselves from the aliens' poison gas. Many reported actually seeing enemy craft. This would never happen today. Science fiction TV shows such as *Star Trek* and *Stargate*, movies such as *Close Encounters of the Third Kind*, *E.T.*, and *Independence Day*, and countless novels and non-fiction books about aliens, abductions, and UFOs have left people far better equipped to deal with anything a broadcast network can throw at them. Conspiracy theorists have it that our governments are working on much the same principle.

Meanwhile, sceptics will continue to deny that aliens exist until they are presented with cast-iron evidence, arguing that they have every right to demand the very highest calibre of proof. Respected astronomer Carl Sagan desperately wanted there to be intelligent life forms elsewhere in the universe but his response to questions about whether it existed was: "It would be an absolutely transforming event in human history. But the stakes are so high on whether it's true or false that we must demand the most rigorous standards of evidence." As far as the kind of activities in which alien creatures might be indulging here on Earth were concerned, his response, as a scientist, was: "Precisely because of human fallibility, extraordinary claims require extraordinary evidence."

The very nature of conspiracy theories means that that kind of extraordinary evidence is neither required nor desirable. As James Lovell might have added to his Santa Claus quip: "All you have to do is believe."

4000 BC
THE SUMERIANS AND THE ANUNNAKI

Aliens regarded as gods visited the ancient world – and are doing so today

The Sumerians were a race of people living in ancient Mesopotamia, an area now mainly in Iraq, from around 4000 BC. At that time most cultures were nomadic, but the Sumerians built cities, developed irrigation, raised crops, kept livestock, and became traders. They built ships to transport goods, invented a form of writing and a system of arithmetic, charted the stars, and, by dividing a circle into 60 segments, devised the basis of our timekeeping. They fought territorial wars, treating their vanquished enemies as slaves. Then, around 2000 BC, the Sumerians were overrun by invaders from the north.

The great advances that were made by the Sumerians have been attributed by some not to man's developing ingenuity but to alien intervention. Conspiracy theorists believe that the gods worshipped by the Sumerians were actually creatures called the Anunnaki from the planet Nibiru. The Anunnaki are supposed to have not only educated the Sumerians but also interbred with them, producing a more advanced human that then dominated the species. The theory further suggests that they are still regularly monitoring the progress of their experiment.

Surviving Sumerian writing, in pictogram form, shows images that have been interpreted by some as aliens descending from above. This "alien gods" theme has been developed most notably by author Erich von Däniken, who followed up his first book, *Chariots of the Gods?* (1968), with over two dozen others in a similar vein.

Ancient drawings, monuments, and texts, including the Bible, can undoubtedly be used as "proof" to support the "alien gods" theory, but they can just as well be seen in other lights, providing as much entertainment as they do evidence of our alien past.

1945
THE BERMUDA TRIANGLE

An area of the Atlantic east of the Bahamas is a hunting ground for alien trophy seekers

The so-called Bermuda Triangle is defined by lines drawn from Bermuda to Puerto Rico, then to the southernmost part of Florida and back to Bermuda. The idea that a disproportionate number of ships and aircraft disappear here in highly unusual circumstances was first suggested over 50 years ago, when the area was dubbed "the Devil's Sea," but became a real talking point with the publication of Charles Berlitz's book *The Bermuda Triangle* (1974). Berlitz catalogued a whole series of disappearances, including that of a flight of five US Navy torpedo bombers in December 1945 – the legendary Flight 19. He reported bizarre compass readings, strange sea conditions, and even a lack of buoyancy in ships, before proposing several theories to account for the mystery. The more outlandish of these (the triangle as a gateway to another dimension; as home to the inhabitants of Atlantis, who were protecting their privacy; as the haunt of aliens, who were kidnapping people, ships, and planes) really captured the public's imagination and the book became a bestseller.

Conspiracy theorists believe that this is a designated area where aliens take specimens for study and that, although the authorities are well aware of this, they do nothing in order to avoid conflict with the extraterrestrials.

There is in fact no proof of any alien involvement in the Bermuda Triangle, even though the pilots of Flight 19 turn up aboard an alien vessel in *Close Encounters of the Third Kind*. There is, however, an abundance of evidence of natural phenomena in the region, including violent tropical storms, seabed gas emissions, and earthquake activity. This is also one of the world's busiest seaways and, statistically, it shows no greater loss of shipping than anywhere else.

1945
FOO FIGHTERS

World War II bomber crews were "buzzed" by glowing alien aircraft

During World War II, Allied aircrews reported seeing strange lights or small, orange-coloured discs flying near their aircraft. Dubbed "foo fighters," these were assumed to be some new kind of German weapon, as they were never seen in friendly airspace. However, the balls of light made no attempt to attack, generally disappearing after a few minutes. Allied soldiers near the front lines in Europe also reported seeing similar lights, as did aircrew operating against the Japanese in the Far East.

Conspiracy theorists believe that foo fighters were alien craft or probes sent to observe the conflict, and that this was known by Allied governments and is being kept a secret to this day.

Military records and even newspaper reports from the time make no mention of aliens. Instead, as the sightings were

Nazi rocket scientist Wernher von Braun, seen here with President John F. Kennedy, later worked on the US space programme.

over enemy-held territory, foo fighters were assumed to be German secret weapons shared with the Japanese – anti-aircraft weapons such as the Wasserfall radio-controlled missile or the Feuerball. The Feuerball was supposedly an experimental remote-controlled rocket or jet-powered device designed to fly alongside an aircraft, emitting signals to disrupt its radio, radar, or engines. The Wasserfall is known to have existed, while the Feuerball may not have, but neither was reported as being successfully deployed.

Natural phenomena such as ball lightning or St Elmo's fire could explain some of the sightings, while ice crystals in the air or the planes' con trails reflecting lights or glowing exhausts could account for others. However, 60 years later there remains no conclusive answer to the mystery of the foo fighters.

1945
NAZI FLYING DISCS

German scientists, instructed by aliens, created advanced flying machines using alien technology

At the end of World War II, as the Allied forces fought their way into Germany from the west and the Soviets swept in from the east, a major priority for the intelligence experts on both sides was the capture of German records and personnel. German scientists and technicians had intricate

knowledge of their country's most advanced weaponry, much of which the Nazis ordered to be destroyed as bases and research facilities were overrun, while intelligence officers held information that would prove invaluable in the years ahead as East faced up to West during the Cold War.

The Allies lagged far behind Germany in the development of military technology, the Germans having fielded the first jet fighter aircraft, the pulse-jet V-1 "cruise missile," the rocket-powered, supersonic V-2 ballistic missile, and the fastest aircraft of the war, the Me 163 rocket plane. Although officially western powers were reluctant to employ Germans who had been prominent Nazis or involved in research where slave labour or human experimentation had been utilized, the option of leaving them free to carry on their work for a new Germany or letting them fall into the hands of the Soviets was not to be countenanced.

The Americans instituted Operation Paperclip in early 1946 to allow Germans captured or under their influence to emigrate to the US. Hundreds of scientists, technicians, and their families were provided with homes, many starting their new lives as US citizens at the military research facility of Fort Bliss in Texas. One such scientist was Wernher von Braun, the rocket engineer who had created the V-2 and surrendered 500 of his staff to the Americans. He and members of his team subsequently worked on US Army missile development and he became a leading light at NASA.

The conspiracy theory
Some people think that German military research and development was so far advanced because of contact between aliens and mystical German secret societies. They claim that it was the aliens who supplied the plans and assistance necessary to build flying saucers and other machines capable of immense speeds.

The evidence
There is plenty of evidence for the existence of secret societies in Germany prior to World War II (the Thule and Krill organizations have already been mentioned, and played a major part in the rise of the Nazi party), but there is no way of proving that they were in contact with aliens.

The verdict
German scientists were working on flying discs and other advanced aircraft designs. At the end of World War I, the Treaty of Versailles banned Germany from building military aircraft. This had a crippling effect on the country's aviation industry and many young aviation enthusiasts instead concentrated their efforts on creating highly unusual aircraft designs for the growing new sport of gliding. Consequently, this meant that they were working to perfect aerodynamics and wing design, and Germany soon became the world leader in this field.

Brothers Walter and Reimar Horten were building V, or delta-winged, gliders in the 1930s and developed tailless "flying wing" jet planes for the Luftwaffe during World War II. Alexander Lippisch designed and built triangular, delta-winged aircraft, and was also involved in the delta-winged Me 163 rocket plane. Arthur Sack built an aircraft with a circular wing, and Professor Heinrich Focke of the Focke-Wulf company patented his own flying-disc design in 1939. The Germans certainly flew prototype triangular and boomerang-shaped aircraft during World War II and reports have emerged to suggest that they may well have tested circular-wing or disc-shaped aircraft as well, powered with new jet or rocket engines. The technology they required to do so already existed and would not have needed any input from aliens.

See also: *The Roswell Incident p.302; Area 51 p.308*

The 1994 US Air Force Roswell report asserts that the aeroshell of a Voyager probe was mistaken for a UFO.

1947
THE ROSWELL INCIDENT
An alien spacecraft crashed in the New Mexico desert and was recovered, but the incident was hushed up

In June 1947, rancher Mac Brazel was working on his sheep farm around 50km (30miles) from Corona, which was 120km (75miles) northwest of Roswell in New Mexico, when he discovered some silvery metallic debris – he described it as being like tinfoil or paper – and sticks scattered over a wide area. He thought no more about it until, three weeks later, having travelled to Corona to sell wool, he heard about the spate of UFO sightings that had been sweeping the country. With no radio or telephone at his ranch, Brazel knew nothing of the UFOs but thought the debris he had found strange enough to report to the Roswell sheriff on July 7th, perhaps hoping there might be some reward. Sheriff George Wilcox reported the find to the Roswell Army Air Field and Intelligence Officer, Major Jesse Marcel, who was dispatched to inspect the wreckage. The headline in the *Roswell Daily Record* of July 8th read: "RAAF [Roswell Army Air Field] Captures Flying Saucer on Ranch in Roswell Region." Marcel had announced that the debris was from a flying saucer and a team from the air base had been assigned to recover any wreckage. This was then flown to Wright Field in Dayton, Ohio, one of the US Air Force's main flight test centres, for examination. At this point the official story changed, with the wreckage being identified as part of a high-altitude weather balloon or radar target, although it may well have been one of the top-secret "Project Mogul" balloons designed to monitor Soviet nuclear weapons tests. Excitement over the find subsided and the whole incident seemed to have been accepted as a false alarm, sparked by a wave of UFO hysteria, and was left well alone for the next 30 years.

The conspiracy theory

Dr Robert Carr, a retired professor at South Florida University, sparked off the Roswell debate once again in the 1970s, when he claimed to have interviewed witnesses to a UFO crash in Aztec, New Mexico, from which a wrecked craft and its alien occupants had been recovered. In 1978, nuclear physicist Stanton Friedman and former teacher William Moore began researching a book, *The Roswell Incident*, which was published in 1980 with Charles Berlitz as co-author. They claimed that debris from an alien craft had been recovered at Brazel's ranch near Corona and that the actual craft had crashed almost 290km (180miles) west of Roswell, where alien bodies were recovered. They maintained that the flimsy "balloon" debris Major Marcel had exhibited to the press was not what was originally found, previous statements having described the silvery metal wreckage as thin but resistant to prolonged attacks with a blowtorch and a sledgehammer, and impossible to cut or tear. The conspiracy theory then grew that the US government was covering up the existence of the alien spaceship and the alien creatures to avoid worldwide panic about an alien invasion. They may also have been concerned to suppress alien technology – engines that ran on water – which could cripple the US economy and make the oil industry a thing of the past.

The evidence

There seems to be plenty of information to prove the story of the crash. In July 1947, Lydia Sleppy, a teletext operator in Albuquerque, was typing out a story about the crashed flying saucer, which was being dictated to her for a news wire service when, according to *The Roswell Incident*, she was interrupted by an incoming message from an unknown source: "Attention Albuquerque. Do not transmit. Repeat, do not transmit this message. Stop communication immediately." At least, that was her recollection in the 1970s. Almost 20 years later she asserted that the message had

said: "This is the FBI. You will immediately cease all communication." This is just one example of how witnesses' stories change, as you might expect, in the course of 45 years. In fact, so many witnesses, rightly or wrongly, have been discredited and so many charlatans exposed over Roswell, including some who produced film of an "alien autopsy," that the truth behind what, if anything, happened is now shrouded in layers of speculation and fabrication.

In 1997, Stanton Friedman published *Top Secret/Majic*, an investigation into Majic-12, a group, according to "leaked" MJ-12 top-secret documents, which was appointed by President Truman in 1947 for the "recovery for scientific study of all materials of a foreign or extraterrestrial manufacture," such items to include EBEs – Extraterrestrial Biological Entities. Having spent 13 years with the material, Friedman was convinced it proved that a crashed alien ship or ships, along with the bodies of the crew, were recovered in 1947. But the documents have been denounced as fakes by debunkers, who point out that, even if they were "leaked" from a government source, they don't necessarily prove that the aliens and their ships exist, only that we are being persuaded that they do, possibly to protect the US's own top-secret aircraft development programme by perpetuating the myth of alien UFOs.

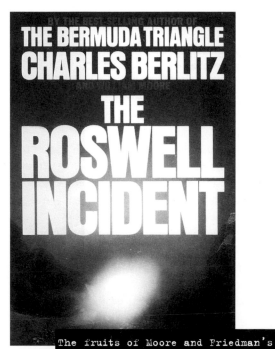

The fruits of Moore and Friedman's research into the Roswell incident, published in 1980.

The verdict

The wreckage that was found at Roswell may well have had a terrestrial origin. Even if a "flying saucer" was recovered, it could have been an experimental US military aircraft rather than an alien spaceship. The whole alien story could just be part of a smokescreen created by the security services to hide the shortcomings of one of their own devices. Somewhere in the Roswell story, the truth has been lost in a morass of lies.

See also: *Nazi Flying Discs p.301*

1947–present day
UFOS HUSHED UP BY POLITICAL POWERS

The world's governments deny the existence of UFOs to protect organized religion and prevent panic

On June 24th, 1947, Kenneth Arnold, an experienced pilot, was flying a light aircraft through the Cascade Mountains in Washington state when he spotted a flight of nine crescent-shaped aircraft flying in formation in the vicinity of Mount Rainier. The aircraft appeared to dip or skip through the air. News of his sighting soon reached the press, who reported the unidentified objects as having travelled at phenomenal speeds impossible for any known aircraft to achieve. There followed a wave of UFO sightings across the US and general panic about whether alien invaders or (perhaps worse) the Russians were violating US airspace.

Kenneth Arnold's sighting is regarded as a classic UFO encounter, with a robust and reliable civilian aviator providing the most credible of witnesses. While many UFO sightings can be dismissed for a multitude of reasons – misidentification of military or civilian aircraft, natural phenomena such as electrical storms, ball lightning, or meteor showers, and even confusion caused by bright stars and planets (Venus is a favourite) – there are many that defy simple explanation. In fact, there were enough for the US Air Force to establish Project Sign UFO research team in 1947. Sign became Project Grudge in 1949 and Project Blue Book in 1952. The Blue Book team, although at times reduced to just a handful of personnel, logged and investigated UFO sightings until it was disbanded in 1969. In the UK, the government set up the Flying Saucer Working Party in 1950 to investigate reports and in the early 1990s British UFO investigator and civil servant Nick Pope, author of *Open Skies, Closed Minds* (1990), was attached to the Secretariat (Air Staff) with a brief to study UFO reports.

Governments, then, appear to take the UFO threat seriously, none more so than the Belgian authorities, who had a major scare in 1990, following hundreds of UFO sightings over a period of some months. The incident culminated on March 30th, 1990, when two F-16s were scrambled to intercept a craft picked up on radar. Despite locating the target on their own radar, the F-16 pilots never made visual contact, describing instead the impossible manoeuvres that were undertaken to evade them. The craft eventually accelerated away over the North Sea at a speed the F-16s, capable of Mach 2, could not match. Thousands of Belgians reported having seen huge triangular aircraft, often low-flying and slow-moving, during the 1989–90 "UFO Wave," creating one of the best-documented series of sightings ever recorded.

The conspiracy theory

Some people believe that the major world powers know that UFOs are alien craft, but keep this a secret to avoid widespread panic about an alien invasion, and to prevent the collapse of the major world religions, which would not accept the existence of creatures from another planet, and because the most powerful nations on Earth can do nothing to prevent the contact.

The evidence

While UFOs most definitely exist, it cannot be said with certainty that they are craft piloted by alien creatures. Most researchers agree that only a tiny percentage of sightings defy explanation, but this does not make the UFOs alien ships. Kenneth Arnold's sighting in 1947 was sensationalized by the media. He never claimed that the aircraft he saw were travelling at unusually high speeds, always believing that they were secret, advanced American planes. He may have been right. What he saw could have been a US development of the German Horten Gotha Ho IX or Northrop YB-49 "flying wings." Their apparently strange flight characteristics might have been caused by haze or other atmospheric conditions distorting Arnold's view.

Similarly, the object pursued by the Belgian F-16s in 1990 could have been a top-secret aircraft such as the Aurora spy plane, said to be capable of Mach 6 – well over 4,800kph (3,000mph). It might also have been an unmanned reconnaissance vehicle, helping to account for the manoeuvres it executed that involved g-forces no human pilot could have survived. Although naturally occurring atmospheric conditions can create radar "shadows," which can then show up as erroneous contacts capable of bouncing around in an unpredictable manner on operators' screens, the Belgian F-16 pilots did not believe they were chasing shadows and their UFO was last reported heading out over the sea towards the English coast. The UK authorities denied that any unknown aircraft entered their airspace, but there are a number of bases in England, including Boscombe Down in Wiltshire and Warton in Lancashire, from which secret, experimental aircraft have been flown. The slower-moving, low-flying Belgian UFOs could have been different but no less secret military aircraft. The Aereon Corporation worked on designs for extremely large, triangular LTA (lighter than air) vehicles for the US military in the 1970s. These aircraft/airship hybrids were intended to have a massive load capacity and to be used as "stealth" transports with the ability to fly very slowly or hover if required.

The verdict

Secret military aircraft may account for many otherwise inexplicable sightings and, in order to preserve their secret status, the military may be happy for witnesses to believe that they have seen something of extraterrestrial origin. That they have done, of course, remains a possibility.

1969
THE MOON LANDING

The landing was either faked by NASA or aliens prevented it from happening

On July 20th, 1969, Apollo 11 astronaut Neil Armstrong became the first man to set foot on the moon. In the eight short Cold War years since Alan Shepard had become the first American in space in May 1961 – Soviet cosmonaut Yuri Gagarin was the first man in space, orbiting the Earth two months earlier – NASA had overcome the USSR's perceived lead in space technology. President Kennedy had pledged, following Shepard's mission: "... this nation should commit itself to achieving the goal, before this decade is out, of landing a man on the moon and returning him safely to Earth." NASA finally made good the president's promise six years after his assassination in Dallas with what they expected the world to see as a demonstration of the superiority of western engineering and ingenuity over Soviet technology. The US had won the race to the moon and Armstrong's triumphant moon walk was watched by a worldwide TV audience estimated at 600 million. After 19 minutes, Armstrong was joined on the lunar surface by fellow astronaut Buzz Aldrin. Including their time inside the lunar module landing craft, the two spent around 22 hours

on the surface before blasting off to rendezvous with the third Apollo 11 crew member, Michael Collins, who was orbiting in the command module. The return journey took three days before they splashed down safely in the Pacific on July 24th.

The conspiracy theory

Some people maintain that the moon landing was faked, using a Hollywood-style film studio, and that NASA perpetrated the elaborate hoax to fulfil Kennedy's promise, to not lose face in front of their Soviet rivals, and to avoid having the US government cut their budget if they had lost the space race. Another even more sinister theory suggests that alien bases had been discovered by previous Apollo orbiting missions, and the aliens then warned the humans to stay away.

The evidence

To support their ideas, conspiracy theorists quote Apollo 8 astronaut James Lovell's quip when his command module, in lunar orbit, emerged from the radio blackout of the "dark side" of the moon on Christmas Day 1968: "Please be informed that there is a Santa Claus." This was said to be a coded message meaning that he had spotted an alien base. The fact that man no longer travels to the moon is also used to support the case, but the theory holds about as much water as the Sea of Tranquility.

The verdict

Sending a 110m (363ft) Saturn V rocket with Apollo 11 perched on top blasting off from Cape Kennedy in Florida, watched by thousands on the ground and hundreds of millions on TV, would make this, even without the special-effects back-up required to create the rest of the mission, the most elaborate hoax ever staged. NASA points out that it would have cost more to fake the Apollo missions, for whatever reason, than to actually stage them. It would have required special effects beyond the powers of the best in the movie business, effects which would have had to sustain not a two-hour cinema feature but film for an entire eight-day mission. Tracking stations and astronomers around the world would have had to be party to the scam if it were to succeed. There were also five other Apollo moon landings up to the end of the programme in 1972 and these would have had to have been faked too. The 1978 movie *Capricorn One*, in which a mission to Mars is faked, apparently has a lot to answer for. Without doubt, Neil Armstrong landed on the moon.

1972

THE SPACE MONOLITH

An alien satellite spotted by Apollo 10 astronauts and Yuri Gagarin, was subsequently retrieved by NASA

In May 1969, Apollo 10 astronauts Tom Stafford, John Young, and Eugene Cernan travelled to the moon in a final "dress rehearsal" for the Apollo 11 landing mission. The Apollo 10 crew were to come within a few thousand feet of the surface of the moon, closer than man had ever gone before, testing equipment, taking photographs, recording data, and surveying landing sites in preparation for the next historic space flight.

Stafford and Cernan descended towards the surface of the moon in the lunar module, while Young maintained a 110km (69mile) high orbit in the command module, just as the crew of Apollo 11 would do two months later. The astronauts encountered several slight problems during the mission, including hydrogen in their drinking water, a fault with the seal on the command module hatch, and intermittent communication failures both between the command and lunar modules, and with Earth, but the mission ran almost exactly to time. They re-entered Earth's atmosphere at the highest ever speed – almost 40,000kph (25,000mph) – and splashed down safely within 35 seconds of their scheduled landing time.

The conspiracy theory

The cover-up that some people believe surrounds the Apollo 10 mission involves an alien satellite, or communication beacon, known as the Monolith. The Apollo 10 crew are said to have approached the beacon, rather like the one in Arthur C. Clarke's *The Sentinel* (the short story on which Stanley Kubrick's 1968 movie *2001: A Space Odyssey* was based), in a clandestine departure from their mission schedule, to film and photograph the message and star map etched on its surface. The energy signals emanating from the Monolith caused various electrical malfunctions and communication failures aboard Apollo 10, which nearly didn't make it back to Earth as a result. The alien artifact had been observed by the first man in space, Soviet cosmonaut Yuri Gagarin, in 1961 and remained in orbit until 1972, when an experimental military space shuttle was sent to retrieve it for study at a top-secret US research centre.

The evidence

As one might expect, there is very little evidence to prove the theory. Gagarin died in a plane crash in 1968, the year

before the Apollo 10 mission, and none of the astronauts ever mentioned the Monolith. The problems that Apollo 10 encountered were more to do with mundane procedural hiccups and faulty or malfunctioning equipment than with interference from an outside source. While they did re-enter much faster than any previous Apollo flight, there is no reason to suspect that there was anything suspicious about this, and the fact that they splashed down within seconds of the mission schedule, which had been meticulously planned months before, means that they could not have spent extra time secretly examining an alien satellite.

Even if they had wanted to approach the Monolith, locating it in space and manoeuvreing towards it would have been beyond the limited capabilities of the Apollo spacecraft, which was intended to go to the moon and back, with very little flexibility in its design to allow it to do anything else. As for the secret military space shuttle recovering the Monolith in 1972, it seems highly unlikely that, if such advanced technology were available in the US, Apollo 17 would have made the perilous journey to the moon that year using the same systems as all of the previous American space flights. In any case, space watchers would certainly have spotted such a craft taking off or landing after its covert space mission.

The first real space shuttle mission, commanded by Apollo 10 astronaut John Young, did not take place until 1981 – nine years after the "secret" shuttle is said to have been in operation. Nine years of research, testing, and operational experience with a military shuttle would surely have helped

Apollo 10 astronauts are believed to have seen the Monolith from their lunar module.

to overcome the problems that plagued NASA's high-profile "civilian" version.

The verdict

It is entirely feasible that astronauts and cosmonauts would have seen discarded parts of our own rockets or satellites orbiting as "space garbage." However, space garbage quickly becomes "alien Monolith" when reports of astronauts having "seen something" reach those who really want to believe that such objects exist. The legend of the Monolith, it seems, owes more to science fiction than to historical fact.

1980
THE DULCE BASE

There is a secret underground facility in New Mexico where aliens and humans share technologies

Since the early 1980s, people living near the small town of Dulce, on the Jicarilla Apache Indian Reservation in New Mexico, have reported strange vibrations in the ground and the regular appearance of military helicopters, jeeps, and personnel in the desert. In this area of northern New Mexico there have also been a large number of UFO sightings and reports of strange lights seen in the desert at night, not to mention many incidences of bizarre cattle mutilations. This last disturbing phenomenon, where dead cattle have been discovered with their udders, sexual organs, and tongues removed with surgical, bloodless incisions, spread throughout the US farming regions in the 1980s and 1990s, although the earliest reported cases may date back to the early 1960s.

The conspiracy theory

Some people believe that there is a secret underground facility in the desert near Dulce where aliens are working with the US military, trading their technology for assistance in their biological experiments on cattle and human specimens. The exact purpose of the aliens' experiments is unclear, but it may involve genetic manipulation aimed at adapting their own physiology to allow them to live on Earth. They may also be working with American scientists to develop advanced weapons for biological warfare. Conspiracy theorists point out that Dulce is only about 150km (95miles) from Los Alamos, home of the Los Alamos National Laboratory, one of the leading scientific institutions involved in genetic research, implying that the two institutions may share information and personnel. They claim that the vibrations felt by people living near Dulce

are caused by either underground testing of new human/alien technology or the blasting required for the excavation of new areas to accommodate the ever-expanding secret facility.

The evidence

Evidence for the existence of the Dulce underground base is sparse. The vibrations in the ground might easily be naturally occurring earth tremors, as this is an area where minor geological activity is not uncommon. What's more, the presence of US military personnel on operation in desert areas over the past 25 to 30 years should not really come as a surprise. The Soviet invasion of Afghanistan in 1979 would have prompted the US top brass to ensure that their combat units' desert and mountain skills were up to scratch, while the fiasco in the Iranian desert during the attempted rescue of personnel from the besieged US embassy in Tehran demonstrated that combined operations training and experience were sadly lacking. From 1980 to 1988 Iran and Iraq were at war, again highlighting the need to be ready for desert operations, and in 1991, of course, US troops went into action against Iraq in the first Gulf War. Day and night, military exercises in the desert throughout this period would have been regarded as priority training, whether the exercises took place in recognized military training areas or in territory testingly unfamiliar to the troops.

Such manoeuvres would certainly account for strange lights at night and even daytime UFO sightings, but they do not explain the cattle mutilations. Police forces throughout the US, as well as in other parts of the world, have investigated these grotesque outbreaks, because many thousands of cattle have been killed. While some inquiries have come close to secretive satanic cults and others have revealed barbaric hoaxes, the cause of the majority of mutilation cases remains a mystery.

The verdict

The precise location of the Dulce base also remains a mystery. Supposedly "leaked" documents and witness testimonies have turned out to be unreliable, providing no conclusive evidence of the whereabouts of the base or even of its existence. In February 1990, a Japanese team from Nippon Television mounted an expedition to Dulce, interviewing people about the strange lights and UFOs seen in the vicinity, and venturing out into the desert area to search for signs of an entrance to the base. In the desert, however, they found nothing but desert. If there is a secret underground base at Dulce, it is a very well-kept secret.

Present day
AREA 51

Alien equipment, bodies, and actual aliens
are housed and tested in secret US facility

In 1955, US President Eisenhower authorized the seizure
of an area of land in Nevada around 145km (90miles) north
of Las Vegas to be set aside for a high-security military base.
The sector of desert land near the sun-hardened bed of the
long-since-dry Groom Lake had been selected by a Lockheed
test pilot as an ideal site for the testing of the new U-2 spy
plane. The area was close to a nuclear test facility and, as
such, would benefit from the "no fly zone" of restricted airspace that already existed there.

Area 51 is actually the invisible box of restricted airspace
above the Groom Lake facility. Over the years, more and
more of the desert area would be cordoned off by the US Air
Force until the Nellis Air Force Range, also known as the
Nellis Range Complex, extended over an area of around
13,000sq km (5,000sq miles). Nellis includes the Nevada
Nuclear Test Site and the Tonopah Test Range for missile
and artillery firing, as well as air force training ranges, the
Groom Lake facility, and at least one other high-security
site at Papoose Lake, 24km (15miles) from Groom Lake. The
base at Groom is sometimes referred to as Paradise Ranch
and, in conjunction with Papoose, Dreamland. The area is
not completely fenced off but is strewn with sophisticated
intruder-detection systems, and security vehicles patrol
the roads around the facility.

It is believed that some 2,500 staff work at Groom and
Papoose lakes, arriving each day on special flights from
McCarran airport in Las Vegas. The Boeing 737 aircraft in
which they make the half-hour flight allegedly file false destinations and flight plans each day, the first leaving at
4.30am and the last returning at 7pm. The Groom Lake complex has been extensively developed over the past 50 years
and now boasts housing and leisure facilities, as well as an
8km (5mile) runway. Up until 1995, it was still possible to
catch a glimpse of the runway and some of the Groom Lake
buildings from a hill called Freedom Ridge, near the perimeter of the secure zone, about 19km (12miles) from the site,
but the authorities then placed a further 650hectares
(1,600acres), including Freedom Ridge, off limits.

The conspiracy theory

It has been widely believed for many years that the
facility known as Area 51 is being used for the evaluation
of alien spacecraft and the "back engineering" of alien

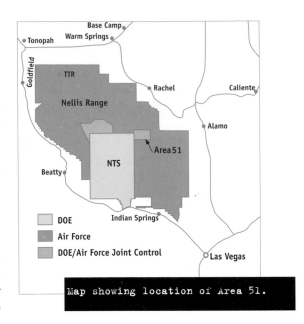

Map showing location of Area 51.

technology so that it can be understood, reproduced, and
made available for use by the US military. Conspiracy
theorists also claim that the bodies of aliens recovered from
UFO crashes, such as the one at Roswell, were ultimately
brought to Area 51 to be studied and stored. Aliens who
survived such crashes are also thought to have been
housed here, either kept as prisoners for examination or
staying voluntarily to help US engineers understand their
spacecrafts' systems.

The evidence

Lights in the sky at night around Area 51, apparently belonging to strange aircraft, have been seen ever since the
base was established. Very few of the many thousands of
people who work or have worked at Groom Lake over the
past half-century are willing to talk about what they have
seen there. Indeed, depending on what their jobs entailed,
many of them may never have seen anything unusual at all.
What is certain is that they, like so many other government
and military personnel, are sworn to secrecy, with dire consequences threatened should they ever breathe a word
about classified projects. Two witnesses are known to have
talked about what they saw in Dreamland. One was Leo
Williams, who died in 1989. He claimed to have been employed by the CIA for 30 years and said that he had worked
inside Area 51 on the evaluation of alien technology, around
which the development of the B-2 stealth bomber was
based. He apparently talked to relatives when dying of cancer, brought on by contact with toxic materials at Area 51,

once he no longer feared the retribution of his old employers. The other was a man named Bob Lazar who openly claims to have worked on alien flying-saucer propulsion systems in Area 51. But doubts have been cast upon Lazar's educational and professional qualifications, making him an unreliable witness. Williams's story is also somewhat flawed. Would someone with life-long experience of the workings of the CIA expose his family to potential danger by revealing secrets to them? It seems unlikely.

The verdict

The various reports of strange lights and aircraft spotted in the vicinity of Area 51 from the time it was established are actually consistent with the known use of the facility. The U-2 was tested and flown from here, as was its replacement, the Mach 3+ SR-71 Blackbird, which entered service in 1966. The F-117 stealth fighter and B-2 stealth bomber flew from Groom Lake, and these are only the secret aircraft about which we have been told. The likelihood that other experimental aircraft – triangular- and circular-winged vehicles with unconventional propulsion systems – have been developed and tested here, by Operation Paperclip personnel from 1946 onwards, is very strong. The chances that aliens have been involved, however, are not so strong.

See also: *Psi-War: Operations Grillflame and Stargate p.153; Nazi Flying Discs p.301*

Present day
CROP CIRCLES

Formations in fields are ridiculed to prevent discovery of alien landing sites

Crop circles have been puzzling experts ever since they first came under serious investigation in the early 1980s. In 1989, Pat Delgado and Colin Andrews published *Circular Evidence*, which became a major bestseller. Their research focused on crop circles found in England, but cases have been documented from across the US and Canada, Brazil, France, Switzerland, Australia, New Zealand, and Russia. Crop circles are flattened rings in fields of growing wheat or corn where the stalks have been pushed over, without breaking, in a swirling pattern. There can be concentric rings or patterns of separate rings up to around 20m (66ft) in diameter and they generally appear during the night.

Conspiracy theorists believe these marks are made when alien spacecraft land and that our governments are aware of this but are keeping the truth from us. As proof, they point to the fact that there is often a military presence and recent UFO activity near circle sites. However, as a large number of British crop circles are found in areas where there are military bases, this is hardly conclusive evidence. Military areas also generate high levels of bogus UFO sightings. That said, no natural phenomenon has been found to produce this precise effect. Experienced investigators can identify hoax circles by their clumsy execution but have been unable convincingly to replicate the patterns in the flattened stalks created when a real crop circle is formed, whatever type of tools are used. The crop circle mystery seems set to endure for some time to come.

Present day
EARTH'S ALIENS

Aliens are living on Earth and travel around in UFOs

In 1946, in the magazine *Amazing Stories*, publisher Ray Palmer presented a series of tales written by author and artist Richard Shaver about meeting demonic, robot-like aliens who lived in underground complexes. Palmer cleverly contrived the stories as fiction based on fact. There followed an overwhelming response from readers with similar claims.

The theory is that these aliens have been living in various underground sites for years, latterly with the collusion of the world's governments. They originally came to Earth from another planet, possibly Mars, when a comet destroyed its atmosphere, forcing them underground. Having developed the technology for space travel, they came to Earth, establishing underground colonies to avoid interfering with the indigenous primitive species – in other words, us.

Believers point to folk tales from cultures all over the world that refer to strange creatures living underground. Satan and hell, after all, are supposed to be "down there." The noise of unfamiliar machinery and strange voices heard by miners working deep underground also suggest the presence of other beings. When one Charles Marcoux set off with directions to find a gateway to Shaver's underworld in the Blowing Cavern near Cushman, Arkansas, in 1981, he was mysteriously attacked and killed by a swarm of bees.

None of this, of course, amounts to concrete evidence. Noises in deep mines can be transmitted, even through solid rock, by machinery being used elsewhere in the mine, and Marcoux's tragic accident would have been a rather clumsy way for an advanced alien race to preserve their anonymity. If they are down there, we won't know for sure until they think we are ready to meet them.

Present day
TAKEN

Humans are being abducted and taken aboard alien craft to become the subject of strange experiments

In September 1961, Betty and Barney Hill were driving home to Portsmouth in New Hampshire late at night after a trip to Canada. Postal worker Barney (41) and social worker Betty (39) noticed a light following them through the White Mountains, so, near North Woodstock, Barney pulled over to see what it was. When he got out of the car several figures approached and, feeling threatened, he jumped back in and drove off. Near Indian Head, the frightened couple heard a loud beeping, appeared to lose consciousness, and awoke two hours later 56km (35miles) closer to home.

The Hills had no proper recollection of what had happened during the "missing" part of their journey but both felt very peculiar. Barney was suffering some discomfort in his genitals while Betty felt extremely disturbed, subsequently having bizarre nightmares in which she and Barney were transported to an alien craft. They were separated and small grey creatures subjected them to medical tests – including, for Betty, having a needle inserted into her abdomen. Barney had no dreams and no memory of anything having happened to him.

After months of anguish, the Hills determined to solve the mystery by undergoing hypnosis. Barney was then able to overcome his memory block, describing how the aliens took a sperm sample from him. Betty gave details suggesting that she had undergone some kind of fertility test. This normal, respectable, church-going couple were appalled by what appeared to have happened to them. They spoke out about it and were contacted by journalist John Fuller, who wrote a book about their experiences, *The Interrupted Journey* (1966). This was the first well-documented account of what were to become known as alien abductions. Soon many thousands of people started to come forwards with their own stories.

Almost 40 years later, researchers have found that some of those who volunteer abduction stories are, unlike the Hills, simply fantasists or attention seekers. There are many more, however, who just want to talk privately to someone who might be able to understand, or explain, the trauma they have suffered. These people won't even talk to their family or friends about their experiences, such are their feelings of embarrassment, shame, and confusion, as well as an understandable fear of ridicule or debasement.

The conspiracy theory

There are a number of broadly similar theories covering the subject of human abduction by aliens. Some theorists belive that creatures from another planet kidnap humans for study, just as we do with sharks: for example, inserting implants under the skin in the same way that human scientists "tag" sharks to learn more about their habits and to help relocate the specimen. Others have it that the aliens are desperately trying to mate with humans, or use humans to help them genetically alter their own species so that they can adapt themselves to be able to survive on and colonize our planet. They may also be intent on creating human/alien hybrids as drone workers, slaves, or soldiers who can operate more freely than they themselves can in Earth's atmosphere.

The evidence

The fact that cases have been reported all over the world, sometimes by people with little or no knowledge of "westernized" society who could not be expected to have been influenced by sci-fi comic books, novels, movies, and TV shows, but whose stories are remarkably similar to those of western abductees, is given as verification of alien abductions. A common element of the abduction experience is the "missing time" which defies explanation, and abductees also often have strange marks on their skin, while some have even produced what they say are implants inserted by the alien surgeons.

The verdict

A fear of the unknown, of being forcibly separated from family and friends by evil strangers, is certainly a common emotion, no matter where we come from. Stories of people being kidnapped, abused, and kept as slaves exist in the history and folklore of every culture, providing plenty of material for the kind of nightmares that will always be open to interpretation as alien abductions. While hallucinations (even joint hallucinations) brought about by fatigue or stress can account for some elements of abduction experiences, the time lapse is more difficult to explain. In many cases, however, including that of the Hills, the time lapse is calculated long after the event, leaving a wide margin for error when relying on a memory clouded by trauma. No evidence of physical wounding has ever been found that could not be otherwise explained and no implant has ever been discovered that could be proved to have come from out of this world.

The strongest evidence in abduction cases is the testimony of the abductees, often given under regressive hypnosis. Not everyone makes an ideal candidate for hypnosis. Research shows that those who do tend to have extraordinarily good memories and a strong ability to visualize events, either real or fantasy. In other words, they have vivid imaginations. Abductees have undoubtedly been through some kind of trauma, but were aliens really the culprits? Clandestine organizations in countries around the world have experimented on their own citizens with substances as diverse as LSD and poison gas. Those who have been abducted for experimentation need not necessarily have been taken by creatures from another planet.

Present day
THEY'RE HERE: THE CHUPACABRA

The chupacabra, and other alien species, are already here and living on Earth

In Puerto Rico in November 1995, at least two dozen people saw what they believed to be a chupacabra, a vicious, sharp-toothed, horned creature that appeared to be able to fly and was blamed for countless attacks on livestock around the countryside, leaving turkeys, rabbits, goats, and even cows drained of blood. The chupacabra is believed to be just one of a whole host of alien species already living among us here on Earth. Others include the more sophisticated 1.5m (5 ft) tall, dark-eyed Greys; the 1.8–2.4m (6–8ft) tall, blond-haired Nordics; and the 2.1m (7ft) tall, lizard-like Reptoids. Then there are Big Foot, Sasquatch, and others who may have the ability to appear human.

Conspiracy theories involving alien entities here on Earth are as many and varied as the species themselves. Some of the more friendly aliens are thought to be cooperating with the major world governments, especially the US government, at secret facilities such as Area 51 (where there is accommodation for thousands, despite the workers being flown in from Las Vegas every day) and the Dulce Base. In return, they expect to be allowed to establish colonies on Earth and settle among the general population once their human disguises are perfected, or for their existence to be gradually introduced and ultimately revealed to the rest of mankind. In short, they want to share our planet as they have no home of their own.

The existence on Earth of vampire creatures, wild animals, or even more civilized beings from other worlds is entirely possible, just as the presence of a monster in Scotland's Loch Ness cannot be entirely ruled out. However, until we have all been properly introduced, there will always be other, more likely explanations involving rare or unknown native Earth species to account for most of these alien sightings.

See also: *Area 51 p.308*

Present day
WAR IN SPACE

The Rendlesham Forest UFO was a casualty of a war between aliens

On the night of December 26–27th, 1980, US servicemen from a base at RAF Woodbridge in Rendlesham Forest, Suffolk, saw strange lights in the trees near the perimeter fence of the base. Given permission to investigate, they went outside and, according to some reports, saw what may have been a shiny, triangular, metallic object. A team from the base later found strange indentations in the ground and scorch marks on tree trunks, and they also recorded unusual radiation readings. That night there were more strange lights observed in the sky.

Many believe that Rendlesham was the site of a UFO crash similar to the Roswell/Aztec incident, only this one was recovered by the aliens themselves in a search-and-rescue operation, being the result of an alien war. The theory is that battle lines may occasionally take in our sector of space, or the war may actually be about us, with "friendly" aliens battling to protect us from domination and enslavement by more malevolent creatures.

Evidence to support the idea of an alien war is about as thin on the ground as debris from a wrecked flying saucer. Battles are not the easiest things to conduct in secret and surely at least one side in the alien war, those who wish to enslave us, would have no reason to fight covertly – they are far more likely to want us to know that they are out there. Too many eyes are trained on the sky today for opposing alien space fleets to manoeuvre around the Earth without being spotted.

See also: *The Roswell Incident p.302*

BIBLIOGRAPHY

AL-QAEDA

Aburish, Said K., *The House of Saud*, Bloomsbury, 1994

Armstrong, Karen, *Islam*, Weidenfeld & Nicholson, 2001

Bergen, Peter, *Holy War, Inc.*, Weidenfeld & Nicholson, 2001

Burke, Jason, *Al-Qaeda*, Penguin, 2003

Clarke, Richard A., *Against All Enemies*, Simon & Schuster, 2004

Gunaratna, Rohan, *Inside al-Qaeda*, Hurst, 2002

Jacquard, Roland, *In the Name of Osama*, Duke University Press, 2002

Meyssan, Thierry, *L'effroyable imposture*, Editions Carnot, 2002

Reeve, Simon, *The New Jackals*, André Deutsch, 1999

Unger, Craig, *House of Bush, House of Saud*, Scribner, 2004

ASSASSINATIONS

Bowden, Mark, *Killing Pablo*, Penguin Books, 1992

Brier, Bob, *The Murder of Tutankhamen: A True Story*, Berkley Publishing Group, 1999

Coleman, Ray, *Lennon: The Definitive Biography*, MacMillan, 2000

de Witte, Ludo, translated by Ann Wright and Renée Fenby, *The Assassination of Lumumba*, Verso, 2002

Donald, David Herbert, *Lincoln*, Pocket Books, 1996

Garrow, David, *The FBI and Martin Luther King Jr.*, Penguin Books, 1981

Guevara, Che, *The Bolivian Diaries*, Pathfinder Books, 1994

Haley, Alex, *The Autobiography of Malcolm X*, Penguin, 2004

Halperin, Ian, and Max Wallace, *Who Killed Kurt Cobain?*, Citadel Press, 1999

Hibbert, Christopher, *The House of Medici: Its Rise and Fall*, Morrow-Quill, 1980

Katz, Robert, *Days of Wrath: The Ordeal of Aldo Moro*, Doubleday, 1980

King, Greg and Penny Wilson, *Fate of the Romanovs*, John Wiley, 2003

Levine, Isaac Don, *The Mind of an Assassin*, New American Library/Signet Books, 1960

Levy, Bernard Henri, *Who Killed Daniel Pearl?*, Melville House Publishing, 2003

Montefiore, Simon Sebag, *Stalin: The Court of the Red Tsar*, Knopf, 2004

Morris, Edmund, *Dutch*, HarperCollins, 2000

Nicholl, Charles, *The Reckoning: The Murder of Christopher Marlowe*, Harcourt, 1994

Sadat, Anwar, *In search of Identity*, HarperCollins, 1979

Cook, Judith, *Who Killed Hilda Murrell?*, NEL, 1985

Shirer, William L., *The Rise and Fall of the Third Reich*, Arrow, 1991

Stich, Rodney, *Defrauding America*, Diablo Western Press, 1998

Thompson, E.A, *A History of Attila and the Huns*, Oxford University Press, 1948

Trachtman, Paul, *The Old West: The Gunfighters*, Time Life Books, 1974

Vellenga, Dirk and Mick Farren, *Elvis and the Colonel*, Delacourt, 1988

Webb, Gary, *Dark Alliance: The CIA, the Contras, and the Crack Cocaine Explosion*, Seven Stories Press, 1999

DISINFORMATION

Dorril, Stephen, *MI6: Fifty Years of Special Operations*, HarperCollins, 2000

Hennessy, Peter, *The Secret State: Whitehall and the Cold War*, Allen Lane, 2002

Hollingsworth, Mark and Nick Fielding, *Defending the Realm: Inside MI5 and the War on Terrorism*, André Deutsch, 1999

Pilger, John, *Heroes*, Vintage, 1986

Stormer, John, *None Dare Call it Treason*, Buccanneer Books, 1990

Thomas, Kenn (ed.), *Popular Paranoia: A Steamshovel Press Anthology*, Steamshovel Press, 2002

GLOBAL CONSPIRACIES

Brackett, D.W., *Holy Terror—Armageddon in Tokyo*, Weatherhill Inc., 1996

Curran, James, *Media and Power*, Routledge, 2002

Elliott, A. Larry and Richard J. Schroth, *How Companies Lie*, Nicholas Brealey Publishing, 2002

Fox, Loren, *Enron*, John Wiley & Sons, 2004

Gott, Richard, *In the Shadow of the Liberator*, Verso, 2000

Harding, Luke, *The Liar: Fall of Jonathan Aitken*, Fourth Estate,1999

Kogut, Bruce, *The Global Internet Economy*, MIT Press, 2004

Laqueur, Walter, *The New Terrorism*, Weidenfield & Nicholson, 2001

Leeson, Nick, *Rogue Trader*, Time Warner, 1997

McLuhan, Marshall, *Understanding Media*, MIT Press, 1994

Mylroie, Laura, *War Against America*, Diana Pub. Co., 2004

Nye, Joseph S., *The Paradox of American Power*, OUP, 2002

INTELLIGENCE

Bailey, Brad, and Bob Darden, *Mad Man in Waco: The Complete Story of the Davidian Cult, David Koresh and the*

Waco Massacre, WRS Publishers, 1993

Blum, William, *The Rogue State*, Zed Books, 2001

Bock, Alan W., *Ambush at Ruby Ridge: How Government Agents Set Randy Weaver Up and Took His Family Down*, Dickens Press, 1995

Bowart, W.H., *Operation Mind Control: Our Secret Government's War Against Its Own People*, Dell, 1978

Boyle, Andrew, *Climate of Treason,* Coronet, 1987

Bernstein, Carl, and Bob Woodward, *All The President's Men*, Pocket Books, 1994

Foot, Paul, *Who Framed Colin Wallace?*, Macmillan, 1990

Hersh, Seymour M., The Coming Wars, *The New Yorker* 2005-01-24 and 31

Hougan, Jim, *Secret Agenda*, Random House, 1984

Langguth, A.J., *Hidden Terrors,* Random House, 1979

Marks, John, *The Search for the Manchurian Candidate*, Times Books, 1979

McMoneagle, Joseph, *Mind Trek*, Hampton Roads Publishing, 1993

Michel, Lou, and Dan Herbeck, *American Terrorist*, HarperCollins, 2001

Morris, Roger, *Partners in Power*, Henry Holt & Co, 1996

Morton, Andrew, *Monica's Story*, St. Martin's Press, 1999

Philby, Kim, *My Silent War*, Ballantine Books, 1983

Picknett, Lynn, and Clive Prince, *The Stargate Conspiracy: The Truth About Extraterrestrial Life and the Mysteries of Ancient Egypt*, Berkley, 2001

Reich, Wilhelm, *The Function of the Orgasm*, Farrar, Straus and Giroux, 1986; *The Mass Psychology of Facism*, Farrar, Straus and Giroux, 1980

Serrano, Richard A., *One of Ours: Timothy McVeigh and the Oklahoma Bombing*, W.W.Norton & Co, 1998

Sterling, Claire, *Thieves World*, Simon & Schuster, 1994

Summers, Anthony, *Official and Confidential: The Secret Life of J. Edgar Hoover*, Putnam Publishing Group, 1993

Vidal, Gore, The McVeigh Conspiracy, *Vanity Fair* September 2001

Wright, Peter, *Spycatcher*, Doubleday, 1988

KEY FIGURES

Chomsky, Noam, *Manufacturing Consent—The Political Economy of the Mass Media*, Seven Stories Press, 2001

Dale Scott, Peter, *The Assassinations: Dallas and Beyond* Penguin, 1978

Kaplan, Fred, *Gore Vidal*, Bloomsbury, 1999

Keel, John, *The Mothman Prophecies,* New English Library, 2002

Keith, Jim, and Kenn Thomas, *Octopus: Secret Government and the Death of Danny Casolaro,* Feral House, 2003

Mailer, Norman, *Harlot's Ghost*, Random House, 1991 *Oswald's Tale*, Little Brown, 1995

Michell, John, *Eccentric Lives & Peculiar Notions*, Cardinal,1984

Moore, Michael, *Stupid White Men*, Penguin, 2001

Pipes, Daniel, *Conspiracy: How the Paranoid Style Flourishes and Where It Comes From*, Touchstone, 1999

Posner, Gerald, *Case Closed: Lee Harvey Oswald and the Assassination of JFK,* Doubleday, 1994; *Why America Slept: The Failure to Prevent 9/11*, Harvest, 2003

Quigley, Carroll, *Tragedy and Hope,* GSG & Associates Inc., 1995

Ronson, Jon, *Them: Adventures with Extremists*, 2001; *The Men Who Stare at Goats,* Macmillan, 2005

Skolnick, Sherman, *The Secret History of Airplane Sabotage*, 1973

Stich, Rodney, *Unfriendly Skies*, Diablo Western Press, 1968; *Defrauding America*, Diablo Western Press, 1995

Sterling, Claire, *The Terror Network,* Henry Holt & Co, 1981

Sterling, Rob, *50 Reasons Not to Vote for Bush*, Feral House, 2004

Thornley, Kerry, *The Idle Warriors*, Atlantic, 1991

Webster, Nesta, *Secret Societies and Subversive Movements*, R.A. Kessinger Publishing Co., 2003

Weisberg, Harold, *Whitewash: The Report on the Warren Report,* (self-published) 1984

MEDICAL CONSPIRACIES

Harris, Robert and Jeremy Paxman, *A Higher Form of Killing: The Secret Story of Gas and Germ Warfare*, Chatto & Windus, 1982

Hooper, Edward, *The River: A Journey back to the Source of HIV & AIDS*, Allen Lane, 1999

Horton, Richard, *MMR Science & Fiction: Exploring the Vaccine Crisis*, Granta, 2004

Reilly, Philip R., *The Surgical Solution: A History of Involuntary Sterilization in the United States*, Johns Hopkins University Press, 1996

MILITARY CONSPIRACIES

Bischof, Gunter, and Stephen Ambrose, *Eisenhower and the German POWs: Facts Against Falsehood*, Louisiana State University Press 1992

Brackman, Roman, *Secret File of Joseph Stalin*: *A Hidden Life,* Frank Cass, 2001

Gehlen, Reinhard, *The Gehlen Memoirs*, Collins, 1972

Hinsley, F.H., *British Intelligence in the Second World War*, Vol. 2, HMSO, 1981

Kilzer, Louis, *Hitler's Traitor: Martin Bormann and the Defeat of the Reich*, Presidio Press, 2000

Laurens, Anne, *The Lindemans Affair*, Allan Wingate, 1971

Moise, Edwin, *Tonkin Gulf and the Escalation of the Vietnam War*, University of North Carolina Press, 1996

Plaster, John, *SOG: The Secret Wars of America's Commandos in Vietnam*, Simon & Schuster, 1997

Sanders, James, *The Downing of TWA Flight 800*, Zebra Books, 1997

Seagrave, Sterling, and Peggy Seagrave, *Gold Warriors: America's Secret Recovery of Yamashita's Gold*, Verso, 2003

Thomas, Hugh, *SS-1: The Unlikely Death of Heinrich Himmler*, Fourth Estate, 2001

Wilcox, Robert, *Japan's Secret War*, William Morrow, 1985

Winterbotham, F.W., *The Ultra Secret*, Weidenfield & Nicholson, 1974

RELIGIOUS CONSPIRACIES

Baigent, Michael, and Richard Leigh *The Dead Sea Scrolls Deception*, Arrow, 2001

Brown, Dan, *The Da Vinci Code*, Corgi, 2004

Cusack, M.F., *The Black Pope* (1896), R.A. Kessinger Publishing Co., 2003

Decamp, John, *The Franklin Cover-up: Child Abuse, Satanism and Murder in Nebraska*, AWT, 1996

Drosnin, Michael, *The Bible Code*, Weidenfeld & Nicholson, 1997

Gardner, Laurence, *Genesis of the Grail Kings*, Element Books, 2000

Lacoutre, Jean, *Jesuits: A Multi-Biography*, Counterpoint, 1995

Lambert, Malcolm, *The Cathars*, Blackwell, 1998

Manhattan, Avro, *The Vatican in World Politics; Vatican Imperialism in the 20th Century*, CA Watts & Co. Ltd, 1949

Marrs, Jim, *Rule By Secrecy*, HarperCollins, 2002

Schonfield, Hugh J. *The Passover Plot*, Element, 1995

Wilson, Ian, *The Blood and the Shroud: New Evidence That the World's Most Sacred Relic Is Real*, Pocket Books, 1999

Winder, Robert, "The Final Prophecies," *New Statesman*, May 2002

ROYAL CONSPIRACIES

Andersen, Christopher, *The Day Diana Died*, Blake, 1999

Burrell, Paul, *A Royal Duty*, Signet, 2004

Clarke, William, *The Lost Fortune of the Tsars*, St Martin's Press, 1996

Cornwell, Patricia, *Portrait of a Killer: Jack the Ripper Case Closed*, Little, Brown, 2002

De Marigny, Alfred, and Mickey Herskowitz, *A Conspiracy of Crowns*, Bantam, 1990

Harrison, Michael, *Clarence: The life of HRH the Duke of Clarence and Avondale, 1864–1892*, W.H. Allen, 1972

Icke, David, *The Biggest Secret: The Book That Will Change The World*, Bridge of Love Publications, 1999

Knight, Stephen, *Jack the Ripper: The Final Solution*, Harrap, 1976

Penrose, Barrie, and Simon Freeman, *Conspiracy of Silence*, Grafton Books, 1986

Spiering, Frank, *Prince Jack*, Doubleday, 1978

SECRET SOCIETIES

Allen, Gary and Larry Abraham, *None Dare Call it Conspiracy*, Buccaneer, 1976

Barrett, David V., *Secret Societies*, Blandford, 1999

Booth, Martin, *The Dragon Syndicates*, Doubleday, 1999

Elliot, Paul, *Warrior Cults*, Blandford, 1995

Ray, James Earl, *Who Killed Martin Luther King Jr?: The True Story by the Alleged Assassin*, Marlowe & Company, 1997

Sifakis, Carl, *The Mafia Encyclopedia*, Facts on File, 1981

UFOs

Brookesmith, Peter, *The Government Files*, Blandford, 1996

Delgado, Pat and Colin Andrews, *Circular Evidence*, Bloomsbury, 1989

Evans, Hilary, *From Other Worlds*, Carlton Books, 1998

Friedman, Stanton T., *Top Secret/Majic*, Michael O'Mara Books, 1997

Matthews, Tim, *UFO Revelation*, Blandford, 1999

Randles, Jenny, *The Complete Book of Aliens and Abductions*, Piatkus, 1999

Sturrock, Peter A., *The UFO Enigma*, Warner Books, 1999

Tuckett, Kate, *The A-Z of Conspiracy Theories*, Summersdale, 1998

INDEX

Figures in italics indicate illustrations

9/11 14, 15, *19*, 24-7, *25*, 76

A

Abdul Aziz, King of Saudi Arabia 106
Abu Ghraib 172, 235
Afghanistan
  attacks on forces in 29
  drug trade 14
  Russian invasion of 12, 18
  US bombing of al-Qaeda training
    camps 22, 23
  US and UKL involvement in war 225-
    6
  US-led invasion of 14, 15, *15*
  war for oil 234
Agca, Mehmet Ali 180
Agent Orange 193, 208, 226-7
AIDS 200-201, *200*
Aitken, Jonathan 128
Ajaj, Ahmed 13
Al-Fayed, Dodi 112, 267, *267*, 273
Al-Fayed, Mohammed 120-21, 273-4
al-Qaeda 77
  9/11 attacks 24-5, 76
  attacks on forces in Afghanistan and
    Iraq 29
  Bali bombing 28
  Bin Laden 13-14
  and Bush family 27
  in Iraq during first Gulf War 20
  Madrid mobs 28-9
  origins 12-13
  Saudi terrorist attacks 21-2
  splintering of 14
  and *USS Cole* 23
  and the West 14-15
Alex Brown, Inc. 26-7
Alexander the Great 34, 264, *266*
aliens 296-9
  abduction of humans 310-11
  Anunnaki 300
  Area 51 308-9, *308*
  Bermuda triangle 300
  chupacabra 311
  crop circles 309
  Dulce base 307
  on Earth 309
  Foo Fighters 300-301
  Monolith 308-9, *308*
  Moon landing 305
  Nazi flying discs 301-2, *301*
  war in space 311

Allende, Salvador 30-31, 60-61, 74,
  120
American Indian Movement (AIM) 152
Ames, Aldrich 163
Ansar al-Islam 29
anthrax 96, *197*, 198
Anti-Defamation League 249-50
anti-Semitism 11, 178, 248-51
Antipater 264
Anunnaki 300
Arafat, Yassar 262-3, *263*
Arbusto Energy 27
Area 51 297, 308-9, *308*
Aristotle 264, *266*
Armstrong, Neil 305
Arrow Airways DC8 crash 156
Asahara, Shoko 232, *233*, 276, 277,
  278
Assassinations Records Review Board
  9
Atahualpa 38-9
Atta, Mohammed 15, *19*, 24, 25
Attila the Hun 35
Aum Shinrikyo/Aleph 96, 232-3, *233*,
  276, *276*, 277, 295
Aznar, ex-Prime Minister 28
Azzam, Dr Abdullah 12, 18

B

Baarma, Sami 27
Baigent, Michael 9
Baker, James 27
Bali bombing (2002) 28
Bank of England 246
al-Banna, Hasan 12, 18
Barbie, Klaus 230
Barings Bank 94, 126
Barrientos, President René 57, 58
Bashir, General 20
Bath, James 27
Batista, Fulgencio 57
Bavarian Illuminati 10, 41, 174, 278,
  284, 285-7
Bay of Pigs Invasion of Cuba 55, 57,
  68, 116
BCCI (Bank of Commerce and Credit
  International) 27, 124-5
Beatles 183
Beck, General Ludwig 48
Begin, Menachem 66
Bell, Art 93
Beria, Lavrenty 50, 51
Bermuda Triangle 300
Berners-Lee, Timothy 89, *89*
Bernhard, Prince, of the Netherlands
  109, 266

Bhutto, Benazir 69
Bhutto, Zulfiqar Ali 69
Bible Code, The 236, 258-9
Bigley, Kenneth 78-9, *79*
Bilderberg Group 108-9, *109*, 112, 279
Billy the Kid 41
Bin Laden, Mahrous 17
Bin Laden, Sheikh Mohammed bin Oud
  17
Bin Laden, Osama 11-14, *14*, 17-25,
  21, 29, 66, 77, 124, 125
Bin Laden, Salem 17, 27
Bin Laden, Shafiq 27
Bin Laden family 16-17, 27, 121
biochemical weapons 96-7, *97*, 128,
  194-5, 197-8, *197*, 208
Birch, John 85
black helicopters 209, 230-31
Black Panther Party 59-60, 75
"Black" Pope 236, 261-2
Blair, Tony 15, 77, 78, 130, 169, 170-
  71
Blavatsky, Helena 289-90, *289*
Bletchley Park 207
Blunt, Anthony 138, 139, 147, 271
Bohemian Club 289
Bolshevik world order 101-2
Bonds, Ron 189
Boorda, Admiral Jeremy 74
Booth, John Wilkes 31-2, 39, 40
Borgia family 37, 38
Bormann, Martin 206, 216-17, *216*
Branch Davidians 160-62, *161*
Brandt, Daniel 187
Braun, Wernher von 301, *301*
Bre-X scandal 127-8
Bremer, Arthur Herman 32
Brighton bombing (1984) 64
British Broadcasting Corporation
  (BBC) 77, 81, 83, 84-5
British Medical Association 193
Brookhaven National Lab 125-6
Brown, Dan: *The Da Vinci Code* 9, 236,
  238, *238*, 247
Bruni, Georgina 296, 297, 298
Brussell, Mae 93, 177, 181-3
Brzezinski, Zbigniew 19, 113
Bull, Gerald 159
Burgess, Guy 138, 139
Bush, George H.W. 27, 65, 118, 137,
  168
Bush, George W. 15, 24, 27, 65, 86,
  95, 99, 100, 106, 124, 131, *137*,
  167, 168, 171, 206, *209*
Bush, Jeb 168
Bush, Neil 65

ADVENTUROUS
WATERCOLOURS

Jenny Wheatley
and Robin Capon

BATSFORD

Long awaited and, as ever, for Lottie

www.jennywheatley.co.uk

First published in the United Kingdom in 2011 by
Batsford
10 Southcombe Street
London W14 0RA
An imprint of Anova Books Company Ltd

ISBN-13: 9781906388744

A CIP catalogue record for this book is available
from the British Library.

10 9 8 7 6 5 4 3 2 1

Repro by Rival Colour Ltd, UK
Printed by 1010 Printing international Ltd, China

This book can be ordered direct from the publisher
at the website: www.anovabooks.com, or try your
local bookshop.

Page 1
Lucca
water-based media on paper
61 x 68.5 cm (24 x 37 in)

CONTENTS

Introduction

Painting has been an important part of my life since childhood. Both of my parents were involved in the printing and advertising business, and my grandmother was one of the first students to study at Camberwell School of Art. Also, my mother was an enthusiastic amateur artist: art materials, paintings and other visual stimuli were always around and available when I was young. My family has strong connections with the theatre and the film industry, and I would often be taken to see shows in London. Talk was often about the arts.

As my love of the theatre grew, so did my fascination with stage set design and the way that scenery flats are used to create the illusion of space and depth. These qualities, together with my subsequent study of printmaking techniques, which essentially are based on building with layers of colour, have greatly influenced the way I like to paint.

For me, painting soon became a need; certainly now it is not just a job, but an entire way of life. I have been fortunate in that, since leaving art college, I have been able to pursue a career as a professional artist – and in fact even more fortunate in that I have always been able to do this by following my own inclinations and inspiration, unaffected by the fashions of the art market. In my view, to paint well, you must paint with integrity, and be true to yourself. All artists have a different view of the world and this should be reflected in the way that they paint, showing a personal insight into the subject matter combined with aspects that reveal something about themselves.

Although I would describe myself as a figurative artist, I never feel that the purpose of painting is simply to capture a faithful representation of a subject. I want each painting to maintain a connection with reality, but equally I think that it should be an expression of my particular response to a subject – what I feel is important about it and preferably something that adds to the experience of what I have seen. Also, I am a firm believer in having a clear objective for each painting and keeping to that. I often think of other ideas for the same subject, and if so I save those for new paintings. Consequently, I might paint the same subject twenty or thirty times.

I travel a good deal and paint and collect a lot of reference material on location. On site I usually start with drawings, to get to know the subject. In these, and perhaps also in paintings, written notes and photographs, I will begin to explore more specific, personal ideas that I often re-examine and develop further in the studio. However, the studio paintings are never just better, more resolved versions of the location work – they are quite separate entities.

I paint in watercolour, mixed media, oils and acrylics, always choosing the medium that I feel is most appropriate for the idea I want to express and the marks that are relevant in that instance. That is an important point to bear in mind, because although this is a book about the way I use watercolour – and I love working in watercolour – I would not choose to torture the medium just because I like using it, when oil or acrylic would do a better job. Once you have discovered the possibilities of every medium, you can choose the best one for the work in hand, and as a result really enjoy it in its own right.

My work is often characterized by strongly coloured pattern, while testing the accepted notion of perspective and space. I enjoy playing with the effects of recession and illusion, focus and ambiguity. For me, the success of a painting depends on a number of factors. It has to work pictorially, as a three-dimensional image on a two-dimensional surface; as an effective design within the format chosen; and in terms of its use of colour,

The artist
Jenny Wheatley in her studio.

Tropical Intention
watercolour
61 x 84 cm (24 x 33 in)
I travel a good deal, and paint and collect a lot of reference material on location. This painting was inspired by my travels in the South Pacific. Typically, it involves a variety of techniques, including the use of an airbrush for the grid system of the birdcage.

texture and other formal qualities.

I am not a purist: my work in watercolour does not follow the conventional approach. I often combine watercolour with other media, including collage. Despite what is generally written about watercolour and the common assumption that it must be used in a certain way – developing the painting with sequential colour washes and working from light to dark, it is in fact an extraordinarily versatile medium, allowing tremendous individuality in technique and result. Now, with a knowledge and understanding of the accepted practices, I feel able to play with the 'rules' and make the medium work very much in the way that I require, exploiting its versatility to the full.

This book has given me the opportunity to appraise and analyse my working methods, and to put into words my thoughts and feelings about painting and about my watercolour technique in particular. In explaining the way I work, rather than presenting it as a model to copy, I hope instead it will encourage you to be adventurous with watercolour. I hope it will help you to find an approach that encourages you to be true to yourself and paint with feeling and resolve.

Old Havana
watercolour
40.5 x 51 cm (16 x 20 in)
Among the many decisions I make prior to painting, the size and shape of the work are always important factors. In this painting I wanted the image to be very much related to the edges of the paper and to convey a slightly ethereal quality.

1 MARKS AND MEDIA

Watercolour is known for its delicacy and transparency. Many artists like to exploit the fluid nature of the medium and the fact that, because the paint is transparent, it allows the white, reflective surface of the paper to shine through the colours, giving them a distinctive luminous quality. Although this makes watercolour the perfect medium for capturing subtleties in light and colour, particularly in landscape painting, it does mean that artists have to be more inventive when it comes to expressing forms and textures. Being essentially a 'flat' medium, it presents more challenges in finding ways to convey depth and different surface effects.

Texture is an important feature in much of my work. I might want to suggest the sense of decay and history in the façade of a building, for example, or to include particular surface textures and effects. To add the illusion of texture, or indeed to actually create a slight texture within the paint surface, I use different mark-making techniques – perhaps working with a brush, or spattering, dribbling or using similarly expressive ways of applying paint. However, while emphatic brushmarks are useful in this respect, they must always be considered in relation to the success of a painting as a whole: technique must not be allowed to take over or become contrived.

Telephone Exchange
water-based media on paper
99 x 94 cm (39 x 37 in)
As here, thoughtful, specific types of marks can infer particular surface characteristics and details without having to labour the point and include all the intricacy. In this painting I haven't put in all the stonework detail – there are just enough brushmarks to convey the style and features of the building, leaving the viewer the opportunity to have their own input as well.

Expressive marks

The way that marks are used in a painting has a significant influence on the way the work is perceived and interpreted. To achieve the impact you have in mind, the mark-making must suit the subject matter and what it is that you want to say about it. These two contrasting paintings illustrate this point.

I always have very clear intentions for a painting and know how I aim to achieve them. In *Ramatuelle*, the aim was to convey the hot, sultry atmosphere of the scene: I wanted to create the feeling of the heat beating down from a heavy sky, pressing down on the buildings and landscape below. It would have been easy to leave the sky as a smooth blue wash, but this would have diminished its impact. Instead, I wanted it to look oppressive and have its own interest. To achieve that effect, I initially painted the sky with a colour very similar to the one used for the hillside, and then I worked over that with thicker, opaque paint and more obvious brushmarks. Similarly, in the foreground area, there is a lot of overpainting with quite decorative textural marks, which help convey a sense of place without getting involved in all the detail.

Ramatuelle
watercolour
26.5 x 30.5 cm (10½ x 12 in)
Particularly in the foreground of this painting, I used quite decorative, textural, overpainted marks to convey a sense of place without getting involved in unnecessary detail.

In contrast, the marks used in *Up the Garden Path* are more decorative and, in a sense, more arbitrary and whimsical. They dance around the painting, moving the interest from one area to another. Much of my work is influenced by my love of traditional set designs for the theatre, and particularly the way that sets are constructed with a sequence of painted screens, or scenery flats, to create the illusion of three-dimensional space – which I characterize as 'layers of space'. This is the way that I develop my paintings, building one layer over another. Thus, the top layer – the one that people see – is not something that has been placed as an entity in its own right; rather, it has a history, it has evolved and has been influenced by the stages that preceded it. This is what I love most about painting – the process, the journey and the passage of time between identifying a subject and its emergence on the paper surface.

I think this is where inexperienced artists sometimes fail – they think only of the top layer (the way they want the completed painting to look), without considering how they are going to reach that conclusion and the importance of the stages leading up to it. The success, excitement, interest and impact of the final layer depend largely on what happens underneath. Every mark, like every experience in life, has one or more consequences; sometimes it is the dismantling and reconstruction of a painting, reviewing subject and intent, which will lead to a successful finished work.

Up the Garden Path
watercolour
81 x 63.5 cm (32 x 25 in)
This subject inspired a much freer approach, so that the mark-making is more arbitrary and whimsical, constantly moving the interest from one area to another.

Mark-making techniques

As with so many aspects of painting, the effectiveness of mark-making techniques depends on experience and the ability to make the right choices regarding the materials and the way they are used. Three factors are always influential: the type of paper; the choice of brush and brush techniques; and the consistency of the paint – whether it is thick, dryish colour perhaps, or very wet and fluid. For example, if you take a lightly loaded bristle brush and drag it across a textured sheet of white paper, the paint will just catch the raised areas of the surface, leaving the hollows untouched, so creating a broken-colour, speckled effect – ideal for suggesting dappled light, the reflected light on

In the Red
water-based media on paper
53 x 61 cm (21 x 24 in)
For the soft, slightly diffused effects in this painting, much of the colour was applied wet into wet.

the surface of water, and so on. But with smoother paper and a softer brush generously laden with wash, the effect is quite different: this will give an even colour flow. However, once that has dried, you could again work over it with drier, dragged paint and, as appropriate, continue to develop other mark-making techniques and effects. Everything depends on your skill in recognizing what is required and making the necessary choices regarding materials and techniques.

I often paint on a wet surface. As in *In the Red* (opposite), I start by drawing on the paper to give me the amount of information I need, which usually means quite a detailed drawing for the more architectural subjects. Then I stretch the paper, if necessary, and apply the first colour wash while the paper is still wet. When a wash is applied to wet paper, the moisture limits the spread of the wash to a large extent, resulting in a soft-edged effect. On the other hand, if you apply a wash to dry paper, there is more scope for the colour to run and perhaps suffuse other colours, creating accidental effects.

When I stretch paper, I like to soak it thoroughly, perhaps for fifteen minutes, depending on the weight (thickness) of the paper. I want it saturated, so that every fibre is totally wet and has expanded. Then I tape the paper to a board and begin painting. I leave the tape in place until the painting is finished. This ensures that it always dries flat. If the tape is removed before the painting is finished, the paper is likely to buckle. With the heavier rag papers, I often work on them without stretching them, because I do not want to lose the beautiful heavy deckle of the outer edges, which I think is an essential quality of these papers.

Villa Navillus at Night
water-based media on paper
91 x 61 cm (35¾ x 24 in)
I often start a painting by wetting the paper with clean water. Here, the paper was only lightly wetted, which allowed me more control with the marks, and I was then able to slowly define shapes as the paper dried. Incidentally, in this painting, I have also used quite a lot of silver and gold pigments.

In order to make my images look simple and spontaneous it is vital that I have a clear plan right from the outset, and then all the mark-making will lead to this objective.

Freedom and control

In my view, successful paintings rely on achieving the right balance between working freely, intuitively and expressively, and maintaining a fair degree of control. I do not find the two approaches to be contrary to each other.

While empathy for the subject is vital – it creates the inspiration and starting point – it is never a matter of just putting something down on paper and seeing what happens. I like to start with observation and analysis: thinking about the subject, what I feel about it, and how best to approach the painting. I keep those thoughts and ideas very much in mind as I am painting. The final marks might look direct and spontaneous – I hope they do – but actually they result from careful planning. I always start with a master plan, although this may be adjusted to some extent to meet the needs of the painting as it develops.

Turkish Cup
watercolour
20.5 x 25.5 cm (8 x 10 in)
This painting includes surprises and visual tricks. I like the way that some decorative elements almost disappear into the background, while others emerge from it.

Exploiting watercolour's strengths

Books and courses often give the impression that there is a certain methodology for watercolour painting – an established process to follow, and rules and limits within which to work. It can be helpful, perhaps, to start by learning the conventional approach to watercolour painting, but in fact the medium is surprisingly versatile and offers immense scope for individual, creative work.

I have always painted in watercolour; it is one of several media that I regularly use. I like the challenge and potential of working with a variety of media, particularly watercolour, acrylics and oils. For me, a special attraction of watercolour is the rich, luminous colour quality that can be achieved: the way that superimposed colours glow through each other, enhanced and reflected from the white surface of the paper beneath. Also, I enjoy exploiting the contrasts that are possible between, for example, flat passages of colour and other areas in which there is an illusion of depth and space, as in a theatrical context, or opaque colour and colour that is reminiscent of stained glass. There is lots of scope to work in an original way and create exciting results.

Sometimes I paint in pure watercolour, but often I combine watercolour with other compatible water-based media, usually white gouache. Many of my paintings are a mixture of watercolour, pigment and gouache, but I might go further and introduce collage and other materials if I think the painting needs this. My watercolours are a combination of purchased paints in tube and pan form, and paints that I have made myself.

Essentially, when I buy pans and tubes, I am looking for certain colours. The other main consideration is the speed with which the colour is released and therefore picked up on the brush. Taking these factors into account, I know from my experience with a wide variety of watercolours

Yialia in Springtime
watercolour
28 x 35.5 cm (11 x 14 in)
I really enjoy paintings like this, in which there is no obvious subject matter and therefore the marks and spaces are all the more significant.

from different manufacturers that with some brands the tube colours work best, while with others my preference is for pan colours. Factors such as staining power and colour quality can vary considerably from one brand to another. Viridian, for example, is sometimes gritty, or it can be perfectly smooth. Manufacturers' charts offer useful information, but by far the best way to find out the strengths and weaknesses of a particular colour is to use it and see how it responds.

The colours you choose can have a profound influence on the outcome of a painting. So, don't be afraid to experiment with new colours and, if necessary, adjust your colour palette. Why not start by choosing the colours that make you tingle? As long as the selection covers the full range of primary colours and their warmer and cooler, more transparent and opaque natures, you can't go far wrong. If they are colours that excite you, you will probably be looking to find them in the subjects that you paint anyway.

As I have said, I also make my own watercolour paints, using raw pigments, gum arabic, glycerine and ox gall. I mix the ground pigment with some gum arabic, which acts as a binder, and then I add a little glycerine to improve solubility and prevent the paint cracking, plus a touch of ox gall to increase the fluidity of the paint. By varying the way the pigment is ground and the ratio of the ingredients, I have the freedom to make the paint thin or thick, coarse or fine, depending on what I need. Sometimes I also work directly on watercolour paper with gum arabic and dry pigment.

Paper

For the same reasons, I think it is a good idea to experiment with different watercolour papers now and again, rather than stick to a few favourites. I really enjoy going to paper manufacturers to see what is available, or sending for samples and trying them out. I use both manufactured and handmade papers, including stocks of paper that I have bought from paper mills which have closed down, and papers that I have had specially made for me. Naturally, all my papers are of archival quality and, as explained on page 13, I always stretch the paper.

Not all watercolour paper is white. There are also tinted papers – for example, the de Nîmes paper, from Two Rivers Mill is available in green, cream, sand, oatmeal and grey. These papers are ideal for subjects in which you want to exploit an underlying tonal or atmospheric quality. Additionally, papers can vary in the degree of surface or internal sizing used and, of course, in their surface texture. Hot-pressed (HP) paper is smooth; Not paper (cold-pressed paper) is a good, general-purpose paper with a medium texture; and Rough paper, as the name implies, has a noticeable texture (and, being more robust, suits techniques such as dry-brushing and lifting out). The experience of using different types of paper will enable you to judge which surface will be best for a subject and the effects you have in mind.

Brushes

Brushes, of course, play the most important part in mark-making. Each type of brush has particular qualities and scope for creating different textures and wash effects, and once again it is a matter of making suitable choices and applying the particular techniques in order to achieve the result you want. Sable hair brushes are often recommended for watercolour painting, but don't feel obliged to use these, and certainly don't overlook the potential of other types. Nylon brushes, for example, are firmer and consequently give a more textural brushstroke, while bristle brushes (normally used for acrylic or oil painting) are ideal for stippled, broken colour or similar effects. Again, my advice is to experiment!

Maltese Mansion
water-based media on paper
68.5 x 74 cm (27 x 29 in)
To some extent, this was a milestone painting for me. I had always been loath to paint without direct reference to subject matter, but it was not possible to paint this subject on site, and so I had to wait until I was back in the UK and then rely on my memory and written notes.

I use a wide variety of brushes, including riggers, large mops, sables and nylon/ sable mix brushes, as well as different sizes and shapes – rounds, flats, filberts and so on. Certainly with the mops and sables, I want a brush that has a good paint-holding capacity and will 'point' well when needed. However, I avoid using good-quality sable brushes for any work involving the direct use of gum arabic, as it is very difficult to get the brushes totally clean afterwards. Similarly, it is best to choose old brushes for applying masking fluid – although this is not something that I ever use.

The importance of mark-making

Maltese Mansion (page 17) is a good example of a painting in which the mark-making plays a crucial role. Here, the techniques include stencilling – using stencils that I made specially – as well as lifting out, rubbing and using resists over the initial colour-wash effects. Interestingly, this proved to be a very important painting in my career: it was the first time that I produced a painting away from the actual subject. I had always been very reluctant to work in this way before, but for this subject there was no alternative, as it was physically impossible to work on site, plus of course it was a night scene! So, I had to wait until I returned to the UK and my studio, and then work from memory and my written notes. However, my mental image of the building was very strong, as it seemed to take on the most bizarre persona at night, and consequently I knew exactly what I wanted to say about it and how I wanted to say it.

Sequential colour washes

The basic watercolour technique is the colour wash, of which there are three main types: the flat wash, graded wash, and variegated wash. The flat wash is ideal for covering large areas, such as part of the background, with a fairly even colour. For this, use a big brush loaded with plenty of colour. Success with a graded wash depends on progressively weakening the colour by adding more water as you work across an area – so creating a gradual transition from dark to light. In a variegated wash, one colour is allowed to run into another, wet into wet. A point to remember with all washes is that colours dry lighter than they look when first applied. Also, the character of a wash is influenced by factors such as whether it is applied to a wet or dry surface, as well as the type of paper and brush used, and the strength and particular characteristics of the chosen colour.

I usually work with a sequence of washes, often ten or more, building up from the general to the specific. I might leave some areas with relatively little paint on, while developing others in a much bolder and more textural way – it depends on the subject matter and my intentions for the painting. I add more graphic, defined and decorative marks over the much softer washes, but equally I might decide to work back into the surface, destroying what is there and repainting it. Whatever the process, I keep the

Watercolour paintboxes
Dry pigments
Mixing colours
I quite often make my own watercolours by putting gum arabic in a plastic container and adding water and the necessary amount of pigment, depending on the strength of colour I want.

whole painting in mind, rather than concentrating on a particular area. Often, the finished painting will involve a lot of layers and adjustments. As I add the washes, I try to make each one the strength that I will finally require, so that my layering is more about colour changes and variations than about tentative starts.

Moathouse demonstrates this approach. I started with a sequence of washes to develop a specific 'history' in the underpainting, knowing what I would eventually paint over this, and considering the whole image as I worked. For me, the colours are quite neutral, deliberately chosen to suit the nature of the subject and the way it seemed to rise out of the moat. Note how, in the sky area, although the final colour is opaque, it nevertheless shows the influence of the olive and ginger colours used in the underpainting.

Moathouse
watercolour
74 x 94 cm (29 x 37 in)
Before beginning any painting, it is essential to consider what you want to achieve and how you are going to do it. This painting is a good example: I began with a series of washes for the underpainting, envisaging how these would help and influence what I planned to paint on top to complete the work.

Witch's House, Keswick
location sketches, pencil

Whites, details and alterations

Traditionally, white and highlights in watercolour painting are achieved by making use of the white paper – either by leaving areas unpainted or by protecting them with masking fluid. Depending on the style of the painting and the subject matter, you can also use white paint or ink; sometimes lifting out colour or scratching through the surface colour with a sharp knife or point is effective. I never use masking fluid: it is a well-known fact that I hate it! I occasionally leave white areas of paper or use white gouache if I want a really strong white mark. Mostly, however, what seems white in my paintings is actually colour. It is colour that appears white in relation to stronger tones or colours that I have used around it.

Detail is always an important consideration, but often the key decisions will relate to what to leave out, rather than what to put in. Many of the buildings that interest me have complex façades and, whether I am working on the spot or in the studio, I will normally make a very careful, intricate drawing. This gives me plenty of information, confidence, and an underlying 'scaffolding' for the painting. It allows me to concentrate on the painting process, to paint with a sense of freedom, because I know I can get back to the drawing if I need to. For example, I might dribble or splash the paint, using it quite freely, but then redraw things or paint around edges where I feel it is necessary to add more definition or detail.

If I am tempted to get too specific and consequently want to simplify an area, I put a colour wash over the whole area or use spattering or a similar technique, destroying some parts and bringing others back into focus. The wash acts rather like a glaze or scumble in oil painting – it half-blocks out the image, leaving a sort of ghostly effect and with it the opportunity to redefine certain aspects and drastically simplify others.

Nothing is assured in painting and, despite the planning and skill and of the artist, sometimes things can go seriously wrong; the only sensible solution is to start something else. You could start on a new sheet of paper, but I quite often like to work over the image I have already attempted, even though I intend painting an entirely different subject. As I have mentioned, I like the idea of a history of colours, marks and effects beneath the surface of a painting, because it adds greatly to the character and impact of the finished work.

Witch's House, Keswick
watercolour
66 x 107 cm (26 x 42 in)
This was very much a tonal subject and although you get the impression of quite a lot of light, the colour washes were much darker than you might think. My aim was to increase the colour content while retaining the tonal contrast.

Birdcage Table
water-based media on paper
48 x 48 cm (19 x 19 in)
If I overwork a painting, I put it in a bath to remove most of the colour.
Some of the 'history' of the painting will remain, which can make an interesting
foundation for a new subject. **Birdcage Table** started out as a Venetian façade!

Having started a painting, that history is always there and provides an interesting basis from which to work. Most will be overpainted, but is still subject to the influence of what was there before, while some areas of the new painting can be enhanced and energized by incorporating parts of the old. I have made paintings that have started as a still life, for example, and finished as a Venetian façade and vice versa – see *Birdcage Table* (page 21). Alternatively, if you find your painting is getting heavy and overworked, don't be afraid to put it in a bath of water to soak off most of the colour. This will leave you with a 'ghost' version of the original painting to develop as you wish.

Some subjects need far more initial planning, thought and analysis than others. The famous Deux Garçons Café in Aix-en-Provence, for example, was a place that I knew very well, and I kept thinking that it should somehow make an interesting painting. But, while there are some subjects that attract my attention and I immediately know what I want to say about them, with this one I had to think for a very long time before I was confident about the way I thought it would work. In *Deux Garçons*, you can see that I wanted to capture the look, light and atmosphere of the subject. Incidentally, you will also notice that it appears to include white sunshades and awnings. However, as explained on page 20, much of this 'white' is in fact soft colour washes.

Deux Garçons
watercolour
25.5 x 30.5 cm (10 x 12 in)
White is always a relative colour in my paintings – it is seldom a true white, but appears so in relation to the colours around it. As in this painting, my 'whites' are usually slightly tinted colour washes.

Combining watercolour with other media

While every medium has its own strengths and characteristics, inevitably it also has certain limitations. With watercolour, although there is plenty of scope to work both in a controlled way, with carefully organized elements and details, as well as in a much freer style, working with subtle colour and an emphasis on mood and suggestion, there are limits to the development of strong surface qualities and textures. For this reason, I often work with watercolour and mixed media, exploiting effects achieved with gouache (body colour: see below), collage, or acrylic paint or dry pigment with gum arabic.

This is not to say that, when using watercolour alone, effects are always limited to the flat wash. There are several techniques, such as lifting out, dry-brushing and scratching through, which will add greater variety and interest to a painted surface. But more dramatic, expressive and colourful textural effects are possible by involving other media.

Pastels, coloured pencils and inks can similarly add to the scope of watercolour and mixed-media work. The inclusion of different media should depend on the specific objectives in a painting. For mixed-media paintings to work successfully, there must be a sensitive and technical affinity between the different media. It is also important to be aware of the quality and conservation issues relating to each medium.

The House of Sticks
water-based media on paper
60 x 101.5 cm (23½ x 40 in)
I sometimes use white gouache mixed with watercolour to make opaque colours or, as in the sky area here, I might scumble gouache over a watercolour wash to create a certain mood or texture.

Acrylic and gouache paint

Acrylic paint, being another water-soluble medium, is perfectly compatible with watercolour; the essential difference is that, once dry, acrylic is water-resistant. Another useful quality is that although most acrylic paint is opaque, when it is applied as a glaze or wash it usually becomes semi-transparent. These are interesting qualities to exploit and combine with watercolour techniques, plus, of course, acrylics can be used to add texture.

I often paint in acrylics, but generally for large-scale works in their own right, painted on canvas, rather than for mixed-media paintings. However, as in *Japanese Interior* here, I occasionally include some acrylic in a watercolour painting when using certain techniques. For example, I might use acrylic to block out an area that I want to modify in some way, and then repaint it in watercolour, or use it as the basis for developing resist textures. Acrylic dries with a slightly shiny surface which, as I have mentioned, is water-resistant. Thus, when watercolour is applied over this, it tends to separate and create a broken-colour, textural effect.

Gouache is made in a similar way to watercolour, except that a white pigment or filler – precipitated chalk or *blanc fixe* – is added to the colour pigment and gum binder. This gives the paint more substance or 'body', and hence the term 'body colour' is often applied to this medium. Gouache colours tend to be more vibrant than their watercolour equivalents, and most are opaque. The paint remains soluble when dry and therefore care must be taken when re-wetting or repainting an area. Mainly because of possible issues with the stability and permanency of gouache, I only use designers' white gouache. Sometimes I use this for specific whites and highlights or, more often, I mix it with watercolour when I need colours that have more body or opacity. In *The House of Sticks* (opposite) for example, to create the slightly smoky, atmospheric feeling across the sky area, I used a scumbling technique with colour mixed from gouache and watercolour.

In conjunction with a mixed-media approach, I often use certain related techniques to help develop interesting and appropriate surface effects. These include lifting out colour in various ways and scratching into and through the surface colour. In

Japanese Interior
water-based media on paper
89 x 61 cm (35 x 24 in)
This painting includes acrylics in places, but these areas were mostly overpainted with watercolour to produce interesting textures.

Talking at Table, as you can see, the area under the table is much lighter in colour than the table, which was achieved by lifting out some of the colour wash that had been applied initially. I liked the idea of having a sort of glow of colour, rather than just leaving it white, which would have looked very stark.

If you are working with good-quality paper and paint, you can lift out colour at any stage in the painting, whether it is wet or dry. There are several methods that I use: a damp sponge; a dry brush (wet the area first, if the paint has already dried); or I cover a wet area of paint with some tissue paper, gently press this in place using a small rubber roller, and then lift off the tissue paper, which will have absorbed some of the colour.

I often use this techniques in a deliberate way to create surface interest – adding colour, lifting it out, adding more colour and lifting it out, and so on, as in *The House of Sticks* (page 24). There are several factors that influence the type of textures and effects with this process: the staining power of the colours used, the degree of absorbency and texture of the paper, and the pressure on the roller.

Alternatively, if you look at the top strip of background colour in *Talking at Table*, you will notice various lines and marks in a lighter colour than the background. These were scratched into the surface of the paint. For this effect I use colour that contains quite a lot of gum arabic and, while it is still wet, I scratch into the surface with the pointed handle end of a brush.

Talking at Table
watercolour
63.5 x 99 cm (25 x 39 in)
Sometimes the right effect is best achieved by removing paint rather than adding it. In this painting I have scratched lines into the top strip of the background colour and also lifted out colour from the bottom area, beneath the table.

Deux Garçons at Night
water-based media on paper
109 x 74 cm (43 x 29 in)
I like doing paintings of buildings at night. The character of the building is quite different from the way it appears in daytime, with contrasts and ambiguity between areas that almost disappear and those that begin to glow.

Adding collage

My use of collage is sometimes experimental, as in *Castles in the Sky*, which includes origami papers, bits of handmade paper and decorative papers; sometimes as a means towards finding the best composition for a painting; and, more generally, as a complementary and essential feature of the painting process. In *House of a Thousand Tiles* (opposite) for example, I worked with pieces of collage cut and torn from specially painted sheets of paper and card, for creating soft and hard edges of particular shapes within the design. Much of the collage was applied to previously painted areas and was then itself repainted, becoming an integral part of the work.

With collage, it is never just a matter of adding a sense of texture or variety by introducing it at one particular stage in a painting: it has to be considered with regard to the ongoing dialogue between painter and painting throughout the development of the work. If you want to emphasize something, bring it forward or create a certain texture, you might add collage. But later, if you find this looks too dominant, you might decide to paint over it, or a part of it. It is a continuous process of assessing and reassessing.

The advantage of using collage to help work out a strong, interesting composition for a painting is that it prevents you from getting involved with unnecessary detail. Also, with torn and cut paper shapes, it is easier to move them around and try different compositional ideas. With collage, you are forced to concentrate much more on the relationship of shapes and the important structural elements of the design. For fixing the shapes in place I use PVA adhesive, which is pH-neutral (acid-free), as are all the types of paper that I use. Sometimes, if I intend to develop a resist-textured effect with colour washes, I apply the PVA over the top surface of the collage as well.

Castles in the Sky
collage and watercolour
18 x 12.5 cm (7 x 5 in)
Here, my use of collage was more experimental and included origami and handmade papers, as well as sequins and scraps of Victorian paper.

Windows on the World
collage and watercolour
18 x 12.5 cm (7 x 5 in)
Working with collage is a good
compositional device, because
it prevents you getting too
involved with detail and
enables you to concentrate on
the essential structural
elements of a painting.

House of a Thousand Tiles
water-based media on paper and collage
109 x 94 cm (43 x 37 in)
I view this type of mixed-media work as a
dialogue between paint and collage. As here, I
often use shapes cut and torn from sheets of
paper that I have painted and prepared myself.

Visual interest

The success and impact of a painting depend on it making a strong visual statement. This is influenced by factors such as use of colour and other formal elements, as well as the design and overall sense of unity and coherence. Each of these factors must be carefully considered so that it achieves exactly the right significance in relation to the rest. Naturally, when using a variety of media, it is more difficult to create a painting that works effectively, although in my view, one rule that always contributes to success is to consider the subject and painting as a whole, and to maintain this approach throughout the development of the work. Keep in mind the qualities that are important about the subject, and your objectives for the painting.

However, there are no guarantees in painting: not every painting will be successful, and this is something that all artists have to accept, whether professional or amateur. We are learning all the time, and this is why I always recommend to students that they should never throw anything away, because there is always something to learn from a painting, no matter how disastrous it is. In fact, I would say that the more you struggle with a painting, the more you will learn from it. So, keep everything as a reference, as a reminder of different techniques, effects and things that worked, as well as what not to do!

Venetian Façade (page 32) results from a painting that I had finished, was very dissatisfied with and had consigned to a drawer, but which I eventually decided to look at again and then managed to create a much more successful version. The original painting was quite colourful and detailed – too much so; it didn't work. So I made it much simpler, building on its 'history' with unifying colour washes and dribbles of paint. This is another reason why I think you should never destroy paintings. Sometimes, with the passage of time and a fresh eye, you can see how to retrieve an idea and turn a failure into a success. Often, the reason that paintings fail is that they lack visual coherence – they are disjointed and so they need unifying in some way.

Venetian Madrigal
water-based media on paper
56 x 76 cm (22 x 30 in)
Here again, I am playing with ambiguity – the fact that the painting can look like a piece of tapestry, with some parts emerging and others less distinct.

Venetian Façade

water-based media on paper
58.5 x 71 cm (23 x 28 in)
This painting was originally very colourful and detailed, but for me it didn't work. When I reviewed it some time later, I felt that it could be more successful if I were to make it much simpler. This I did, with unifying washes and by taking out most of the detail.

Venetian Façade (detail)

Every mark in a painting plays its part, so you have to think very carefully about the marks you use. For the decorative marks that edge the colour and archway in Venetian Façade, as shown in this detail, I chose a particular round brush, put just the right amount of paint on one side of the brush, and used exactly the right degree of pressure.

2 ADVENTUROUS COLOUR

Colour is a vital concern and a powerful force in all my work. For me, it is the quality that has the most emotional impact in a painting and I like to exploit that potential. Often, my colours are high-key and perhaps seem to bear little connection to the actual subject matter. But in fact, I never invent colours. I arrive at a colour scheme through a process of observation and distillation – selecting and emphasizing the colours that will give me the mood and degree of colour saturation that I need for the painting, as well as reflecting the way I have responded to that subject at that particular moment.

Obviously, exciting colour alone is not enough to make paintings that are truly interesting and satisfying. Colour has to work in relation to other elements of a painting, especially composition, which in turn will rely on the choice of subject matter. I start with a subject that inspires me, and which I want to say something about, and the choice of colours will develop from that.

Gentlemen's View of Purgatory, Sicily
watercolour, body colour and pigment
84 x 51 cm (33 x 20 in)
Like the fauvist painters of the early 20th century, I am instinctively attracted to the high-key colour potential of a subject. Having found a subject that interests me, I develop the colour scheme through a process of observation and distillation.

Colour and interpretation

In painting, a personal approach is always important, and for me, colour usually plays the dominant role when I'm interpreting a subject. Naturally, to work successfully with colour, a detailed knowledge of the various processes and colour theories is required, as well as confidence in colour mixing. Essentially, the greater your experience in handling colour, the more ambitious and intuitive you can be in your working methods. Don't forget that there are rules, but once you are familiar with them and appreciate their effects, you should be able to manipulate them in a methodical manner in order to achieve your own ends.

To satisfy my interest in a subject and create work that truly reflects my thoughts and feelings, I very often produce a series of paintings of the same subject. Usually, I start by adopting a fairly realistic response to content and colour – at first I feel morally obligated to include things. But gradually, as I become more familiar and relaxed with a subject, I allow myself to be more selective and I begin to home in on the qualities and colours that I regard as the most significant. I gradually

Cocktail Party
watercolour, pigment and body colour
45.5 x 45.5 cm (18 x 18 in)
Colour and composition must be considered together. As here, I like to explore designs that test our accepted notion of perspective and space, and my choice and use of colour, texture and building up/ knocking back plays a key part in this.

Looking Towards the Mountains, Collioure
watercolour and body colour
38 x 53 cm (15 x 21 in)
I often paint the same subject again and again, gradually distilling the content
and colour until I have a result that satisfies me. Note that in this first painting of
the famous lighthouse at Collioure, I have worked in a fairly realistic way.

distil my thoughts, aims and responses, while ensuring that there is always a sufficient degree of
figurative content and that the painting is not merely decorative. So, while I am always asking
myself what elements I can simplify or eliminate, I still want to retain just enough to communicate
with the viewer.

My three paintings of Collioure – *Looking Towards the Mountains, Collioure* (above), *Collioure
Lighthouse and Boats* (page 38), and *Collioure Lighthouse and Boats 2* (page 39) – demonstrate this
approach. I have painted in Collioure many times over the past thirty years: it is a place that is very
close to my heart and, of course, it has been an inspirational location for artists since the Fauves,
Picasso, and the many other artists whom I greatly admire first painted there.

In my first painting, *Looking Towards the Mountains, Collioure*, you will see that I have worked
in a relatively tonal way, aiming to create a feeling of space by setting the lighthouse tower within
its environment. In fact, this was not how I initially perceived the painting – I had wanted to keep
to slightly tertiary, warm colours and not do too much overpainting. However, although the final
painting was quite realistic and therefore did not fully satisfy my intentions, it did make a good
starting point.

Collioure Lighthouse and Boats
watercolour
25.5 x 26.5 cm [10 x 10½ in]
For my second painting of this
subject, I chose a square format in
order to focus on the strong,
compositional elements of the
lighthouse itself. However, I felt
that the colour was still more
realistic than I wanted.

Collioure Lighthouse and Boats, my second painting, worked better in terms of composition and colour, although – perhaps because there were people watching me – I was still tempted to paint the sky blue and the sea a blue-green. But following this, in *Collioure Lighthouse and Boats 2*, through a process of further evaluation and distillation, I was able to achieve a result that was more true to myself – keeping the actual tonal balance the same, but now concentrating on the emotive pink tones in the subject. Interestingly, if you were to reduce both of the square-format paintings to a monochrome copy, you would see that the tonal values are very similar, although the last painting mainly involves opposite colours to those originally viewed, and everything is kept within a much closer colour-key palette.

Working at a location is always a valuable experience, but subsequently, with the knowledge and understanding you have gained, it can be a more liberating process to work away from the actual subject matter. However, eventually I find that I need to go back and reacquaint myself with a subject: I avoid becoming so removed that I lose the connection with the subject matter. Generally, my aim is for a memory, an evocative sense of a subject, rather than feeling that I must include things simply because they are there.

Collioure Lighthouse and Boats 2
watercolour
25.5 x 26.5 cm [10 x 10½ in]
There was an underlying pink tone to the sky and the sea, and in this third version of the subject, influenced by the fact that I was feeling hot after sitting there for a protracted period of time, I decided to focus on a hot range of colours to try to express this. With its more emotional response to colour, this painting worked much better than the earlier versions in my opinion, and was a truer reflection of what I wanted to achieve.

Colour, mood and impact

Our response to colour is subjective and individual. We see colours differently and this, together with our character, our painting skills and other factors, influences our interpretation of colour. In my view, this personal response to colour is something to exploit. For example, I have a strong inclination to use warm colours – especially reds and pinks – in my paintings, because in fact I often see those colours in the subjects I choose. It is not just that I like reds and pinks the most! I am sure that if we do not worry too much about conventions and the need to follow certain accepted practices, but instead are faithful to our own way of seeing and reacting to colour, this inevitably will lead to the most interesting and successful paintings. In my view, compromise in any form is the kiss of death to a painting.

Akamas, Cyprus
watercolour
35.5 x 53 cm (14 x 21 in)
For this late afternoon pastoral scene, I felt that a cool palette of blues and greens would work best. Where the subject stood against the shimmering sea, I also wanted the colours to be largely translucent and to appear almost like layers of stained glass.

Outcrop, Droushia, Cyprus
watercolour
33 x 51 cm (13 x 20 in)
In response to the hot, arid nature of this landscape subject, I worked with high-key colours – mainly reds, oranges and yellows. The light tones were created by lifting out colour – I rubbed back the wet paint with paper tissue or rag (for this technique, it is important to choose a robust and sympathetic paper to work on).

The first step is observation. Before attempting to interpret the distinctive quality and mood in a subject, it is always a good idea to spend some time just looking and assessing which colours are the most meaningful, the most vital to capture the effect you want. Try to do this without any preconceived ideas as to which colour something should be. Don't assume that the sky is blue, for instance. There might be an underlying warm tone that you want to emphasize to support the mood and interpretation you have in mind.

The Akamas Peninsula in Cyprus is another painting location that I have often visited during my career. *Akamas, Cyprus* (opposite) and *Outcrop, Droushia, Cyprus* (above) are two of my more recent paintings from this area, and they demonstrate contrasting colour and mood effects. I kept to a palette of blues and greens to capture the cool, late afternoon mood in *Akamas, Cyprus*. But for the stark, rocky landscape in *Outcrop, Droushia, Cyprus*, I wanted a much hotter and dustier feel, and so worked with reds, oranges and yellows. Incidentally, in both paintings I have included quite a lot of coloured charcoal drawing over the initial watercolour washes.

San Salute, Evening
watercolour
25.5 x 26.5 cm (10 x 10½ in)
For this version of San Salute, I have chosen a much warmer colour palette to capture the golden glow of the evening light, and have relied mostly on watercolours that offer a wide range of opacity, rather than using so much body colour.

San Salute, Morning
watercolour and body colour
25.5 x 26.5 cm (10 x 10½ in)
Although I often keep to a limited range of colours within a painting, there can be a surprising variety of subtle tonal variations within that range, mixed from a wide selection of colours – as here. To create the necessary brushmark effects in this painting, and the cool, ethereal quality, I have used quite a lot of body colour. I partially applied it while the painting surface was damp, to spread the colour and diffuse the light.

Colour palette

Some artists work from a very limited palette, perhaps using only the three primary colours. By mixing these together in different combinations and quantities, they expand their colour range. My approach is exactly the opposite. I prefer to have an extensive choice of colours available, maybe thirty or more. But I use these to mix a limited number of colours. For example, I might need a lot of close-toned, high-key reds, but to make these I will need to include a wide variety of other colours. Also, I often expand and change the colour washes that I am using by adding other colours to existing washes, thus keeping a continuity. This creates variety with harmony. See *San Salute, Morning* (above) and *San Salute, Evening* (above).

If I want a slightly more opaque colour or a special tint, I add a small amount of body colour (designers' white gouache) to the watercolour wash. I know there are some purists

Owlpen Manor
watercolour, body colour and pigment
45.5 x 58.5 (18 x 23 in)
To create the greatest impact when expressing what I feel is important about a subject, technique and colour must work in unison. Here, I liked the contrast between the colour and formality of the building and the surrounding landscape. I also enjoyed exploiting the ambiguity of space and working with various techniques.

who will shudder at the thought of adding body colour to watercolour, but my own view is that if it is used with integrity, then why not. And, if it was good enough for J. M. W. Turner, Thomas Girtin and Samuel Palmer, it is good enough for me!

Colour and technique

In addition to the relative tonal value of a colour and its extent and interaction within a painting as a whole, its effectiveness will be influenced by the technique or techniques used to apply it – whether, for example, it is applied as a gentle, flat wash or as a more lively broken, resist or textured colour. Also, watercolours vary in their transparency, opacity, granulation and staining power, and these are other factors that play a part in determining the impact of a colour.

In *Owlpen Manor* (below), for example, I have used a wide range of techniques to create

different effects with colour. Essentially, my aim was to link opposite (as found on the colour wheel) colours – the pinks and greens – by adding them to a common and existing mixture. I also wanted to create the impression of the building growing out of the landscape. For this, I used an overall orange/ pink underpainting, on top of which I developed the degree of luminosity that I wanted and a sense of ambiguity – so that you are not quite sure which things should be in front of which. The effect of 'layers of space' in a theatrical stage set has always been fascinating to me, and I often use layers of colour in my work to suggest space and depth.

In fact, although the greens are quite dark in places, they are still reasonably translucent. Another interesting point about this painting is that I have used pigment mixed with some very thick gum arabic in some areas, particularly in parts of the sky, the roof of the building, and the foreground. This created thicker, more opaque colour into which I was able to scratch, using the handle end of the brush, to arrive back at the underpainting and so create a shimmery effect. Such effects are not possible without careful planning: the underpainted colours that you want to reveal have to be sufficiently strong to carry the overpainting and to stand up to it once you work back in.

See also the details from various paintings, shown on page 45, which demonstrate other interesting colour effects.

Chapel by Night
watercolour and water-based media
53 x 63.5 cm (21 x 25 in)
This chapel was derelict at the time I painted it. Seen against the sea and in the moonlight it had a slightly sinister, eerie character, which I tried to emphasize with the use of splatters and very directional marks in the layering process.

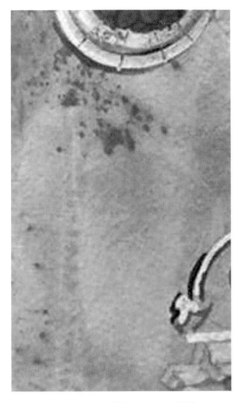

Venetian Madrigal (detail)
watercolour and pigment
The sequence of marks on the right-hand side was made with the flat of a brush, while on the extreme right there is a lot of rigger brushwork and varied layered colour. In other areas, particularly on the left, the texture of the paper was allowed to show through to enhance the broken-colour, textural effect.

Gentlemen's View of Purgatory, Sicily (detail)
watercolour, body colour and pigment
The textural colour effects shown here were made by spattering dry pigment on to a light coating of gum arabic, and by impressing pigment into the surface of the paper using a lino-printing roller. Also, I have exploited the 'cauliflower' effect that happens when wet colour is allowed to push its way into colour that is beginning to dry. These various effects combine to give a sense of the aged and weathered façade of this fascinating building.

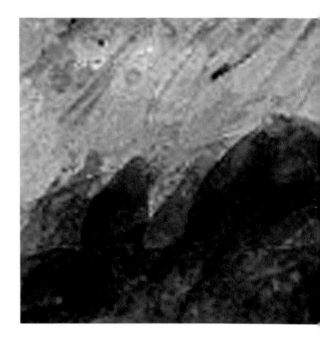

Owlpen Manor (detail)
watercolour, body colour and pigment
You can see, in the upper part of this detail, how I have scratched through the opaque top layer of colour to reveal the more luminous colour beneath. These marks give a contrasting effect to the layered brushmarks in the green area below, and their direction helps to attract the eye down the painting.

Onion Skin Exterior (detail)
watercolour and pigment
Here again there is a combination of drawn brushmarks, suggesting the detail on the shutters, with spattered colour and scratched-out marks.

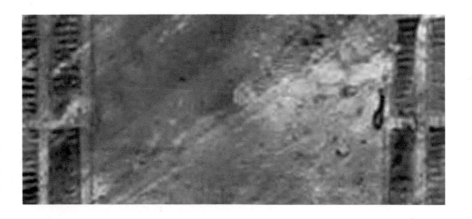

Contrast and harmony

> It would be very easy to lose my way if I did not have a clear approach in mind backed by the necessary knowledge. I always work with a firm idea of the result I want and the sequence of colours and techniques that I need to use to achieve it.

Essentially, success in capturing mood and creating impact in a painting depends on the specific choice of colours and how the different colour masses and intensities interact and work together across the picture. Usually, the selection of colours will relate to a warm or cool colour palette, to suit the mood and produce a sense of harmony in the work. But it will often also include the use of a complementary colour or a more dramatic tone here and there, to give one or two areas of contrast and focus. As in *Cave St Louis* (below) and *Mas Gouge* (opposite), this adds to the drama and impact of the painting.

Cave St Louis
watercolour
86 x 89 cm (34 x 35 in)
The formal architecture of this subject, a combination of buildings I saw in the South of France, demanded a much more graphic and controlled approach. Note how the green of the palm tree creates a useful contrast to the high-key colours of the buildings, and how the initial strong washes, with their soft colour transitions, make a distinct contrast to the hard edges of the detailed architectural overlays.

It is certainly worth studying colour theory, so that you can exploit the full potential of different colours. Each colour has particular attributes, and additionally, you need to know what happens when it is used in colour mixes or placed against other colours. With a good knowledge of colour theory, you can work confidently and quickly to develop the kind of effects you want, but with no understanding of colour theory, you will struggle to find solutions. I find it extremely useful to know how to tone down a particular colour, for example, how transparent or opaque it is going to be, or how I can achieve a certain optical effect with colour. This sort of knowledge is invaluable, and fundamental to sound working practice.

Mas Gouge

watercolour and body colour
38 x 53 cm (15 x 21 in)
One way to create a sense of colour harmony and unity in a painting is to start with an underpainting. Here I have used a varied red/orange colour as the starting point, allowing this to show through in places, especially in the sky area, so the viewer realizes that much of this area was once the same colour as the buildings that were later defined by the paint that edges up to it.

Colour layers

In most of my paintings I build up the colour and surface effects gradually, by applying a succession of subtle colour washes, perhaps as many as twenty, one over another. It is a way of working that has been influenced by my training and interest in various printmaking processes, with their concern for colour overlays and colour separation. Every painting is different, of course; there is no set method. But, having wetted the paper, I quite often start with pigment mixed with gum arabic to establish the basic colours, before building up the colour layers, which may involve various wash, resist, accidental and other techniques.

The process is very much one of building up and knocking back. Subsequently, I add more definition in parts and I may draw in quite firm shapes over the underlying vagueness, so creating an ambiguity about things coming and going.

Onion Skin Exterior (opposite) is a good example of my layering technique, and here the build-up of colours and effects particularly suited the character of the building, with its flaking plaster façade and obvious sense of history. Some of the colour layers were allowed to dry; some were worked wet into wet, or splattered. For others I used gum arabic, sometimes rubbing it away in order to partially lift out the colour beneath, and sometimes using the gum arabic as a resist.

In fact, you can use gum arabic in much the same way that some artists use masking fluid. And it is certainly my preference: I never use masking fluid. I dislike it for various reasons, but principally because it tends to stain the watercolour paper with a slight yellow tone, and with textured papers it can damage the surface. There are better ways to create whites in watercolour, I think!

Passage of Time
*watercolour and
water-based media
56 x 76 cm (22 x 30 in)
For this type of subject, I usually
start with some very careful
drawing. This gives me a sound
structure to get back to, if needed,
when I subsequently begin to
work much more freely.*

Onion Skin Exterior
*watercolour and pigment
74 x 84 cm (29 x 33 in)
This is very much a 'layered' painting, using a lot
of subtle colour washes and involving various
techniques, applied one over another. Equally,
the composition is important – here, based on a
near square within a near square and creating
mostly a flattened space, although with the hint
of the building on the far right and the roof
overhang adding some perspective.*

For *Passage of Time* (page 49), I started by defining the proportions and details of the building in a drawing. I was then able to work quite freely with splattering, textures and so on, because I knew I could revisit that foundation if necessary. I probably used twenty layers of colour. Many of these were very subtle and were made by applying a colour wash and then placing a sheet of absorbent paper over it to lift out some of the colour. Other colours were rag-rolled on or applied with different types of brushes. I defined the details by painting the area around them, rather than painting their actual shapes.

Experimenting with colour

Don't be afraid to be ambitious with colour and test out new ideas and techniques for using it. This is the best way to increase your confidence, experience and skill in handling colour. Also, remember that, while there is a lot of scope for creating interesting, powerful images with watercolour, the potential for expressive work in colour can be greatly enhanced by introducing other media and techniques. Watercolour will combine well with all types of drawing and water-based media, including acrylic paint, acrylic inks, collage and even certain printmaking techniques. Each medium has its own strengths and characteristics, which can be employed to fulfil specific objectives in a painting with regard to colour, texture, translucency, opacity and other qualities.

Making your own watercolours, by mixing pigment with gum arabic and glycerine, also adds to the variety of thickness and texture that can be achieved, rather than just relying on the consistency of ready-made traditional watercolours. These colours are technically the same as tube or pan colours, but have a slight rawness about them.

I often use a mixed-media approach and, as demonstrated in *Cannaregio* (page 52) and *Façade, Barcelona* (opposite), this can include painted and decorative types of paper and card applied as collage. Occasionally I use 'found' papers for collage, as with the angels included in *Façade, Barcelona*, but usually I prepare my own papers. I paint sheets of paper different colours, and then cut out the shapes I need and glue them on to the painting – and so build up various layers and contrasting colour effects. I ensure that any collage papers are completely colourfast before applying them to the painting surface. See also page 28.

If I want softer edges, I work with torn paper shapes, and even the directions and sides that the papers are torn on is important, as it will affect the visual outcome. The layers of collage create different surface and illusionistic qualities within the painting, with a play between parts that come forward and others that stay back. The whole process becomes a continual dialogue of advancing and receding surfaces.

On the right-hand side of *Cannaregio*, for example, I began by painting the whole area, including some of the sky, with the orange/ red colour, applied wet into wet. Over this, I built up parts of the façade with shapes cut from thick card, thus creating quite a three-dimensional effect. These areas were linked to the painted areas by splattering paint across them. A similar approach was used in *Façade, Barcelona*, in which the horizontal orange stripes were cut from thick card.

Sometimes it takes several attempts at a subject before you can clarify what it is that you want to say about it. And each painting might inspire further ideas, other ways of interpreting the subject. For example, I have painted the two buildings shown in *Cannaregio* many times, separately and together (in reality they are not actually situated side by side). But I reached a point where I needed to express the idea more three-dimensionally. There are some subjects that demand that sort of approach, I find. I often make written notes and statements about my subjects to keep myself focused as I produce each successive image. The success of the whole process relies on the ability to see, in your mind's eye, how to develop the painting.

Façade, Barcelona
watercolour, water-based media and collage
96.5 x 62 cm (38 x 24½ in)
When combining other materials and media with watercolour, it is important to make sure that they work as a sensitive and integral part of the painting. With collage, I sometimes partially paint over the paper or card shape, or splatter it with paint, to help link it to the rest of the painting.

Cannaregio
watercolour, water-based media
and collage
61 x 96.5 cm (24 x 38 in)
The impact of colour can be
influenced by surface qualities,
such as very textured paper or, as
here, a surface that has been
modified by gluing on shapes cut
from coloured paper and card. I
then painted over the new layers
to knock back some of the obvious
surface texture.

Interior Conversation
water-based media on paper
109 x 109 cm (43 x 43 in)
Sometimes I create different
textures by offsetting or
imprinting colour on a
previously painted area,
choosing the colour carefully
with regard to its staining or
non-staining quality. To make
the blue texture in this
painting, I rolled soft paper
soaked in colour over the
underlying colours.

Colour and texture

Although watercolour is essentially a
'flat' medium this does not mean that
you cannot involve a sense of texture
– whether this is implied or actual
texture. Mostly I create texture using
different painting techniques,
including lifting out colour, and I also
quite often use collage.

In addition to the emotive and expressive power of colour, the impact of a painting is also
influenced by its surface quality – the texture created by the paint and other materials
used and the way this adds interest, perhaps helps suggest and describe things, and
contributes to a certain mood and means of interpretation. So as well as making decisions
about colour, you must also think about whether that colour should look smooth or
textured in some way. And this often requires planning ahead, because you may need to
apply a particular sequence of colour washes and techniques to achieve the surface
quality you have in mind.

Applied and implied texture

Texture can be introduced in a physical form, as with collage or the impasto technique, or it can be implied, as with stippling, scumbling, dry-brushing and other brushwork techniques. I quite often use both approaches within the same painting, combining collage with different wash and mark-making techniques. For collage, I select appropriate papers from the wide-ranging stock of painted, textured, decorative, handmade, origami and other types of papers and card I have available, using cut or torn shapes glued in place with PVA adhesive – see page 28. In my painting here, while the collage adds colour, texture and decorative elements, equally it has been used in a deliberate way to build an effective composition.

The texture in my paintings often results from the fact that I like to work with many layers of colour, applied in different ways – wet on dry, wet into wet, and so on. Also, as well as adding colour, I might decide to destroy some of the surface colour to reveal something of the history of colours and effects beneath. As in *Interior Conversation* (opposite), particularly in the blue areas on the left-hand side, I sometimes work with tissue paper and a roller to 'lift' colour or add a coloured texture.

I describe how to lift out colour on page 50. But similarly, if absorbent tissue paper (or kitchen roll) is soaked in pigment and then applied to an area of a painting and lightly pressed in place – I use a small rubber roller for this – a certain amount of colour will be offset and so create a broken-colour, textural effect. Use dry paint if you want hard edges, but wet paint if you want a softer, more diffused textural quality.

In contrast, in *Birdcage Interior* (page 56), the paint surface is much smoother, which interestingly has resulted in a slightly disquieting effect. It is quite a tonal painting for me, but I wanted it to be fairly ambiguous and moody. I think the fact that I have used a lot of wet-into-wet washes and soft edges has given the painting its rather eerie quality. Again, it demonstrates the influence that texture can have on the impact of a painting and the fact that you always have to consider which approach will work best for your subject and intentions.

Experimenting with different texturing techniques is a good way to increase your knowledge and confidence in their use. For example, I have looked at all kinds of ways of dropping, throwing and applying paint on various surfaces – trying different heights and implements to see what marks are possible. And don't be afraid to capitalize on chance textures that may occur during the painting process, or to be innovative in your use of texture. You may feel that you don't want to jeopardize the success of a painting by taking risks – but if you don't take risks, how will you know what could be achieved?

In the Pink
collage and watercolour
18 x 12.5 cm (7 x 5 in)
Collage adds texture and can be painted over to complement the surrounding colours; it is also a useful means of adding structure to a composition.

Birdcage Interior
watercolour
74 x 99 cm (29 x 39 in)
The particular surface texture of a painting will play a key role in creating a mood for the work. Here I worked quite tonally and, combined with smooth washes of colour, this has given the painting a slightly ambiguous quality.

Difference of Opinion
watercolour
52 x 70 cm (20½ x 27½ in)
I like to test the boundaries of conventional design, yet find
ways of making it work – as in this painting, which was very
consciously based on a composition of two contrasting halves.

3 RHYTHM, PATTERN, DESIGN

We all make decisions concerning rhythm, pattern and design every
day. Essentially these are decisions about aesthetics, about the way
things look and are arranged – the relationship of shapes, colours
and textures and how these combine to create something that is
pleasing or displeasing in its design. So, we make judgements about
the clothes we are going to wear, the furnishings in our house, our
garden design, and so on.

A similar scenario applies to painting, but in painting these
qualities – rhythm, pattern and design – and the decisions we make
about them are all the more significant, because they are so
fundamental to the success of the work. A painting can have an
exciting concept and be technically very strong, showing much skill
and expression on the part of the artist, but unless the design is
sound, it loses impact.

There are various principles concerning design which are useful
to understand and follow – creating an asymmetrical composition
rather than an evenly balanced one for example, or using lead-ins
and focal points to add rhythm and flow to a design and so direct
attention around a painting in a certain way. However, as in all
aspects of painting having learned the 'rules', it is good to
experiment and find a way of adapting the conventions to arrive at
your own style of working.

Selection

A good design will hold the viewer's interest by involving a variety of elements while managing to organize these in such a way that the painting works as a coherent image.

Whatever the subject matter, in order to express it convincingly as a painting, there must be a certain degree of selection. The extent of that selection – what to include in the painting and what to leave out – will naturally depend on your response to the subject and consequently the qualities you feel are important about it and want to express. Moreover, decisions associated with selection run right through the painting process: with every brushstroke you have to ask yourself whether to accept it or reject it.

Bouquet
watercolour
48 x 48 cm (19 x 19 in)
I wanted this huge bouquet of artificial flowers to create an explosion from the centre outwards, but at the same time see if I could hold all of that together within a successful design.

On the Waterfront, Viareggio
watercolour
63.5 x 84 cm (25 x 33 in)
There is no specific focal point in this painting. My aim was to create a dialogue between the three palm trees and so encourage a constant flow of movement around the painting, but in the process allow the viewer to stop and take a closer look at the different areas.

What I usually find appealing about a subject is not so much the actual content – the fact that it is a fascinating building or a wonderful landscape, for example – although this is obviously an important factor. For me, what is more important is that the subject offers the potential to work with the formal qualities of painting – essentially composition, colour and texture. In a sense the subject matter is only a starting point, a vehicle for exploring ideas with paint, working within a certain format.

For instance, with *Difference of Opinion* (page 58), I did not start by thinking I must do a painting of a table and some flowers. The objective was more to do with the challenge of working with a certain format, playing with the figurative elements and 'rules' but still aiming to create a visually unified composition. With still life subjects, although I work from objects that I have collected and which are available in my studio, I never feel that I must paint something a particular size or colour, or in a particular place, just because that's how it is in reality. The key issue is not representation in terms of the subject matter, but the success and impact of the painting. I believe, more and more, that a painting must live its own life.

For me, it is very important to repaint the same subject again and again – not because I need to make more images of it, but in order to reach the most abbreviated conclusion. In each painting, I leave out or simplify more elements; I keep subtracting marks in each attempt, until it appears that one further subtraction might make the whole image fall apart.

Points of interest

In every design a key consideration is proportion – the relative scale and impact of one area to another and, of course, its place and importance within the whole. Here, most artists in the West are guided by their innate sense of proportion, which interestingly relates to a proportion found throughout nature (and which forms the basis of much of the work by scholars such as the Italian mathematician, Fibonacci), namely the Golden Section or Golden Mean.

This is a principle of proportion in which (for example, when applied to the basic division of a sheet of paper or the canvas) the ratio of the smaller area to the larger is the same as that of the larger to the whole. It is expressed approximately in numerical terms as a ratio of 5:8. It is found in almost all traditional figurative paintings, which tend to be so designed that the most important feature, essentially the focal point, is placed at a point equivalent to the Golden Section proportion – that is a division roughly two-thirds (or one-third) across the picture surface. Artists today often refer to this proportion/division as the 'rule of thirds'.

A successful design never looks imposed or contrived. As discussed on page 59, there are various theories and conventions that can help in creating a design that works successfully, particularly if these are used with some discretion and imagination. Generally, paintings that are full of detail and very busy all over lack the impact of those in which there are contrasts between quiet areas and areas of interest. Essentially, a good design will attract and hold the viewer's attention; it will help him or her discover the painting's meaning and individual qualities, but at the same time leave something to the imagination. Often, to fulfil these objectives, a design is developed around a particularly strong feature, focal point or centre of interest within a piece of work.

However, this approach isn't obligatory, and I frequently make paintings in which there is no specific focal point, as in *On the Waterfront, Viareggio* (page 61). You can also create rhythm and movement within a painting by repeating or echoing certain shapes and colours. Again, this attracts interest, so that the viewer is encouraged to look from one shape or colour to the next. *The Musicians* is a good example of this technique.

The Musicians
watercolour
53 x 71 cm (21 x 28 in)
Here again there is a lot of interest throughout the composition, with one shape played against another. This painting is also rich in narrative and symbolism – the creatures all stand for conversations I have heard or situations that I have experienced.

Planning and design

As I have said, the secret of a good design is that it doesn't look contrived. Sometimes you can find a subject where the composition works perfectly well as seen, and you can use that as the basis for the painting. On other occasions, you might want to place a greater emphasis on interpretation: consequently, in order to create more impact, you will select and reorganize from what you see. Whatever the approach, it is important to start with clear objectives for the design, even if these have to be modified later. To help with these decisions and explore alternatives, many artists like to start with a series of small, simple line drawings or thumbnail composition sketches.

I give a lot of thought to the design of my paintings: they are planned to a much greater extent than is revealed in the final work. But I don't necessarily feel bound by my initial decisions, for the design may have to change to suit the needs of the painting as it develops. Also, I have to admit that sometimes a design doesn't work and I have to start again, or I consider that it could work even better or in a different format, and so I make a second painting. Another factor to consider in relation to design is the viewpoint. *Tabletop I* and *Tabletop II* are a good demonstration of alternative viewpoints. In the first, the viewpoint is from above the table, whereas in the second I decided on a design that included the table legs and some of the space beneath it.

Tabletop I
water-based media on paper
48 x 61 cm (19 x 24 in)
The particular viewpoint chosen can add to the impact of a design. Sometimes it is interesting to make a series of paintings from different viewpoints, exploring different qualities within the subject and other design possibilities. Here, the viewpoint is from above the table.

Tabletop II
water-based media on paper
48 x 61 cm (19 x 24 in)
*I have chosen a lower viewpoint for this painting, although flattening the space somewhat (compare this with **Tabletop I**, above). Note the relationship of the principal shapes in this design, particularly the way that the triangular shape cuts in on the right.*

Passing the Time of Day
watercolour
81 x 84 cm (32 x 33 in)
A square format offers much potential for
interesting designs. Here, I have worked with a
sequence of squares within squares.

Design and impact

Design plays a vital part in how we 'read' a painting and respond to it, with the impact of the work largely determined by the way the subject matter is manipulated, as well as factors such as the shape and size of the final image. For example, I very often choose a square format, which, because of its symmetry, creates greater challenges in arriving at an effective design, although often with more interesting possibilities, I think. In *Passing the Time of Day* (page 65), for example, I have based the design on a number of squares within squares.

The link between interpretation and design is demonstrated in *The Tall Houses, Uzes* and *The Tall Houses, Uzes, Night*, which show two contrasting paintings of the same subject. I have made many drawings of those buildings on site, and they always seem very tall, because you can only view them from close quarters. However, I have emphasized their height by adding an extra storey or two to the house and also, in the night-time version, I have curved the main building slightly, to give it more character and create the feeling that it is looking down on us. The dark windows at the top could be interpreted as two eyes, lending a slightly eerie and otherworldly quality to the painting, which is much more interesting than a formal representation, I think.

As well as the impact created by its design, content and interpretation, a painting can have a physical impact by virtue of its scale. However, it does not follow that large paintings are necessarily more impressive. A small work will often have tremendous impact: it depends on the subject matter and means of expression. *Hidden in Barcelona* (opposite) is a very large painting for watercolour and mixed media, and I made it large because there was a lot to say about this extraordinary subject; also I wanted to create the sense of scale of the tall, towering building. Watercolour paintings don't have to be small and delicate!

The Tall Houses, Uzes
water-based media on paper
84 x 68.5 cm (33 x 27 in)
Inevitably, design and interpretation are closely linked. In this painting, I wanted to emphasize the height of the buildings, so have added a couple of extra storeys to the house to create the feeling that it is gazing benevolently on the viewer below.

The Tall Houses, Uzes, Night
water-based media on paper
99 x 68.5 cm (39 x 27 in)
I often feel that buildings have their
own character. I liked the way that
these tall houses seemed to lean
over slightly to look down on me.

Hidden in Barcelona
water-based media on paper
107 x 68.5 cm (42 x 27 in)
The actual size of a painting is another factor to consider in relation to its design and intention. This
was a large painting to suit the towering height and scale of this impressive building.

Indian Wedding
watercolour
99 x 63.5 cm (39 x 25 in)
Here, the impact relies both on
the design – the viewpoint,
placement and relationship of
the various objects – and on
the strong contrasts between
the glowing colour above and
the darker colours below.

Pictorial space

Paintings can be flat or essentially decorative, with no attempt at implied depth and space, or, between this and the other extreme, photo-realism, involve many variations in the way that they suggest pictorial space. The challenge for artists is in deciding to what extent they want to convey a sense of space, what form of space to convey, and how to convey it, given the limitations when using paint on a flat sheet of paper or canvas. As with composition, there are established techniques for creating pictorial space – in using perspective and changes of scale, for example, or working with tonal variations or warm/ cool colour relationships and different levels of colour saturation. Experience of those techniques can be useful, but here again, I think for more original and exciting paintings it is necessary to find other solutions.

I like the physical process of applying paint and in fact having some fun with this process to see what happens when different effects are tried out. I often test the accepted concepts about space and recession to see if I can make something work when, in theory, it should not work. For instance, although I know that, in reality, a certain object is much nearer than something else, I might make it part of the underpainting and paint other things around it. Consequently, physically, in the relative terms of the paint surface, it is more distant. But it can still look successful, in terms of pictorial space,

Mas Gouge
watercolour
30.5 x 48 cm (12 x 19 in)
When painting on site, my aim is to get to know the subject and the way it fits into its environment. I want to be familiar enough with the subject to be able to go back to the studio and start working in a more personal way.

because I will be considering it in relation to the whole picture area and the interaction of colours, tones and mark-making throughout. My influences and references come from the way that space is defined in a theatrical stage set, rather than from conventional perspectival space.

Before I paint something in the studio, I like to feel confident about the subject – to know how it works and how it fits into its environment, as well as what I want to do with it. To reach this understanding, I make small drawings on site or written notes to remind me of the different qualities and features about the subject that are important. Usually, to get to grips with a subject in this way, I also make paintings on site. *Mas Gouge* (opposite) is an example. These site paintings are often quite representational – analyses of the things before me, my way of learning what I want in the long term and how that something works in reality, before I start playing with it in the studio.

I like to look at a subject quite objectively to begin with, so it follows that there will be a more conventional approach to pictorial space. Subsequently, I am able to use this information in the studio to paint in a much freer and imaginative way. *Lacock* (above) and *La Noria* (right) are examples of paintings that were made after having built up this sort of knowledge. I have focused on mood and atmosphere in the first painting, while in the second I wanted to include more decorative elements.

Pattern and design

It was Ivon Hitchens who said that: 'All great paintings are decorative, but no great paintings are purely decorative,' and I think that is such a true statement. Decorative elements are often important in realizing an idea with maximum effect, as in *Indian Table* (above). But, in my view, to help arrest the viewer's attention and add to the interest and impact, a painting also needs other layers of understanding and more graphic elements. The table in *Indian Table* is one that I have in my studio: it features in a lot of my paintings. In this example, the design plays with contrasts between decorative elements, flattened space and three-dimensional objects, and more graphic, two-dimensional forms. There are hints towards perspective, but only hints!

Indian Table
watercolour
81 x 84 cm (32 x 33 in)
As in this design, I like to explore different possibilities with pattern and space, so that some elements are flattened and others are not.

Similarly, in *Place aux Herbes* (below), which was painted on the spot, I wanted to test less conventional ideas about pattern, space and design to see what would happen. I love the negative spaces that are found with certain tree shapes – interesting pattern effects – and what I wanted to try in this painting was to work in negative, by painting the patterns but leaving as spaces the parts that were much further forward. *Looking Down to St Siffret* (page 74) was also painted directly from the subject – I was aiming to get to know it. Again, it includes a balance between elements that are graphic and representational, and mark-making that is decorative and interpretative. I think that if you find a subject interesting and want to paint it, then you should want to add something to it – something that demonstrates your own particular understanding and response to that subject.

Place aux Herbes
watercolour
30.5 x 35.5 cm (12 x 14 in)
Painted on the spot, this was really
an experiment in handling space
in different ways.

Looking Down to St Siffret

watercolour

33 x 48 cm (13 x 19 in)

This is another example of sitting in front of a subject and trying to get to know it through making a painting. Certain subjects are intriguing and you feel you must paint them. And in fact, this is the only way to see if they are going to make an interesting painting or not!

4 IDEAS AND REFERENCE MATERIAL

Everyone has their own views about painting and their own methods of working, and obviously this is how it should be. For example, some artists never work on location, directly from a subject, but prefer to stay in the studio and paint from photographs or entirely from imagination. While that approach may be successful for them, I know I could not consider painting something unless I had already made drawings, paintings, written notes, or some kind of colour reference on the spot.

I like to start with that direct reaction to a subject and the opportunity to get to know and understand it – my response in terms of how I feel about the subject and how it appears to me. Later, in the studio, with the passage of time and in this more controlled environment, there is the chance to distil ideas and explore the potential of the subject further. For me, there is little point in painting something just because it is an interesting view, building, still life or whatever. There has to be something that I feel I must say about the subject, something that I want to add.

Resplendent Decay
watercolour
107 x 111.5 cm (42 x 44 in)
With reference to drawings made on site, combined with my notes and memories of the subject, this studio painting is a good example of the way that I often work.

Inspiration

I always start by working from direct observation of the subject that interests me – usually by making a sequence of drawings and paintings to help me get to know and understand the subject. Then, from this understanding, I am able to work in a more personal way and explore different possibilities.

I paint a wide range of subjects – landscapes, buildings, still lifes, interiors and so on. However, it is never simply the appearance or content that inspires me to paint something, rather it is the scope it offers me to explore ideas relating to pictorial space and surface qualities. As I have mentioned, I am fascinated by stage set design, with its flat 'layers of space', and this, combined with my training in printmaking, which similarly is concerned with building up effects in layers, has greatly influenced the way that I approach painting. Also – no doubt from my interest in the theatre – I like the sense of illusion that I can create in a painting.

My continued motivation to paint comes partly from the fact that I find painting very rewarding (if at times quite frustrating!), although I think I remain motivated principally because there are always more questions than answers. Were I ever to find all the answers, there would be nothing left to do. In every single painting, I learn from either its good points or its bad points, and this is what helps my work to keep evolving. Keep searching for those answers – that would be my advice to any artist!

Subject appeal

Very often, the quality that first attracts me to a subject will be the colour, or perhaps more accurately the colour relationships and their potential to make an exciting painting. Colour is always important in my work: it will create a certain mood and add to the impact and interpretation I want. However, generally it is the narrative element of a painting that concerns me most, and I use colour and paint handling to help me achieve my particular ideas in that respect.

Tenements, Havana
watercolour
48 x 58.5 cm (19 x 23 in)
This was painted on the spot and, as you can see, I am immediately thinking of the formalities of the painting and the information I need, so that I know what to do in the studio as a result.

Like every aspect of painting, the way we see and interpret colour is a very personal thing. Mostly, I work with a heightened sense of colour. On location, I look at the colours in front of me and aim to accentuate their relationship to each other, noting how they work in context with their surroundings and my feeling about them. In *Tenements, Havana*, for example, I think the colours are very true to the actual scene, although other people would say that in fact the building was not as yellow as that or the sky as blue.

I painted this subject on site and although it looks to be an incredibly tranquil, ordered environment it was in fact a very dirty, noisy and smelly residential square. In order to achieve the viewpoint I wanted, I had to sit wedged between an overspilling refuse tip and a row of idling dumper trucks! I was surrounded by rubbish, but I deliberately chose that viewpoint because I wanted to directly face the building so that the façade would form a slightly off-centre rectangle within the main rectangle of the painting. For me, this is the aim of location work – to get down the necessary information and start thinking about the formalities of the painting, so that I know what I can do in the studio as a result.

Look-Out
watercolour
56 x 76 cm (22 x 30 in)
These buildings were not neighbours in reality: I have brought them together from different reference sources. One of the great things about painting is that you can select and change elements from those observed in the actual subject, and so create something more original and exciting – a summation of your reaction to a certain place and time.

Ideas and locations

Travel is vital to the way I like to work. It is very easy to become complacent in one's familiar surroundings – to take the familiar for granted, or simply stop seeing it with fresh eyes. I am always interested in new places and finding new ideas, and naturally I choose locations that are likely to offer the subjects that will most inspire me. I went to Cuba, for example, because I knew the architecture would be exciting, with lots of decorative, rococo-style and slightly decaying buildings. In the event, it was much more exciting than I had expected. Together with the colours and textures that I had hoped to see, there were influences from the different cultures that had occupied the island. The houses bore the scars of much neglect and seemed almost derelict at first glance. But slowly, the evidence of occupation by many families grew as I noticed the presence of livestock on the balconies, washing propped precariously on ancient verandas and people languidly watching the world pass by through broken shutters or gloomy doorways. The use of sheets of corrugated boarding to patch up walls and openings, along with old crates and any refuse that could serve to mend the crumbling structures, added to the more recent history of the buildings and the continued and good-humoured occupation by the current residents.

Ideally, it helps if you can stay at a location for a reasonable length of time, so that you can really get to know it. I usually have a map and I start by doing a lot of walking, standing and staring. I quite methodically look at each street in turn, at different times of the day, noting the influence of light and any other circumstances that might add to the interest of potential subjects. Then I make lots of drawings or watercolours or, if time is limited, make sketches with added written notes. These are my references for further work later in the studio: they enable me to move on to a more personal response to the subject. I never regard the reference material simply as something to help me create a more resolved version of the idea. Rather, it is an evolving process, and I am always looking for new directions in which to explore each idea.

Back Streets, Uzes
watercolour
30.5 x 25.5 cm (12 x 10 in)
An exploratory painting – I was just trying to find out what happened with the light, shadows and colours, and how these influenced the character of the buildings.

Blue Door, Blue Sky
watercolour
35.5 x 38 cm (14 x 15 in)
I made this painting for a film commissioned for the Royal Watercolour Society archives. I liked the geometry of the subject – the squares and rectangles – and also the quality of light. For me, the essence of the painting was about the two blues of the door and the sky, which were very similar in tone, and the actual space they occupied.

Agriculture in Akamatra
watercolour
25.5 x 28 cm (10 x 11 in)
This is one of a series of small paintings I made on the Greek island of Ikaria. The subject invited a quick, decorative mark-making response, I felt, particularly because of the rapidly moving sun and the lyrical subject matter.

Similarly, I have no set way of painting on site: I adapt the approach to suit my response to a subject. Compare the different techniques used in *Blue Door, Blue Sky* (opposite), *Back Street, Uzes* (opposite, below), and *Agriculture in Akamatra* (below), for example. Of these, *Blue Door, Blue Sky* was the most representational and controlled in technique. I liked the sense of geometry in this subject – the relationship of squares and rectangles – and I wanted to capture that quality quite accurately. For *Back Street, Uzes*, which I viewed as an exploratory painting, I used a looser technique. This subject was full of colour, light and shadow, and I wanted to find out how those elements would work as a painting. And, different again, *Agriculture in Akamatra* inspired a quick, spontaneous approach with quite decorative mark-making, hopefully reflecting the hot and steamy environment in which I was painting.

Statement of intent

Always start with a clear idea about what it is that you want to achieve in a painting. When a painting fails, very often it is because there were too many differing or conflicting objectives included at once or, alternatively, there was no good reason to paint it all! I cannot see how it is possible paint anything unless you know why you are painting it and what your aims are. It is only with that vision for the painting that you can judge which medium will work best and similarly address all the other considerations that play a part in creating the right effects and impact.

For me, it is crucial to have a clear objective for a painting; equally, I think it is crucial to stick to that objective. Of course, other ideas occur to me while I am painting, perhaps better ideas, but were I to keep adjusting the original idea it would never succeed; it would lose the sense of purpose and clarity that I started with. If a painting does not work, I consider why it has not worked and, bearing that in mind and adopting a different approach as necessary, I make a new painting. On location and in the studio I often paint the same subject a number of times, and although the paintings might look quite similar, they will each be considering something different about the subject matter – they will have different intentions.

Starting from observation

The most interesting paintings are original and individual; they show something different and personal about the subject matter. However, in my view, it isn't possible to explore and express a subject in this way without having first got to know and understand it. I find the best way to achieve this is to start by working from observation.

In whatever direction you want to develop your painting – perhaps by simplifying shapes to create an almost abstract result – the process will only succeed if you work from a position of knowledge about the subject matter. Without it, how can you decide how you want the painting to work: how can you decide what to leave out or exaggerate? For example, having started with observation and the sort of information and quite realistic approach shown in the drawing on page 84 and *Sharing Gossip* (opposite), I am then able to move on to a more poetic, imaginative response, as in *Building, Havana* (above), which is the same building.

Building, Havana
watercolour
48 x 38 cm (19 x 15 in)
After completing **Sharing Gossip** (opposite), I made this painting of the same building, working in a freer way with heightened colour, and placing the building in its context.

Sharing Gossip
watercolour
43 x 33 cm (17 x 13 in)
Here, working directly in watercolour, I decided to concentrate on the doorways and more decorative content of the building. See also **Building, Havana** (above).

Drawings and notes

Having found a subject that interests me, I usually start by making a pencil drawing or a sequence of drawings, like the ones shown here. In the drawings I might consider tone, colour, specific decorative elements or the way that the subject fits into its context. I might also add written notes – specific phrases or words to help me remember different features of the subject and why I was attracted to it. In other drawings, I am thinking about how I might want to develop the subject in perhaps a more whimsical way, or by using a particular format; or I might add some colour, again just as a reminder, using the limited colours I'd taken with me. But chiefly, I make these drawings in response to the reason that first attracted me to the subject, rather than a concern for all the detailed figurative elements, while the written notes further distil my thoughts and feelings about the subject.

Eagle House, Havana

location pencil drawing
On site I often start with a drawing like this,
which helps me discover things about the
subject and reminds me of the features that
attracted me to it in the first place – here, the
eagle at the top of the building.

Lacock Abbey

location pencil and wash drawing
This drawing was, unusually for me, a line
drawing to which I added tone to make some
elements melt away in an eerie way that felt
synonymous with the subject.

Well
location pencil drawing
Here, I wanted to analyse and place in compositional context a detail that might come in handy later.

Laid Out in Black and White
location pencil drawing
In this subject, I was fascinated by the transition from light shapes against dark to dark shapes against light.

House on the Edge of the Moor
location pencil drawing
This small drawing shows an analysis of marks that I might make on a painting, at the same time as familiarizing myself with the subject.

Photographs

For many years, I found photographs too inhibiting to use as references for my work; however there was also the frustration, when travelling to a new place, of not having enough time in the day to sketch or paint all the subjects that I wanted to. Ultimately, my solution was to combine whatever practical work I could do on site with a number of photographs which might provide additional useful information later, back in the studio.

I take photographs of the subject, both as a complete image and in detail, from various angles. I am not concerned with making good photographs (I am not a good photographer!), but in collecting enough information to help me pursue my initial intention, while having photographs that I cannot just copy. In the studio I will often scour my sketchbooks for an extra figure, palm tree, window detail or whatever, to 'borrow' to complete a painting. Similarly, I sometimes use a series of photographs of different façades, or details within those façades, to help me complete a painting because they seem to me to capture the essence of the subject.

Using photographic reference

Let's start with some words of caution about photographs. I advise against working solely from a photograph or series of photographs. In my view, it is obvious and detrimental when someone has done so. A photograph is the unselected reproduction of what the camera sees before it, and the better the photograph, the more tempting it is to copy it, without any significant amount of interpretation. A painting, on the other hand, is essentially the selection of elements from a subject, and an extremely personal response and statement about what one has chosen to paint. Also, if photographs are the only source of reference, you are more likely to start considering all the detail in a subject, and in consequence the vigour of the painting process will be lost.

Yet there is obviously a case for taking photographs as a source of reference. For example, you may not have enough time to make a finished drawing or painting on site, or perhaps there is nowhere that offers you a space to work and also gives you the view that you want. Sometimes there are too many people about, or the weather is against you – there can be many reasons why it is difficult to work outside!

The advent of the digital camera makes it so much easier and more financially viable to take thousands of photographs and I find this quite a good way of building up a knowledge of a location and different subjects and, of course, of recording information. But I never rely on photographs alone: I use them in conjunction with location drawings and other material. Another thing I do, to help me make sure that I use photographs only as a reference, is to keep the photographs well away from the painting. When I want to refer to the photographs, I have to walk to the far end of the studio. By the time I have turned around and returned to the painting, the information is distilled as I concentrate on recalling the elements that I need for inclusion in the painting.

I quite often take references from different photographs and combine these within the same painting. Sometimes I do this by working from a number of photographic prints pinned up in the studio, as for *Look-Out* (page 79) *or Rendezvous (*Page 88), or I might work on my computers – I have two screens – and move images or parts of images across to build up a new, composite image that will form the basis of an idea for a painting. You can see from *Rendezvous* (page 88), for which the photographs on the opposite page were a source of reference, that the final painting is never that close to the images in the photographs.

Façades, Havana
When I use photographs, I usually take information from a group of related images, as here.

Façades, Havana
I keep any photographic reference at the other end of the studio, so there is never any temptation to copy it. If I want to take any information from a photograph I have to stop painting, walk to the photograph, and then on my return process that information before using it in the drawing.

Façades, Havana
I often use a computer to combine parts of images from different photographs and so create a completely new image as source material.

Rendezvous
watercolour
56 x 76 cm (72 x 30 in)
Although in this painting I
used the photographs shown
on page 87 as reference, as
you can see, the final image is
quite different.

When painting on site the scope is often influenced by practical considerations and factors such as the weather. However, my aim is to capture those qualities that impress me about the subject, and to do that I adopt whatever approach and techniques seem most suitable.

Painting on site

For location trips, I usually have a good selection of materials and equipment with me and so, if there is time, I will make some paintings on site. Time is always a key factor: I might be limited to working fairly quickly to explore an idea and create some colour reference, or, with the advantage of more time, I might have the opportunity to make larger finished paintings, as with *Leaning Tower in Venice* (opposite).

For this painting, I started with some drawing to ensure that the general proportions, perspective and position of the buildings worked well – not an elaborate drawing but just enough to remind me of the overall shape of things when I came to apply the colour washes. In my view, there is no point in drawing every detail, because this can be done in a much less laboured way with a brush, later on. Also, I don't want the pencil lines to dictate what happens in the painting or the marks themselves to detract from the colour work. As with many of my paintings, this one began with very wet-into-wet washes to give soft edges which I could subsequently define, more and more, as required. The sky was painted with more opaque colour, although allowing some of the warm-toned underpainting to show through in places and so link to the warmth of the buildings and reflections below.

Materials and equipment

When I am going out for the day I take a rucksack packed with all the necessary equipment, plus a lightweight folding stool. It is basic, compact equipment that gives me the choice of making drawings or working in watercolour or oils, whichever medium will best suit the subject and interpretation I have in mind. Incidentally, all this equipment easily fits into a suitcase for long-distance travel.

For watercolours, the equipment includes a watercolour paintbox, paper of various types and sizes, brushes and the necessary accessories, together with a lightweight drawing board/ folder made from two sheets of foam board taped together along one edge. For oils, I take a selection of boards prepared with a really good, absorbent ground (so that the paint will dry quickly during the trip), and a small painting box with paints, brushes and so on. I use strips of Velcro to hold the boards in place at the back of the oil-painting box.

My watercolour travel box
I replenish the colours in this from my stock of tube colours.

Leaning Tower in Venice
watercolour
53 x 33 cm (21 x 13 in)
A subject such as this needs a certain amount of initial drawing to show the main shapes and proportions, but I keep this to a minimum. I don't want the pencil drawing to control what happens in the painting, or to have the pencil marks dirty the clarity of the colour.

Façade, Venice
watercolour
28 x 30.5 cm (11 x 12 in)
Some initial drawing was essential here too, although with this subject I felt that the decorative qualities were most important and also I wanted to explore the idea of working with a square within a square.

Just One Tree
watercolour
25.5 x 30.5 cm (10 x 12 in)
Most of the work in this painting – the drystone wall, for example – relies on drawing with a brush. There is also a certain amount of scratching through the surface colour to let some of the original colours emerge again.

Appropriate techniques

I like to encourage students to be adventurous with watercolour and test its potential and limits. A willingness to experiment will add to your knowledge of the medium and in turn give you more resources to call upon when you are thinking about the best way to interpret an idea.

If you look at the paintings here, all of which were painted on site, you will notice that each one shows a different approach, involving different techniques, to suit the particular subject matter and what impressed me about it.

Façade, Venice looks to be the most formal of the four paintings, and in fact I did start with a certain amount of drawing to ensure that the key elements were in the right place and subsequently worked with a sequence of colour washes. However, the composition is less conventional, in that effectively I started with a square, destroyed it and then brought it back again. Contrastingly, for *To the Castle* I wanted a more decorative, whimsical quality and so the colours are more diffused, applied wet into wet, and the brushwork is much freer.

I believe that drawing and painting are not different disciplines, but different states of mind. In my view, one can draw with a brush or paint with a pencil. The way that one uses those tools dictates the discipline. As you can see in *Just One Tree*, particularly in the way that I have interpreted the drystone wall, I sometimes rely to a great extent on drawing with a brush. In my view, this work is as much a drawing as a painting. Also, I have exploited contrasts between opaque and transparent qualities and, as well as building up effects in paint, I have scratched through the colour in places, such as in the sky area (in fact I used a twig for this), to reveal the colour underneath. And *Collioure from the Gardens* is different again, with various forms of mark-making and in general a more decorative quality.

To the Castle
watercolour
28 x 30.5 cm (11 x 12 in)
I often start a painting by working
wet into wet, as you can see with
the sky effect in this example.

**Collioure from the
Gardens**
watercolour
25.5 x 30.5 cm (10 x 12 in)
The treatment here is more
decorative, involving various
forms of mark-making and an
almost jigsaw-like approach.

Themes and variations

Paintings can so easily become complicated and confusing if you try to say everything about a subject within a single image. I start with the quality that initially attracted me to the subject and I keep to that intention. As I have said, as I work I often see other ways of exploring and expressing an idea and each of these becomes a fresh painting. In this way, I might paint the same subject perhaps twenty or thirty times.

Understandably, sometimes the first painting can look a bit contrived or laboured, because I am still getting to know the subject and it is not always easy to immediately create the right focus and emphasis. For example, I felt that my first painting of *Arundel Castle* here, which was made on the spot, was rather laboured. My second attempt – for which, unusually for me, I used the original painting as the reference (although I did turn it upside down!) – was far more spontaneous in approach, focusing on the essence of the subject, and was consequently much more satisfactory.

Arundel Castle I
watercolour
30.5 x 35.5 cm (12 x 14 in)
With this first painting, which was made on the spot, I concentrated on finding out as much as I could about the subject. However, I felt that the result looked rather laboured.

Away from the actual subject matter I could concentrate on my idea, my distillation of the subject, rather than thinking I must put in every turret and so on.

I also like exploring different themes: taking a similar subject and giving it a different emphasis. The paintings on the following two pages are all based on the theme of looking from one place or area into another.

The starting point for a painting can lie anywhere. The crucial thing is to know what you want to say and keep to the integrity of your initial idea: then the reference material is only an aid and a prop for the intent, rather than something to be copied at the expense of the idea you are trying to convey. So, my advice is, before you start, get out all the reference material that you have and decide what you want to express.

Arundel Castle II
watercolour
30.5 x 35.5 cm (12 x 14 in)
Now in the studio, using **Arundel Castle I** (opposite) as the reference, this painting was far more successful in terms of making a personal response.

Through the Gate, Down the Valley and Out to Sea
watercolour
38 x 28 cm (15 x 11 in)
Another painting made on site in which I am exploring the idea of near and far, together with the relationship between spaces and shapes.

Early Morning View
watercolour
35.5 x 33 cm (14 x 13 in)
The same theme, this time considering the contrast between inner and outer spaces.

Alleyway, Urn and Vine
watercolour
35.5 x 30.5 cm (14 x 12 in)
I enjoy exploring different themes for subject matter. Here, the theme was looking from one space into another.

Alleyway, Crete
watercolour
35.5 x 33 cm (14 x 13 in)
Working from the same location as for **Alleyway, Urn and Vine** (above), I tried a slightly different viewpoint and used bolder colour.

5 RESOLVING OBJECTIVES

Every painting is a different experience, and I don't think you should be totally inflexible if you see that a slight adjustment in approach would help improve the result.

Often, things happen during the course of a painting which suggest alternative solutions, and you have to decide whether to doggedly keep to your original aim or modify it. I would advise against making major changes – save those for a different painting. But if a painting is becoming very laboured and is reaching a point where it is never going to work, you may have to do some drastic reworking, or make a fresh start. My philosophy is to keep to the original intention, exploring that idea to the best of my ability. If it doesn't work, I have learned something from it to take forward to the next painting. And if I can see no future in a painting, I am not averse to washing off the paint, working over the original and incorporating some of its 'history', or turning over and starting again.

Aardvark at the Table
water-based media on paper
48 x 48 cm (19 x 19 in)
This is a very formal painting, very symmetrical in its design, but not taking this approach so far that the work loses its impact and sense of intrigue. In order to achieve this 'simplicity', I had to take away a lot of elements in the painting as it progressed.

Initial decisions

With a positive idea in mind and a vision of how you want a painting to look, you should be able to think 'backwards', as it were, to plan the necessary stages that will enable you to achieve your objective. This sort of focus will also help you make the right choices regarding the type of paper to work on, the colour palette, and so on. As I have stressed, watercolour is a far more versatile medium than is generally thought, and as such there are no particular considerations or restrictions that must be taken into account when making a start. However, if I intend working with sequential layers of colour, I try to keep to the more staining and transparent colours to begin with. Opaque colours tend to sit on the surface of the paper and are more likely to lift off when other colours are applied over them.

Aims

There are general aims in painting and more specific aims governed by the subject matter as the catalyst. Formal qualities, such as composition and the use of colour, are always important. Thereafter the success of a painting will depend on how effectively it conveys a reaction to the subject; and naturally the type of response and the means of expressing it will vary from one painting to the next. In *Aardvark at the Table* (previous page) I wanted to see how little I could leave in the painting and yet still make it work, with a composition that had interest and held together; *Tropical Gathering*, however, is much more complex. Here, I have included a great variety of objects, the aim being to

Butcher's House
watercolour
25.5 x 23 cm (10 x 9 in)
I painted this from a drawing made on site and my objective was as much to do with the narrative, the character of the building, as it was with the formal qualities in terms of design, pattern and warm/ cool colour contrasts.

Tropical Gathering
watercolour
56 x 76 cm (22 x 30 in)
Here, the design is much more complex and my aim was to explore the idea of things emerging and disappearing.

Hay Barn
watercolour
33 x 53 cm (13 x 21 in)
Sometimes, to create the right effect, you need to remove paint rather than continue to add it. Having realized that this painting was getting overworked and heavy, particularly in the sky area, I lifted out a lot of the colour.

exploit the contrasts between things emerging and disappearing. Each new painting has its own objective, and as such the degree of success will always be relative to that particular objective.

Sometimes, in working to fulfil the aims for a painting, it is the paint handling rather than the figurative content that needs simplifying or adjusting in some way, and this is what happened in *Hay Barn* (above). Often, art technique books and demonstration films give the impression that the only option in watercolour painting is to build up effects using a succession of overlaid colour washes. In fact, if you use the right paper you can manipulate the paint in all sorts of ways, including rubbing it back and lifting it off. Removing or partially removing colour is a technique that can be just as important as building up effects with layers of colour. In *Hay Barn*, I wanted the painting to have a lyrical, light and airy quality. But it was becoming heavier and heavier, so I came to the conclusion that I must remove quite a lot of paint, particularly in the sky area. Always it is a matter of finding a means to an end – a means to create the type of painting that you envisaged when you started.

Preliminary work

Back in the studio, having looked at all the reference material collected on location, some artists like to work on a sequence of compositional roughs or preparatory drawings to finalize their thoughts and ideas for the painting before making a start in watercolour. This is a matter of choice, of course, so do whatever works best for you. Personally, once I am in the studio, I prefer to get straight on with the paintings. If I think there are potential alternative designs or ideas for a subject, I will explore those in the form of small thumbnail sketches before I start work on the painting in question. The only word of caution I would add about preliminary work is that if it is overdone, and an idea is planned too thoroughly, there will be very little left to discover in the painting, and inevitably this will lessen its vitality and impact.

Deconstruction and reconstruction

Having trained as a printmaker, I have always been used to thinking very carefully about the process, the sequence of colours and overlays that will be needed in order to achieve the result I want. In screenprinting and lithography, for example, I know that to arrive at certain colour combinations at the end, I must start by deconstructing all of those colour mixtures into their basic elements. I need to know which colour to start with and, from there, which colour to apply next, and so on.

As I build up the image, each new colour will create further colours, depending on where I place it and the particular colours beneath. I apply the same principle to painting: I look at the subject; decide on the image, effects and colours I want to finish with; deconstruct the painting into relevant stages; and then start with the first stage, the underpainting. In effect, I am rebuilding nature.

Starting points

It is a matter of opinion, but perhaps my method isn't a conventional one for painting in watercolour. I work with layers of colour; I take colour away in places as well as add to what is there; and I like to exploit the effects that can be achieved by putting one colour over another or by revealing textures, colours and other qualities within the build-up of a 'history' in the painting. I don't always start by reserving the light areas or necessarily by working from light to dark. Watercolour is versatile and will always allow you to find a way of painting that you are comfortable with.

An understanding of colour theory underpins my approach and essentially, it is only by trying out different colour overlays and colour mixes that you develop this sort of knowledge. It is a good idea, particularly with the more unusual colour combinations and effects, to keep small samples in a notebook, with an explanation of how you made those colours. Similarly, you can learn a great deal by trying several versions of a painting, using different colour sequences. People often comment that my colour work looks loose and intuitive, but in fact it is based on much thought, knowledge, control and experience with colour and composition.

Armenistis
watercolour
33 x 53 cm (13 x 21 in)
As in this painting, often my starting point is a
series of underlying, soft-edged washes of
colours that relate to each other right across the
work. Here, I wanted a strong sense of the
glowing light in the sky and a dance between
the elements in the landscape.

Armenistis in the Heat of the Day

watercolour

30.5 x 35.5 cm (12 x 14 in)

I painted this in the middle of the day and it was extremely hot. I chose colours and marks that would create that feeling – the red sky and the vertical 'melting' brushstrokes on the right-hand side, for example. I started the painting with the idea that this would be the underpainting and that I would add more realistic colours. But as I progressed and I became hotter and hotter myself, the relationship of the hot colours seemed to sum up the atmosphere more adequately.

Vision and response

Although I always set out with a particular intention for the final colour effects, there are times when the colour combinations and relationships begin to work very successfully at an earlier stage than I had anticipated, and so there is no need to add any further layers that I might have planned. In this painting, for example, the sky is red. This is because, having started with a red underpainting relevant to the result I wanted – which was essentially a blue sky but with a heavy, warm undertone to it – I reached a point at which I felt that the relationship of colours and tones worked well just as it was. I liked the warm/cool contrast and the red gave a better sense of the extraordinary heat in the middle of the day, and so there was no need to overpaint it.

The degree of control implicit in working towards a certain objective does not necessarily preclude some freedom in devising ways of achieving that objective. As I have described, I might retain part of what I had initially planned as the underpainting. Equally, later in the process, I sometimes decide that there are areas that are becoming too dominant, graphic or hard-edged and consequently these should be subdued in some way or 'knocked back'. So, I will apply a colour wash over those areas to simplify them and create a better link to the rest of the painting. Then, if necessary, I might work back into that wash to pick out certain elements. This is the technique I have used on the right-hand side of *Tropical Gathering* (page 100) to make some of the objects less obvious.

Birdcage
watercolour
48 x 76 cm (19 x 30 in)
I often make use of colour from the underpainting to define shapes, as here, where in the main I painted the spaces between the bars of the cage, rather than the bars themselves.

Although on location I may start by interpreting the subject in a representational way, I never feel bound by that approach. Indeed, once I have got to know the subject it will often suggest an entirely different interpretation, which perhaps might also involve images or a narrative from other sources.

From general to specific

In watercolours, as in every medium that I use, I like to start by considering the overall flow of a painting and how everything links together. I work from this general concept to increasingly specific marks, and finish with the detail. Not only does this help in creating a strong sense of unity and energy within the design, but it also works entirely in sympathy with my technique of deconstruction and reconstruction using overlaid colour washes.

Therefore, as I develop an underpainting, if for example I want a warm tone in one area, I look to see where else I could use that colour or a very similar colour. In this way, I quickly block in the initial colours and start working towards the harder edges and more specific colours, shapes and marks. And, of course, this approach is essential when working outside, where the light can change very quickly.

Focus and ambiguity

As I apply different colours and gradually construct a painting I am all the time considering where each colour will have an influence, either directly or at a later stage, and consequently how strong or weak to make that colour in relation to its context and the effect I want to achieve. I know that eventually I will subdue some colours and elements within the painting, while leaving other colours to come through in places and so define certain objects, details or qualities.

I use this 'lost and found' technique quite a lot so that, interestingly, it is often the colour from the underpainting that actually defines the things that appear nearest to the viewer.

The Only Shade
watercolour
25.5 x 30.5 cm (10 x 12 in)
This was painted early in the day, observing and recording the effect of light and the low, early morning shadows.

The Only Shade II
watercolour
25.5 x 30.5 cm (10 x 12 in)
A sequel to the painting oppsite, painted later in
the day when the light was more intense and
consequently influenced the colour and tonal values.

Subject and content

I never feel that I have to represent a subject exactly as I see it, although I may start like that when working on location. Instead, the subject will often suggest a quite different interpretation and, in order to achieve that, I might decide to combine images from various sources or work to a narrative inspired by an entirely different context. For example, as in *Birdcage Houses*, I often view buildings as having their own personalities and perhaps engaging in a conversation or argument with each other. And I might use a similar approach with a still life group, creating a situation which is being played out by the objects.

Local Gossip was inspired in that way. I spend a lot of time observing people, perhaps in cafés or in the village where I live, and I sometimes use those situations and interactions as the underlying theme in my paintings. In this painting, the two birds definitely look as though they are having a slight argument or disagreement about something! In *Bittersweet*, on the other hand, the conversation seems much more amicable, the mood more evenly balanced, with the flowers creating a symbolic 'olive branch' between the two birds.

Shopfronts, Ikaria
watercolour
38 x 25.5 cm (15 x 10 in)
The attraction of this subject was the interlocking play of geometric shapes and colours.

Local Gossip
water-based media on paper
48 x 46 cm (19 x 18 in)
These birds are personalities engrossed in discussion, and they reflect my observations of village life!

Birdcage Houses

watercolour

38 x 53 cm (15 x 21 in)

I did not find these buildings next to each other, or even in the same town. This painting was very much a composition from elements that I had seen, liked and wished had lived together, thinking that they combined to produce my idea of the essence of an imagined place.

Bittersweet

watercolour

81 x 84 cm (32 x 33 in)

Here again, the painting is concerned with formal qualities and a narrative.

Painter and painting

I have always been interested in painting, and since I was very young it has been a compelling attraction and challenge, something I must do. What has kept me motivated and eager to express myself in this way is the fact that, as well as the infinite variety of ideas and subjects to paint, there is always something new to discover and learn about the process or techniques.

In my view, a painting can only be successful if it is made to fulfil the feelings and ideas of the artist and, similarly, completed in a manner that is totally in keeping with the approaches and working methods that the artist wants to use. For this reason I do not paint commissions, because I am not willing to compromise regarding the concept or method for any painting. I could not work to someone else's brief: I know I would find that immensely inhibiting and unsatisfactory.

On the Grand Canal
watercolour
25.5 x 30.5 cm (10 x 12 in)
A painting from early in my career. It demonstrates how I used to be much more governed by the subject matter and a concern for showing exactly what was there.

Being bold

To work successfully, artists need various qualities, including perseverance and self-confidence. For each painting, you have to believe in yourself and so develop the idea to the best of your ability. Ideally, each painting will be a positive statement expressed in an original way and, as you gain experience and skills, you will be able to paint with increasing confidence and impact. If you are tentative and indecisive, your paintings will reflect that, so be bold. We all have to make many decisions on a daily basis outside our painting life, and I can never understand why someone should go to pieces the moment they are confronted with a piece of paper and some paints. The worse that can happen is that it ends up a mess, and even from that one can learn something about the intrinsic qualities of the paint!

However, even with a great deal of experience I don't think you can ever be totally confident and this is just as well, because it keeps you aware of the various challenges and conscious of the process and decisions you should be making. Until a painting is finished, you can never be sure how successful it will be, and of course you have to accept that not everyone is going to like what you do or understand it. Painting is a very subjective business.

Every painting will be an expression of something that you want to state at that particular time; that you are willing to put all your faith in at that moment. It won't mean that it is necessarily right or that you won't change your mind about it at some later point. Usually, the best paintings are the ones that you have had to struggle with.

I once had a very good client who bought a lot of my paintings, but he would always buy the paintings that I thought showed less confidence and which were less successful. When I eventually asked him about this, he explained that the paintings he chose were the ones in which he felt I had battled the whole way through and had just about won the battle! So, for him, those paintings were much more interesting, much more telling about the painting process and what I was trying to achieve. This was very perceptive, and I think it is a salutary reminder and lesson for every painter.

Learning from experience

Painting is a constant learning process. We learn from the successes and failures in our own work, and equally we can learn from the paintings and working methods of other artists. *On the Grand Canal* and *Golden Façade* are two paintings from different stages in my career that clearly demonstrate contrasting approaches and how the advantage of experience assists in the creation of images that have greater impact and originality. In the first painting, from the early part of my career, you can see that I was very much influenced by the reality of the subject matter, its actual content and colours. Whereas in *Golden Façade*, a more recent painting, I had the confidence to paint what I felt about the subject and to create an image that has a significance in its own right.

Courses and workshops can be helpful. My advice here is to get the widest possible experience you can – from different tutors and different courses. Initially, you may come across artists whose work you admire and, consequently, whose courses you want to attend. But try other artists as well: a contrasting approach might well inspire you to attempt something quite different and so open up a whole new path of ideas and techniques to explore.

I occasionally take students on painting trips abroad and I find this very rewarding, both from the teaching point of view and with regard to my own work – by having to explain various aspects, it sometimes reveals other ideas that I might want to pursue. Equally, I enjoy events such as Art in Action (www.artinaction.org.uk), where I can meet fellow artists and watch them at work.

Golden Façade
water-based media on paper
48 x 53 cm (19 x 21 in)
Now, with far more experience, I focus on what I feel is important about the subject matter: I want to create images that are original and significant in their own right. Now, perhaps (more than earlier in my career), I have a clearer idea of what a painting is all about before I begin, and I am braver in allowing myself to put this idea down at the expense of other issues that might muddy the waters.

6 WORK IN PROGRESS

I make no distinction between my work as an artist and who I am and how I live. So I am usually involved in some way with the painting process even when I am not actually creating work – perhaps thinking about the paintings in progress or noting other ideas and bits of visual information that might be useful. For example, recently, while waiting in a traffic jam, I noticed a woman in a bright red coat and she was standing in front of an ivy-clad wall. It was a striking colour combination, and one that I know I will want to use in some context in the future.

I have a purpose-built studio, which I have deliberately incorporated into the house. The reason for this is that I like to have my work easily accessible. I would find it very unsatisfactory if I had to make a special effort to go to the studio, even if it just meant walking up the garden path. I like to be able to pop into the studio at any time when I have an idea about something I am working on – day or night. And in fact I don't feel that I must only work in the studio, for in a sense the whole house is my studio. There are paints in the kitchen, drawings on the dining table, paintings and evidence of painting everywhere. Even the dog gets colour on her at times!

The Old School, Marylebone
watercolour
81 x 84 cm (32 x 33 in)
I have painted quite a few London façades. This was one of two studio works based on the Marylebone area and painted from drawings and notes made on site. Originally I thought I would overpaint the sky blue, but once the relationships were already decided in red, I decided that a red sky would add unity to the painting.

My studio work includes paintings that are inspired by resource material – from the drawings, photographs, notes and other information that I have collected on painting trips – as well as paintings based on objects set up in the studio. In both instances, as I have explained, my principal interest is to explore ideas with pictorial space, colour and other formal qualities, rather than be constrained by a particular subject matter.

Studio practice

My studio includes separate areas for water-based media and oil painting, as well as storage for all my materials, equipment and paintings. It has direct access to the outside, via steps leading to the front gate, so that I can move large paintings in and out easily and also, if I wish, have contact with anyone coming to the house. The studio has good natural light and various spotlights, which in fact I often have on, so as to ensure a consistent quality of lighting while I am working. There is also a large bay window with a window seat and a lovely view of the sea.

Usually, I have a number of paintings in progress at the same time. If I am using water-based media and collage, I might work straight through on a painting until it is finished. In contrast, with the oil paintings, which have been my main interest in recent years, there are times when they must be left to dry, and then I will switch to something else. Also, I think it is sometimes an advantage to leave a painting propped up somewhere in the studio, to give time to reconsider it and decide on the next step. Sometimes I will leave a painting for a considerable period: months or even years.

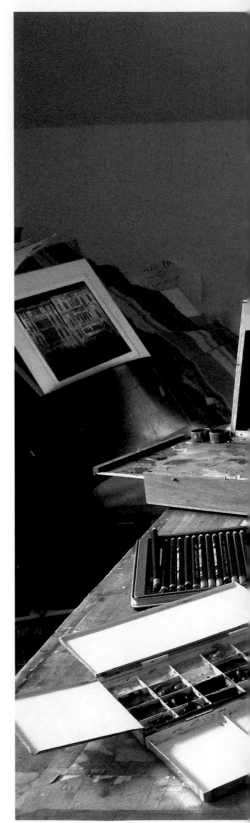

Part of my studio
I have separate areas set up for water-based media and oil painting. They are both constantly accessible, so that I can work on different paintings and ideas in different media concurrently.

Starting from reference material

I have an immense resource of sketchbook drawings, notes, location paintings and photographs from which I can select and develop ideas in the studio. *Neighbours, Nice* is a studio painting made in this way, with reference to paintings and drawings made on site. I often paint composite images, combining ideas from different source material. This painting is an example of that approach. The two buildings are typical of the traditional type of houses found in and around the Nice area on the French Mediterranean coast. They are from different locations, but I chose them deliberately because I thought they would work well together, with their contrasting 'personalities' and the elegant gate in between.

I decided to work on a handmade Indian watercolour paper for this painting. It has quite a waxy surface, almost like fabric, and this tends to hold the paint in place and keep it fresh: the colours don't spread and run, unless you want them to. Its other advantage is that, being a tough surface, it allows you to take colour off. The paper was not stretched, and I used it with the deckle edge showing, as an integral part of the work.

As you can see in Stage 1, I started with a pencil drawing to indicate the principal shapes and details. As I have previously explained, I only need sufficient information in a drawing to help with the painting. The drawing is a guide, rather than something merely to fill in – I don't feel bound to keep to the drawing, but I know it is there if ever I need to add more definition somewhere. Also, I want to lose the pencil lines in the colour as the painting progresses. Too much pencil work will muddy subsequent colour washes.

The first colours were applied to wet paper, see Stage 2, so creating very soft edges and a basis from which to develop the painting. These initial washes were actually much stronger in tone than you might assume. In the final painting they look quite subdued, but this is relative to the much stronger colours placed around them.

In Stage 3, I started to work in a more specific way, both with wet-into-wet and wet-on-dry colour, but all the time considering the whole composition and working with the minimum number of marks to hold it all together. Finally in Stage 4, I concentrated on strengthening some of the tonal contrasts, adding further marks and details where required, and exploiting lost and found edges, but always taking care not to overwork the painting. I wanted the painting to be as ambiguous as it could be, yet still hold on to enough information to convey the intended idea effectively.

Neighbours, Nice: Stage 1
Pencil drawing to indicate the main shapes within the composition.

Neighbours, Nice: Stage 2
I worked on wet paper initially, to give soft-edged shapes.

Neighbours, Nice: Stage 3
Now I am beginning to create more definition and stronger colours where necessary.

Neighbours, Nice
watercolour
35.5 x 51 cm (14 x 20 in)
Stage 4: The final painting has just enough information to make it interesting and lively, yet at the same time slightly ambiguous.

Observation and imagination

An alternative approach is to work directly from a group of objects set up in the studio. Often the chosen objects will relate to some kind of theme or narrative, but here again my intention is not to copy what is there but to explore the possibilities that the arrangement offers for working with different aspects of pictorial space, pattern, colour, texture and design. *In Suspense* is an example of this approach and the actual group of objects is shown in the photograph here.

Having decided what I want to paint and the objectives for the painting, I then 'deconstruct' the idea so that I can establish the sequence of stages that will be necessary. To demonstrate this more clearly, and particularly with regard to the thought process involved, I would like to discuss *In Suspense* by starting with the finished painting and showing how each stage developed from the specific decisions taken previously.

In the finished work, in Stage 7, you will notice that I have used quite a variety of painting and collage techniques and included different elements of perspective and pictorial space. For instance, I have flattened out the tabletop to show a much greater area that I could see in reality. I wanted to keep the content as simple as possible, but at the same time create a sense of energy

Still life arrangement in the studio
My painting titled In Suspense is based on this group of objects, which I set up in the studio.

In Suspense: Stage 7
water-based media and collage
51 x 61 cm (20 x 24 in)
The final painting. I am satisfied that there is sufficient coherence and impact in the completed painting. When using such a variety of elements, media and techniques, one has to spend a lot of time evaluating the whole work as it progresses, in order to be sure of creating a sense of unity throughout the painting.

within the work with the use of colour and texture.

The collage papers include origami, decorative and painted papers, both cut and torn. For example, for the flowers and the plate in the foreground, I used watercolour paper – torn pieces of paper to complement the natural, organic shapes of the flower petals, and more precise, cut-out shapes for the plate. Incidentally, the plate is made up from two separate shapes: the centre and the outer rim. This enabled me to create a shadow between the two shapes and so add the illusion of the plate's three-dimensional form. With both the flowers and the plate, I have painted and drawn over the collaged shapes.

For the bars of the birdcage, I used strips of paper cut from sheets that I had painted with specific colours: yellow, turquoise and blue. The dark lines – the bars on the far right-hand side – were made by painting the edge of a ruler and pressing this down on the paper. Beneath the bird there is a row of collaged shapes, which were cut or torn from a discarded painting. Old paintings can be very useful for collage work, providing some interesting variations in colour and texture.

Going back a stage to Stage 6, you can see how I have been working with contrasts of collage and paint to create ambiguity of space, while choosing marks that are pertinent to each particular element within the composition, and not adding anything more than is necessary. Each stage shows traces of the one before, with clues about the decisions that were taken. Here, you can see that I have redefined the drawing in places by introducing origami paper shapes around the red bird.

The bird is quite a dominant image, so I kept it as a painted shape rather than adding texture and dimension to it with collage. Below the large area of the origami paper, you can just make out some of the red against yellow stripes coming through from the previous stage, with some stronger red lines to the right, made with a rigger. And below that, in Stage 5, the other bird was painted with thick opaque paint, with lines scratched into the paint with the handle end of the brush.

In Suspense: Stage 6
The red bird is a very striking image – I didn't want it to be too powerful, so I kept it as a painted shape rather than developing it with collage and texture.

In Suspense: Stage 5
For this bird, I worked with thick opaque paint and drew into its surface, using the blunt end of a brush.

Deconstructing a stage further, in Stage 4, it is evident that all the main elements are in place, although there is work to do in order to unify the composition and create more impact. The painting needs more detail and definition. For example, the dark areas around the edge are not yet dark enough, the birdcage needs enhancing, there is not enough tonal or decorative detail in the flowers, and there are other elements, such as the yellow jug and the red bird, which I would like to stand out more. Hence, I introduce more collage in the next stage. The whole image is a bit flat at this point.

For the jug on the left-hand side of the painting, shown in Stage 3, the strips of paper were cut and torn from close-up photographic prints of Moroccan tiles that I happen to have in my studio. I printed the photographs on watercolour paper, using my A3 Epson printer. I felt that the tile textures and patterns were exactly right for the jug, and by working with dark and light strips, I was able to suggest its rounded form.

So, back to the very beginning of the painting, see Stage 2. From the start I am thinking about what is happening and where it is happening. In a way it is quite a tentative start, working wet into wet to give soft-edged shapes, although with strong colour. Some of the initial drawing from Stage 1 is still showing through – and acts as a sort of safety valve – but essentially I have established the overall sense of the subject on which to build.

In Suspense: Stage 4
Going back a stage further, you can see how the painting looked before I introduced more collage and decorative interest to the plate and other elements.

In Suspense: Stage 3

Always try to make your marks and media appropriate to the subject matter and the intentions you have in mind. For this jug, I decided to use strips of paper torn and cut from images of Moroccan tiles, which I photographed and printed myself.

In Suspense: Stage 2

Guided by the initial drawing. I applied the basic harmonies, contrasts and tones, wet into wet.

In Suspense: Stage 1

Pencil drawing.

Further ideas and approaches

Being adventurous with different media and techniques is very important, I think. It is the best way to gain a wider understanding and experience of the different possibilities for painting and so add to your confidence, style of work and general development as an artist.

Keep an open mind: don't be afraid to try various types of subject matter or experiment with different techniques and new media. See what works for you. As I have emphasized, watercolour is a surprisingly versatile medium, whether used independently or in a mixed-media context.

Each painting adds to the learning process. In my view, there is no point in being precious about a painting once it is finished, because once I have completed it, I have learned what I am going to learn. Some paintings are successful; others are not. I think one has to accept that and be ready to move on to the next challenge. The worst thing to do is play safe and always work within your comfort zone. As for the choice of subject matter, I tend to be led by an attitude of mind. Sometimes I will make a specific choice – to go to Cuba because I want to paint interesting and decorative architectural subjects, for example. Or, I might want to find subjects that suit a certain type of mark-making or offer the potential to work with strong colours.

I quite like subjects in which there is a limited amount of defined content, as in *Primeval Valley, Cumbria* here. With subjects that are genuinely unique, like this, there is no history of related paintings to influence my response. So, I have to really think about the marks I am going to use, and indeed I can be more inventive with the marks. It is only by trying something out that you gain experience and confidence with different media, combinations and techniques. Also, I am sure you will find that the best-quality materials – the finest, most stable pigments and so on – will help you create the most effective results.

Primeval Valley, Cumbria
water-based media on paper
35.5 x 53 cm (14 x 21 in)
This subject didn't have a lot of obvious content and so I had to really think about the marks I needed to use – both drawn and painted – in order to describe the more abstract and found elements of the subject.

Night Café
water-based media on paper
94 x 68.5 cm (37 x 27 in)
The aim here was to produce an eerie atmosphere. Again, this is a composite image, using buildings from different sources, painted in the studio from drawings made on site in Barcelona. I wanted to create a haunting image, with the café lurking in the half-shadows of this crumbling sector of the city.

Watercolour in context

As well as working in watercolour, and water-based media with collage and other mixed-media techniques, I also paint in oils and sometimes in acrylics on canvas. In fact, in recent years, for the majority of my paintings I have used oils, and this is because at the moment I am particularly interested in surface texture. Although, to an extent, it is possible to create textures in water-based media, oils obviously have a gooey quality that gives you greater scope for texture.

There are lots of advantages to having skills in more than one medium. As with texture, a choice of media creates better opportunities to interpret ideas in the most fulfilling way, while work in one medium can help inform another and, of course, the experience gained from different media will greatly add to your knowledge of painting and your development as an artist. But whatever the medium, as I hope I have shown in discussing my particular approach to painting, the key to success lies in having a defined objective for the work and a considered plan to help fulfil that objective – in other words, a clear understanding of both concept and process. Together with those points, the factor that most determines a good painting is the ability of an artist to express the idea in a personal way. So, in watercolour, as in all painting, be adventurous!

Fishing Trip
oil on canvas
51 x 51 cm (20 x 20 in)
I often paint in oils, particularly when I want more solidity and texture in the colour and surface effects. This was my second painting of this subject, the objective being to subdue most of the decorative detail on the hut, while keeping an interesting relationship of shapes and colours and enough hints of the figurative elements to suggest the feel of a hut selling fishing tackle and offering fishing trips. Compositionally, it was important that the hut was at a slight angle.

Neighbourly Chat
oil on canvas
71 x 71 cm (28 x 28 in)
I enjoy playing with different aspects of pictorial space. With this subject, I have flattened the table
and other foreground shapes, so creating a heightened sense of spatial ambiguity. I wanted to be
able to include the various viewpoints that interested me – all at the same time – in a single painting.